Judaism

A People

Its History

Religion, History, and Culture
Selections from The Encyclopedia of Religion

Mircea Eliade
EDITOR IN CHIEF

EDITORS

Charles J. Adams
Joseph M. Kitagawa
Martin E. Marty
Richard P. McBrien
Jacob Needleman
Annemarie Schimmel
Robert M. Seltzer
Victor Turner

ASSOCIATE EDITOR

Lawrence E. Sullivan

ASSISTANT EDITOR

William K. Mahony

Judaism
A People and
Its History

EDITED BY
Robert M. Seltzer

Religion, History, and Culture
Selections from The Encyclopedia of Religion

Mircea Eliade
EDITOR IN CHIEF

MACMILLAN PUBLISHING COMPANY
New York
COLLIER MACMILLAN PUBLISHERS
London

Macmillan Publishing Company
866 Third Avenue, New York, N.Y. 10022

Collier Macmillan Canada, Inc.

Library of Congress Catalog Card Number: 89–8278

Printed in the United States of America

printing number
1 2 3 4 5 6 7 8 9 10

Library of Congress Cataloging-in-Publication Data

Judaism: a people and its history / edited by Robert M. Seltzer.
    p. cm. — (Religion, history, and culture)
  Includes readings from the Encyclopedia of religion.
  Bibliography: p.
  ISBN 0-02-897374-7
  1. Judaism—History. 2. Jews—History. I. Seltzer, Robert M.
II. Encyclopedia of religion. III. Series.
BM160.J79   1989   89-8278
296—dc20   CIP

CONTENTS

MAPS

PUBLISHER'S NOTE

Since publication of *The Encyclopedia of Religion* in 1987, we have been gratified by the overwhelming reception accorded it by the community of scholars. This reception has more than justified the hopes of the members of the work's editorial board, who, with their editor in chief, cherished the aim that it would contribute to the study of the varieties of religious expression worldwide. To all those who participated in the project we express again our deepest thanks.

Now, in response to the many requests of our contributors and other teachers, we take pride in making available this selection of articles from the encyclopedia for use in the classroom. It is our hope that by publishing these articles in an inexpensive, compact format, they will be read and reflected upon by an even broader audience. In our effort to select those articles most appropriate to undergraduate instruction, it has been necessary to omit entries of interest primarily to the more advanced student and/or to those who wish to pursue a particular topic in greater depth. To facilitate their research, and to encourage the reader to consult the encyclopedia itself, we have thus retained the system of cross-references that, in the original work, served to guide the reader to related articles in this and other fields. A comprehensive index to the coverage of Judaism may be found in volume sixteen of the encyclopedia.

Charles E. Smith
Publisher and President
Macmillan Reference Division

INTRODUCTION

The reader of this volume is offered a selection of articles from *The Encyclopedia of Religion* both as a gateway to the vast and growing body of contemporary scholarship in Judaica and as a point of departure for the study of Judaism in the context of the phenomenology and history of religions. Limitations of space made it impossible to include many other original and informative articles on Judaism from the encyclopedia, but this volume should serve as an appropriate introduction to Jewish history and faith for college students and the general reader. The articles on Judaica in the encyclopedia are interspersed among articles on all aspects of religion; between the covers of this book they can be seen in relation to each other as part of a multidimensional portrait of the Jewish heritage.

An encyclopedia designed to present the entire spectrum of human religiosity must be selective and yet multidimensional in scope. For the editors, the solution was a table of contents composed of diachronic and synchronic cross sections: chronological accounts of a given religion's change through time and nonchronological descriptions of religious behavior, thought, literature, symbolism, and society. Because religiosity is virtually coextensive with human existence—it has been characterized as "the organization of life around the depth dimensions of experience" (*The Encyclopedia of Religion*, vol. 12, p. 286)—a faithful description of a tradition such as Judaism must seek to be as thorough and comprehensive as possible. That which has been called "Judaism" includes formalized prayer and mystical concentrations, chanting and silent meditation, folklore and metaphysics, structures of holy space and time, ethics, and food and dress regulations; it ranges from systems of law and speculation to the achievements of outstanding or typical individuals to intricate social institutions created for a group confronted by the constraints of power politics and the opportunities of migration, survival, and adaptation in sundry parts of the world—and much more besides.

More than thirty-two centuries old, Judaism has survived a series of radically different physical environments, social systems, emotional climates, and levels of philosophical or scientific sophistication. There was an original Israelite (that is, proto-Judaic) religion that sprang from seminomadic patriarchal clans who later formed confederated tribes bound in convenant to a God that had liberated their ancestors from Egyptian bondage. There were the monarchies of ancient Israel and Judah, with their royal cities, armies, temples, priesthoods, and (not infrequently vexing) prophets—kingdoms that were subject to destruction, or at least domination, by the Assyrians, Babylonians, and Persians. There was an increasingly diversified Judaism of the Hellenistic era following the conquest of the Middle East by Alexander the Great: clashing fellowships, schools, and sects in the land of Israel under Ptolemaic and Seleucid rulers, the revolt in the 160s BCE of Judah the Maccabee and his insurgent fighters, an independent state of Judea under Hasmonean priest-kings, a commonwealth indirectly subject to Roman rule at the end of the first century BCE, and a province of the Roman empire from the first century CE on. At the same time, there was already a far-flung and populous Jewish diaspora with its own Hellenized version of Judaism in almost all the cities of Asia Minor, Syria, and Egypt, as well as outlying Jewish communities in Italy, Iberia, Gaul, North Africa, and the northern shores of the Black Sea. Finally, there was a broad network of Jewish settlements to the east in the Persian empire.

Gradually, under the pressure of military defeat, the need for reconstruction, and the opportunity for creative advance, the classic lineaments of rabbinic Judaism took shape. The last centuries of ancient history saw the burgeoning of the Palestinian and Babylonian rabbinic academies. These laid the groundwork for the medieval variations of rabbinic Judaism that flourished in most of the Christian and Islamic lands of the Middle East, North Africa, and Europe. Beyond the sway of medieval rabbinic Judaism were the Karaite rejectors of the Talmud in the Middle East and the Byzantine empire and the Jewries of the steppe frontier, the Caucasus mountains, the caravan cities of Central Asia, and localities in India, China, and Ethiopia. The modern coexistence of a veritable family of Judaisms, each with its own institutions, customary practices, and cultural ideals is not that different from what scholars now understand to have been the multiplex texture of religiosity considered "Jewish" by the branches of the Jewish people throughout most of its history.

Of the various ways in which the inner religious diversity of Judaism can be unified, four powerful religious themes for establishing the coherence of the Jewish phenomenon emerge in the articles presented here. The first is Israelite radical monotheism, a starkly singular conception of divinity virtually unique in ancient times, a concept that remains the lietmotif of Jewish theology. The second is the canonized scriptures, a collection of writings with such a special intensity of holiness that they serve throughout Jewish history as the authoritative account of the formative and archetypal personages and events of the people's past, amplified by later legend and preaching. (The encyclopedia itself contains a whole series of such "biographies" of biblical figures as they were elaborated by Jewish storytellers, preachers, and commentators.) Third is the idealization and the reality of Jewish peoplehood as a collective body standing in a convenantal relationship with God. Fourth is the continuity of sacred law based on divine command, rabbinic interpretation, and communal enactment.

The articles in this volume are grouped into five sections. The introductory overview of the Jewish tradition by Eugene B. Borowitz opens with remarks on the range of present-day views on the nature of Judaism and surveys the essential components of the Jewish way of life. The article by Moshe Weinfeld on Israelite religion defines the roots of the Jewish tradition as transmitted by the Jewish Bible. The second section deals with the historical development and makeup of classic rabbinic Judaism according to the sages and teachers whose views are recorded in the Midrash, Mishnah, and Talmud. This group of articles, representing contrasting scholarly methodologies and points of view, includes an important article on the pivotal concept of Torah, divine *instruction* as interpreted by the human mind, which is the closest authentic Jewish equivalent of the term *Judaism*.

After an overview of the Jewish concept of Jewish peoplehood, including the procedures for entering and leaving Judaism, the third section of this book deals with the Jewish diaspora and the history of regional varieties of the Jewish religion in the lands from the Atlantic to Central Asia, where important self-sustaining diaspora communities were established. These articles indicate the variety of ways in which Judaism accommodated to Islamic, Greek Orthodox, Roman Catholic, and Protestant milieux in the Middle East, North Africa, Europe, and America during periods of ferment, chaos, stability, and stagnation.

The fourth section of the book contains articles that together outline much of the Jewish religious observance. An analysis of the matrix of Jewish religious action in rabbinic Judaism is provided by the article on *halakhah*, the normative "way" including Jewish religious law, followed by articles on the components of Jewish religious life in the liturgy, the religious year, the life cycle of the individual, the home, and in visual symbols. (The reader will want to consult the encyclopedia for articles on specific holy days and other rites of the Jewish tradition.) Judaism is a religion in which deeds (and thinking about possible acts) have a certain priority over theology, but there is a rich Jewish literature on theological and metaphysical issues, as well as innumerable works of biblical commentary, piety, ethics, and mysticism. For the interested reader, the encyclopedia contains extensive articles on the philosophical and quabbalistic traditions and the major medieval and modern forms and proponents of Jewish speculation. As a transition from the integrated world of traditional Judaism to the special tensions of the modern period, the concluding article of this section deals with East European Hasidism, the influential Jewish revivalist movement of the early modern period.

The fifth and final part of the book revolves around the problematic but crucial concept of modernization: Jewish interaction with the ever-changing social and intellectual environment shaped by modern science, technology, economics, and politics since the eighteenth century. The primary transformation of context that has propelled the Jewish people into redefining itself and the fundamentals of its heritage is usually presented as "emancipation," equality before the law for Jews as part of the citizenry of the modern nation-state. The successes and failures of emancipation have generated their own complex of reactions: the need to find modern substitutes for the premodern autonomous Jewish community, a whole series of "anti-Semitic" (that is, anti-Jewish) ideologies and movements that represent a backlash against emancipation, and an unfolding sequence of modern Jewish theologies formulated against the background of ideologies and philosophies from the Enlightenment and Kantian idealism to social Darwinism and existentialism. Yet another variation of Jewish emancipation is Jewish self-emancipation, the guiding principle of the Zionist movement for a rebuilding of Jewish life in the land of Israel, the religious dimension of which is also treated in the encyclopedia.

One distinguished reviewer has observed that, of the comprehensive encyclopedias of religion published during the present century, *The Encyclopedia of Religion* has the most thorough and balanced treatment of Judaism, a treatment that seeks to render the Jewish tradition accessible in its own terms and according to its own structure of faith. Ismar Schorsch observed that "never before has a general encyclopedia devoted so much space to expounding the sundry deposits of Judaism's millennial religious dynamism. . . . A profound respect for the uniqueness of religious phenomena motivated Eliade and his circle to illuminate the central expressions of Judaism, as understood by the best of Jewish scholarship in our day." ("Judaism No Longer a Fringe Religion in New *Encyclopedia of Religion*," *Moment,*

October 1987, pp. 53–55). The articles on Judaism in the encyclopedia and, we hope, this volume, are an indication that the objective, scholarly study of religion is now accepted without embarassment as a integral part of the humanities and that the objective, scholarly study of Judaism is an essential component of the fabric of modern humanistic scholarship.

APRIL 1989   ROBERT M. SELTZER

ONE

ROOTS OF THE TRADITION

1

JUDAISM: AN OVERVIEW

Eugene B. Borowitz

Neither of the sacred Jewish classics, the Bible or the Talmud, speaks of "Judaism." Hellenistic Jews created this Greek word to describe their uncommon way of serving God (*2 Mc.* 2:21, 8:1, 14:38; *Gal.* 1:13–14). All such mediating terms, because they utilize alien categories as the means of self-representation, necessarily distort as much as they explain. Thus, while the Jews of the first century CE integrated their ethnicity and their religion, Paul, writing *Galatians* for gentile readers, must sunder faith from folk in order to communicate.

Contemporary Jewish thinkers radically disagree as to the nature of Judaism and even the advisability of employing the term. Interpretations of Judaism today range from steadfast traditionalism to radical universalism. The traditionalists themselves differ strongly on accommodation to modernity. The right-wing Orthodox resist accommodation, while the Modern Orthodox accept any cultural good not forbidden by God's revelation. Debates over the role of mysticism add further diversity. Other contemporary Jews have rejected Orthodoxy because they deem it incompatible with the practice of democracy and the findings of the natural and social sciences, especially critical history.

Among nonreligious Jews, some are humanists who assimilate their Jewishness to contemporary culture, especially ethics. Others identify Judaism with Jewish folk culture. Zionism and the state of Israel represent the secularization of Judaism at its fullest.

Among liberal—that is, non-Orthodox—religious Jews, four differing emphases occur. (1) Jews who have an ethnic attachment to Judaism often find that it acquires a core of universal spirituality that, in turn, revitalizes their attachment. (2) Jews seeking a more disciplined Jewish religiosity direct their ethnic life through Jewish law, dynamically interpreted, as a historically evolving structure. (3) Jews concerned with the demands of rationality assert that Judaism uniquely comprehends the idea of ethical monotheism, a universal truth that is reinforced by their sense of ethnicity. (4) Jews who adopt a personalist approach conceptualize Judaism as a relationship, a covenant mutually created by God and the Jewish people and re-created in every generation. This article describes postbiblical Judaism in terms of the evolving expression of the Jewish people's covenant with God, understood in liberal religious terms.

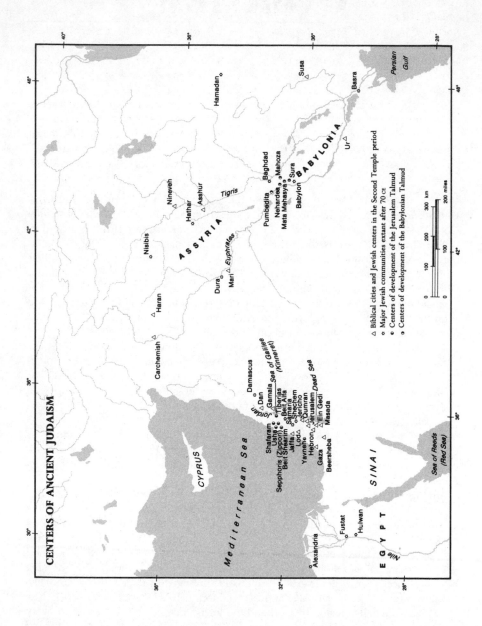

CENTERS OF ANCIENT JUDAISM

△ Biblical cities and Jewish centers in the Second Temple period
○ Major Jewish communities extant after 70 CE
◉ Centers of development of the Jerusalem Talmud
◉ Centers of development of the Babylonian Talmud

From the Bible to Rabbinic Judaism

We have little hard data by which to trace the progress from biblical to rabbinic Judaism, despite some help from the biblical *Book of Daniel.* From Ezra and Nehemiah (Hebrew leaders of the mid-fifth century BCE) to the earliest rabbis (the authorities mentioned in the Talmud) in the first half of the first century CE, the sources in Jewish tradition that are considered authoritative provide little reliable historical information. Learned conjectures can fill this gap, but as their validity rests on hermeneutic foundations that often shift, all such speculations are best left to historians. [*See* Rabbinic Judaism in Late Antiquity.]

The rabbis themselves affirmed an unbroken transmission of authoritative tradition, of Torah in the broad sense, from Moses to Joshua to the elders, the prophets, and thence to the immediate predecessors of the rabbis (*Avot* 1.1). By this they meant that along with the written Torah (the first five books of the Bible, also known as the Pentateuch or Law) Moses also delivered the oral Torah, or oral law, which contained substantive teaching (legal and nonlegal) as well as the proper methods for the further development of the Torah tradition. As inheritors and students of the oral (and written) law, the rabbis knew themselves to be the authoritative developers of Judaism.

Modern critical scholarship universally rejects this view. For one thing, the Bible makes no mention of oral law. Then, too, it is reasonable to think of Torah as undergoing historical development. When, over the centuries, Judaism grew and changed, later generations validated this unconscious process by introducing, retroactively, the doctrine of the oral law.

We may see rabbinic Judaism's mix of continuity and creativity more clearly if we briefly note these same features in their late biblical predecessors. Ezra and Nehemiah believe that God and the Jewish people have an ancient pact, and they seek to be faithful to it by their lives. Though they acknowledge that God rules the whole world, they and their fellow Babylonian Jews manifest a deep loyalty to a geographic center returning from an apparently more prosperous land to resettle Jerusalem and restore God's Temple there. They are ethnic separatists, rejecting offers of help from the Samaritans and requiring Jewish males to give up their gentile wives. They carefully restore the Temple cult and insist on observance of the Sabbath. But their Judaism involves sensibility as well as statute. When Nehemiah discovers people collecting debts in a time of hardship, he denounces such hard-heartedness as incompatible with covenant loyalty, and they desist.

Ezra and Nehemiah also evidence a new religious concern: acting in accordance with "the book of God's Torah" (*Neh.* 9:3). In a great public ceremony, the book is read to all the people, men, women, and children, and explained to them in detail. By the mid-fifth century BCE, then, a written tradition has taken the place formerly occupied by divination, prophecy, and priestly teaching. [*See* Israelite Religion.]

Nearly three centuries later, *Daniel* gives us another glimpse of late biblical Judaism. Daniel, the paradigmatic Jew, lives outside the Land of Israel, among idolaters. He perseveres in the prescribed Jewish patterns of eating, drinking, and praying, despite the threat of severe punishment. A heavy eschatological focus distinguishes this book, as do its bizarre visions and their cryptic interpretations. After calamitous persecutions of the holy people, including wars against them by foreign powers, God intervenes, sending one who defeats their foes and establishes their kingdom forever. A time of cosmic judgment follows that dooms the wicked to eternal reprobation while the righteous live on forever. The biblical prophets' expectations of an ideal king, descended from King David, who would one day establish worldwide justice, compassion, and recognition of God have here been radically extended.

The Judaism of the Rabbis

Rabbinic Judaism appears as a mature development in its earliest datable document, the Mishnah, a compilation of Jewish traditions redacted about 200 CE. [*See* Mishnah and Tosefta.] We can flesh out its sparely written text by consulting the more extensive classic works of rabbinism, the Talmud and the Midrash. The Talmud—essentially a collection of rabbinic discussions on the Mishnah—exists in two forms: the Jerusalem Talmud *(Yerushalmi)*, redacted about 400 CE, and the Babylonian Talmud *(Bavli)*, redacted about 500 CE and considered the more authoritative of the two. [*See* Talmud.] The Midrash is a body of homiletic and other exegeses of the Bible, of which the earliest compilations date from the third to the sixth centuries CE. The rabbis proceed on the assumption that the Temple, destroyed by the Romans in 70 CE, will be rebuilt only in "the days of the Messiah." They refer to the Temple cult mainly as the stuff of memory and hope and as material for study. Their Judaism centers about the Torah, particularly the oral Torah. To the critical eye, the distinctive features of rabbinic Judaism reflect creative development as much as reverent continuity with the past.

A structural innovation of the rabbis provides a convenient entry into their Judaism. They utilize parallel, mutually reinforcing modes of instruction, *halakhah* ("the way," the law, the required pattern of living) and *aggadah* (all else, including lore, preachment, speculation, and theology). Both are considered Torah, which literally means God's own instruction. In rabbinic texts they are often found organically intertwined, but they carry different degrees of authority. When dealing with *halakhah,* the rabbis, for all their disagreement and debate, seek to attain coherence and to decide what constitutes lawful practice. (The rabbis' courts can inflict severe penalties on transgressors.) By contrast, the realm of the *aggadah* is unregulated. The rabbis appear to delight in finding ingenious ways to amaze their colleagues with their imaginative exegeses and dicta. In all their contradiction and contrariety, these teachings too are part of the oral law. [*See* Midrash and Aggadah.]

WAY OF THE RABBIS

For the rabbis, the covenant entails the adoption of a way of life faithful to God more than acquiescence to a specific doctrine. All later varieties of Judaism—including, despite radical differences, the modern ones—have echoed these spiritual priorities. A description of Judaism, therefore, should begin with some highlights of the rabbinic way. What follows represents the norms stated in authoritative rabbinic texts much more than it does the realities of community practice of the rabbinic era, about which we have no direct independent data.

Responsibility of the Individual. The bulk of rabbinic literature concentrates on how the ordinary Jewish man ought to conduct himself so as to sanctify his life.

Feminists have correctly pointed out that the rabbis take men to be the primary focus of God's instruction, with women essentially considered to be their adjuncts. Thus, men make all the halakhic decisions about women's duties, and though any man might qualify to render such decisions, traditionally no woman can. The rabbis did assign women a comparatively high personal and communal status. Nonetheless, by egalitarian standards, the differentiation of women's duties from those of men, which are viewed as the norm, imposes on women a loss of dignity and worth.

The troubling issue of sexism aside, rabbinic Judaism is remarkably democratic. It calls all Jews to the same attainable virtues: righteousness in deed, piety of heart, and education of the mind. It may derogate the wicked and the ignorant, but it never denies they might change and attain the highest sanctity. The sacred elite, the rabbinate, remains open to any man and recognizes no substantial barriers between rabbis and other Jews.

With the Temple destroyed, rabbinic Judaism made the ordinary Jew a "priest" by transforming many rituals once connected with the Temple cult so that they became a way of sanctifying one's everyday life at home or in the marketplace. Before eating or after excreting, one was to wash one's hands ritually and recite an appropriate blessing. Each morning and afternoon—the times of the Temple sacrifices—men worshiped in a prescribed liturgical structure. (An evening service was added later.) In the morning, men said their prayers wearing head and arm phylacteries (Heb., *tefillin*), small leather boxes that contain biblical citations. (The very pious wore them all day.) The doorpost of a Jewish home bore its own small container, the *mezuzah,* which contained Torah texts. A special fringe on the corner of a man's garment served as a reminder of his responsibility to God.

The Jew's table became an altar. What came to it had to be ritually acceptable, *kasher.* The list of foods proscribed by the Torah was amplified by rabbinic interpretation. Animals had to be slaughtered in a religiously acceptable, humane manner, and their carcasses had to be examined for diseases. Rabbinic law extended the biblical prohibition against boiling a kid in its mother's milk to prohibit mixing any meat with any milk product. [See Kashrut.] It also mandated various blessings to be recited prior to eating bread, fruit, grain, vegetables, and other foods. After a meal, a longer, preferably communal grace was to be said.

The recitation of blessings was a constant part of the Jew's day. Hearing good news or bad news; seeing the sea, or a flowering tree, or an odd-looking person, or a meteor; smelling spices; acquiring something new; passing a place where a miracle had been done—all such occasions, and many more, required brief words of prayer.

The conduct of business also exhibited this intermingling of the commonplace with the transcendent. The rabbis spelled out in detail their religious equivalent of what Western civilization calls civil law. The covenant embraced such issues of justice as the proper treatment by employers of workers and the responsibilities of workers to their employers; the definition of reasonable inducements to customers and of illegitimate restriction of trade; the extent of a fair profit and a seller's responsibility in the face of changing prices; the duty to testify in the rabbinic court and the form in which contracts were to be written. Disputes between Jews on any of these matters were to be taken to the rabbinic court, which had detailed standards for administering justice.

The rabbis made daily study—for its own sake and as a ritual observance—a religious responsibility of the highest significance. The minimum requirement could be satisfied by studying selected biblical verses and rabbinic passages, but even the liturgy included numerous study texts and regular Torah readings. Besides, the acquisition of knowledge was a source of community esteem, a typical example of social custom strengthening rabbinic ideals. The rabbis endowed Jewish religiosity with its bookish cast, and their argumentative, analytic form of study made Jewish life uncommonly verbal and cerebral.

Because much that the rabbis valued could not usefully be made law, they surrounded their precepts with their individual opinions about what constitutes the good person and the ideal community. Like the Bible's authors, they abominate lying, stealing, sexual immorality, violence, and bloodshed. They decry gossip, slander, faithlessness, injustice, hard-heartedness, arrogance, and pride. They glorify industry, honesty, compassion, charity, trustworthiness, humility, forgiveness, piety, and the fear of God. Believing in the Jewish community's good sense, they urge individuals to acquire a "good name."

They do not underestimate the difficulties involved in striving to be a good Jew—yet they never doubt that, with God's help, one can be more righteous than wicked. They picture humans as being in perpetual conflict between their *yetser ha-ra'* ("urge to do evil") and their *yetser tov* ("urge to do good"). The former they describe as a relentless, wily, indefatigable foe that seeks to dominate human consciousness and easily infects human sexuality and that can be defeated only momentarily. Realists that they were, the rabbis acknowledge that the evil urge often leads to good. Its driving energy causes people to marry, build homes, engage in useful commerce, and the like. Though one ought never to underestimate its destructiveness or one's own vulnerability, human beings can harness some of its strength for their own good and to do God's work.

One can best fight off or sublimate the "urge to do evil" by studying, remaining pious, keeping good companions, and above all by observing the Torah. However, nothing guarantees its defeat, and self-righteousness practically invites its victory. Death alone terminates the struggle, and only at the "end of days" will the "urge to do evil" be destroyed. Until then, Jews continually beseech God's help, confident that, as the Bible teaches and the rabbis continually reiterate, God will aid them in their striving for purity.

The rabbis do not expect anyone to remain sinless. (Even Moses, their model, was not sinless.) Having sinned, one should do *teshuvah,* "turning" or "repentance." Elaborating on a biblical theme, the rabbis specify the stages by which sinners right their relationship with God. One begins by becoming conscious of having sinned and feeling remorse. That should lead to a confession of one's sin before God and thus to confrontation with one's guilt. But morbidity leaves no energy for sanctification. Instead, guilt should motivate one to recompense those one has wronged and ask their forgiveness. Having firmly resolved never to repeat the iniquity, one may then beseech God's mercy with confidence, for God loves this effort of the human will and graciously accepts each sincere initiative, granting atonement.

One need not be Jewish to do *teshuvah,* and the rabbis directed that the *Book of Jonah* be read on the annual Day of Atonement to remind Jews that even the wicked Ninevites had once done so. Even for Jews *teshuvah* involves no special rites or sanctified personnel. Rather, each day's dynamic of striving but often failing to fulfill the Torah involves the individual in practicing *teshuvah*. (On Yom Kippur, the Day of Atonement, the Jewish people, in a unique sequence of four worship services, carries out a corporate *teshuvah.*) [*See* Atonement, *article on* Jewish Concepts.]

Family in Rabbinic Judaism. The rabbis usually think of individuals not as isolated entities but as organically connected to their families and their people. For the rabbis the Jewish way primarily involves an ethnic group's unique covenant with God and its consequences for the lives of the individuals who constitute the group. The Jewish family replicates in miniature the greater covenant community.

The rabbis consider marriage a cardinal religious obligation, though they tolerate some exceptions. Through marriage one carries out the biblical command to have children. Because marriages were arranged in their era, the rabbis provide much counsel about this important process. They strongly urge that men marry early and that they take a wife from a good family who has a pleasant personality. They favor monogamy but do not require it (it was finally made obligatory by the medieval sages). They subordinate good looks, love, sexual pleasure, and even fecundity—in all of which they delight—to their goal of family well-being, *shalom,* which comes from a couple's mutual dedication to the Torah.

The rabbis hope that a deep love will arise between the spouses, on whom they enjoin sexual fidelity. (Talmudic law defines such fidelity in terms of the wife's behavior; medieval writers tend to apply similar standards to husbands.) They expect male dominance in the household, but counsel the temperate use of power by husbands and fathers. They also display a canny sense of the critical, even decisive, role the wife/mother plays in family affairs.

Despite this exaltation of marriage in their sacred way of living, the rabbis provided for the possibility of divorce. Though they decried the breakup of a family, they did not make divorce administratively impractical. Divorced men and women often remarried.

From biblical times, Jews experienced infertility as grievous suffering. If Jews have no offspring, the covenant expires. Through future generations all prior Jewish devotion hopes to reach completion. Children—particularly sons, in the rabbinic view—therefore come as a great blessing, and if they grow up to be good people, respected in the community, their parents enjoy inestimable fulfillment. Should they be wicked, their parents consider it a major judgment on themselves. Some rabbis identify suffering caused by one's children as the worst of divine visitations.

Only occasionally do the rabbis discuss parents' obligations to their children, perhaps because they believed that natural sentiment, guided by Jewish folkways, would adequately direct them. By contrast, they say much about children's duties toward their parents. The rabbis' amplification of the Fifth Commandment—"Honor your father and mother"—not only reflects their regard for wisdom and experience but testifies to the covenant between the generations that revivifies the covenant between God and Israel. Jewish personal names add to this intimacy, for one is called the "son (or daughter) of so-and-so" and thus carries one's parent in one's personhood all one's life.

These relationships functioned within the Jewish home, the primary scene of ongoing Jewish observance. Particularly since it might also be one's place of business, the home brought the diverse aspects of Jewish life together in mutually strengthening integrity. [*See* Domestic Observances, *article on* Jewish Practices.]

Jewish Community and Jewish People. In rabbinic times most Jews lived away from the Land of Israel, in the Diaspora, and from about the fifth to the tenth century CE, Babylonian Jewry exercised preeminent religious authority. To carry on their faith, the Jews who were scattered across the Parthian and Roman empires found it helpful to live near other Jews. The experience of anti-Semitism also brought Jews together. As always, the social and the sacred interpenetrated.

The responsibility of the Jewish community to uphold the covenant received its most visible expression in the liturgy of the daily worship services at which communal prayer was offered. (Obligatory individual prayer derives from this corporate duty.) A quorum of at least ten adult males, representing the entire Jewish people, was required to be present. At the morning service on Mondays, Thursdays, Sabbaths, and festivals, and on Sabbath afternoons, the group read a portion of the Torah scroll, often followed by a selection from the prophetic books. If a particularly learned man were in the congregation, he might give a sermon.

Any man with the requisite knowledge could lead the service or read from the scroll. Various religious functionaries enhanced the community's life, but a rabbi was not a requirement. Both a ritual slaughterer (so there could be kosher meat) and a teacher for the children took priority. Devoted volunteers attended and buried the dead and took care of other such communal duties.

Rabbis in the Talmudic period were not employed by the Jewish community but, like other Jews, worked at some ordinary occupation. When the community did have a rabbi, he functioned as both scholar and judge. He exemplified the Jewish duty to study and he answered questions about Jewish law, when necessary convening a rabbinical court *(beit din)*. Decisions of the *beit din* were considered part of the oral law and hence carried divine authority, yet they could be appealed by writing to a greater scholar elsewhere who might, by the authority of his knowledge and piety, indicate that the ruling was faulty.

Corporate life turned about several institutions. One, the synagogue, which may have predated the earliest generations of rabbis, was recognized by them as a surrogate for the destroyed Temple, with prayer as a fully adequate substitute for sacrifice and laymen in the place of priests. The rabbis also made it possible for a synagogue to function anywhere a quorum met, including a private home. A populous settlement might have many congregations. A prosperous community would erect an appropriate building to house synagogue activities. [*See* Synagogue.]

Another institution was the study house, where those devoted to learning would find a place to study and to meet with other students of Torah. Often this was a room in the synagogue.

The rabbinical court, which was composed of three learned men, did more than hear significant cases. It bore responsibility for the community's spiritual well-being. In special situations, its executive power had few limits, and it could enact decrees that were binding on the community.

The community's rabbinical authorities shared power with its lay leadership. Jewish communities in the Diaspora often possessed considerable legal independence, and their gentile rulers expected the community leaders to collect taxes, regulate the markets, and generally supervise Jewish internal affairs. All these matters were handled by applying the Torah's teaching to the immediate social and political realities.

Community leaders, carrying out a prime Jewish obligation, collected and disbursed charity (the Hebrew term, *tsedaqah,* literally means "justice"). Every Jew had obligations toward every other Jew, particularly those who needed help. Gathering and distributing the funds were among the most honored community tasks. Many communities so esteemed *tsedaqah* that even its recipients gave to others.

Geography and cultural differences produced variations in Jewish practice between the two leading centers of Jewry, one in the Land of Israel (under Roman rule) and the other in Babylonia (under Parthian and, after 226 CE, Sasanid rule). No single agency existed to enforce uniformity in practice or theory. Instead, a relatively loose pattern of authority emerged. From time to time, certain institutions or individuals arose whose scholarship and piety commanded the respect of many Jews. In time, their teachings established precedents for later Jewry.

Despite the open texture of the Judaism of this era, the rabbis exhibited a clearcut sense of the unity and identity of the Jewish people, who were the sole recipients of God's law and thus bore unique witness to God. They detested the idolatry and immorality they saw all about them. Hence they consciously sought to distinguish and separate Jews from the nations. But most rabbis happily accepted sincere converts. The isolation of the Jews made hospitality to strangers critical: Jews on a journey could always expect to find a welcome in other Jewish communities, which, despite variations in custom, clearly followed the same Torah in the same basic way. [*For further discussion, see* Jewish People.]

Three Rhythms of Jewish Time. Jews live in three interrelated dimensions of time: the personal, the annual-historical, and the eschatological. The critical passages of each individual's life are marked by sacred rites. On the eighth day after his birth, a newborn boy receives the physical sign of the covenant in the ceremony of circumcision. At thirteen he assumes personal responsibility for performing the commandments, becoming *bar mitsvah.* Should he complete the study of a classic text, he marks the occasion with a small celebration. Marriage is preceded by formal betrothal. The wedding itself is as elaborate as the family's means and the community's standards will allow. The birth of children, the experience of bereavement and mourning, the dissolution of marriage in divorce are all social acts that involve community participation; many of them are also sanctified by prayer and ritual. [*See* Rites of Passage, *article on* Jewish Rites.]

Prayer and ritual similarly mark the great moments of each year. The six workdays climax in the rest, worship, study, and feasting of the Sabbath. On Friday eve (in the Jewish calendar, the day begins at sundown) it is traditional that women light the Sabbath candles and say a blessing over them. Before the special Sabbath meal is eaten, a prayer of sanctification is recited over a cup of wine. When the Sabbath has ended, its "holy time" is demarcated from the "profane time" of the weekday by the recitation of blessings over wine, spices, and a multi-wicked flame in a ritual called Havdalah ("separation"). [*See* Shabbat.]

The year begins in the autumn during the period of the High Holy Days. The solemn synagogal rites of Ro'sh ha-Shanah celebrate God's sovereignty, justice, and mercy. The ensuing ten days of penitence are climaxed by the all-day fast and worship service of Yom Kippur, the Day of Atonement, in which the congregation beseeches God's promised forgiveness. In the course of the year there are three

"pilgrimage" festivals, Passover, Shavu'ot (Weeks or Pentecost), and Sukkot (Tabernacles; Feast of Booths). Originally these were agricultural festivals during which
all Jews came on pilgrimage to the Temple in Jerusalem, but they were transformed by the rabbis into historical symbols: Passover celebrates the Exodus from
slavery in Egypt, Shavu'ot the giving of the Torah, and Sukkot God's providential
care of the Israelites in the wilderness. Thus, the undeviating cycle of the year becomes a reminder and renewal of the Jewish people's unique historical experience.

Rabbinic creativity likewise embellished the minor festivals of the year. The rabbis
established a ceremony of special psalms, prayers, and a reading from the Torah
scroll to greet the beginning of each lunar month. For the fast day of Tish'ah be-Av,
commemorating the destruction of the Temple, they enjoined a reading of the *Book
of Lamentations.* They memorialized other tragic events with lesser fasts. The salvation of ancient Persian Jewry, recounted in the *Book of Esther,* is remembered on
the feast of Purim. The Maccabees' rededication of the Temple in 164 BCE, after its
desecration by the Hellenistic ruler of Syria, Antiochus IV, is celebrated as Hanukkah
at about the time of the winter solstice with a ritual that includes the kindling of
lights in the home over the course of eight nights. [*See also entries for each holiday
and* Jewish Religious Year.]

The number of each Jewish year indicates the time since creation, according to
rabbinic calculation, even as the rhythm of the year directs attention toward history's
promised climax, God's manifest rule on earth. A messianic hopefulness infuses all
Jewish observance, for the end might begin at any moment; yet the Jews' heartbreak-
ing experience with premature messiahs—particularly Bar Kokhba in the rebellion
against Rome of 132–135 CE—indicated that the Messiah would come only at the
"end of days."

We can surmise something of the tone and quality of the rabbis' Judaism from
what their traditions tell us about the way they lived. Their teachings show that they
can be wildly playful, though they are usually highly serious; exuberant in celebration, yet careful of minutiae; free in opinion, yet obedient to discipline; guilt-stricken
at sinning, yet confident of forgiveness; desirous of intention in the performance of
mitsvot (the commandments), yet content with the deed itself; highly individualistic,
yet absorbed in community; concerned with the practical, yet oriented toward the
eschatological. They were simultaneously mystic and rationalistic, emotionally de-
monstrative and devoted to order, foolish sinners and pious martyrs. They were
ordinary people who might be one's neighbors, yet they were saintly, endowing
their spirituality with intellect and a communal and personal activism. And the communities that were guided by their teachings seem much like them, human and holy
at once.

Above all, the rabbis have a passion for this mundane life, despite the finer one
to come. They delight in its opportunities to serve God through the routines specified by Torah. Yet they insist that in order to save a life, all the laws of the Torah
could—indeed, must—be broken (except the prohibitions against idolatry, murder,
and sexual sin). Similarly, when the survival of the Jewish people seems to be at
risk, the rabbis find ways to accommodate reality, but not by compromising principle. For they believe, above all, that the world was created for the sanctification of
life, and that only through holy Jewish living can it hope to endure and reach completion.

BELIEFS OF THE RABBIS

It is characteristic of the rabbis that their faith is inseparable from their way of life. Their test for heresy was behavioral, not creedal. Their explicit statements of belief are generally more poetic than precise, more fragmentary than general, and they exhibit little interest in systemic coherence.

While acknowledging the notorious elusiveness of what they call rabbinic theology, some modern scholars have yet found it possible to explicate some of its major themes. The rabbis' theological creativity operates mainly in their reshaping of the multitudinous ideas and images of biblical belief. In this process they continue the millennial Jewish experience of reinterpreting the covenant as times change and as their own intellectuality and religious sensitivity demand.

The primacy of continuity in rabbinic belief helps explain what modern readers often consider the rabbis' surprisingly modest response to the Temple's destruction. Though they were deeply traumatized, the rabbis did not see the loss of the Temple as a disaster requiring major theological reconstruction; rather, they found it a confirmation of the Bible's teaching. God had done what God had promised to do and had done once before (in 587/6 BCE). Sin eventually begets punishment, even to the destruction of God's Temple and the exile of God's people. But the punishment has a covenant purpose, to bring the people back to God's service. In due course, the rabbis believed, God would again restore the holy people and their Temple. Continuing the faith of the Bible as they understood it, the rabbis indomitably transcended profane history.

God. Monotheism anchors the rabbis' faith, just as it anchors the later biblical writings. The rabbis abominate idolatry and passionately oppose the notion that there are "two powers" in heaven. That does not prevent their speaking of God's heavenly retinue, the subordinates by whom God's governance of the universe usually proceeds. Similarly, they exhibit no inhibition about using metaphors to describe God. These may be abstract names, such as "the Place," "the Power," "the Holy," or images drawn from human life, such as references to God's phylacteries, or daily schedule, or emotions.

Another typical rabbinic dialectic moves between the utter greatness and the immediate availability of God. The ineffably glorious Sovereign of all universes attends and responds to a human whisper or fleeting meditation.

Rabbinic theology often pivots about God's justice and mercy. The declaration "There is no Judge and no justice" seems to be the rabbinic equivalent of atheism, but the rabbis give elaborate validations of the reliability of God's justice. They believe that the world could not survive if God were absolutely just: human fallibility and willfulness make such stringency impractical. For people freely to come to righteousness, God must also be merciful and compassionate. But if there were mercy without justice, this same rebellious humankind would never become responsible for its own actions. Undaunted by the paradoxes, the rabbis affirm that the one and only God is both just and merciful, demanding and forgiving, the ultimate idealist and realist in one.

Much of what other people might take to be evil the rabbis steadfastly consider the subtle working-out of God's justice. They do not deny that unmerited suffering occurs. Sometimes they explain this as "chastisements of love," torment given to the pious in this world so that rewards will await them in the afterlife. Sometimes they merely ascribe it to God's inexplicable will, God's "harsh decree." (Parallel reasons are offered by the rabbis for the gift of God's unmerited blessing—that is, it comes because of the "merit of the patriarchs," or simply because God loves or chooses to bless the recipient.) Less frequently, the rabbis will picture God, as it were, as somehow unable to prevent a tragedy or as lamenting its occurrence. With reason or without, they hold God to be the ultimate source of evil as well as good and so call for the recitation of a blessing upon hearing evil tidings. They devoutly trust God, whom they know they cannot hope to understand despite all their study and piety. [See Attributes of God, *article on* Jewish Concepts, *and* God, *article on* God in Postbiblical Judaism.]

Perhaps they evince such confidence because they have a strong, full belief in life after death. Several stages of the afterlife may be identified in rabbinic traditions. At death, the soul is taken from the body for preliminary judgment and purification and stays with God until the general bodily resurrection that will take place at the "end of days." Then the soul, rejoined to its purified body, receives judgment. The wicked are utterly destroyed, and the less culpable receive a limited term of expiatory punishment. Finally, the individual enters the "future to come," the blissful but indescribable reward God has promised the righteous. [See Soul, *article on* Jewish Concepts.]

Humankind and Human Destiny. The rabbis' conception of humankind stands behind their Jewish self-understanding. Human beings literally constitute a family since God created them from one pair of progenitors. And God made and maintains a covenant with all the descendants of Noah. Under it, God promised that there would be no more annihilatory floods and commanded all people to obey seven laws: six negative—not to blaspheme God, or worship idols, or steal, or murder, or commit sexual offenses, or eat the limb of a living animal—and one positive—to set up courts of justice.

Human nature being so torn between its evil and good urges, people regularly transgress these simple laws. So God brought a special nation into being, the Jews, to serve God devotedly by accepting a covenant of 613 commandments. In the rabbinic sociology of religion, people are either Jews, faithful servants of the only God, or part of "the nations," idolaters and therefore sinners. The Jews' experience of anti-Semitism reinforced this view and strengthened the Jewish commitment to separatism for God's sake.

The customary strife between the nations and the people of Israel will greatly intensify as the "end of days" nears. But God will send the Messiah, a human, Davidic king descended from King David, to lead God's people to victory. Once again, the rabbinic accounts grow hazy and irreconcilable. Some see the nations converting to Judaism; others see them accepting Jewish leadership. There is little elaboration of the biblical poems that prophesy a time of universal justice, peace, contentment, and lack of fear. However, the rabbis anticipate that at the final judgment the nations will be found guilty of wickedness and denied entry to the "future to come." Some rabbis mitigate this attitude by teaching that individuals who are "pious among the nations of the world have a share in the world to come."

Of course, any sinner might become righteous by repenting. The rabbis tell—occasionally with considerable envy—of a number of gentiles and Jews who by a heartfelt act of *teshuvah* immediately gained the life of the world to come.

Most of these matters became part of rabbinic law concerning non-Jews. Hence this doctrine, in general, may be said to be authoritative rabbinic teaching.

Rabbinic Theory of Torah. Radical theological creativity appears starkly in the rabbis' doctrine of the oral law. Unlike some of their other distinctive ideas, such as repentance, the Messiah, and resurrection, the notion of the oral law has no explicit biblical foundation. Since it undergirds all of rabbinic Judaism, it may be said to be the rabbis' most characteristic doctrine. To reiterate what has been said above, the rabbis taught that God gave Moses not only the first five books of the Bible (and, by implication, the rest of it) but also unrecorded verbal instructions, including specific duties and the methods for educing further oral law.

The rabbis also delimit the content of the written law in its broader sense of holy scripture, that is, the Hebrew scriptures. They apparently inherited fixed versions of the five books of the Torah and of the Prophets (including *Joshua, Judges, Samuel,* and *Kings*) and they determined what would be included in the Writings, admitting *Ecclesiastes,* for example, but rejecting *Ben Sira.* With these three divisions (Torah, Prophets, Writings; abbreviated in Hebrew as *Tanakh*) they closed the canon, for they believed that revelation ended with *Haggai, Zechariah,* and *Malachi* and that the books of the Writings had preceded these prophetical books. Though the rabbis occasionally hear a "heavenly echo" concerning matters under discussion, they may disregard it. Effectively, therefore, postbiblical Judaism derives from the rabbis' delimitation of the written law and their continuing explication of the oral law.

God excepted, no aspect of Jewish belief arouses the rabbis' awe as does Torah. They describe it as existing before creation, as God's guide to creation, and as God's most treasured possession, one so precious the angels tried to keep it from being taken to earth. The people of Israel, by virtue of having been given and having accepted the Torah, have become infinitely precious to God and central to human history. The rabbis acknowledge that wisdom may be found among the nations, but for them Torah contains God's fullest truth for humankind, making it the arbiter of all wisdom.

The rabbis do not detail the correct means or institutional structure for amplifying the oral law. Rather, the living practice of the master (*rabbi* means "my master") sets the model for his disciples. From time to time various institutions have emerged that temporarily exercised some general authority, but none lasted or created a form that later generations utilized. We have no way of gauging the extent to which Jews accepted the rabbis' leadership even in their own time. It seems paradoxical to seek control and integrity with such lack of structure and tolerance of diversity, but the arrangement has persisted to the present day.

With God's teaching available in verbal form, learning became a major Jewish religious activity. On a simple level, study motivated Jewish duty and specified its content. On a more advanced level, pondering God's instructions—even those of only theoretical relevance, like the rules for the Temple service—enabled one to have intellectual communion, as it were, with God. Gifted men sought to become rabbis, perhaps even to have their teachings cited by others, but always to set a living example for other Jews. Often reports of a master's deeds themselves became part of the oral law.

This heavy intellectual emphasis should not be divorced from its religious context. The intellectually keenest rabbis are also depicted as deeply pious, passionate in prayer, caring and virtuous in their dealings with people, intimately involved in the ordinary activities of life. Many also were mystics, though we have only hints about their esoteric spirituality.

The rabbinic doctrine of Torah brought fresh dynamism to Judaism. By authorizing new and open forms of authority and practice it enabled the Jewish people to keep the covenant vital, no matter what changes were brought by time and dispersion. With Judaism now centered on the individual and communal practice of Torah rather than on the Temple cult in Jerusalem, one could live as a faithful Jew anywhere. And as life created new problems, one only needed to find or become a learned Jew to determine what God wanted now, God's continuing command, and hence feel God's continuing care and concern. This oversimplifies a highly sophisticated process, but also conveys its providential gist. [*For further discussion, see* Torah.]

The Jews as God's Treasured People. The people of Israel uniquely serve the one God of the universe by living by God's teachings. Whatever superiority the people of Israel might claim over the gentiles derives from their faithfulness in living according to the covenant. Having the Torah does not exempt the Jews from God's demand for righteousness; if anything, because they have more commandments to fulfill they bear more responsibility before God. At the same time, God has a special love for the people of the covenant. When the people of Israel sin, God patiently waits for them to repent and helps them do so, sometimes by punishing them to remind them of their responsibilities.

The rabbis directly applied these beliefs to their situation, with the Temple destroyed and Jewish life in the Land of Israel degenerating. They lamented the calamities of their time: their inability to fulfill the commandments regarding God's cult and the material and spiritual distress brought on by dispersion and Roman rule. But their faith did not waver. They held that this people had been justly punished for its sins, though they often pictured God as pained at having had to execute so dire a sentence. To the rabbis, this new exile came because of the covenant and not as its negation; God had fulfilled what the covenant called for in response to egregious iniquity.

The Jews' political and social insignificance in the Roman empire did not negate their faith in their continuing spiritual uniqueness. Rather, the idolatry and immorality of the Romans proved them unworthy of Jewish admiration and God's esteem. To keep their service of God uncontaminated, the Jews set a distance between themselves and the nations. They also lived in the hope that their stubborn loyalty to God would one day be vindicated before all humankind. The eschatological savior described in the *Book of Daniel* had become an important figure in rabbinic Judaism, the King Messiah. One day—perhaps today—God would send him to restore the holy people to its land, defeat its enemies, reestablish its throne, rebuild its Temple and reconstitute its cult, institute a world order of justice and compassion, and usher in a time when all the promise of creation and the covenant would be fulfilled.

This was a human and historical expectation. As a consequence, some Jews would, from time to time, declare one or another figure of their day to be the anticipated Son of David, in the hope that the Jewish people had so lived up to its covenant responsibilities that God had sent the Messiah. Even if the folk did not merit him, it was understood that God would, in God's own time, send redemption. In either case, the rabbis could only fantasize as to what God would then do to transform and perfect creation. They imagined nature pacified and responsive, the nations admiring of the Torah or even converted to Judaism. Diverse as these conceptions were, all the rabbis agreed that this glorious time will be succeeded by the resurrection of the dead, the final judgment, and the climactic but indescribable "future to come."

The rabbis taught the people of Israel to remain confident of God's rule and favor and to await in history and beyond it God's sure deliverance and blessing—a faith that carried them through history until modern times. [*See also* Messianism, *article on* Jewish Messianism.]

From Talmudic to Modern Times

After the editing of the Talmud, countless variations of the rabbis' way appeared as Jews lived in diverse countries, cultures, social orders, and historical circumstances. Mostly they added observances; some of these became generally accepted, such as the holiday of Simḥat Torah (Joy of Torah), which became the ninth day of the festival of Sukkot, and the *yohrtsayt,* the later Ashkenazic practice of memorializing a close relative's day of death. A selective factor also operated, as in the abandonment of the triennial cycle of reading the Torah scroll during worship services in favor of an annual cycle. The range of this cultural creativity was greatly extended by the folk or ethnic nature of the Jews.

Two major cultural streams emerged. The Sefardic tradition (from the medieval Hebrew word *Sefarad* for the Iberian Peninsula) chiefly embraced the Jews of the Mediterranean Basin, many of whom were descended from families exiled from Spain in 1492, as well as those in Arab countries. The Ashkenazic tradition (from the medieval word *Ashkenaz* for northern France and Germany) encompassed the Jews of northern and eastern Europe, from whom most Jews in North America descend. Sefardic rabbis led Jewry throughout the Diaspora from the eleventh through the sixteenth century; meanwhile, the Ashkenazic sages created a halakhic scholarship that eventually brought them to the fore in Jewish life.

Each cultural style encompassed diverse national and local ways of living that changed over the centuries. Sefardic spokesmen have often taken pride in their community's urbanity, its respect for form and decorum, its devotion to liturgy, and its esteem of clear intellectuality. Similarly, Ashkenazic leaders have proudly noted their group's passionate energy, its fierce individuality, its dedication to study, and its love of Talmudic erudition.

DEVELOPING THE RABBINIC WAY

We know little about the actual practices of Jews for much of this period, though we know much about what rabbis said ought to be done. But the quasi-institutional means that evolved to control the development of Jewish life so evidences the spirit of Judaism that it deserves description. In their far-flung Diaspora, Jews recognized no institution or group as universally authoritative. Yet despite the slowness of communication, or lack of it, among the Jewish communities, and the immense diversity in local practice, the Jews remained and recognized one another as one covenant people.

Persecution intensified this sense of identity. With the rise of Islam early in the seventh century, Jews, living mostly in Islamic lands, became a group tolerated, but given second-class social and legal status. Among Christians, the occasional anti-Jewish outbreaks of the early centuries gave way after the First Crusade (1096 CE) to nearly seven centuries of harassment, including economic limitations, forced conversions, pogroms and riots, and communal expulsions, culminating about 1500 CE in the formal creation of the ghetto, the walled-in Jewish quarter of European cities. This pariah status strongly affected Jewish practices and attitudes and helped give rise to an elemental spiritual resistance founded on the certainty of possessing God's revelation and favor. The immediate contrast between their way of life and that of their oppressors empowered Jews to live and die steadfast in their faith. [*See* Anti-Semitism.]

Jewish communities vested authority in those whose learning and piety evoked it. Early on, the geonim, leaders of the Babylonian academies (*yeshivot*) that produced the Babylonian Talmud, began responding to questions addressed to them by distant Jews. This pattern of questions and answers, *she'elot u-teshuvot*, established itself as a way to get and give authoritative guidance. To this day, *teshuvot*, also known as *responsa*, remain the preeminent device for Jewish legal development. The power of a *teshuvah* derives entirely from the prestige and scholarship of its author. Many *teshuvot* became academic additions to the body of Jewish "case law." Others became widely authoritative, like one of Rav Amram, gaon of the *yeshivah* in Sura, Babylonia, from 856 to 874 CE. His lengthy answer to a question from Spanish Jews about liturgical practice established the prototype for Jewish prayer books.

The geonim and other sages sometimes wrote commentaries to portions of the Talmud or composed treatises on an aspect of the law. Eventually, the growing accretion of law led some teachers to compile codes. Each code became the subject of critical commentaries, some of which are printed alongside the code text in modern editions. The *Shulḥan 'arukh* of Yosef Karo (1488–1575), a Sefardic master, published in 1565 CE, became generally accepted among Ashkenazic Jews as well after Mosheh Isserles (c. 1525–1572) wrote glosses to it that reflected Ashkenazic practice. To this day, the *Shulḥan 'arukh* remains the authoritative code of Jewish law, though scholars continue to rework some of its sections. [*For a discussion of the development of Jewish law, see* Halakhah.]

Only one serious internal challenge to rabbinic Judaism emerged in the medieval period: the Karaite (biblicist) movement, which rejected the authority of the oral law and created a pattern of practice based on the Bible alone. Beginning in the eighth century CE in the Middle East, it reached the peak of its appeal and literary productivity in the eleventh and twelfth centuries. By then rabbinic authorities had declared Karaism heretical and prohibited intermarriage with Karaites. Some few thousand Karaites still exist, largely in the state of Israel. [*See* Karaites.]

In many other fields, as well as law, the range of Jewish study continually expanded. Biblical exegesis, homilies, poetry, mystical accounts, chronicles, polemics, explorations of piety, handbooks for good conduct, philosophy—every period produced its books and the students to ponder them. The invention of printing added further impetus to Jewish learning.

NEW IDEAS AND THEIR EFFECT ON PRACTICE

Four particularly significant, if not always distinguishable, intellectual currents moved through much of the Jewish world during the Middle Ages: pietism, mysticism, philosophy, and polemic. It will help to consider pietism, the most popular, first, though mysticism, an elitist enterprise, predates it.

Medieval Pietism. The Talmud and Midrash devote much attention to the virtues a Jew should manifest, but do so only in passing. About the eleventh century, a popular, specifically pietistic literature known as *musar* began to appear. Well into modern times, large numbers of Jews read and sought to live by the high spiritual standards its authors advocated.

The title of the early, exemplary *musar* book, *Duties of the Heart,* written in Arabic by Baḥye ibn Paquda in the late eleventh century, epitomizes the movement's aims. While the Talmud focused on the good Jew's acts, Baḥye stressed the inner life as the basis for action. He and other pietists called attention to the need for intimacy between the individual and God, stressing the humility of the one and the greatness of the other. Consciousness of this relationship, they said, should strongly motivate one to cultivate personal holiness, particularly through loving behavior to others—an emphasis so pronounced that the pietists' writings are often called "ethical" books. [*See* Jewish Thought and Philosophy, *article on* Jewish Ethical Literature.]

Two concerns of *musar* teachers gradually became common in most medieval Jewish writing. First, the pietists strongly contrast the purity of the soul with the grossness of the body. This duality, alluded to in both the Bible and the Talmud, became central and intense in *musar* piety. With corporeality the soul's antagonist, the pietists commend a measure of asceticism and social withdrawal. Yet they do not go so far as to become full-fledged dualists, for they believe that God created the body and ordained social life.

Second, the pietists express great anxiety about sinning and cultivate the fear of incurring guilt. How can anyone who is intensely aware of God's greatness not find the idea of defying God utterly reprehensible? One of the most common *musar* strategies for avoiding or surmounting temptation is to remember the punishment awaiting the wicked in the next world. The *musar* writers therefore urge heartfelt remorse and repentance for every sin, even suggesting compensatory atonements one might undertake. In no small measure, the conflict between the values of modern life and the values of premodern Judaism arose from disagreement over these matters.

Maturation of Jewish Mysticism. Whereas pietism reached out to ordinary Jews, mysticism limited itself to select individuals who were initiated into an esoteric doctrine by masters who often concealed as much as they revealed.

The Jewish mystical writings describe and exhibit phenomena that are associated with mysticism in many cultures: stringent spiritual discipline, bizarre language and exalted spiritual expression, techniques for gaining mystical experience, visions of the heavenly realm, physical images of God coupled with assertions of God's utter ineffability, longing for religious consummation and ways of hastening it—all these and more appear refracted in perplexing and fascinating fashion through sensitive temperaments affected by highly diverse situations.

The main tradition of Jewish mysticism is known as Qabbalah. Developed in response to God's revelation of a holy way of life, it has a highly cognitive content that is concerned with cosmogony and theosophy. Its most significant document, the *Zohar* (Book of Splendor), written primarily in Aramaic in late thirteenth-century Spain, is a commentary on the Torah that elaborates a mystical doctrine of God's complex nature. Ultimately, God is Ein Sof, "without limit," hence the one about whom nothing at all can be said. Yet God is also intimately known, contemplated, and related to through interacting loci of divine energy, the *sefirot* (lit., "spheres" or "numbers"; in qabbalistic terminology, emanations from God's inner being). The mystics speak of the *sefirot* with a freedom of metaphor that is almost limitless, not even excluding sexual anthropomorphisms. Feminine metaphors for God, rare in the Bible and occasional in the Talmud, now come into full use alongside masculine metaphors in explications of God's nature.

The Jewish mystics, for all the immediacy of their relationship with God, believe that Torah—the written and oral law—remains primary to Judaism. They therefore eschew antinomianism—the idea that faith, not law, is sufficient—and cultivate meticulous observance. By ascribing supernal significance to commandments and customs that reason cannot explain, they easily provide absolute justification for them.

Two late developments in Jewish mysticism have had continuing repercussions. The first was the qabbalistic thought of Isaac Luria (1534–1572). According to his cosmogonic explanation of evil, creation began with an act of divine self-contraction that produced an outflow of generative light. God projected this light into the vessels, or material forms, that had been prepared for it. These vessels proved too fragile and shattered, leaving unsanctified shards or husks that contain only sparks of God's creative, transformative light. By observing God's commandments, people can free the heavenly sparks from their husks and mend the broken vessels, thus restoring the world and rescuing it from evil. God appears passive in this process, as it is human action that brings the Messiah—a striking anticipation of modern liberalism. [*See also* Qabbalah *and the biography of Isaac Luria.*]

In the eighteenth century, in southern Poland and the Ukraine, the Hasidic movement transformed qabbalistic tradition through a radical appropriation of God's accessibility (prompting charges by their opponents that the Hasidim were pantheists). To the Hasidim, God's nearness implied that life should be lived with joy and enthusiasm. For cleaving to God, one need not be a spiritual virtuoso but only give God one's heart. This attitude encouraged new practices and fervent observance, though its opponents claimed that its emphasis on spontaneity and inner experience led to laxity in ritual.

Hasidism became a mass movement that carried a dialectical tension. On the one hand, the humblest person could live the mystical life. The Hasidic leaders encouraged this egalitarianism by putting many of their teachings in exoteric form, as tales, stories, and popular preaching, and by promoting a close community life. On the other hand, Hasidism established a religious elite. Each community was led by a *tsaddiq,* or *rebe.* The *tsaddiqim* represent Hasidism's esoteric side, privately practicing an exalted mysticism and serving as the intermediary between their followers and heaven. Their followers believed that the *tsaddiqim* could work wonders and thus beseeched their intercession on every personal problem. Since each community thought its own *tsaddiq* the most powerful, some Hasidic communities isolated themselves even from other Hasidim.

Later, Hasidism became institutionalized around dynasties and antagonistic to modernity. The groups that managed to survive the Holocaust have had a resurgence in the state of Israel and the United States. They have gained recruits from Jews who, disillusioned with secular culture, seek out the intensity of immersion in a separatist Jewish esoteric community.

The Encounter with Philosophy. The Talmud knows nothing of Philo Judaeus of Alexandria (fl. first century CE) or any other Hellenistic Jewish philosopher. Certain that they possessed God's revelation, the rabbis spurned formal Greek philosophy, which they associated with idolatry. In the ninth century CE, Jews encountered Muslim philosophy, which claimed that it taught the purest monotheism because its doctrine of God had been refined through rational argument. For the next seven centuries—that is, as long as cultural involvement with the Muslims persisted—a tiny Jewish intellectual aristocracy created Jewish philosophy. Their work had little direct impact on Jewish life, though some of their ideas—for example, Moses Maimonides' excoriation of anthropomorphism—became widely influential.

The early philosophical thinkers, such as Sa'adyah Gaon (882–942), adduced proofs for God's creation of the world, from which they deduced God's unity and sovereign power. On this basis they sought to give rational justification to such problems as miracles, providence, evil, and why Judaism was the true revelation. The rational defense of certain inexplicable commands of the Torah evoked considerable philosophic ingenuity.

In the course of time, most medieval Jewish philosophical thought came to employ Aristotelian categories. The occasional Neoplatonic voice found little philosophic resonance, though the mystics found the Neoplatonic concept of emanation congenial to their notion of levels of being. Sometimes, as in the case of Yehudah ha-Levi (c. 1075–1141), a thinker became critical of philosophy and subordinated reason to revelation, rather than making it an equal or senior partner.

Modern thought rejects the medieval concept of causality, and the philosophy based on it remains of interest mainly to academic specialists. However, the contemporary clash between reason and faith seems prefigured in the writings of Moses Maimonides (Mosheh ben Maimon, 1135/8–1204), the preeminent Jewish philosopher. The author of the first great code of Jewish law, the *Mishneh Torah* (lit., "Second Torah"), he gained incomparable stature among Jews. He faced an intellectual crisis: the resolution of the Torah's teachings with the views of Aristotle, who had denied the idea of creation and affirmed the eternity of the universe. Maimonides refused to repudiate the demands either of reason or of faith, and his masterful effort to harmonize Judaism with a scientific view of reality became the model for all later rationalist validations of religious faith. But when, at the end of the fifteenth century, the Jews were expelled from Spain and Portugal, where philosophy was an important part of the culture, this fruitful intellectual enterprise came largely to an end.

The intellectual defense of Judaism took a more popular form in the polemics against Christianity that circulated from the twelfth century on. The Talmud contains remnants of earlier polemics, but not until major Jewish centers suffered under Christian religious oppression did Jewish books criticizing Christianity appear. (Fewer polemical works were directed against Islam, whose treatment of Jews as inferiors was based on sociopolitical stratification rather than harassment and was often mitigated by pragmatic considerations. Relatively quiescent relations existed between Muslims and Jews after the early centuries of Muslim conquest.)

Jewish teachers could elaborate their faith without reference to Christianity or Islam, though the Bible and Talmud are replete with attacks on idolatry. Besides, the Christian claim that Jesus of Nazareth was the Messiah seemed, to the Jews, self-refuting, as the world remained radically unredeemed. But as the church increasingly attacked Jewish belief, Jewish leaders found it necessary to refute the church's claims and invalidate its doctrines.

Jewish polemics sought to demonstrate Christian misinterpretation of biblical texts by citing the original Hebrew texts and the traditional Jewish understanding of them. Christian converts from Judaism countered these arguments by citing Talmudic and Midrashic passages that were alleged to prove Jesus' messiahship. The Jewish disputants attacked the credibility of the conflicting gospel accounts of Jesus' life and the evangelists' ignorance of Talmudic law (which they assumed to have been operative in Jesus' time). They also caustically exposed the irrationality of such Christian doctrines as the virgin birth, the incarnation, and the Eucharist. By contrast, they contended, Judaism was a religion a rational man could accept. It was a theme that Jews would continue to find persuasive into modern times. [For further discussion, see Polemics, articles on Muslim-Jewish Polemics and Jewish-Christian Polemics.]

Modernity: Opportunity and Peril

Emancipation, the fitful process by which the segregation and oppression of European Jewry was encouraged to end, began in earnest with the French Revolution. Gradually, as nationality was severed from membership in an official Christian faith, Jews and other minority denominations received equal political rights and social opportunity. As a result, most modern Jews, despite their religious heritage, have avidly supported keeping government and civil society neutral with regard to religion. Because their politics and religion are closely intermixed, the Islamic nations that granted Jews complete equality were among the last states to do so.

After some fifteen hundred years of degradation and centuries of grinding oppression, most European Jews enthusiastically welcomed equality. To those raised in the ghettoes or in the shtetls (Yi., "villages") of eastern Europe, every new freedom, no matter how hedged by limitations or by secularized forms of anti-Semitism, came as a near fulfillment of messianic hopes. A politicized, humanistic hope now became the dominant tone of Jewish existence.

But the price of equality was conformity to the larger culture. European society did not allow for much cultural diversity, and although the accepted social conventions were ostensibly secular, they often reflected their Christian origins.

As emancipation proceeded, the consequences for rabbinic Judaism were devastating. One group of Jews rejected modernization altogether, another group rejected the major doctrines of Judaism. Most Jews found these reactions too extreme, preferring a middle way.

A small minority of traditionalists, rather than surrender anything that they felt God asked of them, spurned modernization. Many pious eastern European Jews long refused to immigrate to America with the hundreds of thousands of Jews who began to do so in the last decades of the nineteenth century. This produced a social situation unique in Jewish history. Elsewhere, long established Orthodox institutions formed the basis of community life. The non-Orthodox movements that arose with the coming of modernity were reactions to them. In the United States, non-Orthodox institutions became well established in the late nineteenth and early twentieth centuries, and only after World War I did Orthodox institutions slowly come to prominence.

Most Jews rejected this strategy of separatism for pragmatic and intuitive reasons. Practically, emancipation offered Jews a dignity they had known only sporadically for two thousand years. Hence their embrace of modernity can be understood as an existentially transformed way of keeping the covenant, arising from the intuition that Western civilization, as evidenced by its movement toward liberation, contained a considerable measure of the universal truth of Judaism.

Some Jews carried this appreciation to the point of urging Jews to assimilate fully and allow their "parochial" faith to die so that they might participate in humankind's emerging universal culture. Again, most Jews demurred. Given their passion for modernity, their insistence on also remaining Jewish has been difficult to explain, especially since no single philosophy of modern Jewish living has ever become widely accepted. Anti-Semitism has kept some Jews Jewish—yet its continuing virulence seems more a reason to defect than to stay. Moreover, even in the absence of overt hatred of Jews, many Jews have refused to assimilate. Modernist believers see this as an act of persistent loyalty to the covenant: Jews remain personally faithful to their ancient pact even if uncertain about how to live it, while God, in some inexplicable but familiar way, does not let them go.

Postemancipation Jewry has chosen to be both modern and Jewish, thus fixing its continuing agenda: first, establishing a less separatistic, more adaptive way of living; and second, validating the authenticity of that way in Jewish and modern terms.

SUNDERING THE UNITY OF THE WAY

Modernity made religion a private affair and defined religious groups in terms derived from Christianity—that is, as communities united by common faith and ritual practice. Nationality was dissociated from religion and subordinated to the nation-state, an arrangement that can still cause social unrest in multinational countries. On both counts, Judaism could not maintain itself as a religio-ethnic entity (the hybrid designation modernity has forced upon students of Judaism). As a result, an unprecedented dichotomy came into Jewish life: one group of Jews defined their Judaism as "religious," while another group defined theirs in secular terms, as an ethnicity.

Religious Ways of Liberal Jews. Faced with the unacceptable options of either staying Jewish but in an isolated manner—as though still within ghetto walls—or joining modern society by converting to Christianity, some early nineteenth-century German Jewish laymen began experimenting with a Judaism adapted to European modes of religiosity. In that spirit, they reformed synagogue worship. Essentially, they adorned it with a new aesthetic, eliminating liturgical repetitions and poetic embellishments and introducing solemn group decorum, vernacular prayers, sermons, and contemporary musical styles (including the use of a pipe organ and female as well as male singers). They also abolished the halakhic requirement of the separation of the sexes at services, allowing families to sit together in worship. [*For* *an overview of the traditional mode, see* Worship and Cultic Life, *article on* Jewish Worship.]

This early version of Reform Judaism paved the way for subsequent non-Orthodox Jewish movements. The early reformers justified their form of Judaism with the notion, derived from contemporary German culture, that eternal essences take on transient forms. The essence of Judaism, in their view, is ethical monotheism, which its rituals and customs serve to transmit and strengthen. When times change and old forms no longer function well, they should be altered or abandoned and new forms created.

Most modern Jews have accepted moral duty as the core of Jewish obligation. Many believe that the Jewish people have a mission to teach humankind the religious primacy of universal ethics. In any case, modern Jews often reduce the teachings of the Torah to ethics and, though allowing much else in rabbinic Judaism to atrophy, devote themselves to the moral transformation of society. This universalized sense of covenant responsibility accounts for the astonishing record of modern Jewish contributions to the improvement of human welfare.

In the latter part of the nineteenth century, a new movement emerged: Conservative Judaism. Many eastern European immigrants to America found that their sense of Jewish modernity was not satisfied by the adaptive tone and the essentially ethical content of Reform Judaism, which had been brought over by earlier immigrants from Germany. While seeking to be modern, these Russian and Polish Jews also wanted to preserve a considerable measure of particular Jewish practice. Devotion to the Jewish people as the dynamic creator of Jewish law was their counterpoise to the Reform concentration on ethics. Over the decades, smaller movements have also arisen, positioning themselves essentially in relation to these central communal groups. The most significant of these is Reconstructionism, a movement which derives from the theory of Mordecai Kaplan (1881–1983) that the Jewish community, acting in democratic fashion, ought to be authoritative with regard to Jewish practice.

By the 1970s, the denominational lines had become blurred. Most American Jews, regardless of affiliation, now follow one of several patterns of liberal Jewish living. These vary in their loyalty to classic observance and spirituality, but show considerable similarity in the cultural activities they integrate into their Judaism—especially participation in higher education, civic affairs, and the arts, music, and literature. But the interplay between Judaism and modernity can best be illustrated by the devotion of Jews to interpersonal relationships. American Jews today express the longstanding rabbinic commitment to family and community by their disproportionate involvement in the helping professions (such as teaching, social work, and psychotherapy) and their intense concern for family relationships. In these areas they demonstrate a dedication lacking in their observance of the halakhic dietary laws and laws governing sexual relations between spouses. They seem to believe that sanctifying life, their covenant goal, now requires giving these general human activities priority in Jewish duty.

Despite this heavy cultural borrowing, American Jews manifest a significant measure of particular Jewish action. Even at the humanist end of the religious spectrum, the concern with ethics and other universal issues is reinforced by an attachment to the Jewish folk. Such Jews invest energy and self in Jewish charity, organized defense against anti-Semitism, support of the state of Israel, and occasional ritual acts, most notably those associated with life-cycle events, High Holy Day services, and the home

Seder, the Passover meal. In this group one sees clearly a problem that continues to bedevil all liberal Jews: the freedom not to be Orthodox is often taken as a license to do and care little about Judaism altogether.

At the other end of the liberal religious spectrum stands a small minority of Jews whose lives are substantially guided by Jewish tradition, interpreted through a modern ethical and cultural sensibility. They exhibit the rabbinic devotion to self, family, people, and God, seeking to live by rabbinic law wherever they can. They constitute the spiritual heart of non-Orthodox Judaism, whose viability depends upon its acceptance of their leadership in combining modernity and tradition.

The outstanding achievements of liberal Judaism derive from its pursuit of a mediating spirituality. It has radically enlarged the horizon of Jewish duty by its dedication to ethics and democracy. It has revolutionized the study of Judaism by its insistence upon the adoption of modern scholarly methods. Above all, it has convinced most of the Jewish community that modernity and Judaism can successfully be integrated. What many in a prior generation passionately feared and fought, most Jews now consider of great benefit to Judaism.

Nothing so well illustrates the continuing promise and problem of liberal Judaism as its response to feminism. Early in the nineteenth century, the German reformers recognized an ethical imperative to break with the Jewish laws and customs that discriminate against women. But it took more than a century for Reform congregations to elect women officers and until 1972 for the first American woman to be ordained a rabbi; women cantors followed quickly. Since then, the Reconstructionist and Conservative movements have accepted both innovations.

Much of the community has welcomed this development, but it is not clear how far it will tolerate alteration of the old patterns—for example, removing the sexist language of the prayer book, or allowing the genuine sharing of power between men and women. If liberal Jewish daring in this matter eventually becomes part of the accepted covenant way, then its experimentation will again have taught Jews a new way of sanctifying Jewish existence. Orthodox critics rejoin that in breaking with the traditional rabbinic understanding of the Torah which defines separate roles for the sexes, the liberals are more likely to dilute Judaism than to win its future.

Religious Ways of Orthodox Jews. As a self-conscious movement, Jewish Orthodoxy arose in response to liberal Judaism with the purpose of correctly delineating Jewish authenticity. Traditional Judaism knows only one standard of faithfulness to God: loyalty to God's law as expounded in the Torah, especially the oral law in its continuing development by contemporary sages. The Torah has absolute primacy. Modernity can come into Judaism only as the Torah allows. Hence the lives of believing Orthodox Jews display religious continuity more than religious change. Variations in observance among Orthodox Jews derive from local custom, from the differences between Ashkenazim and Sefardim, Hasidim and other Orthodox Jews, and from the variety of opinion passed down by various sages.

The major forms of Orthodoxy can be distinguished by the degree to which they are open to modernity. They stand united, however, in defense of the Torah against what they consider the faithlessness of most other Jews. Even innovations permissible under Jewish law are often resisted lest they give credence to other Jews' radical departures from tradition.

Orthodox attitudes toward the acceptance of modernity range from antagonistic to embracing. The Hasidic sects visibly project their hostility to modernity and their distance from the gentile world (and other Jews) by their distinctive dress, hair, and body language. Several Orthodox groups also seek to reconstitute the cultural isolation of eastern European Jewry, but in less separatistic ways—a goal more easily accomplished in the state of Israel than elsewhere. The continued use of Yiddish, the Judeo-German vernacular of eastern European Jewry, characterizes this entire wing of Orthodoxy. Its antagonism to modernity does not prevent the pious from utilizing technological advances that enhance observance of the commandments or from having contacts with gentiles when necessary, as in commerce. Some groups have marginal affiliates who live in more modern fashion but maintain their ties to the group by keeping some of its special customs, visiting its communities, and giving financial support.

Another wing, known as Modern Orthodoxy, contends that Jewish law allows, and many sages exemplify, the virtue of embracing any cultural good that enhances human existence as the Torah delineates it. The Modern Orthodox have been most innovative in creating two new instruments for Jewish education, the Jewish university and day school, which feature the sciences and sports, both once considered un-Jewish. They generally speak the vernacular (English in America, Hebrew in Israel), not Yiddish, and their only distinguishing visual sign is the small, often knitted skullcap (Yi., *yarmulke;* Heb., *kippah*) worn by males. But their disciplined loyalty to the Torah appears in such matters as prayer, diet, study, and Sabbath and festival observance.

Orthodoxy has enjoyed a significant resurgence as the twentieth century moves toward its end. Some Jews have lost their once great confidence in Western civilization and have withdrawn from it somewhat by adopting a more distinctive practice of Judaism. A minority have joined the separatistic Jewish sects. Most Orthodox Jews have rejected self-ghettoization, choosing to live a dedicated Jewish life as part of an observant community so as to differentiate themselves from an ofttimes pagan society. Their approach to living the life of Torah has nonetheless carried a modern overlay their Orthodox great-grandparents would probably have opposed; even so, the movement to greater Jewish authenticity has debilitated Modern Orthodoxy's innovative zeal.

The large number of Jews who are only nominally Orthodox testifies to the continuing influence of modernity. Despite their affiliation, these Jews are only sporadically observant and their faith fluctuates or is inconsistent. They often consider their private preferences in Jewish law to be genuine Judaism, a heresy in the eyes of Orthodox sages.

Orthodoxy has notable accomplishments to its credit. Despite dire predictions of its death from the effects of modernity, it has created a cadre of Jews whose personal piety and communal life demonstrate the continuing religious power of rabbinic Judaism. It has kept alive and advanced eastern European Jewry's exalted standards of the study of Jewish law. Particularly in the field of bioethics, but in other areas as well, it has shown the continuing vitality of the oral law.

As with liberal Judaism, the issue of feminism best clarifies the continuing promise and problems of Orthodox Judaism. In refusing to grant women substantial legal equality, contemporary sages have defended the integrity of God's law as they received and understand it. Considering how modernity has shattered family life, they do not deem it to possess a wisdom superior to that of Torah. Rather, every genuine faith demands some sacrifice, and Judaism, abandoned by so many and in such worldwide peril, deserves the obedient dedication of all who wish it to remain true to itself and God.

Many Orthodox authorities have long acknowledged that some laws regarding women create suffering—for example, the woman who, because she cannot meet certain technical criteria, is barred from receiving a Jewish divorce. Liberal Jews perceive the inability of contemporary Orthodox sages to institute legal remedies for this situation as a telling indication that, good will notwithstanding, the laws' inequities are still operative. Feminists cannot believe that, with most Orthodox Jews committed to the general self-fulfillment of women, Orthodox women will long be content with sex-segregated duties and roles. However, Orthodox Judaism has shown no significant loss of membership from its defense of classic Judaism in this matter.

Culture as "Torah" of Secular Jews. In late nineteenth-century Europe and mid-twentieth-century America, as Jews became university educated and urban dwelling, they secularized. They believed that modernization meant the acceptance of the idea that there is no God and the end of practices that differentiated Jews from their neighbors. Yet, as they became thoroughly secularized, they generally did not do so to the point of assimilation. Large numbers retained a connection with the Jewish people, if only by discovering that many of the humanitarians they enjoyed associating with were also secularized Jews. Two interrelated major patterns of secular Jewish living arose from this process, one cultural, the other political.

The early foes of emancipation argued that the Jews could not modernize because they had no capacity for high culture. Liberal Jews sought to refute them by aestheticizing Jewish worship. Secular Jews did the same by devoting their lives to literature and the arts, often achieving uncommon success in these areas. Existentially, secular Jews made high culture their "Torah," bringing to it the intense dedication they had once given to faith, for it now validated their existence.

To keep the Jewish people alive, some European Jewish secularists suggested that Jews participate in universal culture through the development of a secular Jewish literature, initially in Hebrew, but later in Yiddish as well. This movement toward Haskalah (Enlightenment) revived the Hebrew language, which had long been used only for traditional scholarship and religious purposes. The long-range hopes of the leaders of Haskalah did not survive the realities of anti-Semitism, acculturation, and migration. Only in the state of Israel, where Jews have created a national culture, has the Hebrew language successfully been used as a means for the modernization of Jewish life. In the Diaspora, few Jews now maintain their Jewishness by utilizing Hebrew or Yiddish to pursue humanism. Yet Diaspora Jews and those of the state of Israel commonly consider a positive attitude to culture an integral part of their Jewishness.

Jewish secularity also directed itself to ethical politics, that is, redeeming the world through the achievement of social justice. Jews became advocates of the rights of labor and the virtues of socialism, seeing in the struggles for civil rights and civil liberties their own cause as it affected other minorities. Prayer and piety no longer seemed effective responses to social injustice. Being politically informed and involved therefore became for Jews the modern equivalent of a commandment.

This movement's effects have been felt both in general society and in the Jewish community. Jewish politicians and Jewish activists have been a significant influence in humanizing modern society. Simultaneously, the notion of pluralistic democracy has reshaped Jewish life in America. The American Jewish community now operates on a fully voluntary basis and features a broad inclusiveness, diverse organizations, and a dynamism undaunted by emergency or changing times. It has raised more money for Jewish charity than any other voluntary philanthropic effort in history. In the midst of secularization, the lineaments of the covenant appear.

NATIONALISM: ZIONISM AND THE STATE OF ISRAEL

The cultural and political drives in Jewish secularization climaxed in Zionism, the movement that reinterpreted Judaism as Jewish nationalism. Organized on a world-wide basis by Theodor Herzl (1860–1904) in 1897, the Zionists began a crusade to liberate Jews on two levels. First, they sought freedom from persecution by acquiring a land where the Jewish masses might find economic opportunity and political security. Second, they wanted to create a genuinely Jewish culture that would express, in an untrammeled way, the Jewish people's spirit.

Many liberal and Orthodox Jews initially opposed Zionism for religious reasons. The former found its secularism Jewishly aberrant and its nationalism a threat to Jewish emancipation in the Diaspora. The latter objected to its notion of a Jewish state independent of the Torah and found its nationalistic activism a usurpation of God's role in bringing the Messiah. Vestiges of these anti-Zionist attitudes still exist, but most religious Jews now ardently support the state of Israel.

Before the founding of the state of Israel in 1948, Zionism generated a new form of Jewish living in the Diaspora, one built on political activity, immigration and the preparation for it, and participation in the renewal of Hebrew culture. The barbarity of Nazi Germany and the callousness of the rest of the world toward the Jews in the 1930s and 1940s gave Zionism an additional concern: acquiring one place in the world to which Jews could immigrate without restriction.

With the birth and growth of Israel, Jews could return to a way of living they had not known for nearly two millennia: as a Jewish community living on the Jewish homeland in Jewish self-determination. Israel is a secular state—though Orthodox Judaism retains special rights in it—and its ethos is democratic and welfare-oriented. Its extraordinary effort, amid the most trying political circumstances, to hold itself to ethical standards higher than those pursued by most other nations has won it the admiration and identification of world Jewry. Nothing in postemancipation Jewish life has remotely approached its ability to arouse Jewish devotion and action.

Israeli Jews, the great majority of whom consider themselves nonreligious (that is, non-Orthodox), live by the rhythm of the Jewish calendar and draw their ideals from the Bible, the great national saga. Their everyday language is Hebrew and their culture increasingly reflects the concerns of individuals and a society facing the awesome dilemmas of modern existence. In every human dimension, Jews living in the state of Israel are, even without thinking about it, living Jewishly. And for those who carry on Orthodox Judaism or the tiny minority who are Reform or Conservative Jews, the reconstituted Jewish society provides an incomparable context for religious existence.

Outside the state of Israel, Zionism as a total way of life has virtually disappeared. Most Diaspora Jews do not carry on a Jewish cultural life in Hebrew or plan to immigrate to Israel. They may be deeply emotionally attached to Israel, but it does not provide the essential content of their Jewish lives. Zionism has had an incomparable triumph in the high human and Jewish accomplishment of the state of Israel. Yet Zionism's thorough secularization of the covenant has apparently rendered it incapable of guiding Diaspora Jewish life. [*For further discussion, see* Zionism.]

PHILOSOPHIC GROUNDS OF MODERN JEWISH LIFE

Judaism makes its claims upon the Jew in the name of God and the Jewish people's corporate experience—but modernity radically individualizes authority. A modern philosophy of Judaism must mediate between autonomy and tradition and do justice to each of them.

Contemporary Orthodoxy does not wait for each individual to make a decision about what constitutes Jewish duty. Orthodoxy begins with faith and has felt no pressing need for theoretical expositions of its beliefs. It has therefore largely left to liberal Jews the task of constructing systematic Jewish theologies. Five distinctive intellectual statements have gained continuing attention—six, if Zionist ideology can be considered an equivalent system.

Two Rationalist Interpretations. Rationalism had an irresistible appeal to nineteenth-century Jewish modernizers. It compellingly distinguished between the lastingly valuable essence of Judaism, ethical monotheism, and its transient historical expression in ceremony and ritual. This early liberal criterion of continuity and change first attained sophisticated statement in the work of Hermann Cohen (1842–1918), the famed Marburg Neo-Kantian philosopher.

In rigorous academic works, Cohen delineated the religion a rational person could accept. Cohen sought to demonstrate that rationality requires a philosophical idea of God to integrate its disparate scientific, ethical, and aesthetic modes of thinking. His system was dominated by ethics and he argued that this ethical monotheism appeared for the first time in history in the work of the biblical prophets. As the earliest and purest proponent of ethical monotheism, the Jewish people had a mission to humankind: to teach the universal truth of rational religion. Messianism could no longer be the miraculous advent of God's regent, but became humankind's task of ethically perfecting itself. (This view led Cohen to oppose Zionism as a constriction of the Jewish ethical horizon.) All customs that strengthened Jewish ethical sensitivity or kept Jews faithful to their mission ought to be maintained; those that thwarted them ought to be abandoned. In greatly diluted fashion, Cohen's ethical reworking of Judaism became the accepted ideology of modern Jews. [*See also the biography of Cohen.*]

Leo Baeck (1873–1956), the German thinker who remained closest to Cohen's Judaism of reason, felt the need to supplement reason with the experience of mystery, even though that meant sacrificing Cohen's logical rigor. Baeck pointed to religious consciousness as the deepest foundation of ethical monotheism. He evocatively described the sense human beings have of being creations yet also ethical creators, of being utterly transient yet linked in spirit with that which is eternal.

However, Baeck's rationalism remained sovereign. Fearing the dangers of romanticism, he insisted that religious consciousness should lead to action only as ethics permitted. Thus, while authorizing some nonrational commandments, he ruled out anything that smacked of superstition and bigotry. He also conducted a vigorous polemic against Christianity and Buddhism, finding both of them deficient in their ethics and monotheism. He so closely identified Judaism with a universal rational faith that he alone among modern Jewish thinkers urged Jews to seek converts.

Baeck called for a broad horizon of Jewish obligation. He believed the Jewish people to be so historically identified with the idea of ethical monotheism that should Judaism die, ethical monotheism would also die. The Jewish people, therefore, must survive. To keep it alive, the Jewish people continually create group practices that strengthen and protect the people from the perils it encounters in history. [See also the biography of Baeck.]

Rational Validations for the Primacy of Peoplehood. Zionist ideologists proclaimed the Jews a nation, not a religion, and looked forward to a renewal of Judaism as the communal life of the Jewish folk resettled on its ancient soil. They demythologized the biblical interpretation of exile—which Jewish mystics had applied metaphorically even to God—and made it a purely sociopolitical concept. Redemption would not come by a Messiah but with geographic relocation, cultural self-expression, and political reconstitution.

One early Zionist debate still roils the community: is modern Jewish nationalism rigorously secular, and thus free of religious and ethnic values, or is it distinctively Jewish? No one raised this issue more penetratingly than the essayist Ahad ha-ʿAm ("one of the people," pseudonym of Asher Ginzberg, 1856–1927).

Ahad ha-ʿAm's Zionism drew on the nineteenth-century concepts of folk psychology and cultural nationalism to assert that Jews, like other peoples, had a folk "character" to which they needed to be true. The Jewish national soul exhibited a talent for ethics and high culture with a devotion to absolute justice as the central theme of great literature and other arts, as the Bible indicates. Jewish nationalism, therefore, had to work for the re-creation of an ethically and aesthetically elevated Jewish culture. A renascent Jewish state could serve as its worldwide spiritual center, and Diaspora Jewish communities would survive spiritually by participating in its cultural life.

Most Zionist ideologists simply assumed that Zionism mandated humanistic values and rarely sought to explicate them. Besides, crises in Jewish life followed so hard upon one another in the twentieth century that arguing such abstractions seemed frivolous. But various events in the life of the state of Israel have kept the issue alive. Its very persistence testifies to its unusual combination of secularity and religiosity. The Israeli courts, in rulings on the legal definition of Jewishness and other issues, have refused to sever the connection between Jewish nationalism and Jewish religion. Some thinkers therefore insist that, for all its putative secularity, the state of Israel can best be understood as an eccentric development of classic Jewish ethnic religiosity.

An American thinker, Mordecai M. Kaplan (1881–1983), created another distinctive Jewish rationalism in terms of philosophic naturalism. Basing his thinking on ideas derived from the recently developed science of sociology, Kaplan held that for Jewish life today to be meaningful, it must reflect the scientific worldview and democratic commitment of modernity. Kaplan therefore carried on a vigorous polemic against supernaturalism in Judaism. He inverted the central idea of traditional Judaism: that God gave the Torah to the Jewish people (thus giving it its distinctive character). Kaplan now claimed, arguing from the perspective of sociology, that the Jewish people had created Judaism, which he defined as an ethnic civilization, based on a land, a language, a history, a calendar, heroes, institutions, arts, values, and much else, with religion at its core. Through its concept of God, Jewish civilization expressed its highest values. The Jewish people's health could be restored only by fully reconstructing its folk life; hence Kaplan called his movement Reconstructionism. The involvement of American Jews in Jewish art, music, and other cultural forms owes much to Kaplan. Kaplan also called for the Jewish community to reorganize itself institutionally so that the community, not a given religious movement or synagogue, would be the focus of Jewish affiliation. Though pluralistic, it could then democratically seek to legislate for its members and meet the full range of religious, political, cultural, and social needs of a healthy ethnic group. But no Jewish community has yet so reconstituted itself.

Kaplan proposed a daring definition of God as the power (or process) that makes for "salvation," by which he meant "human fulfillment." Speaking of God in impersonal, naturalistic terms indicates the purely symbolic status of folk anthropomorphisms and the modern rejection of miracles, verbal revelation, and the idea of the chosen people. Equally important, defining God in finite terms—as that aspect of nature that abets human self-development—solves the theological problem of evil. Kaplan's God does not bring evil, only good. We can now maturely see evil as caused by nature and take it as a challenge to our moral creativity.

Kaplan's bold recasting of Judaism won him a small but enthusiastic following. However, his equation of modernity with scientific rationality lost its appeal in the Jewish community as the interest in nonrationalist Jewish thinkers heightened. [*See also the biography of Kaplan.*]

Nonrationalist Jewish Thinkers. After World War I, Franz Rosenzweig (1886–1929), the youthful German author of a magisterial work on Hegel, pioneered Jewish existentialism with his effort to situate Judaism in selfhood rather than in acts or ideas. Rosenzweig connected being Jewish with acting Jewishly—that is, observing the law insofar as one was existentially able to acknowledge it as possessing the quality of commandment. He thus specified, but never fully clarified, a greatly appealing balance between duty and freedom, bequeathing to later liberal Jewish thought one of its central issues.

Martin Buber (1878–1965), an older contemporary and sometime collaborator of Rosenzweig's, created a more extensive system. He suggested that human existence is dynamically relational, occurring either in an objectifying mode he called I–It, or a value-conferring mode of personal openness and mutuality he called I–Thou, which he carefully differentiated from romanticism and mysticism. Romanticism involves an I–It of emotion or experience; mysticism, a loss of self in the One. Buber had in mind something as subtle yet much more common.

Like all significant personal involvements, an I–Thou relationship with God (the "Eternal Thou") evokes responsive action—it "commands." Transgression of such duty involves guilt and the need to atone. All this has a corporate dimension, for whenever two persons truly meet, God is present as well. Consequently, the I–Thou experience directs us to create true human community, a society of Thou's.

Religions arise when relationships with God take on social forms. In time, this process of institutionalization, instead of expediting living contact with God, obstructs it. Institutionalized faiths may designate one sphere of life as holy, leaving the rest to be profane. But the I–Thou relationship knows no limits, and all life should be lived on its terms. Hence Buber opposed all "religion."

According to Buber, the Hebrew Bible recounts the I–Thou experiences of the Jewish people with God, which, over centuries, created an indissoluble relationship between them—the covenant. No other ethnic group has ever so identified its corporate existence with loyalty to God. Because of its covenant, the Jewish folk undertook the messianic task of creating community among its members and thus, eventually, among humankind. While Jews sometimes lost sight of this task, it could never be completely lost, as indicated by early Hasidism and by Zionism. During Buber's decades of residence in Israel, his public insistence that the state should live up to his ideal of the covenant made him a figure of considerable controversy there. [See also the biographies of Rosenzweig and Buber.]

Another great system-builder, Abraham Joshua Heschel (1907–1972), integrated much of twentieth-century Jewish experience in his own life. The scion of a Polish Hasidic dynasty, he took a doctorate in Berlin, escaped World War II by going to the United States to teach at the Reform rabbinical school (Hebrew Union College) in Cincinnati. He later taught a near-Orthodox theology at the Conservative seminary in New York.

Heschel faulted the existentialists for defining religion as the movement of people toward God. Modern Jewry's very skepticism, he said, should make it awestruck at the power Someone has given humankind. When such "radical amazement" opens people to the reality of the giver, it becomes apparent, as the Bible indicates, that God pursues humankind, forcing upon it God's self-revelation, and that the biblical prophets accurately transmit God's message.

The meaning of the prophets, Heschel said, is clear: God is a God of pathos, one who suffers when people transgress and who rejoices when they achieve holiness. To argue that God would be more perfect if God had no feelings reflects a Stoic, that is, a Roman point of view, not that of the Bible. Revelation proceeds by "sympathos," by uncommonly gifted individuals coming to feel what God feels. They may verbalize this understanding in different ways, but they do not interpose themselves between God and humankind. The commandments transmitted by Moses and the sages accurately reflect God's injunctions. They are the divinely sanctioned media for meeting God by doing God's will.

Two themes in Heschel's thought mitigate his absolute acceptance of Jewish tradition. First, he emphasized the paucity of revelation compared with the subsequent plethora of interpretation, thereby suggesting the virtue of continuing development. Second, he carefully documented the prophets' intense ethical devotion, implying, perhaps, that human considerations should predominate in interpreting the Torah. He nobly exemplified this in his participation in the civil rights and antiwar struggles of the 1960s. But he never indicated whether he would advocate changes in Jewish law for these or other reasons. [See also the biography of Heschel.]

Since the articulation of these six positions, much theological writing and discussion has gone on, but no distinctive new pattern has won substantial acceptance.

CONFRONTING THE HOLOCAUST

For reasons still debated, not until the mid-1960s did Jewish thinkers confront the theoretical implications of the Nazi murder of six million Jews. With the emergence of the short-lived "death of God" movement, some Jewish philosophers demanded that a Jewish theology be created that would focus on the reality revealed at Auschwitz, the most notorious of the Nazi death camps and the symbol of the Holocaust. Where the revelation at Sinai spoke of God's rule, God's justice, and God's help to the people of Israel, Auschwitz now spoke of God's absence, of the world's injustice, and of the terrible abandonment of the Jewish people. But it was in the creation of the state of Israel that the Jewish people had given its deepest response to Nazi destructiveness: it was the expression of an intense determination to survive with high human dignity. The Arab-Israeli Six-Day War of 1967 which threatened Israel's (and therefore Jewish) existence catalyzed Jewry worldwide to identify even more intensely with the state of Israel. Israel, therefore, for all its secularity, took on a numinous quality for those who strove to maintain the covenant.

The survival of the Jewish people now became a central preoccupation of Diaspora Jews and a major motive for individuals to assume or extend their Jewish responsibilities. Associated with this was a reassessment of the values of the emancipation. Because of the messianic hope that emancipation had awakened, Jews had surrendered much of their traditional way of life. Now, even as Western civilization began to lose its ultimate confidence in science, technology, education, and culture—in utter human capability—so Jews started to approach their tradition with new receptivity. For some, this partial withdrawal from universal concerns led back to Orthodoxy. Most Jews found that though their social activism could no longer take on redemptive guise, they still could not spurn the ethical lessons of the emancipation, especially with regard to feminism. The critical challenge now facing such chastened liberal Jews is the delineation of their duty and the creation of communities to live it, a concern giving rise to considerable experimentation.

The theoretical response to the Holocaust had an ironic outcome. Experience made substituting Auschwitz for Sinai was unacceptable to most Jews. Despite the mass depravity that continues to plague the twentieth century, the revelation of God's absence and of humanity's depravity in the Holocaust does not constitute the norm of human or Jewish existence. Sanctifying the routine without forgetting the extraordinary remains the Jew's fundamental responsibility, as the revelation at Sinai taught. The primary response to the Holocaust, Jews agree, must be an intensification of human responsibility.

Some Orthodox leaders, like the *rebe* of the Lubavitch Hasidic sect, say, in the tradition of the *Book of Deuteronomy,* that in the Holocaust God grievously punished a sinful generation. Most Jews find it impossible to view the Holocaust as an act of divine justice. Alternatively, rationalist teachers assert that God has only finite power and was incapable of preventing the Holocaust, so humankind must actively help God bring the Messiah. Others have come to a Job-like stance. They remain stunned that God can entrust humans with the freedom to become as heartless as the Nazis did. They admit they do not understand God's ways. Nonetheless, they accept God's sovereignty and seek to build their lives on it. [*For further discussion, see* Holocaust, The, *article on* Jewish Theological Responses.]

All these views of evil circulated in the Jewish community well before the Holocaust, leading some to suggest that what truly died in the Holocaust was the Enlightenment's surrogate god, the infinitely competent human spirit. As a result of the loss of absolute faith in humankind, a small minority of modern Jews have sought answers in Jewish mysticism. [*See* Qabbalah.] For others, Orthodoxy has gained fresh appeal. For most Jews, the emancipation has only been qualified, not negated. Mediating between Judaism and modernity continues to be the central spiritual concern of the people who believe themselves to stand in covenant with God, working and waiting for the realization of God's rule on earth.

[*For further discussion of the mainstream movements in contemporary Judaism, see* Reform Judaism; Orthodox Judaism; Conservative Judaism; Reconstructionist Judaism; *and* Hasidism. *Aspects of Judaism that are not rabbinic in origin are discussed in* Folk Religion, *article on* Folk Judaism. *Jewish religious thought is discussed in* Jewish Thought and Philosophy.]

BIBLIOGRAPHY

The *Encyclopaedia Judaica,* 16 vols. (Jerusalem, 1971), encapsulates contemporary scholarship on Judaism, not altogether replacing the first magisterial survey, *The Jewish Encyclopedia,* 12 vols. (1901–1906; reprint, New York, 1964). Louis Jacobs's *A Jewish Theology* (New York, 1973) provides erudite historical accounts of major Jewish ideas from a believing but nonfundamentalist viewpoint. Robert M. Seltzer's comprehensive survey *Jewish People, Jewish Thought* (New York, 1980) adroitly balances history and religious ideas. The finest recent account of the Jewish religious sensibility of the Bible is Jon D. Levenson's *Sinai and Zion* (New York, 1985).

Reliable, if not altogether comprehensible, English translations of the central rabbinic texts exist: *The Mishnah,* translated by Herbert Danby (Oxford, 1933); *The Babylonian Talmud,* 35 vols. (1935–1948; reprint in 18 vols., London, 1961); and *Midrash Rabbah,* 10 vols., translated by Harry Freedman et al. (London, 1939). An English rendering of the Jerusalem Talmud by Jacob Neusner is under way as *The Talmud of the Land of Israel* (Chicago, 1982–); thirty-five volumes are projected. Current scholarship has raised so many questions about rabbinic Judaism that great care must be exercised in utilizing any single source. A well-rounded overview can be gained from the revised (but not the original) edition of Emil Schürer's *The History of the Jewish People in the Age of Jesus Christ,* 2 vols., edited and revised by Géza Vermès and Fergus Millar and translated by T. A. Burkill et al. (Edinburgh, 1973–1979).

No history of the development of Jewish practice exists. Valuable insights may still be gained from the dated work of Hayyim Schauss, *The Jewish Festivals,* translated by Samuel Jaffe (Cincinnati, 1938), and *The Lifetime of a Jew* (New York, 1950). Menachem Elon treats some central themes of Jewish law in *The Principles of Jewish Law* (Jerusalem, 1975), and an invaluable guide to more specific themes is the presently incomplete *Entsiqlopedeyah Talmudit,* edited by S. Y. Zevin and Meir Bar-Ilan (Jerusalem, 1947–).

The *aggadah,* because of its human appeal, is more readily accessible. Two good anthologies available in English are Louis Ginzberg's *The Legends of the Jews,* 7 vols., translated by Henrietta Szold et al. (Philadelphia, 1909–1938), which follows the organization of the Bible, and C. G. Montefiore and Herbert Loewe's *A Rabbinic Anthology* (1938; reprint, Philadelphia, 1960), which is thematically organized. The most comprehensive anthology, however, is in Hebrew: H. N. Bialik and Y. H. Ravnitzky's *Sefer ha-aggadah,* 3 vols. (Cracow, 1907–1911), often reprinted.

Three valuable, if problematic, introductions to rabbinic thought are Solomon Schechter's *Some Aspects of Rabbinic Theology* (New York, 1909), and George Foot Moore's *Judaism,* 3 vols. in 2 (1927–1930; reprint, Cambridge, Mass., 1970), both of which show apologetic tendencies, and E. E. Urbach's *Hazal* (Jerusalem, 1969), translated by Israel Abrahams as *The Sages,* 2 vols. (Jerusalem, 1975), which unconvincingly seeks to resolve rabbinic inconsistencies by applying a historical hermeneutic. Jacob Neusner's continuing researches in this literature deserve careful attention. For his demonstration of how ahistorical (by Western academic standards) rabbinic "theology" was, see his *Judaism in Society* (Chicago, 1984).

Most of the great Jewish legal works of the Middle Ages await reliable translation according to the standard set by *The Code of Maimonides,* 15 vols. to date (New Haven, 1949–), the now nearly complete translation of Maimonides' *Mishneh Torah.* The burgeoning scholarship on mysticism builds on the paradigmatic researches of Gershom Scholem, whose synoptic statement is *Major Trends in Jewish Mysticism* (1941; reprint, New York, 1961). Many major works of medieval Jewish philosophy have been translated. The older, still useful survey of the field is Isaac Husik's *A History of Mediaeval Jewish Philosophy* (New York, 1916). Its modern successor is Julius Guttmann's *Philosophies of Judaism,* translated by David W. Silverman (New York, 1964).

The documents of the emancipation and its aftermath are bountifully supplied and valuably annotated in Paul R. Mendes-Flohr and Jehuda Reinharz's *The Jew in the Modern World* (Oxford, 1980). Some sense of the reality of modern Jewish life as it is lived in North America can be gained from the ideals projected in the works of some of its leading guides (respectively, Modern Orthodox, far-right-wing Conservative, tradition-seeking independent, and Reform): Hayim Halevy Donin's *To Be a Jew* (New York, 1972); Isaac Klein's *A Guide to Jewish Religious Practice* (New York, 1979); *The Jewish Catalog,* edited by Richard Siegel, Michael Strassfeld, and Sharon Strassfeld (Philadelphia, 1973); and *Gates of Mitzvah,* edited by Simeon J. Maslin (New York, 1979), and *Gates of the Seasons,* edited by Peter Knobel (New York, 1983).

Developments in Jewish law are difficult to track even for seasoned experts, but since its founding, *The Jewish Law Annual,* edited by Bernard S. Jackson (Leiden, 1978–), has been a most valuable guide. Reliable introductions to current Jewish theologies are William E. Kaufman's *Contemporary Jewish Philosophies* (New York, 1976) and my own *Choices in Modern Jewish Thought* (New York, 1983).

For the Holocaust, the early works of Elie Wiesel, fiction and nonfiction, uniquely limn the paradoxes of trying to live and write about the ineffable. Two focal statements about the Holocaust are Richard L. Rubenstein's *After Auschwitz* (Indianapolis, 1966) and Emil L. Fackenheim's *To Mend the World* (New York, 1982).

Modern Orthodoxy is surveyed in Reuven P. Bulka's *Dimensions of Orthodox Judaism* (New York, 1983), but the ideas of its preeminent theoretician, Joseph B. Soloveitchik, are most available in his early, searching essay *Halakhic Man,* translated by Lawrence Kaplan (Philadelphia, 1983). My book *Liberal Judaism* (New York, 1984) explicates the religious positions of much of American non-Orthodox Judaism.

2

ISRAELITE RELIGION

MOSHE WEINFELD

This discussion of the religion of Israel pertains to the religion as presented in the literary sources of the Hebrew scriptures. These sources constitute a selection guided by certain normative principles and therefore do not always reflect the real circumstances of daily life. The religion of Israel described in the Hebrew Bible represents the view of the elite circles of the society of ancient Israel, such as priests, prophets, and scribes, who shaped the image of the ideal Israel. Furthermore, as will be shown below, even this ideal image of the religion of Israel underwent a process of development. However, despite this idealization, a continuous line of development of the religion of ancient Israel can be discerned, and it is this development that I shall attempt to delineate.

General Features

Unique in many ways, Israelite religion is most remarkable for its monotheism. The difference between monotheism and polytheism is not only in number—one god versus a plurality of gods—but in the character and nature of the deity. In contradistinction to the polytheistic system according to which gods are subject to biological rules (the existence of male and female in the divine sphere, which means procreation, struggle for survival, etc.), the God of Israel is transcendent, that is, beyond the sphere of nature and therefore not subject to physical and biological principles. In the biblical descriptions of the deity we never encounter any sexual feature, procreation, struggle for survival, or gaining of status. Theogony (genealogy of the gods) and theomachy (strife among the gods), which are almost indispensable in any polytheistic religion, are completely absent from the religion of Israel.

In what appears to be an exception, we are told that God subdued Rahab, the monster, during the creation period (*Is.* 51:9, *Ps.* 89:11, *Jb.* 26:12; verse citations are to the Masoretic text). However, this does not mean that Rahab existed outside the domain of the creator. Rahab could have been created by God, as were the other creatures, but in contrast to others he rebelled and therefore was crushed and defeated (cf. *Ps.* 74:12-14).

The transcendence of God explains the absence of mythology in the religion of Israel. Mythology, here defined as storytelling about gods and their life, activities, and adventures, is inconceivable in the monotheistic sphere. God's relation to men may be described in an anthropomorphic manner, but nothing is told about God's own self or body or about his personal activities and adventures. His actions, when depicted, are always presented in the framework of God's relationship to people or to his nation.

The transcendent character of the God of Israel explains, too, the objection of Israelite religion to magic, which was so prominent in polytheistic religions. The pagan prophet, according to ancient Israelite perception, resorts to various media in order to reveal the will of gods or to coerce them to do something for men. But the Hebrew scriptures express the Israelite belief that God's will cannot be revealed unless he himself wishes to do so; his will cannot be revealed through magic, which draws its power from mystic powers not subordinated to the deity. Indeed, the Israelite legislator, speaking about pagan diviners and the prohibition against pagan mantic devices (*Dt.* 18:9–12), adds an important explanation: "You must be whole-hearted [*tamim,* "sincere"] with the Lord your God. Those nations that you are about to dispossess do indeed resort to soothsayers; to you, however, the Lord your God has not assigned the like" (*Dt.* 18:13–14). The use of magic presupposes reliance on ungodly forces, and that means "insincerity" toward God.

It is true that the biblical stories as well as the biblical cult contain magical elements. There are many allusions to the marvelous transformation of objects: the staffs of Moses and Aaron become serpents (*Ex.* 4:2–4, 7:9–10); Moses divides the sea with his staff (*Ex.* 14:16); Elisha's staff is supposed to revive the Shunammite's son (*2 Kgs.* 4:29); and the three arrows that Joash, the king of Israel, drove into the ground gave him three victories over Aram (*2 Kgs.* 13:14–19). However, all these acts are considered wondrous signs from God. The wonder is seen as "the hand" and power of God and not as originating in the action itself or in the power of the sorcerer, as was the case in pagan religions (cf. *Ex.* 4:1–4, 7:8–10, et al.). Thus, for example, Elisha's staff performs wonders only when accompanied by prayer (contrast *2 Kgs.* 4:29–31 with 4:32–35).

Another transcendent feature of Israelite monotheism is the prohibition against representing God by visual symbol or image: "You shall not make for yourself a sculptured image [*pesel*] or any likeness" (*Ex.* 20:4, *Dt.* 5:8, et al.). This is explained in *Deuteronomy* 4:15: "Be most careful [not to make for yourself a sculptured image], since you saw no shape when the Lord your God spoke to you at Horeb out of the fire." The god which is beyond nature and cosmos cannot be represented by anything earthly and natural.

It is this feature which makes the Israelite religion philosophical, as conceived by the Greeks. For example, it was the observation of Theophrastus (c. 372–287 BCE), a disciple of Aristotle, that "being philosophers by race, [the Jews] converse with each other about 'the Divine' [*to theion*]" (Menachem Stern, *Greek and Latin Authors on Jews and Judaism,* vol. 1, 1974, p. 10). "The Divine" denotes here the philosophical concept of the one force that governs the world in contrast to the popular belief in various mythical deities.

Historical Development until the Temple Cult

It is hard to know how and under what concrete circumstances the monotheistic belief crystallized and whether at its emergence the religion of Israel was already characterized by the negation of mythology as well as of magic and iconic representation of the deity. According to Yehezkel Kaufmann in *History of the Religion of Israel* (trans. Moshe Greenberg, 1972), the sudden emergence of monotheism cannot be understood unless we suppose a radical revolutionary move under the leadership of Moses. Kaufmann compares this to the emergence of Islam, which, under the aegis of Muḥammad, succeeded in taking control of the whole Middle East in the course of twenty-five years. One must agree with Kaufmann that there is no clear evidence of an evolutionary process in the Israelite religion. The evolutionary approach of the last century supposes that monotheism developed gradually from polytheism through henotheism (belief in one national god while not excluding the existence of gods of other nations) to monotheism. Real monotheism—according to this opinion—crystallized in Israel only during the times of the prophets, in the eighth century BCE. [*See* God, *article on* God in the Hebrew Scriptures.]

However, this supposition has little support in the literary-historical sources of the Bible. The documents and sources of the Bible, which represent a very broad spectrum of opinions and beliefs rooted in various historical periods, do not show any trace of such polytheistic concepts as the origin of God (theogony), God's consort and family, or the gods' battle for survival (theomachy). By the same token, we do not find anything in these sources which alludes to the official religious use of magical devices for mantic purposes—as, for example, hepatoscopy (inspecting an animal's liver) or augury (deriving inferences from the behavior of birds and other omens), which was so prevalent in pagan religions.

It should be stressed that this article is concerned with the offical religious trend and not with popular religious life. In the popular religion, cultic practices prevailed that reflected pagan beliefs, especially beliefs connected with a divine power of fertility that was represented by the female characteristics of the deity. Archaeological excavations in Palestine revealed numerous female figurines that were used as amulets for securing fertility (see J. B. Pritchard, *Palestinian Figurines in Relation to Certain Goddesses Known through Literature,* London, 1943). Similarly, it was found that the Israelites worshiped the female goddess Asherah and the goddess of fertility Astarte (cf. *Jgs.* 2:13, 3:7; *1 Sm.* 7:4, 12:10; *1 Kgs.* 15:13; *2 Kgs.* 21:7, 23:6). In recent years inscriptions that date back to the ninth century BCE were discovered in Kuntillet 'Ajrud (in southern Palestine) in which YHVH is being blessed next to Asherah— a positioning that suggests syncretic religious worship. Moreover, the worship of the Queen of Heaven (Ishtar?) was widespread in Judah during the end of the monarchic period (*Jer.* 7:18, 44:18). [*See* Astarte.]

All of these tendencies toward syncretism were strongly condemned by the prophets of the northern kingdom of Israel and the southern kingdom of Judah, who considered them aberrations from the pure monotheistic faith.

More complicated is the problem of the aniconic characteristics of Israelite religion. Although erection of images is prohibited in the legitimate Israelite cult, as attested in the various legal codes of the Hebrew scriptures (*Ex.* 20:20, 23:24, 34:14, 34:17; *Lv.* 19:4, 26:1; *Dt.* 4:15ff., 5:8; et al.), the practice as such was not unheard of in ancient Israel. It is not the worship of the golden calf as told in *Exodus* 32 and in *1 Kings* 12:28ff. which we have in mind, because, as investigation has shown, this worship cannot be considered idol worship. The iconic art of the ancient Near East shows that the calf or bull usually represented the pedestal of a god and not the deity itself. The latter was usually carved in human form. Indeed, the most appropriate place for an image of the deity, should this have existed, would have been the throne or the chariot of God, both represented by the Ark of the Covenant (cf. especially *Nm.* 10:35– 36). The Ark, which together with the cherubim represented the throne and the footstool of the deity (see Menahem Haran: "The Ark and the Cherubim: Their Symbolic Significance in Biblical Ritual," *Israel Exploration Journal* 9, 1959, pp. 35ff.), actually constitutes an empty throne: the god sitting on it is invisible, which attests to the antiquity of the aniconic principle in the religion of Israel.

On the other hand, the practice of image making in ancient Israel is described in the stories in *Judges* about Gideon and Micah. Gideon, the great judge of Israel, made an ephod (some sort of image) of gold and set it up in his town (*Jgs.* 8:27), and, similarly, the mother of Micah consecrated silver to make a sculptured image *(pesel)* and a molten image *(massekha)* to YHVH (*Jgs.* 17:3). However, it has been suggested that these events might be seen as deviations from the pure legitimate worship, as were other incidents in the history of Israel caused by Cannaanite influence (cf. the worship of Baal during the period of King Ahab [c. 874–853], *1 Kgs.* 19:18 et al.) and should not be considered a reflection of genuine Israelite religion. Indeed, as will be shown below, new evidence about the tribal setting in Sinai, the cradle of Israelite monotheism, tends to confirm the view that Israelite monotheism was aniconic from its beginning.

THE RELIGION OF THE PATRIARCHS

Tradition considers Abraham the father of Yahvistic monotheism but this has no basis in the Bible itself. On the contrary, the biblical documents show an awareness of a gap between the religion of the patriarchs and the Yahvistic national religion of Israel. The name of God, *Yahveh* (preserved only unvocalized in the texts, i.e., *YHVH*) is not known before Moses (*Ex.* 3:13f., 6:2ff.), and the nature of the patriarchal creed is completely different from that of Moses and later Israelites. The god of the patriarchs is tied to person and family; the god is called God of Abraham, Isaac, or Jacob or "the God of the father" (*Gn.* 26:24, 28:13, 31:42, 32:10, 46:3, 49:25), as is appropriate to a wandering family. When *El,* the generic designation of the god, occurs in the patriarchal stories, it is not of a national or universal character, as in later Israel; the name *El* is always bound to the place where the patriarch stays. In Jerusalem God's name is El-'Elyon (*Gn.* 14:18f.); in Beersheba the name of the deity is El-'Olam (*Gn.* 21:33); in Bethel, El-Beit-El (*Gn.* 31:13); and in Shechem, El-elohei Yisra'el (*Gn.* 33:20). The names of the patriarchal family do not contain the Yahvistic component, and there is no trace in the patriarchal religion of an established cult or of official cultic objects. It must be admitted, then, that the national concept of "Yahveh the god of Israel" does not apply to the patriarchal period. The very term *patriarchal period* has to be used with great caution, since Israel as such did not yet exist, and the descriptions of this period are based on anachronisms. At any rate, according to the descriptions themselves, the national creed and cult were still nonexistent.

HISTORICAL CIRCUMSTANCES OF THE BIRTH OF MONOTHEISM

According to the stories of *Exodus,* Mount Sinai or Horeb, which became the mountain of God's revelation to Israel, was hallowed before the revelation to Moses (*Ex.* 3:1; cf. Zeer Weisman, "The Mountain of God," *Tarbiz* 47, 1978, pp. 107–119). It is designated as Mountain of God, a geographical appellation, prior to any connection to Yahveh's theophany (*Ex.* 4:29). Furthermore, it was known as the Mountain of God to Jethro, the Midianite priest, Moses' father-in-law, and he went to this mountain in order to offer sacrifices and to celebrate (*Ex.* 18:12), which points to the fact that the Mountain of God was known to other nomadic tribes of the Sinai area. This is corroborated by the divine epithet "the god of the Hebrews" which occurs only in the stories of *Exodus* discussed here (*Ex.* 3:18, 5:3). This epithet refers to the god to whom the Hebrew tribes paid allegiance before their crystallization into Israel under Moses.

As is well known, the term *Hebrews* (*'Ivrim*) is associated with the term *Habiru,* which designates the nomadic population in the ancient Near East during the second millennium BCE. The "god of the Hebrews" was worshiped by all sorts of nomads in the area of Sinai and the Negev: the Midianites and Kenites, as well as the Israelites. Most important in this respect is the new, extrabiblical evidence which came to light in the last decades. In the Egyptian topographical lists of King Amenhotep III (1417–1379 BCE) discovered in the temple of Amon at Soleb in Nubia as well as in the list of King Ramses II (1304–1237 BCE) discovered at Amarah West, we find "the land of nomads [of] Yahveh," along with "the land of nomads [of] Seir" (see Raphael Gibeon, *Les bédouins Shosu des documents égyptiens,* Leiden, 1971, nos. 6a, 16a). A land of nomads associated with Yahveh alongside the land of Edom (Seir) reminds us of the old traditions of Israel, according to which Yahveh appeared from Sinai, Edom, Teman, Paran, and Midian (*Dt.* 33:2, *Jgs.* 5:4, *Hb.* 3:3–7). The fact that Yahveh's revelation is associated with places scattered over the whole Sinai Peninsula as well as over the Edomite territory east of Sinai seems to indicate that Yahveh was venerated by many nomads of Sinai and southern Palestine and that "the land of nomads of Yahveh" refers to the whole desert to the east of the delta. To be sure, the god revealed to Moses and adopted by the Israelites reflects a unique phenomenon. Monotheism did come out of Israel and not out of Edom or Midian. However, in the light of the new evidence, one must consider the existence of some kind of proto-Israelite belief in Yahveh in the wilderness region of Sinai and Edom (cf. S. Herrmann, "Der Name Jhw in den Inschriften von Soleb." *Fourth World Congress of Jewish Studies,* vol. 1, Jerusalem, 1967, pp. 213–216; B. Mazar, "Yahveh came out from Sinai," *Temples and High Places in Biblical Times: Proceedings of the Colloquium in Honor of the Centennial of Hebrew Union College–Jewish Institute of Religion, Jerusalem, 14–16 March 1977,* ed. A. Biran, 1981, pp. 5–9). The Egyptian inscriptions which speak about nomads living in the land of Yahveh make it easier for us to understand the biblical traditions about the connections between the Israelites, the Kenites, and the Midianites during their wanderings in Sinai. Moses marries the daughter of Jethro, the Midianite priest (*Ex.* 2:16ff., 3:1f.), and it is during his stay with Jethro that he visits the Mountain of God. According to *Exodus* 18:11, Jethro gives full recognition to the god Yahveh and even helps Moses to organize the judicial institutions of Israel (*Ex.* 18:14–27). On another occasion we find Moses proposing to his father-in-law to join him and serve as a guide for the Israelites in the wilderness (*Nm.* 10:29–32). In *Judges* 1:16 we hear that the Kenites of the clan of Jethro settled together with the tribe of Judah in the Negev.

All this shows that there were close relations between the Israelites and other nomads in the desert, and, as we have indicated above, Yahveh's appellation in *Exodus*, "the god of the Hebrews," seems to support this notion. Another important contribution to the problem discussed here is the archaeological findings in the area. Excavations at Timna, some 30 kilometers (19 miles) north of the Gulf of Aqabah, have shown that the Midianites who built a shrine on the top of an Egyptian sanctuary mutilated the statue of the Egyptian goddess Hathor and reused many objects from the original structure. According to the excavator, Benor Rothenberg, there is evidence of a tent-sanctuary the Midianites erected on the place of the Egyptian shrine, and this brings to mind the tabernacle of the Israelites in the desert (B. Rothenberg, "Timna," in *Encyclopedia of Archaeological Excavations in the Holy Land,* ed. Michael Avi-Yonah and Ephraim Stern, vol. 4, 1978).

In this Midianite sanctuary a copper snake was found, which reminds us of the copper serpent made by Moses and mounted on a standard (*Nm.* 21:4–9). This was the only votive object found in the sanctuary. The Egyptian representations of the goddess Hathor were effaced, and the central niche was left empty. All this should be interpreted as a reaction of the Midianite nomads against Egyptian religion and culture, not unlike the Israelite reaction against pagan idols. Israelite monotheism is described in *Exodus,* as emerging out of a wrestling with Egyptian religion and magic (cf. *Ex.* 7:8ff., 8:12f., 12:12). Indeed, the aniconic tendency of Israel's religion is characteristic not only of ancient Israel but also of other nomadic tribes in the wilderness of Sinai and southern Palestine and seems to have persisted down to the period of the Nabateans in the third to second century BCE.

The affinity of Israel's faith with the faith of their nomadic confederates is clearly expressed in the episode about Jehu, the king of Israel (c. 842–815 BCE) who, by his zeal for Yahveh and his opposition to the Canaanite Baal, asked Jehonadab the son of Rechab to cooperate with him (*2 Kgs.* 10:15–16). The Rechabites, who were associated with the Kenites (*1 Chr.* 2:55: cf. 4:12 [Septuagint]), preserved their nomadic way of life for hundreds of years (cf. Diodorus Siculus 9.9 on the first Nabateans). They were persistent in their zeal for Yahvism (see *2 Kgs.* 10:16), which was the faith of their ancestors, the nomads who lived in the land of Yahveh, according to the Egyptian inscriptions. In this connection it should be noted that the ninth-century BCE prophet Elijah who, like Jehu, opposed the Baal worship, made a pilgrimage to Sinai to express his zeal for Yahveh (*1 Kgs.* 19), and, as will be shown below, reestablished the cult of Mount Carmel according to the Mosaic principles and Sinaitic traditions. The trend in the ninth century against Baal stirred a movement which strove for a return to the old Mosaic worship.

EXODUS FROM EGYPT

Among the nomadic tribes in the land of Yahveh (that is, the Sinai Peninsula), the Israelites were under Egyptian control, and, as I have indicated, the religion of Israel actually took shape in the course of a struggle with Egyptian religion and culture. As shown above, the Midianites, who were close in their religion to the Israelites, also fought Egyptian cult and religion. The struggle of the Israelite tribes with the Egyptians comes to full expression in the story about the liberation of Israel from "the house of bondage"—that is, the Exodus, which became the hallowed Israelite epic.

Historical Background. Egyptian documents tell us about constant movements of nomads from Edom and other eastern regions into Egypt as well as of movements from Egypt into the desert. In one of these documents (Papyrus Anastasi VI) we read about the entrance of nomads into the pasturage of the delta: "We have finished letting the Shosu nomads of Edom pass the fortress . . . to keep them alive and to keep their cattle alive," (James B. Pritchard, *Ancient Near Eastern Texts relating to the Old Testament,* 3d ed., Princeton, 1969, p. 259), and in another we are told about the pursuit of runaway slaves (ibid.). This calls to mind the biblical traditions about the Israelite tribes entering Egypt in order to survive a famine (*Gn.* 45:7) and about their subsequent escape from slavery (*Ex.* 13–14). The Exodus stories may perhaps be traced back to a clash between a group of enslaved Hebrew nomads and the Egyptian authorities.

Biblical Account. According to biblical traditions, the leader of the Israelites was Moses, an Egyptian-born man (cf. *Ex.* 2:19) who was at odds with the Egyptian authorities and had been forced to flee to the desert. There he found shelter amongst the Midianites and married the daughter of the Midianite priest Jethro (compare the Egyptian prince Sinuhe, who fled Egypt and found shelter in the house of one of the leaders of an Asiatic tribe). His acquaintance with the Midianites and his previous associations with Egypt enabled him to conceive his plans for the liberation of his brethren from Egyptian slavery. Moses availed himself of his ties with the Midianites and Kenites in order to find his way in the wilderness of Sinai (cf. *Nm.* 10:29–32), and these ties were remembered for hundreds of years among the tribes of Israel (cf. *1 Sm.* 15:6). Furthermore, according to *Exodus* 18:12, Moses and Aaron and the elders of Israel participated in the common sacrificial meal prepared by Jethro, the Midianite priest, and learned from him how to administer justice, which procedure Moses initiated among the Israelite tribes.

Religious Meaning Ascribed. The successful flight of the Israelites and their interpretation of it as divine salvation turned into the main vehicle of national-religious education. The God of Israel was always hailed as the one who redeemed the people from "the house of bondage" (see the prologue to the Ten Commandments, *Ex.* 20:1 and *Dt.* 5:6), and the events of the Exodus were recited to the children of Israel, especially during the festival of Passover, in order to teach them loyalty to God (*Ex.* 12:26–27, 13:8, 14–16; *Dt.* 6:20–25). The events of the Exodus were also recited during religious gatherings of the tribes when they recounted their glorious past and the divine help given them (*Dt.* 29:1–5; *Jos.* 24:5–7; *1 Sm.* 12:6–8; etc.). Individual thanksgiving also opened with praises of God for his deliverance of Israel from Egypt (*Dt.* 26:5–9).

The liberation from Egyptian slavery was the reason behind the divine command for the abolishment of slavery within Israel—"For they are my servants, whom I freed from the land of Egypt, they may not give themselves over into slavery" (*Lv.* 25:22)—and was similarly used as motivation for not oppressing the stranger— "You shall not wrong a stranger or oppress him, for you were strangers in the land of Egypt" (*Ex.* 22:20; cf. *Ex.* 22:9); "You shall love the stranger, for you were strangers in the land of Egypt" (*Dt.* 10:19; cf. *Lv.* 19:34). The liberation from "the house of bondage" was considered an act of grace by the God of Israel for which the people were to express their gratitude by being loyal to God, that is, by keeping his commandments. This loyalty had to be endorsed by a solemn act: a covenant between God and Israel.

EARLY CULTIC WORSHIP

According to Pentateuchal sources, God revealed himself to the people on a specific mountain called Sinai or Horeb. However, ancient poems hail several places in the Sinai Desert as places of theophany. For example, *Deuteronomy* 33 speaks of YHVH coming from Sinai, Seir, and Mount Paran (33:2; cf. *Jgs.* 5:4-8). In *Habakkuk* 3 we read that God comes from Teman and from Mount Paran, and in the continuation of this poem Cushan and Midian are also mentioned. In all of these instances God sets out from his holy abode (on the mountain) to save his people, not to give laws as in the later prosaic sources. Furthermore, in these poems the deity sets out not from a single hallowed place (e.g., Sinai or Horeb) but from various places scattered throughout the Sinai Peninsula and the northwestern Arabian Desert. It seems that there were several holy mountains in this area that served the nomads who venerated YHVH.

This supposition can be supported by the excavations at Mount Karkom in the Negev (see Emmanuel Anati, "Has Mt. Sinai Been Found," *Biblical Archaeology Review* 11, 1985, pp. 42–57). This mountain constituted a sacred site for nearly a thousand years (3000 BCE to 2000 BCE) and displays features that characterize Mount Sinai as it is presented in the Pentateuchal tradition. At the foot of this mountain twelve standing stones were discovered. These stones are placed next to a structure that looks like an altar (cf. *Ex.* 24:4). A cleft was discovered in the mountain that is similar to the cleft in the rock, described in *Exodus* 33:22, in which Moses hides himself.

Such excavational findings suggest that the Sinai Desert was the site of a long tradition of cultic practices; Mount Sinai was only one of many cultic sites. The elaborate biblical descriptions of the cultic practices at Mount Sinai may reveal aspects of worship at such sites throughout the desert. The center of the tribal worship was the Mountain of God, ascent to which was allowed only to the priesthood and the elders (*Ex.* 24:1–2, 24:9, 24:14). Access to the godhead was the privilege of the prophet Moses alone (*Ex.* 3:5, 19:9–13, 19:20–22, 24:15, 33:21–23, 34:2ff.). Beneath the mountain stood an altar and twelve pillars (*Ex.* 24:4), where sacrificial rites were performed.

A reflection of this procedure may be found in the stories of the prophet Elijah, who tried to revive the old nomadic religion in defiance of that brought in by the Phoenicians (*1 Kgs.* 18–19). Like Moses, Elijah ascends Mount Horeb (*1 Kgs.* 19), and the divine revelation to him is similar to God's revelation to Moses in *Exodus* 33. Both stand at the opening of a cave or rock with their face hidden or wrapped (*Ex.* 33:22; cf. *Ex.* 3:6; *1 Kgs.* 19:13) while seeing God's "back" pass (*Ex.* 33:23, 34:6; *1 Kgs.* 19:11). Both fast forty days and forty nights before or during their encounter with the deity (*Ex.* 24:18, 34:28; *Dt.* 9:9ff.). They demonstrate their zeal toward God in a similar manner: Moses commands the killing of the men who violated the covenant and worshiped the golden calf (*Ex.* 32:37–38); Elijah slaughters the prophets of Baal out of zeal for Yahveh and his covenant with the children of Israel (*1 Kgs.* 18:40, 19:10, 19:14).

More instructive is the parallel of the cultic establishment by Moses at Sinai and by Elijah at Mount Carmel. Like Moses, who builds an altar at Sinai and erects twelve stone pillars there in order to mark the bond between God and Israel, Elijah restores the altar of Yahveh at Carmel with twelve stones, which represent the tribes of Israel, and performs the sacrificial rite, which symbolizes the presence of God and the reestablishment of the relationship with him (*1 Kgs.* 18:30ff.). Just as the people at Sinai confirm their bond with God by a solemn declaration of loyalty ("The people declared unanimously: 'Whatever Yahveh commanded we shall do,'" *Ex.* 24:3, 24:7; cf. *Ex.* 19:5), so the people gathered at Mount Carmel declare, "Yahveh alone is God" (*1 Kgs.* 18:39). Furthermore, the establishment of Yahveh's cult at Mount Carmel is strikingly similar to its establishment at the Tabernacle at Sinai. In the Priestly account of the dedication of the Tabernacle (*Lv.* 9:24), we read that when the people saw that the fire of Yahveh consumed the burnt offering, they fell on their faces and shouted (that is, they proclaimed in a hymnic way the praise of God). Similarly, we read of the ceremony at Mount Carmel that when all the people saw the fire of Yahveh consuming the burnt offering, and so on, they fell on their faces and said, "Yahveh alone is God, Yahveh alone is God" (*1 Kgs.* 18:39).

Though not all of these features may be traced to the time of Moses, it seems that most of them are rooted in the ancient nomadic reality of the Israelite tribes reflected in Mosaic tradition. In the Elijah stories there is a conscious tendency to reshape the religion as it was in the Mosaic period, which means that there was a strong awareness in Israel of the period of the Sinai revelation and its importance for the faith of the nation. In the light of the adduced parallels we may say that the Mosaic religion as presented in the Pentateuch was already a living tradition in the northern kingdom of Israel in the ninth century BCE. This implies that the kernel of this tradition goes back to premonarchic times, when tribal religion was fresh and dominant in the life of Israel and historically close to the Mosaic period.

COVENANT BETWEEN GOD AND ISRAEL

The covenant of Sinai, which became so central in the religion of Israel, denotes not a bilateral agreement between the deity and the people but rather a commitment by the people to keep the law of YHVH as it is inscribed on tablets and found in the "Book of the Covenant" (*Ex.* 24:3–8). The word *covenant* (Heb., *berit*) means a bond or obligation that is accompanied by a pledge or oath and that is validated by sanctions, dramatized curses, threats, and the like performed in specific cultic rites.

A very old Mosaic cultic rite not repeated in later periods is the blood covenant as described in *Exodus* 24:3–8. After Moses builds an altar at the foot of Mount Sinai and erects twelve stone pillars, he prepares sacrifices and uses the blood of the animal sacrifices for the covenantal ceremonies. Half of the blood he sprinkles on the altar (and, apparently, on the stone pillars), and the other half he puts into basins in order to sprinkle it over the people. Then he declares: "This is the blood of the covenant that the Lord [YHVH] has cut with you" (*Ex.* 24:8).

Blood covenantal ceremonies are attested in ancient nomadic societies. Herodotus (3.8), writing in the fifth century BCE, tells about covenantal procedures of the ancient Arabs. We read that the covenant was performed by taking blood of the participants' thumbs and smearing it on the holy stones which stood between them. A closer analogy to the Sinaitic blood ritual is found in a Ramesside ostracon of the twelfth century BCE. Here we read about a father reproaching his son for associating himself with the Semites of the delta by eating bread mixed with blood, that is, by making a pact with them (see Jaroslav Černy, "Reference to Blood Brotherhood among Semites in an Egyptian Text of the Ramesside Period," *Journal of Near East-*

ern Studies 14, 1955, pp. 161–163). The fact that the blood ritual is found only in the Sinaitic ceremony may teach us that it belongs to the ancient nomadic reality and therefore reflects a Mosaic background.

REVELATION AT SINAI

In the description of the Sinaitic cult we find a clear distinction between the place of revelation on Mount Sinai and the place of worship below the mountain. This situation is reflected in the tradition about the tent of meeting *(ohel mo'ed)* at Sinai. According to *Exodus* 33:7–11, Moses pitches the tent of meeting outside the camp, and there it serves as a place of encounter between God and Moses. This contrasts with the later description of the Tabernacle by the Priestly source, which conceives the tent of meeting as the sanctuary in the middle of the camp, where Moses meets God (cf. *Ex.* 29:42–43; 40:34–35). The two phenomena, revelation and cult, which previously existed separately, amalgamated here, a situation which prevailed in later times when prophecy and cult joined hands in the Israelite and Judahite temples.

The place of revelation, be it the top of the mountain or the tent outside the camp, was out of bounds to the people. Indeed, according to the Sinaitic tradition it was Moses alone who received the words of God (the Decalogue), and as mediator, he delivered them afterward to the people. Literary criticism shows that gradually the notion developed that all Israel witnessed the theophany at Sinai and received with tremor the Ten Commandments. The rest of the laws were given indirectly; that is, they were transmitted through Moses (*Ex.* 24:3, *Dt.* 5:28ff.). But the distinction between two kinds of divine legislation, a short one written on tablets *(luhot)* and a longer one written on a "book" *(sefer),* always prevailed. As described in *Exodus* 32, the Ten Commandments, the basic constitution of Israel, were written by God on the tablets, which were put into the Ark, which represented the footstool of the deity, as described above. As holy documents they were deposited, as it were, beneath the feet of God, a procedure known to us from other ancient Near Eastern cultures.

That the words written on the tablets of the covenant are identical with the commandments of *Exodus* 20 is explicitly said in *Deuteronomy* 5:19, 9:10, and 10:4, and there is no reason to suppose that this was differently understood in former times. A series of cultic commandments in *Exodus* 23:10–19 (paralleled in *Exodus* 34:10–26) has been considered the original Decalogue by some scholars, who see the traditional Decalogue (*Ex.* 20:1–14) as a later ethical decalogue inspired by prophetic circles. But there is no warrant for this supposition. The division of the series of laws in *Exodus* 23:10–19 and 34:10–26 into ten discrete commandments is highly controversial, and the idea that a "cultic decalogue" should be more ancient than an "ethical" one has no basis at all. There is nothing specifically prophetic in the ethical decalogue; on the contrary, one can show that the prophets drew upon it (see *Hos.* 4:2, *Jer.* 7:9) and not vice versa. The "ten words" written on the tablets (cf. also *Ex.* 34:27) should be seen as identical with the commandments in *Exodus* 20:2–17 (and *Dt.* 5:6–18), while the series of cultic laws in *Exodus* 23:10–19 and 34:10–26 belongs to the Book of the Covenant.

✳ THE TEN COMMANDMENTS: THEIR ESSENCE AND FUNCTION

From the point of view of content and form there is no difference between the Ten Commandments and other laws. The various law codes of the Bible contain the same injunctions which are attested in the Decalogue in both its versions. The prohibitions against idolatry and swearing falsely, the observance of the Sabbath, the honoring of parents, and the prohibitions against murder, adultery theft, and false witness—all these appear again and again in the various laws of the Pentateuch. The only exception is the injunction against coveting a neighbor's property, and this is indeed indicative of the particular nature of the Decalogue.

Let me state the five most particular and most characteristic features of the Decalogue.

1. *Universality.* In contrast to the ordinary laws whose enactment depends on particular personal or social circumstances such as sacrifices offered in various conditions (e.g., priestly dues dependent on income; civil laws dependent on ownership of property; laws of matrimony dependent on family status, etc.), the ordinances of the Decalogue apply to everybody regardless of circumstances. Every Israelite is committed not to practice idolatry and not to swear falsely, to observe the Sabbath and honor his or her parents, not to murder, not to commit adultery, not to steal, not to give false witness, and not to covet, no matter what his or her personal status is or in what society or in which period he or she lives. The commandments have thus universal validity.

2. *Restrictive conditionality.* The commandments are for the most part formulated in the negative, and even the positive, such as observance of the Sabbath and honoring one's parents, are in fact prohibitions. The observance of the Sabbath is explained by way of a prohibition: "Six days you shall work but the seventh day is a Sabbath . . . you shall not do any work" (*Ex.* 20:9– 10). Similarly, the object of the commandment to honor one's parents is to prevent offense or insult to them, as implied by the various other laws concerning parents (cursing and beating in *Exodus* 21:15, 21:17, and in *Leviticus* 20:9; rebellion and disobedience in *Deuteronomy* 21:18–21). These negative conditions determine the moral obligations or restrictions demanded of every member of this special community governed by the Decalogue.

3. *Instructability.* The commandments are concisely formulated and contain a typological number of units (ten) easy to inculcate. Biblical scholarship long held that the original Decalogue was even shorter than the present version and was approximately like this:

1. I am the Lord your God, you shall have no other god beside me.
2. You shall not make for yourself a sculptured image.
3. You shall not swear falsely by the name of the Lord your God.
4. Remember to sanctify the Sabbath day.
5. Honor your father and your mother.
6. You shall not murder.
7. You shall not commit adultery.
8. You shall not steal.
9. You shall not bear false witness against your neighbor.
10. You shall not covet your neighbor's house.

That the present form of the Decalogue is expanded may be learned from the fact that the explanation of the Sabbath commandment in the version of the Decalogue in *Deuteronomy* is completely different from that in the version in *Exodus*. This shows that both authors had before them a short commandment which they expanded, each in his own way. The author of the *Exodus* version added an explanation of a sacral-cosmogonic nature, while the author of *Deuteronomy* added an explanation of a sociohumanistic nature. The terse structure and short form of the Decalogue, the typological number ten divided into two (commandments concerning man versus God and commandments concerning man versus his neighbor), enabled their engraving on two stone tablets and their learning by heart. This intimates that these commandments make up a set of fundamental conditions which every Israelite was obliged to know and to inculcate.

4. *Covenantal, nonlegislative nature.* The commandments are, as indicated, essentially categorical imperatives of universal validity; they are beyond a specific historical time and place and independent of circumstances. Therefore no punishment is prescribed, and no detailed definition of each crime is given. One might ask what kind of theft is meant in the eighth commandment and what would be the thief's punishment, but these questions are irrelevant since the commandments are not intended to represent legislation as such; rather, they constitute the formulation of God's decrees set as conditions for being part of the covenantal community. The tenth commandment, not to covet, is irrelevant for any court legislation since no court could enforce punishment for mere intention (cf. Bernard S. Jackson, *Essays in Jewish and Comparative Legal History,* Leiden, 1975, pp. 212ff.). It is a principle employed by God's justice for the holy community and not by jurisprudence of man. Only under the terms of a covenant with God could man be punished for violation of such a commandment. The commandments are given to the people and not applied to the court. Anyone who does not observe these commandments excludes himself from the community of the faithful.

5. *Personal, apodictic nature.* The commandments are formulated in the second person singular, as if they were directed personally to each and every member of the community. This formulation of "I and thou" is not found in the legal corpora in the ancient Near East and indeed looks strange in human jurisprudence. The latter is usually formulated in casuistic style, that is, stating the objective case (in the third person) and giving the terms of punishment for the violation. On the contrary, in the Decalogue we find the apodictic style, which addresses the listener in the second person and does not mention punishment at all. This bears the character of instructions given by a master to his pupils or by a lord to his vassals. Indeed, this style is prevalent throughout the Bible in the various instructions and adjurations of the highest king to his subjects. (See my "The Origin of the Apodictic Law," *Vetus Testamentum* 23, 1973, pp. 63–75.) It is rooted in the covenantal assembly, where the God of Israel confronts his subjects and addresses them personally.

The Decalogue is, then, distinguished by its concisely worded basic obligations directed at every member of the Israelite community and is an aspect of a special covenant with God. It is an Israelite creed similar to the Shema' declaration (*Dt.* 6:4), which also consists of an easily remembered verse containing an epitome of the monotheistic idea and serving as an external sign of identification for monotheistic believers. It is no accident that both the Decalogue and the Shema' were recited together in the Temple (*Tam.* 5.1). In *Deuteronomy* the whole Decalogue pericope (chap. 5) precedes the Shema' passage (*Dt.* 6:4f.), which opens Moses' discourse, so that the combination of both in liturgy has its roots in the tradition of *Deuteronomy* itself.

Though we do not have clear evidence of when the Decalogue was crystallized and accepted, it seems to be very old. It is referred to by the eighth century BCE prophet Hosea (*Hos.* 4:2) and later by Jeremiah (*Jer.* 7:9) and is cited in two ancient psalms (*Ps.* 50:7, 50:18–19, 81:9–11), and one cannot deny that it might date from the beginning of Israelite history; it may even be traced back to Moses, the founder of Israel's religious polity.

A clear parallel in the ancient world to such a phenomenon as Moses, the prophet who reveals divine commands to the people, is to be found in a Greek document of the Hellenistic period. In a private shrine of the goddess Agdistis in Philadelphia (modern-day Alaşehir), in Asia Minor, an oath inscribed in a foundation stone of the sanctuary was found which contains injunctions similar to the ethical part of the Decalogue: not to steal, not to murder, not to commit adultery, and so on. These were revealed in a dream by the goddess Agdistis to the prophet Dionysius, who inscribed them on the stela of the sanctuary (see F. Sokolowski, *Lois sacrées de l'Asie Mineure,* 1955, no. 20, ll. 20ff.). It is also said in the inscription that whoever will violate one of the mentioned commandments will not be allowed to enter the shrine. Although this document is of late origin (first century BCE), it undoubtedly reveals ancient religious practice which is typologically similar to that of the Decalogue: a concise set of commandments revealed by a god to his prophet, who is to transmit them to the believers.

The tablets containing the Decalogue thus constituted a kind of binding foundation-document for the Israelite community. With the disappearance of the Ark of the Covenant and the tablets of the covenant sometime during the existence of the First Temple, the Decalogue was freed from its connection to the concrete symbols to which it was previously attached. At sacred occasions and every morning in the Temple, the Decalogue was customarily read, and all who were present would commit themselves to the covenant by oath *(sacramentum)* (cf. Pliny's epistle on the Christians who make an oath [*sacramentum*] every morning not to steal, commit adultery, etc., which is, no doubt, an allusion to the Decalogue).

Despite the similarity in background between the Decalogue tradition and the oath of the worshipers at the temple in Philadelphia, there is a decisive difference between them: the basic religious demands that are included in the first pentad of the Decalogue are not found and are not expected to be found in the Philadelphia oath. The first five commandments have a peculiarly Israelite nature: the name *YHVH* is mentioned in each commandment, whereas the last five commandments are of a universal nature and do not mention the name *YHVH*.

THE LAW

Biblical law consists of different literary types, indicating varying backgrounds of formation. In the oldest Israelite law corpus, *Exodus* 21–23, referred to in the Bible as *sefer ha-berit* ("book of the covenant"), we can recognize three types of law: civil law (*Ex.* 21:1–22:16), sociomoral law (22:17–23:9), and cultic ordinances (23:10–19). However, this distinction blurs in the later law corpora, where the laws mingle and blend, leaving little possibility of distinguishing between the various types. Furthermore, civil laws, which account for over half of the Book of the Covenant and make up the larger portions of Mesopotamian law codes, gradually diminish and disappear in the later law codes of the Bible, because the religious legislator in Israel is no longer concerned about them.

This blurring of borders between types of laws is also discernible in the form and formulation of the laws. While in the Book of the Covenant the civil laws use a style known as casuistic ("if . . . then"), which is predominant in the ancient Near Eastern law corpora, and the cultic and moral-ethical laws use primarily an imperative apodictic style ("you shall," "you shall not," "do not," etc.,), in the late collections the styles are mixed. A law commencing casuistically switches in midstream to the apodictic, and no distinction can be made between them (e.g., *Lv.* 22:18–22; *Dt.* 22:23–24).

Furthermore, the later codes, and especially the Deuteronomic code, crystallized in the seventh century BCE, tend to free themselves of their legalistic character and become humanistic, sermonizing, and rhetorical. Thus, explanations given add a moral motivation for obedience to the law, for example:

You shall not oppress a stranger, for you know the feelings of the stranger, having yourselves been strangers in the land of Egypt.   (*Ex.* 23:9)

Six days you shall do your work, but on the seventh day you shall cease from labor in order that your ox and your ass may rest and that you bondman and the stranger may be refreshed.

(*Ex.* 23:12)

You shall not rule over [your servant] ruthlessly, you shall fear your God.

(*Lv.* 25:43)

You shall not take bribes, for bribes bland the eyes of the discerning and upset the plan of the just.   (*Dt.* 16:19; cf. *Ex.* 23:8)

Furthermore, the "laws" themselves sometimes lose their legal character because of their moralistic, sermonizing nature:

You shall not hate your kinsfolk in your heart . . . . Love your fellow as yourself.
(*Lv.* 19:17–18)

Do not harden your heart and shut your hand against your needy kinsman. Rather, you must open your hand and lend him sufficient for whatever he needs.
(*Dt.* 15:7–8)

Such demands, which are directed to one's heart, are in fact moralizing discourses and cannot be considered legislative. Even cultic-ritual laws are explained and motivated by inner religious and moral reasons. For example, the obligation to sprinkle the blood of the sacrifice is explained by the necessity to atone for the shedding of blood (*Lv.* 17:1–7). The prohibition against eating carcass is motivated by the notion of the holiness of Israel (*Dt.* 14:21), and the same motivation is given for the command to ban the Canaanites and to destroy the pagan cultic installations in the Land of Israel (*Dt.* 7:5).

COVENANT BETWEEN GOD AND ISRAEL

The obligation of Israel toward God to keep his law equals the pledge to show loyalty to him. Besides the Mosaic covenant, which is based on the promise to observe the laws, we find in *Joshua* 24 a covenant which stipulates exclusive loyalty to the one God. Joshua's covenant, which took place in Shechem, modern-day Nablus (cf. *Dt.* 27 and *Jos.* 8:30–35), is mainly concerned with the choice of the God of Israel and the observance of strict loyalty toward him: "He is a jealous God. . . . if you forsake the Lord and serve alien gods, . . . he will make an end of you" (*Jos.* 24:19–20). This covenant, which was concerned with loyalty and made at the entrance to the Promised Land, was especially necessary because of the exposure to Canaanite religion and the danger of religious contamination.

In fact, the Shechemite covenant described in *Joshua*, which is associated—as indicated—with the foundation ceremony between mounts Gerizim and Ebal (cf. *Dt.* 27, *Jos.* 8:30–35), is close in its character to the covenant of the plains of Moab, presented in *Deuteronomy*. This covenant takes place before the crossing into the Promised Land and is defined as an act of establishing a relationship between God and Israel (*Dt.* 26:17–19, 27:9–10, 29:12; see expecially *Dt.* 27:9: "This day you have become a people belonging to the Lord your God").

The two covenants presented in the Pentateuch, the one at Sinai (*Ex.* 19–24) and the other at the plains of Moab in *Deuteronomy*, were patterned after the type of covenant prevalent in the ancient Near East between suzerains and vassals. Thus we find treaties or, rather, loyalty oaths between the Hittite suzerain and his vassals that contain the following elements:

1. Title and name of the suzerain,
2. Historical introduction, in which the suzerain tells about the graces he bestowed upon his vassal which justify the demand for the vassal's loyalty,
3. The basic stipulation of allegiance,
4. Stipulations of the covenant,
5. Invocation of witnesses,
6. Blessings for keeping loyalty and curses for disloyalty,
7. The deposit of the cofenantal tablets in the sanctuary,
8. The recital of the covenant before the vassal and his subjects.

All these are reflected in the Pentateuchal covenants. First comes God's introduction of himself, then a historical introduction (*Ex.* 19:4, *Dt.* 1–11; cf. *Jos.* 24:2–13), the statement of the basic postulate of loyalty (*Ex.* 19:5–6, *Dt.* 6:4–7:26, 10:12–22; cf. *Jos.* 24:19–24), covenantal stipulations (*Ex.* 21–23, *Dt.* 12–26), invocation of witnesses (*Dt.* 4:26, 30:9, 31:28; cf. *Jos.* 24:22, 24:27), blessings and curses (*Ex.* 23:16–28, *Dt.* 28), the deposit of the tablets of the covenant and the Book of the Covenant (*Ex.* 25:21, *Dt.* 10:1–5, 31:24–26; cf. *Jos.* 24:26), and the recital of the covenant before the people (*Ex.* 24:7, *Dt.* 31:9–13).

The forms which served a political need in the ancient Near East came then to serve a religious purpose in Israel. The religious use of a political instrument was especially suitable to Israel because the religion of Israel was the only religion that demanded exclusive (monotheistic) loyalty; it precluded the possibility of multiple loyalties, such as were found in other religions where the believer was bound in diverse relationships to many gods. The stipulation in political treaties demanding exclusive loyalty to one king corresponds strikingly to the religious belief in one single, exclusive deity. The political imagery applied to the divine being also helped crystallize the concept of the kingship of God so that in Israel the relations between the people and their God were patterned after the conventional model of relations between a king and his subjects. Thus, for example, political loyalty was generally expressed by the term *love* (see my article, "The Loyalty Oath in the Ancient Near East," in *Ugarit Forschungen* 8, 1976: 383–384). The emperor demanding loyalty of his subjects enjoins: "Love the king of Assyria as you love yourselves" (see Donald. J. Wiseman, *Vassal Treaties of Esarhaddon,* London 1958, p. 49). Similarly, the worldly emperor demands love "with the whole heart and soul," thus placing in context *Deuteronomy* 6:5: "and you will love the Lord your God with all your heart and with all your soul." *Love* here, as in the treaties, means loyalty and absolute devotion.

The notion of exclusive loyalty that is characteristic of the monotheistic belief has been dressed not only in the metaphor of the relationship between suzerain and vassal but also in the metaphor of the relationships between father and son and husband and wife. Just as one can be faithful only to one suzerain, to one father, and to one husband, so one can be faithful only to the God of Israel and not to other gods as well. The prophets elaborated the husband-wife metaphor in describing the relations between God and Israel (*Hos.* 3, *Jer.* 3:1–10, *Ez.* 16, 23).

SPIRITUAL TRANSFORMATION OF CULTIC RITUALS

Cultic acts in pagan religions were performed in order to reenact events of the divine sphere, such as the celebration of the divine marriage *(hieros gamos),* the dramatization of the death of the young god (Tammuz) and his annual resurrection, the ceremonies of awakening the god, and so forth. These are not attested at all in Israelite religion. By the same token, no magic procedure is applied in Israel's ritual. The priest never used spells in order to drive out evil spirits, and no incantations were used in the Israelite cult. It is true, sacrifices and purification rituals were very common in ancient Israel, and the techniques of sprinkling blood and burning incense before the deity were practiced like in the pagan religion. We even find the scapegoat ritual on the Day of Atonement (*Lv.* 16). However, in contrast to the pagan cult, all these are not accompanied by spells and magical formulas, save the confession of sin (*Lv.* 16:21).

The festivals and rituals of the Israelites, many of which derived from the customs and celebrations of ancient Near Eastern peoples, especially those of Hittite-Hurrian origin (cf. Moshe Weinfeld, 1983), underwent a transformation when adapted to the religion of the Israelites. As opposed to the mytho-theogonic explanations of the ancient Near Eastern festivals, the Israelite festivals are given historical explanations. The harvest festival as well as the ingathering festival are, for example, associated with the Exodus (*Ex.* 23:15, *Lv.* 23:42–43). [*See* Sukkot]. Even the first-fruit ceremony, in which one would expect to hear about the god who fertilizes the earth and provides the crops, consists only of a thanksgiving prayer in which the liberation from Egypt and the grant of land by God are hailed (*Dt.* 26:5–10). [*See* Shavu'ot.]

The New Year signifies the creation of the world by God, as in other Near Eastern religions; but in contrast to the latter, the New Year festival in the religion of Israel does not commemorate the combat of the supreme god with his rivals, as we find in the Babylonian epic *Enuma elish,* which was recited in the New Year ritual. The New Year in Israel serves as a day of "rememberance before the Lord," indicating the beginning of God's rule over the world. It is called "day of acclamation" (*yom teru'ah, Nm.* 20:1; cf. *Lv.* 23:24) because of the blowing of the horn, which signifies the coronation of a new king. This is the day of God's ascent to the throne and of his salutation as king (cf. *Ps.* 47, 96699) and therefore bears a cosmic character. In the liturgy of this day there comes to expression the hope that all the nations will recognize the sovereignty of Israel's god-king and will abandon idolatry (see Sigmund Mowinckel, *The Psalms in Israel's Worship,* vol. 1, Oxford, 1962, pp. 101–189).

The severance of the cult from its mythological and magical background transforms the ritual into a series of actions symbolizing spiritual values. The tenth day of the New Year festival, Yom Kippur, whose main purpose was the purification for the sanctuary (cf. the *kuppuru* rites in the Mesopotamian New Year festival Akitu), becomes the Day of Atonement for the sins of the individual. The ceremony of purification itself (*Lv.* 16) has a lot in common with Hittite and Assyro-Babylonian purification ceremonies (see Weinfeld, 1983, pp. 111-114); however, the distinct feature of the Israelite atonement ceremony is the confession of the sins of the children of Israel (*Lv.* 16:30) and the injunction associated with it ot fast on this day (*Lv.* 16:29; cf. *Lv.* 23:27–32). [*See* Ro'sh ha-Shannah and Yom Kippur.]

A similar transformation from a cultic aspect to a spiritual-moral one may be recognized in the Sabbath. The Sabbath was originally seen as a reenactment of God's rest during creation (*Gn.* 2:1–3; *Ex.* 20:11, 31:17). 20:11, 31:17). However, the institution of Shabbat in Israel became a covenantal sign that attested to the establishment of an eternal relationship between God and his people (*Ex.* 31:16–17). Elsewhere we find a moral-humanistic interpretation of the institution of Shabbat: it was instituted in order to give rest to the enslaved and deprived (*Ex.* 23:12) and was motivated by the liberation of Israel from Egyptian slavery (*Dt.* 5:15). The idea of resting every seventh day undoubtedly has roots in the ancient world, where certain days (connected with the lunar cycle) were considered unfit for human activities. In Israel, however, these days were dissociated from their ancient magical background and became sanctified days endowed with deep moral-religious meaning. [*See* Shabbat.]

Other rituals, too, underwent similar transformations. Circumsion, an initiation rite known among various peoples, was explained in Israel as a sign of God's covenant with Abraham and as signifying the bond between God and Israel (*Gn.* 17:7ff.). The act of circumcision was gradually spiritualized and was applied to the heart, as, for example, in *Jeremiah* 4:4: "Circumcise your hearts to the Lord and remove the foreskins of your hearts" (cf. *Dt.* 10:16). Circumcision of heart means repentance, as becomes clear from *Deuteronomy* 30:6: "The Lord, your God, will circumcise your heart. . . .so that you will love him with all your heart and soul."

Two more ancient Near Eastern symbols were transformed within Israelite religion. The amulets worn on the forehead (phylacteries) by the peoples of ancient Egypt and Syria were considered protective symbols of the deity with whom the believer was associated (see O. Keel, "Zeichen der Verbundenheit: Zur Vorgeschichte und Bedeutung der Forderungen von Deuteronomium 6, 8f. und Par.," *Orbis Biblicus et Orientalis* 38, 1981, pp. 159–240). In Israel the signs on the forehead and on the arm were conceived as a reminder of the belief in the uniqueness of God (*Dt.* 6:4–8) and in the gracious act of Exodus from Egypt (*Ex.* 13:9, 13:16). In the same way that these symbols developed into the *tefillin* (a pair of small boxes containing scriptural passages), the tassels of the garments that were worn by aristocratic people in the ancient Near East became the four-cornered *tsitstsit,* a sign of holiness in Israel. Like these two fundamental symbols of the faith, most of the rituals and customs of ancient Israel were explained in a similar manner and thus were freed of their primitive connotations.

Centralization of the Cult: The Great Turning Point

Although there had existed in Israel a central shrine since the times of the Judges (cf. the temple at Shiloh, *1 Samuel* 1–2), small chapels and altars were also allowed. We hear about the patriarchs building altars in various places in the land of Canaan (*Gn.* 12:7–8, 13:18, 26:25), and we also find that during the time of the judges altars were built in the fields and on rocks (*Jgs.* 6:24, 13:19; *1 Sam.* 19:35). These other shrines were not prohibited; on the contrary, from Elijah's words at his encounter with God at Horeb (*1 Kgs.* 19:10, 19:14), we learn that the destruction of an altar dedicated to Yahveh is tantamount to killing a prophet of Yahveh. Elijah himself is praised because of his restoration of an altar to Yahveh on Mount Carmel (*1 Kgs.* 18). We first hear about the liquidation of provincial sites and altars and worship on the one altar in Jerusalem in the time of Hezekiah, king of Judah (715–686 BCE). It was he who destroyed all the altars in the country and commanded the people to offer sacrifices only at the Temple of Jerusalem (*2 Kgs.* 18:4, 18:29). It was the same king who dared to smash the bronze serpent which Moses made in the desert and to which people had burned incense up to that time (*2 Kgs.* 18:4; cf. *Nm.* 21:8–9).

The act of Hezekiah was actually the culmination of a process which started in the northern kingdom of Israel in the ninth century. That was the period of the struggle initiated by the prophets against the Tyrian god, Baal (*1 Kgs.* 17–19, *2 Kgs.* 9–10). From this struggle emerged the polemic against the golden calves erected in Dan and in Bethel (*1 Kgs.* 12:28ff.) and, finally, an iconoclastic tendency which affected the high places and altars all over the country, developing further a tendency to purge Israelite religion of pagan elements. The Canaanite cult involved worship at high places which contained pillars *(matstsevot)* and wooden symbols *(asherot)* next to the altar. Such cultic objects were seen as idolatrous by Hezekiah and Josiah (r. 640–609) and were therefore prohibited for use in Israelite worship. The legal basis for their acts is found in *Deuteronomy,* the only book of the Pentateuch which demands centralization of worship in a chosen place and prohibits erection of altars, pillars, and wooden symbols (see *Dt.* 12, 16:21–22).

The abolition of the provincial sites created the proper atmosphere for the spiritualization of worship as reflected in *Deuteronomy.* Even the Temple in Jerusalem was now conceived not as the physical house of the Lord but as the house in which God establishes his name (*Dt.* 12:11, 12:21, et al.). Furthermore in the reform movement of Hezekiah and Josiah, which is reflected in *Deuteronomy,* there is a shift from sacrificial ritual to prayer. The author of *Deuteronomy* is not concerned with the cultic activities in the Temple, such as daily offerings, burning incense, kindling the lamp, and so on. On the other hand, he is very interested in worship that involves prayer (*Dt.* 21:7–9, 26:5–10, 26:13–15), because he sees in liturgy the most important form of worship. Indeed, the historiographer of *Kings,* who worked under the influence of *Deuteronomy,* describes the Solomonic Temple not as a place for sacrifices but as a place for prayer (*1 Kgs.* 8:30, 8:34, 8:36, 8:39, et al.). This anticipated the institution of the synagogue, which developed during the Second-Temple period.

THE RELIGION OF THE BOOK: SCRIBES AND WISE MEN

Hallowed as the "book of the *torah*" *(sefer ha-torah)* written by Moses (*Dt.* 31:9), *Deuteronomy* became the authoritative, sanctified guidebook for Israel. It was the first book canonized by royal authority and by a covenant between God and the nation, established by the people gathered in Jerusalem in 622 BCE, under the auspices of King Josiah (*2 Kgs.* 23:1-3). Only after other books were appended to *Deuteronomy* did the term *Torah* refer to the whole Pentateuch.

The canonization of holy scripture which started with *Deuteronomy* turned the Torah into an object of constant study. The Israelites were commanded to occupy themselves constantly (day and night) with the written book of the Torah and to teach it to their children (*Dt.* 31:11–13, *Jos.* 1:8, *Ps.* 1:2). It is not by accident that *Deuteronomy* is the only book in the Pentateuch which uses the verb *lamad/limed* ("teach, educate"). The verb is most characteristic of wisdom literature, which was studied in the schools of ancient Israel, and thus reveals the scribal-educative background of *Deuteronomy*. *Deuteronomy* is indeed the only book of the Pentateuch which enjoins the people to act "according to the written *torah*" (cf., e.g., *Dt.* 28:58). This implies that it is not enough to do the will of the Lord; one must comply with the Lord's will as it is written in the book. Hence the importance of studying the written word, which became so important in Judaism, Christianity, and Islam.

The sanctification of the holy writ brought with it the need for scribes and scholars who had the ability to deal with written documents. It is in the period of the canonization of *Deuteronomy* that we hear about scribes *(soferim)* and wise men *(hakhamim)* preoccupied with the written Torah (*Jer.* 8:8). After the return to Judah of many Jews from exile in Babylonia, the man who brought with him the book of the Torah and disseminated it in Judah was Ezra the scribe (*Ezr.* 7:6, 7:11). Since the scribes and wise men were preoccupied with education in general, they did not limit themselves to sacred literature but also taught wisdom literature. The latter consists of didactic instructions on the one hand and speculative treatises on justice in the world (e.g., the *Book of Job*) and the meaning of life (e.g., *Ecclesiastes*) on the other. It is true that wisdom literature is cosmopolitan in nature and therefore addresses man as such and does not refer at all to Israel or to other sacred national concepts. However, this did not deter the scribes and wise men in Israel from incorporating this literature into their lore.

Wisdom literature was canonized and turned into an integral part of the holy writ. Furthermore, it was identified with the revealed Torah (cf. *Sir.* 24). *Deuteronomy,* in which the subject of education plays a central role, defines *torah* as wisdom (*Dt.* 4:6), and as has been shown (Weinfeld, 1972, pp. 260ff.), contains a great many precepts borrowed from wisdom tradition. The amalgamation of the divine word of Torah with the rational values of wisdom turned the law of Israel, especially the Deuteronomic law, into a guide of high moral and humane standards. For example, rest on the Sabbath is explained here as including rest for the slave as well as for his master; similarly, the seventh year *(shemittah)* in *Deuteronomy* is not just for letting the land lie fallow but, also, for the release of the debts of the poor.

THE IMPACT OF PROPHECY UPON ISRAELITE RELIGION

Prophecy was an indispensable tool for any monarchic society in the ancient world. No independent ruler could go out to war or initiate an enterprise of national character without consulting a prophet. Israel was no different in this respect from other nations. The only major difference between Israelite and pagan prophecy was in the way of obtaining the oracle. In the pagan societies the prophets resorted to mechanical devices such as hepatoscopy or augury, whereas in Israel these were forbidden and only prophecy by means of intuition was legitimate.

The prophets were thus serving political and national needs, which is why it is no wonder that most of them were furthering in their prophecies the interests of the king and the people (e.g., *1 Kgs.* 22:12, *Jer.* 14:13–14, et al.). However, the classical prophets, as idealists, managed to free themselves from the professional group (see *Am.* 7:14) and proclaimed, when necessary, messages unfavorable for the king and the people. This made them unique in the ancient world. In their drive for justice and morality, they predicted punishment for the violation of justice, and their words were preserved since their predictions were understood to have been borne out. In their messages the classical prophets came in conflict with popular tradition. They rejected the accepted mode of formal divine worship (*Am.* 5:21, *Is.* 1:13, *Jer.* 7:21–22) and spoke sarcastically and cynically about its conventional institutions (*Am.* 4:4, 5:5; *Hos.* 4:15). They even predicted the destruction of the Temple, which the people considered blasphemous (*Jer.* 26).

However, the prophets also foresaw a new concept of an ideal future in their eschatological visions. Israel was seen as bearing a universal message destined to obliterate idolatry and to bring the gentiles to the one true God, the God of Israel (*Is.* 2:17–18; *Jer.* 3:17, 16:19–21; *Is.* 45:20–25, 56:1–8; *Zep.* 3:9; *Zec.* 2:15, 8:20–23; et al.). In the language of the anonymous prophet ("Second Isaiah") who was active during the Babylonian exile, Israel is designated to become a "light for the nations" so that God's salvation "may reach the ends of the earth" (*Is.* 49:6; cf. *Is.* 42:1–4, 51:4–5). During the same period another prophet envisions that many peoples shall come to seek the Lord in Jerusalem, and "ten men from nations of every tongue will take hold . . . of every Jew by a corner of his cloak and say: 'Let us go with you, for we have heard that God is with you'" (*Zec.* 8:20–23). These idealistic universal visions marked the beginning of a process which culminated in the spread of monotheism through the agencies of Judaism, Christianity, and Islam. They stood in conflict to a particularistic trend which developed during the return from the Babylonian exile in the times of Ezra and Nehemiah (the middle of the fifth century BCE) and which led to Ezra's expulsion of gentile women from the community of Israel (*Ezr.* 9–10).

The particularistic tendency, which expressed a national/ethnic fear of assimilation, was based on scripture enjoining Israel's separation from gentiles (*Ex.* 23:31–33, 34:12–16; *Lv.* 20:26; *Dt.* 7:3–4). These verses refer only to the Canaanite nations, but they were interpreted as being directed against all foreign nations (*Ezr.* 9:12, *Neh.* 13:1–3), and an ideology was based on the idea that the new congregation should represent "the holy seed" (*Ezr.* 9:2), uncontaminated by foreign blood. If this attitude had prevailed, no proselytism would have been possible. Thanks to the universalistic "prophetic" movement, which aspired to admit as many nations as possible into the sphere of Jewish religion (*Zec.* 2:15, 8:23), the particularistic trend was neutralized and proselytism became possible.

An anonymous prophet of this period ("Third Isaiah") even polemicizes with the isolationists and says, "Neither let the foreigner . . . say: 'The Lord will separate me [*navdel yovdilani*] from his people'" (*Is.* 56:3). The prophet employs the same words used by Ezra when revealing his isolationist tendencies: "And the seed of Israel separated themselves [*vayibadlu*] from all foreigners" (*Neh.* 9:2; cf. *Ezr.* 9:1–2). The Judaism of the Second-Temple period managed to reach a synthesis between the two opposing tendencies. Proselytizing was subject to the obligation to keep the law: a gentile could become an Israelite the moment he agreed to take upon himself the precepts of the Israelite religion as embodied in the Torah, especially circumcision (for men) and observance of the Sabbath (see *Isaiah* 56:4: "the eunuchs who keep my Sabbaths, . . . and hold fast to my covenant [through circumcision]").

THE CRYSTALLIZATION OF JUDAISM: THE POSTEXILIC PERIOD

The period of exile and restoration left its deep marks on the people and changed their spiritual character. The severance of the exiles from their land made it easier for them to get rid of the cultic habits associated with the land, such as high-place worship, the burning of incense on the roofs (*Jer.* 7:17–19, 44:15–19), child offering (*2 Kgs.* 23:10; *Jer.* 7:31, 19:5; et al.), and other customs rooted in the Canaanite culture. After the exile, pagan worship never returned to Israel.

Because the exiles were deprived of sacrificial worship as a result of the principle of centralization of worship in Jerusalem, the spiritual, abstract nature of the religion was enhanced. The shift from sacrifice to prayer was facilitated by the very act of centralization, as shown above; however, as long as sacrifice was being practiced in the chosen place in Jerusalem, religion was still tied to the Temple. In the religious vacuum created following the destruction of the First Temple, stress came to be laid on the spiritual side of religion, and thus the way was paved for the institution of the synagogue, which is based on prayer and the recital of holy scripture. We do not know how this institution developed; it is clear, however, that in the times of Ezra and Nehemiah (end of fifth century and beginning of the fourth century BCE) it started its existence in Jerusalem. In *Nehemiah* 8–9 we find all the components of synagogue worship:

1. The recital of scripture with all the pertinent procedure, such as the reader standing on the pulpit (*Neh.* 8:4) displaying the scroll to the people while they stand up (*Neh.* 8:5), the recitation of blessings before the start of the reading (*Neh.* 8:6), and the use of the Targum (an Aramaic translation and explanation of the Torah; *Neh.* 8:8).
2. The reading of the Torah on each one of the holy days (*Neh.* 8:18).
3. The summoning of the people to bless the Lord before starting the prayer (*Neh.* 9:5).
4. Communal prayer (*Neh.* 9:6–14), which contains the elements of the Sabbath and festival conventional prayer.
5. The confession of sin and supplication (*tahanun*; *Neh.* 9:16–37).

All this leaves no doubt that the synagogue service was already taking shape in the fifth century BCE. Since the service as described in *Nehemiah* 8–9 was sponsored by the leadership of the exilic community, it is likely that the exiles brought with them the liturgy as it had crystallized in Babylonia. This suggestion might be supported by the fact that the whole pericope of *Nehemiah* 8–9, which describes in detail the service of the congregation during the first month, the month of the High

Holy Days, does not allude at all to Temple worship, which was undoubtedly quite intensive in this season of the year. The author does not refer to the Temple worship (the Second Temple was in existence since 516 BCE) or comment on this omission since its procedure was performed by priests according to ancient conventional principles.

The relatively newly established synagogal liturgy contained a great deal of edifying material: the doctrines of creation and election (*Neh.* 9:6, 9:7), sin and repentance, and the observance of the Sabbath and the Torah (*Neh.* 9:13–14); thus the liturgy turned into an instrument for the education of the people. Second Temple Jewry was dominated by the Babylonian returnees who, as descendants of the preexilic Judahite aristocracy, managed to preserve the genuine tradition of classical Israel.

Another important factor which shaped the character of Second-Temple Judaism was the impact of prophecy. The fact that prophets of the First-Temple period had predicted the return to Zion after a period of exile added to the glorification of the prophets and to the trust in their words. People began to believe that the prophecies about Jerusalem as the spiritual center of the world would also be realized and that the nations would recognize the God of Israel and finally abandon their idolatrous vanities. This was supported by the exiles' physical encounter with idol worshipers in Babylonia. Convinced of the futility of idol worship (cf. *Is.* 54:6ff.), the exiles apparently tried to persuade their neighbors of it. Some of the enlightened foreigners seem to have been attracted by the peculiar but reasonable faith of the Jews and joined the Jewish congregation (*Is.* 56:1–8; see above), a first step in the spreading of monotheism, and one which prepared the ground for later proselytism and for Christianity. It was during these several centuries that the fundamental elements of Judaism were settled.

Observance of the Torah. The exiles took seriously not only the demand for exclusive loyalty to the God of Israel, which meant complete abolition of idolatry and syncretism, but also the positive commands of God embodied in the law of Moses. They felt obliged not only to fulfill the law in a general sense but to do exactly as written in the book. This demanded expert scribes and exegetes to investigate scripture and explain it to the people (see *Neh.* 8:8).

At this time the Tetrateuch, the first four books of the Pentateuch, was added to the "Book of the Torah," or *Deuteronomy,* which had been sanctified before the exile, with the reform of Josiah in 622 BCE. The Tetrateuch was composed of ancient documents that had already been codified in literary sources, such as the Yahvistic-Elohistic source and the Priestly code. After adding these sources to *Deuteronomy,* the name "Book of the Torah" was extended to the whole of the Pentateuch, namely, the Torah, which was thus also taken as comprising the "Book of Moses."

The Pentateuch, then, comprised various codes representing different schools or traditions and different periods which sometimes contradicted each other. However, all of them were equally obligatory. How then would one fulfill two contradictory laws? According to the Priestly code, for example, one has to set aside a tenth of his crop for the Levites (*Nm.* 18:21f.), while the Deuteronomic code (written after centralization of the cult) commands one to bring the tithe to Jerusalem and consume it in the presence of the Lord (*Dt.* 14:22ff.). These laws reflect different social and historical circumstances, but since both were considered to belong to the law of

Moses, both were authoritative; therefore, in the Second-Temple period two types of tithe were introduced: the so-called first tithe, which was given to the Levites, and second tithe, which was consumed in Jerusalem.

No less a problem was the exact definition of the ancient law in order to apply it to life circumstances. Thus, for example, the commandment "you shall not do any work on the seventh day" (*Ex.* 20:9) is quite vague. What does *work* mean? Is drawing water from the well considered work (as in *Jubilees* 50.8)? Interpretation of the law split the people into sects; the most practical were the Pharisees, who fixed thirty-nine chief labors forbidden on the Sabbath (*Shab.* 7.2), and thus tried to adjust the law to life. The Essenes, however, were much more stringent in their understanding of work forbidden on the Sabbath. Before the Maccabean Revolt (166– 164 BCE), making war was forbidden on the Sabbath; in the Maccabean times, when the nation fought for its existence, the people learned that it could not survive without permitting themselves to fight on the Sabbath.

The struggle for the correct interpretation of the Torah was actually the struggle to fulfill the will of the Lord, and in this goal all Jews were united.

The Fate of the Individual. The problem of individual retribution and the fact of the suffering righteous is mainly dealt with in wisdom literature: *Proverbs, Job,* and *Ecclesiastes.* In *Proverbs* the optimistic view prevails: everybody receives his reward in accordance with his deeds. If one sees a righteous man suffering and a wicked man succeeding, this perception is only an illusion. In the long run the righteous will be vindicated, and the evil will fail (*Prv.* 23:18, 24:14–20, et al.). The wisdom traditions of *Psalms* express this idea most explicitly:

> though the wicked sprout like grass
> though all evildoers blossom
> it is only that they may be destroyed forever.
> (*Ps.* 92:8; RSV 92:7)

> Do not be vexed by evil men;
> do not be incensed by wrongdoers;
> for they soon wither like grass,
> like verdure fade away.
> (*Ps.* 37:1–2)

A similar solution is reflected in the prosaic narrative of *Job*: Job, the righteous one, is restored to his former happiness after long suffering (1–2, 42:7–17).

A different philosophical solution is offered in the poetic section of *Job* (3:1–42:6). In this section the point is made that no one can understand the ways of God and that one should not expect any reward for his deeds. The true faith is one that is independent of material interest. A more skeptical, cynical solution to the problem is found in *Ecclesiastes,* in which everything is said to be predestined by God, and nothing can be changed by man. Hence, one should not complain but enjoy life as long as one can; otherwise everything in life is vanity.

A somewhat mystical response to the problems of seemingly unjust rewards is found in the religious lyrics of *Psalms,* especially in Psalm 73. The Psalmist is perplexed by the problem of the evildoers, "the ever-tranquil who amass wealth" (*Ps.* 73:12), but finds the answer in God's dwelling. Through his trust in God he feels completely secure:

> My body and my mind came to end,
>   but God is my portion forever.
> They who are far from you are lost. . .
> As for me, nearness to God is good.
> I have made the Lord God my refuge.
>
>   (*Ps. 73:26–28*)

The eternal portion (*ḥeleq*) which the pious finds in God reminds one of the expression of later Judaism about the portion in the world to come. That there was in ancient Israel some belief in immortality or blessed posthumous existence may be learned from Psalm 16. The Psalmist opens his prayer with a declaration that he seeks refuge in God, a declaration found also at the end of Psalm 73. Then he speaks about the holy in the earth (the ghosts, *Ps.* 16:3), and in this connection he mentions that he will have no part of their bloody libations, a procedure well attested in the ancient world in connection with necromancy (cf. Theodor H. Gaster, *Myth, Legend, and Custom in the Old Testament,* vol. 2. 1975). Afterward we hear an exclamation, similar to the one in Psalm 73:26–28: "You, Lord, are my alloted portion [*ḥelqi*] . . . Delightful is my inheritance." (*Ps.* 16:5–6). He expresses his hope that his body will rest secure and that God will not let him down into She'ol and will not cause him to see the pit (*Ps.* 16:11). Most instructive here is comaprison of the concept of She'ol with that of the portion of the Lord. She'ol, "the world of shades" (*ref'im*), is here understood in a negative manner, not unlike the Geihinnom (Gehenna) of the Second-Temple period, and is actually the opposite of God's portion and inheritance, which is reserved for the pious. That such ideas prevailed in ancient Israel may be deduced from *Proverbs* 15:24, whre we read: "For the knowledgeable [in God's knowledge] the path of life leads upward, in order to avoid She'ol below." This view is supported by *Ecclessiastes* 3:21, whose author questions the generally accepted premise by asking: "Who knows if the man's spirit does rise upward and if a beast's spirit does sink down into the earth?"

Human Nature and Destiny. The prevalent outlook in the Hebrew Bible is that "man's thoughts and inclinations are always evil" (*Gn.* 6:5); "his inclination is evil from his youth onwards" (*Gn.* 8:21). Yet the fact that man was created in the likeness of God (*Gn.* 1:27, 5:1; cf *Ps.* 8:6) makes him potentially good. God implanted in him the striving toward good or the good inclination (cf. *yetser tov* in rabbinic literature) which complements the evil one (cf. the tree of the knowledge of good and evil in *Gn.* 2–3). Indeed, the prophets envisioned in the ideal future a type of man who is naturally good and, consequently, who will do no evil.

Isaiah describes the ideal man in the framework of his vision of eternal peace (*Is.* 11:1–9). A world of peace between man and animal will be filled with knowledge of the Lord as water covers the sea (*Is.* 11:9). Jeremiah predicted that in the days to come, when the new covenant (*berit ḥadash*) will be established with Israel, there will be no need for teaching one another because every man and child will know the Lord, that is, will know how to behave:

> I will put may law into their inmost being
> and inscribe it up their hearts. . . .
> no longer will they need to teach one another
> and say to one another: "Know the Lord,"
> for all of them, from small to great,
> shall know me.
>
> (Jer. 31:33–34)

Obedience to God and respect for one another will be part of human nature, and force will not be needed to impose God's law.

TRANSFORMATION TO SECOND-TEMPLE JUDAISM

The canonization of the Torah during the time of Ezra brought with it scribal activity and exegesis that marked the beginning of a new period. Over time, the religion gradually shifted away from the domain of the Temple and its functionaries. The will of God, expressed in holy scripture, could not be interpreted not only by the priests but by trained sages (ḥakhamim) and scribes (soferim). This shift was due in part to the fact that after the destruction of the First Temple exiles in Babylonia had begun to base their worship on prayer and the recital of the Torah. Futhermore, Jews living outside the Land of Israel were not subject to many of the purity laws and taboos connected with the land of YHVH (see *Hos.* 9:3–5, *Am.* 7:17b; cf *Jos.* 22:19, *1 Sm.* 26:19). What had been the Israelite religion became less dependent on the physical reality. For Jews living outside the land and for those who had returned, the spiritual dimension of Jewish religious life intensified as stress was laid on institutions of a spiritual nature that were unrelated or only symbolically related to Land and Temple—the Sabbath, synagogal service, religious ethical obligations, and the other fundaments of Judaism as it was to evolve.

[*Related articles include* Biblical Temple; God, *article on* God in the Hebrew Scriptures; Israelite Law; Priesthood, *article on* Jewish Priesthood; *and* Prophecy, *article on* Biblical Prophecy.]

BIBLIOGRAPHY

Albright, William F. *Yahweh and the Gods of Canaan.* London, 1968.

Alt, Albrecht. *Der Gott der Väter: Ein Beitrag zur Vorgeschichte der israelitischen Religion.* Stuttgart, 1929.

Cross, Frank Moore. *The Ancient Library of Qumrân and Modern Biblical Studies.* Rev. ed. Garden City, N.Y., 1961.

Cross, Frank Moore. *Canaanite Myth and Hebrew Epic: Essays in the History of the Religion of Israel.* Cambridge, Mass., 1973.

Eissfeldt, Otto. *The Old Testament: An Introduction.* Translated from the third German edition by Peter R. Ackroyd. Oxford, 1965.

Fohrer, Georg. *History of Israelite Religion.* Translated by David E. Green. Nashville, 1972.

Gaster, Theodor H. *Myth, Legend, and Custom in the Old Testament.* New York, 1969.

Kaufmann, Yehezkel. *History of the Religion of Israel* (in Hebrew). 8 vols. in 6. Jerusalem, 1937–1956. Translated by Moshe Greenberg as *The Religion of Israel: From Its Beginnings to the Babylonian Exile.* New York, 1972.

Mowinckel, Sigmund. *The Psalms in Israel's Worship.* 2 vols. Translated by D. R. Thomas. Oxford, 1962.

Noth, Martin. *Gesammelte Schriften zum Alten Testament*. Munich, 1960.

Pedersen, Johannes. *Israel: Its Life and Culture*. 4 pts. Translated by Aslaug Møller and Annie I. Fausbøll. Oxford, 1926–1947; reprint, Oxford, 1959.

Rad, Gerhard von. *Gesammelte Studien zum Alten Testament*. Munich, 1958.

Rad, Gerhard von. *Old Testament Theology*. 2 vols. Translated by D. M. G. Stalker. New York, 1962–1965.

Vaux, Roland de. *Les institutions de l'Ancien Testament*. 2d ed. Paris 1961. Translated by John McHugh as *Ancient Israel: Its Life and Institutions*. London, 1965.

Vaux, Roland de. *Histoire ancienne d'Israel* (1971). Translated by David Smith as *The Early History of Israel*. Philadelphia, 1978.

Weinfeld, Moshe. "The Covenant of Grant in the Old Testament and in the Ancient Near East." *Journal of the American Oriental Society* 90 (April–June 1970): 184–203.

Weinfeld, Moshe. *Deuteronomy and the Deuteronomic School*. Oxford, 1972.

Weinfeld, Moshe. "Social and Cultic Institutions in the Priestly Source against Their Ancient Near Eastern Background." In *Proceedings of the Eighth World Congress of Jewish Studies*, pp. 95–129. Jerusalem. 1983.

Wellhausen, Julius. *Prolegomena to the History of Israel*. Translated by J. Sutherland Black. Edinburgh, 1885. Reissued as *Prolegomena to the History of Ancient Israel*. New York, 1957.

Zimmerli, Walther. *Gottes Offenbarung: Gesammelte Aufsätze zum Alten Testament*. Munich, 1963.

TWO

POSTBIBLICAL JUDAISM AND CLASSICAL TEXTS

3 PHARISEES

ELLIS RIVKIN

The Pharisees were, along with the Sadducees and the Essenes, one of the three *haereseis* ("schools of thought") that flourished among the Jews from the time of Jonathan the Hasmonean (d. 143/2 BCE) until the destruction of the Second Temple in 70 CE. According to Josephus Flavius, what distinguished them from the other two *haereseis* was their belief that the laws that had been handed down "from the fathers but which were not recorded in the laws of Moses" had to be observed, that there is a delicate interplay between fate and free will, and that every soul is imperishable, with the souls of the good ultimately passing into another body (resurrection) and the souls of the wicked condemned to suffer eternal punishment (cf. *The Jewish War* 2.162–163, 3.374; *Jewish Antiquities* 13.171–173, 18.166). These views, Josephus tells us, were so influential with the masses that "all prayers and sacred rites of divine worship were performed in accord with their exposition" (*Antiquities* 13.298, 18.14–15).

Josephus's description of the Pharisees as the authoritative teachers of the unwritten laws corresponds to Paul's holding up his being "as to the Law a Pharisee" and "as to righteousness under the Law blameless" (*Phil.* 3:4–7) and his precocious commitment as a youth to the *paradosis,* that is, the unwritten laws of the fathers, as justifying his right to speak with authority about the Law (*Gal.* 1:13–17). It also corresponds to Mark's account of the Pharisees' upbraiding Jesus for allowing his disciples to make light of the *paradosis* of the elders (*Mk.* 7:13); to Matthew's affirmation that the scribes (i.e., the Pharisees) sit in Moses' seat, and sit there legitimately (*Mt.* 23:1–3); and to the picture of the Pharisees displayed throughout the Gospels and *Acts of the Apostles* as a class of teachers enjoying an elevated and respected status by virtue of their legal expertise and their religious leadership.

Josephus's description likewise agrees with that of the tannaitic literature (the Mishnah, the Tosefta, and the *beraitot*), the repository of the oral law. Here the Pharisees are found to be identical with the *soferim* ("scribes") and the *hakhamim* ("sages"), who are, as in Josephus and the New Testament, the authoritative teachers of the twofold law (the written and the oral) and, again as in Josephus and the New Testament, juxtaposed to the Sadducees, who rejected the oral law and the authority of the Pharisees.

The name *Pharisees* is derived from the Greek transliteration, with a Greek plural ending, of the Hebrew *perushim,* which means "separatists, deviants, heretics." That the name may have originated as an epithet hurled at these teachers by the Sadducees, who rejected their authority, is indicated by the fact that in the tannaitic literature the term *perushim,* meaning "Pharisees," is used only juxtaposed to *tseduqim* ("Sadducees").

In contrast to the above approach and taking for granted that the Hebrew term *perushim* means "Pharisees" in most tannaitic texts, eminent scholars such as Emil Schürer (1902), Robert Travers Herford (1902), Louis Finkelstein (1962), and, most recently, Jacob Neusner (1971) have constructed a definition of the Pharisees based on a tannaitic text (*Hag.* 2.7) that states that the garments of *perushim* are a source of uncleanness to the *'ammei ha-arets.* According to this text, the *perushim* were pietists who were so scrupulously concerned with the laws of ritual purity that they banded together into a confraternity separating themselves from the less scrupulous masses, the *'ammei ha-arets.* These scholars also identify the *perushim* with the *haverim* ("associates"), who likewise separated themselves from the masses for the same reason (cf. *Dem.* 2.3).

These two attempts to define the term *perushim* are mutually exclusive. The first definition is built on texts that only juxtapose *perushim* to *Tseduqim,* Sadducees, while the second definition is built on texts that only juxtapose *perushim* to *'ammei ha-arets.* Since the definition that juxtaposes the term *perushim* to *tseduqim* conforms not only to certain tannaitic texts but to the testimony of Josephus and the New Testament, it is to be preferred.

ESSENTIAL TEACHINGS AND INSTITUTIONS

The essential core of Pharisaism was its affirmation of a triad of faith that sharply distinguished it from the priestly system of Judaism that had flourished uncontested from the time of the promulgation of the Pentateuch (c. 397 BCE) until the rise of the Pharisees, probably during the Hasmonean Revolt (166–142 BCE). This triad of faith proclaimed that (1) the one God and Father so loved the individual that (2) he revealed to his people Israel a twofold law, one written down in the five books of Moses, the Pentateuch, and the other transmitted orally from Moses to Joshua to the elders to the prophets to the Pharisees (*Avot* 1.1), so that (3) each individual who internalized this twofold law could look forward to eternal life for his soul and resurrection for his body (cf. *San.* 10.1). It would seem that this highly novel triad of faith was rejected by the Sadducees, who reasserted the Aaronic, or priestly, belief that God had revealed a single, immutable written law, which made no mention of eternal life for the individual. On the basis of this triad of faith, however, the Pharisees asserted their authority over the Aaronic priesthood.

The triad of faith likewise generated novel institutions. The first of these was a body called the Beit Din ha-Gadol (Great Court), or the Great Boulē (Gr., "council meeting"). Its function was to legislate new oral laws, to transmit oral laws previously legislated, and to dissolve those oral laws no longer deemed relevant. The Beit Din ha-Gadol consisted of seventy-one authoritative teachers of the twofold law presided over by an elected *nasi'* ("prince"), who represented the majority, and an *av beit din* ("father of the court"), who represented the minority point of view (cf. *Hag.* 2.2). The *nasi'* and the *av beit din* were referred to as a "pair" (Heb., *zug;* pl., *zugot*). The "pairs" flourished from the time of the Hasmonean Revolt until the transformation of the office of the *nasi'* from an elective to a hereditary one, which occurred after the death of Hillel (c. 10 CE). Although during this period debate was mandatory, oral laws once passed were binding on majority and minority alike. When, however, the office of *nasi'* became hereditary, the sages were given the option of following either the oral laws of the school of Hillel or those of the school of Shammai. Following the destruction of the Temple in 70 CE, each authoritative teacher could formulate oral laws that were binding on him and his disciples. [*For another view of the Beit Din ha-Gadol, see* Sanhedrin.]

The institution launched by the Pharisees that proved to be the most durable was the synagogue. [*See* Synagogue, *article on* History and Tradition.] Although many scholars argue that the origin of the synagogue is to be traced back to the Babylonian exile, no source attests to the existence of the synagogue until after the Hasmonean Revolt. Only after the Pharisees proclaimed their triad of faith did prayer and reading from the Pentateuch and the Prophets become mandatory. The individual reaching out for an unmediated relationship with God in his quest for eternal life and resurrection needed a noncultic institution where, in the presence of other co-believers, he could proclaim the Shema' to affirm God's singularity and utter the Tefillah, eighteen blessings that include the statement that God will, with his great mercy, revive the dead. [*For further discussion of the development of the Jewish liturgy, see* Siddur and Maḥzor.]

In addition to novel institutions, the Pharisees developed new notions about God and the peoplehood of Israel. Although God was occasionally conceived of in scripture as a father, it was as the father of his people and not as the father of the individual. The Pharisees, for their part, however, spoke of the father in heaven, who so loves and cares for each individual that he revealed the road by which the individual could reach eternal life and resurrection. The Pharisees further stressed this one-to-one relationship when they coined such new names for God as *Maqom* ("all present, everyplace"), *ha-Qaddosh Barukh Hu'* ("the holy one, blessed be he"), and *Shekhinah* ("indwelling presence").

The Pharisees stressed that God had chosen Abraham to father a people to be a blessing for all the peoples of the earth, and not just for the seed of Abraham. The Pharisees therefore preached that membership in Israel was open to everyone who embraced the triad of faith (cf. *Mt.* 23:15). What defined a true Israelite was his belief that God had revealed a twofold *torah* and that God would reward with eternal life and resurrection the law-abiding individual and punish with eternal suffering those who did not live in accordance with its precepts. A pagan who ascribed to these beliefs was thus a truer member of the house of Israel than was a Sadducee, who, although born into Israel, rejected the twofold law and otherworldly rewards and punishments (cf. Josephus, *Against Apion* 2.210).

As a class, the Pharisees far more resembled peripatetic teachers, such as the Stoics, than either prophets or priests (cf. Josephus, *The Life* 12). As champions of the oral law, they made it a point to formulate their teachings in nonbiblical modes, forms, and language. Thus they wrote down none of their teachings, framed their laws (*halakhot*) and doctrines (*aggadot*) without regard for historical setting, rejected poetic modes of expression even for the prayers and blessings they formulated, cultivated logical (i.e., deductive) modes of reasoning, and introduced proof texts.

HISTORY

None of the sources, not even Josephus, was interested in the history of the Phari-sees, which must, therefore, be reconstructed from indirect evidence. A likely origin for the movement is the Hasmonean Revolt, when the breakdown of traditional priestly authority as exercised by a high priest of the Aaron-Eleazar-Phine-has . . . Zadok line collapsed and the need for new leaders was desperate. Con-fronted by Antiochus's decrees, which threatened with death the Jews who remained true to the Law, and confronted with the question of why one should die for the Law if no reward for such martyrdom could be forthcoming in this world, a group of *soferim* responded to this crisis of survival by proclaiming that God had revealed two laws and not one, and that God would reward with eternal life those who gave up their lives. Support by the majority of the Jewish people enabled the *soferim* to overthrow the Zadokite high priesthood and convoke on their own authority a Great Synagogue, which in 142 BCE invested a non-Zadokite, Simon the Hasmonean, as high priest (cf. *1 Mc.* 14:27–35).

Beholden to the Pharisees for their high priestly office, first Simon (142–134) and then his son John Hyrcanus (134–104) gave their seal of approval to the oral law. But eventually John Hyrcanus broke with the Pharisees, abrogated their unwritten laws, and seeded the soil for the bloody civil war that broke out during the high priesthood and reign (103–76) of his son Alexander Yannai (Josephus, *Antiquities* 13.288–298, 372– 383, 398–404). Alexander Yannai's successor, SalomeAlexandra (76–67), made peace with the Pharisees, restored them to power, and reinstituted the oral law. In order to keep the Sadducees in line, however, the Pharisees sanc-tioned bloody reprisals against the Sadducean leaders (*Antiquities* 13.408–418). Rec-ognizing that the substance of their faith required only that they be free to teach the road to eternal life and resurrection and that all public manifestations of religion, such as the liturgical calendar and worship in the Temple, would be carried out in accordance with the provisions of the oral law, the Pharisees formulated the doc-trine of two realms, secular and divine, with respect to the state and a doctrine of tolerance with respect to the Sadducees and the Essenes. These doctrines were embraced by the political authorities, whether Hasmonean, Herodian, or Roman, and by the other religious groups. Thus when the first Roman procurator, Copon-ius (6–9 CE), ordered a census to determine the size of the tribute to be levied on the Judeans, the Pharisees urged the people to cooperate, since the Romans were not interfering in the religious sphere. And when some of their followers broke with their leaders on this issue, this difference alone was sufficient to mark them off as a fourth philosophy, a *haeresis* in their own right (*Antiquities* 18.2–10, 23–25).

This doctrine of the two realms remained firm until the outbreak of the revolt against Rome, in 65 CE, which the Pharisees sought to head off until the very last moment (*Jewish War* 2.411–414). Some of the leaders of the Pharisees reluctantly gave their support to the revolutionaries; others, however, remained adamant, and one of them, Yohanan ben Zakk'ai, managed to escape from the besieged city of Jerusalem and convinced the Roman general Vespasian that the Pharisees could be depended on to adhere to the doctrine of the two realms.

With the destruction of Jerusalem and the burning of the Temple, the Pharisees emerged triumphant, the unchallenged leaders of the Jewish people. The Sadducees, who consisted preeminently of priests, disappeared as a group, as did the Essenes. The name *Pharisees* fell into disuse, because it had never been used by the group itself but only by its Sadducean opponents.

THE PHARISEES AND JESUS

As the authoritative teachers of the twofold law, the Pharisees were troubled by Jesus' refusal to bow to their authority. They therefore challenged his claim to a singular relationship to God. But this was as far as the Pharisees could go, since they were committed to the principle of religious tolerance. Jesus' teachings were, if anything, even less heretical than those of the Sadducees, whom the Pharisees challenged but did not bring to trial before either the Beit Din ha-Gadol or a lesser body called simply a *beit din* ("court") or *boulē* ("council meeting"). Since all the Gospels are in agreement that Jesus was tried before a Sanhedrin presided over by a high priest appointed by the Roman procurator, which was hence religiously illegitimate and therefore solely a political body, Jesus must have been tried on political, not religious grounds. In Jesus' day the distinction between a political Sanhedrin and the Pharisaic *boulē* was a matter of daily experience, as the Gospels testify (*Acts* 23:1–10, 26–30). Whatever role Pharisees played as members of a political Sanhedrin was strictly political and not religious.

The hostility toward the Pharisees found in the Gospels is thus to be seen as stemming from their authors' anger with these teachers for having rejected Jesus' claims and those of his followers. When put in historical perspective, it is evident that such central Christian beliefs as the Resurrection are rooted in the central beliefs of the Pharisees and that Paul's conversion is inconceivable without his extreme anxiety as to whether he had been sufficiently obedient to the twofold law to merit eternal life for his soul and resurrection for his body. Certainly the Christian triad of faith bears a formal resemblance to that of the Pharisees, with the twofold law of the Pharisees displaced by Jesus Christ. [*See* Christianity and Judaism; Jesus; *and the biography of Paul.*]

HISTORICAL SIGNIFICANCE

The Pharisees transformed Judaism first by elevating themselves to Moses' seat and by proclaiming the twofold law, and not the written law alone, to be normative. The Pharisees' oral law gave birth to the Mishnah, the Palestinian and Babylonian Talmuds, the geonic, medieval, and modern *responsa,* and the various codes of Jewish law—all of which are, for a majority of Jews, still recognized as normative.

Second, by affirming the belief in eternal life and resurrection for every individual who internalizes the twofold law, the Pharisees established a one-to-one relationship with God the Father, strengthened the believing individual, and readied him for martyrdom when need be.

Third, by linking personal salvation to an internalized twofold law and by freeing the individual's salvation from the intermediating role of priest, prophet, or sage, the Pharisees made it possible for Judaism not only to flourish in the Diaspora but to establish centers there that exercised a higher degree of religious authority and influence than did those in the Land of Israel.

Fourth, by their success in winning over the majority of Jews to their belief in eternal life and resurrection, the Pharisees set the stage for Christianity. Had not Jesus and his disciples believed in the resurrection of the dead, it is hardly likely that Jesus' disciples would have been so certain that they had indeed seen Jesus risen from the dead. Thus the New Testament bears witness to the Pharisaic use of proof texts, the Pharisaic system of reasoning, the Pharisaic mode of oral transmission through discrete episodes, items, and dicta, Pharisaic ethical and moral teachings, and Pharisaic abandonment of poetry as a medium for law, lore, and liturgy. Although less direct, the Pharisees' teachings of eternal life and resurrection had a major impact on a central belief of Islam.

Fifth, by absorbing Greco-Roman institutional models, such as the *boulē*, Greco-Roman modes of deductive reasoning, and Greco-Roman examples of lawmakers, sages, and philosophers, the Pharisees enabled their followers to be in congruence with Greco-Roman civilization without loss of their Jewish identity.

Perhaps the most enduring of the achievements of the Pharisees was their focus on the individual and his yearnings for an eternal life for his individual soul and his individual body. By picturing God the Father as so loving every individual that his yearning for immortality might be fulfilled, the Pharisees, and the Christian and Muslim teachers who took up the refrain, enhanced the individual's sense of eternal worth.

[*For another view of this period in Jewish history, see* Rabbinic Judaism in Late Antiquity.]

BIBLIOGRAPHY

The definition of the Pharisees offered above was first articulated in Solomon Zeitlin's *History of the Second Jewish Commonwealth: Prolegomena* (Philadelphia, 1933), pp. 41–56, and spelled out in detail by him in "Ha-Tseduqim ve-ha-Perushim," *Horeb* 3 (1936): 56–89, which appeared in English as "The Sadducees and the Pharisees: A Chapter in the Development of the Halakhah," in Zeitlin's *Studies in the Early History of Judaism*, vol. 2 (New York, 1974), pp. 259–291. It has been further elaborated in my own writings, especially "The Internal City," *Journal of Scientific Study of Religion* 5 (1966): 225–240; "The Pharisaic Revolution," in *Perspectives in Jewish Learning*, vol. 2 (Chicago, 1966), pp. 26–51; "Prolegomenon," in *Judaism and Christianity*, edited by W. O. E. Oesterley (1937–1938; reprint, New York, 1969); "Pharisaism and the Crisis of the Individual in the Graeco-Roman World," *Jewish Quarterly Review* 61 (July 1970): 27–52; "Defining the Pharisees: The Tannaitic Sources," *Hebrew Union College Annual* 40/41 (1969–1970): 205–249; and *A Hidden Revolution: The Pharisees' Search for the Kingdom Within* (Nashville, 1977). Although I am fundamentally in agreement with Zeitlin on the definition of the Pharisees, I diverge radically from him on reconstructing their history; compare Zeitlin's *The Rise and Fall of the Judean State*, vol. 1 (Philadelphia, 1962), pp. 178–187, with my article "Solomon Zeitlin's Contribution to the Historiography of the Inter-Testamental Period," *Judaism* 14 (Summer 1965): 354–367, and my book *A Hidden Revolution*, pp. 211–251.

For the range of scholarly opinion, see especially A. Michel and J. Moyne's comprehensive discussion and extensive bibliography in "Le Pharisiens," in *Dictionnaire de la Bible, supplément*, edited by H. Cazelles and A. Feuillet, fascs. 39–40 (Paris, 1966), and Ralph Marcus's "The Pharisees in the Light of Modern Scholarship," *Journal of Religion* 32 (July 1952): 153–164. Most influential have been the views of Emil Schürer in *A History of the Jewish People in the*

Time of Jesus Christ, 2d div., vol. 2, 2d rev. ed. (New York, 1902), pp. 10–28; R. Travers Herford in *The Pharisees* (1924; reprint, Boston, 1962); George Foot Moore in *Judaism in the First Centuries of the Christian Era,* in vol. 1 (Cambridge, Mass., c. 1927), pp. 56–71; Louis Finkelstein in *The Pharisees: The Sociological Background of Their Faith,* 2 vols., 3d ed. (Philadelphia, 1962); and, more recently, Jacob Neusner in *The Rabbinic Traditions about the Pharisees before 70,* 3 vols. (Leiden, 1971), and *From Politics to Piety: The Emergence of Pharisaic Judaism* (Englewood Cliffs, N.J., 1972).

4 RABBINIC JUDAISM IN LATE ANTIQUITY

JACOB NEUSNER

In its formative period, 70–640 CE, rabbinic Judaism forged a synthesis between two antithetical phenomena in the religion of Israel: first, the messianic movement, with its stress on history's meaning and end, and second, the priestly component, with its interest in enduring and ahistorical natural life, celebrated in the cult. Starting with the Mishnah, the systematic expression of the priestly viewpoint, composed in the aftermath of the two great messianic wars against Rome (66–73 and 132–135), the rabbis of late antiquity so reconstructed the Mishnah's system of law and theology as to join to that system the long-standing messianic and historical emphases. Rabbinic Judaism thus presents a way of life of order and regularity, lived out beyond the disturbances of one-time events of history, but in which Jews looked forward to the end of time and the coming of the Messiah. That is, as a result of their adhering to that same, permanent, holy way of life, the Messiah would come. The thesis of historical and teleological messianism generated its antithesis, the Mishnaic system of the everyday celebration of eternal things, which then fused into the rabbinic synthesis, legal-messianic Judaism as it has been known from late antiquity to our own times.

DEFINITIONS

By *Judaism* we mean a worldview and way of life held by a group of Jews, defining the holiness of their people. Any kind of Judaism will draw upon the Hebrew scriptures (the "Old Testament"), usually called Tanakh, an acronym standing for *Torah* (Law), *Nevi'im* (Prophets), and *Ketuvim* (Writings). Every kind selects and interprets a particular part of the Hebrew scriptures.

By *late antiquity* we mean the first six centuries of the common era, from the destruction of the Jerusalem Temple in 70 CE to the Muslim conquest of the Near and Middle East about 640 CE. The countries in which rabbinic Judaism took shape and flourished were the Land of Israel (Erets Yisra'el, i.e., "Palestine") under Roman, then Byzantine, rule (from before the first century CE to the Muslim conquest nearly seven centuries later) and Babylonia, part of the western satrapies of the Iranian empire (to about 225 under the Parthians, an Iranian people of the northeast; from about 225 to the Muslim conquest, under the Sasanids, an Iranian dynasty from the province of Fārs). [*See map accompanying* Judaism, *overview article.*]

As to sources, rabbinic Judaism is known to us from documents created in the period under discussion: the Mishnah (c. 200 CE) and the two Talmuds (one produced in Babylonia about 500 CE, the other in the Land of Israel a century earlier), which in form constitute commentaries to the Mishnah. Other important rabbinic documents of the time include commentaries on parts of the Hebrew scriptures—in particular *Mekhilta'*, for *Exodus; Sifra'*, for *Leviticus;* and *Sifrei*, for *Numbers* and *Deuteronomy*—and *Bere'shit Rabbah* and *Vayiqra' Rabbah*, compilations of exegeses on *Genesis* and *Leviticus*. The Jewish prayer book *(siddur)* and certain mystical writings come down from this same period. They clearly relate to the larger rabbinic form of Judaism. But the precise definition of that relationship has not been fully clarified.

The adjective *rabbinic* before the noun *Judaism* tells us that we deal with a kind of Judaism named after its principal kind of leader, a rabbi, a supernatural sage. The definition of *rabbi* shifts in ancient times. The title itself was originally quite neutral, and not unique to Jews. It means simply "My lord," and hence no more than *Monsieur* or *Mein Herr*. When Jesus was called "rabbi," the term was equivalent to *teacher* or *master, Sir*. Rabbis in the Mishnah, figures of the first and second centuries, generally give opinions about trivial legal matters; they were considered sages but were never represented as wonder-workers. Representations of rabbis in documents from the third century onward, including discussion of first- and second-century figures in those later documents, by contrast present the rabbi as a supernatural figure. The rabbi then emerges as a lawyer-magician, or supernatural judge-sage-mystic. Accordingly, through the centuries the title *rabbi* has come to refer solely to a distinctive amalgam, within the Jewish nation, of learning, piety, and holiness or supernatural power, associated with the sages of the Talmud and related writings.

"Rabbinic Judaism," then, is the worldview and way of life applied to the Jewish nation by rabbis. The Judaism under discussion also is called "Talmudic," after its principal literary documents. It may be called "classical" or "normative" in reference to its definitive character from its own day to today. In Talmudic times, however, the conception of a systematic *-ism,* a Juda-ism, is not attested in the rabbinical literature. Outsiders, coming after the fact, identify and name a religion. That an abstract system was perceived and named is not likely. We cannot isolate a word, or a concept to be presented by a single word, for "Judaism." The closest verbal symbol for this kind of Judaism is *Torah*. A sage became a rabbi because he knew Torah in the right way, having learned under proper auspices and having given ample evidence of accurate mastery and correct interpretation of the Torah.

It follows that the definitive trait of rabbinic Judaism is stress upon Torah. In fact, we may define the character of this kind of Judaism within three elements: holy faith, holy man, holy way of life. Thus, first is emphasis upon the doctrine of the dual revelation to Moses at Sinai, a written Torah (the Pentateuch) and an oral Torah. Second comes belief in the leadership of the sage, or rabbi (in context, "My lord"). Third, we find stress upon doing the will of God through study of Torah under the guidance of sages and upon living the holy way of life laid down in the Torah as interpreted by rabbis.

THE MYTH

Let us now consider in detail the definitive symbolic structure of rabbinic Judaism, as it emerges from late antiquity. The central myth of classical Judaism is the belief that the ancient scriptures constituted divine revelation, but only a part of it. At Sinai God had handed down a dual revelation: the written part known to one and all, but also the oral part preserved by the great scriptural heroes, passed on by prophets to various ancestors in the obscure past and finally, and most openly and publicly, handed down to the rabbis who created the Talmuds. The "whole Torah" thus consisted of both written and oral parts. The rabbis taught that the "whole Torah" was studied by sages of every period in Israelite history from Moses to the present. It is a singular, linear conception of a revelation preserved only by the few but pertaining to the many, and in time capable of bringing salvation to all.

The Torah myth further regards Moses as "our rabbi." It holds that whoever embodies the teachings of "Moses, our rabbi," thereby conforms to the will of God, and not to God's will alone but also to his *way*. In heaven God and the angels study Torah just as rabbis do on earth. God dons phylacteries like a Jew. He prays in the rab-binic mode. He carries out the acts of compassion called for by Judaic ethics. He guides the affairs of the world according to the rules of Torah, just as he does the rabbi in his court. One exegesis of the creation legend taught that God had looked into the Torah and therefrom had created the world.

The myth of Torah is multidimensional. It includes the striking detail that whatever the most recent rabbi is destined to discover through proper exegesis of the tradition is as much a part of the way revealed to Moses as is a sentence of scripture itself. It therefore is possible to participate even in the giving of the law by appropriate, logical inquiry into the law. God himself, studying and living by Torah, is believed to subject himself to these same rules of logical inquiry. If an earthly court overrules the testimony, delivered through miracles, of the heavenly one, God would rejoice, crying out, "My sons have conquered me! My sons have conquered me."

Before us is a mythical-religious system in which earth and heaven correspond to one another, with Torah as the nexus and model of both. The heavenly paradigm is embodied upon earth. Moses "our rabbi" is the pattern for the ordinary sage. And God himself participates in the system, for it is his image that, in the end, forms that cosmic paradigm. The faithful Jew constitutes the projection of the divine on earth. Honor is due to the learned rabbi more than to the scroll of the Torah, for through his learning and logic he may alter the very content of Mosaic revelation. He is Torah, not merely because he lives by it but because at his best he forms as compelling an embodiment of the heavenly model as does a Torah scroll itself.

The final and generative element in the rabbinic Torah myth concerns salvation. It takes many forms. One salvific teaching holds that had Israel not sinned—that is, disobeyed the Torah—the scriptures would have closed with the story of the conquest of Palestine. From that eschatological time, the sacred community would have lived in eternal peace under the divine law. Keeping the Torah was therefore the veritable guarantee of salvation. The opposite is said in many forms as well. Israel had sinned; therefore, God had called the Assyrians, Babylonians, and Romans to destroy the Temple of Jerusalem; but in his mercy he would be equally faithful to restore the fortunes of the people when they, through their suffering and repentance, had expiated the result and the cause of their sin.

So, in both negative and positive forms, the Torah myth tells of a necessary connection between the salvation of the people and of the world and the state of Torah among them. For example, if all Israel would properly keep two Sabbaths, the Messiah would come. Of special interest here is the rabbinic saying that the rule of the pagans depends upon the sin of Israel. If Israel would constitute a full and complete replication of "Torah"—that is, of heaven—then pagan rule would come to an end. When Israel makes itself worthy through its embodiment of Torah—that is, through its perfect replication of the heavenly way of living—then the end will come.

THE MISHNAH'S LAYER OF RABBINIC JUDAISM

The history of the Judaism expressed in this Torah myth is obscured by the superficially uniform character of the rabbinic compilations of late antiquity. All of them, early and late, appear to wish to say pretty much the same thing. It goes without saying that each rabbinic document finds in scripture ample precedent for its own viewpoint. That is why they all look alike. The documents, moreover, are collective, bearing the names of many authorities in common. Accordingly, when we turn to the sources for the viewpoint just now outlined, we find it everywhere. So it is difficult to trace the history of the ideas shared in common by them. Yet that is not entirely the case, for there is one rabbinic document of late antiquity, the Mishnah, that stands apart from the rest. It ignores scripture and the need for proof-texts, on the one side, and it omits reference to the Torah myth as the critical symbolic element, on the other.

The Mishnah is the first document of rabbinic Judaism, and it constitutes the foundation for the two Talmuds and the law of Judaism thereafter. The Mishnah rarely cites a scriptural proof-text for any of its propositions, even when the laws simply rephrase in the Mishnah's own language the facts supplied by scripture. Except for the tractate *Avot,* distinct in language and character, the Mishnah finds no room in its definitive construction—that is, in the formation of its principal divisions, let alone in its subdivisions (tractates) and their chapters—for extended discussion on the matter of the study of Torah, the place of the sage in the heavenly-earthly continuum, and those other propositions definitive of the Judaism that rests upon the Mishnah.

That is not to say the Mishnah knows nothing of the priority of learning. On the contrary, here and there we find explicit statements that the sage takes precedence. But the issue is this-worldly, not a matter of supernatural consequence, as is the case in equivalent allegations in Talmudic and later writings. An instance of the Mishnah's phrasing of the matter is in *Horayot* 3.5, followed by the Tosefta's gloss of the passage:

> A *priest takes precedence over a Levite, a Levite over an Israelite, an Israelite over a* mamzer, *a* mamzer *over a* natin, *a* natin *over a proselyte, a proselyte over a freed slave.*
> *Under what circumstances?*
> *When all of them are equivalent* [*in other regards*].
> *But if the* mamzer *was a disciple of a sage, and a high priest was an ignoramus, the* mamzer *who is a disciple of a sage takes precedence over a high priest who is an ignoramus.*

The Tosefta adds:

> A sage takes precedence over a king.
> [For if] a sage dies, we have none who is like him.
> [If] a king dies any Israelite is suitable to mount the throne.
>
> (Tosefta, Horayot 2.8)

What we see here is the first stage in the process by which the sage is moved from a merely earthly status as a principal authority to the supernatural position described above. Accordingly, the notion that Torah-learning enjoys priority is not alien to the Mishnah, and indeed begins there. But the Mishnah contains no hint of the view of the sage as a supernatural figure. Furthermore, the Mishnah distinguishes wonder-workers, such as Honi the Circle Maker (Ta'an. 3.8), from the sages, expressing disapproval of the former.

A still more striking trait of the Mishnah's kind of Judaism is the stress, within the Mishnah's system, upon enduring things and the omission of reference to one-time, historical events. The Mishnah presents a world in stasis, in which regularities and orderly patterns govern. It scarcely alludes to the coming of a messiah, the end of days, the meaning of Israel's suffering. The Mishnah offers no explanation or interpretation of Israel's history. If, therefore, we may characterize the first literary evidence of rabbinic Judaism in late antiquity, as of about 200 CE, we describe that Judaism as focused upon the ongoing life of nature, the priesthood, and the Temple, with the sage telling the priests what to do. The Mishnah's simple, descriptive laws indicate how Israelite society, revolving about the cult, is maintained in stasis.

THE TALMUDIC RABBIS' RETURN TO SCRIPTURE AND HISTORY

Now at the other end of the period at hand, about 600 CE, that is not the Judaism that emerges. On the contrary, as we have seen, rabbinic Judaism fully revealed focused upon the meaning of Israel's history, its end in the coming of the Messiah. It was deeply engaged by one-time events and their meaning. Torah was defined by the sage as a supernatural figure who was qualified by constant reference to scripture. The contrast between the Mishnah's statements, divorced from scripture even where repeating scripture's own facts, and the later reception of the Mishnah, is seen in one fact. Both Talmuds systematically supply to Mishnah's laws precisely those proof-texts omitted by the Mishnah's fram ers. Accordingly, the Talmudic authorities will cite Mishnah's passage and immediately ask, "How do we know these things?" What follows will be scriptural proof-texts.

There is further indication that, in the two centuries after the closure of the Mishnah, about 200 CE, a massive reaction against the Mishnah's formulation of an ahistorical Judaism of eternal return took place. The character of other writings produced by the rabbis of those centuries provides important evidence of a renewed interest in history and its meaning. Beyond the two Talmuds and Tosefta, centered upon the Mishnah, we have the formation of compilations of exegetical remarks, systematically laid forth for the Pentateuchal books of Genesis and Leviticus. These are generally supposed to have come into existence in the fifth century, that is, just as the Talmud of the Land of Israel had come to conclusion and the Talmud of Babylonia was coming to closure. Even more striking is the character of Sifra', a systematic essay on the Book of Leviticus. One basic literary form of that exegetical document is the citation of a passage of the Mishnah, or of Tosefta, verbatim or nearly so. The anonymous voice of the document then asks, "Is this not a matter of [mere] logic?" The argument then will unfold to prove that logic alone cannot prove with certainty the proposition of the Mishnah that has been cited. To the contrary, the only foundation of certainty is in a cited scripture, sometimes then subjected to exegetical work to prove the proposition of the Mishnah that stands at the head of the passage. The polemic is unmistakable. The Mishnah's laws, standing by themselves, cannot endure. Only provision of exegetical bases for them will suffice.

MESSIANISM

Beyond the emphasis upon the sage as a supernatural figure and upon scripture as the sole sound basis of truth, the third pillar of rabbinic Judaism as it emerged from late antiquity was its emphasis upon Torah as the means of reaching the messianic fulfillment and resolution of Israel's history. The authoritative expression of the messianic expectation is in the *siddur* (prayer book), emerging from late antiquity and enduring to the present day:

> Sound the great shofar to herald man's freedom;
> Raise high the banner to gather all exiles;
> Restore our judges as in days of old;
> Restore our counselors as in former times;
> Remove from us sorrow and anguish.
> Reign over us alone with loving kindness;
> With justice and mercy sustain our cause.
> Praised are You, O Lord, King who loves justice.

The restoration of the exiles to Zion and the gathering of the dispersed followed naturally by the prayer for good government, government under God's law. Then comes the concrete reference to the Messiah:

> Have mercy, O Lord, and return to Jerusalem, Your city;
> May Your presence dwell there as You promised.
> Rebuild it now, in our days and for all time;
> Re-establish there the majesty of David, Your servant.
> Praised are You, O Lord, who rebuilds Jerusalem.
> Bring to flower the shoot of Your servant David.
> Hasten the advent of the messianic redemption;
> Each and every day we hope for Your deliverance.
> Praised are You, O Lord, who assures our deliverance.

The link between the messianic hope for salvation and the religion of Torah and of rabbinic authority is expressed time and again in rabbinic writings. One example is as follows:

Rabbah [a fourth-century rabbi] said, "When a man is brought in for judgment in the world to come, he is asked, 'Did you deal in good faith? Did you set aside time for study of Torah? Did you engage in procreation? Did you look forward to salvation? Did you engage in the dialectics of wisdom? Did you look deeply into matters?'"   (B.T., Shab. *31a*)

Rabbah's interpretation of the scripture "And there shall be faith in thy times, strength, salvation, wisdom and knowledge" (*Is.* 33:6) provides one glimpse into the cogent life of rabbinic Judaism. The first consideration was ethical: did the man conduct himself faithfully? The second was study of Torah, not at random but every day, systematically, as a discipline of life. Third came the raising of a family. Celibacy and abstinence from sexual life were regarded as sinful. The full use of man's creative powers for the procreation of life was a commandment. But, fourth, merely living day by day according to an upright ethic was not sufficient. It is true that people must live by a holy discipline, but the discipline itself was only a means. The end was salvation, daily expected in consequence of everyday deeds.

When we reflect upon the Talmudic teaching, already cited, that if all Israel only twice will properly keep the Sabbath (as the rabbis instruct), the Messiah will come, we see the true state of affairs. The heirs of the Mishnah took over the messianic hope, so deep in the consciousness of the Jewish nation from biblical times onward, and harnessed its power to the system we now know as rabbinic Judaism, a holy way of life taught by masters of Torah. Accordingly, as stated at the outset, in late antiquity we witness the formation on the disparate foundations of, first, the Mishnah, a law code lacking reference to history, on the one side, and, second, hope for the end of history and the coming of the Messiah, on the other, the kind of Judaism we call rabbinic.

INSTITUTIONS

The institutional forms of rabbinic Judaism as we know them in particular from the Talmuds, are two. The first, not surprisingly, is the figure of the rabbi. The second is the court-school, that is, the place in which the rabbi ruled on certain matters affecting the Jewish community and also taught his apprentices, that is, disciples. Let us speak first of the figure of the rabbi as we know him in the third through the seventh century in the Babylonian Talmud.

The Rabbi. The rabbis of that period conceived that on earth they studied Torah just as God, the angels, and "Moses, our rabbi," did in heaven. The heavenly schoolmen were even aware of Babylonian scholastic discussions. This conception must be interpreted by reference to the belief that the man truly made in the divine image was the rabbi; he embodied revelation, both oral and written, and all his actions constituted paradigms that were not merely correct but actually heavenly. Rabbis could create and destroy men because they were righteous, free of sin, or otherwise holy, and so enjoyed exceptional grace from heaven. It follows that Torah was held to be a source of supernatural power. The rabbis controlled the power of Torah because of their mastery of its contents. They furthermore used their own mastery of Torah quite independently of heavenly action. They were masters of witchcraft, incantations, and amulets. They could issue blessings and curses, create men and animals, and communicate with heaven. Their Torah was sufficiently effective to thwart the action of demons. However much they disapproved of other people's magic, they themselves were expected to do the things magicians did.

The rabbi was the authority on theology, including the structure and order of the supernatural world. He knew the secret names of God and the secrets of the divine "chariot"—the heavens—and of creation. If extraordinarily pious, he might even see the face of the Shekhinah, the presence of God; in any event, the Shekh inah was present in the rabbinical schools. The rabbi overcame the evil impulse that dominated ordinary men and was consequently less liable to suffering, misfortune, and sickness. He was able to pray effectively because he knew the proper times and forms of prayer. Moreover, the efficacy of his prayers was heightened by his purity, holiness, and other merits, which in turn derived from his knowledge of the secrets of Torah and his consequent particular observances. He could bring rain or cause drought. His blessings brought fertility, and his curse, death. He was apt to be visited by angels and to receive messages from them. He could see and talk with demons and could also communicate with the dead. He was an authority on interpretation of omens and dreams, on means of averting witchcraft, on incantations for cures, on knot tying (for phylacteries), and on the manufacture and use of amulets.

A central conception set rabbinic Judaism apart from Manichaeism, Mazdaism, Christianity, and other contemporary cults. It was not expected that the masses would assume the obligations of or attain to the supernatural skills of the Manichaean elect, Mazdean magi, Christian nuns and monks, or the religious virtuosi and cultic specialists of other groups. All male Jews, however, were expected to become rabbis. The rabbis wanted to transform the entire Jewish community into an academy where the whole Torah was studied and kept.

These beliefs aid in understanding the rabbis' view that Israel would be redeemed, the Messiah brought, through Torah. Because Israel had sinned, it was punished by being given over into the hands of earthly empires; when it atoned, it would be removed from their power. The means of this atonement or reconciliation were study of Torah, practice of commandments, and doing good deeds. These would transform each male Jew into a rabbi, hence into a saint. When all Jews had become rabbis, they then would no longer lie within the power of history. The Messiah would come. So redemption depended upon the "rabbinization" of all Israel, that is, upon the attainment by all Jewry of a full and complete embodiment of revelation or Torah, thus achieving a perfect replica of heaven. When Israel on earth became such a replica, it would be able, as a righteous, holy, saintly community, to exercise the supernatural power of Torah, just as some rabbis were already doing. With access to the consequent theurgical capacities, redemption would naturally follow.

The School. Study of Torah was just that: primarily an intellectual enterprise whose supernatural effects were decidedly secondary. The resources of the schools were knowledge of the laws and traditions that for the rabbis constituted the Torah of Moses. The actual method of learning used by the academies had nothing whatever to do with magic. The "Torah" of the rabbis was essentially no more than a legal tradition that had to be studied by the classical legal methods. The rabbis were expected to act as did other holy men, but they themselves respected legal learning and the capacity to reason about cases. Not everyone would achieve such skills of reasoning any more than everyone could make rain, and the academies doubtless attracted many who could only memorize and repeat what they knew. The whole process of learning, not merely its creative and innovative aspects, was, however, regarded as sacred, for the words themselves were holy.

The following exposition from the school of Rabbi 'Anan exemplifies this process:

What is the meaning of the Scripture You that ride on white asses, that sit on rich cloths, and that walk by the way, tell of it (Judges 5:10)?
Those that ride on asses *are the sages who go from city to city and from province to province to study Torah.*
White *means that they make it clear as the noon hour.*
Sitting on cloths *means that they judge a case truly.*
And that walk *refers to masters of Scripture.*
On the way, *these are masters of Mishnah.*
Tell of it *refers to masters of Talmud, all of whose conversation concerns matters of Torah.*   (B.T., Eruv. 54b)

Found in the Song of Deborah, this verse about the victory of Israel over the Canaanites was explained by the rabbis as a description of the triumph of the Lord in the "wars of the Torah," a frequent image of rabbinic Judaism, and the consequent celebration by the people of the Lord. That people included many whose talents were limited but who, added all together, constituted, and celebrated, the Lord's triumph. Some, like itinerant philosophers, would wander in search of teachings. Others had great skill at clarification. Others were able and selfless judges. Still others merely knew scripture, or Mishnah, or Talmud, but spoke of nothing else. Here is the integrated, mature vision of the academies: a whole people devoted to revelation, each in his own way and according to his talent.

RABBIS AND ORDINARY FOLK

What average Jews ordinarily did not know and the rabbis always did know was the one thing that made a common man into a rabbi: *"Torah" learned through discipleship.* It begs the question to speak of the ordinary people as "ignorant of Judaism." One does not have to exaggerate the educational attainments of the community as a whole to recognize that learning in the rabbinic traditions did not by itself separate the rabbi from other people. It would, accordingly, be a gross error to overestimate the differences separating the way of life of the ordinary Jews from that of the rabbinical estate.

In general the rabbis' merely conventional social manners or customs were deepened into spiritual conceptions and magnified by their deeply mythic ways of thinking. In the villages ordinary people regarded the rabbi as another holy man, but still as a man, heart and soul at one in community with other Jews. The rabbinical ideal was antidualistic; the rabbis believed that all Israel, not just saints, prophets, and sages, stood at Sinai. All bore common responsibilities. No one conceived of two ways of living a holy life—two virtues or two salvations—but of only one Torah to be studied and observed by all, and thus the cutting edge of rabbinical separateness was blunted. The inevitable gap between the holy man and the layman was further reduced by the deep concern felt by rabbis for the conduct of the masses. This concern led them to involve themselves in the everyday affairs of ordinary people, and it produced considerable impact upon daily life.

A review of the primary distinctive characteristics of the rabbinical school will show that the rabbis could not have created unscalable walls of social or religious difference. The sages spent a good part of their years in these schools; ordinary

Jews, obviously, did not. Yet the schools were not monasteries. Disciples who left but who remained loyal to the school's way of life did not engage in ascetic disciplines of an outlandish sort, calculated to utterly divide the sages' way of living from that of normal men. They married. They ate regularly and chose edible food, not wormwood or locusts or ref use. They lived in villages, not in the wilderness. They did not make their livelihood through holy vagrancy. Their clothes were not supposed to be tattered or in rags. These differences between rabbis and other types of holy men, such as the Christian monks and the Manichaean elect, are obvious and therefore all the more important. The sages sought the society of ordinary Jews, so they lived in the villages rather than in the countryside ("wilderness"). Not engaged in begging ("holy vagrancy"), they owned property and were glad of it. They occupied important and permanent positions in the administration of communal life, and so came into constant and intimate contact with the common people. Access to rabbinical schools remained open to all, and the rabbis actively proselytized within the community to gain new candidates for their schools. Advantages of birth were minimal. In no way did the rabbis form a caste or a clan; the right marriage counted for little.

What, therefore, did the peculiarities of the rabbinical way of living amount to? A rabbi could eat with any other Jew in Babylonia because the biblical taboos about food were widely observed. Differences between the rabbis' interpretation of taboos about food and those advanced by others gradually diminished, as in time the rabbis' growing domination made their learned exegeses seem more commonplace. For example, although the rabbis said grace at meals and offered intelligible blessings for food, they were willing to teach others just what those blessings and prayers meant. Nothing in the rabbinical ritual of eating was to be kept secret. A person showed himself "ignorant" if he violated the rituals. His remedy was to go to a sage to study and learn, and this was explicitly recommended by the rabbis.

THE RABBI AS JUDGE

What did a rabbi actually do as a community administrator? The following account gives a helpful portrait of the workday function of Rabbi Huna', head of the Sura academy about 300 CE:

> *Every cloudy day they would carry him out in a golden palanquin, and he would survey the whole town. Every wall which looked unsafe he would order torn down. If the owner could rebuild it, he did so, but if not, he [Rabbi Huna] would rebuild it of his own funds.*
>
> *On the eve of every Sabbath, he would send a messenger to the market, and all the vegetables that remained to the market-gardeners, he would buy and throw into the river.*
>
> *Whenever he discovered a medicine, he would fill a jug with it, and suspend it above the doorstep and announce, "Whoever wants to, let him come and take." Some say, he knew from tradition a medicine for [a certain disease caused by eating with unwashed hands], and he would suspend a jug of water and proclaim, "Whoever needs it, let him come so that he may save his life from danger."*
>
> *When he ate bread, he would open his door wide, and declare, "Whoever is in need, let him come and eat."* (B.T., Ta'an. 20b–21a)

The variety of public responsibilities carried out by the rabbi is striking. He had to prevent the collapse of mud buildings during a rainstorm. He had to ensure a constant market by encouraging truck gardeners to provide a steady supply of fresh vegetables. He had to give out medical information, to preserve public health, and to make certain that poor people could benefit from the available remedies. And he had to provide for the poor, so that no one would starve in his town.

These responsibilities reflected the different roles played by the rabbi. Only the first and second duties listed depended upon his political function. As judge he could order the destruction of dangerous property; as administrator he had to supervise the marketplace and use his funds to control supply and prices. But these roles had nothing to do with medical and eleemosynary activities. The former was contingent upon his reputation as a man of learning who had mastered the occult sciences, which then included medicine; the latter was based upon his possession of great wealth, accruing from his positions in politics, administration, and academic life.

Litigations coming before the Jewish courts were not particularly important in the evidence covering 200–500 CE. On the whole they corresponded to those likely to come before a small-claims court in modern society. Thefts involved a book or a few rams. Betrothal cases concerned the exchange of property, such as a few zuz, a willow branch, some onions, or a piece of silk. Settlements of marriage contracts required division of a robe of fine wool, a silver cup. A few cases of alleged adultery were recorded, all of sufficient innocence for the court to rule that no adultery had taken place. The preparation and delivery of proper divorce documents hardly amounted to weighty matters of state. Divorce litigations in any event were provoked by peculiar and exceptional circumstances; normally a man could divorce his wife without court intervention, merely with the help of a scribe who wrote out the writ of divorce in accordance with the law.

The settlement of estates entailed somewhat larger sums of money. A woman's marriage contract stipulated that if she were divorced, she would be given an alimony of four hundred zuz, a round number that probably represented approximately enough capital for two years' maintenance. Provisions by the court for widows (food, wine, clothing) were humble and more typical matters. Even most estate cases pertained to rather small claims, such as a few trees, a slave, or a choice plot of ground. Settlement of debts, collections of mortgages and bonds, and the like did require rulings on somewhat more substantial sums, but the real issues were still relatively inconsequential—a hundred zuz, or whether a pledged spoon or knife had to be returned.

Some commercial litigations were brought before the courts. Questions of contract involved a few ferrymen and sharecroppers, or devolved upon a hired ass, a purchase of wine or poppy seed, a flooded field. Some commercial disputes demanded that the courts decide about a few zuz worth of silk beads, some sour wine, the sale of a wine press or a field. Others concerned a damaged jar or utensil, a dead goat, a stolen purse, a broken ax or wine barrel. Property cases similarly involved alleged fraud in a relatively small plot, the claim of an option to purchase a field, the use of canal water, and, very frequently, squatter's rights over a house or field and the eviction of tenant farmers.

Cases such as these clearly reveal the real substance of issues left in the rabbis' hands. With a few exceptions, strikingly petty sums of money or barely consequential pieces of property were all that the lower classes of society brought to litigation. And it was those classes that were primarily subject to rulings by the rabbinical courts. Large commercial transactions for many thousands of *zuz* worth of silk or pearls, wine or beer; enormous property transactions involving a whole village or town; claims of a considerable number of workers against a single employer, or vice versa; the affairs of large estates, rich landowners, big businessmen, important officials—none of these appears with any frequency, if at all, in extant reports.

The rabbis surely could not have agreed, however, that the humble and petty issues before them were of no consequence. It was their view—a very old one in Judaism—that the least and humblest affairs, as much as the largest and most weighty ones, testified to heaven about the moral state of society. If the prophet Amos had condemned Israel of old because a poor man was cheated of his shoes, then one can hardly be surprised that a later rabbi insisted upon the return of a cooking utensil given in pledge. What was important to the rabbis was that justice should prevail. They knew that if justice did not characterize the street, the trading market, the small farms and shops, then great affairs of commerce and the state would not likely be morally superior. They knew that the ethics of daily life, the life concerned with exchanges of onions and the use of water in a small canal, determined the destiny of Israel.

SUMMARY

The history of Judaism in late antiquity can be summarized very simply. First came the Mishnah, shaped over the first and second centuries CE. Then, second, followed four hundred years in which the legal and theological system of the Mishnah was drastically reshaped into something new. Since the Mishnah's system constituted a reaction against the messianic wars of the time in which it came into being, we see a process by which the messianic "thesis" generated the Mishnah as its antimessianic antithesis, so producing the rabbinic synthesis in the Talmuds. That is to say, the messianic "thesis" rested on prophetic, historical, and apocalyptic passages of scripture. The Mishnah's "antithesis" constructed a system based on priest ly and ahistorical legal passages. The Mishnah's system stood aloof both from biblical proof-texts and from the messianic interest in the meaning and end of history characteristic of its own day. Over the next four hundred years the rabbinic heirs of both the Mishnah and the scripture brought the two back into relationship. They forged them into a messianic and legal synthesis, the one "whole Torah" of "Moses, our rabbi," just as their Torah myth alleged.

[*See also* Pharisees; Tannaim; Amoraim; Mishnah and Tosefta; Midrash and Aggadah; *and* Talmud.]

BIBLIOGRAPHY

The best systematic account of the theology of rabbinic Judaism is George Foot Moore's *Judaism in the First Centuries of the Christian Era: The Age of the Tannaim*, 3 vols. (Cambridge, 1954). The same categories of historical theology are addressed by E. E. Urbach in *The Sages: Their Concepts and Beliefs*, 2 vols. (Jerusalem, 1975), translated from the Hebrew by Israel Abrahams; by Solomon Schechter in *Some Aspects of Rabbinic Theology* (1909; reprint, New York, 1936); and by E. P. Sanders in *Paul and Palestinian Judaism: A Comparison of Patterns of Religion* (Philadelphia, 1977). These three works present a categorically similar picture of rabbinic Judaism's theology. An important anthology of sources is C. G. Montefiore and Herbert Loewe's *A Rabbinic Anthology* (New York, 1974). Two collections of essays on special topics provide guidance into the principal scholarly approaches of the last generation: Jacob Z. Lauterbach's *Rabbinic Essays* (Cincinnati, 1951) and Louis Ginzberg's *On Jewish Law and Lore* (Philadelphia, 1955). A different approach to the description of rabbinic Judaism is provided in my book *Judaism: The Evidence of the Mishnah* (Chicago, 1981). On the mysticism of rabbinic Judaism the most important book is Gershom Scholem's *Major Trends in Jewish Mysticism* (New York, 1954); on messianism, Scholem's *The Messianic Idea in Judaism* (New York, 1971). On the liturgy of Judaism in this period, the two definitive books are Joseph Heinemann's *Prayer in the Talmud* (Berlin and New York, 1977) and Lawrence A. Hoffman's *The Canonization of the Synagogue Service* (Notre Dame, Ind., 1979). On the archaeology of Judaism in this period one should consult, as a start, Eric M. Meyers and James F. Strange's *Archaeology, the Rabbis, and Early Christianity* (Nashville, 1981) and Lee I. Levine's edition of *Ancient Synagogues Revealed* (Jerusalem, 1981). On rabbinic Judaism viewed historically, there is my own *History of the Jews in Babylonia*, 5 vols. (Leiden, 1965–1969).

5   TORAH

E. E. URBACH
Translated from Hebrew by Akiva Garber

Torah is a term that is used in many different ways. Of the etymologies suggested for the word, none has been proved, but most of them derive from the use of the word in the Hebrew scriptures. In *Genesis* and *Exodus* the plural of *torah, torot,* is usually coupled with other words, as in "mitsvotai huqqotai ve-torotai" ("my commandments, my laws, and my *torot,*" *Gn.* 26:5), and "mitsvotai ve-torotai" (*Ex.* 16:28). Even when the word occurs in these books in the singular, it refers to specific commandments. In *Leviticus* and *Numbers* the word *torah* denotes specific groups of ceremonial rules for the priests; sometimes the word occurs when the rules are introduced, as in *Leviticus* 6:1 ("This is the *torah* of the burnt-offering") and *Numbers* 19:2 ("This is the law of the *torah*"), and sometimes it serves as a summary and conclusion, as in *Leviticus* 11:46–47 ("This is the *torah* of the beast and the bird . . . to distinguish between the ritually impure and the ritually pure"). In *Deuteronomy* the word *torah* is used with the emphatic *he'* ("the") as a general term including not only the laws and rules, but also the narrative, the speeches, and the blessings and the curses of the Pentateuch. All these are written in "this book of the *torah*" (*Dt.* 29:20, 30:10).

In the prophecies of Hosea, Amos, and Isaiah the word *torah* carries a broad meaning that includes cultic, ethical, and legal matters. The concept of *torah* in *Jeremiah* is likewise broad and all-inclusive, while in *Ezekiel* the use of the plural returns, referring to groupings of laws and rules (*Ez.* 44:24).

In the historical books one finds exhortations encouraging observance and study of the Torah, as in *1 Kings* 2:2–6, along with a clear allusion to the "book of the *torah* of Moses," in *2 Kings* 14:6, citing *Deuteronomy* 24:16. In *Chronicles,* changes made by the kings in both the cult and the legal system are said to have been carried out "according to all that is written in the *torah* of God" (*1 Chr.* 16:40, 22:11–12; *2 Chr.* 14:3, 17:9).

In *Ezra* and *Nehemiah* a number of citations from the Torah appear together with exegetical activity of the scribes and the Levites (*Ezr.* 9:11; *Neh.* 8:14, 10:35). Of Ezra himself it is said that "he prepared his heart to expound the *torah* of God and to do and to teach among the people of Israel law and justice" (*Ezr.* 7:10), while the Levites "read from the book, from the *torah* of the Lord, clearly, and gave the sense, so the people understood the reading" (*Neh.* 8:8).

In private and communal prayers and in the psalms, the word *torah* exhibits a broad range of meanings in accordance with the various literary types and historical circumstances represented in them. In *Proverbs* the word *torah* is used as a parallel for the terms *musar* ("instruction," *Prv.* 1:8), *mitsvah* ("commandment," *Prv.* 3:1, 6:20), and *leqah tov* ("a good doctrine," *Prv.* 4:2), and thus it is also used to refer to the person who draws upon the wisdom found in international wisdom literatures. Nevertheless, the word still preserves the primary religious connotation that characterizes its use in the rest of the books of the Hebrew scriptures, by referring to the totality of the commandments of the covenant between God and his people.

CONTENT OF THE PENTATEUCH

The collection of writings that we call "Torah" or "the Torah of Moses" comprises the first five books of the Bible (the Pentateuch) but in fact has been considered one unified work, unlike the Prophets and the Hagiographa (or Writings), which together with it make up scripture. In content the Pentateuch is a continuous composition reporting history from the creation of the world until the death of Moses—when the people of Israel are arrayed in the plains of Moab—interspersed with groups of laws and rules. More precisely, in consideration of the central purpose of the Pentateuch, one ought to say that it is a collection of several groups of laws and commandments that were given to the people of Israel, set in a framework of stories that explain the special status of the people before God.

As is usual in Hebrew, the books of the Pentateuch are referred to by the first significant word in each book. The first book, *Bere'shit* ("in the beginning")—opens with a description of the creation of the world—whence the designation *Genesis*—and the genealogy of mankind and continues with the genealogy of Noah and his descendants after the great flood. The book emphasizes the covenant that God makes with Abraham ("the covenant of the parts") in which he promises Abraham that he will bring his descendants out from Egypt, where they will sojourn, and will give them the land of Canaan.

The second book, *Shemot* ("names"), contains the description of the events from the time of the bondage in Egypt until the revelations at Mount Sinai, where God establishes his special covenant with Israel, gives the Torah, and prescribes the tabernacle and the ceremony in which it is to be consecrated. This book is also known as "the book of the departure from Egypt," while in Greek and other languages it is called *Exodus*.

The third book, *Vayiqra'* ("and he called"), is known in tannaitic literature as *Torat Kohanim* ("*torah* of the priests") and in Greek as *Leuitikon*. Other translations, following the Latin, call the book *Leviticus*. It includes laws relating to worship in the Temple and the laws of sacrifices; special commandments of sanctity applicable to the priests and commandments of sanctity incumbent on the entire people of Israel; laws of ritual purity and impurity and of incest and other forbidden sexual relations; laws about the sanctity of particular times, festivals, and holidays; and laws about the sanctity of the Land of Israel, the Sabbatical year, and the Jubilee year.

The fourth book of the Pentateuch is usually called *Bemidbar* ("in the wilderness"), after the first significant word, but is sometimes referred to by the first word in the book, *va-yedabber* ("and he said"). The sages called it *Humash ha-pequdim,* while it was designated in the Septuagint as *Arithmoi* and in the Vulgate as *Numeri*

("Numbers"). It records the history of the people of Israel in the desert from the second year after they left Egypt until the death of Aaron. Thus it includes the description of the censuses and journeys of the people of Israel and a recounting of their complaints, the sending of spies to the land of Canaan, the rebellion of Korah, and the episode involving Balaam. Intermixed with these accounts are various legal sections, namely, the trial by ordeal of the unfaithful wife (5:11–31); the rules of the Nazirite (6:1–21); the laws of tithes (18:25–32), the red heifer (19:1–22), and inheritance (27:6–11, 36:1–9); the commandments of sacrifices, daily sacrifice, and additional sacrifices (28:1–29, 39); and the laws of oaths (30:3–17), manslaughter, and cities of refuge (35:9–37).

The last of the five books of the Pentateuch is *Elleh ha-devarim* ("These are the words"), or *Devarim* ("words"). The original designation of this book in the literature of the sages is *Mishneh Torah* (in the Septuagint *Deuteronomion*), which connotes the nature of the book as "a repeated Torah." In a series of speeches before his death, Moses summarizes the history of the people, intermixing his account with ethical teachings, warnings, and reproof. At the end of the book (chap. 32) is a poem that begins with the word *ha'azinu* ("give ear"), followed in chapter 33 by the parting blessings pronounced by Moses on all the tribes of Israel.

LITERARY AND HISTORICAL CRITICISM

Comparison of *Deuteronomy* with parallels in the other books of the Pentateuch reveals numerous inconsistencies between both the narratives and the collections of laws as well as linguistic and stylistic differences. This fact stimulated the growth of an extensive exegetical literature that attempts to reconcile the discrepancies. Modern biblical scholarship has attempted to uncover different sources upon which the five books of the Pentateuch are based. It is true that allusions to works more ancient than the Pentateuch are not lacking. In the Torah itself there is a reference to the *Book of the Wars of the Lord (Nm.* 21:14), which according to some medieval commentators and modern scholars was a specific book that served as a source for the narrative parts of the Pentateuch.

In the second century CE, tannaim attempted (*Mekhilta' de-Rabbi Yishma'e'l,* Bahodesh, chap. 3) to identify the nature of the "book of the covenant" from which Moses read to the people (*Ex.* 24:7). Yose ben Yehudah said, "From the beginning of *Genesis* until here," while Yehudah ha-Nasi' considered this a reference to a collection of laws that the people had been commanded to observe up until that time. Two generations earlier, however, the tanna Yishma'e'l ben Elisha' identified this "book of the covenant" with *Leviticus* 25:1–26:46, a section that opens, "And God spoke to Moses at Mount Sinai saying," and concludes with the verse, "These are the laws and the judgments and the *torot* which God gave, between him and the people of Israel at Mount Sinai by the hand of Moses." This identification is in agreement with a principle of interpretation transmitted in the name of the same tanna, that is, "No strict order as to 'earlier' and 'later' is observed in the Torah" (*Mekh. de-R. Y.,* Shirah, chap. 7), which means that the chapters and verses of the Torah are not necessarily recorded in the order in which they were given or the order in which they happened. This interpretative principle and the identification of the "book of the covenant" can be explained only if one assumes that the Torah was not given all at once. Indeed, the amora Yohanan bar Nappaha' (fl. first half of the third century

CE) transmits in the name of the tanna Bana'ah that "the Torah was given section by section" (B.T., *Git.* 60a). *Midrash Tanhuma'* tells that while the people of Israel were still enslaved in Egypt, "they possessed scrolls, in which they delighted from Sabbath to Sabbath, which said that the Holy One, blessed be he, would redeem them" (Va'eira' 1). Opposed to these opinions I have mentioned were tannaim and amoraim who held that "there is an order to the sections of the Torah" and expounded passages based on their proximity. Thus 'Aqiva' ben Yosef (fl. beginning of the second century CE) is cited as saying, "Every passage which is next to another learns from its neighbor" (*Sifrei Nm.*, 131).

A concerted effort to reconstruct the process that brought into being the books of the Torah as we have them was begun only in the middle of the eighteenth century. This effort resulted in the hypothesis that there are four sources or documents, given the designations J, E, P, and D. The distinction between J and E is based primarily on the different usages of the names of God (JHVH, or YHVH, and Elohim) and the names Jacob and Israel. Similar criteria were used to differentiate passages based on the priestly source, P, and the Deuteronomic source, D.

Besides the discernment and differentiation of these sources, there were also attempts to establish a chronology among them. A pioneer in this research, Wilhelm de Wette (1780–1849) proposed that *Deuteronomy,* which emphasizes the concentration of the cult in one place, reflects the situation that began to crystallize during the reign of Hezekiah, who concentrated the cult in Jerusalem (*2 Kgs.* 18:3–6), and that concluded in the time of Josiah, during whose reign Hilkiah discovered "the book" (*2 Kgs.* 22:8). This book, according to de Wette, was none other than the *Book of Deuteronomy,* which stands at the end of the development of the sources, as it is the only one in which there is any demand for the centralization of the cult.

Julius Wellhausen, in his studies during the second half of the nineteenth century, perfected and consolidated this type of historical criticism, according to which the Torah did not exist during the early part of the history of the people of Israel in their land, but rather reflects the historical circumstances of later generations. To de Wette's assertions Wellhausen added others appertaining to other aspects of the worship of God among the people of Israel, such as the nature of the sacrifices and the holidays and the status of the priests and Levites. In all of these subjects Wellhausen discerned a movement in the priestly sources from the natural to the abstract and non-natural. He concluded that the P source dated only from the time of the Second Temple, when the priests wielded political power.

Objections to and criticism of this approach were voiced already in the time of Wellhausen, and they have increased in recent decades. Even scholars who accepted the documentary hypothesis (Hermann Gunkel, Hugo Gressmann, and others) tried to discover ancient traditions in the Torah and investigate their nature and source. Using knowledge of other civilizations of the ancient Near East and their literatures, they turned their attention to the form and structure of the traditions and the way in which they became established in cultic life. Without intending to, these scholars significantly undermined the documentary hypothesis, for they showed that all those institutions that Wellhausen considered artificial and late had existed in the ancient Near East centuries before the people of Israel appeared on the scene. Thus comparison of the biblical account with Mesopotamian, Hittite, and Ugaritic cultures weakened Wellhausen's claims about the late development of the Priestly source. Wellhausen's theories were also undermined by the work of scholars who stressed the central role of oral traditions and the accuracy of their transmission in ancient times (Johannes Pedersen, Sigmund Mowinkel, Henrik Nyberg, Ivan Engnell). They claim that oral transmission influenced the sources even after they were reduced to writing. While this approach has not been accepted in its entirety, it has served as a restraining influence (e.g., for Roland de Vaux). Some have expressed doubt about the independent status of the P source (e.g., R. von Rentdorf), while others doubt the validity of the entire documentary hypothesis (David Hoffmann, Umberto Cassuto, Benno Jacob, F. Dornseiff).

Even those who adopt the critical view, which sees the Pentateuch as a work compiled from different sources that reflect differing trends and styles, are nevertheless forced to admit its function and influence as a single, unified book. Every law and commandment in it is presented as the word of God to Moses, and taken together these laws form for Judaism an authoritative code whose authority infuses even the narrative sections with which they are intermixed. [*See also* Biblical Literature, *article on* Hebrew Scriptures.]

WRITTEN TORAH AND ORAL TORAH

We hear of the Torah in the documents of the return to Zion: "The Torah of the Lord which he gave by the hand of Moses" and is accepted by all Israel (*Ezr.* 7:10; *Neh.* 8:1, 9:3, 10:30). The book of the Torah is a complete and sealed scripture, and every innovation in legislation or exegesis of the commandments of the Torah, many of which are stated without specification of details or directions for their implementation, has become a companion tradition, an "oral Torah." The word *torah* returns in this usage to its basic meaning, "teaching," as in the Mishnah: "These and those come to the Great Court which is in the Chamber of Hewn Stone, from which Torah goes out to all Israel" (*San.* 11:2). In *Ben Sira*, the *torah* of Moses and the *torah* of wisdom join to form a single concept. The remnants of the myth of preexistent wisdom and its necessity for the creation of the world, which are found in *Proverbs* (8:22–31), were transferred to the Torah. Thus it is said of Torah that it existed before the creation of the world (*Sifrei Dt.* 37, *Gn. Rab.* 4, 3, p. 6), and El'azar ben Tsadoq (fl. beginning of the second century CE) and 'Aqiva' speak of Torah as "the instrument used to create the world" (*Sifrei Dt.* 48, *Avot* 3.14).

During the Hellenistic period, prior to the Hasmonean rebellion, the word *torah* had two distinct referents. On the one hand, it included not only the commandments but also the teachings of the prophets and the wisdom of the elders, while on the other hand, it meant the *torah* of Moses in its entirety. This duality explains the fact that Paul and the author of the *Gospel of John* refer at times to verses from the Prophets and the Hagiographa as *nomos*. They thereby reflect a more ancient tradition, which is already traceable in the words of Daniel: "the *torah* of Moses the servant of the Lord," yet also, "His *torot* which he put before us by the hand of his servants and prophets" (*Dn.* 9:10–13, *2 Chr.* 29:25, *Ezr.* 9:10–14).

It would seem that for the Jews of Alexandria, *torah* was an institution that embodied the covenant between the nation and its Lord, reflecting a system of commandments, laws, customs, and traditions connected with the history of the people and the activities of their judges, kings, and prophets. If this was really the meaning of *torah*, then the translation *nomos* is in fact appropriate. Thus the translator of *Isaiah* 1:10 interpreted *torah* in the passage "Hear the *torah* of our Lord, people of

Gomorrah" as *nomos,* for such prophetic statements as "I cannot suffer injustice together with public assemblies" and "Wash and purify yourselves; remove from yourselves your evil deeds" are also *torah.*

The term *oral torah* first appears in a story said to be from the time of Hillel and Shammai (fl. first century BCE–first century CE). In response to a prospective convert's question about how many *torot* exist, Shammai answered, "Two: the written Torah and the oral *torah*" (B.T., *Shab.* 31a). The answer of Gamli'el of Yavneh (in the next generation) to a Roman consul who asked the same question was the same (*Sifrei Dt.* 351, p. 408). Thus it seems that even gentiles and prospective converts were aware that besides the written Torah there was a "tradition of the ancestors" that was also considered *torah.*

The term *oral torah* does not imply a *torah* precedent to and more valuable than the written Torah, unlike the Greek *agraphos nomos* ("unwritten law") which is not legislated by god or man but like nature simply exists, so that whether it is written or not makes no difference at all. In contrast, the characteristic feature of the oral *torah* is precisely the fact that it is not written. Still, the oral *torah,* like the written Torah, is not natural law but, rather, revealed law. Philo Judaeus (d. 45–50 CE) though, accepted and identified with the Greek conception and therefore identified the unwritten tradition *(agraphos paradosis)* with the unwritten law *(agraphos nomos)* (Philo, *On the Special Laws* 4.149–150). This explanation of *torah* not only paved the way for allegorical exegesis; it even led some hellenized Jews to the conclusion that precisely the allegorical interpretation, which reveals the inner meaning, is primary. It is true that Philo himself opposed extreme allegorists, who explained the commandment of circumcision allegorically and felt that their inner understanding of the commandment sufficed; still, in his own words one can see the influence of such a conception (*On the Migration of Abraham* 92–95). This same idea is echoed in Paul's writings: "For he is not a Jew, which is one outwardly . . . but he is a Jew inwardly, and circumcision is that of the heart, in the spirit and not in the letter" (*Rom.* 2:28–29). For Paul, however, all the tension between the letter *gramma* and the spirit *pneuma,* which is intended to bring about the abrogation of the Torah, derives from his belief in the Messiah. Allegorical exegesis enables him to provide the justification for and evidence of the belief that "the Messiah is the end of the Torah, that everyone who has faith may be justified" (*Rom.* 10:4). In contrast, the saying of Eli'ezer ha-Moda'i in *Avot* 3.11 that "he who denies the covenant of our father Abraham [i.e., circumcision] and he who exposes inner meanings in the Torah are denied a portion in the world to come" seems to be directed against such extreme allegorical interpretations—the one "who exposes inner meanings in the Torah" is he who explains allegorically, thereby causing the abrogation of commandments and the denial of the covenant of Abraham.

Among the Jews of the Land of Israel understanding of the meaning of *torah* developed differently. Along with the written Torah, the ancestral traditions, legislation, and decrees all became *torah.* The expositions and explanations of the sages also became oral *torah.* Among the sects, such as the Dead Sea sect, *halakhot* (the laws in the Covenant of Damascus Scroll and the Manual of Discipline) and exegesis (the *pesharim* of Habakkuk, Isaiah, Jeremiah, Micah, Nahum, and others) were written in scrolls, and interpretations were even interpolated among verses of the Torah (the Temple Scroll). The Sadducees had a "written and sealed book of decrees." However, the Pharasaic sages preserved the distinction between the Torah and everything else that had been added to it—legislation and decrees, homilies and interpretation—by forbidding the writing of the latter category. This very distinction made possible a great measure of freedom in interpretation. On the one hand, scriptural support was found for *halakhot* whose sources were actually tradition, custom, testimonies, and firsthand reports; on the other hand, "the details of biblical exegesis and whatever new interpretations the sages will establish in the future" (J.T., *Meg.* 4.1, 71d) were claimed to have been given to Moses at Sinai.

'Aqiva' saw the oral *torah* as implicit in the written Torah, in its words and in its letters, whence it is recorded that he expounded: "'These are the laws and the rules and the *torot*' [*Lv.* 26:46]—from which we learn that two *torot* were given to Israel, one written and one oral. . . . 'On Mount Sinai by the hand of Moses' [ibid.]—from which we learn that *torah* was given complete with all its laws, details of interpretation, and explanations by the hand of Moses at Sinai" (*Sifra'*, Behuqqotai 8, p. 112c). In light of this, one can understand the term "*torah* from heaven"; the statement of 'Aqiva' was in response to those who said, "*torah* is not from heaven" (*Sifrei Dt.* 102, p. 161), meaning that they denied the revealed nature of the oral *torah.* In *Sanhedrin* 10.1 such people are among those excluded from a portion in the world to come.

The third *Sibylline Oracle* (sec. 256), which dates from around 140 BCE, says that "Moses . . . [led] the people . . . to Mount Sinai, then God gave them the *torah* forth from heaven, writing all its ordinances on two tablets." For the school of 'Aqiva' and in the Mishnah, though, *torah* does not refer solely to the Ten Commandments. Furthermore, the revelation included not only the Torah and its interpretations, but also the assertion of the authority of the interpretation. Thus the amora Rav (Abba bar Aiyvu, fl. beginning of the third century) summed up the conception of oral *torah* held by 'Aqiva' and his disciples in a paradoxical story about Moses: "When Moses ascended on high and the Holy One, blessed be he, showed him 'Aqiva' expounding, Moses had no idea what he was saying, but nevertheless his mind was set at rest when he heard 'Aqiva' answer a student's question, 'Teacher, how do we know?' by saying 'It is a *halakhah* ["law"] given to Moses at Sinai'" (B.T., *Men.* 29b).

According to the method developed by 'Aqiva' and his school, the Torah scholar and exegete, by application of the principles used for the interpretation of the Torah and through his reasoning, can uncover within the Torah those same laws, details of interpretation, and explanations that were given together with it. In adopting this doctrine they follow Yehoshu'a ben Hananyah, teacher of 'Aqiva', who refused to admit the continued intervention of divine forces in the determination of halakhic matters. This contrasts with the position of Eli'ezer ben Hyrcanus and others, who refused to discount the possibility of further revelations, whether in the form of a heavenly voice or through prophecy. According to the understanding of Yehoshu'a and his disciples, "Torah is not in the heavens, so we do not listen to heavenly voices" (B.T., *B.M.* 59b). Those who adopted this position even denied that earlier prophets could have established innovations on the basis of their gift of prophecy. Rather, the exposition and expansion of the Torah were severed from any and all dependence on supernatural forces.

The desire to confine revelation to a single, unique event is already found in tannaitic sources (*Sifrei Nm.* 78, 111, 133). The amoraim Yitshaq and Shim'on ben Laqish (fl. c. end of the third century) even went so far as to say that not only is no prophet permitted to establish any innovations after the giving of the Torah (*Sifra'* Behuqqotai 13), but that the prophecies of the prophets of every generation were already included in the voice heard on Mount Sinai; the words already existed from antiquity, and only their articulation occurred at various times. Thus the prophets turn out to be no different from the sages of each generation, "each of whom received his portion from Mount Sinai" (*Ex. Rab.* 28.6, *Tan.* Yitro 11). The only difference between the words of the prophets and those of the sages is that the former are written while the latter remained oral. This distinction does not necessarily reflect well on the prophets, who only appeared among the people of Israel in response to the sins of the people, whereas "had Israel not sinned, they would have received only the Pentateuch and the *Book of Joshua,* which emphasizes the value of the land of Israel" (B.T., *Ned.* 22b).

This is not true of the oral *torah.* According to Yoḥanan bar Nappaḥa', "the covenant at Sinai was established only for the sake of the oral *torah*" (B.T., *Giṭ.* 60b; *Shav.* 39a), for the explanation and understanding of the written Torah is dependent on the oral *torah.* Furthermore, one who learns and explains the Torah can merit a renewed "revelation at Sinai." In *Leviticus Rabbah* (16.6) it is told of Ben 'Azza'i, a disciple of 'Aqiva', that as he expounded, a fire burned around him. When 'Aqiva' was informed of this fact, he asked his pupil whether he was occupying himself in mystical endeavors. Ben 'Azza'i answered, "No, but I am joining the words of the Torah to the Prophets and the Prophets to the Writings and the words of Torah are happy as on the day they were given from Sinai, and were they not given at Sinai primarily in fire? as it says, 'And the mountain is burning with fire unto the heart of the heaven' [*Dt.* 4:11]."

Many of the meanings of the word *torah* developed from polemics against different approaches and conceptions. One of the last amoraim, Yehudah bar Shalom, explained the prohibition of writing oral *torah* thus: "When the Holy One, blessed be he, told Moses to 'write yourself [this book of the Torah],' Moses wanted to write down the Mishnah also, but since God saw that the nations of the world would eventually translate the Torah and read it in Greek and claim 'I am Israel,' and up to this point the scales of judgment are balanced, he told the nations: 'You say you are my children, but I recognize only he who possesses my mystery; they are my children.' And to what does this refer? To the Mishnah" (*Tan.* Vayeira' 5, Tisa' 34). Clearly this saying defines the preference of the oral *torah* as a response to the claims of Pauline Christianity that the church is the true inheritor of Israel because it is the son of the free woman, while Israel is of the flesh, at best the progeny of the maidservant (*Gal.* 3:26, 4:21; *Rom.* 2:28). Following Paul, the church fathers from Justin through Augustine claimed scripture was no longer the property and heritage of the Jews (Justin, *Apologia* 1.53; Augustine, *Against the Jews,* 4.8). The oral *torah* supposedly refutes such claims.

Contradictions between various sayings about the relationship between Torah and the books of the prophets can be explained if one views these statements in a polemical context. Levi in the name of Hanina' said: "The eleven psalms which Moses composed are set down in the books of the prophets. And why were they not included in the books of the law? Because the latter are words of *torah* and the former are words of prophecy" (*Midrash Tehillim* 90.4). According to this statement, even the words of prophecy by Moses himself are distinct from *torah.* In this saying and in others like it the revelation at Mount Sinai is restricted to a single, unique, all-inclusive event, thereby making impossible any additional revelation that could challenge the completeness of Torah. However, there were also sects that did not recognize the authority of the prophetic books at all. (The church fathers ascribed this position to the Sadducees; it was also adopted by Christian gnostic sects.) The words of the following Midrash were directed against these groups:

> When Assaf came, he began to say, "Listen, my people, to my Torah" [Ps. 78:1]. Similarly, Solomon said, "For I have given you a good teaching, my Torah, do not abandon it" [Prv. 4:2]. Israel said to Assaf, "Is there some other torah, such that you say, 'Listen, my people, to my torah?' We have already received it at Sinai." He answered them, "The sinners of Israel say that the Prophets and the Writings are not torah and that they do not believe in them, as it says: 'For we did not listen to the voice of God, the Lord, to go in the way of his torah which he put before us in the hands of his servants, the prophets' [Dn. 9:10]. Behold, the Prophets and Writings are torah, as it says, 'Listen, my people, to my torah.'"
>
> (Tan. Re'eh 1)

Still, beyond all polemic, the books of the Prophets and Writings were sanctified as parts of the tripartite Torah (B.T., *Shab.* 88a; *Tan.* Yitro 10): the Pentateuch (Torah), Prophets (Nevi'im), and Writings (Ketuvim). Readings from the Prophets and some of the books of the Writings (*Esther, Lamentations,* and, according to some customs, the other three *megillot,* i.e., *Song of Songs, Ruth,* and *Ecclesiastes,* as well) are included in the synagogue service, preceded and followed by blessings. Nevertheless, the distinction between them and the Pentateuch is preserved, for the sanctity of the rest of the books is not equal to that of the Torah scroll: it was forbidden to join together the Torah and prophetic books in a single scroll (*Sofrim* 3.1) or to lay a prophetic book on top of the Pentateuch (B.T., *Meg.* 27a).

THE TEN COMMANDMENTS

There are also differing understandings of the relationship between the Ten Commandments and the rest of the Torah. Philo saw the Ten Commandments as the principles and sources, while the rest of the commandments of the Torah are only specific details. Thus he organized the specific commandments, grouping them according to their roots—that is, according to their agreement with the Ten Commandments. Yet Hananyah, nephew of Yehoshu'a, and others following him asserted that "the details of the Torah were written in the intervals between the commandments of the decalogue" (J.T., *Sheq.* 6.1, 49d; *Sg. Rab.* 5, 14). Thus these sages were interested in deemphasizing the Ten Commandments and denying them any special status, in order to prevent people from claiming that they alone were given from Sinai and not the rest of the commandments (J.T., *Ber.* 1.8, 3c). This approach is intended to reject an antinomian orientation, which would limit observances to ethical commandments alone. [*See also* Ten Commandments.]

CONCEPT OF TORAH AMONG THE MEDIEVAL PHILOSOPHERS

Jewish philosophy in the Middle Ages in the lands under Muslim dominance stood before two challenges: philosophical justification of Torah as a religion of divine revelation and rejection of the Muslim claim that the revelation to Israel was superseded by the revelation to Muḥammad. For Saʿadyah Gaon (882–942), who is considered the father of medieval Jewish philosophy, the divine revelation is identified with the content of reason. Reason can recognize both the speculative and the ethical content of revelation, which is nevertheless necessary to reveal truth in a universally accessible form, making it available to the common man, who is incapable of thinking for himself, and also to the philosopher, who is thereby presented *a priori* with the truth that he could otherwise discover only through great effort. Still, it is a religious duty to come to truth also through the use of reason (Saʿadyah Gaon, *The Book of Beliefs and Opinions,* translated by S. Rosenblatt, New Haven, 1961). Out of this conception Saʿadyah developed the distinction between the commandments of reason, which revelation simply repeats, and the traditional commandments, which are known only through revelation. The latter category includes the sacrificial and ceremonial orders of the Torah (ibid., treatise 3, sections 1–3). Saʿadyah applied this conception in composing a liturgical poem in which he attempted to fit all 613 of the commandments into the framework of the Ten Commandments (*Azharot* in *Siddur Rav Saʿadyah Gaʾon,* 1941, pp. 185ff.), which as in Philo can be considered general principles. This undertaking also answers those who claim that numerous divine revelations are possible: there was no such multiplicity of revelation to Israel, and the divine will is certainly not prone to change or to cancel the content of the true revelation (*The Book of Beliefs and Opinions,* treatise 3, sec. 7).

Maimonides (1135/8–1204) ascribed two purposes to *torah:* to order communal life and to enlighten the spirit of men by revealing to them the truth. The political laws, ethical commandments, and ceremonial and sacrificial laws of the Torah are all means toward the attainment of these two goals. All the laws that serve to educate the people ethically work toward the achievement of the first goal, while all the laws that strengthen certain specific beliefs advance the second goal. Maimonides attempted to demonstrate this point by developing an elaborate system of explanations of reasons for the commandments, some of them rationalistic and some historical, presenting certain commandments and prohibitions as protection against polytheistic ideas and customs of worship (Maimonides, *Guide of the Perplexed* 3.29–3.44). With great consistency Maimonides stressed in all of his works the uniqueness of the revelation of the Torah of Moses. For him the role of the prophets was not to create a religion: "As for the prophets from among us who came after Moses our master, you know the text of all their stories and the fact that their function was that of preachers who called upon the people to obey the Torah of Moses. . . . We likewise believe that things will always be this way, as it says, 'It is not in heaven'" (ibid. 2.39; translation by Shlomo Pines, Chicago, 1963). [*For further discussion, see* Biblical Exegesis, *article on* Jewish Views.]

VIEW OF THE QABBALISTS

Qabbalistic literature, which is mostly made up of commentaries on the Torah, emphasizes the absolute virtues of the Torah over the rest of the books of the Bible. The conceptions of the qabbalists about the Torah are in part a radical development of ideas found in *midrashim* of the sages and in part bold innovation. A saying ascribed to the amora Elʿazar, which appears in *Midrash Tehillim* 3.2, explains a verse in *Job* (28:13) as follows: "The sections of the Torah were not given in order, for had they been given in order, anyone reading them would be able to resurrect the dead and to perform wonders. Therefore the order of the Torah was hidden, but it is revealed before the Holy One, blessed be he, as it says, 'And who is like unto me? Let him read and declare it and set it in order for me [*Is.* 44:7].'" The author of this saying hints at the possibility of use of the Torah for magic, but he rejects that possibility. Nevertheless, such magical use was described in the work *Shimushei Torah,* which apparently dates from the geonic period.

Nahmanides (Mosheh ben Nahman, c. 1194–1270) mentions reading the Torah "in the manner of the names," which was transmitted to Moses verbally, "for we possess a true tradition that the entire Torah is made up of the names of the Holy One, blessed be he" (Introduction to Nahmanides' commentary on the Torah). Similarly, the *Zohar* (Yitro 87.1) says, "The entire Torah is the holy name, for there is not a word in the Torah which is not included in the holy name." Based on this idea, Me'ir ibn Gabbai wrote in the beginning of the fourteenth century that Torah is called "the Torah of God" because it is in fact the name of God. This supposition relates to the preexistent reality of the Torah, in which it was used to create the world. The fact that the Torah is thought to have been made up by the interweaving of divine names implies that the Torah has multiple meanings. The different kinds of interpretations were summed up in the *Zohar* in the acronym *PaRDeS,* standing for *peshat, remez, derash,* and *sod. Peshat* includes the understanding of scripture evinced in the oral *torah; remez* includes allegory and philosophy; *derash* is the homiletic approach; while *sod* is made up of the qabbalistic explanations. In the qabbalistic exegesis, precisely those verses and words that seem unimportant are raised to the level of profound symbols.

The qabbalists propounded a distinction between the *torah* of the names of the messiah and the revealed Torah. In so doing they diverged from the saying of Yohanan that "the books of the Prophets and the Writings will in the future be canceled, but the Pentateuch will not be canceled in the future" (J.T., *Meg.* 3.7, 70d) as well as from the *midrashim* in which one may uncover hints of the possibility of changes, like: "The *torah* that a man learns in this world is empty in comparison with the *torah* of the Messiah" (*Eccl. Rab.* 11.8) or "'*Torah* will go out from me' (*Is.* 51:4)—a renewal of the Torah will go out from me" (*Lv. Rab.* 13.3). In these *midrashim* the innovative nature of the Torah is not specified, but the qabbalists explained the nature of the change in the light of their conceptions: the Torah will be understood in accordance with its spirituality, and its letters will join together to form a different reading.

Qabbalistic literature of the thirteenth century explained that in the dictum of Shim'on ben Laqish, "the Torah which the Holy One, blessed be he, gave to Moses was white fire engraved on black fire" (J.T., *Sheq.* 6.1); "white fire" refers to the Torah itself, while "black fire" refers to the oral *torah.* Thus the written Torah is hidden in the white parchment, but in the future the blank spaces in the Torah will reveal their letters.

The Hasidim of the eighteenth century essentially adopted the qabbalistic understanding that the elevated religious value of the Torah is found in its inner essence rather than in its exoteric manifestation. The simple meaning of the Torah is a symbolic expression of divine truths. In keeping with the individualistic tendency within

Hasidism, achieving understanding of the secrets of Torah was considered to depend on the mending of the individual's specific personal soul and on his attempts to cleave to God in every aspect of his being.

An opponent of Hasidism, Eliyyahu ben Shelomoh Zalman (1720–1797), known as the Vilna Gaon, emphasized the all-encompassing, eternal nature of Torah. Everything that ever was, is, or will be existent is included in the Torah. The specific details of every person, animal, plant, and inanimate object are included in the Torah from the word bere'shit until the phrase le-'einei kol Yisra'el (the words that close Deuteronomy). He studied qabbalistic literature in the same way in which he studied the books of the Bible and halakhic works. Rather than expecting personal revelations as a result of occupying himself with Qabbalah, he anticipated that his devotion and absolute dedication to Torah study would aid him in understanding the Qabbalah.

TALMUD TORAH ("TORAH STUDY")

Alongside the demand that one must uphold the commandments written in the Torah, there is also in the Torah an explicit requirement to study, learn, and teach it (Dt. 6:6–7, 11:18–20; see also Jos. 1:8). This commandment from the start related to every part of the Torah. During the time of the First Temple, the priests were the main group encharged with teaching the Torah (Jeremiah 2:8 mentions together with them "those who handle the Torah"). In the time of the Second Temple, the sofrim ("scribes") were the teachers and explicators of torah, while the authority for halakhic instruction and legal determination was invested in the Great Court. The legislation and decrees, reports of the acts of the courts, and explanations of the words of the Torah all become part of the oral torah, and the commandment of talmud Torah was considered to apply also to them. The tannaim and amoraim and scholars of subsequent generations dealt at length with the commandment of talmud Torah, considering its meaning and nature and ways of fulfilling it.

The desire to know how to fulfill accurately the commandments of the Torah is only one of the justifications for talmud Torah. Also significant is the desire to gain understanding of the Torah, its intentions, and the way in which it develops and expands. Already the author of Psalm 119 emphasizes repeatedly the intellectual enjoyment that the study of torah provides, and he says, "Were not your torah my pleasure, I would have perished in my affliction" (verse 91). The requirement to study torah is incumbent on every man, whatever his situation. The Babylonian amora Rav, describing God's daily schedule, declared that during the first three hours of the day he "sits and engages in torah study" (B.T., 'A.Z. 3b).

The requirement of talmud Torah is one of the four "things which have no limit, and a person enjoys the fruits of it in this world, while the capital is laid up for him in the world to come" (Pe'ah 1.1). The students in yeshivah, the main institution for the study of torah, are expected to devote the bulk of their time to study, even in conditions of financial distress and even if doing so entails living a difficult life (Avot 6.4). At the time of the Hadrianic persecutions, the sages continued to reach and learn torah despite the actual risk to their lives.

The content of the studies, their breadth, and the method of study varied in different times and places. There were times when the study of the rest of the biblical books was not included together with the study of the Torah itself. Some students concentrated only on the study of *halakhah*, while others preferred the *aggadah*. There were those who included the study of philosophy and Qabbalah, while some stressed attention to *musar* ("ethical teachings"). Within the study of *halakhah* itself there were various methods of study: some emphasized casuistry and sharp-wittedness, while others stressed the importance of broad knowledge of the sources and drawing conclusions for practical application. Still, everyone recognized that the requirement to study *torah* is incumbent on the entire community in some form or another. Thus public homilies in the synagogues on Sabbaths and holidays were instituted. Starting in the first century BCE, a framework of schools for children was established. Besides, every man was required to fulfill the commandment to recite the Shema' morning and evening. This recital includes references to the requirement of *talmud Torah*, and a blessing similar to the blessing over the Torah was instituted, to be said prior to the Shema'. Nevertheless, in most times Jews were not satisfied to fulfill their obligation to study in this minimal fashion. Instead, communities saw that there would be people spreading *torah* among the masses, while workers, merchants, and clerks all organized themselves in groups whose designated purpose was to fix times for *torah* study.

The stress on *talmud Torah* as an ultimate value found expression in the dispute between Tarfon and 'Aqiva' concerning whether learning or deeds is more important. The dispute ended in general agreement with the position of 'Aqiva' that "learning is greater for learning leads to deeds" (B.T., *Qid.* 40b). [*See also* Halakhah; Midrash and Aggadah; *and, for a discussion of the history of the study of Torah,* Yeshivah.]

READING THE TORAH IN THE SYNAGOGUE

Today the reading of the Torah occupies a central role in communal prayer. Public reading of the Torah is mentioned three times in the Bible, but always on special occasions. The first mention is in *Deuteronomy* 3:10–13: Moses commanded the reading of "this Torah before all Israel" in the Sabbatical year during the festival of Sukkot (Tabernacles). In the opinion of tannaim (*Sot.* 3.8, *Sifrei Dt.* 160), the king was commanded to read *Deuteronomy* with certain abridgments during this ceremony. Another reading is mentioned in *2 Kings* (23:1–2), where King Josiah is said to have "read in their ears all the words of the book of the covenant which was found in the house of God." It seems reasonable to assume that this account served as a source for the aforementioned tannaitic description.

Nehemiah (8:1–8) tells how Ezra the scribe brought the scroll of the Torah before the congregation on the first day of the seventh month and read from it "in the ears of the entire people clearly, and he gave the sense." In this reading the people found "written in the Torah which God commanded by the hand of Moses that the people of Israel sat in tabernacles during the festival of the seventh month" (8:4). When they then celebrated this festival of Sukkot, they again read "in the book of the Torah of the Lord every day, from the first day until the last day" (8:18). This account can be viewed as the start of the custom of reading the Torah publicly on festivals.

Reading the Torah on the Sabbath is mentioned by Philo (*Moses* 2.216; see Eusebius's *Praeparatio evangelica* 8.2) and Josephus (*Against Apion* 2.175) and in the *Acts of the Apostles* (15:21) as an ancient custom. In *Megillah* 3.6 the requirement to read the portion about each festival at the time of that festival is deduced from the verse "And Moses spoke the festivals of God to the people of Israel" (*Lv.* 23:44). The tannaitic Midrash *Sifra'* ascribes the institution of this custom to Moses himself: "This teaches us that Moses told them the *halakhot* of Passover at Passover time, those pertaining to Shavu'ot (Pentecost) at the time of Shavu'ot, and those pertaining to Sukkot at Sukkot time." In the description of the ceremonial rite of Yom Kippur, the Mishnah (*Yoma'* 3.1) reports that the high priest read sections of the Torah appropriate to the day (*Lv.* 16:1–34, 23:26–32; *Nm.* 29:7–11). In addition to the readings on Sabbaths, festivals, and the holidays mentioned in the Torah, the Mishnah also fixes public readings for Hanukkah, Purim, New Moons, public fast days, Mondays and Thursdays (which were market days), and during the afternoon service on the Sabbath (*Meg.* 3.6, 4.1) as well as during *ma'amadot,* assemblies of the watches that gathered in the Temple and in their towns to pray and read from the Torah while the priests and Levites from their region performed the rites in the Temple (*Ta'an.* 3.4). The tannaitic *midrash* notes that "the prophets and the elders established for them the requirement to read from the Torah on Sabbaths, Mondays, and Thursdays" (*Mekhilta',* Va-yehi 1). However, the Jerusalem Talmud ascribes to Moses the readings on Sabbaths, holidays, New Moons, and the intermediate days of the festivals (*Meg.* 4.1, 75a), and Ezra is credited with establishing the readings on Mondays and Thursdays and on the afternoon of the Sabbath. The Babylonian Talmud attempts to reconcile the two traditions (*Meg.* 32a).

The Mishnah specifies only the portions to be read on festivals, on the four special Sabbaths between the beginning of the month of Adar and Passover, on public fast days, and during *ma'amadot* (*Meg.* 3.5–6). Thus the order of the portions of the Torah and their division among the Sabbaths of the year are not mentioned at all in the Mishnah. The Babylonian Talmud reports that in the Land of Israel it was customary to complete the reading of the Torah scroll once every three years (*Meg.* 29b). Indeed, this custom is reflected in the *midrashim* composed in the Land of Israel and in the masoretic division of the Torah into between 153 and 167 *sedarim* ("sections"). There were as well those who divided the Torah into 54 *parashiyyot* ("portions") so that they could complete it once yearly. This was the custom in Babylon. The one-year cycle supplanted the three-year cycle, which remained in use in just a few places. In 1170 the traveler Binyamin of Tudela found the three-year cycle still in use in the synagogue of the Palestinian Jews in Cairo.

In the one-year cycle the reading of the Torah is completed each year on the last day of the festival of Sukkot, which came to be called Simhat Torah ("Rejoicing of the Torah"). On every Sabbath afternoon and on Mondays and Thursdays, one reads from the beginning of the *parashah* of the following Sabbath, in accordance with the opinion stated by Yehudah bar Il'ai in a *baraita'*. According to Me'ir, however, one ought to start reading at the Sabbath afternoon service at the place in the scroll where the reading left off in the morning; on Monday, where the Sabbath afternoon reading ended; on Thursday, where the Monday reading ended; and on the following Sabbath, where the Thursday reading left off. This opinion does not allow for a three-year cycle.

The Mishnah also fixes the number of people who go up to read from the Torah on each occasion. On Mondays, Thursdays, and Sabbath afternoons, three people read; on New Moons and the intermediate days of the festivals, four; on holidays, five; on Yom Kippur, six; and on the Sabbath, seven (*Meg.* 4.1–2). The first two people to go up to read are a *kohen* (one of priestly descent) and a Levite (*Git.* 8.8), if such are present. In Mishnaic times, the first person to go up pronounced the blessing before reading the Torah and the last person recited the afterblessing, while everyone who went up in between read without making a blessing (*Meg.* 4.1). Subsequently the custom was changed so that each reader recited a blessing before and after reading (B.T., *Meg.* 21b). The accepted wording of the first blessing is "Blessed are you Lord our God, King of the universe who chose us from among the nations," which is the version adduced in the Babylonian Talmud (*Ber.* 11b), but other conclusions of the blessing were also extant such as ". . . who gives Torah from heaven" (*Sofrim* 13.8) and ". . . who chose this Torah" (*Dt. Rab.* 11).

The Mishnah mentions the custom of translating each verse into the language spoken by the people—that is, Aramaic—at the same time as it was read in Hebrew (*Meg.* 4.4). This custom is apparently very ancient, perhaps as old as the custom of public Torah reading itself. In places where the vernacular was Greek, it was customary to begin and end the reading in Hebrew but to read the intermediate portions in Greek so that the congregation could understand the portion (Tosefta, *Meg.* 3.13). The emperor Justinian in 553 CE decided a dispute between two groups within a certain community who argued about whether one ought to read the Septuagint or the translation of Aquila. Over an extended period of time the translation of Onqelos was read in most communities, but nowadays only the Yemenite Jews continue this custom.

The public Torah reading was supplemented with a reading from the prophetic books. This reading from the Prophets is called the *haftarah.* Generally the portion chosen to be read as the *haftarah* parallels in some way the content of the *seder* or *parashah* read from the Torah on the same occasion.

SEFER TORAH

Only a scroll including the five books of the Torah written on parchment may be used for public reading. A whole system of *halakhot* fixes the procedures for the preparation of the parchment and the ink as well as the details of the proper form of the letters of the square Hebrew script in which the scroll must be written. *Sefer Torah,* one of the minor tractates from the period of the geonim, deals with these *halakhot,* and they also found their place in the codes of the decisors. The Torah scroll and everything connected with it are treated with an exceptional measure of sanctity. In the Mishnah the holy ark with the scrolls of the Torah in it is referred to as the *teivah* ("chest") (*Ta'an.* 2.1). It is considered more holy than the synagogue building (*Meg.* 3.1). The name *aron ha-qodesh* ("holy ark"), which calls to mind the Ark of the Covenant referred to by that name in *2 Chronicles* 35:3, is already used in the Talmud (B.T., *Shab.* 32a). The name *heikhal* ("palace") is also commonly used in rabbinic literature, and it was adopted by the Sefardic and Eastern Jews.

When the Torah scroll is removed from the ark, it is customary to recite the verse "And when the ark moved . . ."; as it is returned, the congregation recites, "And when it rested, he said . . ." (*Nm.* 10:35–36). One stands when a Sefer Torah is displayed and kisses the cloak or case in which it is wrapped. The cover and cloak in which the Torah scroll is tied and wrapped, as well as the finials and crown that ornament it, are all considered secondarily sanctified articles. While it is totally forbidden to illustrate the Torah scroll itself, or even to change in any way the form of the letters written in it, the holy ark and the religious articles connected with the

Torah have throughout history been fashioned and adorned artistically, in accordance with the economic status, cultural level, and artistic taste of the various Jewish communities of the world.

BIBLIOGRAPHY

Content and Historical-Critical Research

Childs, Brevard S. *Introduction to the Old Testament as Scripture.* Philadelphia, 1980.
Hahn, Herbert F. *The Old Testament in Modern Research.* 2d expanded ed. Philadelphia, 1966.
Kraus, Hans-Joachim. *Geschichte der historisch-kritischen Erforschung des Altern Testaments von der Reformation bis zur Gegenwart.* Neukirchen, 1956.
Leiman, Sid Z. *The Canonization of Hebrew Scripture: The Talmudic and Midrashic Evidence.* Hamden, Conn., 1976.
Rendtorff, Rolf. *Das überlieferunggeschictliche Problem des Pentateuch.* Berlin, 1977.
Sanders, James A. *Torah and Canon.* Philadelphia, 1972.
Segal, M. H. *The Pentateuch: Its Composition and Its Authorship.* Jerusalem, 1967.
Sellin, Ernst. *Introduction to the Old Testament.* Translated by David E. Green; revised and rewritten by Georg Fohrer. Nashville, 1968.
Weinfeld, Moshe. *Deuteronomy and the Deuteronomic School.* Oxford, 1972.

The Concept of Torah in Later Judaism

Davies, W. D. *Torah in the Messianic and/or the Age to Come.* Philadelphia, 1952.
Heschel, Abraham. *Torah min ha-shamayim ba-aspaqelaryah shel ha-dorot.* London, 1965.
Scholem, Gershom. "The Meaning of the Torah in Jewish Mysticism." In his *On the Kabbalah and Its Symbolism,* translated by Ralph Mannheim, pp. 32–86. New York, 1965.
Urbach, E. E. *The Sages: Their Concepts and Beliefs.* 2 vols. Translated from the second expanded Hebrew edition by Israel Abrahams. Jerusalem, 1979. See the index, s.v. *Torah.*

Torah in Service and Ritual

Elbogen, Ismar. *Der jüdische Gottesdienst in seiner geschichtlichen Entwicklung* (1924). Hildesheim, 1962.
Gutmann, Joseph. *Jewish Ceremonial Art.* New York, 1964.
Kanof, Abram. *Jewish Ceremonial Art and Religious Observance.* New York, 1971.

6 TALMUD

Robert Goldenberg

In form, the Talmud is an extended, multivolume elaboration of selected tractates of the Mishnah, but it must be emphasized that the contents of the Talmud go far beyond its ostensible base. No subject of interest to the ancient rabbis failed to find its way into this immense body of teaching, and for that reason no question arising in later centuries was deemed outside the range that Talmudic teaching might legitimately claim to resolve. A document that seemed merely to elucidate an older text eventually became the all-embracing constitution of medieval Jewish life.

As noted, the Mishnah supplied the overall format for the Talmud. Like the former, the Talmud is divided into tractates, which in turn are divided into chapters and then into paragraphs. Each phrase of the Mishnah is discussed, analyzed, and applied for as long as the editors of the Talmud have materials to supply; when such materials are exhausted (sometimes after very long and quite wide-ranging digressions), the discussion simply moves on to the next phrase or paragraph. The digressions can be such that one loses track of the Mishnaic passage under discussion for pages at a time, but the Talmud always picks up again from its base text when the next section begins.

ORIGINS AND DEVELOPMENT

Very soon after it began to circulate, the Mishnah of Yehudah ha-Nasi' (compiled c. 200 CE) assumed a central place in rabbinic study. As time went on, the structure and content of the Mishnah—the meaning and the sequence of its paragraphs—determined the manner in which the growing accumulation of rabbinic lore was organized. Non-Mishnaic legal materials (the so-called outside traditions; Aram., *baraitot*) were studied primarily in connection with their Mishnaic parallels, and an entire supplementary collection (Tosefta) that followed the Mishnah's own sequence of orders, tractates, and chapters was compiled. Similarly, post-Mishnaic rabbinic teachings—of law, morality, theology, and so forth—were remembered and discussed primarily as the consecutive study of Mishnaic tractates called them to mind, so that most such teachings eventually came to be linked with one or another specific passage (or, occasionally, several) in the earlier collection.

In this way, great compilations of rabbinic teaching, each in the form of a loose exposition of the Mishnah, came into being. Evidence suggests that various centers of rabbinic study developed their own such collections, though in the end only one overall collection was redacted for the Palestinian centers and one for Babylonia. For several generations, the collections remained fluid. Materials were added, revised, or shifted. Free association led to the production of extended discourses or sets of sayings that at times had little to do with the Mishnaic passage serving as point of departure. Early materials tended to be brief explanations of the Mishnah or citations of parallel texts, but later rabbis commented as much on remarks of their predecessors that were not included in the Mishnah or were subsequent to it as on the Mishnah itself. Numerous recent scholars have seen in the developing tradition two sorts of material: brief, apodictic statements of law and much longer dialectical explanations of the specific laws and their underlying principles. Such discussions in turn eventually gave rise to a new generation of legal dicta, and these in turn provoked new efforts at dialectical complication. Thus the Talmudic tradition grew.

The Hebrew word *talmud* and its Aramaic equivalent, *gemara'*, both mean "study." Each term had other meanings at various times, but in the end *gemara'* came to be the name of the vast Mishnah commentary that had taken shape, and *talmud* the name of the combined text (Mishnah plus *gemara'*) that eventually emerged. The rabbis of the immediate post-Mishnaic period (third to fifth centuries CE) are called amoraim (from the Aramaic *'mr,* "say, discuss"), because their characteristic contribution to the developing tradition was the extended discussion of the Mishnah they produced.

Through a process that can no longer be traced with certainty, the text of the *gemara'* underwent periodic reshaping until finally the two Talmuds as we now know them came into being. It should be emphasized that early rabbinic Torah study was oral, so that the *gemara'* was not so much a fixed text as a more-or-less accepted formulation of accumulated lore. There is therefore no reason to assume that there ever was an authorized "original text" of the Talmud, although there may have been parallel recensions of these collections from the earliest stages of their history preserved in different localities. There is still no altogether accepted standard text, and even the relatively uniform wording of recent centuries has much to do with the eventual predominance of European over Asian and North African Jewry and the standardization that inevitably followed the invention of printing.

The Jerusalem, or Palestinian, Talmud. The so-called Jerusalem Talmud (Heb., *Talmud Yerushalmi*) is really the work of the rabbinic academies of the Galilee; it was substantially completed by the middle of the fifth century. The Jerusalem Talmud covers the first four orders of the Mishnah with the exception of two tractates (*Avot* and *'Eduyyot*); in the last two orders, only half of tractate *Niddah* has Palestinian *gemara'*. The Jerusalem Talmud is characterized in general by brevity and an absence of editorial transitions and clarifications. Its discussions frequently seem laconic and elliptical and often take the form of terse remarks attributed to one or another amora with no connective phrasing at all between them. Occasionally, however, such comments are built up into a more integrated dialectical treatment, with objections raised and answered, contradictions cited and resolved, and biblical proof texts adduced as the editors see fit.

The Babylonian Talmud. According to tradition, the redaction of the Babylonian Talmud (Heb., *Talmud Bavli*) was completed by the amoraim Ashi and Ravina' around the year 500. It is clear, however, that the distinctive features of this Talmud in contrast to the other are the work of several generations of rabbis who came after these authorities and are collectively known as the savoraim (from the Aramaic root *svr*, "consider, hold an opinion"), that is, those who reconsidered the Talmudic text and established its final version. Thanks to the labors of these latter revisers, the Babylonian Talmud is far more thoroughly worked out than the Palestinian. Its arguments are replete with a sophisticated technical terminology for introducing source materials, considering objections and counterobjections, offering refutations and defending against them, and so forth. In addition to their detailed contributions, the savoraim also composed entire sections of the Talmud; in particular, the first extended discussion, at the beginning of many tractates, is attributed to them. In general, the literary superiority of the Babylonian Talmud, its far greater logical clarity, and its considerably larger bulk can be attributed to the savoraim of the sixth and seventh centuries. The Talmud as we now have it did not exist until these had done their work.

While the Jerusalem Talmud treats the entire first order of the Mishnah, the Babylonian Talmud has *gemara'* only for the first tractate (*Berakhot*), which deals with liturgy; the rest of the order treats agricultural rules that were not considered applicable outside the Holy Land. On the other hand, and harder to explain, the great bulk of the fifth order, which regulates the Temple cult and is not to be found in the Jerusalem Talmud, has very substantial Babylonian *gemara'*. Otherwise, with minor exceptions, the two Talmuds cover the same parts of the Mishnah.

LATER DEVELOPMENTS

Over the several centuries following the appearance of the two Talmuds, the Babylonian Talmud gradually eclipsed the other. This predominance was rationalized by the claim that the Babylonian Talmud was the more recent, so that its editors already knew the Jerusalem Talmud and could include its acceptable teachings in their own work and suppress those portions for any reason found unworthy. In retrospect, however, it is clear that such a claim was part of the propaganda of the Babylonian geonim of the last centuries of the first millenium CE in favor of their own authority and against the rival authority of the rabbis of the Land of Israel. The eventual predominance of the Babylonian Talmud throughout the Diaspora and even in the Land of Israel probably is to be explained through reference to such factors as the relatively stronger ties of the rising communities of North Africa and Spain to Babylonian Jewry and the relatively more severe decline of Palestinian Jewry, especially under the onslaught of the Crusades. Those parts of Europe, especially Italy, that retained strong ties with the community in the Land of Israel apparently maintained a tradition of study of the Jerusalem Talmud, but by the beginning of the second millenium this process had run its course. From then on, "the Talmud" always meant the Babylonian. It was taken for granted that issues of Jewish law should be resolved by reference to the Babylonian Talmud, not the Palestinian, and that the latter could provide rulings only in cases where the Babylonian Talmud was silent or ambiguous.

Once the primacy of the Babylonian Talmud was established, it was continually reinforced. The Babylonian Talmud received more attention. It was studied by more scholars, it became the subject of more and of better commentaries; it was copied more often and more carefully by larger numbers of scribes. The result is that modern scholars have a more solidly established text of the Babylonian Talmud and a more fully developed exegetical tradition with which to work. Modern critical study of the Jerusalem Talmud has much more fundamental analytical and restorative work to accomplish before a reliable and comprehensible text becomes available.

It should be noted as well that the power of the medieval Christian church affected the development of the Talmud in two important ways. Periodic waves of seizure and destruction reduced the number of Talmud manuscripts available in certain parts of Europe. The most important of these waves took place in thirteenth-century France and in Italy at the time of the Counter-Reformation; the last burning of the Talmud occurred in Poland in 1757. Occasionally thousands of copies of the Talmud or of Talmudic digests and commentaries were destroyed at a time. In addition, Jewish efforts to avoid such destruction often led to voluntary or involuntary submission of the Talmud to censorship by church authorities. As a result, much early rabbinic discussion of Jesus or the Christian religion has been lost or must now be recovered from scattered manuscripts.

TALMUDIC RELIGION
Despite its vast size and scope, the Talmud is not without focus. Certain themes and certain styles of argument and discourse strongly predominate in its pages, and as a result both the religion of the Talmudic sages themselves and the forms of Judaism based on the Talmud that flourished during the Middle Ages are more compatible with certain types of spirituality than with others.

The Role of Law. Well more than half of the Babylonian Talmud and more than three quarters of the Jerusalem Talmud are devoted to questions of law. The Mishnah itself takes the form of a law code, and Talmudic discussions are chiefly concerned with clarifying, extending, and finding new applications for the provisions of Mishnaic law. This concentration on law is related to the ancient rabbis' role in their communities where they usually served as judges, teachers, or public administrators. Rabbinic piety came to be organized around gratitude for the law and joy in its fulfillment. The law was understood to be a divine gift, and observance of its provisions was seen as the appropriate response to this generosity. To observe the law meant to strengthen one's link to its giver, and in developing the law into a huge accumulation of detailed regulations covering all aspects of day-to-day living, rabbinic teachers were seeking to multiply occasions for strengthening this link. Study of the law was both the highest intellectual activity in which a Jew might engage and also a practical activity designed to further this expansion of opportunity. Enlarging the scope of the law was not felt to be adding to an already heavy burden; on the contrary, it increased the portion of one's life that could be conducted in response to the voice of God.

The Role of Study and Intellect. While the Mishnah looks like a law code, in fact it is probably something other; its numerous unresolved disputes, its sporadic use of biblical proof texts, and its occasional narratives all reflect the value of study as a religious ritual in its own right, and eventually the activity of studying God's law was as important in Talmudic religion as was the content of that study. With respect to Talmudic law, this enhancement of study as religious rite led to the creation of an elaborate set of legal corpora, most of which are identified by the name of the master to whom the discrete opinions in each corpus were attributed. The well-known Talmudic penchant for hair-splitting dialectics reflects the rabbis' concern that each of these sets of teachings be internally consistent on the one hand and significantly different from any other such set on the other. Hence the frequency with which the Talmud records the chains of transmission by which individual sayings were passed on. Hence the steadily growing integration of teachings from widely disparate fields of law into a single web, and the often forced effort to find unifying principles behind teachings that seem to have nothing to do with one another. Hence, as well, the relative lack of personal interest in the personalities of early masters, except, paradoxically, for those few who became the subject of frequently incredible legends.

This intellectual tendency had several important consequences for Talmudic religion. It gave rabbinic studiousness a scholastic tinge that continued to sharpen as later centuries wore on. It made text commentary an important genre of religious literature; a standard edition of the Talmud even today contains several classical commentaries on the page along with the text and many, many more at the back of the volume. Rabbinic intellectualism turned into disciplined argument; the interplay of proof and refutation, into a holy activity. It also gave primacy to the correct formulation of the wording of sacred texts and recitations over the manner or the circumstances in which they were pronounced; this in turn had important effects on Talmudic and post-Talmudic conceptions of prayer, meditation, and inward spirituality.

TALMUDIC LEARNING AND RELIGIOUS AUTHORITY

In the ancient rabbis' view there was a connection between their emphasis on learning and the role of leadership to which they aspired. It was taken for granted that only the Torah, when properly and sufficiently studied and understood, could enable the people of Israel to become the "kingdom of priests and holy nation" (*Ex.* 19:16) that God intended them to be. This in turn meant that only those properly and sufficiently learned in Torah should be allowed to assume leadership over the community, since only such leaders could be trusted to guide the people in a divinely ordained direction.

Inherent in Talmudic and post-Talmudic Judaism is the assumption that Torah learning (once the Talmud was complete, this meant Talmudic learning) is the only proper criterion by which the leaders of the community should be selected. Whenever conditions permitted, rabbis sought to institutionalize their authority over the community. In the early period, this meant reaching an accommodation with the real rulers of the community (e.g., the Roman empire or, in Babylonia, the allegedly Davidic dynasty of the exilarchs). Later, it meant assuring that internal Jewish courts should be dominated by rabbis and that Talmudic law should govern those aspects of life where Jews maintained internal autonomy (marriage and divorce, religious ritual, educational institutions). Although rabbinical authority was not without challengers, it was never overthrown in principle until the breakdown of Jewish self-government, which began in the late eighteenth century and continued into the nineteenth.

TALMUD STUDY AS RELIGIOUS EXPERIENCE

Rabbis saw their own teaching as "oral Torah." They believed the contents of the Talmud represented a part of the revelation to Moses that had been kept oral but faithfully transmitted for centuries before its inclusion in the text of the Talmud. The name *Talmud,* in fact, can be understood as a short form of the common phrase *talmud Torah,* or "Torah study." Thus to study Talmud was in fact to let oneself hear the word of God, and to add to the accumulation of commentaries, digests, codes, and the like was to make one's own contribution to the spread of divine revelation in the world. To learn Torah was thus a kind of sober mysticism, a reliving of the events at Sinai, while to add to the growing body of "oral" law was to share in a divine activity. Already in the Talmud God is depicted as studying Torah several hours a day (B.T., *A.Z.* 3b), but the kinship between the rabbi and God was felt to be even stronger. By increasing the amount of Torah in the world, the rabbi could do what previously only God had been held able to accomplish.

Thus the text of the Talmud became the center of an activity believed to be the most Godlike available to human experience. Everyone could study some Torah, and no one was considered incapable of adding a few original thoughts to a study session. In this way, Talmud study became a widespread activity among later Jewish communities. The degree of commitment to this activity might vary, from the ascetic twenty-hour-a-day devotion of the closeted scholar to one-hour-a-week popular learning on Sabbath afternoons. The climax of a boy's education was the point at which he was ready to learn *gemara'.* Such "learning" continues even in our time, even after the functioning authority of Talmudic law has all but disappeared. It represents the most powerful and the longest-lived inheritance of classical Judaism.

[*See also* Mishnah and Tosefta; Biblical Exegesis, *article on* Jewish Views; *and, for a survey of the development and structure of Jewish law,* Halakhah.]

BIBLIOGRAPHY

The history and current state of critical scholarship about the two Talmuds is comprehensively review in two essays in *Aufstieg und Niedergang der römischen Welt,* vol. 2.19.2 (Berlin and New York, 1979): Baruch M. Bokser's "An Annotated Bibliographical Guide to the Study of the Palestinian Talmud," pp. 139–256, and David Goodblatt's "The Babylonian Talmud," pp. 257–336. Both have been reprinted in *The Study of Ancient Judaism,* vol. 2, edited by Jacob Neusner (New York, 1981). These two surveys should be understood as successors to Hermann L. Strack's *Introduction to the Talmud and the Midrash* (Philadelphia, 1925). This work is a dated classic but a classic nonetheless. Several of Neusner's students also produced longer examinations of the work of particular modern scholars; he collected these in *The Formation of the Babylonian Talmud* (Leiden, 1970).

Neusner has also investigated the religious implications of conceiving of Torah study as a holy activity and the theological implications of rabbinic intellectuality; see his concise *The Glory of God Is Intelligence* (Salt Lake City, 1978). A more popular effort of the same sort is Morris Adler's *The World of the Talmud* (New York, 1958). See most recently my own "Talmud," in *Back to the Sources,* edited by Barry W. Holtz (New York, 1984), pp. 129–175.

7
MIDRASH AND AGGADAH

Judah Goldin

Regardless of what specifically the Hebrew word *midrash* stands for in its two oc-currences in a postexilic book of the Hebrew scriptures (*2 Chr.* 13:22, 24:27), where the reference is clearly to something written or written in (Heb., *ketuvim;* Gr., *ge-gramménoi*), by the last century BCE it stands for oral interpretation, that is, interpre-tation of the Torah, the Law of Moses; and one who interprets the Law is referred to as *doresh ha-torah.* This we learn from the literature of the Dead Sea sectarians (*Damascus Covenant* 6.7, 7.18f., 8.29; *Manual of Discipline* 6.6, 8.15; see also *Eccle-siastes* 1:13). Indeed, it is possible that already at the beginning of the second century BCE there were in existence schools where Torah interpretation was going on. In the Hebrew of *Ben Sira* (c. 200–180 BCE), the author, Simeon ben Joshua ben Sira, or Sirach, by whose time "wisdom" is already equated with the Torah, speaks as follows: "Turn to me, you who are untaught, and lodge in my school [*beit midrash;* literally, 'house, or place, of *midrash*'; *en oikō paideias*]." *Midrash* is therefore a school activity. In the *beit ha-midrash,* the school, learning is to be found, wisdom is to be acquired, there is a master, and there are disciples; through interpretation, understanding of the Torah is attained: "The book of the covenant of the Most High God, the Law (Torah) which Moses commanded us . . . fills men with wisdom, like the Pishon, and like the Tigris at the time of the first fruits. It makes them full of understanding like the Euphrates, and like the Jordan at harvest time" (*Sir.* 24:23–26)—and there is more to this effect.

ORIGINS OF THE MIDRASH

A question that may never be answered satisfactorily is that of when, precisely, the interpretation of the Torah began. For from the moment any text is adopted as a rule or guide of life, some interpretation—added explanation, commentary—inevi-tably becomes necessary. In scripture itself, though most commandments are lucidly drawn up, there are four occasions when even Moses was in need of further instruc-tion regarding procedures for laws already established (*Lv.* 24:10–23; *Nm.* 9:4–14, 15:32–36, 27:1–11). The Midrash also calls attention to Moses facing difficulty in understanding specifically what God has ordered (*Mekhilta',* ed. Jacob Lauterbach, 1.15; cf. *Sifrei Zuta',* ed. Saul Lieberman, 6.16; but see also Harry Fox in *Tarbiz* 49,

1980, 278ff.). In scripture such cases are reported probably to underscore that no human legislator, not even Moses, is the originator of biblical laws, that Moses only transmits what the Lord ordains; the Law of Moses is God's law which he communicates through Moses. But these cases at the same time illustrate that no written code can be operative without supplementary instruction. And supplementary instruction is what *midrash* provides.

There is therefore a measure of justice to the traditional view that the written Torah had to be accompanied from the outset by expository teachings of some kind, transmitted and inherited orally (the oral Torah). But we are in no position to fix the time when precisely such very ancient supplementary teaching began. In legendary lore there are views that, for example, statutory prayer services were first established by the patriarchs (B.T., *Ber.* 26b); that benedictions of the grace after meals were added by Moses, Joshua, David, and Solomon (ibid., 48b); and that already at Sinai at the giving of the Ten Commandments interpretation was taking place (*Mekhilta'* 2.267). But such statements have no historical value and perhaps are not meant to be taken as history in the strict sense. They represent a tendency to project later institutions farther and farther back in time in order to suggest high antiquity and that these are not recent unauthorized inventions.

Whatever very ancient interpretation may have been like (reflected also in glosses, popular etymologies, and parables within the Hebrew scriptures themselves; cf. I. L. Seeligmann in *Supplement to Vetus Testamentum,* vol. 1, 1953, pp. 150–181), it is unquestionable that from roughly 250 BCE, when the Pentateuch was translated into Greek (as the Septuagint), and continuing for seven hundred years and beyond, when major collections of Midrashic literature continued to be redacted, *midrash* flourished in the Jewish academies of Palestine. From the end of approximately the second century CE, *midrash* flourished to a lesser extent in the Babylonian Jewish academies as well, though it was principally a Palestinian creation.

Hellenistic-Roman influence on intellectual and cultural life in Jewish Palestine affected Midrashic activity, as can be seen in the penetration of Greek (and other foreign) terms, the terminology for some rules of interpretation, the circulation of tales and epigrams, the parables drawn from royal and imperial establishments, a few cultic details, and the significance given to the numerical value of Hebrew words (*gimatriyyah*). In short, while it would be inexcusably uncritical to assume that wherever there is influence there is simultaneously direct dependence and borrowing, the rich and constant intellectual preoccupation with explanation of the language and content of scripture by teachers to students in the schools, and to the public at large by means of sermons in the synagogues, is an echo of the stimulation provided wherever—not only in Palestine—the spirit of Greek learning and letters came to the attention of the learned classes. Native traditions were not necessarily abandoned; indeed, they might now be held onto more tightly, but they would also be interpreted in ways comprehensible to those who lived in an age when Greek models of thinking and expression dominated the overall intellectual climate.

AGGADIC MIDRASH

Midrash (i.e., interpretation, commentary, exegesis, amplification) was applied to all of scripture, and in tannaitic times (approximately the first two centuries CE), especially to four books of the Pentateuch, *Exodus* through *Deuteronomy,* because these contained the bulk of biblical *halakhah,* the regulations governing the conduct of society as well as individual practice. However, even in these books there is considerable nonhalakhic material, what is called *aggadah,* and the first book of the Pentateuch, *Genesis,* is almost entirely *aggadah.* Aggadic subject matter was therefore also commented on in the tannaitic *midrashim,* and some of the leading masters of *halakhah* were also leading masters of *aggadah.* Thus we have aggadic *midrashim* not only on *Genesis* but also in the midrashic compilations on the other Pentateuch books as well, and aggadic discussion is thus included not only in the tannaitic *midrashim* but in subsequent works devoted to all the books of the Hebrew Bible.

The word *aggadah* may be rendered as "narrative, recitation, account based on scripture," but the term, the concept, implies and refers to very much more in the Midrashic and Talmudic corpora. By *aggadah* is meant that which strictly speaking is not classified as *halakhah,* as required, normative practice. *Aggadah* includes narratives, historical composition, poetry, speculation, genealogical records, fanciful interpretation, moral exhortation—in short, the exposition of the whole variety of scriptural contents beyond the codified, legislative, and juristic, prescribed courses of action which constitute *halakhah.*

There are instances where a sharp line between aggadic comment and halakhic cannot be drawn easily; see, for example, *Keritot* 6.3 (and cf. Eli'ezer in *Keritot* 6.1). On the whole, however, a halakhic discussion is easily distinguished from an aggadic one. In the former, legalistic concern is uppermost, norms of practice are sought, there is close attachment to what the sages regard as literal meaning, argument by authorities is erudite and acute, there is constant resort to tradition, rules of interpretation are followed with due regard for their function (those of Hillel in the first century, those of 'Aqiva' and Yishma'e'l in the second century), and casuistry is employed as in all legal and scholastic disciplines. On the other hand, *aggadah* is unrestrained contemplation and interpretation associated with the vocabulary and themes of all parts of the Bible. There is free application of the subject of one verse in scripture to another verse far removed from it, so that, for example, in undertaking to comment on *Leviticus* 1:1, the teacher or preacher introduces *Psalms* 103:20 and by skillful adaptation can demonstrate that the *Psalms* verse explains the intention of the *Leviticus* verse. *Aggadah* is very often sermonic, interpretation for the benefit of the folk in the synagogue, and therefore, though there are, so to speak, rules of interpretation for *aggadah* as well, they do not really confine the *aggadot* within strictly drawn hermeneutical perimeters.

Considerable liberty of interpretation was permitted to and practiced by the authors of *midrash aggadah,* who employed all the rhetorical devices common among textual scholars of their time, used, for instance, in the interpretation of Homer. Thus much is made of punning, of homophones, of methods of dream interpretation, of figures of speech, and of acronyms. A frequent form of interpretation is the parable of kings and their subjects. Verses receive not just one but many interpretations, which indictes not the rejection of previous explanation but the simultaneous legitimacy of a number of meanings which the biblical, divinely revealed text contains and hence, also, beneath-the-surface lessons. *Midrash aggadah* is employed for polemic purposes, against internal challengers as well as antagonists from the outside. For example, when Pappos interprets *Job* 23:13 as a statement of God's omnipotent and arbitrary power, 'Aqiva' hushes him up by means of an alternative interpretation that every decision of God is just, (*Mekhilta'* 1.248). Or when Israel is mocked because the Temple was destroyed (presumably, a sign of God's rejection of Israel), one sage declares that this was, on the contrary, a sign of God's love for Israel, in that he let out his wrath on the sticks and stones of the structure (his own habitation) rather than on the people themselves (*Lam. Rab. on Lam.* 4:11 ed. Buber, 74b). Comments like these were obviously made as a consolation after profound tragedy. And they reveal too the ready resort to paradox: even misfortune may be for the good (see also *Genesis* 45:5–8; for paradox in *halakhah,* see *Tanhuma'* on *Numbers,* ed. Buber, 52a–b).

Along with polemics, *midrash aggadah* does not hesitate to indulge in varieties of apologetics. Thus examples of questionable behavior of the patriarchs and Israel's heroes (the twelve sons of Jacob, David, and Solomon) are frequently excused and presented in a positive light, while their enemies' characters are in almost all respects regarded as wicked—typical folkloristic treatment. Events in scripture are identified as foreshadowings of experiences later in the sages' own times and of the age to come. By means of *midrash* the protests and resentments of later generations find eloquent outlet, and this in turn leads to attempts at theodicy. In the retelling of biblical narratives legendary lore is drawn upon in order to emphasize particular values and ideals; so, too, to contrast the ways of the nations of the world with Israel's ways. And in virtually all interpretation, especially where more than immediate, literal meaning is sought, the aim of aggadic *midrash* is moral and didactic. This is particularly noteworthy in the stories told about famous sages: in these, fancy and fact are so closely intertwined it is rare that the one can be separated from the other.

Aggadic *midrash* also preserves evidence of gnostic speculation by certain rabbis on the theme of creation, on the chariot spoken of by Ezekiel, on the overpowering reality of the godhead and his celestial retinue, on major historic experiences of Israel (at the sea after the redemption from Egyptian bondage and at the Sinai revelation), on the contrast between the fate of man after the Fall and before it and what might have been otherwise.

With such latitude available to aggadic *midrash,* all aspects of life come under review—the relations of man to God and of man to fellow man. Piety of conduct (in the light of the law and in action surpassing legal prescription) and piety of thought are exemplified. Public virtue and private virtue are discussed in the light of moral expectation, related to biblical verses, which are quoted and given novel interpretation, and interrelated with the particular theme in the mind of the teacher or preacher.

For example, scripture (*Ex.* 19:1–2) reports that "On the third new moon after the Israelites had gone forth from the land of Egypt, on that very day, they entered the wilderness of Sinai. Having journeyed from Rephidim, they entered the wilderness of Sinai and encamped [here the verb is plural: *va-yahanu*] in the wilderness. Israel encamped [here the verb is singular: *va-yihan*] there in front of the mountain."

To draw the moral of these verses the homilist first invokes a verse from *Proverbs* in which the subject is the excellence of wisdom, which for the homilist and his audience is already understood as the Torah. Then *Proverbs* 3:17—"Its [wisdom's] ways are ways of pleasantness, and all its paths are peace"—is made to shed light on the *Exodus* report. Thus the Holy One, blessed be he, actually wished to give the Torah to Israel at the time they left Egypt, but the Israelites kept quarreling with each other, saying all the time, "Let us head back to Egypt" (*Nm.* 14:4). Note what is written (*Ex.* 13:20): "They set out from Succoth and encamped at Ethan"—both verbs are in the plural, for as the Israelites moved on ("set out"), they quarreled, and as they halted ("encamped"), they quarreled; but when they reached Rephidim, they all made peace and became a united assembly (a single band). (And when is the Almighty exalted? When Israel forms a single band, as it is said [*Am.* 9:6], "His band he founded on the earth" [*Lv. Rab.* 30.12, 710]—possibly an appeal not to break up into conflicting sects.) How do we know that they all became a united assembly? For the verse (*Ex.* 19:2) says, "Israel encamped there in front of the mountain," and this time the verb is in the singular: *va-yiḥan*; it is not written, "they encamped," with the verb in the plural, *va-yaḥanu*. Said the Holy One, blessed be he, the Torah, all of it, is peace (-loving); to whom shall I give it? To the nation that loves peace. Hence (*Prv.* 3:17), "and all its paths are peace" (*Mekhilta'* 2.200; *Lv. Rab.* 9.9, 188; *Tanḥuma'* on *Ex.*, ed. Buber, 37b, 9).

A number of elements, typical of *midrash* as a whole, appear in this passage. To begin with, there is the association of a verse "far removed" (in *Proverbs*) with the particular verse (in *Exodus*) to be interpreted—which is meant to demonstrate that all parts of scripture endorse each other and that it can be shown, when necessary, that they are not in conflict. Second, there is meticulous attention to minutiae—the significance even of shifts from plural to singular (by dropping one consonant)—from which an important lesson can be derived. Third, verses are cited at every opportunity to serve as proof text; in many *midrashim* this feature is even more lavishly exhibited than in our passage, and there is no trace of their authors' possessing concordances to help them in their search for apt quotations. Finally, of course, there is the chief theme with which the *midrash* may be concerned, in our case, the theme of peace (which may be a warning against sectarianism or even an exhortation not to contemplate rebellion against the ruling powers). That study of the Torah thrives on peace and leads to peace is what the Midrashic and Talmudic sages frequently tried to stress.

GOALS AND THEMES OF THE MIDRASH

There are very many *midrashim* even more complex in their structure and content, but basically it may be said that all Midrashic teaching undertakes two things: (1) to explain opaque or ambiguous texts and their difficult vocabulary and syntax thus supplying us with what we would call literal or close-to-literal explanation or, for lack of that, purely homiletical guess; (2) to contemporize, that is, so to describe or treat biblical personalities and events as to make recognizable the immediate relevance of what might otherwise be regarded as only archaic. As we have seen, a scene from the account of the revelation of the Ten Commandments becomes a homily on Torah and peace. Patriarchs will be described as mourning for the destruction of the Temple. Esau comes to represent the Roman empire. The twelve sons of Jacob become extraordinary military heroes. And so it goes for the rest of scripture: the past addresses the present, directly or indirectly, and drops hints of the future. There are Midrashic interpretations that grow out of both a lexical problem in the verse and the desire to apply the explanation to the thinking and need of the later age. For example, for *ve-anvehu* ("and I will glorify him" [*Ex.* 15:2]) Abba' Sha'ul says, "Take after him [*ani ve-hu';* lit., "I and he"], even as he is gracious and compassionate, so should you be gracious and compassionate"; thus a meaning of the problematic *anvehu* is provided and along with that the moral lesson of *imitatio dei* (*Mekhilta'* 2.25).

Although, as I have said earlier, the Midrash takes into account whatever scripture refers to, there are at least three themes to which much reflection and commentary are devoted. The first is the absolute unity and incomparability of God. The cue for this is of course in scripture (*Dt.* 6:4 and elsewhere), but the kind of emphasis given is essentially postbiblical—that is, that no dualism or plurality of gods is to be tolerated; no worship of God is to be modeled after pagan worship; that regardless of what overtakes Israel, God's justice is not to be denied; that unlike frequent frivolous treatment of their gods by the pagan world, Israel must love God absolutely, with no reservations, come what may. In the Midrash God may be spoken of anthropomorphically; this does not embarrass the sages; they know that such speech is metaphorical and inevitable (therefore its presence in scripture itself); what they fear is blasphemy and anything that can lead to the desecration of God's name.

A second recurring theme is Israel—that is, Israel of the biblical past, Israel of the present, and the ideal Israel of the age to come. To the patriarchs of Israel there had already been the promise that God would maintain a unique relationship with their descendants. And though God may grow angry at them and visit them with punishments and disasters, the bond between God and their people is a permanent one (see also *Ezekiel* 20:30–44). Israel is under obligation to carry out his commands, and in Midrashic and Talmudic centuries this meant not merely the commands as formulated "briefly" in the scriptures but as interpreted at length by the sages: "'If you do not hearken unto me' (*Lv.* 26:14), that is, if you do not hearken to the interpretation, the instruction [*midrash*] of the sages" (*Sifra'* 111b; see also *Sifrei, Dt.* 49, ed. Finkelstein, 114f.). Along with this fundamental view come all sorts of promises of ultimate reward for adherence to the terms of the covenantal relationship and all sorts of regulations concerning how Israel is to remain distinct from the nations of the world in whose midst Israel of the present must live. The self-consciousness demanded by the original covenant and its subsequent reaffirmations is not merely taken for granted or left implicit; it is repeatedly articulated.

No less pervasive is the third theme, that of Torah, which has two meanings, often simultaneous but often also distinct, and it is not always easy to decide which is intended. The word *torah* can stand both for the study of the Torah and for putting into practice the teachings of the Torah. While obedience to the commands of the Torah is already a frequent biblical injunction, what especially characterizes the demands of the sages in the Midrash is their tireless exhortation that all must study Torah, that neglect of study is not just a sign of a poor education but a deficiency in one's role in life. The sages do not deny that one may merit a share in the life of the world to come even if he is not a scholar or student. But this hardly satisfies them, and ever and again they return to the duty and privilege of Torah study. It is a person's required curriculum from the time he begins scripture study at the age of five—from the time he begins to speak, he should be taught selected verses on the theme of Torah—until the day of his death. Many hyperbolic sayings occur in this connection, and these are indicative of the lengths to which the sages were prepared to go in order to impress on all classes in society, rich and poor, the supreme obligation and value of Torah study. It is the emphasis on Torah study, indeed, that gradually transformed the originally prophetically oriented religion of Judaism into an intellectually directed religious experience in which scholars are the elite. [*See also* Torah.]

THE PROCESS OF COMPOSITION
The bulk of aggadic *midrash* commentary which we possess very likely came into being as homilies in connection with the Torah reading as part of synagogue worship. Unfortunately, it is still impossible to fix the time when public Torah reading was first institutionalized. It was certainly in existence by the end of the last century BCE and the first century CE, for Philo Judaeus, Josephus Flavius, and the New Testament all refer to the study and exegesis of Torah (and prophetic selections) as a weekly Sabbath program. The weekly reading (in Palestine, according to a three-and-a-half-year cycle) served as the principle of organization, the scheme of arrangement for the Midrashic homilies.

The different Midrashic compilations display a certain variety of composition—there are *midrashim* that comment on the biblical text verse by verse (exegetical *midrashim*; e.g., *Genesis Rabbah*) and those that comment only on the opening verse or verses of the pericope and then move on to the next biblical unit (homiletical *midrashim*; e.g., *Leviticus Rabbah*) In these exegetical and homiletic *midrashim*, before the principal Midrashic interpretation there may be an introductory homily or homilies, *petiḥta', petiḥata',* or proems, as a kind of overture to the principal interpretation; perhaps (as suggested by Joseph Heinemann in *Scripta Hierosolymitana,* 1971) these served as brief sermons before the Torah reading. Tanḥuma' Yelammdenu *midrashim* tend to introduce the aggadic discourse by citation of a halakhic question and answer, doubtless not only to convey a rule of practice but to underscore that *halakhah* and *aggadah* are one in aim. There are Midrashic texts drawn up for the round of special days in the year, feasts and fast days and other appointed occasions (e.g., *Pesiqta' de-Rav Kahana'*). There are still other compilations, but what is significant is that in all these texts, regardless of stylization, there is created an intellectual, didactic, hortatory tone which all the *midrashim* share, and thus all the *midrashim* sound as though they all were in manner or approach alike. At a later time (from about the seventh century on), Midrashic views are combined to create a literary composition—for example, on the sacrifice of Isaac or Abraham, on the rabbinic martyrs of the Hadrianic period, on Abraham's discovery of and commitment to the one God, on the death of Moses, and so forth.

There seem occasionally to have existed books of *aggadah* even in rabbinic times, but the rabbis disapproved of them. Like all other branches of study, except for scripture, aggadic *midrash* was delivered and attended to as part of the oral law, that branch of the total tradition that was not to be put in writing: Midrash, Mishnah, Targum, Talmud, the *halakhot* and the *aggadot*—in other words, what the rabbis taught.

The creators of the aggadic *midrashim* were the rabbis, but this does not mean that they drew only on scholarly sources or had only scholarly exposition in mind. The rabbis did draw on these, especially when biblical terms were difficult; but they also drew on folklore, on popular legends, on anecdotes, on deliberately imaginative identifications which would make the passage they were interpreting intelligible and also surprising to their audience. They might use current Greek words and epigrams to add special vividness to their interpretation. They might adopt allegorical methods of explanation. Everyone, including women and children, attended the synagogue to hear the preacher. Midrashic method became so popular that even nonscholarly men could express themselves in the form, or so the Midrash relates. For example, a rabbi's ass driver undertakes to refute a Samaritan when the rabbi himself is at a loss for a proper retort (*Gn. Rab.* 32.10, 296f.); an unlearned man offers an interpretation of a verse the rabbi had not thought of, and the rabbi promises the man that he will use that interpretation in a sermon in the man's name (ibid., 78.12, 932f.). When a homily is admired, one might praise it as "a precious gem."

Exposure and attention to aggadic *midrash* were certainly widespread, especially when the hearts of the people craved comforting. But aggadic *midrash,* as I have mentioned, was also part of the oral law and was also a subject of the *beit hamidrash,* the academy. There is no lack of comments emphasizing the value of this study, but the very repetitions in favor of *aggadah* create the impression that scholars had to be encouraged again and again not to neglect it. Early allegorists said, "If you wish to recognize him who spake and the world came to be [i.e., if you wish to have correct thoughts about the creator of the universe], study *aggadah,* for it is thus that you will recognize him who spake and the world came to be and cleave to his ways (*Sifrei Dt.* 49, ed. Finkelstein, p. 115). The superlative estimate of *aggadah* is here evident: what leads one to a proper knowledge of God and to attachment to his ways is to be found not in pursuit of halakhic studies (alone?) but in reflection on the acts of God as described in many places of the *aggadah.* But the feeling is inescapable that such sentiments imply a criticism of those scholars who, because they are chiefly masters of the law, experts in the complex disciplines of dialectic and halakhic subtleties, tend to regard *aggadah* condescendingly. The very freedom of speculation it permits and its very lack of fixed rules of mandatory conduct probably make the sages uncomfortable. Moreover, the exacting analytic exercises demanded by *halakhah* may have made single-minded halakhists feel superior to that which appealed to popular taste. On the other hand, for the folk as a whole the *aggadah* was a perennial refreshment of spirit and of the courage to endure. This the scholars did not deny, and that experience of refreshment remained true for centuries to come.

PRINCIPAL COMPILATIONS

The following is a list of the principal Midrashic compilations and treatises; critical editions are listed briefly within parentheses. Particular but noncritical editions are listed without parentheses.

First are the tannaitic *midrashim;* these are essentially halakhic, but they contain a good deal of aggadic material as well:

1. *Exodus: Mekhilta' de-Rabbi Yishma'e'l* (edited by Jacob Lauterbach; a second edition was edited by Hayyim Horovitz and Israel Rabin) and *Mekhilta' de Rabbi Shim'on bar Yoḥ'ai* (edited by Jacob Epstein and Ezra Melamed).
2. *Leviticus: Sifra',* edited by I. H. Weiss. There is also an edition by Meir Ish Shalom [Friedmann] that is critical but only a beginning; Louis Finkelstein has published Vatican Manuscript Codex Assemani LXVI of the treatise with a long and instructive introduction. Finkelstein's critical edition of *Sifra'* has begun to appear.

3. *Numbers: Sifrei de-vei Rav,* and *Sifrei zuṭa'* (both edited by Horovitz).
4. *Deuteronomy: Sifrei* (edited by Finkelstein) and *Midrash Tanna'im,* edited by David Hoffmann.

The following are aggadic *midrashim* from the amoraic period (c. third through fifth or sixth century) to the thirteenth century:

1. The collection known as Midrash Rabbah on the Pentateuch and the Five Scrolls *(Song of Songs, Ruth, Lamentations, Ecclesiastes,* and *Esther).* The individual works were drawn up in different times: *Genesis Rabbah* (edited by Julius Theodor and Chanoch Albeck), from the late fourth to early fifth century, is the earliest, and just a little later is *Leviticus Rabbah* (edited by Mordecai Margulies). For *Deuteronomy Rabbah,* see also the edition by Saul Lieberman. On this collection as a whole, see Zunz (1892).
2. *Tanḥuma'* on the Pentateuch and *Tanḥuma',* edited by Solomon Buber.
3. *Pesiqta' de-Rav Kahana'* (edited by Bernard Mandelbaum).
4. *Midrash Tehillim* (Midrash of the Psalms), edited by Buber.
5. The Yemenite *Midrash ha-gadol* on the Pentateuch, by David ben Amram Adani (thirteenth century), which draws on earlier Midrashic compilations (some no longer extant) and even Maimonides to form a collection of its own:
   Genesis and *Exodus* (edited by Margulies)
   Leviticus (edited by Nahum Rabinowitz and Adin Steinsalz)
   Numbers (edited by Solomon Fisch; a second edition was edited by Tsevi Rabinowitz)
   Deuteronomy (edited by Fisch)
6. *Yalqut Shim'oni,* also of the thirteenth century, by a rabbi Shim'on, which gathers its material from many earlier *midrashim* and covers the whole of Hebrew scriptures.

[*See also* Biblical Exegesis, *article on* Jewish Views.]

BIBLIOGRAPHY

On all this literature see the classic presentation by Leopold Zunz, *Die gottesdienstlichen Vorträge der Juden* (1832; 2d ed., Hildesheim, 1966) but even better the Hebrew translation thereof, *Ha-derashot be-Yisra'el* (Jerusalem, 1947), which is brought up to date and corrected by Chanoch Albeck in the light of later research. Other Midrashic collections not listed here, albeit of considerable importance, are also described and discussed in this work.

The best presentation of the sages as aggadic teachers is Wilhelm Bacher's *Die Agada der Tannaiten,* 2 vols. (1884–1890; reprint, Berlin, 1965–1966); *Die Agada der palästinischen Amoräer,* 3 vols. (Strasbourg, 1892–1899); and *Die Agada der babylonischen Amoräer* (Strasbourg, 1878). Bacher introduces each of the principal teachers separately, organizes the teachings around major categories as embodied in many scattered sayings, and comments on them. This work is also available in Hebrew translation by A. Z. Rabinowitz). See also E. E. Epstein-Halevi's *Ha-aggadah ha-historit biyyogerafit le-or meqorot Yevaniyim ve-Latiniyim* (Jerusalem, 1973).

The nature of Judaism as a religion as it emerges from aggadic Midrash especially (but not exclusively) is best represented by Solomon Schechter's *Some Aspects of Rabbinic Theology* (London, 1909), reprinted as *Aspects of Rabbinic Theology* (New York, 1961); George Foot Moore's *Judaism in the First Three Centuries of the Christian Era, the Age of Tannaim,* 3 vols. (1927–1940; reprint, Cambridge, Mass., 1970); Joseph Bonsirven's *Palestinian Judaism in the*

Time of Jesus Christ, translated by William Wolf (New York, 1964); and E. E. Urbach's *The Sages: Their Concepts and Beliefs,* 2 vols., translated from the second Hebrew edition by Israel Abrahams (Jerusalem, 1975). For additional reading one may consult the selected titles listed below.

Albeck, Chanoch. "Introduction." In *Genesis Rabbah.* Edited by Chanoch Albeck and Julius Theodor. Berlin, 1931. Reprinted under the title *Midrash; Rabbath Genesis.* Jerusalem, 1965.

Bickerman, Elias J. "La chaîne de la tradition pharisienne." *Revue biblique* 59 (1952): 44–54.

Fischel, Henry A. *Rabbinic Literature and Greco-Roman Philosophy: A Study of Epicurea and Rhetorica in Early Midrashic Writings.* Leiden, 1973.

Ginzberg, Louis. *Legends of the Jews.* 7 vols. Translated by Henrietta Szold et al. 1909–1938. Reprint, Philadelphia, 1946–1955.

Goldin, Judah. *The Song at the Sea.* New Haven, 1971.

Halperin, David J. *The Merkabah in Rabbinic Literature,* American Oriental Series, no. 62. New Haven, 1980.

Heinemann, Isaak. *Darkhei ha-agadah.* Jerusalem, 1970.

Heinemann, Joseph, ed. *Derashot ba-tsibbur bi-tequfat ha-Talmud.* Jerusalem, 1970.

Heinemann, Joseph, "The Proem in the Aggadic Midrashim: A Form-Critical Study." In *Studies in Aggadah and Folk Literature.* Edited by Joseph Heinemann and Dov Noy, pp. 100–122. *Scripta Hierosolymitana,* vol. 22. Jerusalem, 1971.

Kasher, M. M. *Torah sheleimah.* 37 vols. New York, 1927–1982.

Lieberman, Saul. *Hellenism in Jewish Palestine.* New York, 1962.

Marrou, Henri I. *A History of Education in Antiquity.* Translated by George Lamb. New York, 1956.

Scholem, Gershom G. *Jewish Gnosticism, Merkabah Mysticism, and Talmudic Tradition.* 2d ed. New York, 1965.

Spiegel, Shalom. "Introduction". In *Legends of the Bible* by Louis Ginzberg. New York, 1956.

Spiegel, Shalom. *The Last Trial.* Translated by Judah Goldin. New York, 1964.

Stern, David M. "Rhetoric and Midrash: The Case of the Mashal." *Prooftexts* 1 (1981): 261–291.

Strack, Hermann L. *Introduction to the Talmud and Midrash.* 5th ed., rev. Philadelphia, 1931.

THREE

THE JEWISH PEOPLE AND ITS IDENTITY

8

THE JEWISH PEOPLE

ROBERT M. SELTZER

The Jews are both a historical people in their own right and a social body required and sustained by the Jewish religious tradition. In what sense the Jewish people is to be considered a nation or ethnic group depends on how these terms are defined—the traditional Hebrew concepts for nation, *goi, le'um,* and above all *'am,* apply to the Jews collectively, but the extent to which the peoplehood of the Jews is amenable to definition by nineteenth- and twentieth-century concepts of nationality has been a matter of controversy, to be discussed later. This article seeks to explore the meanings attributed to Jewish peoplehood from ancient to modern times, with special attention to the relationship of Jewry to other faith communities that have emerged from the Israelite religious matrix.

That the Jews are at the same time a people and a religious fellowship is attested by the complex interplay between nationhood and religion in the course of Jewish history. Historical circumstances have periodically intruded on the parameters of membership and the idealized meaning of collective Jewish existence. During periods of rapid change affecting contemporaneous branches of the Diaspora differently, uncertainty and even conflict have emerged as to who is a Jew and what religious actions or principles of faith are required of a Jew. Jewish religious authorities have been forced to take up the task of clarifying the criteria for inclusion in the people and the theological significance of Jewish survival as a group "like all the nations" (*1 Sm.* 8:5), yet "a people dwelling alone and not reckoning itself among the nations" (*Nm.* 23:9). Eventually these confusions subside, only to reappear in later historical eras.

The nature of Jewish religious peoplehood can in part be illuminated by comparative considerations. A similar congruence of peoplehood and religion is found in certain national forms of Christianity (e.g., the Armenian and Coptic churches) and in the "nation" of Islam as corporate body and subject of religious law, especially in the early history of Islam, when it was a religion of the Arabs only and before it became the religion of the Persian, Turkish, and other peoples. Unlike the Christian instances, however, Judaism stands quite separate from its scions and siblings. The line between Judaism and Christianity has remained firm, despite occasional allusion to a "Judeo-Christian" tradition, and, in contrast to Christianity, Judaism has resisted definition by creedal formulation. The centrality of salvation through Christ and related creedal and doctrinal formulations facilitated the theological idea of a multi-national church quite different from the bonds that maintained the unity of the Jewish people. In its emphasis on the centrality of law rather than salvation through faith in Christ and sacramental grace, Judaism shows a much closer structural affinity to Islam. The cultural variation between the various branches of Jewry for many centuries was virtually as great as that of Christendom and Islam, but the political situation of Judaism and the Jews was overall quite different. The Jewish people was a nation before its religion achieved its mature form, and the religious tradition maintained the integrity of the people's identity when the Jews were a minority in all the lands of their residence.

Other peoples and religions have had diasporas, but the Jewish Diaspora is re-markable for its global dispersion and its ability to survive. At least since the end of antiquity the Jews were essentially a diaspora people. After the Israelite and Judean kingdoms of the eleventh to the sixth century BCE and the Hasmonean kingdom of the second and first centuries BCE, and despite exceptional situations where the rul-ing class of a society converted to Judaism, there was not a Jewish state until 1948; for almost nineteen centuries, the political factor in Jewish history has been more indirect, involving semiautonomous communal institutions and leaders of various types not possessing absolute sovereign power but buttressed by the gentile state and by Jewish figures accorded authority in matters of exegesis and legal interpre-tation. The need to adjust to the objective status of a Diaspora minority has surely contributed to Jewish unity and continuity.

During the long course of Jewish history in the Diaspora, common destiny and cohesiveness were maintained by external and internal forces working in tandem. Consciousness of living in *galut* ("exile") and awaiting ultimate redemption has been a key subjective element in the self-identity inculcated by the tradition and constantly reinforced by the Jewish liturgy. At the same time, however, this distinc-tive identity has been maintained by the conspicuous presence of the Jewish people in the formative narratives of Christianity and Islam. In the New Testament the Jew-ish people is depicted as having rejected Jesus as the Messiah, even though he and his disciples were Jews; in the Qur'ān the Jews are depicted as having rejected Mu-ḥammad as the "seal of the prophets" even though he acknowledged the divine source of their sacred book and certain other features of Jewish worship. (In both cases these charges have a historical basis.)

Acknowledgment by Christianity and Islam that the Jewish people has played an extraordinary role in the history of salvation, even when accompanied by doctrines that God rejected the Jews and bestowed grace on another elect people, expressed the ambivalent attitudes toward Jewry of Christian and Muslim religious authorities: confirmation of Jewish specialness and anger at "stiff-necked" Jewish obstinate de-nial of the (Christian or Muslim) truth. Conviction of possessing the truth and anger at the Jews lay behind the social and legal restrictions on Jewish status and were easily available to rationalize anti-Jewish persecutions. But the peculiar conspicuous-ness of the Jewish people also serves to confirm the singularity of the Jewish people, which is a cardinal element of the Jewish tradition itself and a main reason for Jewish survival.

Another issue sometimes raised in connection with Jewish peoplehood is whether Judaism should be characterized as a universal or an ethnic faith. Judaism—more properly, Torah in its broad sense as holy teach-ing and action—is both universalistic and particularistic. Gaining ultimate authority from the conviction that it is derived from divine revelation, Torah includes all forms of Jewish religious practice (*mitsvot,* or commandments; *halakhah,* the correct way, or religious law; and *minhag,* or custom)—but Torah also comprises the values inculcated by Jewish law and preaching, as well as the understandings of reality and the human situation expressed in Jewish religious literature. Torah articulates concepts about the nature of deity in relation to cosmos and history: that deity is one, eternal, creative, transcendent as well as immanent, revelatory, and personal—although Jewish religious thought has brought forth a variety of sometimes quite complex formulations of these and other fundamental principles of faith.

At the same time, the very idea of Torah requires that there be a certain people among the nations of the world that is to study and practice Torah as the *raison d'être* of its existence (and of the existence of the universe, at least in its present form). The notion of a people elected by God to receive the commandments of the Torah hallows the people and locates its special role in the context of world history. The Jewish tradition conceives of this election not solely as a preordained, passive reception of revelation but as an active electing by the people to accept the "yoke" of the commandments. Thus Jewish religious thought transforms the mundane historical fact of the people's social existence into a joyful, voluntarily assumed obligation and responsibility. These introductory remarks indicate some of the complexities of Jewish peoplehood as fact and ideal, which will be dealt with separately in the following.

NAMES FOR THE JEWS AND JUDAISM

In the Jewish tradition, the Jewish people as a socioreligious entity is designated *'am Yisra'el* (the "people of Israel"), *benei Yisra'el* ("children of Israel," Israelites), *beit Yisra'el* ("house of Israel"), *keneset Yisra'el* ("assembly of Israel," in rabbinic literature), or simply as *Yisra'el* (Israel). The biblical patriarch Jacob, renamed Israel in *Genesis* 32:28, is the eponymous ancestor of the people of Israel through his sons, who are considered the founders of the twelve Israelite tribes. In contrast, a native of the modern state of Israel *(medinat Yisra'el),* which possesses Christian and Muslim, as well as Jewish, citizens, is usually rendered by the modern Hebrew adjective *Israeli (Yisra'eli).* The term *Jew* (Heb., *Yehud*) is etymologically derived from *Judah (Yehudah),* the eponym of the biblical tribe of Judah.

After the death of King Solomon around 922 BCE, when the majority of the Israelite tribes rejected his son as ruler and formed a kingdom called the kingdom of Israel *(mamlekhet Yisra'el),* the southern kingdom of Judah, comprising the tribal territories of Judah and Benjamin and the Davidic capital of Jerusalem, remained loyal to the Davidic dynasty. The northern kingdom of Israel came to an end in 722 BCE; the southern kingdom of Judah *(mamlekhet Yehudah)* was destroyed in 587/6 BCE, but the Aramaic cognate *yahud* remained the name for the region around Jerusalem in the Persian empire. (In *Esther* 2:5 the term *Jew* refers to a member of the whole people, even someone of the tribe of Benjamin; in *Esther* 8:17 and 9:27 it refers to the act of gentiles joining the Jews in some unspecified way.) The Greek form *Ioudaia* was used by the Ptolemaic and Seleucid kingdoms and for the independent commonwealth established by the Hasmoneans in the second century BCE. The latinized form was Judaea.

By Hellenistic times the term *Jew* (Gr., *Ioudaios,* Heb., *Yehudi*) had become a name not only for subjects of the Hasmonean state but throughout the Diaspora for those who were members of the Jewish people and adherents of its religious tradition. While accepting the term *Yehudi,* the rabbinic literature continued to prefer *Yisra'el, benei Yisra'el,* and so forth. (In the context of the Jewish liturgy, an "Israelite" is a Jew called to the reading of scripture who is not a priest or a Levite.) Yet another relevant term is *'Ivri* ("Hebrew"), which probably at first referred to a social status rather than to ethnic or gentilic identification (this primary usage of *Hebrew,* as, for example, in *Exodus* 21:2, may have had a philological relationship to the second-millennium social category called in Akkadian the *habiru*). Several biblical instances when *Hebrew* can be construed as referring to an Israelite or to the ancestor of an Israelite (*Jon.* 1:8, *Gn.* 4:13) and as recalling Eber, a descendant of Noah's son Shem (*Gn.* 10:21, 11:14), may have led to its eventually becoming a synonym for the Israelites and their language. In the nineteenth century in some European countries, *Hebrew* became a polite equivalent for *Jew,* which had acquired negative connotations; in the twentieth century the positive force of *Jew* has been regained in English, German, and other languages.

CORPORATE EXISTENCE IN ANCIENT ISRAELITE RELIGION

The Hebrew scriptures represent a selection of the literature produced by and for the people of Israel, mainly in the Land of Israel and over as many as eight or ten centuries. A main theme of the Pentateuch is how the people came into being, a chain of narratives that sets the stage for the enumeration of Israel's corporate duties to its God, YHVH (probably vocalized as *Yahveh*). Accordingly, the ancestors of the children of Israel had lived in the land of Canaan as patriarchal clans for several generations until they settled in Egypt, were enslaved, and, after Moses' confrontation with Pharaoh, were redeemed by YHVH, who brought them to the wilderness of Sinai. There they entered a binding agreement with their God—a covenant that included a taboo against worshiping other gods (*Ex.* 20:2–6). The modern historiography on the origins of the people in the context of the nations and social movements of the second millennium BCE involves many speculative uncertainties: the exact relationship of the direct ancestors of the Israelites to such ancient groups as the Amorites and the Hyksos; whether the proto-Israelites worshiped YHVH before the Exodus (compare *Exodus* 6:3 with *Genesis* 4:26); the extent to which Canaanite peasants or tribes joined the Israelite federation in the thirteenth or twelfth centuries BCE, accepted its God, and were absorbed in the people.

The exclusive divine authority of YHVH in relation to the collective existence of Israel is reflected in various and fundamental aspects of ancient Israelite religion. For example, Israelite tradition went to considerable lengths to disassociate ownership of the land of Canaan from the right of conquest as such. Israelite settlement was said to have been made possible by YHVH as Israel's supreme ruler; the Land of Israel was a territory on which the people could become a nation akin to other nations but devoted to carrying out its covenantal duties. The corporate aspect of land ownership can be seen in the provision that land sold by individuals was to be returned periodically to the family to whom it was "originally" allocated (*Lv.* 25:2, 25:23).

Moral and legal obligations included many stipulations that regulated individual behavior as well as relations between sectors of Israelite society, but the framework and a substantial portion of the covenantal duties preserved in the Pentateuch refer to Israel as a collective entity. In addition to sacrifices to be offered by Israelites as expressing personal thanksgiving or contrition, an elaborate series of sacrifices is to be offered to God by the priests on behalf of the people to express collective gratitude or to expiate collective sin (e.g., *Nm.* 28:2, *Lv.* 16:30). Besides ethical duties incumbent on the Israelites individually and as members of families, there are responsibilities to the "widow, orphan, and stranger" for which Israel as a whole is responsible (*Ex.* 22:21–22).

Throughout the history of the Israelite kingdoms prophetic messengers warned the people that if these collective obligations were not fulfilled, YHVH could take away the land he had given them and force them into exile (e.g., *Am.* 3:2, 7:11). The destruction of the northern kingdom of Israel by Assyria in 722 BCE was interpreted in this manner by the so-called Deuteronomic movement, which probably acquired the opportunity to carry out an extensive program of religious reforms in the kingdom of Judah in the 620s (*2 Kgs.* 22–23, *2 Chr.* 34). The heart of the *Book of Deuteronomy* very likely reflects the position of this group, which emphasized that the corporate responsibility of Israel that had been voluntarily accepted at Sinai was binding on all generations of the people: to love YHVH, obey his commandments, avoid any taint of idolatry, worship him in the place—Jerusalem—that he would "cause his name to dwell," where his only house and sacrificial altar were to be constructed (e.g., *Dt.* 6:4–5, 12:1–14).

When Judah was destroyed by Babylonia in 587/6 BCE, the explanation offered was that the idolatry of the past had condemned the people to exile but that God continued to love them and held out a sure promise of redemption (*2 Kgs.* 24:3–4, *Jer.* 29). The experience of Babylonian exile brought to the fore the prophetic theme of the eternal nature of the covenant between YHVH and Israel. The religiosity of the exilic community was most likely marked by an acceptance of the divine causation for the people's exile, a pervasive regret for the sins of the ancestors, and a heightening of the idealized role of the people in history. While sustaining the concepts of a specific holy mountain (e.g., *Jl.* 4:1), city (*Is.* 2:3), and land of YHVH, that is, of Zion (*Is.* 10:24), a precedent emerged for autonomous Israelite survival outside the precincts of sacred space. (Contrast David's complaint that Saul banished him so that he could no longer serve YHVH, *1 Sm.* 26:19.) The exilic prophecies in the latter part of the *Book of Isaiah* portray the people as God's servant, as "light to the nations" (*Is.* 49:6) that God's salvation be known to the ends of the earth, and they anticipate that gentiles will worship YHVH, the author of good and evil (*Is.* 2:1–4; *Mi.* 4:1–4; *Is.* 45:14, 45:22–24, 56:3–8; *Zec.* 8:20–23).

The decisive difference between Israel's historical evolution and that of other ancient Near Eastern peoples was Israel's elevation of its God to the status of the sole deity, creator of heaven and earth, ruler of the world, and judge of all history. Pre-Mosaic sources of the Israelite cult of YHVH are quite uncertain, and perhaps unlikely. Unlike other Near Eastern deities (Sin, Adad, Ishtar, and so forth), YHVH did not have temples and shrines dedicated to him in various widely scattered localities around the Near East, and he was not incorporated into any other pantheon, confirming the attitude of the biblical authors that YHVH's name and reputation in the world depended solely on Israel. The dating of a full-fledged biblical monotheism is a matter of considerable scholarly controversy. For our purposes, determining when in Israelite history "other gods" came to be viewed as nondivine (in the biblical terminology, mere "idols") is less important than the fact of the eventual emergence, in the course of the intellectual development of ancient Israel, of an explicit, sweeping, and radical demotion of other deities and elevation of one God, an action unprecedented in the history of religion (*Is.* 45:5–7). This transformation was accompanied by the reinterpretation of traditions concerning the past from a monotheistic perspective rather than an abrupt break with the received traditions concerning that past.

The final redaction and reworking of the traditional material concerning human origins and the formative eras of Israelite history from the standpoint of radical monotheism may not have occurred until the postexilic period. The return to Zion of a large portion (but not all) of the Babylonian exiles in the late sixth century and again in the mid-fifth century BCE laid the groundwork for the revival of Jerusalem, its Temple, and the land of Judaea in late Persian and Hellenistic times. By then Judaism had become a world religion, centered on a scripture that defined the Jews as God's treasured possession, "a kingdom of priests and a holy people" (*Ex.* 19:4–6), necessary for his universal plan and goals. [*For further discussion, see* Israelite Religion.]

FROM BIBLICAL ISRAEL TO THE CHRISTIAN AND RABBINIC ISRAELS

Both the corporate and the individual dimensions of Israelite faith were to be extensively developed in succeeding centuries. Closely associated with the corporate aspect of salvation is the messianic idea (buttressed by various scriptural verses and prophecies concerning the End of Days, the permanence of the Davidic dynasty, and the kingship of God) that there would be a completely just, God-inspired king to rule Israel and establish everlasting peace and harmony in the world.

The individualistic dimension of postscriptural Judaism took the form of each person's accountability to carry out the *mitsvot,* including many that had primarily been the duty of the priesthood earlier. Individual immortality became a central doctrine of Judaism perhaps in the second century BCE (a late biblical allusion to the resurrection of the dead is *Daniel* 12:2, most likely dating from the Maccabean Revolt; compare *2 Maccabees* 7:9, 7:14, 9:29). Personal immortality was soon absorbed into most branches of Judaism (except the Sadducees) and was made binding in the second of the Eighteen Benedictions (Shemoneh 'Esreh or 'Amidah) that Jewish males are to recite three times daily. Jewish eschatological teachings of the last centuries BCE and the first century CE, for all their flux and uncertainty, emphasized the crucial significance of Israel ("And the kingdom and the dominion and the greatness of the kingdoms under the whole heaven shall be given to the people of the saints of the Most High," *Dn.* 7:27) and the transcendent value of membership in it ("All Israel has a share in the world to come" with some notable exceptions, *San.* 10.1). This world *(ha-'olam ha-zeh)* of history will be climaxed by the coming of the King-Messiah and a utopian messianic age. And this world is transcended by another realm, the world to come *(ha-'olam ha-ba'),* where the guilty will be consigned to a merited punishment for their sins and the righteous of all generations will be eternally rewarded with the radiance of the divine presence.

Not only theology but also membership in the people of Israel was enlarged during the last centuries BCE and the first century CE. By the time of the Jewish revolt of 66–70 CE against the Romans in Judaea, a majority of Jews were probably residing in the Diaspora, either in Persia under the Parthians (the Jewish community of Babylonia, dating from the exile of the sixth century BCE) or in communities in the Hellenistic kingdoms and later the Roman empire (Antioch, the cities of Asia Minor and European Greece, Alexandria and elsewhere in Egypt, as well as Rome and other locations around the Mediterranean). These new communities had been founded by Jewish settlers who had left Judaea for a variety of political and economic reasons, but they had been augmented by a considerable number of conversions to Judaism in the Diaspora.

Formal conversion to Judaism was a new phenomenon in Jewish life. Previously, non-Israelites had been accepted into Israel on an individual basis (the *Book of Ruth,* which may date from postexilic times, contains one such account). A contrary instance of the rejection of "foreigners" is given by Ezra and Nehemiah, who demanded that the Judahites of their time separate themselves from their non-Israelite wives (*Neh.* 9:2, 13:3) and who rejected the inhabitants of Samaria (the heartland of the former northern kingdom of Israel) who worshiped YHVH but were considered by the Bible not to be of the seed of preexilic Israel (*2 Kgs.* 17:29–34). (The Samaritans became the first religious tradition that stemmed from the biblical matrix but was separate from the Jewish people. [*See* Samaritans.]) At the turn of the common era, however, proselytism seems to have become a common occurrence (see, for example, *Mt.* 23:15, *Acts* 2:5, and B. T., *Shab.* 31a). In addition to formal conversion, which probably entailed circumcision for males, immersion, and the offering of a special Temple sacrifice, there is reference to pagans who followed one or another element of the Jewish tradition (Josephus, *Against Apion* 2.39; Tacitus, *Histories* 5.5).

The last two centuries BCE and the first century CE was a period of intense Jewish religious ferment, when new schools of thought and new elites competed with each other: Pharisees, Sadducees, Essenes, Zealots, early Judeo-Christians, apocalyptic visionaries and sects in Judaea, and hellenized "philosophies" in the Diaspora. By the end of the first century CE or at least by the late second century after the last of the Jewish revolts against the Romans, the rabbinic Judaism that had developed out of the Pharisaic movement had become predominant, and Christianity had become fully separated from the Jewish people. By the end of the first century CE, the rabbis had added a benediction against sectarians *(birkat ha-minim),* apparently to indicate that Christians were unwelcome in the synagogue. Christian writings held that the Jews ignored the messiah and were collectively responsible for his death (*Mt.* 13:57, 27:25). In any event, by then most Christians were not of Jewish descent but were converted pagans.

After the Samaritans, Christianity was the second religious tradition that remained loyal to the witness of the Hebrew scriptures but came to constitute a distinct community of faith. A crucial element in the parting of the ways between Judaism and Christianity was the former's rejection of Jesus of Nazareth as Messiah and the latter's rejection (after a few years of uncertainty) of Jewish law. In what became the dominant Christian formulation, Torah law was held to have been divinely inspired but superseded by the coming of the Messiah, who made available a full salvation that had been prophesied in the Hebrew scriptures and that was not possible under "the law" (*Gal.* 3 and 4). [*For further discussion of the emergence of Christianity from Judaism, see* Judaism *and* Christianity *and the biography of Paul.*]

This principled negation of Jewish law, especially ritual law, ceremonial practice, and *kashrut,* meant that the experience of Jesus, accompanied by baptism, was a sufficient portal into the Christian people, now defined as the "new Israel" of the spirit (e.g., *Acts* 10, *Rom.* 9–11). In particular, the Jewish requirement of circumcision was rejected and baptismal immersion redefined as one's spiritual rebirth as a Christian. (According to rabbinic law, conversion is also a rebirth; the convert to Judaism terminates former family ties and is considered in the category of a newborn child. See *Gerim* 2.6.) For rabbinic Judaism, the Torah as divine law was a permanent feature of creation, a dynamic and ongoing process of articulating the tasks of God's people in history. In the New Testament, Christianity viewed the Hebrew scriptures through the concept of its fulfillment in Christ. Judaism viewed the written law of the Hebrew scriptures as part of a more comprehensive Torah that contained an oral law as well—an oral law that was partly redacted in the Mishnah, God's "mystery" given only to Israel (*Pesiqta' Rabbati* 14b). [*For discussion of this revelation in Judaism, see* Torah.]

Eventually Christianity did not reject the idea of religious law as such (it developed its own religious law to regulate creeds, holy days, family status, religious hierarchies, and so forth), but the Christian theological rejection of the eternally binding character of Torah law meant the sharp separation of 'am Yisra'el by the Jewish self-definition and the "new Israel" according to the Christian viewpoint. The two conceptions of holy peoplehood thus reflect the two contrasting modes of relating to the Hebrew scripture as holy; Christianity pushed much further than Judaism the figural, allegoric, and symbolic interpretation of Old Testament figures, institutions, and prophecies.

PEOPLEHOOD IN RABBINIC JUDAISM AND MEDIEVAL JEWISH THOUGHT

According to rabbinic Judaism, the Jews were the direct, physical descendants of the remnant of preexilic Israel, augmented by those who had accepted the commandments and were adopted into the Jewish people through the rituals required by Torah as interpreted by the rabbis. The biblical term *ger* ("stranger, resident alien, sojourner") was understood to refer to a proselyte—a *ger tsedeq* in contrast to a *ger toshav,* who had rejected idolatry but not accepted the full burden of the *mitsvot.*

Conversion remained a legitimate mode of acquiring the status of Jew, even though most Jews were Jews by birth. Despite traditions that some of the most eminent rabbis were proselytes or their descendants and that God had special love for *gerim,* there were also Talmudic sages who expressed suspicion of the motives and behavior of proselytes. For their own good, prospective converts were to be warned that "this people was debased, oppressed, and degraded more than all other peoples." Only if they persisted were they to be accepted with joy: "To whom are you cleaving? Happy are you! To him who spoke and the world came into being" (*Gerim* 1.1–5).

From the early fourth century on, Jewish proselytizing was anathema to the christianized or islamicized state; the Roman emperor Constantine made conversion to Judaism punishable by death according to Roman law, and a similar prohibition was part of the so-called Pact of Omar defining the status of Christians and Jews under Islam. Certainly external obstacles were determinative in discouraging large-scale conversion to Judaism from the early Middle Ages until recently.

There were also, however, internal factors. Christianity viewed proselytism as its mission in the world with a far greater intensity than did Judaism, and the church fathers insisted with far more rigor that there was no salvation outside the church. The rabbinic doctrine held that only the Jewish people had knowledge of, and was bound by, the full complement of divine commandments, but that there were seven Noahic laws binding on all humanity (usually enumerated as the prohibitions of idolatry, blasphemy, bloodshed, sexual sins, theft, and eating a limb of a living animal, together with a positive commandment to establish a legal system; B.T., *San.* 56a). On the salvation of non-Jews, the normative Jewish doctrine became the opinion of Yehoshu'a that the "righteous of all nations have a share in the world to come" (Tosefta, *San.* 13.2).

According to rabbinic law since the second century CE, the child of a Jewish mother and a gentile father is a Jew, but the child of a gentile mother and a Jewish father is a gentile. This matrilineal principle is alluded to in the Mishnah (*Qid.* 3.12), which deals with marriages valid and invalid according to *halakhah* and the status of the offspring thereof. The relevant Talmudic ruling was Yonatan's that "thy son by an Israelite woman is called thy son, but thy son by a heathen woman is not called thy son but her son" (B.T., *Qid.* 68b); the commentators emphasize the positive conclusion that the offspring of a Jewish woman is a Jew (see Moses Maimonides' *Code of Law,* Forbidden Intercourse 12.7). Various explanations, sociological and historical, have been offered for this principle of matrilineal descent. Apart from the influence of Roman law or the impossibility of confirming paternity, in premodern times the ruling most likely was not often of widespread practical consequence, since it was unlikely that many Jewish men would marry non-Jewish women who did not formally convert yet would rear their children as members of the people of Israel.

What of abandoning the status of Jew? Jews who converted to another religion were still considered Jews, although there are differences of opinion among the authorities over their specific halakhic rights. The relevant Talmudic principle was that such a person was a sinful Jew: "An Israelite, even though he sinned, remains an Israelite" (B.T., *San.* 44a). Thus the Jewish community accepted the return of Jews who had been forcibly baptized during the First Crusade in Europe, but acts of penitence and rituals of purification were required.

Impossible as it was in theory to leave the Jewish people, it was not so in fact. Although there might be psychological costs in apostasy, there were tangible advantages to leaving a group that was of subordinate legal status and subject to persecution. Individual Jewish converts were welcomed by Christian and Muslim authorities. Only in certain situations when large numbers of Jews were pressed into converting, such as in the Iberian Peninsula in the 1390s and again in the 1490s, was there a backlash against these New Christian, or Marrano, families, whose Christian faith was for many centuries considered suspect by virtue of their Jewish bloodline.

Supplementing the halakhic problem of who was and was not a Jew was the aggadic problem of why there was a people of Israel. The determination to idealize the chosenness of the Jewish people is quite evident in this material, epitomized in the benediction recited in the synagogue before the reading of the Torah: "Blessed art thou, Lord our God, ruler of the universe, who chose us from all the nations and gave us the Torah."

The sheer givenness or brute factuality of being a Jew—that Jews found themselves thrown into a Jewish destiny—was acknowledged in some coolly realistic Talmudic statements. Expounding the biblical verse "And they stood at the nether part of the mount" (i.e., Israel at Mount Sinai; *Exodus* 19:17), Avdimi bar Hama' bar Hasa' explained that the Holy One, blessed be he, tilted the mountain over the Israelites like a cask and said, "If you accept the Torah, well and good; and if not, there shall be your burial" (B.T., *Shab.* 88a). Most other scholars reject this notion on the grounds that receiving the Torah under coercion could nullify the obligation to observe it. The rabbinic *aggadah* continues in the line of a theological idealization of the people by emphasizing the collective responsibility of all members of the people both to each other and to God and the absolute centrality of Israel's collective presence in universal history. In a discussion concerning divine punishment, the principle is proposed that "all Israel is surety one for the other" (B.T., *Shav.* 39a). Israel conciliates God only when it is one unity (B.T., *Men.* 27a). The Jewish people fulfills God's plan that his presence indwells in the world.

A homily in *Ruth Rabbah* (1.1) ascribes to God the statement that if Israel had not accepted the Torah, he would have caused the world to revert to void and destruction. A homily in *Exodus Rabbah* (47.3) attributes to God the statement that if this people had not accepted his Torah, he would not look upon them more than other idol worshipers. (The Talmudic dictum that "anyone who repudiates idolatry is called a Jew" [B.T., *Meg.* 13a], based on the biblical identification of Mordecai of the tribe of Benjamin as a *Yehudi* [Judean] in *Esther* 2:5, uses the term *Jew* in a theologically idealized, nonethnic, purely homiletic sense.) It was a merit for the Jews to have accepted the Torah, but ever since Sinai it was Israel's *raison d'être* to obey the 613 commandments it contained. In contrast to the distinction in Christianity of late antiquity and the Middle Ages between the "religious" and the laity, the goal of rabbinic Judaism was to raise all Israel to the level of masters of Torah, transforming the community into an academy, as it were, for the study and practice of Torah.

Despite a Diaspora stretching from the Atlantic to Central Asia and eastward, and from the Baltic to the Sahara and beyond to Ethiopia, medieval Judaism did not become a multinational religion in the sense that Christianity or Islam did. (Christianity was transformed into a multinational faith after becoming the religion of the Roman empire in the fourth century and the conversion of the Franks, the Germanic, Nordic, and Slavic peoples in the Middle Ages; Islam after the conversion of the Persians and Turks. There were only two medieval instances where Judaism was adopted as the religion of a state: sixth-century Yemen briefly and the Khazar kingdom on the Volga between the eighth and tenth centuries.) A wide diversity of Jewish subcultures did emerge: Jewries in the Middle East that were largely the continuation of the ancient homeland and Diaspora communities; Iranian and Kurdish Jews; Jewish tribal groups in the Caucasus Mountains; the various Jewish communities of India and China; Berber Jews in the Maghreb; Sefardic Jews in the Iberian Peninsula; Provençal and Italian Jews; Ashkenazic Jews in northern France, the Rhineland, and later in eastern Germany, Poland, and Lithuania; and other communities with their own distinctive customs, dialectics, liturgies, and halakhic practices.

As a result, in daily life medieval Jews spoke a wide variety of languages—Greek and Aramaic; Persian and Arabic; Spanish, French, and German—and they developed distinctive Jewish dialects of these languages, such as Ladino (a Jewish form of Spanish) and Yiddish (a Jewish form of Middle High German), Hebrew being maintained for literary and liturgical purposes.

Some branches of medieval and early modern Jewry produced sophisticated courtier and banking classes and intellectual elites trained in the natural sciences and Aristotelian and Neoplatonic philosophies, whereas other Jewries were folk cultures of a population overwhelmingly engaged in menial occupations. Although in some regions the Jewish population was large, compact, and had a sizable agricultural or village component (e.g., the Galilee and Babylonia in late antiquity), political conditions under Christian and Muslim rulers necessitated that Judaism sustain itself increasingly as the religion of an urbanized minority mostly limited to crafts and trade (the specific list of the economic roles open to Jews differed widely from land to land and from era to era). In certain areas, such as northwest and eastern Europe, Jewish communities were founded or augmented by Jews invited to settle in frontier areas where the rulers considered them to be economically useful. However, given the interweaving of religion and the state in the countries in which medieval and early modern Jews resided, a Jewry could maintain itself only if permitted considerable legal autonomy—although the extent to which the Jewish leadership was dependent on the gentile rulers or derived its authority solely from the consent of local Jewish communities varied considerably.

The principal cause, therefore, of the mononational character of the Jewish people was not cultural or economic homogeneity. The national unity of the Jews was conditioned by the common psychological situation of being a minority everywhere: a minority with a profound, if disputed, connection to the formative narratives of the ruling religion; a minority enjoying a precarious social status inasmuch as it was always susceptible to persecution but was for considerable stretches of time better off than the local peasants and serfs; a minority with considerable training (especially through the Babylonian Talmud) in adjusting to living under gentile governments while preserving the continuity of Jewish law; a minority possessing a far-flung Diaspora network linked together by traders, scholars, and other Jewish travelers, and a steady stream of Jewish migration, sometimes westward, sometimes eastward; and, above all, a minority that defined itself as central to the history of creation.

The religious self-definition of the Jewish tradition, transmitted through scriptures, rabbinic law and lore, and the *siddur*, reiterated the sanctity of being *Yisra'el, 'amkha* ("your people," as addressed to God who "has chosen his people Israel in love"). This God, who "because of our sins exiled us from our land," nevertheless "remembers the pious deeds of the patriarchs and in love will bring a redeemer to their children's children for his name's sake." He will "gather the dispersed of your people Israel . . . break the enemies and humble the arrogant . . . rebuild Jerusalem as an everlasting building and speedily set up therein the throne of David" (from the Shemoneh 'Esreh, basic to the Jewish liturgy) and "will remove the abominations from the earth, and the idols will be utterly cut off when the world will be perfected under the kingdom of the Almighty and all the children of flesh will call upon your name, when you will turn unto yourself all the wicked of the earth . . . for the kingdom is yours and to all eternity you will reign in glory" (from the 'Aleinu prayer at the conclusion of each service).

Indicative of the force of religion in maintaining Jewish peoplehood until modern times is the major instance of Jewish schism involving the Karaite movement of the eighth and ninth centuries in the Middle East. Calling for a return to the literal meaning of the scriptures and denying the authority of the Talmud and rabbinic law, the Karaites became a distinct tradition separate from mainstream Judaism, with their own religious law based on biblical precedents. Religious authority and the sources of divine law were the cruxes of the Karaite-Rabbinite conflict, although there may have been socioeconomic forces operating as well. There were attempts, by Maimonides and others, to encourage close contacts between the two religious communities. In modern times some Karaite groups have closely identified with the Jews (the Karaites in Egypt), whereas others emphatically disassociated themselves (the Karaites in Russia).

Theorizing about the nature of Jewish peoplehood was not an especially important theme in medieval Jewish philosophy, but it was implied in various formulations of the purpose of Jewish existence. Speculative Jewish thought, with a few outstanding exceptions, moved as far away as possible from the idea of the Jewish people as a natural ethnic bond to its being a group embedded in a theology. In the rationalist stream Judaism was treated as an eminently logical faith, its doctrines of the oneness of God, the createdness of the universe, the rational component of prophecy, and the reasonableness of the commandments all being justified by categories and arguments derived from ancient Greek philosophy and glossed by Jewish, Muslim, and Christian writers. For Sa'adyah Gaon, "our nation of the children of Israel is a nation only by virtue of its laws" that, because they are divine, can never be abrogated; "the Creator has stated that the Jewish nation was destined to exist as long as heaven and earth would exist, its law would, of necessity, have to endure as long as would heaven and earth" (*The Book of Beliefs and Opinions,* trans. Samuel Rosenblatt, New Haven, 1948, p. 158). Torah, as consonant with right reason and authentic revelation, provided the most reliable, expeditious, and truthful means to serve God.

Maimonides presented Judaism as derived from Abraham's great insight into the divine nature:

> *His father and mother and the entire population worshiped idols . . . but his mind was busily working and reflecting until he had attained the way of truth, apprehending the correct line of thought, and knew that there is One God, that He guides the celestial Sphere and created everything. . . . When the people flocked to him [in the land of Canaan] and questioned him regarding his assertions, he would instruct each one according to his capacity till he had brought him to the way of truth. . . . And so it went on with ever increasing vigor among Jacob's children and their adherents till they became a people that knew God.*
>
> (Mishneh Torah, *Idolatry 1.2*)

Addressing a proselyte who asked if he could pray to the God of Abraham, Isaac, and Jacob as the "God of his fathers" (the first of the Eighteen Benedictions), Maimonides wrote that "Abraham our Father, peace be with him, is the father of his pious posterity who keep his ways, and the father of his disciples and of all proselytes who adopt Judaism" *(Letter to Obadiah the Proselyte).* He who believes in the basic principles of the Jewish faith, as Maimonides defined them, "is then part of that 'Israel' whom we are to love, pity, and treat, as God commanded, with love and fellowship"—otherwise he is an atheist, heretic, and unbeliever (Introduction to Pereq Heleq [*Sanhedrin* 10.1]). For Maimonides, those who affirm the unity of God as the cause of causes come as close as humanly possible to grasping divinity as such.

A second tendency in medieval Jewish thought was to emphasize the supermundane nature of Jewish peoplehood. In the philosophical tradition the exemplary exponent of this position was Yehudah ha-Levi, who suggested that "Israel among the nations is like the heart amid the organs of the body," at once the sickest and the healthiest of entities, exposed to all sorts of diseases and yet possessing through its relationship to the "divine influence" a unique proclivity that manifested itself as the gift of prophecy (*Kuzari,* trans. Hartwig Hirschfeld, New York, 1964, p. 109). In another of ha-Levi's images, Israel is the seed "which transforms earth and water into its own substance," carrying this substance from stage to stage until it brings forth fruit capable of bearing the divine influence, so that the nations who at least follow part of God's law pave the way for the Messiah and will become God's fruit (ibid., p. 227).

This version of Israel reached its apogee in Qabbalah, the medieval mystical tradition. Thus, in a discussion of the *mitsvot* in the basic qabbalistic text, the *Zohar,* circumcision is a prequisite for carrying out the surface meaning of the divine regulations (although to be circumcised only and not carry out the precepts of the Torah is to be like a heathen); the deeper mystery is to understand that Torah, God, and Israel are indissolubly linked together (*Zohar, Leviticus,* 73b). Drawing on the ancient Midrashic teachings about Israel's central role in the cosmos and on medieval Neoplatonic metaphysics, the qabbalists taught as esoteric doctrine that Israel's carrying out of the commandments has direct, puissant effects on the highest spheres of being as such. When Israel fulfilled the commandments with the proper intention (*kavvanah*), they overcame forces making for cosmic disharmony, effecting unifications (*yihudim*) in the realm of divinity itself. After the expulsions from the Iberian Peninsula in the 1490s, Qabbalah spread like wildfire, protecting Judaism against loss of morale and providing a solace in times of outward degradation. In the sixteenth-century Lurianic version of Qabbalah, the exile of Israel reflected the tragic exile of God, while the ingathering of the sparks of divinity achieved by fulfilling the *mitsvot* was the metaphysical analogue of the eventual ingathering of Israel at the climax of history. The implications of these qabbalistic doctrines were felt in the seventeenth-century messianic movement surrounding Shabbetai Tsevi and, in a different way, in eighteenth-century Hasidism. [*See* Qabbalah *and* Hasidism.]

THE MODERNIZATION OF JEWISH PEOPLEHOOD

The crisis of traditional Jewish peoplehood coincided with the overwhelming transformation of modernizing societies and the drastic shift in meaning of the term *nation* in Western and westernized societies. Previously, *nation* in many Western languages had loosely designated a community connected by ties of birth and common geographical origin. Toward the end of the eighteenth century and especially during the era of the French Revolution, *nation* acquired a more specific connotation in relation to sovereignty and citizenship: the *nation* came to apply to the citizenry as a whole, in contrast to the "political nation" of the *ancien régime,* which was limited to the wellborn and the elite.

Inasmuch as revolutionary France and, later, other modernizing countries forged the unity of the nation by dissolving the remnants of traditional estates and semiautonomous corporate entities, the extension of legal equality to all citizens had profound implications for the Jews. As modern nationalist movements and ideologies called for the self-determination of one nation after the other on geographical, cultural, linguistic, and historical grounds, the status of the Jews, now on the road to legal and political emancipation and, apparently, to economic and social integration, became exceptional and problematic. The almost seamless web of sociology, *halakhah,* and *aggadah* that had supported traditional Jewish peoplehood for centuries began to unravel.

The French Revolution acknowledged the citizenship rights of all French Jewry in September 1791. In 1807 Napoleon invited a body of lay leaders and rabbis to clarify the status of the Jews of his realm with respect to the accusation that they were a "nation within the nation." In defense of their rights, the Assembly of Jewish Notables (and the following year a group given the grandiloquent title of Sanhedrin) distinguished between the religious requirements of Judaism, which were held to be timeless and absolute, and the political dispositions of biblical society, which were held not to be applicable "since Israel no longer forms a nation." In effect, large areas of Torah law that dealt with civil and criminal matters were declared inoperative, and the fiscal and semipolitical autonomies that the Jewish communities had been awarded were acknowledged as no longer feasible—all this occurring at a time when the assumptions in which traditional religious faith was grounded could no longer be taken for granted.

The course of Jewish emancipation in one Western country after another had to overcome considerable opposition by those who held to the Christian basis of the state or who continued to insist on the alienness of the Jews. During the first three-quarters of the nineteenth century, Jews in Central Europe tended to define Jewry as a purely religious body whose positive mission in the Diaspora was to preserve the doctrines of pure ethical monotheism. The national or ethnic component seemed to many, especially in Germany, to be obsolete. In their rejection of the traditional messianic notion of a particularistic Jewish redemption (the ingathering of the exiles to Zion, the rebuilding of the Temple in Jerusalem, the reinstitution of the Davidic monarchy), the German Jewish Reformers preferred to eliminate these symbols from the liturgy, just as they preferred the language of the land in worship at the expense of Hebrew and otherwise sought to assure Jews and their neighbors that they were "Germans of the Jewish faith."

To support this redefinition it was argued that nationhood had been a necessary aspect of the emergence of ethical monotheism in biblical times and had been the preservative of the truths of Judaism in the Middle Ages, but in an enlightened age, when Judaism would come into its own as a progressive, universalistic faith, it did not need an ethnic integument. Jewish unity was not of a political but of a spiritual character that in no way contravened the loyalty of Jews to their secular fatherlands. Such ideas were echoed in almost all the trends of nineteenth-century Jewish thought in Europe and America that welcomed emancipation as a just and humane move to rectify the humiliation and segregation inflicted on Jewry for centuries and recognize the historical role and intrinsic worth of Judaism. [*For discussion of the Jewish Enlightenment movement, see* Haskalah.]

These conceptions of Jewish peoplehood were influenced not only by the new political situation of the Jews but also by the growth of Jewish historical scholarship that accompanied the emergence of *Wissenschaft des Judentums*. Having gained an appreciation of how Jewish religious institutions and ideas had undergone development in the course of time, some historians, and especially Jewish intellectuals in eastern Europe toward the end of the nineteenth century, turned to the Jewish collectivity as a social fact in its own right. Just as the earlier phase of modern Jewish thinking had been influenced by the struggle for emancipation, so this phase was influenced by the rise of modern anti-Semitism, the growth of nationalist movements among the peoples of eastern Europe, and the emergence of modern Zionism.

The term *anti-Semitism* was coined in the 1870s to indicate that dislike and fear of the Jews supposedly was not the result of religious reasons but a defense against the Jews as "Semitic" aliens acting as a corrupting, dominating force in the national organisms of Europe. Drawing on the medieval negative image of the Jews as Christ-killers and allies of Satan, the new anti-Semitic ideologies assumed a variety of forms, economic, political, and cultural; racist anti-Semitism insisted that the sinister characteristics of the Jews could not be improved through cultural or theological reform because these traits were psychobiological in origin and that Christianity itself was infected with the Jewish virus. [*See* Anti-Semitism.]

The period between 1881 and 1914 also saw the reappearance of physical attacks on the Jews (the pogroms in Russia), restrictive quotas in education, blood libels in which Jews were accused of killing Christian children for ritual purposes, and anti-Semitic congresses and political parties. These and other elements were to be synthesized by Adolf Hilter's National Socialist German Workers' Party (Nazis), which was founded in Germany and came to power in 1933, with fatal results for the six million European Jews caught in the Nazi Holocaust during World War II. [*See* Holocaust, The.]

Zionism gained urgency from the spread of modern anti-Semitism, but it had deep roots in the Jewish tradition as well. Zionism can be considered a recovery of Jewish peoplehood in a tangible sense rather than in the ethereal theological sense of much previous nineteenth-century Jewish thought. Zionist ideologues argued that Jewishness was not based on the mission of Israel to convey pure ethical monotheism to the world but a natural pride in one's heritage and a healthy desire to identify with one's people rather than assimilating to one or another of the chauvinistic nationalisms of Europe. [*See* Zionism.]

This reassertion of Jewish ethnic unity in a secular rather than religious sense produced a broad continuum of movements in eastern Europe by the turn of the century. It engendered a Jewish socialist movement that championed economic justice as well as emancipation for the Jewish working class and came to advocate secular Jewish cultural rights; an ideology of Diaspora Jewish nationalism that called for legally recognized rights of the Jews as a European cultural minority; a Jewish "territorialist" organization that looked for a land other than Palestine as the setting for a Jewish state; a new interest in Jewish social and economic history and in the folklore of east European Jews and of the Sefardic communities; and a literary renaissance in Hebrew and Yiddish that produced a rich body of novels, drama, poetry, and prose in those languages.

In 1897 the world Zionist movement was established by Theodor Herzl to create a modern Jewish commonwealth in the ancient land of Israel. Zionism embraced the ideas that a Jewish homeland would serve as a creative center for the revitalization of Jewish cultural values in modern form; that anti-Semitism was a symptom of the abnormality of Jewish life in the Diaspora that could only be cured with the self-emancipation of a Jewish state; that cooperative Jewish farming communities and the labor movement in the Land of Israel was the expression of a social revolution among the Jewish masses. In post–World War I Europe, and especially after the Nazis came to power in Germany, the need for a Jewish refuge—a home that the Jews could go to by right when threatened with political persecution, economic discrimination, or physical extermination—became a dominant concern.

The thrust of modern thinking around the theme of Jewish peoplehood of Israel in the twentieth century has been marked, therefore, by a recovery of the notion of *kelal Yisra'el* (the wholeness of the people of Israel). An influential Jewish ideology that emphasizes cultural pluralism, Judaism as a civilization, and the centrality of Zion together with the international character of the Jewish people is that of Mordecai Kaplan, who insisted on the continued relevance of Jewish religious values but denied on principle the notion of the Jews as a chosen people. [*See the biography of Kaplan.*] Most Jewish theologians have rejected the effort to normalize fully the Jewish tradition by stripping it of its supernatural uniqueness and mystery. Since World War II the power of ethnicity has been acknowledged as a positive force in Jewry in and of itself, as it has among other groups, while Jewish identity has assumed a far more voluntaristic character, which can be expressed in a wide range and intensity of ways. With the decline of anti-Semitism after the Holocaust has come noticeable improvement in Jewish-Christian understanding. And with the greater acceptance of Judaism and the social integration of Jews has come a considerable increase, at least in America, in the numbers of converts to Judaism.

As a result of the establishment of the state of Israel in 1948 a new series of issues has come to the fore concerning Jewish membership and meaning. Will Israel, as a secular Jewish state, be recognized as a legitimate member of the international society of nations? And in what does the Jewishness of the state of Israel consist? What is to be its relation to the religious dimension of the Jewish heritage? The question of personal Jewish status has been raised several times in Israel's courts of law in connection with the Law of Return, which grants all Diaspora Jews immediate Israeli citizenship upon their immigration there. In the case of Oswald Rufeisen, a born Jew who became a Catholic priest, the supreme court of Israel ruled that although Rufeisen was a Jew by *halakhah* his acceptance of Catholicism excluded him from the Jewish people and therefore he was not to be granted automatic Israeli citizenship. In the 1968 Shalit case, involving children of a non-Jewish mother who were raised as nonreligious Jews, it was not allowed that the children be registered, on purely secular grounds, as Jews on their identity cards.

The current definition of "who is a Jew" in Israel reflects a precarious mix of halakhic principles and Jewish folk attitudes. Yet another issue involves whether the state of Israel will continue to recognize as authentically Jewish those Jews converted in the Diaspora not according to Orthodox authorities or strict halakhic procedures, that is, by Reform and Conservative rabbis. This in turn directs attention to the legitimacy of religious pluralism within the Jewish people—a conspicuous fact in parts of the Diaspora but not in the state of Israel. In America the question of who is a Jew has been raised in connection with children of intermarriages where the non-Jewish mother does not convert to Judaism; the Reform and Reconstructionist movements, but not the Conservative and Orthodox, have argued for a recognition of patrilineal descent under certain circumstances. Underlying the question of who is a Jew is the issue of the authority of *halakhah* in contemporary Jewish life: how, to what extent, and by whom will Jewish religious law be adapted to modern times. Behind all these specifics, however, is the question of the transcendent meaning of Jewish peoplehood, which will surely remain a delicate and profound subject for Jewish theologians.

[*For further discussion of groups that were offshoots or branches of the Jewish people, see the independent entries* Essenes; Karaites; Marranos; Pharisees; Sadducees; Samaritans; *and* Zealots.]

BIBLIOGRAPHY

Three classic histories of the Jewish people are Heinrich Graetz's *Geschichte der Juden von den ältesten Zeiten bis auf die Gegenwart,* 11 vols. (Leipzig, 1853–1876), translated by Bella Löwy and others as *History of the Jews,* 6 vols. (Philadelphia, 1891–1898); Simon Dubnow's *Vsemirnaia istoriia evreiskogo naroda* (1924–1939), 10 vols., translated by Moshe Spiegal as *History of the Jews,* 5 vols. (South Brunswick, N.J., 1967–1973); and Salo W. Baron's *A Social and Religious History of the Jews,* 2d ed., 18 vols. to date (New York, 1952–). An overview of the historiography of the origins of the people up to and including the settlement in Canaan is George W. Ramsey's *The Quest for the Historical Israel* (Atlanta, 1981).

The uniqueness of Israelite monotheism is defended by Yehezkel Kaufmann in his *The Religion of Israel: From Its Beginnings to the Babylonian Exile,* translated and abridged by Moshe Greenberg (Chicago, 1960). An earlier work by Kaufmann explains the primary role of religion in Jewish survival until modern times: *Golah ve-nekbar,* 2d ed., 2 vols. (Tel Aviv, 1954). On Jewish and Christian self-definition in antiquity, see Lawrence H. Schiffman's *Who Was a Jew?: Rabbinic and Halakhic Perspectives on the Jewish-Christian Schism* (Hoboken, N.J., 1985). On biblical, Jewish, and Christian uses of the name *Israel,* also see Samuel Sandmel's *The Several Israels* (New York, 1971). Early halakhic aspects are treated by Shaye J. D. Cohen in "The Origins of the Matrilineal Principle in Rabbinic Law," *Association for Jewish Studies Review* 10 (Spring 1985): 19–53. The theological views of classic rabbinic Judaism are thoroughly treated in E. E. Urbach's *The Sages: Their Concepts and Beliefs,* 2d enl. ed., 2 vols. translated by Israel Abrahams (Jerusalem, 1979), in which see especially chapter 16.

Medieval Jewish views of Jewish identity in a Christian environment are discussed in Jacob Katz's *Exclusiveness and Tolerance: Studies in Jewish-Gentile Relations in Medieval and Modern Times* (Oxford, 1961). A history of Jewish proselytism is found in Joseph R. Rosenbloom's *Conversion to Judaism: From the Biblical Period to the Present* (Cincinnati, 1978). The branches of the Jewish people around the world are surveyed in Raphael Patai's *Tents of Jacob: The Diaspora; Yesterday and Today* (Englewood Cliffs, N.J., 1971). Among the books on Jewish modernization are Jacob Katz's *Out of the Ghetto: The Social Background of Jewish Emancipation, 1770–1870* (Cambridge, Mass., 1973), Calvin Goldscheider and Alan S. Zuckerman's *The Transformation of the Jews* (Chicago, 1984), and Simon N. Herman's *Jewish Identity: A Social Psychological Perspective* (Beverly Hills, 1977).

Secular approaches to Jewish nationhood are defended in the following ideological works, among many: Simon Dubnow's *Nationalism and History: Essays on Old and New Judaism,* edited by Koppel S. Pinson (Philadelphia, 1958), and Ben Halpern's *The American Jew: A Zionist Analysis* (New York, 1956). A gamut of Zionist views, secular and religious, can be found in *The Zionist Idea: An Historical Analysis and Reader,* edited by Arthur Hertzberg (Philadelphia, 1959). Most books that treat the main aspects of Jewish faith discuss the religious significance of Jewish peoplehood, but among the few important Jewish works that have taken it as their central theme are Mordecai Kaplan's *Judaism as a Civilization: Toward a Reconstruction of Jewish-American Life* (New York, 1934), and Michael Wyschogrod's *The Body of Faith: Judaism as Corporeal Election* (New York, 1983). A scholarly account of peoplehood in twentieth-century American Jewish religious thought is Arnold M. Eisen's *The Chosen People in America: A Study in Jewish Religious Ideology* (Bloomington, Ind., 1983). For a collection of statements on "who is a Jew," as this question has come to the fore since the establishment of the state of Israel, see *Jewish Identity: Modern Response and Opinions,* edited by Baruch Litvin (New York, 1956). A philosophically sensitive, coherent picture of the nature of Judaism is Leon Roth's *Judaism: A Portrait* (New York, 1960). A succinct treatment of Judaism in the context of the dilemmas of modernizing religions is R. J. Zwi Werblowsky's "Sacral Particularity: The Jewish Case," in his *Beyond Tradition and Modernity: Changing Religions in a Changing World* (London, 1976).

9

JUDAISM IN THE MIDDLE EAST AND NORTH AFRICA TO 1492

MARK R. COHEN

Judaism is indigenous to the Middle East. There in antiquity the Israelite people formed its unique identity. There the Bible came into being, and there by late antiquity Israelite religion was transformed into normative rabbinic Judaism. The basic texts of rabbinic Judaism—the halakhic *midrashim,* the Mishnah (compiled c. 200 CE), the two Talmuds, that of Palestine and that of Babylonia (compiled in the fifth and sixth centuries), and the first compilations of rabbinic lore *(aggadah)*—were all written in the Middle East. In the formative period of rabbinic Judaism, sectarian groups such as the religious communities of Qumran (the Dead Sea sects) manifested other varieties of Judaism. An esoteric mystical trend within rabbinic Judaism itself also grew in the Middle East of late antiquity. In Egypt in the first century CE, the Greek writings of Philo Judaeus of Alexandria gave voice to a hellenized philosophical trend within Judaism.

Jews carried their religion to North Africa in late antiquity, where some form of Judaism penetrated the native Berber population, and to Arabia, where, in the seventh century, Judaism had some influence on the formation of the new religion of Islam. After the Middle East and North Africa were brought under the dominion of Islam, following the Arab conquests, and the centuries-old separation of Jewry into two branches, one living under Sasanid-Zoroastrian rule, and the other living under a Roman-Christian regime, was brought to an end, Judaism underwent further change. Under Islam, rabbinic Judaism, faced with the unification of North African and Middle Eastern Jewry under one empire, became consolidated. In addition, as Jews adopted Arabic in place of Aramaic as both their written and spoken language, the intellectual culture of their host society became accessible to all layers of Jewish society for the first time in history. Responding to the challenge of dynamic Islamic civilization, perceived with unmediated intensity by Arabic-speaking Jewry, Judaism also experienced new developments in sectarianism, philosophy, and mysticism. These characteristic developments in Judaism between the Muslim conquests and the end of the fifteenth century will form the focus of this article.

THE BABYLONIAN CENTER

In the middle of the eighth century the capital of the Muslim caliphate was moved from Syria (where it had been located since 661 CE) to Baghdad. Under the Abbasid dynasty, Iraq became the center from which power and scholarly creativity radiated to the rest of the Islamic world. In this setting, the institutions of Babylonian Judaism were able to consolidate their own authority and religious leadership over the Jews living within the orbit of Islam. Successive waves of Jewish (as well as Muslim) migration from the eastern Islamic lands, long subject to the religious guidance of the Babylonian Talmud, to the Mediterranean and other western provinces of the caliphate, contributed substantially to this process.

The main instrument of this consolidation was the *yeshivah*. Though usually translated "academy," the *yeshivah* then was actually more than a center of learning. It was, as well, a seat of supreme judicial authority and a source of religious legislation. In pre-Islamic times there were already three *yeshivot,* one in Palestine, headed by the patriarch (the *nasi'*), and two in Babylonia, named Sura and Pumbedita. The Palestinian (or Jerusalem) and Babylonian Talmuds were redacted, respectively, in the Palestinian and Babylonian *yeshivot.* [*See* Yeshivah.]

After the middle of the eighth century the Babylonian *yeshivot* began to outshine their counterparts in Palestine. The heads of the *yeshivot* (first of Sura, later of Pumbedita, too) acquired a lofty title, "gaon" (short for *ro'sh yeshivat ge'on Ya'aqov,* "head of the *yeshivah* of the pride of Jacob," see *Psalms* 47:5). In an effort to assert the authority of Babylonian Judaism throughout the caliphate, the geonim developed many types of halakhic (legal) literature. They were undoubtedly influenced by the intense efforts to consolidate Muslim legal traditions that were going on at the same time in Iraq. However, owing to the centrality of *halakhah* in Jewish life the consolidation of legal authority in the hands of the Babylonian geonim also served the political purpose of endowing the Babylonian gaonate with administrative hegemony over Islamic Jewry.

One of the most important literary vehicles used to this end was the system of questions and answers *(responsa).* Like its analogue in Roman and in Islamic law, a *responsum* (Heb., *teshuvah*) is an answer to a legal question. It can be issued only by a scholar of recognized authority. Something like the *responsa* seems to have existed in pre-Islamic Palestine, but the Babylonian geonim developed the legal custom into a major enterprise for the extension of their spiritual and political domination over the communities of the Islamic empire. Queries dispatched to Babylonia were accompanied by donations, which constituted one of the chief means of support for the *yeshivot* there.

A large number of *responsa* are extant from the mid-eighth century onward. They were sent to places as far away as North Africa and Spain and were transmitted mainly by Jewish merchants. In communities along the trade routes through which they passed, copies of the geonic rulings were often made. In Old Cairo, for instance, a major commercial crossroads of the Islamic Middle Ages, many such *responsa* were discovered in the famous Cairo Genizah, where they had lain undisturbed for centuries owing to the Jewish custom of burying, rather than physically destroying, pages of sacred writings. Once a *responsum* reached the community that had sent the question, it was read aloud in the synagogue, a procedure that strengthened local reverence for the spiritual as well as the political authority of the geonim.

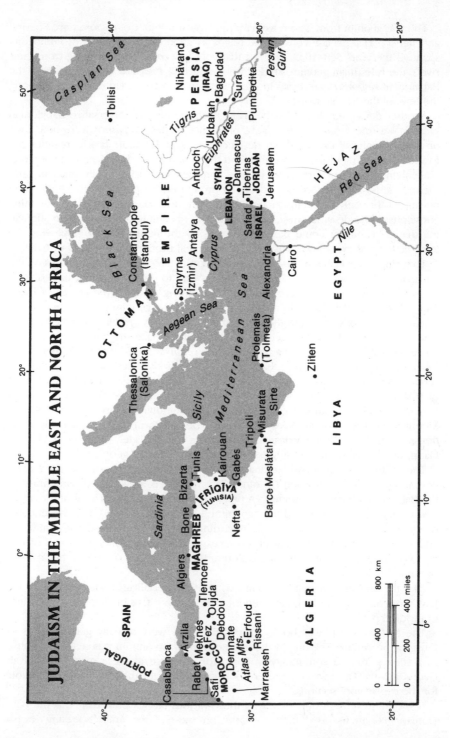

JUDAISM IN THE MIDDLE EAST AND NORTH AFRICA

The two geonim from whom we have the largest number of *responsa* are Sherira' and his son H'ai, whose consecutive reigns as gaon of the *yeshivah* of Pumbedita spanned the years 968–1038. The fact that very few *responsa* emanating from their rivals, the Palestinian geonim, are known is a further measure of the success of the Babylonian *responsa* enterprise in creating a strong Babylonian orientation among the Jews of the Islamic world.

Another device employed by the Babylonian geonim to universalize Babylonian Judaism was the *taqqanah* (legislative ordinance). These *taqqanot* were new laws, or modifications of existing laws, designed to adapt Talmudic law to realities not foreseen by the rabbis of the Mishnah and the *gemara'*. For instance, with the large-scale abandonment of agriculture by Jews and their increasing involvement in commerce, the issue of collection of debts by proxy became problematic. The Talmud permitted this only in conjunction with transfer of land. The Babylonian geonim, conscious of the de-agrarianization of Jewish life, promulgated a *taqqanah* stipulating that debt transfer could be effected even by the nonlanded by employing the legal fiction that every Jew owns four cubits of real property in the Land of Israel.

To further their ecumenical authority the geonim also wrote commentaries on the Mishnah and Talmud. These originated as answers to questions about unclear passages in the Talmud that were posed by Jews living far from the center of living Talmud study in Babylonia. In their commentaries, the geonim gave pride of place to halakhic sections, owing to the juridical priorities of the *yeshivot* and to the practical needs of the Jews. The geonim also sought to make the Babylonian Talmud more accessible to those lacking training at the *yeshivah* itself. To this end they wrote introductions to that literature, explaining the methods, rules, and terminology of rabbinic jurisprudence. One type of introduction consisted of a chronological survey of Mishnaic and Talmudic teachers. This established their historical relationship and linked the rabbinic authority of the geonim with the divine source of Jewish law at Mount Sinai. The most famous work of this type, which in form was actually a *responsum* sent to a North African questioner, is the "Epistle" *(Iggeret)* of Sherira' Gaon, which forms our best single source for the history of geonic rule.

The geonim also compiled the first post-Mishnaic codes of Jewish law. The *Halakhot pesuqot* of Yehud'ai Gaon (in office 757–761 CE) is an abridged paraphrase of the Babylonian Talmud in Aramaic. A practical book, it omits nearly all of the *aggadah* (non-legal literature) and the agricultural and sacrificial laws and concentrates on such practical subjects as precepts regarding festivals, commercial law, family law, and synagogue and other ritual observances. A more comprehensive work of this type was the *Halakhot gedolot* of Shim'on of Basra (c. 825), a student at the *yeshivah* of Sura.

Like the Muslim legists, the geonim composed specialized codes, extracting for handy reference Talmudic laws of inheritance, of deposit, of buying and selling, and of juridical procedure.

The first written prayer books in Jewish history were actually geonic codes of liturgical procedure. The one by the ninth century gaon Amram was sent in response to a request from a community in Spain for guidance in these matters. Sa'adyah Gaon (882–942) also wrote a prayer book, one which, for the first time, used Arabic for the explanatory sections.

It was, however, not only by way of these various literary endeavors that the Babylonian geonim imposed their authority on most of the Arabic-speaking Jewish world and universalized their form of Judaism; they further consolidated their spiritual and political sovereignty by training and licensing judges and by teaching Talmud to Jews who came from afar to hear lectures at the *yeshivah's* semiannual conclaves *(kallot)*. By the beginning of the eleventh century the process had been successfully completed. The Palestinian gaon Shelomoh ben Yehudah (in office 1026–1051) had to send his own son to the Baghdad *yeshivah* to complete his Talmudic education. Shelomoh's successor as gaon in Jerusalem, Daniyye'l ben 'Azaryah, was a Babylonian scholar and a member of the family of the Babylonian exarchs, the descendants of the Davidic royal house who were living in Babylonian exile and were recognized by the caliph, as they had been by the pre-Islamic rulers of Persia, as "heads of the Diaspora." Ben 'Azaryah, who died in 1062, brought Babylonian learning for a brief time to the *yeshivah* of Jerusalem.

NEW CENTERS IN NORTH AFRICA AND EGYPT

In the course of time, the very universalization of Babylonian Judaism and the dispersal of Babylonian-trained judges and scholars throughout the Diaspora in Islamic lands created a foundation upon which new independent centers of religious learning and authority could be built. This happened in North Africa in the tenth and eleventh centuries and in Egypt somewhat later.

Kairouan. In the ninth and tenth centuries, the Jews of Kairouan, the capital of Muslim Ifrīqiyā (modern Tunisia), were firmly within the camp of the Babylonian geonim. Indeed, most of the Jewish settlers in Kairouan had originated in Iraq and Iran, the heartland of geonic authority. But in these two centuries, Muslim Kairouan achieved considerable prosperity and became a major center of Islamic legal studies. Against this background, the local Jewish community began to create its own center of Talmudic scholarship. The first mention of a formal house of study in Kairouan— the term used was *midrash* rather than *yeshivah*—occurs at the end of the century. Led by Ya'aqov bar Nissim ibn Shahin, who belonged to a family whose origins lay in the East (probably Iran) and who was a loyal adherent of Babylonian Judaism, this *midrash* was not yet a rival institution to the Babylonian *yeshivot*. Detachment from Babylonian religious sovereignty became pronounced a generation later, following the arrival in Kairouan of a scholar, believed to have hailed from Italy, named Hushi'el. Italian Jewry had been influenced more by Palestinian than by Babylonian traditions, so when Hushi'el opened a second *midrash* in Kairouan, some Palestinian traditions were taught alongside Babylonian Talmudic scholarship.

In the first half of the eleventh century two of Hushi'el's students placed native North African religious scholarship on a firm literary footing: his son, Hanan'el ben Hushi'el, and Nissim, the son of Ya'aqov bar Nissim (who had died in 1006/7). Hanan'el wrote *responsa,* commentaries on the Torah, on *Ezekiel,* on the dietary laws, and, most importantly, a comprehensive commentary on the Babylonian Talmud. In innovative fashion, this last-mentioned work employed material from the Palestinian Talmud to explain passages in the text, though, like the commentaries of the Babylonian geonim, its primary focus was juridical.

Nissim (d. 1062) maintained his father's loyalty to the Babylonian geonim. However, like his contemporary Hanan'el, he too wrote a fresh commentary on the Talmud utilizing material from the Palestinian text. Duplicating Babylonian geonic efforts to disseminate knowledge of the Talmud, Nissim composed in Arabic his own

"Introduction" entitled *The Book of the Key to the Locks of the Talmud*. Other religious writing of his include a chain of transmission of rabbinic tradition reminiscent of Sherira' Gaon's "Epistle," *responsa* (of which many are extant), and a "Secret Scroll" *(Megillat setarim)*, written in Arabic, that consisted of a potpourri of miscellaneous ritual laws. None of Nissim's rabbinic works has been preserved in its entirety and its original form; they are known of only from fragments or through quotations in the works of others.

Hushi'el's disciples completed the process of fashioning an independent center of religious creativity in North Africa. Their period of activity coincided with the decline of the Babylonian gaonate following the death of H'ai Gaon in 1038. However, the budding new center of rabbinic Judaism in North Africa was cut off abruptly in 1057 when Kairouan was destroyed by bedouin tribes sent by the Fatimid ruler of Egypt to punish his disloyal vassals, the Zirids, in that city.

Fez. Another creative center of Judaism in North Africa developed in Fez (present-day Morocco). *Responsa* addressed to Fez by the geonim of Sura and Pumbedita testify to the presence of learned scholars in that distant North African city. The most famous rabbinic master from Fez, Yitshaq ben Ya'aqov Alfasi (c. 1013–1103), wrote an abridged version of the Talmud that later became part of the apparatus of the standard printed Talmud text. He also wrote many *responsa*.

Egypt. In Egypt a local school of advanced religious study (a *midrash*) was established at the end of the tenth century by Shemaryah ben Elhanan, a scholar educated at one of the Babylonian *yeshivot*. Egyptian Jewry at that time was subject to the political authority of the gaon of the Palestinian *yeshivah*, who was recognized by the Fatimid caliph in Cairo as head of the Jews in his empire (Egypt and Palestine). When Shemaryah's son and successor Elhanan began to expand the activities of the Egyptian *midrash* by soliciting donations even from Palestine and by assuming some of the religious and political prerogatives of the Palestinian gaon, he was excommunicated by the Jerusalem *yeshivah*. This put a temporary halt to the growth of native Egyptian religious scholarship until, in the latter part of the eleventh century, several distinguished scholars settled in Egypt.

As in the case of Nissim ben Ya'aqov of Kairouan, the writings of these scholars are known from fragments, from quotations in later works, and medieval book lists. One notable author was Yehudah ha-Kohen ben Yosef, who wrote commentaries on the Bible and on portions of the Talmud, a code of regulations concerning ritual slaughtering, liturgical poems, and a commentary on the mystical *Sefer yetsirah* (Book of Creation). Another was a scholar from Spain named Yitshaq ben Shemu'el, who wrote an Arabic commentary on some if not all of the Former Prophets, a commentary on at least one Talmudic tractate, *responsa,* and liturgical poems. Though neither of these scholars opened an academy of learning, they gave Egyptian Jewry a renewed sense of independence from the traditional sources of religious leadership in Babylonia and from the political dominion of the *yeshivah* in Palestine.

Related to the activity of these respected rabbinic scholars in Egypt toward the end of the eleventh century was the emergence there of a new Jewish institution of central leadership. This was the office of "head of the Jews" (Arab., *ra'īs al-yahūd),* more commonly known in Hebrew as the office of the *nagid*. The scholarly family of court physicians headed by the brothers Yehudah and Mevorakh ben Sa'adyah was the first to hold this position of dignity. The office of head of the Jews, inheriting the sovereignty formerly reserved for the Palestinian gaon, was invested with supreme religious as well as political authority over the Jews in the Fatimid empire.

In the third decade of the twelfth century the Palestinian *yeshivah,* which had been located outside the borders of Palestine since the Seljuk conquest of Jerusalem around 1071, transferred its own headquarters to the capital of Egypt. With this move the office of head of the Jews temporarily passed into the hands of the newly arrived Palestinian gaon, Matsliaḥ ha-Kohen ben Shelomoh. How much teaching went on in the relocated Palestinian yeshivah we do not know. However, the arrival of Moses Maimonides (Mosheh ben Maimon) in Egypt around 1165 established Egypt as a respectable center of Jewish religious scholarship. Maimonides attracted a circle of students and substituted the study of his own code of Jewish law, the *Mishneh Torah,* for the study of the Babylonian Talmud in the curriculum of Jewish higher education. The Babylonian gaonate voiced opposition to Maimonides, who was seen as a threat to its efforts to reassert its former supremacy over world Jewry. Nevertheless, the Maimonidean tradition of learning in Egypt, modified by a distinctive mystical bent, was continued by his son Avraham and by a succession of Maimonidean descendants until the beginning of the fifteenth century.

Yemen. A center of Jewish learning much influenced by Moses Maimonides was to be found in Yemen. Already in late antiquity there was a small Jewish presence in South Arabia, as we know from the evidence of Hebrew inscriptions and from stories about the conversion to Judaism of rulers of the South Arabian kingdom of Ḥimyar (the last of these Jewish kings of Ḥimyar, who was also the last Ḥimyarī ruler, died in 525 CE). In the Islamic period the Jewish settlement was considerably strengthened by the migration of Jews from Babylonia and Persia. Naturally, from the outset the Yemenite community maintained loyalty to the Babylonian geonim and the Babylonian exilarch, supported the Babylonian *yeshivah* financially, and adhered to the Babylonian interpretation of rabbinic Judaism.

In the eleventh and twelfth centuries, however, Yemen and Yemenite Jews became closely connected with Egypt as a result of general political and economic developments. Thus, they identified in the twelfth century with the *yeshivah* of Matsliaḥ ha-Kohen in Cairo and especially with Maimonides after his arrival in Egypt. In the later Middle Ages a considerable indigenous religious literature developed among the Yemenite Jews, much of it consisting in commentaries on various works of Maimonides. In Yemen, moreover, Maimonides' *Mishneh Torah* became the principal code of Jewish practice. Among Yemenite works from the later Middle Ages that cite passages from Maimonides' oeuvre is the voluminous anthology of homiletic and legal *midrashim* on the five books of the Torah compiled in the thirteenth century by David ben ʿAmram of the Yemenite port city of Aden, entitled *Midrash ha-gadol.*

KARAISM

Not long after the Muslim conquest, the most important religious schism in medieval Judaism, known as Karaism, occurred in the Middle East. The Karaites rejected the jurisdiction of the Talmud and of rabbinic Judaism in general, claiming exclusive reliance on the Bible. Some scholars believe that Karaism actualized a latent anti-Talmudism that had existed beneath the surface since the time of the Sadducees, who centuries earlier had denied the validity of the oral Law. Others identify in

Karaism affinities with the religion of the Dead Sea sects, notably the asceticism shared by these two religious movements.

It is difficult to prove the influence of one sect on another separated from it in time by so many centuries. What is certain, however, in terms of immediate causes is that Karaism arose in opposition to the extension of the authority of rabbinic Judaism by the Babylonian geonim in the early Islamic period and out of resentment towards the power wielded by the Jewish aristocracy of Iraq through the Davidic exilarchate.

The Iranian Plateau, fertile ground for sectarian rebellion in early Islam, spawned several antirabbinic Jewish revolts prior to the crystallization of a cohesive Karaite movement. One example was the sect of Abū 'Īsā al-Isfahānī, whose period of activity is variously given as 685–705, during the reign of the Umayyad caliph 'Abd al-Malik ibn Manṣūr, or at the time of the transition from Umayyad to Abbasid rule, between 744 and 775. His ascetic, anti-Talmudic program included the prohibition of divorce and a change in the daily liturgical cycle from three to seven prayers. Abū 'Īsā was also driven by his belief in the imminent coming of the Messiah to take up arms against the Muslim government.

Abū 'Īsā's sect was but one of many groups whose antirabbinic halakhic practices were collected together in the eighth century by 'Anan ben David, an important link in the chain leading to the consolidation of Karaism in the ninth and tenth centuries. 'Anan may have hailed from the Iranian Plateau, but he operated in the center of geonic-exilarchal territory in Babylonia. He was, in fact, said to have been a member of the exilarchal family. A biased Rabbinite account of his sectarian rebellion ascribes his motives to personal disappointment after being passed over for appointment to the office of exilarch.

'Anan's principal achievement was to assemble scattered bits of sectarian *halakhah* into a code called *Sefer ha-mitsvot* (Book of Commandments). In this book, he employed Talmudic methodology for his own end: his biblical exegesis served to lend credibility and respectability to the deviant practices that he codified. This use of rabbinic methods and language to establish the legitimacy of nonrabbinic Judaism constituted a serious challenge to the authority of the geonim.

'Anan seems to have envisaged the creation of separatist communities of nonrabbinic Jews living in various locales within the Diaspora. One scholar has even proposed that he wished to gain government recognition for a second legitimate school of law within Judaism, coexisting with the school of the Babylonian geonim much like the different *madhhabs* (schools of jurisprudence) in Islam.

Later Karaites attributed to 'Anan the formulation of a principle, expressed as an apothegm: "Search thoroughly in the Torah and do not rely upon my opinion." This legitimated, in theory at least, the exclusive reliance on the Bible that distinguished Karaism from rabbinism and sounded the call for individualistic exegesis in place of slavish adherence to rabbinic tradition. It also justified a proliferation of non-'Ananite sects in the ninth and tenth centuries, such as the sect of Ismā'īl al-'Ukbarī (from 'Ukbara, near Baghdad), the sect of Mishawayh al-'Ukbarī, the sect of Abū 'Imrān al-Tiflisī (from present-day Tbilisi, U.S.S.R.), and the sect of Malik al-Ramlī (from Ramleh, Palestine). Much of our information about these groups comes from the law code, *Kitāb al-anwār wa-al-marāqib* (Book of Lights and Watchtowers), by the tenth-century Karaite thinker Ya'qūb al-Qirqisānī, which contains an introduction on the history of sects in Judaism. Not surprisingly, for Qirqisānī it is the Rabbinites, begin-

ning with the Pharisees, rather than the Karaites, who were the real religious deviants. 'Anan ben David's role as reformer was to rediscover the long-suppressed
true path.

The first to employ the term *Karaites* (*Benei Miqra'*, "children of scripture") was
the ninth-century Binyamin al-Nahāwandī (of Nihāvand, Iran). He was known for his
tolerance of observance of rabbinic laws, especially where biblical legislation failed
to answer practical questions of everyday life. This liberalism with respect to Talmudic law was matched by an insistence on the right of every individual to interpret
scripture as he saw fit. Troubled by the rationalist critique of biblical anthropomorphisms, Binyamin taught that the world was called into being by an angel created by God, and that all anthropomorphic expressions in the Bible were to be
ascribed to that angel. A judge by profession, Binyamin wrote a *Sefer mitsvot* (Book
of Commandments) and a *Sefer dinim* (Book of Laws). He also wrote biblical commentaries.

Daniyye'l al-Qūmisī, another Karaite thinker of the end of the ninth century, was
a messianist who settled in Jerusalem in order to mourn for Zion (the group he
headed was called Avelei-Tsiyyon, "Mourners for Zion") and to pray for redemption.
In his approach to the Bible he rejected the liberal individualism of Binyamin al-
Nahāwandī and the latter's theology of the creator angel. However, in his own exegesis, he was, according to some sources, a rationalist.

By the tenth century Karaism was sufficiently consolidated to pose an active threat
to the Babylonian geonim. Sa'adyah Gaon took up the cudgels of defense on their
behalf, writing a refutation of 'Anan *(Kitāb al-radd 'alā 'Anan)* and opposing Karaite
views in others of his writings. Sa'adyah's hostility inspired a Karaite counterattack.
Indeed, he was the polemical object of much of the rich Karaite literature of the
"golden age" of the tenth and eleventh centuries.

Several important figures of this Karaite golden age bear mention here. Ya'qūb al-
Qiriqisānī (tenth century) composed, in addition to the code of law, the *Book of
Lights and Watchtowers,* commentaries on several books of the Bible, a refutation of
Muhammad's claim to prophecy, and a treatise on God's unity. Salmon ben Yeroham
(tenth century) wrote a poetical tract against the Rabbinites, *The Book of the Wars
of the Lord,* that bristles with polemic against Sa'adyah, and among other works,
biblical commentaries on *Psalms* and the *Song of Songs.* Yefet ben 'Eli wrote commentaries in Arabic on the entire Hebrew Bible, accompanied by translations of
Hebrew text into Arabic. Sahl ben Masliah composed a *Book of Commandments,*
only partly extant, and a letter to a Rabbinite disputant in Egypt extolling Karaism at
the expense of rabbinism. Yūsuf alBasīr (Yosef ha-Ro'eh, from Basra) wrote a *Book
of Commandments* and important *responsa,* and initiated a liberalization of Karaite
marriage laws which, on the basis of literal interpretation of the Bible, had multi-
plied the number of incestuous (and therefore forbidden) marriage combinations,
thus threatening the biological continuity of the sect. Like al-Basīr, Yeshu'ah ben
Yehudah composed a treatise refuting the Karaite laws of incestuous marriage. He
also penned commentaries on books of the Bible. [*For further discussion, see* Karaites.]

REVIVAL OF JEWISH RELIGIOUS PHILOSOPHY

Several factors converged to bring about a revival of Jewish religious philosophy,
dormant since Philo, among the Jews of the Muslim world, Rabbinites and Karaites

alike. Most important were the new availability of Hellenistic philosophy in Arabic translation; Jewish awareness of the application of rationalist inquiry to theological questions in Islam; the critique of biblical anthropomorphism; the attack on the Bible by Jewish skeptics like Ḥiwi al-Balkhī; and the desire to prove that Judaism embraced the same universalistic truths as Islam. The lion's share of Jewish religious philosophy was written in Spain. However, the founder of Judeo-Arabic philosophy, Saʿadyah Gaon, and the most important philosopher of them all, Maimonides, wrote in the Middle East.

The earliest venture by Arabic-speaking Jews into rationalism followed the lead of the Muslim science of *kalām*. *Kalām* means "speech" and refers specifically to discussion of theological problems. The most rationalistic trend in the *kalām* was that of the Muʿtazilah, which originated in Iraq in the cities of Basra and Baghdad, and it was from this doctrine that Saʿadyah, who lived in Baghdad, drew the inspiration for his pioneering work of Jewish religious philosophy, *Kitāb al-amanāt wa-al-iʿtiqādāt* (The Book of Beliefs and Convictions). Like the Muʿtazilah, he began his treatise with an epistemological discourse establishing the indispensability of reason as a source of religious knowledge. To this he added the category of reliable transmitted knowledge—doubtless in response to skeptics and Karaites who discredited the reliability of biblical stories and laws. The idea that reason and revelation lead to the same religious truths remained a cornerstone of all medieval Jewish religious philosophy after Saʿadyah. Like the Muʿtazilah, Saʿadyah placed the discussion of the creation of the world out of nothing *(creatio ex nihilo)* at the head of his treatise, since from the premise of creation flowed the belief in the existence of God and hence all other religious convictions.

The Muʿtazilah struggled with two major challenges to rationalism: scriptural anthropomorphisms that seemingly denied God's unity, and the question of the existence of evil in this world that appeared to contradict God's justice. [*See* Muʿtazilah.] Like the Muslim Muʿtazilah, Saʿadyah devoted separate chapters to these two subjects in his philosophical treatise. Divine unity was defended by invoking the principle that the Torah uses metaphor to describe God in terms understandable to human minds. The problem of divine justice was resolved with the Muʿtazilī solution of claiming freedom of the human will. Saʿadyah took other leads from the Muʿtazilah, for instance, in drawing a distinction between laws knowable through reason and laws knowable only through revelation, as well as in his treatment of retribution. In addition, he addressed Jewish eschatology in his chapters on resurrection and redemption.

The Muslim *kalām* influenced other Jewish writers in the Middle East. Before the time of Saʿadyah, David ben Marwān al-Muqammiṣ (ninth century) combined Muʿtazilī views with Greek philosophical notions. So did the Babylonian gaon Shemuʾel ben Ḥofni (d. 1013) in his commentary on the Bible. Nissim ben Yaʿaqov of Kairouan showed familiarity with Muʿtazilī teaching in his commentary on the Talmud. Finally, the Karaites, liberated from the commitment to tradition as a valid source of religious knowledge, adopted Muʿtazilī rationalism with even less reserve than its Rabbinite exponents. Prominent among the Karaite rationalists were the above-mentioned Yaʿqūb al-Qirqisānī, Yūsuf al-Baṣīr (eleventh century), and Yeshuʿah ben Yehudah (mid-eleventh century).

These Karaites went beyond the principle of the equivalence of reason and revelation and gave primacy to the former. It was, in fact, among the Karaites of Byzantium alone that Mu'tazilī *kalām* continued to have influence on Judaism after the eleventh century. In contrast, among the Rabbinites, Neoplatonism and especially Aristotelianism took over the role that Mu'tazilī thought had played during the pioneering phase of Jewish religious philosophy in the Islamic world.

Neoplatonism and Aristotelianism flourished mainly among the Jews of Spain. However, the first Jewish Neoplatonist, Yitshaq Yisra'eli (c. 850–950), was born in Egypt and composed philosophical works in Arabic while serving as court physician to the Muslim governor in Kairouan. Of his works the *Book of Definition* and the *Book on the Elements* (extant only in Hebrew and Latin translations) and a commentary on *Sefer yetsirah* (Book of Creation), revised by his students, show how he tried to incorporate the Neoplatonic doctrine of emanation into Judaism. Though he did not abandon the biblical premise of divinely willed creation out of nothing for a pure Neoplatonic cosmogony, he adopted the Neoplatonic conception of progressive emanation of spiritual substances in the supraterrestrial world. As with the Islamic Neoplatonists, some aspects of Yisra'eli's philosophy of religion show the influence of Aristotelian ideas. For instance, his concept of reward for ethical conduct is based on the ascent of the human soul toward its final reunification with the upper soul. The phenomenon of prophecy, a problem for Muslim religious philosophers, similarly occupied Yitshaq Yisra'eli; his theory employs the naturalistic explanation offered by the Islamic Aristotelians but leaves a place for divine will in connection with the form of the vision accorded prophets.

The most important full-fledged Jewish Aristotelian was Maimonides. Born in Spain, where in the twelfth century Aristotelianism replaced Neoplatonism as the preferred philosophy, Maimonides did most of his writing, including his philosophic magnum opus, the *Guide of the Perplexed,* in Egypt, where he lived out most of his life as a refugee from Almohade persecution in Spain and North Africa. Maimonides sought to achieve a workable synthesis between Judaism and Aristotelianism without glossing over the uncontestably incompatible elements in each of those systems. Writing for the initiated few in the *Guide,* he took up troublesome theological questions. He argued for the existence of God, which he demonstrated, not in the by-then-unsatisfactory manner of the old *kalām,* but by exploiting scientifically and logically more credible Aristotelian philosophical concepts. He upheld the unity of God, not by accepting the identity of God's attributes with his essence, as *kalām* would have it, but by combining the metaphoric interpretation of scriptural anthropomorphisms with the doctrine of negative attributes, which leaves the fact of God's existence as the sole bit of positive knowledge of divinity available to believers. He even addressed the problem of the creation of the world, which forced him to suspend Aristotle's doctrine of the eternity of the world in favor of the biblical account of the miraculous creation by the will of God.

Maimonides also attempted to bring an Aristotelian conception of Judaism within the reach of the philosophically uninitiated. This he did with a philosophical introduction to, and other occasional rationalistic comments in, his *Mishneh Torah* (Code of Jewish Law); with an Aristotelian ethical introduction to the Mishnah tractate *Avot;* and by formulating a philosophic creed for Jews in his commentary on the Mishnah.

PIETISM AND JEWISH SUFISM

A new religious development in Judaism began in the Middle East in the twelfth and thirteenth centuries. Individual Jews began to be attracted to the pious asceticism of the Muslim Sūfīs. In his introduction to the Mishnah tractate *Avot,* called "The Eight Chapters," Maimonides chastises such people for engaging in extreme self-abnegation, thereby straying from the more moderate path advocated by Judaism.

In the thirteenth century in Egypt, some representatives of the Jewish upper classes (physicians, government secretaries, judges, and scholars) joined together in pietistic brotherhoods akin to the Sūfī orders that were then flourishing in Egypt under the patronage of the Ayyubid dynasty of Muslim rulers founded by Salaḥ al-Dīn (Saladin). These Jews called themselves *ḥasidim,* using the regular Talmudic word for the pious. They fasted frequently, practiced nightly prayer vigils, and recited additional prayers accompanied by bowings and prostrations more typical of Islam than of Judaism. Rather than exhibiting their pietism in public they maintained a private place of worship where they followed their special path. Rather than wearing wool outer clothing like the Muslim Sūfīs, they designated as the symbol of their asceticism the turban that they all wore (Arab., *baqyār* or *buqyār*). [*For comparison see* Sufism.]

The most illustrious member of this circle of *ḥasidim* was the *nagid* (head of the Jewish community) Avraham, the son of Moses Maimonides. He wrote a long code of Jewish law entitled *Kifāyat al-'ābidīn* (The Complete Guide for the Servants of God), which, in its fourth and final book, contains a program of mystical piety for the Jewish elite based on the ethical tenets of Sufism.

The *ḥasidim* in Avraham Maimonides' brotherhood made attempts to influence the general Jewish public to adopt some aspects of their pietism. Earlier, Moses Maimonides himself had introduced reforms in the Egyptian synagogue service aimed at imitating the more decorous environment of the mosque. Driven by pietistic zeal, his son went further. He tried to introduce the kneeling posture of Islamic prayer into the synagogue; he insisted that worshipers face the direction of prayer even while seated; and he required people to stand in straight rows during the Eighteen Benedictions, in imitation of the orderly, symmetrical pattern of the mosque. These and other pietistic reforms aroused much opposition, and some Jews actually denounced Avraham to the Muslim authorities for attempting to introduce unlawful innovations into Judaism. In response, Avraham wrote a vigorous defense of pietism, which has been found in the Cairo Genizah.

Avraham Maimonides' son 'Ovadyah wrote his own Sūfī-like book. Called *Al-maqālah al-ḥawḍīyah* (The Treatise of the Pool), it attempted to impart intellectual respectability to Jewish Sufism. In the later Middle Ages, some Jews in Egypt imitated the style of life of the Sūfī convents in the hills surrounding Cairo. In Egypt, too, Jewish thinkers, outstanding among them the descendants of Maimonides, continued to compose treatises in the Sūfī vein. This turn towards mystical piety in the Jewish world, at just about the time when Jewish religious philosophy reached its climactic stage in the Middle East in the writings of Maimonides, recalls the replacement of philosophy by Sufism as the dominant religious mode in Islam in the later medieval period. Possibly Jewish interest in Sufism similarly reflects a dissatisfaction with the answers given in the past by Jewish rationalism to religious questions. Only when the study of Jewish Sufism, still in its infancy, has progressed further will it be possible to gain a clear sense of its place in the history of Judaism in the Islamic world and of the influence it might have had on the Lurianic Qabbalah that sprouted in Muslim Palestine after the expulsion of Jews from Spain in 1492.

[*See, for context and comparison,* Islam, *overview article and article on* Islam in Spain. *Further discussion on the earliest period covered by this article can be found in* Rabbinic Judaism in Late Antiquity. *Related articles include* Jewish Thought and Philosophy, *article on* Premodern Philosophy, *and* Polemics, *article on* Muslim-Jewish Polemics. *See also the independent entries on important figures mentioned herein.*]

BIBLIOGRAPHY

The most thorough general work on Jewish history and religion is Salo W. Baron's *A Social and Religious History of the Jews,* 2d ed., rev. & enl., 18 vols. (New York, 1952–1980). A good introduction to Jewish life under Islam is to be found in *The Jews of Arab Lands: A History and Source Book,* compiled and introduced by Norman A. Stillman. An older but still valuable book on Jewish history and literature under early Islam is Simḥa Assaf's *Tequfat ha-ge'onim ve-sifrutah* (Jerusalem, 1955).

Regional studies include Jacob Mann's *The Jews in Egypt and in Palestine under the Fāṭimid Caliphs,* 2 vols. in 1 (1920–1922; reprint, New York, 1970); my *Jewish Self-Government in Medieval Egypt: The Origins of the Office of the Head of the Jews, ca. 1065–1126* (Princeton, 1980); Eliyahu Ashtor's *Toledot ha-Yehudim be-Mitsrayim ve-Suryah taḥat shilṭon ha-Mamlukim,* 3 vols. (Jerusalem, 1944–1970), which concerns the Jews of Egypt and Syria; his *The Jews of Moslem Spain,* translated by Aaron Klein and Jenny Machlowitz Klein, 3 vols. (Philadelphia, 1973–1984); and H. Z. Hirschberg's *A History of the Jews in North Africa,* 2d rev. ed., 2 vols. (Leiden, 1974–1981). On the Yemenite Jews see S. D. Goitein's *Ha-Teimanim* (Jerusalem, 1983) and David R. Blumenthal's edition and annotated translation of *The Commentary of R. Hōter ben Shelōmō to the Thirteen Principles of Maimonides* (Leiden, 1974). Goitein's magisterial work, *A Mediterranean Society,* 5 vols. (Berkeley, 1967–1983), presents a detailed portrait of Jewish life, in both its worldly and religious aspects, in the Mediterranean Arab world of the High Middle Ages. On Karaism, see *Karaite Anthology,* edited and translated by Leon Nemoy (New Haven, 1952), and the introduction to Zvi Ankori's *Karaites in Byzantium* (New York, 1959). Julius Guttmann's *Philosophies of Judaism,* translated by David W. Silverman (New York, 1964), and Georges Vajda's *Introduction à la pensée juive au Moyen Age* (Paris, 1947) offer excellent introductions to the subject of the revival of religious philosophy in medieval Judaism in the Islamic world. The major Jewish philosophical works mentioned in this article exist in partial or complete English translation, such as the selection of Yitshaq Yisra'eli's philosophical writings translated into English in *Isaac Israeli: A Neoplatonic Philosopher of the Early Tenth Century* by Alexander Altmann and Samuel M. Stern (Oxford, 1958); *Saadia Gaon: The Book of Beliefs and Opinions,* translated by Samuel Rosenblatt (New Haven, 1948); and Maimonides' *Guide of the Perplexed,* translated by Shlomo Pines and introduced by Leo Strauss (Chicago, 1963). On pietism and Jewish Sufism, see the introduction to Paul Fenton's translation of Obadiah Maimonides' *Treatise of the Pool* (London, 1981) and Gerson D. Cohen's "The Soteriology of R. Abraham Maimuni," *Proceedings of the American Academy for Jewish Research,* 35 (1967): 75–98 and 36 (1968): 33–56.

For additional bibliography on the general subject of Jewish life and culture in the medieval Islamic world, consult the *Bibliographical Essays in Medieval Jewish Studies,* edited by Yosef H. Yerushalmi (New York, 1976), especially my chapter, "The Jews under Medieval Islam: From Rise of Islam to Sabbatai Zevi," reprinted with a supplement for the years 1973–1980 as "Princeton Near East Paper," no. 32 (Princeton, 1981); and that by Lawrence Berman, "Medieval Jewish Religious Philosophy."

10 JUDAISM IN THE MIDDLE EAST AND NORTH AFRICA SINCE 1492

JANE S. GERBER

The year 1492 marks a turning point in the history of the Jewish people. The expulsion of the Jews from Spain closes a brilliant and complex chapter in Jewish history, releasing a massive group of talented and despondent refugees upon the shores of the Mediterranean. They were soon followed by other waves of Jewish émigrés from Portugal, France, Provence, and the various Italian states as a result of the forced conversions or expulsions in those countries in the late-fifteenth through mid-sixteenth centuries. Even within the tragic annals of the Jews, rarely had the contemporary scene appeared so bleak. With most of the gates of Europe closed, the refugees of western Europe fled to the world of Islam, injecting new life and much controversy into the Jewish communities there that had been living in a state of decline for at least two centuries. The emergent period was marked by fervent yearnings for redemption, painful attempts at evaluating why the Spanish Jewish experience had ended in such ignominy, a brief but brilliant renaissance of Jewish life in Turkey, the outburst of antinomianism in seventeenth-century Ottoman Jewry and a final period of increasing intellectual stagnation of Jews in Muslim lands. Beginning in the nineteenth century, winds of change swept the Near East, propelled by the influence of the European powers. Jews were especially receptive to the attempts of western Jews to reform the eastern Jews and their situation, unleashing a chain of events and attempts at modernization whose effects are still being felt.

JEWISH LEGAL STATUS IN MUSLIM LANDS

From its inception, Islam exhibited an ambivalent attitude toward non-Muslims. The prophet Muḥammad had clearly enunciated his indebtedness to the faith of his monotheistic predecessors in the Qur'ān, tolerating their continued existence with certain provisos. Jews and Christians were to be recognized as possessors of scripture, *ahl al-kitāb* ("people of the Book"), were not to be forcibly converted, and were to be afforded a modicum of protection. Implied in the status of protection,

150

dhimmah, or of protected peoples—*dhimmīs*—was the right of the Jews to exercise their Judaism provided they accepted a position of subordination.

Over the centuries Muslim jurists worked out elaborate codes of what constituted subordination and "signs of humiliation." Typically, Jewish and Christian houses of worship were to be inconspicuous, Jews and Christians were to wear distinguishing garments, such as special headgear or footwear and clothing of designated colors. They were prohibited from riding horses or engaging in occupations that would place them in a position of authority over Muslims. In addition, they were required to pay special discriminatory taxes on produce of the land and a special head tax *(jizyah).*

Implementation of the discriminatory decrees was never uniform; the earlier Middle Ages exhibited a far greater degree of tolerance than the later Middle Ages. On the peripheries of the Muslim empire, moreover, in Morocco, Persia, and Yemen, the Muslim regimes tended to enforce discriminatory codes much more rigorously than in the heartland. By the nineteenth century, the entire system of carefully balanced toleration tempered by discrimination had broken down and Jews increasingly turned to the European powers for protection. In general, however, Middle East society was marked by public displays of religiosity, which found particular expression in the family or clan unit. Judaism, too, was a family and communal tradition strengthened by generations of relative economic, social, and political isolation in Muslim lands. Known in Turkish as a *millet* ("nation") in the Ottoman realm (from the mid-fifteenth century), Jews and Judaism enjoyed a relatively self-contained and protected position in the lands of Islam.

JEWISH DEMOGRAPHY IN MUSLIM LANDS: PRE- AND POST-1492

Population estimates of Jews in Muslim lands are extremely risky, since even at the height of the Muslim state its records of tax collection are partial and incomplete at best. It is generally accepted by historians that between 85 and 90 percent of world Jewry lived in the Muslim world in the period from the eighth through the tenth century. As that world became increasingly anarchic in the twelfth century, and as a result of the pogroms unleashed by the Almohads after 1147, Jewish population migrations to Christian lands increased. By the mid-seventeenth century, there were approximately three-quarters of a million Jews in the world, half of whom lived in the Muslim realm and half in Christian Europe (primarily Poland and Lithuania). During the sixteenth century acme of population growth in the Ottoman empire, the Jewish population in Istanbul alone reached forty thousand. At least as many Jews resided in contemporary Salonika. Perhaps as many as ten thousand Jews resided in Fez in Morocco, fifteen thousand in Iraq, and as many as fifteen thousand in the city of Safad (in Palestine) in the sixteenth century.

The Jewish population in the Ottoman empire began to decline dramatically in the seventeenth century as a result of fires, earthquakes, infant mortality, and increasing political insecurity. By the eve of World War II, Jews from Muslim lands numbered approximately one million out of the global Jewish population of approximately eighteen million. Since the Holocaust, Sefardic Jews (of Spanish origin) and Oriental Jews (of Middle Eastern and North African origin) have increased in demographic importance, both absolutely and relatively, since they constitute a majority of the Jewish population of Israel and France, the second and third largest Jewish communities in the free world. (The term *Sefardic Jews* hereafter may include Oriental Jews, when their distinction is not necessary.)

THE EXILES FROM SPAIN TO THE MAGHREB

Jewish flight from Spain began as a mass movement, not in 1492, but in 1391. In that year, waves of violence inundated the Jews of Spain and the Balearic Islands, and while many Jews were martyred, others converted, and still others fled. One of the most important places of refuge of Spanish and Majorcan Jewry in 1391 was Algeria. Sefardic Jews met a mixed reception from the fearful indigenous Jews but quickly assumed leadership positions in the community, providing a new élan to North African Jewish life. The scholar refugee leaders Yitshaq ben Sheshet Perfet (1326–1408) and Shim'on ben Tsemah Duran (1361–1444) have left a voluminous collection of rabbinic decisions and correspondence *(responsa)* revealing that Sefardic Jewry was troubled, not simply by the arduous task of communal reconstruction following flight, but also by very difficult questions of ritual and law as a result of the large-scale apostasy that had accompanied the waves of persecution. Questions of marital, ritual, and dietary law could not easily be resolved as demands for compassion clashed with real issues of communal continuity and Jewish identity.

The wave of refugees rose, and the question of secret Jews and forced converts (Marranos and *conversos*) grew more complex after 1492, as over 150,000 left Spain in haste. [*See* Marranos.] One of the favored refuges was Morocco, where Jews found asylum in the kingdom of Fez after a journey made perilous by unscrupulous captains and pirates. Chroniclers such as Avraham ben Shelomoh of Ardutiel, Avraham Zacuto, and Shelomoh ibn Verga dramatized the hazards of the flight from Spain. In Fez, Meknes, Marrakesh, Safi, Arzila, and smaller towns the Sefardic refugees injected new leadership and frequent controversy into the midst of small indigenous communities. In the coastal regions they exploited their connections with the Iberian Peninsula, serving as commercial agents for the Spanish and Portuguese.

Wherever the Spanish refugees came, they brought with them great pride, loyalty, and nostalgia for their cities of origin. Many of their customs were unfamiliar to the local Jews, particularly the halakhic leniencies that they had devised in response to the religious persecution they had endured. But they considered their customs to be sacrosanct, and controversy raged among the Spanish Jews and between the Spaniards (known as *megorashim,* "expelled ones") and the indigenous Jews (known as *toshavim).* In Morocco, these communal divisions were reflected in a duplication of many communal institutions and a protracted communal debate in Fez that required Muslim intercession.

In Tunisia, divisions between the refugees and the indigenous population were also institutionalized. They were aggravated by the influx of Jews from Livorno, Italy, who reinforced the separatism of the Spaniards. Two communities were established and the divisions between the newcomers (known as the *grana)* and the natives *(touansa)* persisted until the twentieth century. (This internecine struggle enabled local Turkish governors to exploit the Jews more easily.)

Jewish life in the Maghreb bore a number of distinctive features in the period following the advent of the Jews from Spain. On the one hand, most communities were torn by division as Sefardim attempted to impose their customs upon the local

Jews. Given their large numbers, superior educational level, and self-confidence, Spanish Jewry assumed the helms of power in most of the Maghreb. New Jewish intellectual centers emerged in Fez (Morocco) and Tlemcen (Algeria), and the ordinances *(taqqanot)* of the Jews of Castile soon became the guide for natives as well as newcomers. In matters of personal status as well as questions of communal leadership, inheritance, and ritual slaughtering, the Sefardic way became the standard mode of behavior for most Maghrebi Jews.

North Africa was not, however, a mere replica of pre-1492 Spain. Local customs, such as worship at the tombs of saints, the special celebration at the end of the festival of Passover known as the Mimuniah, and belief in the efficacy of amulets and talismans became part and parcel of Maghrebi Jewry as a whole. [*See* Pilgrimage, *article on* Jewish Pilgrimage.] The special role of the emissary from Palestine, the *ḥakham kolel,* in the intellectual life of the Maghreb was already discernible by the fifteenth century. Through the *ḥakham kolel* the mystical movements of sixteenth-century Palestine spread rapidly in North Africa. North African Judaism was characterized by a melding of the study of Talmud with that of Qabbalah or mysticism, and this blending lent a special flavor to the scholarship that emerged there in a long line of teachers, jurists, judges, and mystics.

THE AFTERMATH OF 1492: THE OTTOMAN EAST

Even before the expulsion of 1492, Jews in the West began to hear that the Ottoman empire was welcoming Jewish immigration. Yitshaq Tsarfati reportedly addressed the Jews of northern Europe under the reign of Murad II (1421–1451):

> *Brothers and teachers, friends and acquaintances! I, Isaac Sarfati, though I spring from French stock, yet I was born in Germany, and sat there at the feet of my esteemed teachers. I proclaim to you that Turkey is a land where nothing is lacking and where, if you will, all shall yet be well with you. The way to the Holy Land lies open to you through Turkey.*

Indeed, Ottoman might appeared to be invincible for over one hundred years. By the reign of Süleyman I ("the Magnificent," 1520–1566) the Ottoman borders extended from Morocco in the west to Iran in the east, from Hungary in the north to Yemen in the south.

Throughout the sixteenth century, while the empire was reaching its acme, successive boats brought Jewish refugees ashore in the eastern Mediterranean, particularly to its fairest port on the Aegean, Salonika. Some of the refugees came directly from the Iberian Peninsula while others arrived after an initial stop in Italy or North Africa where many succeeded in recouping their assets. They were eagerly welcomed by the sultan Bayezid II (1481–1512), especially since many were reputed to be skilled munitions-makers who would undoubtedly be helpful allies in the repeated wars against the Habsburgs.

The newcomers to the Ottoman empire displayed a degree of separatism and individualism that surpassed that of their Sefardic coreligionists in the Maghreb. They tended to divide along geographic lines so much so that before long there were more than forty congregations in Istanbul and Salonika each. The very names of the congregations—Catalan, Castile, Aragon, Barcelona, Portugal, Calabria— evoked identification with their origins. Distinctive identities were reinforced by the separate formations of self-help societies of all sorts. The very mixture of Jews, not only various groups of Sefardim, but also Ashkenazim from Germany and Hungary, Greek-speaking Jews from the Balkans (known as Romaniots), and Italian Jews created strains and tensions. It was not long before the preponderance of Sefardim overwhelmed the smaller native communities and the Castilian language, with an admixture of Hebrew, Turkish, and Slavic words known as *Ladino,* became the primary language of Ottoman Jewry and it remained such until the twentieth century.

The city of Salonika emerged as the preeminent Jewish community of the sixteenth century. The fame of its Talmud Torah (a rabbinic academy) spread far and wide, as did the rabbinic decisions of its rabbis Shemu'el de Medina (1505–1589) and his contemporary Yosef Taitasaq. The sixteenth-century Jewish historian Samuel Usque called Salonika in 1545 "a true mother in Judaism." Salonika's preeminence as a city of Sefardic culture remained down to its last days when, in 1943, the community was destroyed by the Nazis, its vast library sacked, and its four-hundred-year-old cemetery desecrated and dismantled.

One of the salient characteristics of the generation of exile was its melancholy brooding on the meaning of the tragic history of Israel, and especially of its Sefardic standard-bearers. A series of historians emerged among the Jewish people to record and comment upon the recent events. In his *Consolations for the Tribulations of Israel,* Samuel Usque, writing in Portuguese, adumbrated a lachrymose view of Jewish existence. His comtemporary, Yosef ha-Kohen (d. 1578) in his *'Emeq ha-bakhah* compared Jewish history to a journey through a "valley of tears." A third sixteenth-century Sefardic commentator, Shelomoh ibn Verga, also sought to decipher the reasons for Jewish suffering in his *Shevet Yehudah* (Scepter of Judah). It has been suggested that this unparalleled outpouring of Jewish historical writing during the sixteenth century not only represented an intense intellectual attempt to understand what had happened but was also perceived by the very writers themselves as a *novum* in Jewish history. Jews were now seeking for the first time to understand the ways of oppressive nations, not only the ways of God. The chronicle *Seder Eliyyahu zuta'* by Eliyyahu Capsali of Crete is devoted in large part to discussions of Ottoman history. The events of the time also called forth two more enduring reactions in the mystical and messianic meanings ascribed to the Spanish Jewish tragedy.

Spanish Jews brought not only their contentiousness and tragic vision but also their critical intellectual and technological skills to the Ottoman realm. Among the most important of the technological skills was the fine art of printing. Soon after the expulsion, a Hebrew press appeared in Fez, and it was followed soon thereafter by Hebrew printing presses in Salonika (1500), Constantinople (1503), Safad (1563), and Smyrna (1764). Hebrew printing spread from there to Baghdad, Calcutta, and Poona and eventually to Jerba, Sousse, Algiers, and Oran. (Not until more than two hundred years after the establishment of the first Hebrew printing press in Turkey was the first Ottoman Turkish press established.) A large number of the works printed by the Jewish presses were tracts dealing with practical Qabbalah or mysticism. Indeed, the rapid spread of mysticism from sixteenth-century Safad throughout the Mediterranean world, as well as the *Zohar*'s dissemination as a popular Sefardic text, can be attributed to the introduction of Hebrew printing in the Ottoman empire. [*See* Qabbalah.]

United under the umbrella of one dynamic and expansive empire, the Jews of Muslim lands enjoyed a cultural renaissance and an era of prosperity in the sixteenth century. Jewish physicians emerged in the royal courts of Constantinople to reassert their special role as courtiers and diplomats. Mosheh Hamon (1490–1554), the personal physician to Süleyman I, managed to outlast the intrigues of the harem to excel as a physician, medical scholar, bibliophile, and protector of Jews against the blood libel (false accusation that Jews have committed a ritual murder). Rabbis Mosheh Capsali (1453–1497), Eliyyahu Mizrahi (1498–1526), and Yosef ben Mosheh di Trani (1604–1639) held considerable sway over the Ottoman Jews through their reputation as scholars rather than through any official position.

Two personalities of sixteenth-century Ottoman Jewish history embody many of the qualities of the Sefardim in this generation. Gracia Nasi' (d. 1568?), a Portuguese Marrano (whose *converso* name was Beatrice Mendès), Jewish banker, entrepreneur, and patron of scholars and schools, arrived in Constantinople amid great splendor. Her many activities in the Ottoman empire included the rescue of Marranos from the Inquisition, the restoration of Jewish learning through enormous charitable donations, and the judicious use of diplomatic levers to assist foreign Jews in distress. Gracia was assisted in her spectacular business undertakings by her nephew Yosef Nasi' (1514–1579; that is, Joseph Mendès). Yosef was also adviser to Selim II, the sultan who awarded him a dukedom over the island of Naxos and a permit to recolonize the city of Tiberias. The awards were apparently made in recognition of the astuteness of Yosef's advice, particularly concerning the conquest of Cyprus in 1571.

Jewish life in the Arab provinces of the Ottoman empire also began to quicken as a result of the Ottoman conquests in the first quarter of the sixteenth century. Egypt produced David ibn Abi Zimra (1479–1573), one of the most prolific *responsa* writers of his day. Despite the Ottoman conquest of 1526, Iraq did not succumb to Ottoman control until the seventeenth century. Its small Jewish community, however, emerged from isolation and resumed contact with the outside Jewish world, turning, for example to the rabbis of Aleppo, Syria, for religious guidance. The Ottoman conquest of Arab provinces did not necessarily improve the lot of the Jews. For the Jews of Yemen, Ottoman incursions and conquest in 1546 destabilized an already precarious situation. Caught between warring Muslim forces, the Jews of Sanaa were subjected to severe discriminatory legislation, culminating in the destruction of synagogues and expulsions in the seventeenth century. Literarily, the community underwent a period of cultural flowering, despite these hardships, during the career of the Yemenite poet Shalom Shabbazi (1617–1680?).

SAFAD AS A CENTER OF SEFARDIC SEARCH AND JEWISH MYSTICISM

The Sefardic refugees of the sixteenth century were a melancholy and restless generation, torn by guilty memories of community apostasy, perplexed by their continuing suffering and exile, and fevered by expectations of imminent salvation. Messianism ran deep in the community, easily aroused by flamboyant pretenders such as David Reubeni who went to Clement VII and other Christian leaders with the offer of raising Jewish armies to help them recapture Palestine from the Ottomans. One of his most illustrious followers, a Portuguese secret Jew, Shelomoh Molkho (1501–1532), heeded Reubeni's call, circumcised himself, and set out for Italy preaching the advent of the Messiah. Ultimately he fell into the hands of the Inquisition and was burned at the stake in Mantua in 1532. His influence, however, spread as far as the settlement of Safad in Palestine.

After the Ottoman conquest of Palestine in 1516, Jewish migration to the Holy Land increased. Soon a remarkable galaxy of scholars and mystics emerged in Safad. Three generations of extraordinary mystics engaged collectively and individually in ascertaining practical means of hastening the redemption of the Jewish people while providing mythic formulations for comprehending the Sefardic catastrophe. These mystics were not recluses but were, rather, legal scholars actively engaged in history. One of their giants, Ya'aqov Berab (d. 1546), arrived in Safad after wanderings in North Africa and Egypt. Believing the time ripe for the messianic redemption of the Jewish people, Berab set out to restore the ancient rite of rabbinical ordination (semikhah) in 1538 as a prerequisite for the reestablishment of the Sanhedrin which was, in turn, prerequisite to the proper repentance of the Jewish people that would bring redemption. While his disciples eagerly accepted the new charge placed upon them, Berab's movement was ultimately thwarted by the forceful opposition of Levi ibn Habib of Jerusalem.

Another towering intellectual figure of that generation who eventually found his way to Safad after many years of wandering was Yosef Karo (1488–1575). Karo's halakhic authority was established by his major work *Beit Yosef.* He is remembered by posterity, however, through the utility of his comprehensive legal handbook *Shulḥan arukh.* In the *Shulḥan arukh* Karo presented numerous Sefardic as well as Ashkenazic practices in a readily accessible fashion, rendering his work one of the most useful codes for subsequent generations of Jews. Karo also possessed a mystical bent that emerges in his work *Maggid mesharim,* a mystical diary of angelic revelations, and he served as mentor to the remarkable cluster of mystics and pietists in sixteenth century Safad. [*See the biography of Yosef Karo.*]

With the arrival of Isaac Luria at Safad in the 1560s, Jewish mysticism reached its greatest heights. A charismatic personality with a stirring effect on his followers, Luria decisively influenced the development of Jewish mysticism in the following generations. Lurianic Qabbalah, with its doctrines of a cataclysmic scattering of divine sparks at creation and the unique role of Israel in liberating and reunifying these sparks, together with a belief in metempsychosis and new mystical modes of prayer, deepened the expectation of messianic redemption and altered the way many Jews thought about themselves for at least a century and a half. [*See the biography of Isaac Luria.*]

The mystics of Safad delved into the vast corpus of Jewish literature, frequently using the *Zohar* as their point of departure. Many unusual personalities in this group were characterized by their frequent walks in the Galilee and fervent embellishment of the Sabbath and daily ritual actions. One of the participants was the poet Shelomoh Alkabets. He is best remembered for the poem *Lekhah dodi,* a Sabbath invocation welcoming the Sabbath as bride and queen that has been included in the Friday evening Sabbath services in all Jewish communities.

After Luria's death in 1572, his disciple Hayyim Vital (1543–1620) began to disseminate a version of the teachings of the Lurianic school of Safad. The prominence of the city itself did not last much longer. In 1576 the Ottoman sultan ordered the deportation of one thousand Jews from Safad to repopulate the newly conquered island of Cyprus. The order was rescinded soon thereafter, but many Jews had already left the city. The vitality of Safad's Jewish community was further sapped by the corruption of Ottoman provincial governors, the impact of devastating earthquakes, and the periodic depredations of local Arabs. In the seventeenth century

Safad reverted to its former role as an inconspicuous settlement in a backwater province while the qabbalistic ideas that had emerged there spread rapidly throughout the Diaspora.

INFLUENCE OF SHABBETAI TSEVI

The decline of the Jewish communities in Muslim lands was a slow process caused by a number of external factors. An especially prominent symptom of this decline is the bizarre and tragic career of Shabbetai Tsevi. Shabbetai Tsevi was born in the city of Smyrna in 1625, began to engage in mysticial studies in 1648, and fell under the spell of Natan of Gaza in 1665, pronouncing himself the Messiah in that year. An anarchic outburst of antinomian activity and frenzy ensued as news of Shabbetai's bizarre behavior spread. Even his conversion to Islam in 1666 did not discredit the movement, but rather accelerated the tendency of that generation to perceive the Spanish experience as one with messianic overtones. The fact that Tsevi converted shook Marrano circles everywhere. Scholars in Italy and Amsterdam were agitated; poets in Kurdistan wrote poems on Shabbetean themes; Jewish followers of Tsevi, known as *Donmeh,* converted to Islam and continued to believe in Tsevi as the Messiah for generations after his death. The energy, confusion, guilt, and false hopes with which the Shabbatean movement had tried to break out of the mold of Jewish suffering left a hyperagitated Jewry deeply depressed. [*For further discussion of this major event, see the biography of Shabbetai Tsevi.*]

Ultimately the messianic storm subsided, rabbis, especially in the Ottoman empire, began to destroy books with references to Shabbetai Tsevi, and concerted efforts were made once again to integrate mystical studies into rabbinics. Ultimately, Near Eastern Jewry repressed Shabbeteanism while retaining traces of it in its particular fondness for an integration of Judaism with such practices as saint worship and visiting holy sites *(ziyārah),* and a strengthened belief in the efficacy of practical Qabbalah such as the casting of lots or the interpretation of dreams.

Ottoman Jewish decline accelerated after the debacle of Tsevi. It was temporarily halted in 1730 when the first volume of the multivolume encyclopedia *Me'am lo'ez* appeared. This popular compendium of Oriental Sefardic lore by Ya'aqov ben Mahir Culi instructed while entertaining the masses with a vast array of legends, anecdotes, customs, and laws. Compositions in Ladino as well as Hebrew continued to be recited in the salons of Salonika, but the once vibrant Jewry of Ottoman lands found itself enfeebled by a series of natural catastrophies and by the mounting hostility of Ottoman Christians as well as Muslims. While some of this hostility was the product of economic rivalry, some of it can also be traced to the influx of anti-Semitic notions from the West alongside the growing influence of Western, particularly French, power among the Christians.

NEAR EASTERN JEWRY ON THE EVE OF THE MODERN ERA

Jewish life in the easternmost part of the Ottoman empire did not share in the renaissance of sixteenth-century Ottoman Jewry. Persian Jews were particularly endangered by the campaign of forced conversion that the Shī'ī Safavid dynasty (1501–1732) undertook in the seventeenth century. Isolated from Ottoman Jewry, the forty thousand Jews of Persia were subjected to an especially harsh code of discriminatory legislation, known as the Jami Abbasi, which was operative until 1925. Even the increasing influence of the European powers couldn't spare the Jews of Mashhad from a forced conversion during the nineteenth century.

Ottoman rule in Yemen (1546–1629) was succeeded by a harsh succession of independent imams of the Zaydī sect. Despite the frequent expulsions from villages and towns and the implementation of the policy of kidnapping Jewish orphans to raise them within Islam, Yemenite Jews continued to produce a significant poetic and qabbalistic tradition during this period. Males were largely literate, the printed prayer books of the period attesting to the spread of Lurianic Qabbalah into the remote corners of the Hejaz. By the nineteenth century, even some of the tenets of Haskalah, European Jewish Enlightenment, had reached such communities as Sanaa. Change brought with it conflict and the Jews of Yemen were internally split. It was the worsening status of the Jews in Yemen, however, and not the ideological conflicts, that precipitated their mass migration from Yemen to Palestine in the 1880s. By the early twentieth century, Yemenite Jews formed a significant community in the city of Jerusalem.

Jews in the East had never ceased their close contact with other Jews even in the age of Ottoman military and political decline. Jews in the Ottoman realm (especially Sefardic Jews) continued to serve as merchants, diplomats, commercial agents, and interpreters throughout the period of Ottoman ascendancy and decline, reinforcing their ties with coreligionists. But by the nineteenth century, the Jewish position in Arab and Turkish lands was one of abject poverty, extreme vulnerability, humiliation, and insecurity. Pressures on the Ottomans to reform were brought to bear by the European powers, not so much to assist the Jews as primarily to assist the Ottoman Christians. Under these pressures the Ottoman reform movement, Tanzīmāt, ended special discriminatory taxation, agreed to protect the legal rights of non-Muslims, and granted civil equality to them. Reforming legislation, however, could not restore the Ottoman empire to good health. Jewish well-being came increasingly to depend upon the intervention of Western powers and Western Jews. No incident highlighted this vulnerability and dependency more clearly than the Damascus blood libel in 1840. When the Jews of Damascus were falsely accused of murdering a Christian for ritual purposes, the community of Damascus, as well as other Syrian communities, faced grave danger. Through the intervention of Moses Montefiore of London and Adolphe Crémieux of Paris, the Jews of Damascus were rescued and the Sublime Porte was forced to publicly repudiate the blood libel accusation. Despite this intervention, Near Eastern Jewry was subjected to a host of unfortunate blood libel accusations at the hands of the Greeks, Arabs, and Armenians in the nineteenth century. More than once the indefatigable Montefiore went to the Near East and the Maghreb to intercede personally on behalf of Jews. [*For discussion of the blood libel and other false accusations, see* Anti-Semitism.]

In 1860 the Alliance Israélite Universelle was founded in France. Among its guiding principles was the goal of protecting the Jewish communities of Muslim lands and modernizing and uplifting them from their abject state of poverty and ignorance. The altruistic goals of French Jewry dovetailed well with the political and imperial goals of the French government. The Jews of France set out with almost missionary zeal to transform the face of Near Eastern Jewry and to forge a community that would embody some of the cherished ideals of the French Revolution. Beginning with the establishment of their first school in Morocco in 1860, the Alliance Israélite Universelle proceeded to introduce modern, secular notions and technical skills to a new generation of Jews throughout the Near East. By World War I, over one hundred Alliance schools teaching the French language and secular subjects had been set up in Morocco, Algeria, Tunisia, Libya, Egypt, Iran, Turkey, and the Balkans. The Alliance schools succeeded in undercutting poverty and Jewish female illiteracy and, introducing secular studies to all Jews, prepared a new generation of Jews for entry into modernity.

The introduction of Western-style education among Near Eastern Jews did not result in a parallel movement of religious reformulation and the building of a new, modern Jewish identity there. This was partially because Near Eastern Jews, unlike the Jews of Europe, were not presented with the option of entering their majority society provided they refashioned themselves since religion remained a fundamental basis of social and political organization in the Middle East. Many Jewish autonomous institutions ceased to exist as a direct result of European colonial legislation. For example, early in their administration, the French authorities in Algeria abolished the independent Jewish system of courts. While Jews were granted French citizenship in Algeria in 1870, elsewhere they adopted European culture without attaining the benefits of European citizenship. Their cultural identity with the European powers, especially in North Africa, ushered in a period of confusion when Arab nationalism began to flower. In some parts of the Arab world, such as Iraq, the Jewish minority became one of the segments of the population most active in creating modern Arabic literature. Yet, at the same time that they pioneered in the language, press, and modernization of the economy of the Arab states, Jews were increasingly isolated from the pan-Arab and pan-Islamic culture then capturing the hearts of the masses. For Middle Eastern Jews, however, the modern period of Western encroachment did not result in indigenous Jewish attempts to form new self-identifying modes of expression. Even the Zionist movement of national self-determination, a late nineteenth-century European Jewish response to emancipation and modernity, echoed only faintly in Muslim lands.

Jewish life in Muslim lands came almost to a complete end in the wake of the creation of the state of Israel and the emergence of Arab nationalist states in the post–World War II period. Fewer than 10 percent of the Near Eastern Jews living in Muslim countries in 1948 still reside in those countries in 1986. Only 17,000 of the former 250,000 Moroccan Jews remain in Morocco. All other Jewish communities have virtually disappeared except the communities of Turkey and Iran. The Judaism of the more than one million Jews who fled their ancestral homes for Israel or the West is a Judaism still in flux. Middle Eastern Jewish religiosity was always anchored in familial and communal action, especially in the post-1492 period. In the Muslim world, people had stayed in their communities for generations, passing on hereditary communal offices from father to son. Although these lines of tradition have been irrevocably cut with the great migration to Western, technological, modern societies, the Judaism of the Middle Eastern Jew has retained some remnants of former times. Among those remnants must be included the fervent love of the land of Israel with its messianic and mystical overtones, the expression of religiosity within a familial context, and the special pride and quality imparted by a specific link with the Sefardic tradition.

Just as 1789 set in motion a crucial reorientation of Jewish identities and Judaism in western Europe, and just as 1881 set in motion a process of change that eventually led to a permanent transformation in the structure of Jewish politics among Ashken-

160   Judaism: A People and Its History

azim, especially in eastern Europe, so too, one suspects, 1948 will be found to have marked a transforming date in the lives of Middle Eastern Jews. With the end of living on the fringes of Muslim society, the Jewish communities from the world of Islam have embarked upon a new path in Jewish history.

[*For further discussion of the religious beliefs and customs of the Jews of North Africa and the Middle East, see* Folk Religion, *article on* Folk Judaism. *For various messianic movements mentioned, see* Messianism, *article on* Jewish Messianism. *For a discussion of Judaism in the state of Israel and the history of Jewish immigration there, see* Zionism. *One dimension of the historic relationship between Jews and Muslims is explored in* Polemics, *article on* Muslim-Jewish Polemics.]

BIBLIOGRAPHY

The best introductory volume on the subject is S. D. Goitein's survey *Jews and Arabs: Their Contacts through the Ages,* 3d rev. ed. (New York, 1974). Norman A. Stillman's *The Jews of Arab Lands: A History and Source Book* (Philadelphia, 1979) provides a fine introductory essay and a large collection of documents translated from Arabic and Hebrew and a variety of Western languages. More recently, Bernard Lewis's *The Jews of Islam* (Princeton, 1984) has offered a fresh interpretation of the broad sweep of Middle Eastern Jewish history. André N. Chouraqui's *Between East and West: A History of the Jews of North Africa,* translated by Michael M. Bernet (Philadelphia, 1968), gives a balanced survey of the Jews of the Maghreb and is particularly informative for the modern period. For a more detailed examination of the Maghreb, see H. Z. Hirschberg's *Toledot ha-Yehudim be-Afriqah ha-Tsefonit,* 2 vols. (Jerusalem, 1965), translated by M. Eichelberg as *A History of the Jews in North Africa,* vol. 1, *From Antiquity to the Sixteenth Century* (Leiden, 1974) and vol. 2, *From the Ottoman Conquests to the Present Time* (Leiden, 1981). Hirschberg analyzes the political history of the Jews in Arab lands and the Maghreb extensively in his article "The Oriental Jewish Communities,"in *Religion in the Middle East: Three Religions in Concord and Conflict,* edited by A. J. Arberry (Cambridge, 1969), pp. 119–225.

Older multivolume studies of Ottoman Jewry such as Solomon A. Rosanes' *Divrei yemei Yisra'el be-Togarma,* 6 vols. (Jerusalem, 1930–1945) and Moïse Franco's *Essai sur l'histoire des Israelites de l'Empire Ottoman depuis les origines jusqu'à nos jours* (Paris, 1897) still contain valuable material culled from rabbinic sources. Volume 18 of Salo W. Baron's exceptionally important *A Social and Religious History of the Jews,* 2d ed., rev. & enl. (New York, 1983), updates these earlier studies, extending the geographic scope to include the Jews of Persia, China, India and Ethiopia as well as the Ottoman empire. Especially useful is Baron's discussion of demography.

The problem of the general question of the legal status of the Jews under Islam has been treated by A. S. Tritton in *The Caliphs and Their Non-Muslim Subjects* (London, 1930). While Tritton is still the standard reference work on Muslim theories regarding the *dhimmī*s, a methodical discussion can be found in Antoine Fattal's *Le statut légal des non-Musulmans en pays d'Islam* (Beirut, 1958).

Four monographs of varying value treat the specific problems of individual Jewries based on rabbinic *responsa.* These studies are sill useful as the sole English source on significant rabbinic figures and their age. Isidore Epstein's *The Responsa of Rabbi Simon B. Zemah Duran as a Source of the History of the Jews in North Africa* (1930; reprint New York, 1968), Israel Goldman's *The Life and Times of Rabbi David Ibn Abi Zimra* (New York, 1970), Morris S. Goodblatt's *Jewish Life in Turkey in the Sixteenth Century as Reflected in the Legal Writings of*

Samuel de Medina (New York, 1952), and Abraham M. Hershman's *Rabbi Isaac ben Sheshet Perfet and His Times* (New York, 1943) each explores the major problems of an age of transition and the response of a leading rabbinic luminary.

A delightful account of the city of Safad and its Qabbalistic circles is Solomon Schechter's essay "Safad in the Sixteenth Century," which can be found in his *Studies in Judaism* (1908; reprint, Cleveland, 1958) and in *The Jewish Expression,* edited by Judah Goldin (New York, 1970). The Qabbalistic movement of Safad also can be seen in the excellent biography *Joseph Karo: Lawyer and Mystic* by R. J. Zwi Werblowsky (London, 1962). For an exhaustive and monumental treatment of the life and times of Shabbetai Tsevi, see Gershom Scholem's *Sabbatai Sevi: The Mystical Messiah, 1626–1676* (Princeton, 1973).

Hayyim Cohen's *The Jews of the Middle East, 1860–1972* (New York, 1973) is one of the few books in English on recent trends among the Jews in the Arab world. Michael Laskier's exhaustive study *The Alliance Israélite Universelle and the Jewish Communities of Morocco, 1862–1962* (Albany, 1983) is a thorough monographic consideration of the educational role of the alliance.

The latest studies on Jews in the Middle East can be found in such Israeli publications as *Sefunot* (Jerusalem, 1956–1966), *Pe'amin* (Jerusalem, 1979–), and *Mizrah u-ma'arav* (Jerusalem, 1919–1932). Interdisciplinary approaches can be fruitfully employed in this field, and the works of contemporary anthropologists such as Moshe Shokeid, Harvey Goldberg, Shlomo Deshen, and Walter Zenner have been especially illuminating in analyzing Middle Eastern Jewish communities in Israel. These studies frequently begin with considerations of individual Near Eastern Jewish communities in their traditional milieu and historical structure.

11 JUDAISM IN SOUTHERN EUROPE

Martin A. Cohen

Despite a differential development, Judaism in southern Europe's many communities has been united geographically by the Mediterranean Sea and historically by a common heritage. The heritage has informed its creativity, while the sea has fostered its communication. As with other areas, the sources on Judaism in southern Europe tend to portray Judaism as conceived by leadership rather than as practiced by laity. Within this region, with its wide variations of time, place, and circumstance, popular Judaism ran the gamut from paradigmatic devotion to listless ignorance, exhibiting also elements of syncretistic blending with indigenous folklore, superstitition, and magic. Jewish sources from Renaissance Italy, for example, document the use of amulets, charms, fortune-telling, witchcraft, and prayers to repel evil spirits. Such often widespread practices are deprecatorily recorded by rabbis, heads of *yeshivot,* and other religious leaders in sermons, *responsa,* and ethical treatises.

The Judaism of all these communities thus reveals two strata: (1) a continuing complex of practices and beliefs, diversely syncretized with alien elements and followed by the majority, and (2) the idealized religion of the intellectual leadership, expressed in a variety of approaches often in conflict with one another, always reflective of the surrounding environment and ultimately influencing the tone of Judaism in the society as a whole. A description of Judaism in all these communities must necessarily focus on the creativity of its leadership, with the caveat that the individuals directly involved were more significant tonally than numerically. One must also bear in mind that the religious creativity of these areas varied greatly from time to time and place to place.

The history of Judaism in southern Europe embraces the experience of Jews on the Iberian Peninsula, in southern France, in Italy, and in the Greek territories. It is divisible into four occasionally overlapping chronological eras: the origin of Jewish settlement until approximately 700 CE; the medieval world (700–c. 1500); the Renaissance and Enlightenment (c. 1300–c. 1850); and the modern and contemporary world (beginning about 1800). The great period of Jewish productivity in the Greek territories, which occurred under Ottoman rule, is outside the scope of this study.

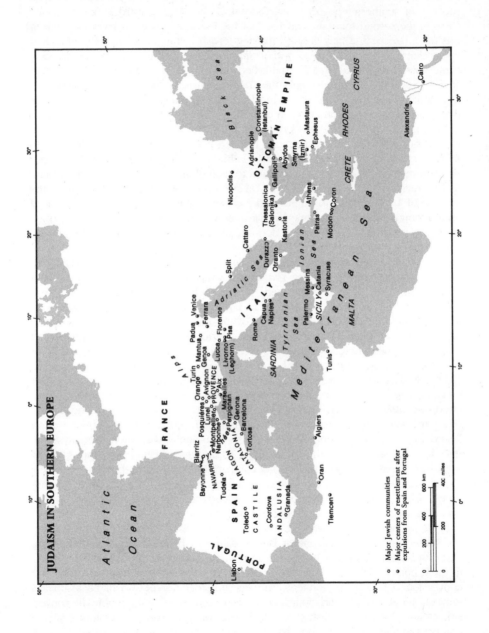

JUDAISM IN SOUTHERN EUROPE

Atlantic Ocean

FRANCE

Alps

PORTUGAL

Lisbon

SPAIN

NAVARRE
Bayonne
Biarritz
Tudela
ARAGON
CASTILE
Toledo
Cordova
ANDALUSIA
Granada
Tlemcen
Oran
Algiers
Tunis

CATALONIA
Tortosa
Gerona
Barcelona
Perpignan
Pyr
Narbonne
Lunel
Montpellier
PROVENCE
Avignon
Orange
Posquières
Aix
Marseilles

Turin
Mantua
Genoa
Padua
Venice
Ferrara
Lucca
Florence
Livorno
(Leghorn)
Pisa

ITALY
SARDINIA
Rome
Capua
Naples
Tyrrhenian Sea
Palermo
Messina
SICILY
Catania
Syracuse

Adriatic Sea
Split
Cattaro
Durazzo
Otranto
Ionian Sea
Modon
Coron
Patras

MALTA

Mediterranean Sea

Black Sea

OTTOMAN EMPIRE
Constantinople
(Istanbul)
Adrianople
Gallipoli
Abydos
Smyrna
(Izmir)
Ephesus
Mastaura
Nicopolis
Thessalonica
(Salonika)
Kastoria
Athens

CRETE
RHODES
CYPRUS

Cairo
Alexandria

○ Major Jewish communities
● Major centers of resettlement after
    expulsions from Spain and Portugal

0   200   400   600 km
0   200   40C miles

ORIGINS

Legends locate Jews in early biblical times in places as remote from the Land of Israel as the Iberian Peninsula, but the inscriptions that constitute the earliest Jewish records of southern European Jewry do not antedate the third century BCE for Greece, the second for Italy, and the first for Iberia and southern France. During this time, Greece and Italy enjoyed thriving Jewish cultures; the Greek regions had the greatest Jewish population, with communities in places like Cyprus, Rhodes, Crete, Kos, and Sparta already established during the Hasmonean period (*1 Mc.* 15:23). Probably from Rome comes the *Collatio legum Mosaicarum et Romanarum,* a work compiled at the end of the third or the beginning of the fourth century CE that contains a comparison between biblical and Roman law.

Little is known about the Jew's religious life in the early centuries of their settlement. Prior to the Hasmonean Revolt (168–165 BCE), Jews most likely brought with them only a form of Pentateuchal Judaism, while later arrivals were likely influenced by proto-rabbinic institutions. In addition to its diplomatic tasks, the patriarch Gamli'el of Yavneh's embassy to Rome (95–96 CE) may have intended to reorganize the substantial Jewish population there under closer rabbinical control. The account of an academy established in Rome by Matya' ben Heresh (early second century) appears historical (B.T., *Me'il* 17a), as does the purported guidance offered him by the sages Shim'on bar Yoḥ'ai and El'azar ben Yose on their visit to Rome.

Prior to the advent of modern secular states, Jews in southern Europe lived with quasi-autonomy under Jewish law *(halakhah)*, which in turn was subject to the laws of the host society. These societies generated harsh legislation against the Jews, from *ad hoc* decrees to major compilations of law such as the Theodosian Code (438) and the *Siete Partidas* (Seven Sections) of the Castilian king Alfonso X (r. 1252–1284). This legislation, however, was often overlooked or minimally implemented in those societies where such actions suited the rulers' needs. Within the bounds of this legislation, the range of Jewish autonomy varied; at times it included even the right to inflict capital punishment. Accordingly, Jewish communities maintained their own separate legal and communal institutions; foremost among them were the local court *(beit din)*, synagogues (often there were separate synogogues for practitioners of a particular craft or members of a certain guild), and cemeteries. Though it followed traditional Jewish models, the Jewish community was often formally influenced by the structure of the surrounding society: its officers often bore Hebrew titles that directly translated the titles of comparable positions in the general society or utilized the language of the society, as in the case of the ancient Greek communities, where we find the titles of *archisynagogos* for the community head, *gerousiarch* as head of the synagogue council, and *presbyter* for elder.

Evidence of numerous synagogues exists for the early centuries CE, particularly for Rome and Greece; the one at Delos (dating to before 69 BCE) is among the earliest discovered. Various sources, from the New Testament and rabbinic literature to the canons of the Council of Elvira (c. 305), attest to a continuing interest in, and conversion to, Judaism by non-Jews. The official recognition of Christianity as Rome's imperial religion in the early fourth century spurred efforts at the wholesale conversion of Jews. If authentic, Bishop Severus's letter on the forced conversion of Minorca's Jews in 418 constitutes the earliest record of mass conversions, which were in any case definitely ordered by several Merovingian and Visigothic kings in the sixth and seventh centuries. Continuous reports on Jewish religious life begin in the mid-tenth century in two centers: Iberia and Italy.

ISLAMIC IBERIA (SPAIN AND PORTUGAL)

Iberia, conquered by the Muslims between 711 and 715, stood at the beginning of the medieval period on the threshold of a golden age. Iberia's Jewish community of approximately 250,000, the largest at the time, shared this development. Organized politically under the *nasi'* ("prince") Hasdai (or Hisdai) ibn Shaprut (c. 915–c. 970) and constitutionally under Talmudic law, the Jews inaugurated a golden age that continued long after Islamic Iberia splintered into some thirty polities in the early eleventh century.

Pervading the high culture of Jewry under Islam was a broadly rationalistic tone. Rationalism encouraged the centralization of *halakhah,* a process signified by the *Sefer halakhot* (Book of Laws) composed by Yitshaq ben Ya'aqov Alfasi (1013–1103) in Fez and brought by him to Lucena. It led ultimately to the magisterial *Mishneh Torah* (Repetition of the Torah, or Code of Law) in 1180 by Moses Maimonides (Mosheh ben Maimon), though this work also was composed outside of the peninsula, in Egypt. The rational spirit also helped produce scientific studies of the Hebrew language, by Menahem ibn Saruq (mid-tenth century), compiler of the first Hebrew dictionary; his rival, Dunash ibn Labrat, who projected a Hebrew grammar; their contemporary, Yehudah ibn Hayyuj, who discovered the triliteral nature of Hebrew roots; and the prolific Yonah ibn Janah (early eleventh century), whose *Kitāb al-tanqīh* (Book of Minute Research) is the oldest extant complete work on Jewish philology.

The same spirit also facilitated the ingress of Greek thought, especially Neoplatonism and Aristotelianism, into Judaism. These philosophies challenged critical doctrines of the revealed tradition—those concerning revelation, creation, providence, prophecy, miracles, immortality, resurrection, and God's attributes. In response, some Iberian thinkers rejected philosophy and others, revelation. Still others created syntheses, the foremost among them given in *Keter malkhut* (The Crown of Royalty), by the Neoplatonist Shelomoh ibn Gabirol (mid-eleventh century); *Kitāb al-hidāyah ilā farā'id al-qulūb* (The Duties of the Heart), by the Neoplatonist Bahye ibn Paquda (second half of the eleventh century); the *Kitāb al-radd wa-al-dalīl fī al-dīn al-dhalīl* (Book of Refutation and in Defense of the Despised Faith), commonly called in Hebrew the *Kuzari,* by Yehudah ha-Levi (eleventh to twelfth century), who combines elements of Neoplatonism and Aristotelianism; and in *Al-'aqīdah al-rafiyah* (The Exalted Faith), by Avraham ibn Daud of Toledo (twelfth century) and Maimonides' *Dalālat al-hā'irīn* (Guide of the Perplexed), both of which draw on medieval Aristotelianism. Except for Ibn Gabirol's work in Hebrew, these were all composed in Arabic with Hebrew characters. Though differing by school and bent, these philosophers all rationalized belief innovatively and at times controversially. For them, God was neither anthropomorphic nor anthropopathic, and the contrarational was tempered by rational explanations. For the Neoplatonists, the soul's ultimate aim was union with the upper world, while for the Aristotelians it was the rational faculty's approximation to the Active Intellect that was of ultimate value. Unlike most of these philosophers, who focused primarily on the individual, ha-Levi dwelt on corporative Israel, its election and receipt of God's revelation.

The rational-philosophical atmosphere also pervaded other religious creativity, including the biblical commentaries of Mosheh ibn 'Ezra' (c. 1055–after 1135) and Avraham ibn 'Ezra' (c. 1089–c. 1164) and the religious poem, or *piyyut,* written especially for the Sabbath and holiday liturgy. Born in Talmudic times, the *piyyut* had developed with the fixing of the liturgy. Iberian Jewry played an important role in this process. Responding to a question from the Lucena community, Natron'ai, the gaon of the Babylonian academy of Sura from 853 to 858, listed the one hundred daily blessings prescribed in the Talmud. To another query, apparently from Barcelona, Natron'ai's successor, 'Amram bar Sheshna (known as 'Amram Gaon, d. 875), sent a complete order of prayers, along with corresponding *halakhah* for the entire year. *Seder 'Amram* ('Amram's Order), the oldest in Judaism, spurred liturgical creativity through the *piyyut.*

Iberian poets, like Ibn Gabirol, Mosheh ibn 'Ezra', ha-Levi, Yosef ibn Abitur (tenth to eleventh century), and Yitshaq ibn Ghayyat (1038–1089), further developed the conventional categories, emphasizing the penitential poems, and conceived new ones for Havdalah, the Sabbath table, and other private occasions, as well as *reshuyyot* ("introductory poems") for public recitation. Their *piyyutim* are distinguished by lucid style, biblical vocabulary, and a special meter of their own creation, though at times they employ Arabic meter and rhyme. Their themes are manifold: God's nature and creation; the human soul and life's meaning; sin, repentance, redemption, and the Messiah; ethical virtues; the Torah and its saintly teachers; and the longing for God's proximity and favor. Noteworthy are ha-Levi's poems on his migration to Zion (especially the *Ode to Zion*), and Ibn Gabirol's philosophical-religious paean to God, the *Crown of Royalty,* which is still recited by Sefardic Jews on the eve of Yom Kippur.

The same themes inform the sermons of this era, which, while no longer extant, can be reconstructed from biblical commentaries like those of David Kimhi (c. 1160–c. 1235), Avraham ibn 'Ezra'; from philosophical works, notably Ibn Paquda's *Duties of the Heart* and ha-Levi's *Kuzari;* and from ethical treatises, like Maimonides' introduction to the Mishnaic tractate *Avot,* known as the *Shemoneh Peraqim* (Eight Chapters). These works evince an intensive religious life, a flourishing synagogue, and a passion for sermonic instruction. Maimonides even recommended a resident preacher for each community (before local rabbis were the rule), while his son Avraham compiled a treatise on traditional rabbinical sermons.

No synagogues remain standing from communities under Muslim rule during this period, but those constructed contemporaneously in the Christian sectors of the peninsula, as in Toledo, for example, unmistakably reveal the influence of Islamic architecture. Equally impressive was the effect of Islamic music upon the Iberian synagogue chant.

MEDIEVAL CHRISTIAN EUROPE

The second center of Jewry was the medieval Christian world. Here, despite chronic disabilities, many Jewish communities were religiously creative. Jewish learning was regularly accompanied by secular knowledge: Talmudists were physicians and scientists conversant with Latin, Greek, Arabic, and their local vernaculars. Their creativity began in tenth-century Italy, in theology with Shabbetai Donnolo (913–c. 982), in history with the anonymous author of the *Yosippon* (Pseudo-Josephus), and in lexicography with Natan ben Yehi'el (1035–c. 1110). Donnolo was a physician and theologian acquainted with Hebrew, Greek, and Latin literature as well as colloquial Italian, and he was the first person in Christian Europe to write on medicine in Hebrew. He sought scientific explanations for creation and asserted that man was created not in God's image but in the image of God's creation. The author of *Yosippon* wove a Latin version of the writings of Josephus Flavius and other works, including the apocryphpal and Talmudic literature, into an imaginative and historiographically perceptive narrative. Natan's *'Arukh,* a lexicon of Talmudic and Midrashic literature, became influential because of the quality of its readings, etymologies, and explanations.

By the thirteenth century, religious culture flourished in southern France, especially Provence, and in the expanding Christian sector of the Iberian Peninsula, the kingdoms of Castile, Aragon, and Navarre. There the rationalist philosophical tendencies that had developed in Islamic Iberia clashed with the traditional view of Judaism regnant in Christian feudal Europe. According to the traditional view, God, usually conceived anthropomorphically and anthropopathically, repeatedly interrupted the processes of nature to reward and punish and to make possible revelation, resurrection, prophecy and other miracles.

The most dramatic ideological battles between the two worldviews revolved around Maimonides' *Guide of the Perplexed.* Maimonideans, such as Shem Tov ibn Yosef Falaquera (c. 1225–1295), Yosef ibn Kaspi (1279–1340), and Moses of Narbonne (Mosheh Narboni, d. after 1360), upheld Maimonides' reconciliation of philosophy and faith and even defended the eternity of matter. In 1305 these controversies culminated in a ban by Shelomoh ben Avraham (c. 1235–c. 1310), rabbi of Barcelona, against the study of Greek philosophy by any Jews under twenty-five years of age. Anti-Maimonideans, like Avraham ben David (c. 1125–1198) of Posquières and Shelomoh of Montepellier (thirteenth century), attacked the *Guide.* Like the courtier physician Yehudah ibn Alfakhar (d. 1235) and the polymath Moses Nahmanides (Mosheh ben Naḥman), who defended Judaism at the disputation of Barcelona (1263), the anti-Maimonideans accepted biblical literalism, divine anthropomorphism, and miracles.

Stemming from the traditional Jewish worldview were the luxuriant developments in Jewish mysticism in Provence and Iberia. By the middle of the twelfth century, the study and practice of Qabbalah flourished in Provence. From this period comes *Sefer ha-bahir,* the earliest work, properly speaking, of qabbalistic literature. Appearing in southern France at the end of the century, *Sefer ha-bahir,* written in Hebrew, reveals recent Iberian influence but may be a composite work harking back to the geonic period. Its ideas are couched in short statements discussing or explaining biblical verses. The most eminent early practitioner of Qabbalah was Yitshaq, son of Avraham ben David, known as Isaac the Blind (d. about 1235), who inspired numerous followers in both Provence and Catalonia. The renowned qabbalistic circle bearing his influence developed in the northern Iberian town of Gerona; the sages of Gerona, dating from the beginning of the thirteenth century, include, among distinguished others, the great Nahmanides. An eminent disseminator of the qabbalistic thought of this period was Bahye ben Asher, a popular author whose commentary on the Pentateuch and whose *Kad ha-qemah,* an alphabetically organized work on faith and ethics, enjoyed wide circulation.

Due in no small measure to the prevalence of philosophical learning, Iberian Qabbalah possessed a philosophical orientation, an awareness of the Neoplatonists,

Aristotle, and, among earlier Iberian Jews, the writings of Ibn Gabirol, ha-Levi, Avraham ibn 'Ezra', and Maimonides. The philosophical bent is patent, for example, in the writings of Yitshaq ben Avraham ibn Latif (c. 1210–c. 1280), who follows Neoplatonism in his identification of God with the primoridal will of Aristotelianism in his concepts of form and matter. The more colorful qabbalist Avraham ben Shemu'el Abulafia (c. 1240–after 1291), who once tried to convert Pope Nicholas III to Judaism, conceived of both philosophy and Qabbalah as propaedeutics to the attainment of a "prophetic Qabbalah."

From this period also is the most important work of Qabbalah, the *Zohar,* composed in Aramaic with many Hebraisms and unusual foreign terms. The *Zohar* is a commentary on the weekly sections of the Torah (preponderantly on *Genesis* and *Exodus*), interrupted by a number of small connected treatises. Though attributed to the second-century sage Shim'on bar Yoh'ai, who appears as its chief teacher, the *Zohar* was actually compiled in the main by the Iberian Moses (Mosheh ben Shem Tov) de León (c. 1240–1305).

Rationalist and antirationalist philosophizing also continued, throughout the Middle Ages, apart from any overt disputation between the views. Hillel ben Shemu'el (d. 1295), an early Jewish philosopher in the Italian Peninsula, learned in Aristotelianism, Neoplatonism, and Christian Scholasticism, wrote a commentary on the twenty-six Aristotelian propositions in Maimonides' *Guide.* Subsequent Jewish philosophers shared Hillel ben Shemu'el's interest in the soul, and some in the fourteenth century, like Narboni, shared his interest in the related question of freedom of the will. Second only to Maimonides as an exponent of Aristotelianism was the philosopher, scientist, and biblical commentator Levi ben Gershom (Gersonides, 1288–1344), author of *Milhamot Adonais* (Wars of the Lord). On the other hand, in *Or Adonai* (Light of the Lord), Hasdai Crescas (d. 1410) presented a critique of Aristotle and offered positive attributes for God. Crescas's pupil Yosef Albo (fifteenth century), who represented Iberian Jewry in the disputations of Tortosa and San Mateo (1413–1414), attained considerable vogue with his *Sefer ha-'iggarim* (Book of Theological Dogmas).

Concern for the strengthening of tradition also informed authors of *responsa* (Heb., *teshuvot*), exemplarily Ibn Adret, who was also versed in Roman and Aragonese law, and Asher ben Yehi'el (known as the Ro'sh), (c. 1250–1327), a German Talmudist who became rabbi in Toledo in 1305. Asher's traditionalism also appears in his compilation of Jewish law, *Pisqei ha-Ro'sh* (Decisions of the Ro'sh), which follows Yitshaq ben Ya'aqov Alfasi's model and offers an alternative to the *Mishneh Torah,* and in Shemu'el Sardi's *Sefer ha-terumot,* (1225), the first comprehensive systematization of civil law following the order of the Talmud. Sardi in turn influenced the epoch's principal code, the *Arba'ah turim* (Four Columns), known simply as the *Tur,* written by Asher's son Ya'aqov (c. 1270–1343).

Jewish religious experience in this epoch is often reflected in great detail in its sermons, *responsa,* and ethical and other literature. These include the deftly crafted collection of Hebrew homilies *Malmad ha-talmidim* by Ya'aqov Anatoli of Provence (thirteenth century), a rabbi schooled in Plato, Aristotle, Maimonides, and Michael Scot (whom he met in Naples at the court of Emperor Frederick II); ethical works, like *Higgayon ha-nefesh ha-'atsuvah* (Meditation of the Sad Soul) by the Barcelonese Avraham bar Hiyya' (d. about 1136); works of social criticism, like the *Iggeret musar* (Epistle on Morality) composed in Portugal by Shelomoh Alami (c. 1370–1420); and even halakhic codes, like the *Tseidah la-derekh* (Provision for the Way) by Menaḥem ibn Zeraḥ of Navarre (c. 1310–1385). Similarly, *'Aqeidat Yitsḥaq* (Binding of Isaac), a compendium of one hundred and five consummately artistic sermons by Yitsḥaq Arama (1420–1499), reveals interest in philosophy, polemics, and history. Its many editions attest to its popularity. Prevailing religious customs, especially prayer and other synagogal activities, are also to be found in descriptions by travelers, beginning with the *Universal Guide* by Avraham ben Natan of Lunel (c. 1155–1215), which describes Iberian Jewry, and the *Sefer minhagim* (Book of Customs) by Asher ben Sha'ul of Lunel (early thirteenth century), an account of travels in Narbonne and Lunel. Such sources reveal increasing communal and regional deviations in liturgical practice within the two major rites—the Palestinian, dominant in Greece and Corfu (the Romaniot rite) and in Italy (the Roman, or Italian, rite) until subordinated by the Sefardic (Spanish-Portuguese) rite in the sixteenth century; and the Babylonian rite followed with distinctive nuances in Catalonia, Provence, and, except for an identical daily service, Aragon and Castile. Responding to this variety, *Sefer Abudarham,* written in 1340 by David Abudarham of Castile, comments on prayers and rituals and includes treatises on various subjects, like the Passover Haggadah, the *halakhah* regarding various benedictions, and the weekly Pentateuchal and Prophetic readings, as well as astronomical and calendrical tables. In addition to the Talmud, *responsa,* and the works of Avraham ben Nathan of Lunel and Asher ben Sha'ul, Abudarham cites much Ashkenazic, French, Provençal, and Iberian material that he was apparently the last author to consult.

The centuries of relative security for Jewish communities and good relations with the Christian rulers came to an end with persecutions and the expulsion of the Jews from nearly all of France (in 1306 and 1394) and Spain (in 1492) and the forced conversion of those in Portugal (in 1497). The synagogues, where not destroyed, were often converted into churches, including the two great sanctuaries of Toledo: the first, dating from around 1200, became Santa María la Blanca; the other, constructed around 1357 by the financier Shemu'el ha-Levi Abulafia, became Nuestra Señora del Tránsito, or simply El Tránsito.

Though officially proscribed, Judaism continued clandestinely among some of the New Christians, as Jewish converts to Christianity and, at least theoretically, all their descendants, were called. Isolated from authentic Jews (though some transient Jews were permitted on the peninsula) and Hebrew learning, the New Christian judaizers, often called Marranos, developed a distinctive Judaism out of some surviving rabbinic traditions and the Vulgate translation of the Hebrew Bible that was read in church and studied in seminaries. Traces of Marrano practice persist to this day among some Catholics of Spanish and Portuguese descent. [*See* Marranos.]   Subject to persecution for judaizing, many New Christians fled in the sixteenth century to three havens in southern Europe: southern France, where they could not live openly as Jews until the eighteenth century; the Ottoman empire, where they could not live as Christians; and the Italian states, where they could choose their identity. In Italy and the Ottoman empire, they found established Jewish communities, augmented by refugees from the expulsion of the Jews from Spain in 1492. At the end of the century, Amsterdam too became an important refuge.

RENAISSANCE AND EARLY MODERN ITALY

The Renaissance influence on Jewish culture and religion is divisible into three periods. The first, from the early fourteenth century to the mid-sixteenth, was one of considerable freedom and manifold interaction with non-Jewish intellectuals. The second, after the burning of the Talmud in 1553 and the creation by the city-states of the ghetto in 1555 and for at least a century thereafter, was characterized by chronic insecurity and sporadic oppression; in this period, varied Jewish creativity nevertheless continued. The third, from approximately 1650 to the middle of the nineteenth century, witnesses an increasing inwardness of Jewish life and thought.

In Italy the refugees from the Iberian Peninsula entered a native community proud of its ancient Italian roots and already augmented by Ashkenazi newcomers from northern Europe in the previous century. Italy became a religious microcosm of western European Jewish life, with each language group retaining its distinctive customs and synagogue rituals. By the middle of the sixteenth century Rome had nine synagogues, including separate congregations of French, Castilian, Catalonian, and Barcelonese Jews. The most notable of all the recent Sefardic immigrants was Isaac ben Judah Abravanel (1437–1508), ethicist, exegete, philosopher, historian, mystic, and diplomat and unsurpassed in his Jewish devotion. By example and philosophy, Abravanel sought to stimulate faith in Judaism and its future. In this he was joined by others notably the grande dame, the former New Christian Doña Gracia Mendès Nasi'. Perhaps her most dramatic effort in this regard was her support of the so-called Marrano press at Ferrara. Established by the former New Christian Yom Tov ben Levi Athias (also known as Jerónimo de Vargas), it was continued by his associate, Avraham Usque. Following Athias's plan, Usque between 1552 and 1555 published works of religious interest in Hebrew, like Menaḥem ben Zeraḥ's spiritual vade mecum; in Spanish, like the Ferrara Bible; and in Portuguese, like Samuel Usque's classic of Jewish historiography, Jewish apologetics, and Portuguese prose, the *Consolation for the Tribulations of Israel* (1552).

Jews played a significant role in the early capitalist economy of the various Italian states. Numerous Jewish savants were humanists at home in the classics and in the vernacular cultures. Exemplary were Eliyyahu Delmedigo (c. 1460–c. 1497), head of Padua's rabbinical academy and lecturer on philosophy to general audiences; Yehudah Moscato (c. 1530–c. 1593), rabbi at Mantua, whose knowledge of Platonism, Neoplatonism, Arabic philosophy, the sciences, astronomy, and rhetoric adorns his influential commentary on the *Kuzari;* Leone da Modena (1571–1648), rabbi in Venice, musician, polemicist, scholar, and author of works in Hebrew and Italian; 'Azaryah dei Rossi (c. 1511–c. 1578), an outstanding classicist and the era's greatest Hebraist, whose empirical investigations and utilization of non-Jewish sources revolutionized Jewish scholarship; Simone Luzzatto (1583–1663), Leone's rabbinical successor in Venice and author of a treatise in Italian pleading for Jewish rights, a work later translated into English by John Toland; and Mosheh Ḥayyim Luzzatto (1707–1747), who was steeped in classical, Italian, and Jewish culture and whose *Mesillat yesherim* (Path of the Upright) remains one of the most influential works in Judaism's ethical literature.

Renaissance humanism stimulated the fourteenth-century philosopher and translator Yehudah Romano to compare the prophet Isaiah to Cicero. It affected biblical commentaries, like those of 'Ovadyah Sforno (c. 1470–c. 1515) and the classical Mishnah commentary of 'Ovadyah ben Avraham yareh of Bertinoro (c. 1450–1515). It touched the Hebrew poetry of Devorah Ascarelli (c. 1600), Yesha'yah Bassani (d. 1739), and Bassani's son Yisra'el (d. 1790). It spurred translations of classics, like Delmedigo's of Ibn Rushd (Averroës) into Latin and that of *Ecclesiastes* into Italian by David de' Pomis (1525–1593), who also prepared a Hebrew-Latin-Italian lexicon. It led to efforts by Yehudah Romano to acquaint Jews with non-Jewish thought and to Delmedigo's defense of philosophical study in his *Beḥinat ha-da'at* (Examination of Religion; 1496). It fostered philosophy in biblical commentaries, like those of Eliyyahu, "the Philosopher," of Crete (fifteenth century), and, among others, the *Ets ha-da'at* (Tree of Knowledge) by Shimshon Marpurgo (1681–1740), rabbi, halakhist, and humanitarian physician. It linked Christian and Jewish savants in intellectual pursuits, with Christian humanists being influenced by Jewish scholars, like Cardinal Domenico Grimani by the grammarian Avraham Balmes (c. 1440–1523) and the famed Cardinal Egidio da Viterbo by the grammarian Eliyyahu ben Asher Levita (1469–1549), who lived in the cardinal's home for thirteen years. Other Christian humanists were influenced by Jewish qabbalists. Yehudah Romano was reported to have guided the king of Naples, Robert II of Anjou (r. 1309–1343), in his studies of the Bible in Hebrew.

Italian humanism provided models for Jewish belles lettres, as in the *Moḥbarot* (Notebooks) of 'Immanu'el ben Shelomoh of Rome (c. 1260–1328?) and *Miqdash me'aṭ* (The Small Sanctuary) by Mosheh of Rieti (1388–1460?), both at least in part inspired by Dante's *Com media*. Numerous Renaissance dialogues also show humanist influence, including David de' Pomis's *Discourse on Human Suffering and How to Escape It* in Italian; the Neoplatonic classic *Dialogues of Love* by Judah Abravanel (known as Leo Ebreo, c. 1460–after 1521); and Simone Luzzatto's *Socrates, or Concerning Human Reason* (1651). The Renaissance stimulated sixteenth-century apologetic histories by Samuel Usque, Yehudah ibn Verga *Shevet Yehudah* (Scepter of Yehudah; 1553), Yosef ha-Kohen *'Emeq ha-bakhah* (The Vale of Tears), and Gedalyah ibn Yaḥya *Shelshelet ha-qabbalah* (The Chain of Tradition). Though diversely oriented, the secular learning and the historical concerns of their time inform the works of these writers.

In addition to the poetry of the synagogue's liturgy, the Renaissance also inspired its architecture, which was especially distinguished in the Baroque period. Salomone Rossi (1570?–1630?), the most renowned of many Jewish court musicians, composed settings such as his *Ha-shirim asher li-Shelomoh* (Songs of Solomon; 1622/3) for sacred services; his polyphonic choral works show the influence of Palestrina and Gabrieli. The Renaissance also promoted the homiletical virtuosity of brilliant preachers Yehudah Moscato, 'Azaryah Picho (also known as Figo, 1579–1647), rabbi of Pisa, and Simone Luzzatto. Their sermons, along with ethical texts like *Degel ahavah* (Banner of Love) by Samuel Archivolti (1515–1611) or the *Path of the Upright* and a panoply of *responsa*, especially those of Me'ir ben Yisra'el Katzenellenbogen of Padua (1473–1565), provide insight into the life of the individual and the community—the divergences in belief and practice, the zeal for faith and quiet devotion on the one hand and the flaunting of wealth and flouting of morality on the other—and into a range of community issues, including the redemption of Jewish captives, integration of former New Christians, individual as against community rights, and the permissibility of a polyphonic chorale and a community theater, swaying during prayer, and playing ball or riding in a gondola on the Sabbath.

The conclusion of this era witnessed the publication of two towering works: *Yad Malakhi,* a systematic compilation of Talmudic methodology, codifiers, and laws, by Malakhi ha-Kohen (d. 1785/90) and *Paḥad Yitsḥaq,* the fullest and most renowned encyclopedia of *halakhah* ever composed, by Yitsḥaq Lampronti (d. 1756), a rabbi, physician, and educator who strongly advocated an education in the humanities as well as Torah.

MODERN ITALY

In Italy the way to Jewish emancipation was paved dramatically by two brief French occupations (1796–1798 and 1800–1815), and thereafter desultorily and differentially in the various Italian states. On the one hand, emancipation stimulated the modern study of Jewish tradition by such scholars as Graziadio Coen (1751–1834), pioneer in the study of the sources of Mishnaic Hebrew and especially Hebrew poetry; Isacco Samuele Reggio (1784–1855), translator into Italian of biblical books and the Mishnaic tractate *Avot* (Ethics of the Fathers), and Shemu'el David Luzzatto (1800–1865), a disciple of Moses Mendelssohn, philosopher, commentator on the Bible, translator of the liturgy into Italian, and staunch champion of traditional beliefs. Luzzatto served as the first rector of the modern, yet traditional, seminary, the Collegio Rabbinico Italiano, founded in Padua in 1829. Scientific journals appeared, like *Il Vessillo Israelitico,* founded in Turin 1874 as successor to the *Educatore Israelita,* and the strongly Zionist *Rassegna Mensile di Israel,* edited from 1922 to his death by Dante Lattes (1875–1965), distinguished biblical commentator, educator, and journalist.

On the other hand, as elsewhere, emancipation led to the dissolution of Jewish corporative life, the diminution of religious study and observance, and accelerated assimilation. The blandishments of new opportunities also contributed to the demographic and religious desiccation of many rural communities. The construction of beautiful urban synagogues did not stem the tide of apathy and defection. An impressive if limited revival of Jewish identification and education initiated by Samuel Hirsch Margulies (1858–1922), rabbi of Florence from 1890, and his disciples was curtailed by the Nazis.

From the Enlightenment on, the Italian synagogues have been at least nominally orthodox. The Reform movement from across the Alps, particularly Germany, made few inroads in the peninsula because of Italy's conservative Catholic environment and the suppleness of Italian Judaism, which permitted variation without prescribing change. Internal tendencies toward liberalism at least as strong as elsewhere hark back to the Renaissance and beyond and include the nineteenth-century figures Reggio, Samuel David Luzzatto, and Marco Mortara (1815–1894), who in 1866 proposed a convention of Italian rabbis to effect reforms in Jewish practices.

CONTEMPORARY JEWISH LIFE IN SOUTHERN EUROPE

After World War II, Jewish life returned to all of southern Europe. In Greece the reconstituted community of some ten thousand has experienced increasing religious apathy and intermarriage. Italy, with its thirty thousand Jews augmented by nearly as many refugees, experiences similar erosions. But it has also demonstrated a strong affirmation of Jewish life, especially in its larger communities like Rome and Milan. This affirmation may be seen in support for seminaries, like the Collegio Rabbinico Italiano, located in Rome since 1934 (though closed for part of the Fascist period), and the Samuel Hirsch Margulies Seminary in Turin; in the creation of umbrella organizations with religious dimensions, notably the Union of Italian Jewish communities; in the continuance of Jewish day schools, attended by some 60 percent of

Italian Jewish children; and in strong communal ties with the state of Israel. Among the dramatic chapters of Jewish religious life in modern Italy was the conversion to Judaism by most of the Apulian village of San Nicandro between 1930 and 1944, during the Fascist regime. Led by a winegrower named Donato Menduzio, the group displayed distinctive customs, including hymns utilizing the local dialect and local melodies. After Menduzio's death in 1948 many of these Jews moved to Israel.

Spain has witnessed the establishment of the first Jewish community since 1492. From the late nineteenth century on, Jews had been tolerated only as individuals. Many Jewish refugees had passed through Spain during World War II, and many abroad with Spanish citizenship had been protected by Spain. A statute promulgated in December 1966 guaranteed Jews equal rights with all other citizens, including the right of their own corporative institutions. Two years later, the Spanish government formally repealed its 475-year-old Edict of Expulsion. In 1985 Spain had some nine thousand Jews, over 80 percent Serfardic, a dozen synagogue communities, five synagogue buildings, and five active rabbis. Since 1940 Spain has evinced an intense interest in its Jewish heritage, as witnessed by the erection of statues to native sons, like that of Binyamin of Tudela (twelfth century), rabbi and world traveler, in his native city and that of Maimonides in Cordova, and by burgeoning scholarship, exemplified by the creation of various chairs in Judaica at universities, a Sefardic center in Toledo, the Arias Montano Institute of Jewish and Near Eastern Studies in Madrid and its organ, *Sefarad,* a distinguished quarterly in Judaica.

Portugal, too, had allowed Jews to settle by the beginning of the nineteenth century, but not until 1892 were they recognized as a community and permitted to hold religious services. Their numbers were small and by the beginning of World War II barely reached one thousand, of whom 650 were refugees. During the war, Portugal protected its Jewish nationals, aided Hungarian Jews, and initiated a liberal immigration policy. Since World War II, the Portuguese Jewish community has numbered approximately 650, with now two traditional synagogues and one rabbi.

After World War I, a military officer of New Christian descent, Artur Carlos de Barros Basto (1887–1961), inaugurated a revival of the Jewish identity among New Christian families when he became a Jew, built a synagogue at Oporto, organized a community, and established a journal to promote Judaism among the Marranos. (His efforts, though short-lived, attracted attention to the history of Iberian Jews and their manifold contributions to Western civilization.)

[*Many of the figures and topics mentioned herein are the subjects of independent entries. For further discussion of the literature and religious trends described here,* see Jewish Thought and Philosophy, *article on* Premodern Philosophy.]

BIBLIOGRAPHY

Adler, Israël. *La pratique musicale savante dans quelques communautes juives.* 2 vols. Paris, 1966.

Adler, Israël. *Hebrew Writings concerning Music, in Manuscripts and Printed Books.* Munich, 1975.

Ashtor, Eliyahu. *The Jews of Moslem Spain.* 3 vols. Translated by Aaron Klein and Jenny Machlowitz Klein. Philadelphia, 1973–1984.

Ashtor, Eliyahu. *Levant Trade in the Later Middle Ages.* Princeton, 1983.

Avni, Haim. *Spain, the Jews and Franco.* Translated by Emanuel Shimoni. Philadelphia, 1982.

Baer, Yitzhak. *A History of the Jews in Christian Spain*. 2 vols. Philadelphia, 1961–1966.

Dozy, Reinhart. *Spanish Islam*. Translated by Francis G. Stokes. London, 1913.

Hilberg, Raul. *The Destruction of the European Jews*. Chicago, 1961.

Marcus, Jacob R. *The Jew in the Medieval World: A Source Book, 315–1791*. Cincinnati, 1938.

Milano, Attilio. *Storia degli Ebrei italiani nel Levante*. Florence, 1949.

Milano, Attilio. *Storia degli Ebrei in Italia*. Turin, 1963.

Molho, Michael, and Joseph Nehama, eds. *In Memoriam: Hommage aux victimes juives des Nazis en Grèce*. 2d ed. 3 vols. Thessaloniki, 1973.

Netanyahu, Benzion. *Don Isaac Abravanel, Statesman and Philosopher*. Philadelphia, 1953.

Netanyahu, Benzion. *The Marranos of Spain from the Late Fourteenth to the Early Sixteenth Century*. New York, 1966.

Parkes, James. *The Conflict of the Church and the Synagogue* (1934). Reprint, New York, 1969.

Reitlinger, Gerald. *The Final Solution: The Attempt to Exterminate the Jews of Europe*. London, 1953.

Roth, Cecil. *The History of the Jews of Italy*. Philadelphia, 1946.

Roth, Cecil. *The Jews in the Renaissance*. Philadelphia, 1959.

Starr, Joshua. *The Jews in the Byzantine Empire, 641–1204*. Athens, 1939.

Usque, Samuel. *Consolation for the Tribulations of Israel*. Translated by Martin A. Cohen. Philadelphia, 1965.

12 JUDAISM IN NORTHERN AND EASTERN EUROPE TO 1500

IVAN G. MARCUS

Although Jews lived in the northern European provinces of the ancient Roman empire, long-lasting communal settlements began only in the tenth century, when Christian monarchs promoted the economic vitality of their domains by inviting Jewish merchants into the newly developing towns.

SETTLEMENT AND EARLY INSTITUTIONS

A pattern of early royal support followed by royal opposition and instability characterized Jewish political life first in western Europe and then later in the East. The earliest royal policy toward the Jews in northern Europe dates from Charlemagne and, especially, from his son, Louis the Pious, who issued three private charters *(privilegia)* to individual Jewish merchants in about 825. These texts indicate that Jews were among the international merchants doing business in the Carolingian empire and were granted protection of their lives, exemption from tolls, and guarantees of religious freedom. This Carolingian policy toward Jewish merchants was also pursued by subsequent rulers of the German empire, and it encouraged the Jewish immigration that became a factor in the demographic and urban expansion of early medieval Europe.

The first communities developed gradually in the Rhineland towns, where various family groups settled and intermarried. Of special significance were the Qalonimos family from Lucca, Italy; the descendants of Abun, a rabbi from Le Mans in northern France; and other families from France, which became the nucleus of the Mainz Jewish elite. Cut off from the Jewish political and religious authorities in Palestine and Babylonia, as well as Spain, the leaders of the Mainz community had considerable room to improvise and experiment with new patterns of autonomous local governance.

From the beginning, communal leadership assumed two overlapping but distinct forms. On the one hand, legal decisions were rendered by religious judges or rabbis who acquired expertise in the Talmud. On the other hand, communal control over nonlegal public affairs devolved upon the "elders," whose authority derived from their age, wealth, family lineage, and other personal qualities. They maintained pub-

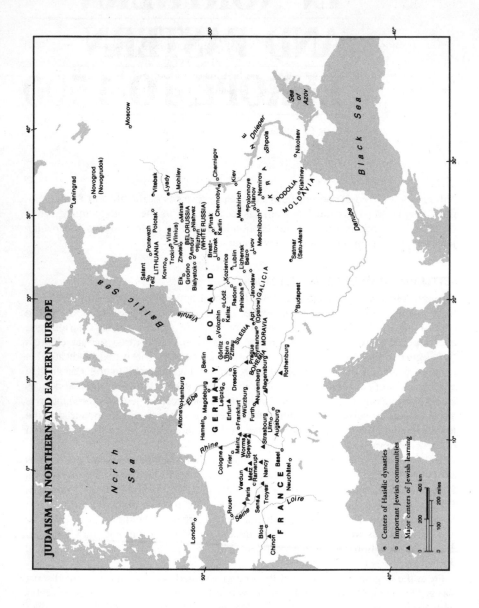

JUDAISM IN NORTHERN AND EASTERN EUROPE

● Centers of Hasidic dynasties
○ Important Jewish communities
▲ Major centers of Jewish learning

0   200   400 km
0   100   200 miles

lic order, collected taxes for the Christian authorities and for support of Jewish social services, and were the liaison between the community and the gentile rulers.

In the period of first settlement the rabbis were merchants, like the rest of the community, and were among the elders who decided public policy. As communities grew in size and complexity, communal roles became more differentiated. A paid rabbinate gradually developed only in the thirteenth century.

The location of the early northern Jewish communities on a frontier prompted religious leaders and elders alike to be innovative. We see this in the legal decisions of Gershom ben Yehudah (d. 1028), the first major rabbinical figure in Mainz. Gershom functioned as an appeals judge on matters of Jewish law, and his legal opinions rarely mention the decisions and precedents of the Babylonian geonim. Rather, he answered questions by interpreting Talmudic or even biblical passages, thereby imitating rather than following the geonim. His ordinances against polygyny and a woman's involuntary divorce became binding precedents.

We also find signs of improvisation in the actions of the early community board (*qahal*) and communal leaders (*parnasim*) contemporary with Gershom, who undertook to maintain law and order, supervise the weights and measures in the market, and provide for the indigent. The institution of *ma'arufyah*, an individual Jewish merchant's trade monopoly with a specific Christian client, was widespread in the Rhineland, and boards adopted measures to protect it. As the Jewish population grew in the eleventh century, local community boards placed a ban on new settlement (*herem ha-yishuv*) to prevent excessive economic competition.

By the middle of the eleventh century, questions about the limits of local autonomy had arisen in newer areas of settlement, like the duchy of Champagne. Yehudah ha-Kohen, Gershom's successor, decided that in the area of general public welfare and security each local Jewish community was completely autonomous, but if a community violated religious law, another community or outside religious authority could hold it accountable.

An additional sign of new communal development occurred in 1084, when some of the Mainz Jews moved to Speyer, where they were welcomed by Bishop Rüdiger, who issued them a formal charter. Modeled on the early Carolingian *privilegia*, this charter extended to the new community guarantees of life, religious protection, and exemption from tolls. Confirmed by the German emperor Henry IV in 1090, this continued the Carolingian policy of royal or imperial legal protection of European Jews until the late thirteenth century. The patterns of royal protection and local Jewish self-rule that had first developed in the German towns became the model for local Jewish communities in the regions of royal France, England, and central Europe.

DEVELOPMENTS IN THE HIGH MIDDLE AGES

The late eleventh and twelfth centuries were a time of social and cultural consolidation in northern Europe. New religious orders were founded; the popes renewed the claims of canon law to establish the primacy of the church over the empire in spiritual and even temporal affairs; and in Paris the university attracted students who eagerly came from all over Europe to sit at the feet of popular scholars like Peter Abelard. It is possible that the Christian Schoolmen were in part motivated to restate Christian doctrine in a clear and logically consistent way because Jews were raising doubts about Christianity in the minds of Christian townsmen. In return, an awareness of Christian religious innovation and ferment stimulated reappraisals of Judaism.

The First Crusade precipitated the first major crisis of Jewish cultural identity in northern Europe. Urban II's call for an armed pilgrimage to Jerusalem in the spring of 1095 led local German peasants and petty knights on their way to the Holy Land to riot in the towns of Mainz, Worms, Cologne, and Speyer. According to the Latin and Hebrew chronicles that recount what happened on this Peasants' Crusade, just before and during the Jewish holiday of Shavu'ot in the spring of 1096, the righteous Jews of Mainz and Worms ritually slaughtered their families and themselves in order to prevent the Christian rioters from forcibly baptizing or killing them. The victims included leaders of the rabbinical elites of Mainz and Worms as well as hundreds of innocent men, women, and children.

Many Jews escaped or were subjected to baptism by force, but the survivors' guilt only heightened the loss of the saintly martyrs, whose memory now cast a shadow over the following generations of German Jews. Among the liturgical memorials they instituted in Europe was the earlier geonic prohibition of celebrating Jewish weddings between Passover and Shavu'ot, still observed as an annual period of collective mourning. New prayers were written to recall the righteousness of the slain and to invoke God's vengeance on the guilty Christians. Each spring the martyrs' names were recited in the Rhenish synagogues in order to keep alive the memory of the sacrificed dead and to invoke their merit as a form of vicarious atonement for the living.

Two other important northern Jewish ideals emerged in the twelfth century; the first of these was the *hasid,* or pietist. By the second half of the twelfth century, an ascetic, pietistic movement emerged in Speyer, the one Jewish community that did not suffer major losses in 1096. It was led by descendants of the branch of the Qalonimos family that survived the riots of 1096. The pietists placed special emphasis not only on punctilious observance of Jewish law but also on certain spiritual exercises including concentrated prayer, physical self-denial, and the mystical and magical manipulations of Hebrew letter combinations that represent the secret names of God. One of the mottos of Shemu'el ben Qalonimos the Elder (fl. mid-twelfth century) is "be resourceful in the fear of God," a Talmudic dictum (B.T., *Ber.* 17a) that he reinterpreted to mean that the pietist, or truly God-fearing Jew, must search scripture resourcefully in order to infer additional prohibitions and higher degrees of self-discipline.

In *Sefer hasidim* (Book of the Pietists), written by Shemu'el's son Yehudah the Pietist (d. 1217), we find a sectarian fellowship of pietists, led by their own sages, who are constantly challenged and tested by their inner passions and by the harmful presence of nonpietistic Jews, whom the author calls "the wicked." Among Yehudah's innovations is the requirement that pietists who sin should confess their sins to a sage and receive penances proportional to the sinful act and to the pleasure experienced while sinning. [*For further discussion of the pietists, see* Ashkenazic Hasidism.]

This new Jewish pietistic ideal, incorporating ancient Jewish mystical and ascetic practices, began as a regimen for religious virtuosos but became a commonplace of European Jewish spirituality after the late twelfth century and continued to define the dominant style of Jewish piety in eastern Europe even after it was challenged by the eighteenth-century revival movement of Hasidism.

The second new mode of Jewish spirituality that developed in the twelfth century in northern France was the Talmud scholar who excelled in intellectual prowess by discovering new interpretations of difficult passages. At the very time that Christian Schoolmen were reconciling the logical inconsistencies in authoritative theological texts and scholars of canon and Roman law were resolving contradictions by making new distinctions, rabbinical scholars began to study systematically the entire Talmudic corpus and apply canons of logical consistency to it. This activity developed in northern France and not in the Rhineland for two reasons. On the negative side, the older academies of Mainz and Worms suffered a loss of leadership in the riots of 1096. On the positive side, the newer schools in Champagne were able to build on the foundations in Hebrew Bible and Talmud interpretation established by the late-eleventh-century rabbinic master Rashi (Shelomoh ben Yitshaq, 1042–1105).

In the duchy of Champagne, another Jewish frontier, the master of Troyes taught generations of students who were geographically and culturally removed from the living oral culture of rabbinic studies in Mainz and Worms. For them Rashi produced the first comprehensive running commentary on almost the entire Hebrew Bible and the Babylonian Talmud, the canon of the Ashkenazic curriculum. Because of his extraordinary sensitivity to the biblical usage of language and his knowledge of the Talmudic corpus, he succeeded in providing the one gloss to both the Hebrew Bible and the Babylonian Talmud that has remained standard for all students of those texts to this day.

The next generation's scholars, who glossed Rashi's commentary (ba'alei ha-tosafot), introduced a synoptic method of dialectical study designed to discover and resolve potential contradictions among different parts of the Talmud and between the Talmud and Jewish life in Christian Europe. [See Tosafot.] The shift from the piecemeal to the synoptic study of the Talmud resulted in an expansion of the scope and detail of Jewish law. The new distinctions that resolved contradictions between divergent traditions added conceptual subtlety to categories of law that had been created for a Mediterranean society. Adjustments were also made to accommodate the Talmudic traditions, a product of ancient pagan and medieval Muslim societies, to the actual practices of the Jews living in Latin Christendom.

The Judaism that resulted from these encounters with Christian Europe in the twelfth century was more complex than the relatively homogeneous religious culture of the eleventh. The righteous self-image, the reverence of the dead martyrs, German Hasidism, and the scholasticism of the tosafists were part of a twelfth-century transformation of classical Judaism into a "traditional" Ashkenazic Judaism. Paralleling these developments were the creative philosophical synthesis of Moses Maimonides (d. 1204) in Egypt and the writing down for the first time of qabbalistic mystical traditions in southern France. [See Qabbalah.]

EXPULSION AND RESETTLEMENT IN THE LATER MIDDLE AGES

The pattern of royal support in return for Jewish economic usefulness appears in England in the twelfth century. Henry I (r. 1100–1135) issued a charter, no longer extant, similar to the continental ones, offering the Jews protection of life and toll exemptions backed by royal justice. Henry II (r. 1154–1189) extended Jewish privileges to include self-government under Jewish law. By this time, sizable Jewish communities existed not only in London but also in Norwich, Lincoln, and Oxford.

In addition to obtaining funds on demand from the community, the English kings turned to especially wealthy Jews, such as Aharon of Lincoln, for major loans. When Aharon died, in 1185, he had outstanding loans of fifteen thousand pounds, three quarters of the annual receipts of the royal exchequer. To protect the safety of these financial records, Jewish and Christian officials were appointed to see to it that duplicate copies of loans were drawn up and deposited in chests *(archae)*. By 1200 the office of exchequer of the Jews was filled entirely by Christians, called the justices of the Jews. Another centralized official of the end of the twelfth century was the *presbyter Judaeorum,* not a chief rabbi but a wealthy Jew appointed by the king to serve as the liaison between the court and the Jewish community.

Jewish money lending at immoderate interest, or usury, became a major factor in the decline of the Jewish communities in England and France in the thirteenth century. Although papal policy condoned Jewish lending at moderate rates of interest, canon lawyers opposed it absolutely, and in the late thirteenth century the English and French kings implemented policies based on the stricter position. These measures against usury were neither economically nor politically motivated; rather, they were successful royal efforts at spiritual reform undertaken at a time of waning papal authority.

In royal France, money lending with interest was made illegal in 1230. To support his crusade, Louis IX (r. 1226–1270) confiscated Jewish loans, as provided by the Council of Lyon (1245), expelled only Jewish usurers from France in 1248/9, and confiscated their property. In England, Edward I (r. 1272–1307) issued his Statute on the Jews (1275), which outlawed Jewish lending completely, and in 1290 the Jews were expelled from his kingdom. Philip the Fair (r. 1285–1314) expelled the Jews of royal France in 1306.

Whereas royal policy toward the Jews shifted from support in the period of settlement to antagonism in the late thirteenth century, papal policy remained relatively constant and supportive. But when heretical movements posed a threat to the church itself, measures adopted to fight heresy sometimes were directed against the Jewish infidel as well. Thus papal approval of the new urban reforming orders of the Franciscans and, especially, the Dominicans as disciplinary arms of the church in the early thirteenth century created a source of new pressure against Jewish distinctiveness. Individual friars, sometimes zealous apostates from Judaism, actively sought to persuade Jews to convert.

At the same time that the Jewish communities were eliminated in England and royal France in the late thirteenth and fourteenth centuries, organized Jewish life in the north shifted increasingly eastward to the politically fragmented German empire, the central European territories of Bohemia, Moravia, and Hungary, and Poland and Lithuania. The thirteenth and early fourteenth centuries were a time of continuous demographic expansion in Europe, and the Jewish communities in central and eastern Europe were augmented by natural increase and new immigration from the West.

The major turning point for central European Jewry was the Black Death of 1349, a trauma that reduced the population of some areas of Europe by as much as 50 percent. Unable to explain a catastrophe of such magnitude, the popular mind personalized the agents of destruction by blaming the Jews for poisoning the wells of Europe. Aside from being subject now to unpredictable waves of violence, whole Jewish communities were routinely expelled. The theme of death began to play an increased liturgical role in the religious sensibilities of Ashkenazic Judaism. In particular, the annual anniversary of a parent's death (Yi., *yahrzeit*) is first attested at the end of the fourteenth century. The regular recitation by mourners of the Qaddish prayer also seems to have begun around the fourteenth century, in this period of increased Jewish martyrdom and random violence.

As a gradual demographic and economic recovery slowly began, Jews were readmitted for specified periods into towns of early settlement, like Speyer, and into newer Jewish communities in Austria and Bohemia. The decline of imperial authority over and protection of the Jews is reflected in the growing influence of the Christian burghers, who reserved the right to expel "their" Jews at will. The elimination of effective royal protection added to the Jewish communities' increased political vulnerability in the later Middle Ages in the West.

In the late fourteenth and fifteenth centuries, Jewish legal authorities generally lost prestige and control in their communities. No intercommunal councils were established in the German empire after 1350, and local rabbis complained that the wealthy members of the community ignored them. To be sure, masters like Mosheh Mintz and Yisra'el Isserlein of Austria continued in the fifteenth century to exert their authority as great sages of the age, as had Gershom in the late tenth, but the influence of local rabbis declined after 1350.

Politically the proliferation of independent principalities and cities in the German empire constituted a safety valve for the Jews there. Whenever residents of one particular community were expelled, they could find refuge in another until the edict was rescinded. But as economic instability reduced the demand for Jewish money lending in the towns, some Jews began to settle in villages and on rural estates. Gradually they entered new occupations as agricultural merchants and middlemen. The decline in economic opportunities in the empire also led many Jews to join the eastward emigration of German Christian burghers attracted by new opportunities in Poland and Lithuania, still another frontier.

Although Jews had been settling gradually in the duchies of Poland and Lithuania for some time, official recognition of their communities appeared only in the thirteenth century. In 1264, Prince Bolesław granted the Jews of Great Poland a charter modeled on those issued by Frederick II, duke of Austria, in 1244; Béla IV, king of Hungary, in 1251; and Otakar II, king of Bohemia and Moravia, in 1254. Unlike the Carolingian-type charters issued to Jewish merchants from the ninth through twelfth centuries, these were designed for Jews whose primary occupation was money lending. But like the earlier ones, the Polish charters provided for Jewish self-government and royal protection. In 1364, Casimir III (r. 1133–1170) issued a confirmation of these regional charters that was valid in the unified kingdom of Poland. Some Jews served the kings or dukes as money lenders and bankers; others managed estates forfeited to them for bad debts, lived in towns that the nobles founded, or farmed tolls. Jews were also prominent in the export trade of agricultural products to the German empire and the Crimea.

The Jews who migrated to Poland from Germany, Austria, and Bohemia brought along their familiar forms of communal government. The frontier model applies to Poland as it had before to the first settlements in western Europe, but with one important difference. The eastern immigrants could rely on support and spiritual guidance from their former homeland in the German empire.

The arrival of Ya'aqov Polak in Cracow, where he opened his innovative Talmudic academy, marks the beginning of advanced Jewish religious study in Poland and with it the first condition for cultural independence from the West. In 1503, Alexander I (r. 1501–1506) appointed him rabbi of Jewry there. Symbolically, a new era of centralized Jewish self-government and cultural ferment was about to begin.

[*Major developments in European Judaism of this period are discussed further in* Halakhah; Rabbinate; Polemics, *article on* Jewish-Christian Polemics; *and* Jewish Thought and Philosophy, *article on* Premodern Philosophy. *See also the biographies of the major historical figures mentioned herein.*]

BIBLIOGRAPHY

Detailed critical discussions of the rich bibliography on this period can be found in my "The Jews in Western Europe: Fourth to Sixteenth Century" and Kenneth R. Stow's "The Church and the Jews: From St. Paul to Paul IV," both in *Bibliographical Essays in Medieval Jewish Studies* (New York, 1976).

Despite its tendency to emphasize Jewish persecution in the Diaspora, parts of chapters 25–41 in *A History of the Jewish People,* edited by H. H. Ben-Sasson (Cambridge, Mass., 1969), contain important discussions of medieval Jewish communal life and also refer to many of the primary sources. On the Jewish communities of England, one still must turn to Cecil Roth's *A History of the Jews in England,* 3d ed. (Oxford, 1964), chaps. 1–5, and the more solid study by H. G. Richardson, *The English Jewry under Angevin Kings* (London, 1960). On northern France, Louis Rabinowitz's *The Social Life of the Jews of Northern France in the Twelfth to Fourteenth Centuries,* 2d ed. (New York, 1972), and Robert Chazan's *Medieval Jewry in Northern France* (Baltimore, 1973) should be supplemented by the pertinent studies of Gavin Langmuir, such as "'Judei Nostri' and the Beginnings of Capetian Legislation," *Traditio* 19 (1963): 183–244, and William Chester Jordan, such as "Jews on Top," *Journal of Jewish Studies* 29 (Spring 1978): 39–56. A synthetic scholarly treatment of German Jewry still does not exist but readers may consult with profit Guido Kisch's *The Jews in Medieval Germany,* 2d ed. (New York, 1970). Important trends in the early years of the European Jewish community are discussed by Avraham Grossman in "On 'The Early Sages of Ashkenaz'," *Immanuel* 15 (Winter 1982–1983): 73–81, a summary of his book *Hakhmei Ashkenaz ha-ri'shonim* (Jerusalem, 1981).

The history and institutions of the medieval Jewish community are treated in depth in Salo W. Baron's *The Jewish Community,* 3 vols. (1942; reprint, Westport, Conn., 1972), which is out of date in some areas. On the major intellectual and religious trends discussed above, see Haym Soloveitchik's "Three Themes in the *Sefer Hasidim,*" *AJS Review* 1 (1976): 311–357, especially on the influence of the Tosafists, and my book *Piety and Society: The Jewish Pietists of Medieval Germany* (Leiden, 1981) on German (Ashkenazic) Hasidism.

Two important studies on the deterioration of Jewish life in the thirteenth century are Kenneth R. Stow's "Papal and Royal Attitudes toward Jewish Lending in the Thirteenth Century," *AJS Review* 6 (1981): 161–184, and Jeremy Cohen's *The Friars and the Jews* (Ithaca, N.Y., 1982).

For Jewish life in central Europe during the late Middle Ages, see Shlomo Eidelberg's *Jewish Life in Austria in the Fifteenth Century* (Philadelphia, 1962) and Eric Zimmer's *Harmony and Discord* (New York, 1970). A basic work on eastern European Jewry that deals with the early period is Bernard D. Weinryb's *The Jews of Poland* (Philadelphia, 1972).

13 JUDAISM IN NORTHERN AND EASTERN EUROPE SINCE 1500

Steven J. Zipperstein

As a result of a series of Jewish expulsions and of Poland's increasing economic attractiveness, in the sixteenth-century Ashkenazic world Poland was widely recognized as the most promising of the European communities.

POLAND AND LITHUANIA

The expulsion of Jews from numerous German cities and secular principalities and from much of Bohemia and Moravia, coupled with the final division of Hungary (previously relatively hospitable to Jews) into Habsburg, Ottoman, and Transylvanian sections, encouraged Jews to look eastward. Poland's rapid commercial expansion, the relative weakness until the late sixteenth century of its craft and trade guilds, and the religious toleration that characterized crown policy reinforced these migratory trends. Jewish adjustment to the new surroundings was eased because of German influences in the cities, which (despite the rapid polonization of the German immigrants) may have encouraged the retention by Jews of Yiddish. Greater occupational diversity was possible here than in Germany. Most Polish Jews worked in domestic trade, moneylending, and artisanry but some Jews also captured important roles in the trade between Constantinople and western and central Europe and in the export of Polish textiles, grains, and cattle. Others acquired the leases over minting and other crucial fiscal and administrative functions.

The increasing impact and militancy of the Roman Catholic church in the wake of the Counter-Reformation and the rising antagonism of burghers toward Jews led to the partial expulsion of Jews from about fifty Polish cities by the end of the sixteenth century. Rarely were they completely barred; most often they were forced to move to suburban enclaves or to the *jurydyki* within the municipal boundaries but under the jurisdiction of the nobility. Jews continued to live in the same neighborhoods with Catholics in the cities where they were freely permitted to reside. However, the introduction of clauses permitting *non tolerandis Judaeis* and the effective unification of Poland and Lithuania with the Union of Lublin in 1569 encouraged Jewish migration to the southeastern Ukrainian expanses of Lithuania.

The *pacta conventa* of 1573, which confirmed the gentry's accumulation of considerable power at the expense of the crown, cemented close relations between the upper *szlachta* ("the magnates") and the Jews. The magnates frequently favored Jews as their commercial agents and lessees. Commerce, artisanry, and, in the southeastern regions, leaseholding (often tied to trade in agricultural goods) became the most common Jewish occupations. By the middle of the seventeenth century—when the Jewish community of Poland and Lithuania numbered, according to varying estimates, somewhere between 250,000 and 450,000—nearly 40 percent of the Jews lived, according to Samuel Ettinger, in the Ukrainian area.

Jewish participation in the Polish nobility's colonization of the Ukraine involved Jews in a system of pledges where Jewish lenders received a part of the income from estates pending the repayment of loans. What evolved was a more direct system of leaseholding, called the *arenda,* in which Jews leased agricultural properties from the nobility, generally for a period of three years, at a designated price. Profits would be extracted from taxes and fees on the local peasantry. The acquisition of a lease frequently constituted the beginning of a new Jewish community, since lessees would encourage other Jews to settle with them to run inns, flour mills, and so forth. Poland's rapidly growing population required ever-increasing supplies of agricultural and meat products, and the colonization of the Ukraine—in which Jews played an important and visible role—ensured a steady supply to domestic (and foreign) markets.

Jewish Communal Autonomy in Poland. A highly ramified system of Polish-Jewish autonomy with a centralized consultative council was created as Jews settled in Poland in large numbers. It was the product of several factors, including the Jewish community's wide geographic dispersion, the example of Jewish communal institutions in Bohemia and Moravia, pressures from the crown for a centralized Jewish leadership, and the diminishing power of the king, which motivated many sectors of Polish society to claim a measure of self-government. On the bottom tier of Jewry's system were the *qehalim,* or Jewish communal councils, which functioned alongside and were structured similar to the municipal councils of Polish cities. Above them were the district councils composed of representatives from the *qehalim.* At the uppermost tier were the super-councils, which met, beginning in 1569 and perhaps even earlier, at the fairs of Lublin and less frequently at Jaroslaw. Representatives from all parts of Poland and Lithuania participated in these meetings of the Council of the Lands of Poland (until a separate Lithuanian council was established, for fiscal reasons, in 1623), where *taqqanot* ("regulations") were issued, individual and communal grievances were aired, and protests against *qehalim* were reviewed. The Council deliberated on halakhic matters and, perhaps most important, intervened on behalf of the community before the authorities. From the vantage point of the state, the Polish Council was a tax-farming body but even the state recognized, at least tacitly, the Council's more extensive functions.

Talmudic Study in Poland and Lithuania. At the same time, the challenge posed by the distinguished Talmudist Mosheh Isserles of Cracow (1520–1572) in numerous works, particularly his *Darkhei Mosheh* to the Sefardic codification of Jewish law, the *Beit Yosef* of Yosef Karo, consolidated Poland's standing as the preeminent center of Ashkenazic learning. Isserles promoted the legitimacy of Polish-Jewish customs along with a rationalist-mystical understanding of *mitsvot*. The rich rabbinical literature of the period—which, in addition to Isserles, was represented by Shelomoh Luria, Yom Tov Lippman Heller, and many other Talmudic masters—was efficiently disseminated by the rapid expansion of printing in the sixteenth century.

Pilpul, a casuistic method based, in Poland, on the application of principles of logical differentiation to reconcile apparent Talmudic contradictions, was the focus of much of the *yeshivah* curriculum. This method was increasingly criticized beginning in the fifteenth century for its alleged obfuscation of the plain meaning of the texts. But it only declined in importance and was supplanted by an alternative pedagogical system in the early nineteenth century. Polish Jewry's wealth helped promote the spread of *yeshivah* study, but Polish-Jewish moralists, preeminently the late-sixteenth-century preacher Efrayim Luntshitz, argued that wealth was a certain sign of corruption and hypocrisy. By the seventeenth century the study of Torah was widely disseminated in Poland and Lithuania—though the Ukraine still provided fewer opportunities for serious study than more settled regions of eastern Europe. [*See* Yeshivah.]

The Khmel'nitskii Uprising. Religious, economic, and ethnic tensions in the Ukraine erupted in 1648, and for the next twelve years the Polish state was faced with a series of Cossack uprisings (initially with Tartar support) and with invasions from Sweden and Muscovy. The Cossacks, led by Bogdan Khmel'nitskii, massacred rural and urban Jewish communities on both sides of the Dnieper river. Hatred of Jews—which had little influence in sparking the Deluge (as both Polish and Jewish accounts refer to it)—resulted nonetheless in the killing of large numbers of Ukrainian Jews and in the evacuation of nearly all the remainder. The Jews of Ukraine quickly rebuilt their communities after the uprising was put down, but it left its mark on the increasingly deleterious fiscal standing of the *qehalim* and the councils.

MOVEMENT WESTWARD

A westward trend in Jewish migratory patterns was now apparent. In particular, Jews from areas of Poland devastated by the Swedish invasion moved in large numbers to Silesia, Moravia, and elsewhere in central Europe. (To be sure, Germany had retained Jewish communities in the intervening period, despite the widespread expulsions, particularly in areas under imperial and ecclesiastical protection and in the central and southern parts of the Holy Roman Empire.) Small numbers of Polish Jews also found their way in this period to Amsterdam and London. Some joined the growing ranks of the central European *Betteljuden* or *Schnorrjuden* (Jewish beggars), but most were absorbed, if only marginally, into the economic life of the Empire, which offered greater opportunities for Jews after the Thirty Years' War.

The skill of Jewish agents and contractors during the war and the rise of absolutist and mercantilist tendencies in government policy helped improve the economic and even the social standing of German Jewry. Jews moved into new localities (especially noteworthy were the Sefardic settlement in Hamburg and the Ashkenazic enclave in suburban Altona) and, with the support of rulers, were permitted to participate in an increasingly wide range of occupations, particularly commerce. German princes, concerned about competition from Atlantic ports better able to trade with the New World, saw wealthy Jews as useful commercial allies. Central European armies had benefited from Jewish contacts with Poland during the Thirty Years' War, and the experience (and wealth) gained by some Jews in this period helped contribute to the eventual emergence of court Jews who served local princes.

Humanist appreciation for Hebrew and the gradual laicization of European culture that accompanied the appearance of humanism in the fifteenth and sixteenth centuries set the stage for some cultural collaboration between Jews and Christians. In the Ashkenazic world, the influence of humanist trends was most clearly reflected in a moderation of anti-Jewish sentiment in certain small but influential intellectual circles. In Johannes Reuchlin's (1455–1522) defense of the Jews against the anti-Talmudic charges of Johannes Pfefferkorn, for instance, he referred to Jews and Christians as "fellow citizens of the same Roman Empire [who] live on the basis of the same law of citizenship and internal peace." The religious wars, which culminated in treaties which acknowledged that religious toleration—at least toward other Christians—was essential if only to save Europe from ceaseless strife, led to arguments for tolerance. More important in this regard, however, were the Protestant sects, most of them marginal, which began to question the connection between religious truth and political rule and showed an often intense interest in the biblical constitution and an attachment to the people and language of the Bible. Such trends were most apparent in Cromwellian England, where the impact of the Judaizers, the growing appreciation for Hebrew, the spread of millenarianist sentiment, and the renewed search for the Ten Lost Tribes with the discovery of the New World created a suitable cultural climate for a receptiveness to Menasseh ben Israel's mission to promote Jewish readmission to England.

Around the time of the Whitehall conference of 1655, which considered the readmission of Jews to England but left the matter undecided, small numbers of New Christians as well as Ashkenazic Jews settled in England, mostly in London. This small community came from Amsterdam, where an increasingly sizable and economically prominent Jewish community had lived since the unification of the northern provinces of the Netherlands and their declaration that the new state would be free from religious persecution.

Within the Ashkenazic sphere, Jewish thought remained largely indifferent to indications (however uneven and contradictory) of changes in Christian attitudes toward Jews. Indeed, a renewed sense of cultural segregation, as Jacob Katz (1961) has characterized it, was apparent in the sixteenth and seventeenth centuries, as reflected in a complete lack of Jewish interest in anti-Christian polemics and in the formation of a set of Jewish attitudes toward non-Jews that saw differences between the two as inherent rather than doctrinal. This case was argued most coherently by Yehudah Löw ben Betsal'el (c. 1525–1609). Yet the same period saw the promulgation of important halakhic decisions that permitted Jews to trade in gentile wine and even in rosaries (in contrast to earlier rabbinic prohibitions against such trade) on the grounds that the Talmudic prohibitions against trade with idol worshipers were not relevant to Christians, who, at least for practical purposes, did not fall under this category.

A stratum of well-placed Jews had, since the religious wars, played a significant role in the centralizing administrations of the absolutist German states. Jewish moneylenders, minters, and agents were selected to perform important administrative, fiscal, and even diplomatic functions because their loyalty to the princes was unaffected by guild attachments or local enmities. Close links were forged between Polish-Jewish agricultural exporters and wealthy Jewish importers in Leipzig, Frankfurt, and Hamburg. Court Jews, as some of these magnates were called, emerged as a group relatively free from Jewish communal and rabbinical control and with independent access to the gentile authorities.

The wealth of the court Jews, their relatively easy access to the Christian elite, and the example of the acculturated Sefardim of Hamburg and elsewhere in central and western Europe encouraged some Ashkenazim to imitate Sefardic and even non-Jewish social patterns. In certain well-to-do German-Jewish circles in the early eighteenth century, dance lessons, the study of French, and even the cutting of beards was common. In the same circles, Polish Jews were frequently characterized as superstitious and culturally inferior.

However, until the late eighteenth century and the spread of the Enlightenment and emancipatory movements, distinctions between German and Polish Jews remained fluid. This essential fluidity was reflected, for instance, in the careers of Ya'aqov Emden and Yonatan Eibeschutz, the eminent rabbinic figures at the center of the most vociferous Jewish polemical battle of the eighteenth century, which spanned the major Jewish communities of eastern and central Europe. Cultural unity was also apparent in the response of Ashkenazic Jewry in the 1660s to the news of Shabbetai Tsevi, whose claim to be the Messiah was received with the greatest enthusiasm by Sefardim but who was supported, according to Gershom Scholem, by most of European Jewry. [*See* Shabbetai Tsevi.]

Shabbetai Tsevi's conversion to Islam in 1666 led to the disintegration of the movement and to its rebirth, on a much smaller scale, as a secret network of sects. In Podolia, where the Frankist movement arose out of this Shabbatean network in the second half of the eighteenth century, it attracted the support of only small numbers of Jews, and its leader, Ya'aqov Frank (1726–1791), along with about six hundred followers, eventually converted under some duress to Catholicism. The teachings of Ya'aqov Frank, which combined an eclectic reliance on Qabbalah and an intense fascination with worldly power, had a limited impact outside Poland when Frank moved to Brno, Offenbach, and elsewhere in central Europe in the last years of his life. The sect served as a syncretistic pathway for some poor as well as rich Jews to a less insular, larger world.

HASIDISM

In contrast to Frankism, the Hasidic movement, which also arose in Podolia, gradually spread beyond the Ukraine after the death of its founder Yisra'el ben Eli'ezer (1700–1760), known as the Besht, and won widespread support in Poland, Belorussia, and, to a more limited extent, Lithuania. Completely devoid of the Christological tendencies that would attract some acculturated Jews to Frankism, Hasidism embraced qabbalistic concepts and built on Jewish spiritual yearnings stirred by the heretical mystical movements. At the same time, it effectively neutralized the potentially subversive elements of Lurianic Qabbalah.

The concept of *devequt* (cleaving to God), for instance, was shorn by Hasidism of its cosmic and elitist features and placed within a mundane framework. Hasidism promoted a strategy whereby Jews might focus on the prosaic and even the patently

profane in order to transform and elevate them. Cosmic elements in Lurianic Qabbalah were transformed into individualized landmarks in the psychology of faith and
repentance.

Hasidism's moderation helped it eventually gain the acceptance of rabbis sympathetic to mysticism. Its halakhic innovations were minor: the introduction of a
sharper knife for ritual slaughter (perhaps to capture Hasidic control over a crucial
communal sphere) and some liturgical changes, such as use of the Lurianic liturgy
and a less punctilious attitude toward the traditionally designated times for prayer.
Moreover, though Hasidism has come to represent for some modern interpreters a
democratized form of Judaism, it promoted no concrete social program and, indeed,
did not attract the support of the urban artisans who constituted at the time the
severest critics of Jewish communal authority. Among its most ardent and earliest
supporters were rural Jews, particularly arendators, who were unhappy with the
inability of the *qehalim* to defend their traditional right of *hazaqah* (protection from
competition) and whose interests were frequently protected by the Hasidim. In this
respect communal decline helped to fuel the movement, and it is unlikely that it
would have spread as quickly or widely—by 1800 close to one half of the Jews of
east Europe flocked to its banner—had the Polish and Lithuanian councils not been
abolished by the state in 1764. When challenged, for instance, by a charismatic
spokesman of the communal elite, as in Lithuania by Eliyyahu ben Shelomoh Zalman, known as the Gaon of Vilna (1720–1797), Hasidism's momentum was temporarily checked.

Rather than introducing a new egalitarian note into Jewish religious life, Hasidism's most influential innovation was the promotion of a new elite that differed from
both the traditional rabbinic scholars and the qabbalistic ascetics. The Hasidic *tsaddiq* forged a link between the qabbalistic master and the Jewish masses by emphasizing his communal responsibilities (in contradistinction to the asceticism of the
qabbalist). The eighteenth century witnessed a marked decline in rabbinical stature.
Jewish popular sentiment, rather than feeling alienated from the rabbis because of
their self-imposed scholastic isolation, criticized them for their inability to live up to
their own austere and still widely accepted standards.

HASKALAH

The German-speaking lands produced at the same time a westernized, acculturated
elite. It was shaped by the emphasis of enlightened absolutists on the state as a
secular rather than a Christian polity; the compulsory education system introduced
(briefly) into Austria; the Enlightenment's vision of a neutral society where religious
distinctions were rendered irrelevant or, at least, subordinate to other considerations; and the French Revolution, which emancipated the Jews of France in 1791.
Most central European Jews, particularly after the Polish partitions (1772–1795)
when Galicia was absorbed by Austria and east Poznań was added to Prussia, were
Yiddish-speaking and religiously traditional and remained so until the mid-nineteenth century. But the self-consciously "enlightened" elite that emerged emphasized the sensualist rather than the divine source of knowledge, the ultimate importance of earthly existence, and a revised understanding of the relationship between
religion and state. As the leading German-Jewish Enlightenment figure, Moses Mendelssohn (1729–1786) argued that Judaism was able (better than Christianity) to fit

into a new order constructed on the basis of natural truth, rationalism, and a clear distinction between the functions and tools of church and state.

RUSSIAN JEWRY

The Prussian state did not repudiate Jewish autonomy as anticipated by Mendelssohn, but in Austria, France, and even, if somewhat ambiguously, in Russia, the unity of Jewish society had to be maintained despite the lack of support and even the hostility of the government. Russia had prohibited Jewish settlement before the Polish partitions but it absorbed in the late eighteenth century approximately eight hundred thousand Jews. The regime was unwilling, and perhaps unable, to integrate Jews into the existing estates, disinclined to believe that Jewish assimilation was possible, and suspicious of the potentially deleterious impact that the Jews might have on the Russian peasantry. The result was the creation of a large area in which Jews were permitted to live, called the Pale of Settlement, in the fifteen provinces of Lithuania, Belorussia, the Ukraine, and so-called New Russia (on the northern littoral of the Black and Azov seas). Jews were also allowed to live in the ten provinces of central Poland, although these were formally excluded from the Pale. Jews constitued an average of 12 percent of the total population in this area of west and south-western Russia (and often the majority of the urban population) by the late nineteenth century. The classification of Jews as *inorodtsy* (in 1835), the legal category created for the semi-autonomous primitive and nomadic tribes at the periphery of the empire, highlighted their essentially anomalous status in Russian law, since the regime abolished the *qehalim* soon afterward, in 1844. Indeed, despite intermittent governmental attempts to assimilate Russia's Jews, the regime continued to share an abiding preoccupation (sometimes more and sometimes less acute) with their irredeemable separateness.

There was little intervention by the Russian state into the communal life of the Jews until the 1840s. Even after the *qahal* was abolished, a separate Jewish judiciary continued to function and many of the duties of the *qahal* were subsumed by other representative Jewish bodies (though Jewish autonomy was now checked by municipal supervision). The Russian Jewish community grew rapidly over the course of the century and by 1880 numbered four million; it increased in size to more than five million in 1897 despite the mass migration to the west in the same period. Rapid demographic increase, the legal discrimination suffered by Russian Jewry, and the sluggishness of those sectors of the Russian economy in which most Jews were employed contributed to the eventual politicization of the community and to its migratory trends in the late nineteenth and early twentieth centuries. At the turn of the twentieth century, more than 40 percent of the world's fourteen million Jews lived in the Russian empire; 7.5 million Jews lived in eastern Europe as a whole, including Galicia and east Prussia.

Rapid urbanization and economic change in the nineteenth century challenged the foundations of Russian Jewish social and economic life. Repeated expulsions from villages, moves against rural Jewish innkeepers, and the concentration of the liquor trade (which employed about 30 percent of prepartition Polish Jewry) in the hands of a small number of wealthy contractors contributed to the community's urbanization. Petty trade, on the other hand, was undermined by the decline of fairs, the rise of permanent markets, and the government's war on smuggling. Eventually the construction of railway lines destabilized previously crucial commercial and banking centers which were bypassed by the railroad. The decline of the commercial sector led to an overcrowding in others, such as artisanry, where Jews tended to concentrate in the garment trade and in shoemaking.

At the same time, improved transportation, renewed efforts at the exploitation of the agriculturally rich Ukrainian steppe, and the construction of major grain exporting ports (the most important being Odessa) where Jews played prominent economic roles all produced a stratum of successful Jewish entrepreneurs and merchants. Jews made substantial contributions to industrial manufacturing (particularly in Bialystok and Lódź), to the sugar trade (where Jews revolutionized marketing techniques), and the construction of railways. By 1851, 20 percent of the members of Russia's wealthiest merchant guild were Jews, though they constituted only about two or three percent of the total Russian population.

Jewish Communal Authority. In the absence of a state-recognized body that represented Russian Jewry (except for the infrequent, government-convened delegations of Jewish deputies and later the tepid rabbinical commissions), considerable pressure and responsibility was placed in the hands of *qehalim* and private associations. The authority of the *qehalim* was undermined by the 1827 statute which instituted the conscription of Jews and which placed responsibility for the draft in the hands of local *qahal* officials. This led to widespread abuse: the exemption of the rich, the forced conscription of the poor, the drafting of boys of twelve and younger who were subjected, once they were drafted and handed over to the military, to intense pressure to convert to Russian Orthodoxy. Protests by Jews against the *qahal* oligarchy erupted in Podolia, Minsk, Mogilev, and elsewhere, and the rabbinical elite—whose *yeshivah* students were protected by communal officials from the draft—mostly remained silent in the face of these abuses, which further eroded their popular stature.

Russian Haskalah. Nineteenth-century Russian Jewry nonetheless retained a traditional profile. There was little scope in Russia for acculturation; the multiethnic character of the empire mitigated assimilation; and anti-Jewish sentiment remained pervasive among liberals and conservatives alike. Yet the introduction by the state in the 1840s and 1850s of a network of schools where secular as well as Jewish subjects were taught, the liberalization of government policy (and the emancipation of the serfs) under Alexander II (1855–1881) which excited Jewish hopes, and the example of an acculturating western and central European Jewry helped create a Russian Haskalah, or Jewish enlightenment movement. Haskalah stressed those aspects of Jewish life that non-Jews presumably considered positive: the purity of biblical Hebrew, the stability of Jewish family life, the Jews' financial aptitude, their agricultural past, and Judaism's philosophical legacy. On the other hand, the movement denounced aspects of contemporary Jewish life at variance with the beliefs of the larger society (and presumably with the true character of Judaism), such as mystical speculation, disdain for secular study, and ignorance of the vernacular.

In contrast to the exponents of the German-Jewish enlightenment in the decades after Moses Mendelssohn's death, Russian *maskilim* (Jews who subscribed to the goals of the Haskalah) hoped to see Jewry rendered acceptable to its neighbors without relinquishing its distinctive social or religious character. In their view, Judaism was to be purified but not entirely stripped of its idiosyncratic tendencies. The Haskalah movement gave rise to efforts to promote a secular Hebrew literature and periodical press and new types of philanthropic and self-help institutions, and it later had a decisive impact on Jewish nationalist and socialist movements. Its promotion of secular study also helped contribute (especially after the 1870s) to the precipitous rise in the number of Jews enrolled in Russian and secular Jewish schools.

Musar. The Musar movement was one response to modernizing trends within the traditional camp. It stressed self-discipline (an echo of the highly influential system of Eliyyahu ben Shelomoh Zalman, which saw the prodigious study of Torah as taking precedence even over the performance of *mitsvot*) but Musar's founder, Yisra'el Salanter (1810–1883), promoted a pedagogical system in which communal meditation and introspection were integrated into the traditional Talmudic curriculum. At the same time, a series of relatively well-funded and prestigious *yeshivot* were established in Lithuania to counter the inroads made by the Haskalah and secular education. Charismatic rabbinic figures, perhaps most prominently Yisra'el Me'ir Kagan (known as the Hafets Hayyim, 1838–1933), continued to represent the community's highest ideals in their personal piety, humility, and devotion to learning.

INTEGRATION AND EMANCIPATION

Nineteenth-century German and Austrian Jewry—with the major exception of the Jews of Galicia—eventually entered the middle class, discarded Yiddish for German, and produced ideologies of Reform and Neo-Orthodoxy which minimized or rejected aspects of Judaism considered as sacrosanct in the east. Joseph II's *Toleranzpatent* (1782) attempted to legislate against Jewish separatism while opening up new economic and educational options for some Jews. The long and contentious debate in Germany over the feasibility of Jewish emancipation made its small Jewish community (which constituted about 1.75 percent of the total population in 1871 when emancipation was finally granted) highly visible and particularly sensitive to the vagaries of public opinion. In Prussia, 58,000 of its 124,000 Jews were in fact emancipated by 1815; elsewhere in Germany restrictions on employment in the public and private sectors and limitations on Jewish residence were abolished, or at least substantially modified, by the 1850s. To be sure, the 1848 uprisings were followed by new restrictions in Austria and Bavaria, and they were also accompanied by a new anti-Semitic argument which identified Jews with the most disruptive and oppressive features of modern society.

In Galicia, where over 800,000 of Austria's 1.2 million Jews lived in 1900, 85 percent of the Jewish population, according to one report, subsisted at substandard conditions and worked as petty moneylenders, agents, and innkeepers. Yet the majority of Germany's Jews, who were concentrated until the mid-nineteenth century in petty trade, small retailing establishments, and artisanry had by 1871 entered the middle and upper-middle classes. The most telling indication of their social mobility was the disappearance of the *Betteljuden* (many of whom immigrated to the United States), who had, together with day laborers and domestic servants, made up 15 to 20 percent of the German-Jewish population in the late 1830s. German Jews continued to be concentrated in a cluster of occupations, but now these were wholesale trade, commerce, the money market, the professions, and journalism.

Emergence of Reform. Attempts at integration by German Jews produced ideologies of religious reform that accepted the diminution of the national traits of Judaism as espoused by the larger society and emphasized those aspects of Judaism most conducive to cultural symbiosis. Abraham Geiger (1810–1874), Germany's major Reform exponent, saw Judaism as having evolved historically and asserted that every generation had to determine for itself what religious practices and concepts retained a contemporary relevance. Geiger identified monotheism and the teachings of the prophets as the quintessential message that had characterized Judaism throughout the ages and that constituted the basis for its ethical system. In a radical departure from the traditional understanding of *galut,* Geiger saw the Jewish dispersion as a positive condition, since it helped Jews promote the universalistic teachings of their faith. This emphasis on mission served to justify continued Jewish peculiarity and helped to reinforce, albeit within a substantially modified context, traditional assumptions of Jewish specialness and chosenness. The fundamental principles of Reform were elaborated in a series of rabbinical conferences held in the 1840s, and these assemblies constituted the culmination of a long period in which Reform promoted a substantially modified Jewish educational curriculum and alterations in synagogue service and decorum.

Emergence of Orthodoxy. The response of Pressburg's (modern Bratislava) influential Mosheh Sofer (Hatam Sofer, 1762–1839) to the emergence of Reform was summarized in his pithy "Hadash asur min ha-torah" ("everything new is forbidden by the Torah"), which denounced all change as undermining Judaism. The call for traditional Jews to segregate themselves from the increasingly Reform-dominated communities of Germany was promoted by many Orthodox rabbis, most prominently by Samson Raphael Hirsch (1808–1888), who argued for the universalizing of Judaism and, at the same time, for an uncompromising affirmation of its traditional commitment to *mitsvot.* Traditional Judaism in Germany, and elsewhere in Europe, began to employ the tools—and in Hirsch's case also the terminology—of the larger, secularizing world in order to combat Reform, and this led to the creation of Orthodox newspapers and political parties. The first such party was established in Hungary in 1867.

ACCULTURATION AND RESPONSES TO ANTI-SEMITISM

European Jewry's acculturation led, to be sure, to a diminution of the importance that Jewish concerns played in the lives of many Jews, but it also provided an increasingly westernized Jewry with new and sophisticated tools with which to promote Jewish interests. Jewish liberals and a small number of political radicals played a prominent role in the 1848 revolutions, in contrast to the political passivity of the Jews of France in 1789; another indication of the tendency of westernized Jews to employ new and innovative means to promote Jewish causes was the creation of a highly diversified Jewish press mostly published in European languages.

Jewish assimilation, whose goal was the fusion of Jewry into the majority culture, was most feasible in settings were Jews formed a small percentage of the population in large urban areas; where acculturation was widespread but anti-Semitism prevalent, the promotion of social integration was thwarted. A precipitous rise in anti-Semitism in societies where Jews had experienced substantial acculturation often contributed to an increase in the incidence of conversion. On average, 145 Jews converted annually in Prussia between 1880 and 1884 while, in the wake of the anti-Semitic agitation of the last decade of the century, the number doubled to 349 between 1895 and 1899.

Of the smaller Jewish communities of western and northern Europe, about 35,000 Jews lived in England in the 1850s, 80,000 in France, about 52,000 in Holland (in the 1840s), 64,000 in Belgium, and fewer than 1,000 in Sweden. In France and England, Jews were concentrated in the largest cities (a process that had begun earlier in England than in France). In both societies, despite the emancipation of French Jewry more than half a century before the Jews of England were admitted into the House of Commons in 1858, acculturation preceded the complete abrogation of Jewish restrictions. An absence of denominationalism was another feature common to both English and French Jewish life, and in the two communities Reform tendencies were absorbed or neutralized by the dominant religious institutions and they did not precipitate the sectarianism characteristic of German Judaism. The absorption into the middle class of most English and French Jews by the late nineteenth century helped encourage a privatization of Jewish identity, which was eventually challenged by the east European migration. Between 1881 and 1914 the English Jewish population increased, mostly as a result of the immigration of Russian Jews, from sixty-five thousand to three hundred thousand. Thirty thousand immigrants settled in Paris in the same period (arriving in particularly large numbers after 1905), and they introduced into the western urban Jewish milieu an ethnic dimension previously unknown. Indeed, between 1881 and 1924, about 2.5 million east European Jews (mostly from Russia) migrated to the West; two-thirds of them left their homes between 1903 and 1914 and the vast majority of immigrants moved to the United States. About 10–15 percent settled in western and central Europe. Russian Jews in particular emigrated in large numbers because of the oppressive tsarist legislation of the 1880s and 1890s, shrinking economic prospects, and often exaggerated rumors of economic prospects in the West.

East European Jewish immigrants became a special focus of attack by the anti-Semitic movement that erupted in western and central Europe in the late nineteenth century. This movement was the product of a general anti-liberal reaction which promoted romantic conservatism over constitutionalism, a free market economy, and freedom of speech and assembly. Anti-Semitism (the term was coined in the 1870s) provided a seemingly plausible target for a wide range of social and economic frustrations. Its literature drew on secular (and often scientific) rather than religious terminology and sometimes, as in Edouard Adolphe Drumont's *La France juive* (1886), it drew on left-wing ideology in its case for the illegitimacy of Jewish wealth and position. Influential anti-Semitic parties appeared in Germany and Austria. Anti-Semitism became a cultural code, in Shulamit Volkov's characterization, for a wide range of groups that stressed militant nationalism, imperial expansion, racism, anticolonialism, antisocialism, and respect for authoritarian government.

The rise and resilience of the anti-Semitic movement compelled some European Jewish leaders to reassess their communal and political strategies. In Germany this gave birth in 1893 to the *Centralverein deutscher Staatsbürger jüdischen Glauben,* which departed from the classical Mendelssohnian stance both in its promotion of a conspicuously Jewish (as opposed to philo-Semitic, liberal, and gentile-led) response to anti-Semitism and in its insistence that the Jewish case be aired and vindicated in courts of law. In Russia, as in the West, before the 1880s Jewish politics was seen as predicated entirely on the goodwill of gentiles and its goal was the encouragement of Jewish emancipation. A new understanding took hold after the 1881–1882 pogroms, best encapsulated in the title of Odessa physician Leon Pinsker's *Auto-Emancipation* (1882), which called upon the Jews to cease their efforts to adapt themselves to the larger environment and to create instead a new one outside of Russia. A new type of Russian Jewish leader emerged in the same period: young, russianized (or partially so), who came to compete with the communal magnates of St. Petersburg and the rabbinical elite.

Zionism. Two major ideological currents emerged: Zionism and Jewish socialism. Zionism drew its constituency and vitality from eastern Europe but the Austrian journalist, Theodor Herzl (1860–1904), gave the small and Russian-based movement a measure of stature and international recognition in the 1890s and early twentieth century. Herzl's most important Zionist adversary was the Odessa intellectual Asher Ginsberg (better known as Aḥad ha-ʿAm, 1856–1927), who provided Zionism with influential ideological underpinnings very different from those of Herzl. From Herzl's perspective, the promotion by Zionism of a Jewish homeland would undercut the growth of anti-Semitism, restore Jewish economic productivity, and provide Jews throughout the world (as well as the threatened liberal order) with renewed stability. Ginsberg, on the other hand, saw Zionism as a framework that could allow Jewry to absorb Western values without having them submerge Jewish identity. He stressed the cultural benefits of the rebuilding of a Palestinian Jewish homeland and minimized its immediate economic impact.

Jewish Socialism. A second Jewish political movement emphasized the need to transform Russia itself—a goal Russian Zionists also eventually adopted in their Helsinki platform of 1906—and the Jewish Socialist Labor Bund, established in 1897, charted a course between the two poles of nationalism and Marxism. Jewish socialism's following, not surprisingly, expanded in moments of revolutionary turmoil and contracted with rapidity in times of relative quiescence. But the heroism of the Jewish revolutionaries, their organization of self-defense groups during the pogroms, their participation in widespread philanthropic endeavors, and even their conspiratorial form of internal organization came to infuse them with an almost legendary respect in the Pale of Settlement.

WORLD WAR I AND ITS AFTERMATH

The war seemed at first to present a singularly unfavorable scenario for Jewish political activity but was, ironically, followed by a series of outstanding victories for Jewish leaders in the diplomatic sphere and by a new and apparently more encouraging political order. The Russian Revolution of 1917 brought down the imperial regime and emancipated Russia's Jews; the Balfour Declaration, issued by the British the same year, was Zionism's first concrete diplomatic achievement and it would serve, until the state of Israel was established in 1948, as a central focus of the movement's strategy. Moreover, the adoption of international guarantees for the observance of national minority rights in the new states of east central Europe (along with prewar Romania) was largely the product of the maneuvering of British and American Jewish leaders. The mass evacuation of hundreds of thousands of Galician and Russian Jews in 1914–1915 (the Russian ones evacuated under particularly degrading conditions) lent Jews a special visibility, which was reinforced by the fact that much of the war was conducted in regions heavily populated by Jews. Misperceptions of the strength and dimensions of Jewish influence (suppositions which gained worldwide notoriety after World War I with the dissemination of the anti-Semitic tract *Protocols of the Elders of Zion*) helped Jews wrest major political concessions for themselves. The Balfour Declaration, in which the British declared sympathy for Zionist aspirations in Palestine, resulted partly from the Allies' belief that Russian (and American) Jewish support was crucial in bolstering the war effort. The Russian liberalization of Jewish residence restrictions in 1915 was the product of a misperception that Jewish-controlled Western loans would be denied to Russia if it continued to be seen as brutally anti-Semitic. Western support for national minority rights in east central Europe was given special impetus in the wake of the Ukrainian pogroms of 1918–1919 in which more than five hundred Jewish communities were attacked and about seventy thousand Jews were killed. The effort of the Bolsheviks—who in November 1917 had overthrown the liberal anti-tsarist government that had been in power in Russia since the fall of the Romanovs earlier that year—to put down the anti-Jewish disturbances and to pacify the Ukrainian separatist movement won widespread (if somewhat equivocal) support for them among Russia's Jews.

The new Soviet government associated anti-Semitism with tsarist reaction and fought it vigorously, but Bolshevism also denied Jewish demands for national recognition on the basis of its authoritative statement on minority nationalism, *Marxism and the National Question* (1913). Nonetheless, Jewry's distinctive cultural and, implicitly, also its national needs were acknowledged by the regime, which was interested in consolidating Jewish support. Secular cultural activity in Yiddish was encouraged; Hebrew was barred as bourgeois and religious institutions and functionaries were harassed. By the early 1930s even Yiddish-language publishing, research, and pedagogical activity were restricted. At the same time, the Soviet Jewish population as a whole—which numbered about three million in 1926—benefited from the expanding economy, became urbanized (it was eventually concentrated in Moscow, Leningrad, and a few other large cities), and was absorbed, despite the existence of a residual popular as well as institutional anti-Semitism, into the industrial working class, the bureaucracy, the professions, and the sciences.

The Jews of interwar Poland (who numbered just under 2.9 million in 1921, 10.5 percent of the total population) underwent a process of acculturation different from that of Soviet Jewry. Ravaged as Poland was by the war and separated from its natural markets and sources of energy by the boundaries of the new Polish state, its postwar economic development was sluggish before 1929 and singularly depressed in the 1930s. Poland's depressed economic state reinforced a widespread integral nationalism that persuaded many Poles that the Jews, as members of a faith inimical to Christianity, had no place in Poland. Particularly after 1936, nationalist xenophobia, church-sponsored anti-Semitism, and economic decline combined to persuade Poles of varied political persuasions that anti-Jewish policies were a necessary cruelty. About one-third of Poland's Jews retained a largely traditional religious profile and promoted Orthodox interests with tenacity and some sophistication. Jewish acculturation was also vividly reflected in the growth of secular Jewish culture and widely diversified socialist and Zionist political activities, which took on different forms in various regions of Poland, Galicia, central Poland, and Lithuania-Belorussia.

THE HOLOCAUST

The vast majority of Germany's approximately 600,000 Jews (constituting about one percent of the population in the early 1920s) were solidly based in the middle class, though one-fifth of the Jewish population were foreign-born and maintained a less prosperous occupational profile. Anti-Semitic sentiment—which reached ferocious levels in the immediate post-World War I period when wide segments of the population associated the sudden loss of the war with the treachery of the Jews—was marginalized during the economic prosperity of 1923–1929. Anti-Semitism regained a mass following with the onset of the worldwide depression. Once Hitler was appointed Chancellor in 1933, German Jewry was gradually segregated from the larger population, denied employment, and those who did not emigrate by 1939 were eventually deported and either worked to death or gassed in labor and death camps. Germany's invasion of Poland led to the effective segregation of its large Jewish community, and Jews elsewhere in Nazi-occupied or Nazi-dominated western and east central Europe were placed in ghettos where they too were starved, brutalized, and, in the end, sent to death camps. More than one million Soviet Jews were killed by Nazi mobile killing units during the German invasion of 1941; the introduction in 1942 of highly efficient means for mass extermination led to the construction of a series of death camps designed expressly for the extermination of European Jewry. Over the course of World War II during the Nazi Holocaust about 6 million Jews were killed: 4.5 million in Poland and the Soviet Union; 125,000 German Jews, 277,000 Czechs, 402,000 Hungarians, 24,000 Belgians, 102,000 Dutch, 40,000 Romanians, 60,000 Yugoslavs, 85,000 French, and tens of thousands in Greece and Italy.

POST-HOLOCAUST JEWISH COMMUNITY

The resilience of postwar anti-Semitism in Poland encouraged most Holocaust survivors to emigrate, and the Polish Jewish community, numbering about 30,000 in the late 1950s, was further decimated following the migration of large numbers of Jews in the wake of the 1968 anti-Semitic governmental campaign. Germany's 25,000 Jews in the late 1960s experienced a high rate of intermarriage (72.5 percent among males in the years 1951–1958) and a death rate that far exceeded its birthrate. The most culturally vibrant Jewish community of east central Europe was Hungary, where between 80,000 and 90,000 Jews in the 1960s maintained, eventually with government support, a wide range of religious and philanthropic institutions, including a rabbinical seminary. The post-1967 resurgence of Jewish nationalist sentiment among Soviet Jews led to a revival of (largely clandestine) cultural activity and helped precipitate a large migration of Jews to Israel and the United States. The centers of European Jewish cultural life in the postwar period were England and France. The French Jewish community, in particular, has demonstrated a marked vitality, encouraged by the migration of North African Jews, primarily from Algeria, in the 1960s.

[For *further discussion of the historical movements and events discussed herein,* see Messianism, *article on* Jewish Messianism; Haskalah; Hasidism, *overview article;* Musar Movement; Agudat Yisra'el; Zionism; Orthodox Judaism; Reform Judaism; *and*

Holocaust, The, *article on* History. *Many of the principal historical figures mentioned in this article are the subjects of independent entries.*]

BIBLIOGRAPHY

Early Modern Period. The most authoritative work in English on the Jews of Poland and Lithuania in the sixteenth and seventeenth centuries is volume 16 of Salo W. Baron's *A Social and Religious History of the Jews,* 2d ed., rev. and enl. (Philadelphia, 1976). For a sociological analysis of Jewish communal autonomy in eastern and central Europe, see Jacob Katz's *Tradition and Crisis* (New York, 1961). On Jews in the late medieval Germanic empire, see Selma Stern's *Josel of Rosheim* (Philadelphia, 1965). Useful methodological questions are raised in an article by Gershon David Hundert, "On the Jewish Community in Poland during the Seventeenth Century: Some Comparative Perspectives," *Revue des études juives* 142 (July–December 1983): 349–372. On the seventeenth century, there is interesting material in Jonathan I. Israel's "Central European Jewry during the Thirty Years' War," *Central European History* (March 1983): 3–30. The best treatment of Polish-Jewish cultural life in the same period is H. H. Ben-Sasson's *Hagut ve-hanhagah* (Jerusalem, 1959). Jewish migratory trends in the seventeenth and eighteenth centuries are studied in Moses A. Shulvass's *From East to West* (Detroit, 1971). On the readmission of English Jewry, see David S. Katz's *Philo-Semitism and the Readmission of the Jews to England, 1603–1655* (Oxford, 1982).

Modern Period. An incisive analysis of the social features of Hasidism may be found in Samuel Ettinger's "The Hassidic Movement: Reality and Ideals," in *Jewish Society through the Ages,* edited by H. H. Ben-Sasson and Samuel Ettinger (London, 1971), pp. 251–266. For a discussion of French Jewish identity, see Phyllis Cohen Albert's "Nonorthodox Attitudes in Nineteenth-Century French Judaism," in *Essays in Modern Jewish History: A Tribute to Ben Halpern,* edited by Frances Malino and Phyllis Cohen Albert (Rutherford, N.J., 1982), pp. 121–141. Michael Stanislawski's *Tsar Nicholas I and the Jews* (Philadelphia, 1983), and Hans Rogger's "Russian Ministers and the Jewish Question, 1881–1917," *California Slavic Studies* 8 (1975): 15–76, study imperial Jewish policy. The essays in *Revolution and Evolution: 1848 in German-Jewish History,* edited by Werner E. Mosse, Arnold Paucker, and Reinhard Rürup (Tübingen, 1981), examine nineteenth century German Jewry, with particular emphasis on the community's socioeconomic transformation. Todd M. Endelman's *The Jews of Georgian England, 1714–1830* (Philadelphia, 1979) is a skillful social history. The political responses of east European Jews are studied in Jonathan Frankel's *Prophecy and Politics: Socialism, Nationalism and the Russian Jews, 1862–1917* (Cambridge, 1981). Ezra Mendelsohn reviews the interwar period in *The Jews of East Central Europe between the World Wars* (Bloomington, Ind., 1983). The best study of Soviet Jewry is Zvi Y. Gitelman's *Jewish Nationality and Soviet Politics* (Princeton, 1972). A particularly insightful essay in Yehuda Bauer's *The Holocaust in Historical Perspective* (Seattle, 1978) is his "Against Mystification: The Holocaust as a Historical Phenomenon."

14 JUDAISM IN THE WESTERN HEMISPHERE

Leon A. Jick

If the records of the Inquisition are to be believed, Jews were among the earliest settlers in the Western Hemisphere. They were Marranos, Spanish and Portuguese Jews who had been coerced to convert to Christianity, but continued to practice their religion secretly. While Jews had been expelled from Spain in 1492 and were, of course, forbidden to settle in the Spanish colonies, not until 1523 did a royal decree exclude even the New Christians, that is, recent converts to Christianity. The first auto-da-fé at which New Christians alleged to be Marranos were burned at the stake was held in Mexico City in 1528. [See Marranos *and* Inquisition.] Independent tribunals of the Holy Office of the Inquisition were established in Mexico City in 1571 and in Lima in 1572 and thereafter Inquisitorial trials and executions of "judaizers" *(judaizantes)* were held regularly. In the great auto-da-fé of Lima on 23 January 1639, sixty-two suspected heretics were convicted and twelve hundred unrepentant victims were burned at the stake. While it is impossible to know how many of the accused were in fact Jews and to ascertain the nature of their Jewish practices, it is clear that the continued existence of the Inquisition in Central and South America into the nineteenth century prevented the emergence of an openly Jewish community until the last decades of that century.

JEWISH SETTLEMENT IN THE NEW WORLD

The earliest Jewish community in the Western Hemisphere was established in Recife, Brazil, during the brief period of Dutch rule there between 1630 and 1654. Holland, following its independence from Spain in 1579, had become a center of commercial capitalism as well as of toleration. The combination of religious freedom and economic opportunity had attracted Sefardic Jews to Amsterdam, and in the late sixteenth century a thriving Jewish center arose there that played a significant role in trade with the New World.

In 1630 the Dutch captured the settlement at Recife and Jews arrived among the earliest settlers. As long as the Dutch retained control of the colony, the Jewish community there flourished. At the peak of its prosperity in 1645 the community is reported to have numbered 1,500—about 50 percent of the European civilian population. In 1654, the Portuguese recaptured the city, and Dutch and Jewish inhabitants were given three months in which to depart. Most returned to Amsterdam; others moved to islands in the West Indies where they joined existing groups of Jewish settlers. One band of twenty-three landed in New Amsterdam (present-day New York) in September 1654. The end of the first Jewish community in South America coincided with the establishment of the first such community in North America.

Settlement of North America. As may be seen from letters from the directors of the Dutch West India Company to Peter Stuyvesant, the presence of this group was grudgingly accepted by the local authorities on condition that "the poor among them shall not become a burden to the [Dutch West India] Company or to the community but be supported by their own nation." Subsequently the rights of Jews to settle, trade in real estate, and practice their religion "in all quietness within their homes" was granted (Max Kohler, "Beginnings of New York Jewish History," *Proceedings of the American Jewish Historical Society* 1, 1905, pp. 47–48). In 1656, a group of Jewish petitioners was granted a cemetery, the first institution signifying that a community of practicing Jews had been established. In 1644, English conquerors replaced the Dutch. They renamed the city New York and confirmed the atmosphere of toleration in what was already a mosaic of religious and ethnic diversity.

During the century that followed, a small but steady trickle of immigration led to the establishment of Jewish congregations along the eastern seaboard in Newport, Philadelphia, Charleston, and Savannah, as well as New York. All followed the Sefardic (Spanish-Portuguese) rite in their worship. Because of the small size and informal organizational pattern of the community, little information has survived concerning the details of institutional practice. During the colonial era, no ordained rabbi served in America; not a single Jewish journal of any kind was established, nor was there any other instrument for the exchange of ideas or information. Colonial American Jewry, sparse in numbers and weak in intellectual resources, left only a meager documentary record.

Despite the difficulties and shortcomings, Jewish religious life, conducted by devoted but often poorly educated laymen, sustained itself. In 1682, a Dutch cleric recorded that the Jews "hold their separate meetings in New York." That same year, the Jewish community purchased its second cemetery, a burying ground that exists in lower New York to this day and is one of the oldest historic sites in the city. In 1695, an English clergyman noted in his memoirs that the approximately 855 families in New York included 20 Jewish families. On a map of the city, he marked a site as "The Jews Synagogue." A subsequent real estate document describes a house on Mill Street as "commonly known by the name of Jews Synagogue." These references offer no information concerning the life of the community, but they do testify to the existence of a small congregation that had established its right to public worship, had rented a building for this purpose, and had made its presence palpable in the city. In 1728, the Jewish citizens of New York purchased a lot and undertook the erection of a building intended specifically for use as a synagogue.

Throughout the eighteenth century, Jewish immigrants were few in number. It is estimated that in 1790 no more than 2,000 to 2,500 Jews resided in the United States. The masses of Jews lived in east-central and eastern Europe and in the Near East in areas not yet awakened to the possibility of migration. An increasing percentage of those who did come were Ashkenazim—Jews of northern European origin. Despite the differences in Ashkenazic and Sefardic religious custom, without exception the Ashkenazim joined the established Sefardic congregations. Colonial American Jewry remained Sefardic in its formal religious practice.

Americanization of Colonial Jewry. At the same time, the style of life in this small community underwent significant changes. Encouraged by the atmosphere of toleration and the openness of the society, colonial Jews became americanized and entered into general social life to a degree that would have been inconceivable in Europe. Although the ritual practices in the synagogue were preserved without change, Jewish knowledge and practice became increasingly attenuated. In the traditional community, an all-pervasive pattern of Jewish thought, action, outlook, and association had been punctuated by occasional excursions into the general society primarily in pursuit of economic ends. In the newly developing American Jewish mode, a distinctively American style of thought, action, outlook, and association was punctuated by occasional excursions to the synagogue for the performance of increasingly marginal ceremonial functions.

In 1761, the *hazzan* (cantor) of Shearith Israel congregation in New York, Isaac Pinto, published the first Jewish book to be printed in the Western Hemisphere. It was a translation of the Sabbath prayer book into English. In his introduction, Pinto explained that Hebrew was "imperfectly understood by many, by some not at all" and expressed the hope that an English translation would "tend to the improvement of many of my Brethren in their Devotion." A report from Philadelphia to Amsterdam in 1785 concludes that "most of the sons of this province are not devoted to Torah and do not understand our holy tongue [Hebrew]. Despite accounts clearly demonstrating that the American Jewry that emerged in the early decades of the nineteenth century was highly acculturated and substantially transformed, no account can deny the achievement of this isolated Jewish group in maintaining its identity at all.

When George Washington was inaugurated president in 1790, Gershom Mendes Seixas, the American-born *hazzan* of Shearith Israel congregation in New York, was recorded as one of the clergymen in attendance. Small as it was, the Jewish community was unable to agree on sending one letter of felicitations to the president, and three letters were dispatched. In a gracious response, Washington reciprocated the good wishes of the "children of the stock of Abraham" and expressed his confidence in their continued well-being in a society which "happily gives to bigotry no sanction, to persecution no assistance and requires only that they who live under its protection should demean themselves as good citizens" (Joseph L. Blau and Salo W. Baron, eds., *The Jews of the United States, 1790–1840: A Documentary History,* New York, 1964, vol. 1, p. 9). American Judaism was recognized as a component in the mosaic of American religious pluralism.

AMERICAN JEWRY IN THE NINETEENTH CENTURY

In the early years of the nineteenth century, revolution and war in Europe reduced immigration to a trickle. American Jewry, small in numbers and weak in intellectual resources, entered a phase of steady attrition. The new American version of Judaism was viable but it never succeeded in becoming vital. "Alas," wrote Rebecca Gratz of Philadelphia, the founder of the Sunday school movement for Jewish children, "it is thought among our degenerate sons and daughters of Israel that only its women and priests acknowledge the force of patriotism and zeal for Judaism" (ibid., vol. 8, p. 955).

Large-scale immigration to America resumed after 1815 when the return of peace restored normal transportation across the Atlantic. A large proportion of these immigrants originated in central European provinces, and among them were increasing numbers of Jews. In 1818, Mordecai Manuel Noah, New York journalist, playwright, and Jacksonian politician, estimated the Jewish population of the United States at three thousand. By 1826, Isaac Harby, a Charleston schoolmaster, put the number at six thousand. The presence of immigrants and the prospect of further immigration stirred signs of life in the near-moribund American Jewish community.

In 1823, the first Jewish periodical in North America appeared. It was a monthly called *The Jew* and devoted solely to reporting the conversionist polemics of Christian missionary societies, especially the so-called Society for Ameliorating the Condition of the Jews. In its two years of publication *The Jew* did not include a single reference to events in the Jewish community of its time. The circumscribed contents of the journal reflect the meagerness of Jewish life; however, the very existence of such a publication is a token of awakening enterprise and growing awareness of need and opportunity.

Grandiose schemes for encouraging immigration proliferated in America during these years. English, German, Swiss, and French groups attempted to establish semi-independent national settlements beyond the Appalachian mountains in what was then the "West." In 1825 Mordecai Noah proposed the establishment of a Jewish settlement on Grand Island in the Niagara River, proclaiming himself as "Judge and Governor of Israel." Nothing came of the proposal; it was dropped after a flurry of publicity without Noah ever having set foot on Grand Island. The significance of the scheme lies in its testimony to Noah's consciousness of the renewed Jewish immigration which had already begun and of the prospect of an increased flow in the future.

The growth in numbers and in diversity of background created strains within the Jewish community. Newcomers from northern Europe soon outnumbered the settlers of the prerevolutionary period. It was inevitable that they would establish their own synagogues. The first synagogue to follow the Ashkenazic (German) rite in worship had been established in Philadelphia possibly as early as 1795. The congregation, however, did not succeed in establishing itself on a sound footing until the late 1820s, when the influx of new immigrants reinforced its ranks. At the same time two new Ashkenazic congregations were established—one in Cincinnati and one in New York. In new areas of settlement, as well as in old established centers, immigrants were forming congregations in accord with their own mode of worship. In 1828, a third synagogue was established in New York.

The most common explanation for the proliferation of congregations was the increasing resistance of Ashkenazim to the Sefardic manner of conducting the ritual. In fact the motives were far more complex. Acculturated native American Jews found the newcomers alien, abrasive, and uncouth, while immigrants found their americanized fellow Jews lax in religious observance. Established citizens wanted an orderly and undemanding "Jewish church" that would affirm their respectability; insecure newcomers sought an environment of involvement and interaction reminiscent of the intimate village gathering place they had known, where they could pray in their accustomed way among sympathetic peers and find acceptance by God and men. The bewildered newcomers of one decade became the solid and settled bourgeoisie of the next. Each succeeding wave of immigration brought a repetition of the pattern.

By 1840, before the largest influx of immigrants had begun or a single rabbi had yet arrived, the number of congregations in New York had risen to six. The pace of institutional growth accelerated sharply in the 1840s with congregations organized in cities from Boston to San Francisco. In 1848, Isaac Leeser, editor of *The Occident and American Jewish Advocate* in Philadelphia, observed that "synagogues are springing up as if by magic. . . . From the newly gotten Santa Fe to the confines of New Brunswick and from the Atlantic to the shores of the Western sea, the wandering sons of Israel are seeking homes and freedom" *(The Occident and American Jewish Advocate* 4, 1848, pp. 317, 366). Before the end of the decade two or more congregations existed in cities with substantial Jewish populations, such as Albany, Baltimore, Cincinnati, New Orleans, Philadelphia, Richmond, and Saint Louis. New York had fifteen congregations, with more in the process of formation.

Beginnings of Communal Structure and Leadership. The voluntarism and pluralism of America, the lack of a Jewish communal structure, and the absence of religious or intellectual leadership together combined to foster an atmosphere of chaos in American Jewish life. Well-intentioned but poorly educated laymen assumed leadership in seeking to establish the rudiments of community. However, they lacked the credentials to interpret Jewish law or to render decisions concerning modifications in religious practice in response to changed conditions. [*See* Rabbinate *and* Halakhah.] No one had the power to enforce traditional norms even within the synagogue. Every congregation and indeed every individual was free to act or refrain from acting according to his own inclination. Authority was absent and unity in dealing with common concerns seemed unattainable.

The earliest manifestations of national communal consciousness came in response to a perceived threat from the outside. In 1840, the ancient blood libel—the false accusation that Jews had murdered a Christian child for ritual purposes—was revived in Damascus. The specter of revived medieval bigotry even in far-away Damascus shook native-born as well as immigrant Jews. "If such calumny is not nipped in the bud, its effect will not be limited to any particular place but will be extended to every part of the globe," wrote Abraham Hart, president of the Sefardic Mikveh Israel congregation in Philadelphia. Disparate Jewish groups in major urban centers joined together with each other, with Jews in other American cities, and with communities in Europe in expressions of mutual concern. The response signified an awakening of group consciousness.

The quickening sense of mutual concern led to the first proposals for a permanent link between Jews in various cities and for an attempt to address the deficiencies and improve the quality of Jewish religious life. Impoverished immigrants struggling to make their way in a strange new land were eager to preserve their Jewish practices and to give their children a Jewish education. They established not only synagogues but also day schools in which Hebrew as well as English and sometimes German were taught. But individual congregations and communities lacked the financial and cultural resources to fulfill the aspirations of their constituents. In an attempt to overcome the inadequacies, Isaac Leeser, then *hazzan* of the Mikveh Israel congregation in Philadelphia, took the initiative and prepared a detailed plan for a national union of American Jewish congregations, which he circulated in July 1841. Leeser, himself of German Jewish background, had emigrated to the United States as a young man in the 1820s. His formal educational background was modest and in the European setting would have qualified him to be no more than an elementary-school teacher. However, he was bright, ambitious, and energetic, and was soon elected to serve as *ḥazzan* of the established old Sefardic congregation. The absence of religious functionaries with more impressive credentials enabled Leeser to assume a national-leadership role. His proposed "Union for the Sake of Judaism" projected the establishment of a "Central Religious Council" consisting of three "gentlemen of undoubted moral and religious character" to be elected by congregational representatives. The council was to "watch over the state of religion," certify the competence of ritual slaughterers and cantors, and oversee the quality of religious schools (for both sexes). The schools were to be established "in every town where Israelites reside" but were not to "interfere directly or indirectly in the internal affairs of the congregations." The proposal—modest as it was—did not elicit a single positive response. American voluntarism and Jewish congregational autonomy combined to subvert any attempt to achieve unity or to establish authority.

Leeser may have been disheartened, but he was not daunted and proceeded at once with other ventures. The following year he announced plans for publishing a monthly journal, and in April 1843 the English-language *Occident and American Jewish Advocate* appeared. Leeser proposed "to give circulation to everything which can be interesting to the Jewish inhabitants of the Western Hemisphere." American Jewry not only had a spokesman; it now had a forum for exchange of information and ideas.

In 1844, Leeser contributed an article entitled "The Jews and Their Religion" to *An Original History of the Denominations at Present Existing in the United States*, edited by Daniel I. Rupps (Philadelphia, 1844). Leeser is described in this volume as "pastor of the Hebrew Portuguese Congregation of Philadelphia" and as the "most prominent divine" among American Jews. In his essay, Leeser states:

> We *have no ecclesiastical authorities in America other than the congregations themselves. Each congregation makes its own rules for its government, and elects its own minister, who is appointed without any ordination, induction in office being made through his election.* (p. 368)

Within American Judaism, as experienced and explained by Leeser, the traditional scholar-rabbi was marginal, at best.

At the time Leeser wrote, the first ordained rabbis had arrived in America, but they had not yet found a recognized place or function for themselves in the new environment. Abraham Rice, who arrived in 1840 and served for a time as rabbi of the Baltimore Hebrew Congregation, wrote to his teacher in Germany: "I dwell in complete darkness, without a teacher or a companion. . . . The religious life in this land is on the lowest level. I wonder whether it is even permissible for a Jew to live in this land." Rice's gloom was not shared by Isaac Leeser, who wrote:

> *In America, where the constitution secures to every person the enjoyment of life, liberty, and the pursuit of happiness without anyone having the right to question him concerning his religious opinion or acts, the Children of Jacob have received a new home.*

Leeser proceeded in 1845 to establish an American Jewish Publication Society to publish material on Jewish subjects in English and to make it possible "to obtain a knowledge of the faith and to defend it against the assaults of the proselytemakers [sic] on the one side and of infidels on the other." Among its first publications was an edition of the Pentateuch with an English translation printed parallel to the Hebrew text.

That same year, Max Lilienthal arrived in America. Lilienthal was the first rabbi with unquestioned credentials and prior reputation to settle in America. In his earliest endeavors he sought to introduce traditional Jewish practices and to promote "decorum" in worship. Lilienthal further undertook to organize a *beit din,* a rabbinical court, that would render, in his words, "beneficial service to the Jewish congregations of America" (David Philipson, *Max Lilienthal, American Rabbi: His Life and Writings,* New York, 1915, p. 55). In deference to the autonomy of American congregations, Lilienthal stipulated that the *beit din* would not assume any "hierarchical authority" but would act "only in an advisory capacity." The effort was unsuccessful, and Lilienthal soon withdrew from congregational life and established a Jewish day school, which he operated for a number of years with considerable success.

A year after Lilienthal settled in America, another rabbi arrived who was to assume a significant leadership role. He was Isaac Mayer Wise. Wise, who had served as a rabbi in a provincial town in Bohemia, lacked reputation or credentials, but he was energetic, ambitious, and ideologically flexible. He was also an effective orator and a competent organizer. He secured a position in Albany and began at once to project himself onto the national scene and to establish himself as an aspirant to leadership.

In December 1848, Wise published a call for a union of congregations addressed "To Ministers and Other Israelites" in the *Occident.* Although both Leeser and Lilienthal associated themselves with this call and nine congregations responded favorably, no meeting was held. Wise was not discouraged. Five years later he was elected rabbi of a synagogue in Cincinnati, and promptly set about convening a conference to organize a "Union of American Israel" whose aim would be to establish a "regular synod consisting of delegates chosen by congregations and societies." At the same time Wise began publication of an English-language newspaper, *The Israelite,* and in Cincinnati established "the first Hebrew college in the United States and England," which he called Zion College.

The college closed after one year. The newspaper, however, flourished, and the conference did take place, in Cleveland in October 1855. A series of resolutions were adopted that straddled ideological issues and attempted to bridge the growing conflict between traditionalist and reformist factions. Unfortunately, personal rivalries, sectional antagonism between the Eastern "elite" and Midwestern "yokeldom," and residual hostility between the older native "aristocracy" and newer immigrant "upstarts" proved more intractable and less amenable to compromise than did ideology. A second conference was scheduled but never convened.

The Reform Movement. During the early decades of the central European immigration there was little evidence of the struggle over religious reform that was stirring German Jewry during these years. Of the scores of synagogues established between 1825 and 1860, only three were founded with the avowed intention of introducing "reforms," and actual changes introduced even in these congregations were relatively modest. On the contrary, most immigrants, in the period immediately following their arrival, seemed more interested in preserving the synagogue un-changed as a refuge from the compromises with observance in their private lives often dictated by economic necessity. In Europe, the Jewish religious Reform move-ment had radical overtones and consequences. It was linked to the struggle for political emancipation and for the elimination of feudal disabilities. It therefore came to be regarded as a challenge not only to the traditional Jewish communal structure but to the established social and political order as well.

In America, precisely the opposite dynamics were at work. When Jewish refor-mism emerged, it reflected a desire not to change the established social and political order but to join it. Jewish religious Reform in nineteenth-century America began with a series of modest ritual changes and shifts in emphasis that were primarily concerned with appearances and social conformity. Ideology in the European sense played a minimal role and a predetermined program was virtually absent. In Ger-many, Reform was viewed as a precursor of acculturation and integration. In America acculturation and integration proved to be precursors of Reform.

The earliest reformist attempt had been made in 1825 in Charleston, South Caro-lina, by a native-born, thoroughly americanized group. Their proposal stressed de-corum and intelligibility to worshipers who no longer understood Hebrew or Ger-man rather than substantive revisions of either faith or practice. The effort expired after a few years and exercised no influence on subsequent developments. When "Reform" emerged again as an issue in the 1850s, it was once more primarily con-cerned with issues of decorum and the use of English rather than with principles. The group most interested in Reform were upwardly mobile immigrants whose eco-nomic advance and americanization were rapidly progressing.

In 1855 David Einhorn arrived in America and took up a rabbinical post in Balti-more at the Reform Har Sinai congregation. Einhorn had been a leader of the radical faction at the German rabbinical conferences of the 1840s. In his pulpit and in *Sinai,* theGerman-language monthly magazine that he established in America, Einhorn es-poused intellectually consistent Reform and ridiculed piecemeal efforts to achieve decorum. He denounced both Wise and Leeser and expressed his contempt for the level of intellectual life in America, which he called "a land of humbug." Einhorn was never at home in America. His continued stress on the use of the German language (which he called the "carrying case of Reform") was disregarded by his eagerly americanizing congregants. Ultimately many of Einhorn's ideas were ac-cepted but they did not derive from the intellectually rigorous reform he had es-poused. Rather, they provided an *ex post facto* justification for a patchwork of prac-tices that had been accepted for pragmatic reasons.

As the decade of the 1850s drew to a close, American Jewry was gaining in vigor and self-confidence. Without a formal change in ideology, ritual practice, or institu-tional structure, a basic transformation of image and outlook had taken place. As Isaac M. Wise wrote in 1859: "We are Jews in the synagogue and Americans every-where." Formal commitment to Reform was still minimal. I. J. Benjamin, the German Jewish traveler who completed his tour of America in 1861, reported that "in a land that numbers more than two hundred Orthodox congregations, the reform congre-gations number eight." A decade later, there were few congregations in which sub-stantial reforms had *not* been introduced.

The Civil War experience accelerated the americanization of all immigrant groups, and economic growth stimulated upward mobility. American Jewry was moving from margin to mainstream; Isaac M. Wise became a member of the board of directors of the Free Religious Association alongside Ralph Waldo Emerson. Sumptuous new edifices arose in all the major cities of the land to house affluent congregations now eager for an elegant, decorous style of worship compatible with the new setting.

In 1869, David Einhorn convened a conference of rabbis in Philadelphia to formulate a statement of principles that would serve as a platform for the reformation of Judaism in America. Twelve rabbis, most of them recently arrived in America, participated. The brief credo which was adopted disavowed the hope for the restoration of Zion or for a personal Messiah, stressing Israel's "universal mission" and the goal of a messianic age that would "realize the unity of all rational creatures and their call to moral sanctification." The statement was issued in German; not surprisingly, it had little discernible impact.

Four years later, in 1873, Wise succeeded in organizing a "Union of American Hebrew Congregations" in Cincinnati with thirty-four congregations participating. In 1875, this Union became the sponsoring organization of the Hebrew Union College, the Reform seminary that has ever since trained and ordained rabbis.

With the exception of the old-line Sefardic synagogues, most of the well-established congregations in the country had become affiliates of the Union by the end of the decade. Reform had carried the day. Without any formal action or specific reformulation, Jewish doctrine had been redefined to conform to the presumed dictates of reason. Jewish ritual practice had been modified to reflect the tastes of an increasingly acculturated constituency in search of "respectability." For a brief period it seemed as though an increasingly homogeneous American Jewry of 250,000 had achieved what it regarded as a generally accepted "American Jewish" pattern.

The formal platform of American Reform Judaism was adopted after the reformation had been achieved. In 1885, Kaufmann Kohler, son-in-law and intellectual heir of David Einhorn, convened a conference of rabbis in Pittsburgh at which he proposed adoption of a platform "broad, compassionate, enlightened, and liberal enough to impress and win all hearts and also firm and positive enough to dispel agnostic tendencies or those discontinuing the historic thread of the past." An eight-point resolution was adopted by the seventeen rabbis who assembled. It hailed "the modern era of the universal culture of heart and intellect [and] the approach of the realization of Israel's great Messianic hope for the establishment of the kingdom of truth, justice, and peace among all men." All ceremonies regarded as "not adapted to the views and habits of modern civilization" were rejected. The traditional hope for national restoration was repudiated: "We consider ourselves no longer a nation but a religious community." Judaism emerged, in the words of the resolution, as a "progressive religion ever striving to be in accord with the postulates of reason."

THE IMPACT OF THE NEW IMMIGRATION

By the time this platform was adopted the situation of American Jewry was being radically altered by the influx of eastern European Jewish immigrants. Beginning in 1881, a flood of immigrants virtually inundated the existing community. By 1900 more than a half million had arrived and between 1900 and 1914 another million and a quarter. Reform was reduced to a marginal position representing only a fraction of American Jews of an upper social and economic level.

The new immigrants were poor, spoke Yiddish (derided as "jargon" by Jewish speakers of "pure" German and English), and, in large part, traditional in their religious practices, though few of them were highly educated or sophisticated in their religious training. They were mostly simple people from towns and villages whose folk religion and natural piety were not easily transplanted to the turbulent industrial urban environment of America. The surviving representatives of traditional Judaism in the established American Jewish community attempted to respond to the new constituency and in 1885 organized the Jewish Theological Seminary of America in New York to train rabbis. The gap between the decorous, acculturated, English-speaking Orthodoxy and the new immigrants was too great to permit communication, and the seminary failed to gain a following among the new immigrants until it was reorganized in 1901.

An attempt was made by the immigrants to transplant their European religious pattern to the New World. In 1888 a group of eastern European synagogues in New York joined together to bring Jacob Joseph, a well-known scholar from Vilna, to New York to serve as "chief rabbi." But the effort was undermined by the indifference of the majority of Orthodox congregations, which were not involved in the project, by opposition from Reform rabbis and the americanized Orthodox, and by the antagonism of secular and radical immigrants. Jacob Joseph, confused and disheartened, was never able to assert rabbinical authority in the fragmented and increasingly heterogeneous American Jewish community.

Traditional Judaism remained weak and disorganized in the years before and after the turn of the century. The few attempts to raise the level of religious study, to maintain standards of observance, and to exercise authority met with little success. The Rabbi Isaac Elchanan Theological Seminary—the first *yeshivah* to be established in America—was founded in 1897. Decades later it became the basis for the development of Yeshiva University, but at the time, it remained small and exercised little influence. In 1898, Henry Pereira Mendes, the rabbi of the Sefardic Shearith Israel Congregation in New York, organized a Union of Orthodox Jewish Congregations, and in 1902, a Union of Orthodox Rabbis was formed. Both remained marginal and their influence at the time was negligible. No institution emerged to serve as a center for the religious life of eastern European Jewry. An impoverished immigrant community, struggling to establish itself and to deal with problems of poverty, social dislocation, and linguistic adjustments, could not yet deal with the challenge of a new and radically different religious environment.

In response to the circumstances and opportunities of American life, new institutions emerged that in part fulfilled the vacuum created by religious inadequacy. *Landsmannschaften*—fraternal organizations of Jews from the same European town or province—flourished. To the extent of their ability they addressed problems of mutual aid and provided support in the face of illness and death. Jewish trade unions assumed functions not only in conducting labor negotiations but also in providing cultural and educational opportunities for workers. A vigorous Yiddish press provided a forum for disseminating ideas and giving circulation to literature. The flourishing Yiddish theater served as a vehicle for the expression and release of shared emotions and experiences. Political organizations of all shades and hues competed for the allegiance and support of the Jewish masses. In the midst of poverty and struggle one irrepressible characteristic flourished: vitality.

After the turn of the century, leaders of the americanized and largely native-born community took increasingly effective measures to deal with the problems of the immigrant element. Jacob Schiff and Louis Marshall were two who exercised leadership in organizing communal agencies that dealt with social welfare and civil rights. Among their endeavors was the reorganization of the Jewish Theological Seminary of America (JTSA) in 1901 to serve as a center for the creation of an American version of traditional Judaism. Their financial support made it possible to bring Solomon Schechter from England to serve as president of the seminary.

Schechter was a distinguished scholar who had both eastern European rabbinic training and a German university education. In addition he served as reader in rabbinics at Cambridge University in England. Schechter created a seminary in which traditional Jewish learning was combined with critical scholarship and use of the English language. Like the pragmatic reformers fifty years earlier, he emphasized decorum and dignity in religious worship.

Schechter and his associates accepted the idea that Judaism would change in response to modern conditions but believed that the necessary changes must be made within the framework of the Jewish legal tradition. The type of modified americanized traditionalism espoused at the Jewish Theological Seminary came to be known as Conservative Judaism—a position between Reform and Orthodoxy. In 1909, a Teachers Institute was established at the seminary. By 1913, Schechter was able to form the United Synagogue of America with sixteen congregations identified as Conservative and with the participation of the association of Conservative rabbis called the Rabbinical Assembly.

When the eastern European immigration grew enormously in the 1890s, an effort was organized by the Jewish Colonization Association to divert a portion of the immigrant stream to Argentina. The Jewish population of Argentina was then 6,085. By 1914, it was estimated as 100,000–117,000. The Jewish settlers who went to Argentina were predominantly secular in their outlook, and religious life remained at a low level. Not until 1910 were Jews there able to acquire their own cemetery. Not until the late 1930s did religious institutions of significance emerge in Argentina.

CHANGES AFTER WORLD WAR I

The outbreak of World War I interrupted the mass immigration to the United States. After the war it was briefly resumed and then was permanently reduced by Congress's adoption of stringent immigration quotas in 1921 and 1924. The process of americanization was accelerated as Jews moved out of immigrant ghettoes into second areas of settlement and up into the middle class. By the mid-1920s, the Jewish population of the United States was estimated at about four million.

The increase in affluence and acculturation resulted in a rash of synagogue building, especially in areas of new settlement. New structures were often elaborate and contained classrooms, auditoriums, and occasionally gymnasiums. Mordecai Kaplan (1881–1983), a Conservative rabbi and dean of the Teachers Institute of the Jewish Theological Seminary, developed the idea of a "synagogue-center" and established such an institution in New York.

The United Synagogue grew rapidly during the 1920s and 1930s. Conservative Judaism provided a combination of traditional ambience with English-language readings and sermons that appealed to the acculturated immigrant and the second-generation Jewish citizen for whom Reform was too cold and old-fashioned Orthodoxy too chaotic. Men and women sat together, the prayers were slightly abbreviated, and individuals whose attachment was more directed to the Jewish people than to religion could feel at home.

The Reform movement during this decade was at a virtual standstill. Its institutions were located in Cincinnati, now far from the centers of Jewish life, and its mode of worship attracted few of eastern European origin. Moreover, the prevailing anti-Zionism of the movement antagonized secularists with Zionist sentiments. To counter this trend, Stephen S. Wise, a Reform rabbi and leading Zionist, established the Jewish Institute of Religion in New York in 1922. In 1947, the institute was united with the Hebrew Union College and maintained as the New York branch of the combined Reform seminary.

The state of Orthodoxy in the 1920s is less clearly defined. On the one hand, americanized immigrants and their children were becoming less and less observant and many were abandoning religious practice and affiliation altogether. At the same time, small but significant steps were taken to develop an American form of Orthodoxy that might confront the challenge. In 1915 in New York, Bernard Revel became head of the Rabbi Isaac Elchanan Theological Seminary, which merged with Yeshivat Etz Chaim. Secular studies were introduced, and in 1928 Yeshiva College was established as the first general (nonrabbinic) institution of higher education under Jewish sponsorship. In 1923, the Rabbinical Council of America, in which alumni of American *yeshivot* predominated, was formed.

The restriction of immigration to the United States in the 1920s diverted a significant number of immigrants to Canada. Prior to 1900, the Jewish population of Canada numbered less than 16,000 and most of these were recent immigrants. By 1930, the population had increased to 140,000. The predominance of eastern European Jews who were recent immigrants and the multilingual nature of Canadian society resulted in a stronghold of Yiddish language and Jewish secular culture. The progress of the Reform movement there was slow whereas the Conservative movement made rapid strides. Both Conservative and Reform congregations and their rabbis are affiliated with the movements in the United States.

In the 1930s the rise of Hitler and the resurgence of anti-Semitism brought a radical change in the outlook and orientation of American Jewry. The Reform movement reassessed its attitude toward Jewish peoplehood, Zionism, and traditional practices. In 1937, the Reform Central Conference of American Rabbis (CCAR) adopted a new platform embracing these changes which stressed the "group-loyalty of Jews" and affirmed "the obligation of all Jews to aid in the rebuilding [of Palestine] as a Jewish homeland by endeavors to make it not only a haven for the oppressed but also a center of Jewish culture and spiritual life." The Union of American Hebrew Congregations (UAHC) unanimously passed a resolution urging restoration of traditional symbols and customs. In 1940, a revised version of the Reform movement's *Union Prayer Book* appeared; it restored some ceremonies and moved closer to the traditional prayer book.

The Conservative movement was energized by the ideas of Mordecai Kaplan, who described Judaism as a "religious civilization," and who stressed "peoplehood" and the totality of Jewish culture. In 1935, Kaplan founded the Reconstructionist movement as an ideological tendency within American Jewry in general and within the Conservative movement in particular. His theological emphasis on religious naturalism was less influential than his sociological emphasis on Jewish communality.

Orthodoxy in America was strengthened by the arrival of distinguished European scholars and rabbinic leaders at the end of the 1930s. Joseph Soloveitchik (1903–) became the leading rabbinical figure among the "enlightened Orthodox" associated with Yeshiva College and the religious Zionists. Moshe Feinstein (1895–1986), one of the leading rabbinical authorities in *halakhah* (Jewish law), became an outstanding figure in right-wing Orthodoxy and in the Agudat Yisra'el movement. The presence of these and other rabbinical leaders together with numbers of refugee *yeshivah* students paved the way for a revival of Orthodoxy in the postwar period.

The flow of refugees in the 1930s, seeking admission to any haven in which they could find respite, led to the strengthening of small Jewish communities in Central and South America. Immigration restrictions everywhere in the Western Hemisphere held the number of immigrants to a minimum, and religious life south of the border remained diffuse and disorganized. However, communal organizations stressing mutual aid and defense against anti-Semitism did emerge in countries such as Mexico, Brazil, and Chile. In 1982 the Jewish population of Latin America was estimated as 464,700. Of this total, 233,000 resided in Argentina, 100,000 in Brazil, 35,000 in Mexico, and 20,000 in Chile (*American Jewish Yearbook,* vol. 85, 1985, p. 55).

AMERICAN JUDAISM SINCE WORLD WAR II

As a consequence of the destruction of European Jewry during World War II, the center of gravity of Jewish life shifted to the United States and to the newly founded state of Israel. The catastrophe in Europe and the struggle for the establishment of Israel had drawn hundreds of thousands of Jews into Jewish fund-raising and rescue activity. The heightened sense of Jewishness, combined with rapid suburbanization and the stimulus of the general religious revival in America, resulted in an unprecedented growth in Jewish religious institutions. The Reform movement, which claimed 290 temples and 50,000 families in 1937, reported 520 congregations and 255,000 families in 1956. The Conservative movement, with 250 synagogues and 75,000 member families in 1937, claimed over 500 congregations and 200,000 families in 1956. Both Reform and Conservative seminaries opened branches in the Los Angeles area. Synagogue affiliation—if not personal observance—had become a central element of Jewish identification in America.

New influences exerted themselves on Jewish religious life. Rabbis like Joshua Loth Liebman (1907–1948) led the way in reconciling religion with psychology. Will Herberg, sociologist and philosopher, and himself a returnee from Marxism to Judaism, led the way in redefining Judaism in terms of religious existentialism. Herberg also proposed a revision of the "melting pot" theory of American pluralism in which the three major religious traditions—Catholic, Protestant, and Jewish—would become the vehicle for preserving diversity in American society in what he described as a "triple melting pot." Abraham Joshua Heschel (1907–1972), a refugee rabbi and scholar from eastern Europe who became an influential member of the faculty of the Jewish Theological Seminary, espoused a Neo-Orthodox, neo-mystical approach to Judaism that proved to be extremely appealing to rabbis and laity alike.

Orthodoxy, which suffered numerical losses in the large-scale move from city to suburbs, nonetheless showed remarkable vigor. In 1945, Yeshiva College became Yeshiva University, and in subsequent years expanded to include Stern College for Women, Revel Graduate School, and Einstein Medical College. Jewish all-day schools on both the elementary and high school levels proliferated, primarily under Orthodox auspices.

Post–World War II immigration greatly strengthened the ultra-Orthodox segment of American Jewry, especially its Hasidic branch. Survivors of Hasidic Jewish communities, uprooted by Hitler, emigrated together with their rabbinic leaders *(rebeyim)* and settled in enclaves primarily in New York City and its vicinity. The branch of Hasidism known as Habad (Lubavitch) established a network of schools and centers and adopted a policy of outreach to secular and non-Hasidic Jews. In contrast, the extremist Satmar Hasidic sect maintained its isolation and its vigorous opposition to Zionism and the state of Israel on the grounds that the re-creation of a Jewish commonwealth must await the coming of a supernatural messiah sent by God. [*See* Hasidism.] From the left wing of Reform to the most extreme right wing of Orthodoxy, Judaism in the United States and Canada grew in institutional strength and in vitality.

The Jewish religious revival of the 1950s seemed to wane in the early 1960s when the Jewish community, like the general society, was swept up in a wave of social action. While the "God is dead" movement never exercised significant influence within Judaism, there was a palpable diminution of involvement in religious institutions and a loss of influence by religious leaders. This tendency was sharply reversed in the late 1960s. The changing mood of the general community fueled a revival of ethnicity that strengthened Jewish identity and motivated increased Jewish communal involvement. At the same time, the threat to Israel's existence prior to the Six Day War in 1967 evoked strong emotions of commitment and solidarity among American Jews. The energies that were generated led to new initiatives within all religious movements in Judaism, especially on the part of young adults.

Among the results of this revival was a significant increase in the number and quality of Jewish day schools under Conservative and Reform, as well as Orthodox, auspices. A new form of religious fellowship called the *havurah* emerged as a significant factor. These self-generated, intimate groups of intensely committed Jews were sometimes independent and sometimes to be found within large synagogues. In either case, they generally functioned without rabbinical supervision. Despite the informal structure and the absence of rigid institutional or ideological affiliation, *havurah* groups grew sufficiently to form a network of their own and in 1979 established a National Havurah Committee which serves as a vehicle for exchange of ideas and experiences. In 1985, this committee estimated that between fifteen hundred and two thousand *havurot* functioned regularly with membership ranging from twenty to eighty participants. Approximately 30 percent of these were affiliated with synagogues.

At the same time, the study of Judaism and Jewish subjects on the college campus expanded rapidly, often stimulated by student interest and by communal support. Together with these formal developments, a movement of *ba'alei teshuvah*—"penitent returners," who might be characterized as "born-again" Jews—gained strength. The returnees were to be found in all of the movements, but most visibly among the Orthodox.

While the general tendency in all branches of Judaism in recent years has been toward increased observance, the gap between the Orthodox and non-Orthodox has been widened by the conflict over women's rights. The Orthodox have resisted demands for changes in status in Jewish law by women in their own ranks and have maintained the traditional role of women as mothers and homemakers. The Reform and Reconstructionist movements have ordained women as rabbis and as cantors. The Conservative movement engaged in a lengthy struggle on this issue that was resolved only in 1984. The movement decided by a split vote to begin the ordination of women. Despite ongoing opposition by a "traditionalist" minority, the decision is being implemented.

Perhaps the most serious challenge faced by the community as a whole is the growing rate of intermarriage and the low birthrate. This tendency has been even more pronounced in the relatively small Jewish communities of Central and South America. Demographic projections envision a substantial reduction in the size of the Jewish community of the Western Hemisphere unless these tendencies can be reversed or at least contained. The Reform movement has reacted to this problem by initiating a program for converting non-Jewish spouses and integrating them into the community. It has also modified the traditional Jewish law that maintains that the child of a Jewish mother is a born Jew while the child of a Jewish father and a non-Jewish mother is not. Such changes have widened the gap between the movements and threaten to produce a schism within the Jewish community over the question "Who is a Jew?"

The prognosis for the future of American Jewry is subject to widely differing assessments. Optimists point to the increase in observance among significant numbers of American Jews; pessimists point to the large and growing number who are not affiliated with a synagogue or with any Jewish communal organization. Optimists point to the growth of Jewish day schools and their emergence in the Conservative and Reform branches of American Jewry; pessimists decry the decline in numbers and quality of supplementary afternoon and weekend schools and the sharp decline in enrollment. Optimists point to the development of programs of Jewish studies in universities, to developments in Jewish ritual art and cultural programs, and to innovative experiments in liturgy, music, and drama; pessimists view the increase in intermarriage and the low birthrate among Jews as symptoms of a decrease in numbers and vitality. Given the complexity and uncertainty of conditions in the last decades of the twentieth century, both points of view are plausible. American Jewry in 1986 remains a vigorous, densely organized, diverse community of 6.2 million, 45 percent of whom are affiliated with more than three thousand synagogues that encompass a wide variety of institutional and ideological options.

[*For further discussion of the four main movements in America, see the independent entries on* Orthodox Judaism; Reform Judaism; Conservative Judaism; *and* Reconstructionist Judaism. *See also the biographies of the leading figures mentioned herein.*]

BIBLIOGRAPHY

Blau, Joseph L. *Judaism in America.* Chicago, 1976.
Eisen, Arnold. *The Chosen People in America: A Study in Jewish Religious Ideology.* Bloomington, Ind., 1983.

Glazer, Nathan. *American Judaism*. Chicago, 1972.

Halpern, Ben. *The American Jew: A Zionist Analysis*. New York, 1956.

Jick, Leon A. *The Americanization of the Synagogue, 1820–1870*. Hanover, N.H., 1976.

Koltun, Elizabeth. *The Jewish Woman in America*. New York, 1976.

Korn, Bertram Wallace. *American Jewry and the Civil War*. New York, 1970.

Liebman, Charles S. *The Ambivalent American Jew: Politics, Religion and Family in American Jewish Life*. Philadelphia, 1973.

Marcus, Jacob R. *The Colonial American Jew, 1492–1776*. 3 vols. Detroit, 1970.

Marcus, Jacob R. *The American Jewish Woman, 1654–1980: A Documentary History*. New York, 1981.

Sherman, Charles Bezalel. *The Jews within American Society: A Study in Ethnic Individuality*. Detroit, 1961.

Sidorsky, David, ed. *The Future of the Jewish Community in America*. New York, 1973.

Sklare, Marshall. *America's Jews*. New York, 1971.

Sklare, Marshall. *Conservative Judaism: An American Religious Movement*. New York, 1972.

Teller, Judd L. *Strangers and Natives: The Evolution of the Jew from 1921 to the Present*. New York, 1968.

FOUR

TRADITIONAL PATTERNS OF JEWISH LIFE

15 JEWISH WORSHIP

LAWRENCE A. HOFFMAN

Beyond the spontaneous prayer, petition, and thanksgiving that individual Jews may appropriately offer at any time to God, Judaism formally prescribes both private and public worship. Private worship is particularly to be found at home, where it is dependent on set occasions (especially meals) but may also be evoked spontaneously by the normal or the miraculous in life (e.g., seeing a rainbow, recovering from illness) or by the anticipation of performing divine commandments (e.g., kindling lights on Shabbat). In all such cases, Jewish tradition specifies standardized benedictions linking God (as sovereign and benefactor or commander) to the specific circumstance of the moment.

Public prayer is similar, in that it too is fixed by time (thrice daily and additionally on holy days), and is constructed around the literary style of the benediction. The contents of public prayer are relegated to prayer books (the *siddur* and the *mahzor*), and their recitation is directed by a prayer leader called the *sheliah tsibbur*. The normal locus of public worship is the synagogue sanctuary, where Judaism's primary religious symbol, the Torah scroll, is prominently displayed.

Synagogue worship defies comprehension without a prior understanding of the ancient sacrificial cult, which preceded it and which constituted the central institution of Jewish worship until the Temple's destruction in 70 CE. This Temple cult consisted of a series of sacrifices arranged in scrupulous detail and allotted according to a sacred calendar: the Passover offering, for example, by which one recapitulated one's place in the formative Exodus experience; or the high priest's meticulous attention to his sacred Yom Kippur task in order to cleanse the people from sin and reinstate them to their rightful position of covenantal trust. This service, then, was highly structured and dependent on the expertise of a specific class—in this case, the priests—who represented the entire people as a collective covenantal partner and who based their activity on the single, central manifesto of Israel's pact with the divine, the Torah, which they preserved and interpreted.

By the first century CE, at least, we find an alternative locus for worship, the synagogue. Its origins are unknown, as are the details of its pre-70 worship patterns. But after 70, it filled the vacuum left by the defunct Temple cult. The most outstanding feature of synagogue worship was its dependence on a detailed system of legislation, frequently patterned explicitly after the cult. For example, the prime prayer (the Tefillah) was likened explicitly to sacrifice (B.T., *Ber.* 26b, 32a) and was scheduled to coincide with the precise times that animal offerings had once taken place. Even terminology was transferred intact; the terms *minḥah* and *musaf,* for example, which originally denoted the afternoon and additional Temple sacrifices, were used to name their equivalent synagogue prayer services instead. The synagogue was thus likened to a *miqdash me'at,* a "Temple in miniature" (B.T., *Meg.* 29a), in which words were offered as animals once had been, according to carefully adumbrated rules of time, place, and procedure.

This service too was dependent on a class of experts: rabbis schooled in oral interpretation of the written Torah. Any qualified person—traditionally, an adult male possessing proper ritual cleanliness, knowledge, and personal piety—might presume to lead worship. This was the *sheliaḥ tsibbur,* literally, "a [legal] agent of the worshiping community," who, like the priest, presented offerings (of words, however, not animals) on the people's behalf to God.

The ideological fulcrum for the whole rabbinic system, worship included, was still the Torah. A serialized reading of scripture was itself presented as an integral part of the public act of worship, so that eventually the entire scroll would have been proclaimed publicly. This event was accompanied by Simḥat Torah, a holiday that celebrated the completion of one cycle and the simultaneous beginning of another, so that, symbolically speaking, no time elapsed during which the community was not engaged in studying holy writ as an integral part of equally holy devotion. Elsewhere too, early each morning, for example, descriptions of sacrifice were recited as if they were prayers addressed to God, so that study itself emerged here as a licit mode of worship.

We may summarize the classic rabbinic worship mode, therefore, by describing it as centered on the word: the people's words (as offerings) were presented to God, and God's word (as *torah,* "law") proclaimed in return. This took place in a representative community (a quorum of ten or more worshipers, called a *minyan*) and was led by agents who directed the presentation of the appropriate words in carefully delineated ways.

This classical pattern, however, represents only the rabbinic ideal, not the totality of Jewish practice extant in the formative post-70 years, nor its demonstrable variety through the centuries. Today the same activities and roles may predominate, but their original connection to the cult goes unrecognized, at least on a conscious level. While retaining its word-oriented focus, therefore, as well as its dependence on Torah, its utilization of the *sheliaḥ tsibbur,* and so on, Jewish practice has added layer after layer of later interpretation to its act of worship, and these are no less authentic than the original stratum.

Four specific examples without which today's totality of Jewish worship is hardly imaginable demonstrate this diversity:

1. In the same early rabbinic Jewry that developed the ideal worship patterns described above, it was common to pattern the linguistic structure of prayers and the manner of their recitation after the model of gnostic cosmology, so that much worship proceeded in a deliberate attempt to propel the worshipers to an immediate apprehension of God seated in a chariot of light and surrounded by praising angels. The angels' presumed antiphonal mode of recitation became the

normative synagogue practice (to this day), as *sheliaḥ tsibbur* and worshiping assembly took turns expressing God's praise.

2. Sixteenth- and seventeenth-century qabbalists saw their devotion as a necessary step to the reparation of a fragmented universe in which God, no less than humanity, is cast in a state best likened to the exile of a people from its home, or a husband and wife from each other, and even invented the now-popular service welcoming the Sabbath with its outstanding hymn, *Lekhah dodi* (Come, My Beloved), to express that motif.

3. Hasidism of the eighteenth century elaborated upon qabbalistic theory but introduced the novelties of quietistic contemplation, on one hand, and ecstatic communal singing and dancing, on the other. [*See* Hasidism, *overview article.*]

4. Reform Judaism began in the nineteenth and early twentieth century as a movement whose members looked askance at both Qabbalah and Hasidism. Instead, they emulated the cultic model of antiquity by outfitting the architecture of their synagogues (which they called "temples") with accoutrements typical of the Temple of old (the seven-branched lampstand, or *menorah,* for example) and by accenting the theological notion of a priestly people whose rabbinical leaders were awarded uniquely sacerdotal roles in prayer. Yet they differed fundamentally from that same cultic model, emphasizing instead a prophetic ideal, whereby prayer is seen as the highest spiritual activity, designed in part to render human beings morally sensitive to God's will.

Depending on time and place, Jews have been known to sing, to chant, to meditate, to cry out, and to read in unison; they have prayed sitting, standing, swaying, bowing, facing Jerusalem, or lying prostrate. Their prayers have begged, demanded, praised, petitioned, and thanked. They have worshiped for ends transcending the act of worship and for the sake of worship itself. The efficacy of prayer has been entrusted to adult males through most of Jewish history; to a specific *rebe* descended from the group's founder, in the case of certain Hasidic sects; and to all adult men and women in liberal American Judaism of today. Almost universally, men have worn specialized prayer garb, but the rules governing these items have varied considerably; in most Reform synagogues, to take one modern movement, for example, men do not wear them at all, while in others some men and also some women do. Most modern synagogues feature sermonic commentaries on the weekly Torah reading.

In the face of all this flux, constants in Jewish public worship are harder to find than one would expect. But they include (1) the congregation as a symbolic representation of Israel, the covenanted community; (2) the ritual reassertion of that community's link to a covenanting God, who gave Torah, promised life beyond death, and guaranteed ultimate meaningfulness to human history and to whom, therefore, words of praise, petition, and thanks are appropriately offered, nowadays in a fixed verbal form codified in prayer books; (3) stipulated rules of procedure that are directed by specially designated leaders who represent the congregation and who achieve their status by knowledge of Torah; and (4) a symbolization of the Torah's centrality, insofar as it is studied, read publicly every week, and ritually presented as the mediating symbol between Israel and its God.

[*For further background to synagogue-centered worship, see* Biblical Temple *and* Priesthood, *article on* Jewish Priesthood. *For normative Judaism, see* Synagogue, *article on* History and Tradition, *and, for the development of the liturgy,* Siddur and

Mahzor. *See also* Domestic Observances, *article on* Jewish Practices; Folk Religion, *article on* Folk Judaism; Rites of Passage, *article on* Jewish Rites; *and individual entries on Shabbat and Jewish holidays.*]

BIBLIOGRAPHY

The determining features of the rabbinic system of worship are most clearly defined in Richard S. Sarason's "Religion and Worship: The Case of Judaism," in *Take Judaism for Example,* edited by Jacob Neusner (Chicago, 1983), pp. 49–65. See also Sarason's translation of Joseph Heinemann's *Prayer in the Talmud* (Berlin, 1977), which, although preeminently a form of critical study of the liturgy itself, necessarily deals also with the tannaitic life of prayer as it arose through early rabbinic institutions. In *Understanding Jewish Prayer* (New York, 1972), Jakob J. Petuchowski has collected a series of essays on such topics as prayer in Hebrew versus prayer in the vernacular, the conflict between spontaneity and tradition, and the role of synagogue poetry. The conflict between spontaneity and tradition is also addressed in H. G. Enelow's " 'Kawwana': The Struggle for Inwardness in Judaism," in *Studies in Jewish Literature Issued in Honor of Professor Kaufmann Kohler* (Berlin, 1913), pp. 82–107. Other relevant essays on specific topics appear in several collections: my own *Gates of Understanding,* vol. 1 (New York, 1977), in which see especially pages 111–168; Asher Finkel and Lawrence Frizzell's *Standing before God: Studies on Prayer in Scriptures and in Tradition* (New York, 1981); and Daniel F. Polish and Eugene Fisher's *Liturgical Foundations of Social Policy in the Catholic and Jewish Traditions* (Notre Dame, Ind., 1983).

The perspective of early Jewish mysticism emerges clearly in Gershom Scholem's *Jewish Gnosticism, Merkabah Mysticism, and Talmudic Tradition,* 2d ed. (New York, 1965), and in my essay "Censoring In and Censoring Out: A Function of Liturgical Language," in *Ancient Synagogues,* edited by Joseph Gutmann (Chico, Calif., 1981), pp. 19–37. There are few serious studies of mystical prayer in the medieval period, but for all schools of Jewish mysticism generally, see Scholem's classic book *Major Trends in Jewish Mysticism* (1941; reprint, New York, 1961), in which see the index, s.v. *Prayer.* For sixteenth-century Lurianic Qabbalah, see Scholem's essay "Tradition and New Creation in the Ritual of the Kabbalists," in his *On the Kabbalah and Its Symbolism* (New York, 1965), pp. 118–157. For the earlier twelfth-century German mystics, the *hasidei Ashkenaz,* see Ivan G. Marcus's "The Politics and Ethics of Pietism in Judaism," *Journal of Religious Ethics* 8 (1980): 227–258, and *Piety and Society: The Jewish Pietists of Medieval Germany* (Leiden, 1981). Later Polish Hasidism (eighteenth century and beyond) is described in Louis Jacobs's *Hasidic Prayer* (New York, 1972); in Rivka Schatz's "Contemplative Prayer in Hasidism," in *Studies in Mysticism and Religion Presented to Gershom G. Scholem,* edited by E. E. Urbach et al. (Jerusalem, 1967), pp. 209–226; and in Arthur Green's *Tormented Master: A Life of Rabbi Nahman of Bratslav* (University, Ala., 1979), in which see the index, s.v. *Prayer.*

16 THE STRUCTURE OF HALAKHAH

David Novak

Halakhah, in the general sense of the word, is the entire body of Jewish law, from scripture to the latest rabbinical rulings. It is a complete system of law governing every aspect of human life. It has been traditionally viewed as wholly rooted in God's revealed will (B.T., *Hag.* 3b) but subject to the ongoing interpretation of the Jewish jurists (B.T., *B.M.* 59b).

In its more specific sense *halakhah* (pl., *halakhot*) refers to those laws that were traditionally observed by the Jewish people as if they were scriptural commandments *(mitsvot)* even though they were nowhere explicitly found in scripture. The term itself, according to Saul Lieberman in *Hellenism in Jewish Palestine* (New York, 1962), seems to refer to the statement of a juristic norm as opposed to actual case law. The task of much rabbinic exegesis, especially during the tannaitic period (c. 70–200 CE), was to show that through the use of proper hermeneutics the *halakhot* could be derived from the text of scripture, especially the Pentateuch. When this could not be done, the specific *halakhah* was termed "a law of Moses from Sinai."

ORIGINS

Concerning the origins of *halakhah* there are three main theories.

The first, the traditional, rabbinic approach, is founded on the literal meaning of "a law of Moses from Sinai," namely, that Moses received two sets of teachings at Mount Sinai, one written (the Pentateuch) and the other oral *(torah she-be'al peh),* and that the oral Torah is the authoritative explanation of the written Torah (B.T., *Ber.* 5a). Thus all subsequent interpretation is in effect recollection of what had already been revealed at Sinai (J.T., *Meg.* 4.1,74d). This theory explains that the constant rabbinical disputes over virtually every point of *halakhah* are due not to any inherent ambiguity in the tradition itself but, rather, to insufficient mastery of the tradition by the rabbis (Tosefta, *Sot.* 14.10).

The second theory is that of Moses Maimonides (Mosheh ben Maimon, 1135/8–1204). Although he too reiterated the literal meaning of the totally Mosaic origin of *halakhah,* in his specific treatment of the constitution of halakhic authority he states that *halakhah* is based on scripture and, equally, on the rulings of the Great Court in Jerusalem (*Mishneh Torah,* Rebels 1.1ff.). This is Mosaic law in that the members of the Great Court are Moses' authoritative successors. Maimonides explains the fact of constant rabbinical disputes in *halakhah* as due to the loss of political sovereignty, which led to the demise of the Great Court's jurisdiction. By this theory Maimonides places both rabbinical legislation and traditional *halakhah* on the same level.

The third theory is that of Zacharias Frankel (1801–1875). Expanding certain medieval comments into a more general theory, Frankel, in *Darkhei ha-Mishnah* (Leipzig, 1859), saw the term "a law of Moses from Sinai" as primarily referring to ancient laws that had become widespread in Jewish practice and whose origins were obscure. They were regarded as if they had come from the actual time of Moses. Frankel's theory, which received severe criticism from more orthodox scholars, reflected the growing historical consciousness of nineteenth-century Jewish scholarship and, also, stimulated research into the different historical origins of various *halakhot.* Frankel, then, along with other scholars of his time, laid the foundation for the historical understanding of *halakhah* as a developmental phenomenon.

SCRIPTURAL EXEGESIS

Because of the Pharisaic and rabbinic emphasis on the essential unity of the written Torah and the *halakhah,* in contradistinction to the Sadducean, which accepted only the former as authoritative (B.T., *Hor.* 4a), an elaborate hermeneutical system was worked out to derive as many of the *halakhot* as possible from the words of scripture, which was considered normatively unintelligible without the process of specifically relating it to the *halakhah* (B.T., *Shab.* 31a). This entire process was called *midrash,* literally meaning "inquiry" into scripture. The most important statement of this rabbinic hermeneutic is the "Thirteen Methods of Rabbi Yishma'e'l" (*Sifra',* intro.). The most widely used of these methods and the most typical was the *gezerah shavah;* namely, the process by which a word in one scriptural context was interpreted according to its meaning in another context. Since this type of interpretation was only for buttressing already normative *halakhot,* what it accomplished was a much wider latitude for tradition to determine the meaning of scripture (J.T., *Pes.* 6.1, 33a). However, not only did such hermeneutical methods support already normative *halakhot,* but they also led to the formulation of new norms. The most prominent proponent of this constructive exegesis was the second-century sage 'Aqiva' ben Yosef, although his oftentimes daring interpretations elicited the criticism of his more conservative teachers and colleagues (B.T., *Men.* 89a).

In tannaitic texts a distinction is made between direct scriptural exegesis (*derashah*) and indirect exegesis. In a purely normative sense, however, it is difficult to see any authoritative difference between laws buttressed by the latter as opposed to the former. Both sets of laws were regarded as traditional *halakhot;* the only difference is that the former were more satisfactorily based on scripture.

RABBINIC LAW

In the amoraic period (c. 220–c. 500) there emerged a more clear-cut distinction between laws considered scriptural (*de-oraita'*) and laws considered rabbinic (*de-rabbanan*). The difference between scriptural law and rabbinic law by this time was that the latter was considered to be evidently rational. As for scriptural law, despite attempts to discover "reasons for the commandments" *(ṭa'amei ha-mitsvot),* God's will was considered sufficient reason for it. "I have made a statute; I have decreed a decree; you are not permitted to violate my decrees" *(Nm. Rab.* 19.1). This phrase was used to refute any suggestion that only those laws whose reasons were evident were authoritative. In fact, certain scriptural laws were admitted to be rationally incomprehensible, but their authority was nevertheless emphasized as being because "my father in heaven has decreed such for me" *(Sifra',* Shemini, ed. Weiss, 93b).

Rabbinic law, although occasionally justified by indirect scriptural exegesis *(asmakhta'),* was then usually justified as being for the fulfillment of some religious or social need (B.T., *Ber.* 23b). This developed to such an extent that it was claimed that there were only three rabbinic laws for which no reason could be immediately discerned (B.T., *Giṭ.* 14a). Furthermore, the lines between direct and indirect exegesis were considerably blurred (B.T., *Pes.* 39b). Finally, Rava', a fourth-century Babylonian sage who became the most prominent advocate of rational jurisprudence, indicated that the rabbis actually had more legislative power than even scripture (B.T., *Mak.* 22b). Nevertheless, although in theory the punishment for the violation of rabbinic law could be even more severe than that for the violation of scriptural law *(San.* 11.3), in reality it was almost always more lenient *(Naz.* 4.3). In case of doubt, in matters concerning scriptural law the benefit of the doubt favored the law, but in rabbinic law it favored the accused (B.T., *Beits.* 3b).

The question of the extent of scriptural law versus rabbinic law was deeply debated among the medieval Jewish jurists. Maimonides, following the Talmudic opinion that scriptural law is limited to 613 Pentateuchal commandments (B.T., *Mak.* 23b), considered any other laws, whether traditional or formulated through exegesis or rabbinical legislation, as having the status of rabbinic laws *(Sefer ha-mitsvot,* intro., sec. 2). Moses Nahmanides (Mosheh ben Naḥman, c. 1194–1270), on the other hand, was of the opinion that anything designated by the rabbis as scriptural law, especially those laws derived hermeneutically in rabbinic literature, has the status of scriptural law. Only those laws specifically designated by the rabbis as rabbinic are to be considered as such. This difference of opinion concerning the very character of *halakhah* is philosophical. Maimonides' prime concern seems to have been with the process of legislation, that is, with the ability of the duly constituted authorities to make new laws and repeal old ones. Nahmanides' prime concern seems to have been with a revival of the whole process of rabbinical exegesis. This distinction can be seen in the fact that Maimonides' chief halakhic contribution was that of a highly innovative codifier, whereas Nahmanides' was that of an exegete. This difference of approach can be seen in the Talmud and throughout the history of the *halakhah,* namely, the apodictic approach (B.T., *Nid.* 73a) as contrasted with the expository approach (B.T., *B.M.* 33a).

Rabbinical legislation was considered the original prerogative of the Great Court in Jerusalem *(Sifrei,* Shofṭim, ed. Finkelstein, no. 144). With the diminution of its powers even before the destruction of the Second Temple in 70 CE and its full demise at that time, how much of its power could be transferred to subsequent courts became the subject of considerable discussion.

Sometimes Jewish juridical power was limited because of the lack of political sovereignty; however, internal Jewish political considerations played an even more important role in determining the extent of juridical authority in certain times and places. Despite the destruction of the Second Temple and the demise of the Great Court, there was a strong attempt to retain prime rabbinical authority in the Land of Israel. Thus unqualified rabbinical ordination *(semikhah)*, which was seen as an institution originating with Moses himself, was limited to those rabbis who functioned in the Land of Israel. When in the third century Rav (Abba' bar Ayyvu) left Israel for Babylonia, where he led the revival of the Jewish community, he was granted a qualified ordination, with authorization to adjudicate only in certain questions of law (B.T., *San.* 5a). Nevertheless, with the exception of adjudicating in the area of scripturally fixed fines *(qenasot,* B.T., *B.Q.* 84b), as the Babylonian community grew and developed its own institutions, its rabbis began to claim virtually all of the halakhic prerogatives of the rabbinate of the Land of Israel (B.T., *Git.* 88b). Generally, this set the pattern for subsequent rabbinical authority, namely, that the rabbis in every time and place exercised as much halakhic authority as political and religious conditions both allowed and required (Tosefta, *R. ha-Sh.* 1.18). Moreover, it was recognized that in emergency situations the rabbis had the right to override existing laws temporarily *(hora'at sha'ah)*, even scriptural ones (B.T., *Yev.* 90b). Finally, it was recognized that the rabbis even had the power to abrogate certain aspects of scriptural laws, although this power was considerably qualified (ibid., 89b).

Types of Rabbinical Legislation. Rabbinical legislation can generally be divided into two classes: decrees *(gezerot)* and enactments *(taqqanot)*.

Decrees were justified by the principle traced back to the period of Ezra (sixth century BCE) that "a fence is to be made around the Torah" *(Avot* 1.1). This "fence" consists of prohibitions designed to protect scriptural law from probable transgression. Thus, for example, numerous additional restrictions *(shevut)* were enacted to protect the thirty-nine scriptural prohibitions of Sabbath labor from being carelessly violated, to enhance the overall sanctity of the day, and to guard against behavior that the rabbis saw as inconsistent with the spirit of the law *(Beits.* 5.2). However, to distinguish rabbinical legislation from scriptural law and to prevent an infinite multiplication of strictures, the rabbis emphasized that laws were not to be enacted to protect their laws (B.T., *Beits.* 3a).

Rabbinical enactments were justified by the scriptural prescription that "you not deviate from what the judges will tell you" *(Dt.* 17:11). Although this probably refers to the simple necessity of applying scriptural law, the rabbis saw it as mandating their power to add to it if circumstances warranted doing so. These enactments were of three kinds.

1. Enactments were made to commemorate postbiblical Jewish events. Thus, for example, the recitation of the liturgical formula "Blessed are you, Lord . . . who has commanded us" was justified for the ritual of kindling Hanukkah lights on the grounds that the rabbinical legislation that mandated it is itself prescribed by scripture (B.T., *Shab.* 23a). As the rabbis often put it, "It is a commandment to listen to the words of the sages" (B.T., *Yev.* 20a).
2. Enactments were made to alleviate hardships arising from the widening gap between scriptural law and social and economic realities. Thus, for example, the scriptural law prescribing the cancellation of debts every seventh year *(Dt.* 15:1ff.) proved to be a deterrent to lending money to those who needed it most in a commercial

economy, where long-term loans were becoming more and more common. To alleviate this situation, in accordance with the overall purpose of the Torah, that is, to promote social justice and well-being, Hillel the Elder (first century CE) enacted the institution of *prozbul,* whereby a creditor handed over his note to a court. Since the court collected the debt, the lender avoided the prohibition of personally collecting the debt after the Sabbatical year (*Giṭ.* 4.3).

3. Enactments were made to curtail individual rights, the exercise of which was seen as contrary to the common good. Thus, for example, the third-century Babylonian sage 'Ula' ruled that although scripture permitted repayment of a debt with merchandise of any quality (*Dt.* 24:11), the debtor must repay a debt with at least medium-grade merchandise so as not to discourage lending (B.T., *Giṭ.* 50a). This same type of curb on what was perceived to be the antisocial exercise of individual privileges was the basis of the numerous laws enacted in medieval communities (*taqqanot ha-qehillot*). The most famous of these was the ban on polygyny issued for Ashkenazic (northern European) Jewry by Gershom ben Yehudah of Mainz (c. 965–1028) even though both the Bible and the Talmud permit the practice.

Rabbinic Legal Procedures. Rabbinical legislation was conducted according to a number of procedural rules. Although the reason for a specific rabbinical enactment did not have to be immediately publicized (B.T., *'A.Z.* 35a), there certainly had to be a clear and compelling religious or social need for it to be enacted. Rabbinical legislation was considered general in scope and was not to be formulated as case law (B.T., *'Eruv.* 63b).

The question of how long a rabbinical enactment was considered binding and what power of repeal subsequent rabbis have is a complicated one and is debated by scholars. Thus an important passage in the Mishnah states that "one court may not repeal [*mevaṭel*] the decrees of a fellow court unless it is greater than it in wisdom and in numbers" (*'Eduy.* 1.5). Some scholars have interpreted this as applying to a contemporary court only. Others have interpreted it as applying to a subsequent court. "Greater in numbers" has been interpreted to mean a greater number of disciples. However, it was highly unusual for a subsequent court to regard itself as wiser than an earlier one. The rabbis generally were too reverent of tradition to attempt to repeal it overtly. The Talmudic statement "If earlier generations were angels, we are but men" (B.T., *Shab.* 112b) reflects this typical attitude. Therefore, repeal usually took the form of more subtle reinterpretation of earlier enactments. However, even when the reason for an enactment was no longer extant, it was still considered binding unless there was a strong reason for reinterpretation.

The question of rejection of a rabbinical enactment by the people was debated in the Middle Ages. The Talmud states that "a decree is not to be made unless the majority of the community are able to abide by it" (B.T., *'A.Z.* 36a), and this was interpreted to mean that it had to have been accepted as normative by the majority of the community. (There does not seem to have been, however, any procedure for an actual plebiscite.) Rashi (Rabbi Shelomoh ben Yitshaq, 1040–1105) restricts this right to the generation of the enactment itself; that is, if they accept it the enactment is binding irrespective of the possible rejection by subsequent generations. Maimonides, on the other hand, extends the right of rejection even to subsequent generations; that is, if an earlier rabbinical enactment had fallen into disuse, then a subsequent court may regard it as no longer binding (*Mishneh Torah,* Rebels 2.7). Following the same logic, in another ruling Maimonides opts for the ancient Babylonian practice of publicly reading the Torah in the synagogue in an annual cycle over the ancient Palestinian practice of reading it in a triennial cycle, simply because the former practice had acquired universal Jewish acceptance.

CUSTOM

Minhag ("custom") is the third constituent element in *halakhah,* after scriptual exegesis and rabbinic law. It basically has three functions.

1. Custom is invoked when the law itself is ambiguous. If there are two reputable opinions as to what a law is, then there are two ways of deciding what is to be done. Either the majority view of the sages is followed (B.T., *Hul.* 11a), or the popular practice of the people is consulted and followed (J.T., *Pe'ah* 8.2, 20c). In the latter situation custom does not establish law but distinguishes between which law is considered normative *(halakhah le-ma'aseh)* and which law is considered only theoretical *(ein morin ken,* J.T., *Yev.* 12.1, 12c). Popular acceptance of one practice over another is considered a valid criterion of juridical choice because "if the people of Israel are not prophets, they are the children of prophets" (J.T., *Pes.* 6.1, 33a). In other words, popular practice is indicative of an unbroken chain of tradition.

2. Custom is considered a valid form of law, supplementing scriptural commandments and formal rabbinical legislation. Certain customs are considered universally Jewish. For example, the Orthodox objection to the modern practice of men and women sitting together in non-Orthodox synagogues, although some have attempted to find formal halakhic objections to it, is actually based on the fact that theretofore separation of the sexes in the synagogue was undoubtedly universal Jewish custom. Earlier in the nineteenth century the same invocation of the authority of custom was used to object to the introduction of the organ into synagogues in western Europe, with the additional point that such a practice constituted "walking in the ways of the gentiles."

Other customs are considered local and binding only on members of a particular locality. Generally, the rule is that if one is in a different locality from one's own, one should do nothing there to cause any scandal or controversy (*Pes.* 4.1). The force of the authority of local custom can be seen, especially, in the diversity of liturgical rites among Jews even to this day. These differences of custom to a large extent reflect differences of local environment and the social, political, and economic conditions within the respective Jewish communities. In new localities, where there are Jews from varying backgrounds, the general approach is to attempt to devise a unified rite so that there not be numerous groups (B.T., *Yev.* 13b). More frequently than not the rites of the more dominant group in the new locality prevail over everyone.

3. Custom sometimes takes precedence over established Jewish practice even when it has no foundation in *halakhah.* Usually this power of custom was used to rescind privileges the *halakhah* had earlier granted (Elon, 1978, pp. 732ff.). However, sometimes custom even had the power to abrogate, *de facto,* scriptural law. For example, the law that certain portions of slaughtered animals be given to descendants of Aaronic priests irrespective of time and place was not considered binding because of customary neglect.

EXTRAHALAKHIC FACTORS

The role extrahalakhic factors have played in the development of the *halakhah* is one of considerable debate among scholars. Aside from the question of the influence of history and general philosophy, which could be seen as extraneous modes of thought, there is the question of the influence of the nonlegal body of rabbinic thought, largely theological, known as *aggadah*. Generally it was held that one could not decide the law based on *aggadah* alone. Nevertheless, it can be shown that aggadic factors were influential in formulating halakhic opinions. This becomes evident when the views of the various rabbis, who were both halakhists and aggadists, are examined.

Thus, for example, 'Aqiva', in a discussion of capital punishment, states that had he been a member of the Sanhedrin when capital punishment was practiced, no one would have ever been executed (*Mak.* 1.10). The Talmud attempts to find a legal basis for this opinion inasmuch as capital punishment is prescribed by scripture for a number of crimes. The halakhic conclusion (written long after the time of 'Aqiva') is that he would have interpreted the laws of evidence so strictly as to make conviction for a crime punishable by death a practical impossibility (B.T., *Mak.* 7a). However, one can find an aggadic statement, recorded in the name of 'Aqiva' himself, that "whoever sheds human blood diminishes the divine image" (Tosefta, *Yev.* 8.7). Since even a convicted criminal has not forfeited that divine image (Tosefta, *San.* 9.7), one can see that 'Aqiva' had theological objections against any sort of bloodshed. It would seem that his theology was the authentic influence on his halakhic opinion, although subsequent legalists had to find a halakhic reason for it lest the authority of the law be reduced to theological opinion, something that was generally avoided (J.T., *Hor.* 3.9, 48c).

One can see further evidence of this in the relation between *halakhah* and Qabbalah (Jewish mystical literature), especially if Qabbalah is taken to be a subsequent development of *aggadah*. On the one hand, despite the growing popularity in the Middle Ages of the *Zohar* (the most important qabbalistic text), there were halakhists who regarded it as nonauthoritative, whether or not they approved of its theology. On the other hand, there were legalists who regarded it as divine revelation and *ipso facto* authoritative. A compromise was reached between these two opinions by David ibn Avi Zimra' (1479–1573), who ruled that when the Talmud was inconclusively divided on a certain law, the *Zohar* could be invoked to decide in favor of one of the Talmudic opinions. However, the *Zohar* could not be so invoked when the Talmud was conclusive.

SUBDIVISIONS OF HALAKHAH

For descriptive purposes it is helpful to see *halakhah* as divided into the following areas: (1) ritual law, (2) law of familial and personal status, (3) civil law, (4) criminal law, and (5) law pertaining to non-Jews.

Ritual Law. Although including inoperative laws pertaining to the Temple cult and most matters of ritual purity, ritual law can be seen today as confined to matters of worship, the Sabbath and festivals, diet, clothing, and sex. In the four-part *Shulḥan 'arukh* of Yosef Karo (1488–1575), which has become the most authoritative halakhic code, ritual law is the subject of all of the first part, *Oraḥ ḥayyim,* and most of the second part, *Yoreh de'ah.*

One of the most important principles to emerge in the development of ritual *halakhah* is that in cases where the observance of the law poses a distinct danger to human life, the law is not to be observed. The origins of this seminal principle can be seen as early as the Maccabean revolt against the Seleucid rulers of the Land of Israel (166–164 BCE). In that revolt the pietists refused to fight on the Sabbath. This led to their being frequently massacred on the Sabbath by their enemies, who quickly became aware of this restriction. It was argued (*1 Mc.* 2.39–42) that this insistence on unqualified Sabbath observance would lead to the total extermination of the Jewish people. In the early second century, under similarly oppressive circumstances, the rabbis meeting secretly at Lod ruled that one was to transgress the law rather than die a martyr's death. The only exceptions were if one were ordered on pain of death to practice idolatry overtly, commit murder, or initiate an act of adultery, homosexuality, or bestiality (B.T., *San.* 74a). All of this was based on the scriptural command "You shall live through them" (*Lv.* 18:5), which was interpreted to mean "You shall live through them but not die because of them" (*Sifra',* Aharei-mot, 86b). This principle, in one form or another, was invoked on numerous occasions and led to such corollaries as "Danger to life takes precedence over a ritual infraction" (B.T., *Hul.* 10a).

Law of Familial and Personal Status. The law of familial and personal status is the subject of *Even ha-'ezer,* the third part of the *Shulḥan 'arukh,* and of some sections of *Yoreh de'ah,* the second part. In this area of *halakhah* the question that has become the subject of widest discussion and deepest controversy since 1948 is that of who is a Jew.

Jewish Identity. According to scriptural law it would seem that Jewish identity is patrilineal, as suggested by such statements as "The whole community were registered by the clans of their ancestral houses [*le-veit avotam;* lit., "the houses of their fathers"]" (*Nm.* 1:18; J.T., *Qid.* 64d). Furthermore, when Ruth the Moabite married the Israelite leader Boaz, without specific mention of any formal conversion, her descendants were automatically considered as following her husband's patrimony (*Ru.* 4:21–22). Nevertheless, according to the Talmud Jewish identity is considered matrilineal (B.T., *Qid.* 68b). The origins of this approach can perhaps be seen in the beginnings of the postexilic period (c. 516 BCE), when at the urging of Ezra the people banished not only their non-Jewish wives but also "those born of them" (*Ezr.* 10:3).

Once one is born of a Jewish mother, or he or she has properly converted to Judaism, that status is considered irrevocable (B.T., *San.* 44a, *Yev.* 47b). However, the community can revoke various privileges of Jewish status from apostates and other persons as well who have removed themselves from basic Jewish identification and observance.

Marriage and Divorce. The subject of the most extensive halakhic structure is marriage and divorce. Marriage originally consisted of two parts. The first part, *erusin* ("betrothal"), was initiated when the man, with the consent of the woman, designated her as his wife before at least two bona fide witnesses, usually by giving her an article of stipulated value (*Qid.* 1.1). The woman, however, continued to live with her parents; her father now had joint responsibility for her, along with her husband. After a period of time, usually one year, the bride left her parental home and went to live with the groom *(nissu'in)*, and the couple consummated the marriage. The status of the woman was greatly enhanced by the marriage contract *(ketubbah)*, which provided a considerable payment in the event of her being divorced or widowed (Epstein, 1927).

Divorce required that the husband present his wife with a formal bill of divorce *(get)*, drawn up at his instigation by a rabbinical court. Although the school of Shammai made adultery the only grounds for divorce, the *halakhah* followed the more lenient view of the school of Hillel, which made virtually any incompatibility sufficient for divorce to be effected *(Giṭ.* 9.10). Although the woman herself could not instigate divorce proceedings, she could, nevertheless, when there was clearly sufficient incompatibility, request that a rabbinical court force her husband to grant her a divorce *(Ket.* 7.10). Indeed, nonfulfillment of the basic husbandly duties of support and regular sexual intercourse obligated a man to do so *(Ket.* 5.6).

Civil Law. Jewish civil law regulates all areas of life involving property. It is the subject of the greatest discussion in *Hoshen mishpaṭ,* the fourth part of the *Shulḥan 'arukh.*

Of all the areas of *halakhah,* civil law has been the most flexible. The underlying basis of this flexibility is perhaps best expressed in the rabbinic dictum "The Torah cares about property of Israel" *(Neg.* 12.5). In other words, although there was a consistent commitment to general principles of justice, it was understood that the law, especially in the unstable and diversified area of economics, must be responsive to the needs of the times. This characteristic, it might be added, was limited to the area of civil law, and for this reason one could not apply most of the principles developed there to the more conservative area of ritual law (B.T., *Ber.* 19b).

Although the *halakhah* developed its own standards for various commercial activities, the operative principle is "Everything is according to the practice [*minhag*] of the locality" *(B.M.* 7.1). Thus, even conditions contrary to the law of the Torah, which under all other circumstances are null and void, in monetary matters are considered valid if freely agreed upon by both parties to a contract (B.T., *Qid.* 19b), except where the prohibition of one Jew taking interest from another Jew is involved. However, even here the *halakhah* eventually evolved a procedure *(hetter 'isqa')* whereby interest could be charged for commercial loans using the legal fiction of designating the creditor as a partner of the debtor in a joint venture (Elon, 1975, pp. 504–505). Furthermore, flexibility in this area of *halakhah* is evidenced by the fact that in monetary disputes informal arbitration was encouraged in lieu of formal adjudication.

Private property was not considered an absolute right by the *halakhah.* Although there is an elaborate system of adjudicating claims and counterclaims between private parties in such areas as torts and contracts, the court had the power to declare private property ownerless *(hefqer)* if this was in the interest of the common good (B.T., *Yev.* 89b). It must be added, however, that this principle was used sparingly, and it seems as though for the *halakhah* a limited free-enterprise system is considered both the norm and the desideratum.

Criminal Law. Jewish criminal law, also dealt with in *Hoshen mishpaṭ,* is concerned with capital and corporal punishment. Capital punishment is mandated for such interpersonal acts as murder and adultery as well as for such ritual acts as public violation of the Sabbath. Corporal punishment (lashing) is mandated for various ritual infractions (*Mak.* 3.1ff.). Most personal injury, however, was treated as a civil tort rather than as a criminal act per se. Thus the scriptural *lex talionis* ("an eye for an eye," *Ex.* 21:24) was interpreted by the rabbis as prescribing monetary compensation for the victim rather than the actual mutilation of the perpetrator.

Even after the Roman rulers of the Land of Israel had removed the power of the Jewish courts to administer capital punishment, sometime before 70 CE, the rabbis were sharply divided about its desirability. Although the institution itself, because it was scripturally prescribed, could not be explicitly abrogated, a number of rabbis were obviously opposed to it in practice if not in principle (B.T., *San.* 71a). This tendency to oppose capital punishment is also seen in the rabbinic institution of *hatra'ah,* according to which one could not be convicted of a capital crime unless he or she had been explicitly forewarned by the same two witnesses who actually saw the crime and the criminal had explicitly indicated that he or she was aware of both the criminal status of the act to be done and the exact type of capital punishment it entailed (B.T., *San.* 40b–41a). Such an institution would seem to limit sharply the number of legal executions. Whether *hatra'ah* was actually practiced when the Jewish courts had the power of capital punishment is questioned by some modern scholars. Nevertheless, it does reflect a definite tendency in rabbinic theory if not in actual practice.

On the other hand, a number of prominent and influential halakhists expressed the view of the second-century sage Shim'on ben Gamli'el II that capital punishment is necessary to maintain social order (*Mak.* 1.10). Indeed, the Talmud is followed by many subsequent authorities in advocating capital punishment even for crimes not specified as capital crimes in the legal sources if the court believed that "the hour required such" in cases of gross public provocation. In the thirteenth century the important halakhist Shelomoh ben Avraham Adret stated that were all the traditional qualifications of capital punishment in the *halakhah* to be followed, "society would be destroyed." His statement, furthermore, was probably not just theoretical in that it is known that Spanish Jewish communities at that time did have the power to execute criminals (Elon, 1978, p. 9).

The actual practice of Jewish criminal law, and to a large extent Jewish civil law as well, has frequently required the type of political sovereignty that Jews did not have. Thus in the third century the Babylonian authority Shemu'el of Nehardea formulated the seminal juridical principle that "the law of the kingdom is the law" (B.T., *B.B.* 54b). This principle was justified in several ways; the most cogent is that the Jewish court has the power to transfer its authority in civil and criminal matters. Historically this relegated all Jewish criminal law and much Jewish civil law to the realm of the theoretical. Thus some medieval authorities seem to have thought that this principle was too radical in that it gave away too much Jewish legal sovereignty. It is still too early for the most part to see if and how Jewish criminal and civil law can be revived in the state of Israel, which, at the present time at least, is constituted as a secular state not subject to the authority of the *halakhah* except in limited areas (see below).

Law Regarding Non-Jews. The area of Jewish law pertaining to non-Jews has been called "the seven commandments of the sons of Noah" (Tosefta, *'A.Z.* 8.4). These commandments are (1) the obligation to adjudicate cases according to defined statutes and the prohibitions of (2) blasphemy, (3) idolatry, (4) homicide, (5) adultery, homosexuality, and bestiality, (6) robbery, and (7) eating a limb torn from a living animal. A number of commentators saw these seven commandments as seven general legal categories rather than seven specific norms.

One of the most important historical questions about this area of *halakhah* is whether or not it was actually enforced among non-Jews. Some scholars consider this highly unlikely inasmuch as no actual case is reported in the rabbinic sources, where these laws were the basis of adjudication, and there do not seem to have been free gentiles living under Jewish legal jurisdiction in the rabbinic period. Indeed, only in Maimonides' *Mishneh Torah* (Code of Law), which deals with every area of *halakhah,* even those no longer (if ever) operative, are the Noahic laws systematically presented and discussed (Kings and Wars 8.10ff.). It is, moreover, important to note that non-Jewish slaves, who were certainly owned by Jews at that time, were subject to a body of law containing many more distinctly Jewish practices and prohibitions than the Noahic laws (B.T., *Hag.* 4a).

Nevertheless, the concept of a law governing non-Jews, which was considered to have been normative for Jews as well before the Sinaitic revelation of the 613 commandments of the Mosaic Torah, had a profound effect on the development of Judaism. In terms of *halakhah* the Noahic laws were considered to be the minimal normative standards upon which the Mosaic Torah was based. Thus the Talmud in more than one place states that "there is nothing prohibited to non-Jews that is permitted to Jews" (B.T., *San.* 59a). In another place it states that Jewish law must be stricter lest it appear as "a lower form of sanctity" (B.T., *Yev.* 22a).

In terms of Jewish-gentile relations the Noahic prohibition of idolatry became the basis of determining which non-Jewish societies were actually idolatrous and which were merely following "ancestral custom" (B.T., *Hul.* 13b). This distinction had great practical importance in that Jewish dealings with confirmed gentile idolators were proscribed in many areas, including in various business transactions ('A.Z. 1.1). In the Middle Ages the Noahic prohibition of idolatry became the standard for determining the Jewish view, both theoretical and practical, of Christianity and Islam. Islamic monotheism was, of course, much easier to justify on Jewish grounds than were Christian incarnationism and trinitarianism. Indeed, a number of medieval halakhists, usually themselves living under Muslim regimes, considered Christianity a form of idolatry entailing all the Talmudic proscriptions pertaining to idolatry and idolators. However, other legalists, usually living under Christian regimes, drew upon earlier Talmudic distinctions between stricter criteria for Jews than for gentiles, especially in areas of religious conviction, and so considered Christianity a mediated monotheism.

In those democratic countries where Jews are full participants, there has been renewed interest in this area of *halakhah* as a source for determining "the Jewish point of view" on various issues of public concern as widely divergent as abortion, capital punishment, and prayer in American public schools. How pertinent, however, many of these sources are to the areas of public concern to which they have been related, without thorough critical historical and philosophical examination and reinterpretation, is itself a source of great difference of opinion among contemporary Jewish thinkers.

CURRENT ROLE OF HALAKHAH

Although *halakhah* is a system of law governing every aspect of personal and communal life, there is no Jewish community in the world today where *halakhah* is the sole basis of governance. This inherent paradox—namely, a total system of law forced by historical reality to share legal authority with another system of law, if not to be actually subordinate to it—has led to a number of tensions both in the state of Israel and in the Diaspora.

Halakhah in the State of Israel. In the state of Israel, *halakhah,* as adjudicated by the rabbinical courts, is recognized as the law governing all aspects of public Jewish religious ritual and all areas of marriage and divorce. (The same privilege is extended to the respective systems of law of the various non-Jewish religious communities there.) This political arrangement has led to a number of areas of tension. Thus many secularist Israeli Jews object to having to submit in questions of personal and familial status to the authority of religious courts, whose very religious justification they do not accept. This conflict has manifested itself in the demand by many secularist Israelis for civil marriage and divorce in the state of Israel, something that *halakhah* rejects as unacceptable for Jews. Even more profound is the fact that there is a conflict between *halakhah* and Israeli law on the most basic question of Jewish identity, that is, who is a Jew. According to *halakhah,* anyone born of a Jewish mother or himself or herself converted to Judaism is considered a Jew. According to the Israeli Law of Return (Hoq ha-Shevut), any Jew (with the exception of one convicted of a crime in another country) has the right of Israeli domicile and Israeli citizenship. However, in 1962 in a famous decision the Israeli Supreme Court ruled that Oswald Rufeisen, a Jewish convert to Christianity and a Roman Catholic monk, was not entitled to Israeli citizenship as a Jew because in the popular sense of the term he was not a Jew even though he was one in the technical, halakhic sense. On the other hand, in 1968, in another famous decision, the Israeli Supreme Court ruled that the wife and children of an Israeli Jew, Binyamin Shalit, were not to be considered Jews for purposes of Israeli citizenship because they had not been converted to Judaism, even though they identified themselves as Israeli Jews in the secular sense of the term. In this case, unlike the earlier one, the court accepted a halakhic definition of who is a Jew.

At the present time, furthermore, there is considerable debate in the state of Israel and the Diaspora about what actually constitutes valid conversion to Judaism. All Orthodox and most Conservative halakhists have rejected the conversions performed under Reform auspices because in the great majority of such cases the objective halakhic criteria of conversion—circumcision for males and immersion in a ritual bath *(miqveh)* for both males and females (B.T., *Yev.* 47b)—have not been fulfilled. Even the conversions performed under Conservative auspices, although fulfilling these objective criteria, are also rejected by many Orthodox legalists, who claim that Conservative rabbis lack the requisite commitment to *halakhah* to function as acceptable rabbinical judges. All of this is evidence of the widening division among the branches of contemporary Judaism.

Halakhah in the Diaspora. In the Diaspora, where adherence to *halakhah* is a matter of individual choice in practically every country that Judaism may be freely practiced, there is little ability to enforce the communal authority inherent in the halakhic system itself. This has led to a number of vexing problems. For example, the Talmud empowers a rabbinical court to force a man to divorce his wife for a variety of objective reasons that make normal married life impossible. When Jewish communities enjoyed relative internal autonomy, such enforcement could be carried out regularly. However, today, because of the loss of such communal autonomy, such enforcement is impossible, and many Jewish women, although already civilly divorced and no longer living with their former husbands, are still considered married according to *halakhah* and are unable to remarry because of the refusal of their former husbands to comply with the order of a rabbinical court.

This growing problem in societies where mobility and anonymity are facts of life has led to basically three different approaches. Many in the Orthodox community have attempted to resort to legal measures in the civil courts to force compliance with *halakhah*. In addition to a lack of success heretofore, this has raised, especially in the United States, the constitutional issue of governmental interference in private religious matters. On the other hand, the Conservative movement since 1968 has revived the ancient rabbinical privilege of retroactive annulment (B.T., *Git.* 33a) in cases where it is impossible to obtain a Jewish divorce from the husband. The Reform movement, not being bound by the authority of *halakhah,* accepts a civil divorce as sufficient termination of a Jewish marriage. These three widely divergent approaches to a major halakhic problem are further evidence of the growing divisiveness in the Jewish religious community in both the state of Israel and the Diaspora.

Reconstitution of the Sanhedrin. The only chance for effecting any halakhic unanimity among the Jewish people would be the reconstitution of the Sanhedrin in Jerusalem as the universal Jewish legislature and supreme court. This proposal was actually made by the first minister of religious affairs in the state of Israel, Judah Leib Maimon (1875–1962). However, considering the fact that this reconstitution itself presupposes much of the very unanimity it is to effect, it would seem that it is rather utopian, something the Talmud euphemistically called "messianic *halakhah*" (B.T., *Zev.* 45a).

BIBLIOGRAPHY

Considering the enormous quantity of halakhic literature, it is most unlikely that even a considerable portion of it will ever be translated into English or any other non-Hebrew language. However, some of the classic sources and some excellent secondary sources are available in English translation.

The Mishnah translation most widely used and accepted is that of Herbert Danby (Oxford, 1933). The Babylonian Talmud has been completely translated in the usually adequate Soncino edition (London, 1935–1948). The Palestinian Talmud is now being translated by Jacob Neusner under the title *The Talmud of the Land of Israel* (Chicago, 1982–); several volumes have already appeared. The Tosefta is also being translated by Neusner (New York, 1977–), and a number of volumes have appeared so far. Most of Maimonides' *Mishneh Torah* has been published as *The Code of Maimonides,* 13 vols. (New Haven, 1949–), in a uniformly excellent translation.

The most comprehensive treatment of halakhic institutions in English is *The Principles of Jewish Law,* edited by Menachem Elon (Jerusalem, 1975), although more detailed questions are dealt with in Elon's Hebrew work, *Ha-mishpaṭ ha-'ivri,* 2d ed. (Jerusalem, 1978). Another helpful work, especially regarding Jewish civil law, is Isaac H. Herzog's *The Main Institutions of Jewish Law*, 2 vols., 2d ed. (New York, 1965). Still the best treatment of the history of *halakhah* is Louis Ginzberg's "Law, Codification of" in the *Jewish Encyclopedia* (New York, 1905). Ginzberg's "The Significance of the Halachah for Jewish History," translated by Arthur Hertzberg in *On Jewish Law and Lore* (Philadelphia, 1955), is a fascinating but controversial treatment of early *halakhah* from a socioeconomic point of view. Another important general treatment is the article "Halakhah" by Louis Jacobs and Bert De Vries in *Encyclopaedia Judaica* (Jerusalem, 1971).

The number of good monographs on halakhic topics in English is steadily growing. One can read and consult with profit the following finely researched and written works: Boaz Cohen's *Jewish and Roman Law: A Comparative Study*, 2 vols. (New York, 1966); Louis M. Epstein's *The Jewish Marriage Contract* (1927; reprint, New York, 1973); David M. Feldman's *Birth Control in Jewish Law* (New York, 1968); Solomon B. Freehof's *The Responsa Literature* (Philadelphia, 1955); Aaron Kirschenbaum's *Self-Incrimination in Jewish Law* (New York, 1970); Isaac Klein's *A Guide to Jewish Religious Practice* (New York, 1979); Leo Landman's *Jewish Law in the Diaspora* (Philadelphia, 1968); Samuel Mendelsohn's *The Criminal Jurisprudence of the Ancient Hebrews* (Baltimore, 1891); and my own *The Image of the Non-Jew in Judaism* (New York, 1983).

The articles in *The Jewish Law Annual*, vols. 1–4, edited by Bernard S. Jackson (Leiden, 1978–1981), generally represent some of the best critical scholarship on halakhic topics in English today. A good sampling of the current theological debate over the authority and scope of *halakhah* can be found in a symposium in *Judaism* 29 (Winter 1980).

17 THE RELIGIOUS YEAR

Louis Jacobs

The Hebrew word *ḥodesh,* used in the Bible for "month," means "that which is renewed" and refers to the renewal of the moon. Hence the Jewish calendar is lunar, the first day of each month being Ro'sh Ḥodesh ("head of the month"). Some months have twenty-nine days, others thirty. When the previous month has twenty-nine days, Ro'sh Ḥodesh is celebrated as a minor festival for two days; when the previous month has thirty days, it is celebrated for one day. In the Pentateuch (*Ex.* 12:2), the month on which the Israelites went out of Egypt is counted as the first month of the year, so when the Bible speaks of the third month, the seventh month, and so on, these are counted from the month of the Exodus. But the festival of Passover, celebrating the Exodus, is said in *Deuteronomy* 16:1 to fall in the month Aviv ("ripening"). This is understood to mean that Passover must always fall in spring, and thus the Jewish lunar calendar presupposes a natural solar calendar like that used in most ancient societies. A process of intercalation was consequently introduced to enable the lunar year to keep pace with the solar. The method is to add an extra month to seven out of nineteen lunar years. During the Babylonian captivity, after the destruction of the First Temple, the Babylonian names of the months were adopted and are still used. These are Nisan, Iyyar, Sivan, Tammuz (its origin in the name of a Babylonian deity was either unknown or ignored), Av, Elul, Tishri, Marheshvan, Kislev, Tevet, Shevat, Adar. When, in a leap year, an extra month is introduced at the end of the year, there is an Adar Sheni, or "second Adar."

THE DEVELOPMENT OF THE CALENDAR
There was no uniform method of dating years until the Middle Ages, when the current practice was adopted of reckoning from the (biblical) creation of the world. The French commentaries to the Talmud (*tosafot* to B.T., *Gittin* 80b) observe that in twelfth-century France it was already an established practice to date documents from the creation. In the Talmudic literature it is debated whether the creation took place in Nisan (the first month) or in Tishri (the seventh month), but for dating purposes the latter view is followed, so that the new year begins on the first day of Tishri. This day is the date of the festival Ro'sh ha-Shanah (New Year). Thus the year 1240 CE is the year 5000 from the creation. Thus 1986 CE from 1 January to 3 October is

235

the year 5746 from the creation; from 4 October (the date of Ro'sh ha-Shanah) it is 5747. This method of dating is used in legal documents, letters, and newspapers but has no doctrinal significance, so that it does not normally disturb traditionalists who prefer to interpret the biblical record nonliterally to allow for a belief in the vast age of the earth implied by science.

It is generally accepted in the critical study of the Bible that the recurring refrain in the first chapter of *Genesis*—"and it was evening and it was morning"—means that when daylight had passed into evening and then night had passed into morning, a complete day had elapsed. But the Talmudic tradition understands the verses to mean that night precedes the day. For this reason the day, for religious purposes, begins at nightfall and lasts until the next nightfall. The Sabbath begins at sunset on Friday and goes out at nightfall on Saturday. The same applies to the festivals. The twilight period is a legally doubtful one, and there is also an obligation to extend the Sabbaths and festivals at beginning and end. Jewish calendars, consequently, give the time of the Sabbath as beginning just before sunset and as ending when it is fully dark. Pious Jews, in the absence of a calendar, will keep the Sabbath until it is sufficiently dark to see three average-sized stars in close proximity in the night sky.

Before the present fixed calendar was instituted (in the middle of the fourth century CE), the date of the new moon was arrived at by observation. If witnesses saw the new moon on the twenty-ninth day of the month, they would present their testimony to the high court and that day would be declared Ro'sh Hodesh, the beginning of the next month. If the new moon had not been observed on the twenty-ninth day, the thirtieth day automatically became Ro'sh Hodesh. Since the festivals falling in the month are counted from Ro'sh Hodesh, there was always some doubt as to which of two days would be the date of the festival. Except on Ro'sh ha-Shanah, which falls on the actual day of the new moon, special messengers could always inform the Jews of Palestine of the correct date of the festival. But for the Jews of the Diaspora, who resided in lands too distant for them to be informed in time, it became the practice to keep both days as the festival and thus avoid any possibility of error. Even after the calendar was fixed, the Talmudic sources state, the Jews of the Diaspora were advised by the Palestinian authorities to continue to hold fast to the custom of their ancestors and keep the "two days of the Diaspora." A post-Talmudic rationale for the two days of the Diaspora is that outside the Holy Land the extra festival day compensates for the absence of sanctity in the land. The practice in the state of Israel is thus to keep only one day (with the exception of Ro'sh ha-Shanah), whereas Jews living elsewhere keep two days. There is much discussion in the legal sources on the practice to be adopted by a Jew living outside Israel who visits Israel for the festival or vice versa. Reform Jews prefer to follow the biblical injunctions only, and they do not keep the two days of the Diaspora. Some Conservative Jews, too, have argued for the abolition of the second day because of the anomaly of treating as a holy day a day that is not observed as sacred in Israel.

THE HOLY DAYS

Similar festivals in the ancient Near East suggest that the biblical festivals were originally agricultural feasts transformed into celebrations of historical events. The most striking aspect of the Jewish religious calendar is this transfer from the round of the seasons to the affirmation of God's work in human history—the transfer, as it were, from space to time.

The holy days of the Jewish year can be divided into two categories: the biblical and the postbiblical, or the major and the minor. (Purim, though based on *Esther,* a book from the biblical period, is held to be a postbiblical festival from this point of view and hence a minor festival.) The first and last days of Passover and Sukkot, Shavu'ot, Ro'sh ha-Shanah, and Yom Kippur are major festivals in that all labor (except that required for the preparation of food and even this on Yom Kippur) is forbidden. On the days between the first and last days of Passover and Sukkot, necessary labor is permitted. All labor is permitted on minor festivals such as Purim and Hanukkah.

Each of the festivals has its own rituals and its own special liturgy. On all of them the Hallel ("praise"), consisting of *Psalms* 113–118, is recited in the synagogue, except on Ro'sh ha-Shanah, Yom Kippur, and Purim. Only part of Hallel is said on Ro'sh Hodesh, when labor is permitted, and the last six days of Passover, it being held unseemly to rejoice by singing the full praises of God since the Egyptians, who were also God's creatures, were destroyed. Festive meals are the order of the day on the festivals (except, of course, on Yom Kippur), and the day is marked by the donning of one's best clothes. It is considered meritorious to study on each festival the relevant passages in the classical sources of Judaism. On the fast days neither food nor drink is taken from sunrise to nightfall (on Yom Kippur and Tish'ah be-Av, from sunset on the previous night).

Following are major dates of the religious year, month by month.

- 15–22 Nisan (15–23 in the Diaspora): Passover, celebrating the Exodus from Egypt.
- 6 Sivan (6–7 in the Diaspora): Shavu'ot, anniversary of the theophany at Sinai.
- 17 Tammuz: Fast of Tammuz, commemorating the breaching of the walls of Jerusalem at the time of the destruction of the First Temple (587/6 BCE) and the Second Temple (70 CE).
- 9 Av: Tish'ah be-Av (Ninth of Av), fast day commemorating the destruction of the First and Second Temples and other national calamities.
- 1–2 Tishri: Ro'sh ha-Shanah, the New Year festival.
- 3 Tishri: Tsom Gedalyah (Fast of Gedaliah), commemorating the slaying of Gedaliah as told in *Jeremiah* 41:1–2 and *2 Kings* 25:25, an event that marked the end of the First Commonwealth.
- 10 Tishri: Yom Kippur (Day of Atonement), the great fast day.
- 15–23 Tishri (15–24 in the Diaspora): Sukkot (Feast of Tabernacles), celebrating the dwelling in booths by the Israelites in their journey through the wilderness after the Exodus.
- 25 Kislev: first day of Hanukkah (Feast of Rededication), celebrating the victory of the Maccabees and the rededication of the Temple. Hanukkah lasts for eight days.
- 10 Tevet: 'Asarah be-Tevet (Fast of the Tenth of Tevet), commemorating the siege of Jerusalem by Nebuchadrezzar before the destruction of the First Temple in 587/6 BCE.
- 15 Shevat: Ro'sh ha-Shanah le-Ilanot (New Year for Trees), a minor festival reminiscent of the laws of tithing in ancient times. Nowadays, this is a celebration of God's bounty, of thanksgiving for the fruit of the ground.

- 13 Adar: Ta'anit Ester (Fast of Esther), based on the account in *Esther* (4:16).
- 14 Adar: Purim (Lots), the festival celebrating the victory over Haman, who cast lots to destroy the Jews, as told in *Esther*.
- 15 Adar: Shushan Purim (Purim of Shushan), based on the account in *Esther* (9:18) that the Jews in the capital city of Shushan celebrated their deliverance on this day.

MAJOR FESTIVALS AND FAST DAYS

The three festivals of Passover, Shavu'ot, and Sukkot form a unit in that, in Temple times, they were pilgrim festivals, when the people came to worship and offer sacrifices in the Temple. The connection between these three festivals is preserved in the liturgy in which there are references to the place of each festival in the yearly cycle. Thus, on Passover the reference is to "the season of our freedom," on Shavu'ot to "the season of the giving of our Torah," and on Sukkot to "the season of our rejoicing," since Sukkot, as the culmination of the cycle, is the special season of joy. The three major festivals of the month of Tishri have been seen as a unit of a different kind. Ro'sh ha-Shanah, the first of the three, is seen as the festival of the mind, when man reflects on his destiny and resolves to lead a better life in the coming year. Yom Kippur, the day when the emotions are stirred, is seen as the festival of the heart, because it is the day of pardon and reconciliation with God. Sukkot, the third in this triad, involves active participation in the building of the booth and eating meals there, and is seen therefore as the festival of the hand. Thus, head, heart, and hand are demanded in the service of God.

The days between Ro'sh ha-Shanah and Yom Kippur, inclusive, are known as the Ten Days of Penitence. This is a solemn season of reflection on life's meaning and sincere repentance. Similarly, the whole month of Elul, the last month of the old year, is a penitential season in preparation for the solemn period at the beginning of the new year. Ro'sh ha-Shanah and Yom Kippur are consequently known as Yamim Nora'im, the Days of Awe.

MINOR FESTIVALS AND FAST DAYS

In the annual cycle there are two periods of mourning during which marriages are not celebrated and tokens of mourning are observed. The first of these is the three-week period from the seventeenth of Tammuz to Tish'ah be-Av, the period of mourning for the destruction of the Temple and the sufferings of the people in subsequent ages. In many places the period becomes more intense from the first of Av in that the consumption of meat and wine is proscribed. The other, lesser, period of mourning is known as the 'Omer period, forty-nine days from the second day of Passover to the festival of Shavu'ot (though, of course, there is no mourning during Passover itself). The 'omer was a measure of meal brought as an offering in Temple times, and there is a biblical injunction to count these forty-nine days (*Lv.* 23:9–16; known as "counting the 'Omer"). It has been suggested that the custom of mourning during the 'Omer has its origin in the ancient belief, held by many peoples, that it is bad luck to marry during the month of May. The traditional sources state that the mourning is over the death by plague of many of the disciples of 'Aqiva' ben Yosef in the second century CE. The mystics introduce a different note. There are seven lower potencies or powers in the godhead, the *sefirot,* that become flawed as a result of human sin. Each one of these contains the others as well, so that each of the forty-nine days of the 'Omer calls for repentance for the purpose of putting right these flaws. The mystics of Safad in the sixteenth century held that the eighteenth of Iyyar, the thirty-third day of the 'Omer—Lag ba-'Omer—is the anniversary of the death of the great mystic Shim'on bar Yoh'ai, a disciple of 'Aqiva' and the alleged author of the *Zohar*. The belief that at the saint's death his soul became united with its source on high is referred to as "the marriage of Shim'on bar Yoh'ai." This day, then, became a minor festival, and marriages are celebrated on the day.

The day of the new moon, Ro'sh Hodesh, is also a minor festival. From the juxta-position of Ro'sh Hodesh with the Sabbath in a number of biblical passages, many biblical scholars conclude that in ancient times Ro'sh Hodesh was a major festival on a par with the Sabbath. Nowadays, however, the day is marked only by festivities in a minor key and by liturgical additions. An old custom frees women from the obligation to work on Ro'sh Hodesh, and this might be a vestige of the ancient sanctity the day enjoyed. The official reason given is that women refused to partici-pate in the making of the golden calf and were, therefore, given an extra holiday. In the mystical tradition the moon symbolizes the Shekhinah, the female element in the godhead, the counterpart on high of the community of Israel, awaiting the re-demption of the Jewish people and of all mankind with harmony restored through-out all creation. The waxing and the waning of the moon is thus a powerful mytho-logical symbol. The Safad mystics consequently introduced a new ritual for the eve of Ro'sh Hodesh. This day is known as Yom Kippur Qatan (Minor Yom Kippur). As the name implies, it is a time of repentance and, for some, fasting.

There are a number of other lesser feasts and fast days. The Fast of the Firstborn has its origins in the early Middle Ages. In *Exodus* (13:1–16) it is related that the firstborn of the Israelites have a special sanctity because God spared them when he killed the firstborn of the Egyptians. Thus the custom of fasting on the eve of Pass-over, 14 Nisan, developed. Generally, nowadays, the firstborn, instead of fasting, attend a study session during which a tractate of the Talmud is completed. To par-take of a festive meal on this occasion is held to be a religious obligation that over-rides the obligation to fast.

Some pious Jews fast on the Monday, Thursday, and following Monday after the festivals of Passover and Sukkot—Beit He' Beit ("Two, Five, Two," referring to the days of the week). The reason given is that it is to atone for any untoward frivolity during the lengthy festival period.

In many Jewish communities the burial of the dead is attended to by a voluntary organization, whose membership is granted only to the most distinguished appli-cants. This organization is known as the *hevrah qaddisha'* ("holy brotherhood"). The members of the *hevrah' qaddisha'* observe a fast on the seventh of Adar, the anni-versary of the death of Moses, to atone for any disrespect they may have shown to the dead. But on the night following the fast they celebrate their privileged position by holding a special banquet.

There are also minor festivals observed by particular groups. For instance, on the analogy of Purim, many communities delivered miraculously from destruction cele-brate ever after their day of deliverance as a "Purim." For example, the Hasidic master Shne'ur Zalman of Lyady (1745–1813), founder of the Habad school of Ha-sidism, was released from prison in Russia on the nineteenth of Kislev, after his arrest on a charge of treason, and his followers observe this day as a festival.

Two modern institutions are Yom ha-Sho'ah (Holocaust Day) on 27 Nisan, marking the destruction of six million Jews during the Nazi period, and Yom ha-Atsma'ut (Independence Day) on 5 Iyyar, the celebration, especially in the state of Israel, of the Israeli declaration of independence on that date. In many religious circles this day is treated as a full *yom tov,* and the *Hallel* is recited.

[*For more detailed discussion of specific Jewish holidays, see* Shabbat; Ro'sh ha-Shanah and Yom Kippur; Passover; Shavu'ot; Sukkot; Purim; *and* Hanukkah. *For non-Western Jewish traditions, see* Judaism, *article on* Judaism in Asia and Northeast Africa.]

BIBLIOGRAPHY

The articles "Calendar, History of" and "Calendar" in the *Jewish Encyclopedia* (New York, 1906) are still the best general accounts. The article "Calendar" in *Encyclopaedia Judaica* (Jerusalem, 1971) contains more detail but is so technical as to be incomprehensible to all but the experts, who will have no need for it. Hayyim Schauss's *Guide to the Jewish Holy Days,* translated by Samuel Jaffe (New York, 1962), is a survey, from the rationalistic standpoint, with critical and historical notes. More traditional are Abraham P. Bloch's *The Biblical and Historical Background of the Jewish Holy Days* (New York, 1978) and Abraham Chill's *The Minhagim: The Customs and Ceremonies of Judaism, Their Origins and Rationale* (New York, 1979). A useful introduction to the traditionalist mood of thought on the significance of the festivals is *Seasons of the Soul: Religious, Historical and Philosophical Perspectives on the Jewish Year and Its Milestones* (New York, 1981), edited by Nisson Walpin. Similar meditations on the Jewish calendar year by a famous nineteenth-century Orthodox theologian are to be found in *Judaism Eternal: Selected Essays from the Writings of Rabbi Samson Raphael Hirsch,* vol. 1, translated from the German original by Isidor Grunfeld (London, 1956), pp. 3–152. *Ha-mo'adim ba-halakhah* (Jerusalem, 1980) by Shlomo Y. Zevin is a particularly fine and popular treatment of the legal principles behind the observances of the festivals and fast days. Part of this work has been published in English translation: *The Festivals in Halachah,* translated by Meir Fox-Ashrei and edited by Uri Kaploon (New York, 1981). Solomon Ganzfield's *Code of Jewish Law (Qitsur Shulhan 'arukh): A Compilation of Jewish Laws and Customs,* vol. 3, annot. & rev. ed., translated by Hyman E. Goldin (New York, 1961), is a comprehensive and clearly written but very pedestrian account.

18 RITES OF PASSAGE

Peter S. Knobel

Judaism has a highly developed series of rites that mark both initiatory and transformative moments in the lives of Jews. The rituals permit both the individual and the community to experience in an orderly and regulated manner the changing status of the Jew's relationship to other individuals and to society as a whole. Although some of the rites may have originated in other neighboring cultures, once adopted they were thoroughly judaized. Their meaning for the Jewish people is to be sought not in their origin but in their function in Jewish society. Some rites have changed little in the millennia since their introduction. Others have been radically transformed. In this article I describe the rites as they are currently practiced, with special emphasis on the Jewish community of North America.

In general, the rites are rooted in biblical regulations (*mitsvot*, "commandments") that were refined and standardized in the Talmudic and medieval periods. Although Jewish law *(halakhah)* defines the essential elements in each rite, local customs *(minhagim)* provide some degree of variation from community to community.

During the last century and a half, Judaism became divided into four streams, Orthodox, Conservative, Reform, and Reconstructionist, and this has created an increased divergence in the liturgy and ritual of life cycle ceremonies. The greatest divergence from standard traditional practice as defined by the Talmud and the later legal codes occurs in Reform and Reconstructionist Judaism. In addition, the growth of the feminist movement in the 1960s and 1970s has had a significant impact on life cycle ceremonies in the non-Orthodox movements: new rituals have been created specifically for women and some standard rituals have been made more egalitarian by the inclusion of women as equal participants or by the removal of sexist language.

CIRCUMCISION, NAMING, REDEMPTION OF THE FIRST-BORN

The male initiatory rite is *berit milah* ("covenant of circumcision"). It involves the surgical removal of the foreskin of the penis and the recitation of prayers that welcome the infant into the Jewish people by initiating him into the covenant of Abraham (*Gn.* 17:11ff.). The rite takes place on the eighth day after birth, counting the day of birth as the first day. So significant is the eighth day that even if it falls on the Sabbath or a festival, the circumcision is not postponed.

241

Circumcision was practiced by other ancient Near Eastern peoples, probably as a fertility rite, but among Jews it became the physical sign of belonging to the Jewish people. [*See* Circumcision.] In the Hebrew Bible, circumcision is first mentioned in the injunction proclaimed by God to the ninety-nine-year-old Abraham, that instructed him to circumcise himself and the male members of his household:

> *God further said to Abraham, "As for you, you and your offspring to come throughout the ages shall keep my covenant. Such shall be my covenant between me and you and your offspring to follow which you shall keep: every male among you shall be circumcised. You shall circumcise the flesh of your foreskin, and that shall be the sign of the covenant between me and you. And throughout the generations, every male among you shall be circumcised at the age of eight days. . . . Thus shall my covenant be marked in your flesh as an everlasting pact."*
>
> (*Gn.* 17:9–13)

In Jewish law, it is the father's responsibility to circumcise his son. As a practical matter, however, it is rare for a father to perform the actual operation. Generally, he appoints a specially trained ritual circumciser, a *mohel,* to perform the rite in his stead. Jewishness does not depend on being circumcised, since any child born of a Jewish mother is a Jew. (In Reform and Reconstructionist Judaism, a Jew is anyone born to either a Jewish mother or father, who is raised exclusively as a Jew.) However, because over the millennia the rite has assumed an ethnonational significance in addition to its religious one, it is observed almost universally even by highly assimilated and secular Jews, though the latter may have their sons circumcised by a physician without any particular ceremony.

The preferred time for *berit milah* is in the morning, to demonstrate that the parents are as eager as Abraham was to fulfill the commandment. Although circumcision is never performed before the eighth day, it may be postponed or in rare cases omitted for medical reasons. If, however, the child was circumcised before the eighth day or was born without a foreskin, the ceremony of *hatafat dam berit* (taking a drop of blood) is mandated for the eighth day.

Whereas the circumcision ceremony used to be held in the synagogue, it is now commonly held at the home of the new parents. The rite proceeds as follows: the infant is taken from his mother by the godmother and brought to the room where the circumcision is to take place. She hands the infant to the godfather, who in turn hands him to the *mohel.* As the child is brought into the room, he is welcomed by those present with the greeting (usually in Hebrew) "Blessed be he that comes." The father then formally declares his willingness to have his son circumcised in fulfillment with the divine commandments. The *mohel* takes the child and places him on the lap of the *sandaq* ("holder"). (When circumcisions were regularly performed in the synagogue there was a special chair for the *sandaq* called the Chair of Elijah. The symbolism of this chair derives from a legend based on the identification of the angel of the covenant in *Malachi* 3:1 with Elijah, according to which the prophet is present at every circumcision and is considered to be the guardian of the child as he enters the covenant of circumcision.)

The surgical procedure consists of three steps: (1) *milah,* the removal of the foreskin, (2) *peri'ah,* the tearing off and folding back of the mucous membrane to expose the glans, (3) *metsitsah,* the suction of the blood from the wound. During this procedure, the infant's legs are held firmly by the *sandaq.* In some places, the infant is placed on a surgical restraining board, which renders the *sandaq*'s role only symbolic. The *mohel* removes the foreskin and recites the blessing over the rite of circumcision. The mucous membrane uncovered, it is torn down the center as far as the corona. *Milah* and *peri'ah* may take place in a single step. After the blood is suctioned from the wound *(metsitsah),* the father recites the blessing: "Blessed are you, O Lord our God, Ruler of the Universe, who has sanctified us with your commandments and commanded us to bring our sons into the covenant of Abraham our Father." Those present respond: "Just as he entered the covenant, so may he enter into the study of Torah, into marriage, and into the performance of good deeds." A blessing is then recited over wine, and a prayer is said for the well-being of the child and his family. The child is given a little wine and is formally named, and the wine is then given to the parents. The child is returned to his mother, and the ceremony is concluded. In the Reform ritual, either parent or both parents together may take the role traditionally assigned to the father.

It is customary to name a boy at the *berit milah* ceremony and a girl in the synagogue. However, in the 1970s, Reform Judaism, in accord with its long-held principle of the equality of men and women and in response to the growing desire on the part of parents to formally initiate their infant daughters into the covenant, adopted a new rite called *berit ha-hayyim,* "covenant of life." It follows the liturgical outline of the traditional *berit milah* service, but involves no surgery. The ceremony, as described in the Reform movement's *Gates of the House* (1977, pp. 114–115) proceeds as follows: the infant is welcomed with the words, "Blessed is she who comes." Her mother lights a candle and recites the blessing: "Blessed is the Lord our God, Ruler of the Universe, by whose *mitsvot* we are hallowed, who commands us to sanctify life." The father then lights a candle and recites the blessing, "Blessed is the Lord, whose presence gives light to all the world." The parents both say, "Blessed is the Lord our God, Ruler of the Universe, for giving us life, for sustaining us and enabling us to reach this day of joy." After a prayer invoking the covenant is said, the child is formally named. Although only Reform Judaism has adopted a specific ritual, many individuals of the other movements have written and performed their own initiation service.

There are no normative rules regarding the naming of children in Judaism. Although it is customary among Ashkenazic Jews to name a child after a deceased relative but not after a living person, among Sefardic Jews a child can be named after a living person. Outside the state of Israel, it is common to give a child two names—a secular one, which is used for most purposes, and a Hebrew or Yiddish name, which is used for occasions of religious significance, for example, when one is invited to read from the Torah in synagogue or when a marriage contract *(ketubbah)* is written. Hebrew or Yiddish names take the following form: for a boy, name, *ben* ("son of"), father's name; for a girl, name, *bat* ("daughter of"), father's name. In non-Orthodox naming ceremonies, it is becoming common practice to include the name of the mother as well as the name of the father.

Pidyon ha-ben, the rite called Redemption of the Firstborn, takes place on the thirty-first day following the birth of a firstborn male child. To qualify for the rite, the male child must literally be the firstborn child of his mother. A child born by

Cesarean section is not eligible, because he has not opened his mother's womb. The firstborn son of a *kohen* or a Levite (descendants of the ancient priestly class) is exempt from the rite, as is the firstborn son of the daughter of a *kohen* or a Levite.

The requirement to redeem the firstborn son is found in the Bible: "The first issue of the womb of every being, man or beast, that is offered to the Lord, shall be yours; but you shall have the firstborn of man redeemed. . . . Take as their redemption price, from the age of one month up, the money equivalent of five shekels by sanctuary weight" (*Nm.* 18:15–16). The present ceremony was already well established in Mishnaic times (c. 200 CE). The father makes a declaration affirming that the child is the firstborn son of the mother. A *kohen,* selected by the father, asks him whether or not he wishes to redeem his son. The father responds that he does, then holds five silver coins in his hand and recites the following blessings: "Blessed are you, O Lord our God, Ruler of the Universe, who has sanctified us with your commandments and commanded us concerning the redemption of the firstborn son. Blessed is the Lord our God, Ruler of the Universe, for granting us life, sustaining us, and permitting us to reach this occasion." The father gives the coins to the *kohen,* who passes them over the child, declaring that the coins are the price of redemption. The *kohen* then raises his hands and recites what is known in Jewish tradition as the Priestly Benediction: "May the Lord bless you and keep you. May the Lord let his countenance shine on you and be gracious to you. May the Lord lift up his countenance to you and grant you peace" (*Nm.* 6:24–26). After the rite, the *kohen* returns all or part of the money, which is then usually given to charity. In the United States, it is customary to use either silver dollars or silver medals minted in the state of Israel specially for use in the redemption ceremony. Reform Judaism has eliminated redemption of the firstborn from its standard practice, because it does not recognize a hereditary priesthood or believe that firstborn sons should be differentiated in any way from firstborn daughters. Some individuals have created a rite for firstborn daughters, but no movement has adopted such a rite.

BAR AND BAT MITSVAH, CONFIRMATION

A boy reaches religious majority, becoming *bar mitsvah,* on his thirteenth birthday according to the Hebrew calendar. A girl reaches religious majority, becoming *bat mitsvah,* on her twelfth birthday according to the Hebrew calendar. The term *bar/bat mitsvah* ("son/daughter of the commandment") means a person who is subject to the commandments *(mitsvot),* that is, a person responsible for observing them. The term also refers to the ceremony marking the child's coming of age. The ages of thirteen for a male and twelve for a female were chosen because they mark the onset of puberty. Most congregations perform the ceremony at age thirteen for both boys and girls.

For males, *bar mitsvah* is usually celebrated by the boy's formal participation in the public worship service. Usually, he is invited to read from the Torah and to recite the blessings over the Torah reading and passage from the prophets *(haftarah).* The boy is often assigned the *maftir,* the final brief reading of the weekly Torah reading. Depending on the boy's training and skill, as well as on local custom, he may be invited to conduct all or part of the service, to recite an original prayer, or to give a learned discourse on some biblical or Talmudic subject. The occasion is then usually celebrated with a festive meal or party.

In the post-World War II period, Conservative, Reform, and Reconstructionist Jews developed the celebration of a girl's becoming a *bat mitsvah* in counterpart to that of a boy's becoming a *bar mitsvah*. The exact nature of the girl's participation varies widely from synagogue to synagogue and community to community. There is a general egalitarian trend in non-Orthodox Judaism, so that in many communities *bar* and *bat mitsvah* are indistinguishable.

Among the Orthodox, where women are not counted in the *minyan* (quorum of ten) necessary for public worship, and are not permitted to lead the service or to read from the Torah at a public worship service where men are in attendance, no *bat mitsvah* celebration has developed.

In the nineteenth century, Reform Judaism in Germany instituted the ceremony of confirmation as a substitute for *bar mitsvah*. It is a group ceremony for boys and girls together, which takes place either on or near the festival of Shavu'ot. Shavu'ot was chosen because it celebrates the Jewish people's receiving and acceptance of Torah, and was seen, therefore, as an appropriate time for young people to affirm their commitment to Judaism. The age of confirmation was set at sixteen or seventeen, because at that age the confirmands are better able to understand the implications of the commitments they are affirming. In the 1950s and 1960s, as *bar* and later *bat mitsvah* were reintroduced as standard practices in Reform congregations (in addition to confirmation), many Conservative and Reconstructionist congregations added confirmation to their life cycle ceremonies.

MARRIAGE: QIDDUSHIN AND NISSU'IN

In Judaic tradition, marriage is the ideal human relationship, ordained by God in the creation narrative: "The Lord God said, 'It is not good for man to be alone; I will make him a fitting helper for him'. . . . Hence a man leaves his father and his mother and clings to his wife so that they shall be one flesh" (*Gn.* 2:18, 24). Marriage in Judaism is a legal contractual relationship. Therefore, even though it is a sacred relationship with spiritual significance, it may be dissolved through divorce.

In the Bible, the marriage ceremony is not described in any detail. In the Talmudic period, marriage took place in three stages: engagement *(shiddukhin)*, betrothal (called either *erusin* or *qiddushin*), and wedlock *(nissu'in)*. Engagement *(shiddukhin)* was a formal commitment to marry at which time a document called *tena'im* ("conditions") was drawn. It was a legally binding agreement which stipulated such things as the time and place of the wedding as well as the dowry and maintenance. Today engagement has become largely a social occasion at which the intention to marry is announced. Originally the act of betrothal and wedlock were separated by a year. They have since been joined into a single marriage ceremony and are thus enacted at the same time. In Orthodox Ashkenazic tradition, immediately prior to the formal wedding ceremony, the groom, in the presence of his and the bride's immediate families, covers the bride's face with a veil in a ceremony called *bedeken*. The officiant then says, "Our sister, may you grow into myriads" (*Gn.* 24:60), and concludes with the words, "May God make you like Sarah, Rebecca, Leah, and Rachel," and recites the Priestly Benediction. The bride and the groom are then led to the wedding canopy *(huppah)* by their parents, where words of greeting are recited by the officiant. Next, two betrothal blessings are recited over wine:

Blessed are you, O Lord our God, Ruler of the Universe, creator of the fruit of the vine. Blessed are you, O Lord our God, Ruler of the Universe, who has sanctified us by your commandments and commanded us concerning forbidden relationships, who has forbidden unto us those to whom we are merely betrothed, but has permitted us to those who are married to us by means of the wedding canopy and the sacred rites of marriage. Blessed are you, O Lord our God, who sanctifies his people Israel by means of the wedding canopy and the sacred rites of marriage.

The groom, in the presence of two witnesses, gives the bride an object, usually a ring worth at least a *perutah* (the least valuable coin of the Talmudic period) and recites the formula: "Behold, you are consecrated unto me with this ring as my wife according to the law of Moses and Israel." Next, the marriage contract *(ketubbah)*, previously signed by both partners, is read. The marriage itself proceeds with the recital of the *sheva' berakhot* (Seven Wedding Blessings) over a second cup of wine:

1. Blessed are you, O Lord our God, Ruler of the Universe, creator of the fruit of the vine.
2. Blessed are you, O Lord our God, Ruler of the Universe, who has created all things for his glory.
3. Blessed are you, O Lord, our God, Ruler of the Universe, creator of man.
4. Blessed are you, O Lord our God, Ruler of the Universe, who has made man in your image, after your likeness, and has prepared for him, out of his own being, a building forever [i.e., Eve]. Blessed are you, O Lord, Creator of man.
5. May she who was barren [i.e. Zion] rejoice and exult when her children will be gathered in her midst in joy. Blessed are you, O Lord, who makes Zion rejoice through her children.
6. Grant perfect joy to these loving companions, even as of old you gladdened your creation in the garden of Eden. Blessed are you, O Lord, who makes bridegroom and bride rejoice.
7. Blessed are you, O Lord our God, Ruler of the Universe, who created joy and gladness, bridegroom and bride, mirth and exultation, pleasure and delight, love, harmony, peace, and companionship. Soon, O Lord our God, may there be heard in the cities of Judah and in the streets of Jerusalem the voice of joy and gladness, the voice of the bridegroom and the voice of the bride, the jubilant voice of bridegrooms from their wedding canopies and of youths from their feasts of song. Blessed are you, O Lord, who makes the bridegroom rejoice with the bride.

The ceremony concludes with an address by the rabbi, and with the breaking of a glass. According to the Talmud (B. T., *Ber.* 31a), the purpose of breaking a glass is to temper the joy of the occasion and to engender proper decorum. Another explanation relates the breaking of a glass to the destruction of the First and Second Temples in Jerusalem in the years 587/6 BCE and 70 CE which reminds all assembled that the world is not yet perfect and that joy can be suddenly terminated. Today, the breaking of the glass signifies the conclusion of the ceremony and draws applause and songs of joy.

Reform Judaism omitted the two betrothal blessings and the formal reading of the marriage contract, but recently there has been a tendency to reintroduce the reading of a new, egalitarian marriage contract into the Reform ceremony. In the Orthodox ceremony, it is only the groom who acquires the bride, by presenting her with a ring and reciting the marriage formula. At Reform weddings, the bride may also present the groom with a ring, and then she, too, recites the marriage formula. The "double ring" ceremony is also used by Reconstructionist and many Conservative rabbis.

The two essential prerequisites of marriage are the mutual consent of the bride and the groom and the writing of a *ketubbah*. The *ketubbah* sets forth the obligations of the husband to his wife. By Jewish law, he is required to provide her with food, clothing, and other necessities, which include a commitment to engage in conjugal relations with her. He also stipulates a fixed amount of money that will be paid to her in the event of a divorce.

In addition to changes in the marriage contract that have been made for ideological reasons, new language has been introduced to deal with the circumstances created by the reestablishment of the state of Israel and by the changing conditions of contemporary life. For example, in order to remedy the problem of the woman whose husband refuses to grant her a Jewish divorce *(get)*, the Conservative movement has added a clause to the marriage contract. This clause gives the rabbinical court of the Rabbinical Assembly (the organization of Conservative rabbis) the authority to summon the husband and wife at the request of one of them, to provide counseling, and to impose sanctions if its decisions are not obeyed. Orthodox authorities have also used the addition of new language to the marriage contract to solve problems in Jewish marriage and divorce law.

DEATH AND MOURNING

In Judaism, the mourners and the mourning rites are clearly defined. Mourners are those who have an obligation to observe the rites of mourning, that is, father, mother, brother, sister, son, daughter, and spouse of the deceased. Mourning itself is divided into three clearly defined periods: (1) *aninut*, from death to burial, (2) *shiv'ah*, the seven days following burial, (3) *sheloshim*, from the end of the seven days until the thirtieth day. These are fixed periods, and they apply to all relatives for whom one is required to mourn. An additional mourning period is observed only for a parent; it extends until the year anniversary of the day of death. It is referred to simply as mourning *(avelut)*. Each of these periods has its own set practices and restrictions.

From death until burial, mourners are exempt from the observance of all positive religious obligations, such as reciting morning prayers or donning phylacteries *(tefillin)*. Mourners are also forbidden to engage in pleasurable activities, such as eating meat, drinking wine, attending parties, or engaging in sexual intercourse. The purpose of the exemptions and restrictions are to permit the mourners to attend to the needs of the deceased and to fulfill their obligation to make appropriate preparations for the funeral and burial. This is based on the principle of respect for the dead *(kevod ha-met)* and the Talmudic principle that one who is engaged in a religious obligation *(mitsvah)* is exempt from other religious obligations (B.T., *Suk.* 26a; B.T., *Sot* 44b).

The body of the deceased is prepared for burial through a process of washing *(taborah,* "purification"), which is performed by members of the Jewish burial society *(hevra' qaddisha',* "holy society"). After the washing, the deceased is dressed in plain linen shrouds *(takhrikhim)*. This practice, which levels distinctions of wealth, was established to avoid embarrassing the poor at the time of death. In addition, funerals were considered inappropriate times to display one's wealth. A man is usually buried with his prayer shawl *(tallit)*. Reform Jews often omit the ritual washing, and they dress the deceased in street clothes. After the body has been properly prepared and dressed, it is placed in a plain wooden coffin in preparation for burial in the ground. The use of wooden caskets and burial in the ground is in fulfillment of the biblical verse, "For dust you are, and to dust you shall return" *(Gn.* 3:19). Jewish tradition prohibits both embalming (except when secular law or circumstance requires it) and cremation. Reform Judaism permits both cremation and the entombing of the deceased in a mausoleum, but burial remains normative Jewish practice.

Jewish tradition recommends that burial take place as soon as possible, preferably on the day of death. Today, this is often not possible, because members of the family may not live in close proximity to one another; therefore, burial may be delayed out of respect for the dead, to permit a mourner who lives at a distance to attend. Timely burial is still the rule, however.

Part of the mourning ritual is the rending of a garment *(qeriy'ah)*. In some instances, the actual rending of a garment has been replaced by the symbolic rending of a special black ribbon, which is attached to the mourner's clothing for this purpose. The rending is done standing, and is preceded by the blessing, "Blessed are you, O Lord our God, Ruler of the Universe, Judge of Truth."

Today, funerals often take place in special funeral chapels or at graveside. In some communities, funerals are also held in synagogues. The liturgy for a funeral usually consists of the recitation of several psalms, a eulogy, and the memorial prayer El Male' Raḥamim ("God full of compassion"):

> *O God full of compassion, you who dwell on high! Grant perfect rest beneath the sheltering wings of Your presence, among the holy and pure who shine as the brightness of the heavens, unto the soul of . . . [the deceased] who has entered eternity and in whose memory charity is offered. May his/her repose be in the garden of Eden. May the Lord of Mercy bring him/her under the cover of his wings forever and may his/her soul be bound up in the bond of eternal life. May the Lord be his/her possession and may he/she rest in peace. Amen.*

After the funeral, the deceased is transported to the cemetery. The casket is borne to the grave by the pallbearers, who make seven stops along the way while Psalm 91 is recited. The coffin is then placed in the grave and covered with earth. Most Reform rabbis omit the practice of stopping seven times during the procession to the grave and do not have the casket lowered and covered with earth until after the interment service is completed. The interment service consists of the recitation of Tsidduq ha-Din, which is an acclamation of God's justice; a memorial prayer; and Qaddish, which is a doxology reaffirming the mourner's faith in God in the face of death. A tradition based on a story about a condemned man's soul rescued from the punishment of Gehenna by 'Aqiva' ben Yosef's recitation of Qaddish has assigned an intercessary role to the recitation of Qaddish. After the service has concluded, the people in attendance form two lines through which the mourners pass. Those present comfort the mourners as they pass, saying, "May God comfort you among the rest of the mourners of Zion and Jerusalem."

The completion of the funeral marks the end of the first mourning period, *aninut,* and the beginning of the second period, *shiv'ah.* On returning home (usually to the home of the deceased), the mourners kindle a candle, which is kept burning for the whole seven-day period. The flame is a symbol of the human soul. ("The soul of humankind is the lamp of the Lord," *Proverbs* 20:27.) Then the mourners are served a meal of consolation *(se'udat havra'ah),* which is prepared by friends and relatives; it traditionally includes round foods such as eggs, a symbol of life and hope.

During *shiv'ah* the mourners remain at home and do not attend to business or engage in social activities. Traditionally, they sit on special low benches, refrain from shaving, cutting their hair, bathing, or anointing themselves for pleasure (though they may do so for hygienic reasons). They do not wear leather shoes or engage in sexual intercourse. (Most of these practices of abstinence have been abandoned by Reform Jews.) A *minyan* (quorum of ten) gathers at the house of mourning for twice-daily services—morning and evening. During *shiv'ah,* friends and relatives have an obligation to visit the mourners to comfort them. When *shiv'ah* ends, the mourners return to work but continue to avoid social gatherings until the thirtieth day after burial. When one is mourning the death of a parent, the restrictions are observed for one year.

Yahrzeit, the yearly anniversary of a person's death, is observed by the mourners' lighting a memorial light, which is kept lit for twenty-four hours; by giving charity in the deceased's memory; and by attending services to recite Qaddish.

The erecting of a tombstone is an ancient custom. Usually the mourners wait one year following the death before having the monument put in place at the gravesite. A common practice is for the mourners to dedicate the tombstone in a brief ceremony, popularly called an "Unveiling," because as part of the ritual a cloth covering the tombstone is removed by the family.

Four times a year—on Yom Kippur (the Day of Atonement), on the last day of Pesah (Passover), on Shavu'ot (Feast of Weeks), and on the last day of Sukkot (Tabernacles)—a memorial service, popularly called *yizkor,* is held as part of the holy day observance. A memorial light is lit at home, and the deceased is remembered at the service. (Most Reform congregations have a memorial service only on Yom Kippur and on the last day of Passover.)

CONVERSION

Conversion may be considered a rite of passage since through the process a person changes his or her status from being a non-Jew to a Jew. The history of proselytism in Judaism is complex and is beyond the scope of this discussion (see Bernard Bamberger's classic study, *Proselytism in the Talmudic Period,* Cincinnati, 1939). Candidates for conversion must come of their own free will without ulterior motive. Therefore, a person who comes for the purpose of marriage is automatically disqualified. However, this stricture is observed only by the Orthodox. Once the sincerity of the prospective convert is ascertained, there is a period of instruction during which the candidate is taught the basic principles and practices of Judaism. Once the prospective convert has completed this education and accepts the obligation to observe *mitsvot* (commandments), the candidate is examined by a *beit din* (a rabbinical court consisting of three rabbis or other observant Jews). Male and female converts are then immersed in a *mikvah* (ritual bath) and males are circumcised by a *mohel.* If the male had been previously circumcised by a doctor as a child, then only a symbolic circumcision *(hatafat dam berit)* is required. The Reform movement does not require immersion or circumcision although an increasing number of Reform rabbis require the traditional rites. In addition to the appearance before the rabbinical court, immersion, and circumcision, a public ceremony of welcome has been introduced into many Reform, Conservative, and Reconstructionist congregations.

[*For further discussion of the development of Jewish law and tradition concerning these rites, see* Conservative Judaism; Orthodox Judaism; Reconstructionist Judaism; *and* Reform Judaism.]

BIBLIOGRAPHY

The best general book on Jewish rites of passage, which contains both popular practices and historical development, is Hayyim Schauss's *The Lifetime of a Jew throughout the Ages of Jewish History* (New York, 1950).

Orthodox Practice. Standard Orthodox practice is explained in H. Halevy Donin's *To Be a Jew* (New York, 1972), which has a good bibliography but lacks extensive source references. The Orthodox rabbi's manual, Hyman E. Goldin's *Hamadrikh, the Rabbi's Guide,* 2d ed. (New York, 1956), contains the liturgy and an excellent summary of the laws. The liturgy and extensive explanatory notes can also be found in Joseph H. Hertz's *The Authorized Daily Prayer Book,* 2d ed. (New York, 1963). Maurice Lamm has two extensive studies on the Orthodox view of death and marriage, *The Jewish Way in Death and Mourning* (New York, 1969) and *The Jewish Way in Love and Marriage* (San Francisco, 1980).

Conservative Practice. The most comprehensive study of Jewish practice available is Isaac Klein's *A Guide to Jewish Religious Practice* (New York, 1979). In addition to a detailed description of the practices from a traditional Conservative point of view, he provides extensive reference to the Talmud and later legal codes. The book contains an extensive bibliography. *A Rabbi's Manual,* new rev. ed., edited by Jules Harlow (New York, 1965), provides the liturgical texts for rites of passage according to Conservative Judaism's interpretation.

Reform Practice. *Gates of Mitzvah: A Guide to the Jewish Life Cycle,* edited by Simeon J. Maslin (New York, 1979), explains the Reform practice. It contains source reference notes and explanatory essays. The Reform liturgical texts are found in *Gates of the House,* edited by Chaim Stern (New York, 1977), and *A Rabbi's Manual* (Cincinnati, 1928), edited and published by the Central Conference of American Rabbis. A recent version of the liturgical texts are contained in *Ma'aglei Tsedeq,* edited by David Polish with notes by W. Gunther Plaut (New York, forthcoming).

New Rituals. *The Jewish Catalog,* edited by Richard Siegel, Michael Strassfeld, and Sharon Strassfeld (Philadelphia, 1973), and *The Second Jewish Catalog,* edited by Michael Strassfeld and Sharon Strassfeld (Philadelphia, 1976), are excellent sources for traditional and creative rituals of observance. *The Jewish Woman: New Perspectives,* edited by Elizabeth Koltun (New York, 1976), contains two essays, "On the Birth of a Daughter" by Myra Leifer and Daniel Leifer, and "On Writing New *Ketubbot*" by Daniel Leifer, which describe some of the egalitarian tendencies in non-Orthodox rites of passage.

19 DOMESTIC OBSERVANCES

Shlomo Deshen

Besides the synagogue, the home has traditionally been a main focus of religiosity both for the Jewish family as a unit and especially for women. Women were traditionally excluded from the duty of Torah study, which for men was, and to some extent remains, a major focus of spirituality. Moreover, women were not obligated to observe many of the religious practices that bound men. In particular, their place in public synagogue ritual was minimal. Consequently, domestic rituals, and especially-those governed by women, are important focuses of their spirituality. For all Jews, certain ritual customs *(minhagim)* and rabbinic laws *(halakhot)* actually require a domestic setting. These rituals may be divided into those that are held on specific occasions of the Jewish calendar and those that are a constant presence in daily life.

PERIODIC DOMESTIC OBSERVANCES

The annual festival cycle begins in the spring with Passover, which focuses on two major domestic activities: the thorough cleaning of the home to remove leavened food, and then the Seder, the Passover eve feast, which has traditionally been led by the father and requires the participation of the children. Shavu'ot, in early summer, is accompanied by only minor domestic customs, such as decorating the home with greenery and partaking of dairy foods. The period of mourning for the destroyed Temple, which follows in midsummer, affects the home in a fashion opposite to that of the festivals: enjoyment of music, food, new clothing, and vacations, and joyfulness in general, are restricted. The fall holy days start with Ro'sh ha-Shanah and Yom Kippur, which are primarily synagogue-centered occasions but which include secondary domestic activities. On Ro'sh ha-Shanah, foods symbolizing good fortune are served at the family meal, and on Yom Kippur, family elders bless the young. During the week-long Sukkot festival the domestic focus is again pronounced. Temporary booths or huts *(sukkot)* are erected near or adjacent to each family home. Meals are eaten there, and some males follow the rabbinic tradition of sleeping in the booths at night. People entertain guests and generally pass time in the family *sukkah*. Hanukkah, in early winter, is focused domestically as well. Lights are ritually kindled in the home, and special holiday foods are prepared. Hanukkah also has indoor child-centered activities (gift-giving and living-room games). In late winter, Purim requires a formal feast at home, and women and children become particularly involved in the traditional sending of gifts of food to friends.

PERENNIAL DOMESTIC OBSERVANCES

Besides seasonal events, the Jewish home also has perennial ritual activities, primarily on the Sabbath, when the routine of the home is transformed. Domestic rituals are observed on the Sabbath: candles are lit by the housewife on Sabbath eve; the Qiddush ("sanctification of the day") is chanted at the first of the three mandatory festive meals; families sing Sabbath songs *(zemirot)* and sometimes study Torah together. Of these customs, candle-lighting is a major rite for women, a virtual symbol of female religious identity. In recent times, with the attenuation of many more-burdensome Jewish customs, candle-lighting has remained vital and thus has become more prominent. According to some traditions, parents formally bless their children on Sabbath eve, and Sabbath night is a preferred time for conjugal relations. In the home the Sabbath ends with the ceremony of *havdalah* ("separation" of the Sabbath from the week), which involves the use of wine, spices, and a special braided candle, and at which a new fire is lit. Another perennial domestic ritual element is the display of religious artifacts. Foremost of these is the mandatory *mezuzah* inscription of biblical verses, encased on all doorposts. Brass or silver candelabra, wine goblets, and collections of Judaica books are common in the more prosperous homes. It is a custom to leave a section of wall in the home (about one square foot) unpainted, as a symbol of pain over the destruction of ancient Jerusalem *(zekher le-ḥurban)*.

The celebration of rites of passage spills over into the home through the holding of festive meals. Domestically, the most marked rites of passage are mourning rites, which restrict the bereaved to their homes and require them to receive condolence visits. Memorial candles for the dead are lit at home. In the past, marriages in Mediterranean countries were patrilocal and some marriage observances paralleled mourning rites. The bridal couple were restricted to their new home for seven days of festivity, and daily rites were held in the presence of visitors. In our time, owing to the attenuation of patrilocality, the practice among many young Orthodox bridal couples, both in Israel and elsewhere, is to travel distances to visit their kin, and to be hosted in different homes where rites are held for the duration of seven days.

In Orthodox and traditionally observant families, the home is the scene of innumerable daily acts of individual piety: the ritual washing of hands upon arising, before meals and after voiding; the uttering of grace after meals, and of shorter benedictions before and after the partaking of any food. Prayers are recited upon waking and upon retiring at night, and three daily prayer services *(shaharit,* in the morning, *minḥah,* in the afternoon, *ma'ariv,* in the evening) are required of all adult males. In recent times, because of the weaker hold of the community, weekday prayers are frequently said at home rather than at the synagogue; hence, the role of the home in daily prayer has increased.

The most pervasive home observances are those that concern food and conjugal relations. Observance of the rules of *kashrut* (maintaining a ritually pure, kosher kitchen), is dependent upon the foods introduced into the home, and on the separation of various categories of foods in the kitchen and dining area. *Kashrut* also requires the services of extra-domestic agents, such as a *shoḥet* (ritual slaughterer), and of manufacturers of kosher foods. The maintenance of "family purity" *(ṭaharat ha-mishpaḥah)* depends to a greater extent on the privacy of domestic practice. "Family purity" consists of the maintenance of a monthly schedule of conjugal separation and reunion based on the menstrual cycle, and on the woman's periodic immersion in a *miqveh* (ritual bath). While the availability of an external agent, the *miqveh,* is required here as well, the element of domestic autonomy in this area of intimacy is nonetheless very strong. The autonomy of the home in this area was curtailed in traditional times (in Northern Europe roughly until the mid-nineteenth century, in Mediterranean lands until close to the mid-twentieth century). Decisions concerning the proper timing of immersion were not handled exclusively by the woman then, but rather in conjunction with a circle of elder females, family and neighbors. If there was any physiological irregularity, male rabbis were consulted. In contemporary Orthodoxy, middle-class sensitivities concerning the privacy of sexual matters have eliminated the role of the outside female circle; rabbis are consulted only in the most unusual cases. But it is in the maintenance of *kashrut* that the role of the home has increased most in contemporary times, and has assumed a novel symbolic weight. The affective term "kosher home" is now commonly used in reference to *kashrut* observance, which has gained much greater prominence in relation to its historical place in Jewish practice and thought. Over time, additional domestic practices have become more prominent (contemporary domestic Sabbath practices are innovations of the late sixteenth century). Most recently in the West, the pressure of Christmastime commercialism has encouraged Jewish families to elaborate the observance of Hanukkah, especially with parties, gift giving, and the decoration of the home, as an ethnic counterpoint to Christian symbols such as the tree and Santa Claus.

There are two major exceptions to this development (i.e., the increasing emphasis on Jewish domestic ritual). One is the virtual disappearance of the *ḥallah*-separation rite. Married women baking their bread used to separate and burn a small portion of the dough, as a symbol of the tithe that was due the priests in Temple times. *Hallah*-separation used to be a major female responsibility, similar to Sabbath candle-lighting and to the maintenance of family purity *(niddah).* But as bread production has shifted from a domestic to a commercial setting, the rite has become uncommon. Another exception is in practices of the Hasidic movement, which encourages male groups to congregate by themselves, or at the court of the *rebbe,* the sect leader. In these congregations, adult males eat the third of the three required meals together, away from their families, on the Sabbath afternoon. Hasidism also encourages men to spend some of the holy days and Sabbaths at the distant court of the *rebe,* again separating them from their families.

[*See also* Kashrut *and entries on individual Jewish holy days and festivals.*]

BIBLIOGRAPHY

For a masterly, though brief, overview of the position of formal *halakhah,* see Aaron Lichtenstein's "Ha-mishpaḥah be-halakhah" in *Mishpeḥot Yisra'el: Divrei ha-kinus ha-shemonah-'asar le-maḥshavah Yehudit* (Jerusalem, 1976), pp. 13–30. On Ashkenazic Jewry, Jacob Katz's *Tradition and Crisis: Jewish Society at the End of the Middle Ages* (New York, 1961) provides a fine sociological overview; much pertinent information is scattered in the chapters on the family, religion, and Hasidism. In a shorter monograph, *Tsibbur ve-yiḥidim be-Maroqo: Sidrei ḥevra ba-kehillot ha-Yehudiyot ba-me'ot ha-18–19* (Tel Aviv, 1983), I describe eighteenth- and nineteenth-century Moroccan Jewry and thereby provide documentation for a section of Sefardic Jewry; some of this material appears in English in "Women in the Jewish Family in Pre-Colonial Morocco," *Anthropological Quarterly* 56 (July 1983): 134–144. A comprehensive ethnographic survey of religious and other home feasts in a village of Moroccan immigrants in Israel is given in Moshe Shokeid's "Conviviality versus Strife: Peacemaking at Parties among Atlas Mountains Immigrants in Israel," in *Freedom and Constraint: A Memorial Tribute to Max Gluckman,* edited by Myron J. Aronoff (Assen, Netherlands, 1976). One such feast is described in detail in my *Immigrant Voters in Israel: Parties and Congregations in a Local Election Campaign* (Manchester, 1970), pp. 140–147. The qabbalistic sources for some of the comparatively recent domestic Sabbath customs are cited in Gershom Scholem's *On the Kabbalah and Its Symbolism,* translated by Ralph Manheim (New York, 1965), pp. 142–146. In an overview of United States suburban Jewry, *Jewish Identity on the Suburban Frontier* (Chicago, 1979), Marshall Sklare and Joseph Greenblum analyze the novel weight of Hanukkah child-centered activities.

ICONOGRAPHY

MOSHE BARASCH

Jewish iconography, whether actually represented in works of art or existing only as traditional imagery (and occasionally referred to in literature), was determined from the first by the biblical "prohibition of images." This prohibition, transmitted in the Bible in several versions, could be understood (1) as forbidding, in a religious context, all images, regardless of their subject matter (*Ex.* 20:4, *Dt.* 4:15–18), or (2) specifically forbidding the depiction of God and the ritual use of such a depiction as an idol (*Dt.* 27:15). While the first interpretation of the prohibition did not prevail (the Bible itself provides evidence of this in *1 Kgs.* 6:23–29, *Ez.* 8:5–12), the other was consistently implemented. Possibly the most striking feature of Jewish iconography throughout the ages is the systematic avoidance of any depiction of the figure of God. To a large extent this is also true for saintly personages: though hagiographical literature emerged in Judaism, it was not accompanied by any visual imagery of saints. From the beginning, then, Jewish religious iconography developed in marked contrast to the traditions predominant in the Christian West. Since the loss of political independence in 71 CE, Jewish imagery could not be formed within the framework of a state art and did not enjoy any official support for its symbols. As the art and imagery of a religious minority, however, it flourished in the Diaspora throughout the ages. The iconography that emerged within these limitations developed mainly in a few periods and thematic cycles.

HELLENISM

The meeting between Judaism and the Greek world—a process that lasted from early Hellenism to late antiquity (roughly, second century BCE to fifth century CE)—resulted in a body of religious images. While the Mishnah and Talmud were being compiled (roughly second to sixth centuries CE) Jewish communities produced a large number of representations, which have been uncovered in Jewish remains (mainly synagogues and burial places) from Tunisia to Italy and eastward to the Euphrates; sites in Israel are particularly rich. [*See* Synagogue, *article on* Architectural Aspects.] Occasionally this imagery includes human figures, either in biblical scenes (see figure 1) or in pagan myths (frequently the image of Helios, the Greek sun god).

FIGURE 1. *Wall Painting.* Dura Synagogue; Dura-Europos, mid-third century CE. This depiction of Ezekiel's vision of the resurrection of the dry bones (*Ez.* 37:1–14) is part of an extant cycle of fifty-eight figurative episodes in some twenty-eight panels.

More often, however, these survivals show objects with definite ritual connotations (see figure 2). Most prominent are the seven-branched *menorah* (candelabrum), Aron ha-Qodesh (the Ark of the Covenant), *lulav* and *etrog* (palm branch and citron), and shofar (ceremonial animal horn). These objects (which reflect the crystallization of Jewish ritual) have no strict hierarchy, but the *menorah,* and the Ark of the Covenant, representing the law itself, are more important than the others. When both are shown together, they always occupy the central place. Besides such explicitly ritual objects, Jewish remains abound in artistic motifs, taken over from Hellenistic art, whose symbolic character is obscure. A good example is the vine, most likely derived from contemporary Dionysian imagery and often found in Jewish cemeteries. But whether in Jewish communities it carried the meaning of salvation that it had in the pagan world is a matter of dispute. Some modern scholars tend to see these motifs as "decoration" devoid of articulate symbolic meanings; others, especially Goodenough, attribute established symbolic meanings to them.

MIDDLE AGES

In the European Middle Ages, especially between the thirteenth and fifteenth centuries, Jewish religious imagery developed further. The illumination of manuscripts is the central aesthetic medium of the period; of particular significance are the manuscripts produced in Spain, Italy, and Germany. All these manuscripts are of a ritual nature, the most important groups being the Haggadah for Passover and prayer books for the holidays, the *mahzor.* The illuminations (and later, printed illustrations) represent many ritual utensils, but they also include, more often than in Jewish art of other periods and media, human figures, especially in biblical scenes (see figure 3). The iconographic repertoire is enlarged by mythical motifs, attesting to messianic beliefs. Among these motifs are the legendary beasts (such as the *shor habar,* a kind of wild ox), on which the just will feast on the day of redemption; these are particularly prominent in manuscripts produced in Germany. The future Temple that, according to common belief, is to be built after the redemption, is another frequent mythical motif, especially in Spanish and German manuscripts; it is sometimes patterned after contemporary Christian models. Both the temple building and the ritual utensils (the latter sometimes rendered on the opening folios of Bible manuscripts produced in Spain) may be taken as expressions of "the ardent hope and belief" to see the "restored Temple in the messianic future." In countries under Islamic rule, Jewish art readily adapted the aniconic attitude and the repertoire of

FIGURE 2. *Mosaic Floor.* Beit Alfa' Synagogue; Palestine, 518–527. At the top is the Ark of the Covenant (with eternal light above), lions, a seven-branched *menorah*, a *lulav*, an *etrog*, a shofar, and censers. In the middle appears a zodiac with the four seasons at the corners and the sun at the center. The bottom portion depicts the binding of Isaac, with the hand of God above and Abraham's servants and donkey at left.

FIGURE 3. *Illustrated Page from Printed Passover Haggadah.* Executed by Gershon Cohen; Prague, 1526–1527. Inset within the text is a picture of Elijah mounted on his donkey. The border contains representations of Judith carrying the head of Holofernes (left) and Samson with the gates of Gaza (right). Adam and Eve are above.

decorative motifs common among the Muslims, although in literature, visual imagery continued to thrive in the form of metaphors and descriptions. [*See* Biblical Temple.]

QABBALISTIC SYMBOLISM

The qabbalistic tradition is a special field of iconographic creation. Qabbalistic literature abounds in visual metaphors, since the authors often tend to express (or to hide) their thoughts and mysteries in visual images and descriptions of supposed optical experiences. Since the beginnings of Jewish mysticism in late antiquity, a continuous tradition of visual symbols has persisted. Considerably enriched in the

Middle Ages, and in the seventeenth century, this tradition remained unbroken up to, and including, Hasidic literature. The central image of qabbalistic symbolism is the Tree of Sefirot. The godhead is imagined as structured in ten spheres, each of them representing a "divine quality" (Heb., *sefirah*). The shape and place of the spheres, and the spatial relationships between them, are firmly established in the qabbalistic imagination. The overall pattern vaguely resembles a tree (hence the name), but the basic character of the image is abstract rather than figurative. Though the Tree of Sefirot has frequently been depicted (mainly in simple form, primarily in popular printed editions) and has exerted some influence on contemporary Jewish painters, the image is not primarily an artistic one; rather, it is still widely known from the literary sources.

Qabbalistic literature produced other visual symbols, among them the images of broken vessels, scattered sparks, Adam Qadmon (primordial man) as a figure of God, and so forth. Scholem has also shown that an elaborate color symbolism emerged in the qabbalistic literature. [*See* Qabbalah.] In modern civil societies, Jewish iconography is still in the process of formation and has not yet been properly studied.

BIBLIOGRAPHY

For the imagery of the Hebrew Bible (though not necessarily in art only) still useful is Maurice H. Farbridge's *Studies in Biblical and Semitic Symbolism* (1923; reprint, New York, 1970). Erwin R. Goodenough's *Jewish Symbols in the Greco-Roman Period,* 13 vols. (New York, 1953–1968), has a rich collection of photographs; the text is stimulating, albeit sometimes arguable. Mainly for the Middle Ages, see Jacob Leveen's *The Hebrew Bible in Art* (1944; reprint, New York, 1974). For early modern times, see *Beauty in Holiness: Studies in Jewish Customs and Ceremonial Art,* edited by Joseph Gutmann (New York, 1970), a catalog of Jewish artifacts from the Prague Museum shown at the Jewish Museum in New York.

Much can be learned from the discussion of single problems. See, for example, *The Temple of Solomon,* edited by Joseph Gutmann (Missoula, Mont., 1976). Another individual problem is discussed by Zofia Ameisenowa in "The Tree of Life in Jewish Ico-nography," *Journal of the Warburg and Courtauld Institutes* 2 (1938–1939): 326–345. Qabbalistic imagery is best discussed in Gershom Scholem's *Major Trends in Jewish Mysticism,* 3d rev. ed. (New York, 1954), esp. pp. 205–243. A highly interesting study of a particular subject in qabbalistic symbolism is Scholem's "Farben und ihre Symbolik in der jüdischen Überlieferung und Mystik," *Eranos Yearbook* 41 (1974): 1–49, *The Realms of Colour* (with English and French summaries).

FIVE

JEWISH MOVEMENTS
AND ISSUES

21 HASIDISM

JOSEPH DAN

Hasidism is the common appellation of a Jewish pietistic movement that developed in eastern Europe in the second half of the eighteenth century, became, before the end of that century, a major force in modern Judaism, and has remained as such into the twentieth century. Previous Hasidic movements in Jewish history—mainly the Ashkenazic Hasidism of medieval Germany (twelfth–thirteenth centuries) and the early *hasidim* of the tannaitic period (first–second centuries CE)—will not be discussed here. Rather, the movement at hand is that called, in the writings of the opponents of Hasidism and some historians, "Beshtian Hasidism," a sobriquet that refers to the movement's founder, Yisra'el ben Eli'ezer, known as the Besht (an acronym for Ba'al Shem Tov, "Master of the Good Name").

ROOTS OF THE MOVEMENT

Hasidism did not emerge, as most other Jewish religious movements did, from the schools of the higher social strata and leading intellectuals. Its first teachers belonged to a social group of popular preachers who used to wander from one community to the other, usually among the smaller and poorer Jewish communities in Podolia and the neighboring areas. Many of these preachers were suspected of Shabbatean tendencies, and they found their audience among the small merchants and the poor in peripherial areas. This fact influenced the later development of the Hasidic movement. Even after Hasidism grew dominant in larger communities, it remained faithful to the social groups that supported it in its early beginnings, and an awareness of the religious needs of the uneducated and the poor became one of the traits of the movement.

Attempts to describe Hasidism as a movement of social rebellion of the poor against the rich, the downtrodden masses against the leaders, have failed. There is no evidence that the Hasidic teachers intended to change the social structure of Jewish communities. But Hasidism did emphasize the ability of the lower social groups to actively participate and achieve a high position in Jewish religious practice.

The religious background for the appearance of the Hasidic movement is the Shabbatean crisis. While various historians differ in their descriptions of the main reasons for the emergence of Hasidism and in their evaluation of the social and cultural reasons for its success, there is little doubt that the movement served as an answer to the most profound religious crisis that affected Judaism from the late seventeenth through the eighteenth centuries. Gershom Scholem described Hasidism as the neutralization of the messianic element in Judaism after the Shabbatean crisis, and while some scholars insisted that there are messianic elements in Hasidism, none disputed the direct relationship between Hasidic theology and the Shabbatean sects that flourished in eastern Europe in the eighteenth century.

Jewish theologians of the seventeenth and eighteenth centuries, many of whom persisted in believing in the messianism of Shabbetai Tsevi, had to develop a theology that would explain the paradox of a messiah committing the worst possible transgression against orthodox Judaism—Shabbetai Tsevi's conversion to Islam in 1666. Various theologies were developed, some of which called upon the believers to follow the messiah and convert to Islam, thereby creating a "coalition" between Judaism and Islam against Christianity; others maintained that belief in Shabbetai Tsevi could be continued within Judaism provided the believer express his attachment to the new messianic, redemptive period that began with the appearance of Shabbetai Tsevi. These expressions eventually covered a whole range of possibilities, from the most anarchistic, antinomian ones of the Frankist movement in Poland in the middle of the eighteenth century to the mild celebrations of Tish'ah be-Av (the ninth day of the month of Av, the day of the destruction of the Temple and a day of fasting, which the Shabbateans turned into a celebration of Shabbetai Tsevi's birthday).

Among the various expressions of the continued belief in Shabbetai Tsevi as the Messiah, two are of interest in understanding the beginnings of Hasidism: the most radical one and the most orthodox one. The radical Frankist movement, which proclaimed that in the new messianic world the way to preserve the Torah was to destroy it, was regarded as a sign of a deep crisis in Jewish religion and education. The Frankists, before converting to Christianity, participated in a religious dispute (in Kamenets in 1757 and in Lvov in 1759) during which they were reported to have directed a blood libel (accusation of a murder for ritual purposes) against their Jewish coreligionists. This aberrational movement, which included some very tempting ideas that captured the hearts of many, signified the need for a reformulation of Jewish organized religious life as well as for the formulation of new answers to basic theological questions, especially the interpretation of qabbalistic symbols from the thirteenth century *Zohar* and from the teachings of Isaac Luria of Safad (1534–1572) that were used extensively by the Shabbateans.

The other side of the Shabbatean response to the conversion was a retreat to ultraorthodoxy or cryptoorthodoxy, often with some pietistic ("Hasidic") elements. Explaining that the crisis of the Shabbatean endeavor was caused by the insufficient spiritual support the messiah received from his followers, these Shabbateans adopted a way of life that emphasized continued practice of repentance, self-negation, and insistence on strict adherence to every detail of Jewish religious law. Groups of such *hasidim* appeared in several Jewish communities in eastern Europe that were the centers for spiritual seeking. Not all of their members were Shabbateans, and the Shabbateans themselves were divided in many ways. But when the new Hasidic movement emerged, it did so against the background of several groups or sects of *hasidim* that had already become a common phenomenon in the major centers of Jewish culture in eastern Europe.

The relationship of Hasidism to Shabbateanism and the Frankist movement is complicated. On the one hand, an early Hasidic legend tells how in the Besht's participation in the Lvov disputation of 1759, he defended Judaism from the accusations of the Frankists. On the other hand, another Hasidic tradition quotes the Besht as lamenting the conversion of the Frankists following that disputation, claiming that as long as a limb is connected to the divine body of the Shekhinah it can be cured, but once severed it is lost forever. In a similar vein, we find motifs of understanding and closeness to the Shabbatean experience coupled with fierce negation and rejection of the Shabbatean message. The Besht is described as trying to save the soul of Shabbetai Tsevi from Hell, where he saw him stretched out on a table with Jesus Christ; Shabbetai Tsevi then tried to pull the Besht down, and only by a great effort did the Besht succeed in extricating himself. It seems that though the condemnation of Shabbateanism by the Hasidim was absolute, the idea that the Shabbateans could and should be saved also persisted in Hasidic circles. Members of the Bratslav sect of Hasidism believed that their leader, Nahman of Bratslav, was destined to correct the religious damage done by the Shabbatean movement.

HISTORY

The history of the early Hasidic movement can be divided into four main periods, each a major step in its development.

1. *The circle of the Besht (c. 1740–1760).* The Besht seems to have been in contact with a group of wandering preachers, like himself, who in their homiletics preached a new kind of worship and presented a new conception of the role of the elect in Jewish religion. They were qabbalists, following the main mystical symbols of the Lurianic school but emphasizing the achievements of the individual and his ability to assist his brethren in religious matters. *Devequt* (communion with God) was one of the main subjects they preached, stressing man's ability to attain constant communion with God. It is possible that parallel to the Besht's circle of adherents there were other pietistic groups in some of the major centers of Jewish culture in eastern Europe. Some of these circles were influenced by various Shabbatean ideas; all were aware of the Shabbatean crisis.

2. *The first Hasidic center in Mezhirich (1760–1772).* After the Besht's death, the leadership of the Hasidic movement was assumed by his disciple, Dov Ber of Mezhirich (now Międzyrzecz, Poland). He held "court" in his home, where many young Jewish intellectuals as well as common people gathered to listen to his sermons. These were transcribed by his disciples and later published in several versions. The court of Dov Ber (called the *maggid,* i.e., "preacher") was described, among others, in the autobiography of Salomon Maimon, who had visited it in his youth. In this period begins the history of Hasidism as an organized movement, led by an accepted authority.

3. *The disciples of Dov Ber (1773–1812).* This is the most important period, in which Hasidism became a major force within Judaism. Several of Dov Ber's disciples created "courts" like that of their teacher, and led *'edot* ("communities"), around which thousands, and then tens of thousands, of adherents gathered, accepting the

leadership of that disciple and making their community an alternative social and religious organization of Jews, distinct from the hegemony of the traditional rabbinate. Elimelekh of Lizhensk (now Lezajsk, Poland), Shne'ur Zalman of Lyady (Belorussia), Menaḥem Mendel of Vitebsk, and, to some extent, Naḥman of Bratslav belong to this category. In this period of Hasidic theory of the *tsaddiq* was developed and began to shape both Hasidic thought and social organization. At this same time the Hasidim became a distinct group, not only because of the internal development of Hasidism, but also because of the growing opposition to it from the school of Eliyyahu ben Shelomoh Zalman, the "Gaon of Vilna," which published several pamphlets against Hasidic ideology and practice, denouncing them as heretics and excommunicating them, even trying to enlist the help of the Russian government against their leaders (especially Shne'ur Zalman of Lyady, founder of the Habad sect). This fierce opposition was motivated both by fears that the Hasidim were going to undermine the traditional Jewish social structure, which was based on the prestige of the scholars and Talmudists, and by the fear of another Shabbatean movement. There is no doubt that the growing opposition to Hasidism contributed significantly to the internal cohesion of the Hasidic communities and created clear lines of demarcation between areas in which the Hasidim became dominant and areas governed by their opponents.

It was in this period that Hasidic literature was initially published. The first works were those of Ya'aqov Yosef of Polonnoye, the Besht's greatest disciple, whose voluminous collections of sermons include most of the material we have concerning the teachings of the Besht (the first Hasidic work published was Ya'aqov Yosef's *Toledot Ya'aqov Yosef,* Korets, 1780). These were followed by the sermons of Dov Ber, published by his disciples, and then many other collections of sermons by his followers. The only work published in this period in the form of an ethical work and not the usual collection of sermons was Shne'ur Zalman's *Tanya'* (see below). By the beginning of the nineteenth century the Hasidic movement had an organized leadership, prolific literature, well-defined communities and areas of influence, and an established standing in the general framework of Jewish life.

4. *The development of Hasidic "houses" or "lines of succession" (shoshalot).* To a very large extent this process has continued to the present. Many of Dov Ber's disciples served as founders of several Hasidic communities when their disciples scattered and each established his own "house" and community. The custom of passing Hasidic leadership from father to son or, in some cases, son-in-law, became more and more frequent, until it was universally accepted that the new leader had to be from the family of the previous leader. These "houses" usually bore the names of the towns in which they were established, even after the center was moved to another country—Poland, for instance, where many centers were located in Warsaw before the Second World War—or to another continent such as to the United States or Israel, where many of the centers are today. The history of Hasidism has since fragmented into the separate histories of various houses or schools. Only two of the communities have preserved their specific ideological and organizational profile, remaining distinct from all others, throughout this period—Habad Hasidism, founded by Shne'ur Zalman of Lyady, and Bratslav Hasidism, the followers of Naḥman of Bratslav, the Besht's great-grandson. The rift between Hasidim and their opponents has obtained until this day; most Jews of east European descent belong to family lines of either Hasidim or *mitnaggedim* ("opponents").

SPREAD OF THE MOVEMENT

The spread of Hasidism after the death of Dov Ber in 1772 occurred at the same time that the opposition to the emerging Hasidic movement was growing. After that year, for a period of nearly fifty years, their opponents orchestrated repeated declarations excommunicating the Hasidic leaders and several times enlisted the help of the Russian government in their efforts, claiming that the Hasidim, as heretics, were undermining the foundations of the state. The documents concerning this organized opposition have been collected by Mordecai Wilensky and analyzed in a detailed, two-volume study.

The persecution by their opponents did not halt the spread of the movement, which gathered momentum and gained new communities and adherents in the end of the eighteenth century and the first half of the nineteenth century. The disciples of Dov Ber and their disciples established the great Hasidic houses. Levi Yits-haq established an important Hasidic community in Berdichev, while Menahem Nahum built the house of Chernobyl, which was continued by his son, Mordechai Twersky, and went on for many generations. Yisra'el of Rizhyn (now Ruzhin, Ukrainian S.S.R.), a descendant of Dov Ber, built the Rizhyn-Sadigora house; his four sons who followed him made it into one of the most important and eminent Hasidic communities in Russia. Mosheh Hayyim Efrayim of Sedlikov (now Sudylkow, Poland), a grandson of the Besht, did not lead a community, but his book, *Degel mahaneh Efrayim,* a work of Hasidic sermons that often relies on direct traditions of the Besht, was influential. In Poland and Lithuania Hasidism became a major force through the work of Shelomoh ben Me'ir of Karlin and Hayyim Haiqel of Amdur (Indura). Hasidic communities in the Land of Israel were established in Safad and Tiberias by Menahem Mendel of Vitebsk and Avraham ben Aleksander Kats of Kalisz who migrated to the Land of Israel in 1777. In the beginning of the nineteenth century a group of great leaders gave renewed impetus to the spread of Hasidism, among them Ya'aqov Yitshaq ("the Seer of Lublin"), Ya'aqov Yitshaq ben Asher of Pshischa (now Przysucha, Poland), and Avraham Yehoshu'a Heschel of Apt in Moldavia (now Opatow, Poland). Menahem Morgenstern established the great house of Pshischa-Kozk, and Shalom Rokeah the Belz Hasidim. Mosheh Teitelbaum, a disciple of Ya'aqov Yitshaq of Lublin, created the powerful and influential Satmar Hasidism in Hungary. By the middle of the nineteenth century Hasidism was the dominant force in most Jewish communities in eastern Europe, and most Hasidic houses continued their existence and development until the Holocaust. [*For location of the major Hasidic courts, see the map accompanying* Judaism, *article on* Judaism in Northern and Eastern Europe to 1500.]

THEOLOGY AND ETHICS

It is nearly impossible to describe Hasidic theology and ethics as being distinct from previous Jewish ideologies because Hasidic teachers preached their ideas in the form of sermons, which included all layers of earlier Jewish thought. Almost all the main ideas and trends found in early-eighteenth-century Hebrew homiletical literature also appear in Hasidic thought, and attempts to define specifically Hasidic ideas, or even emphases, usually fail because similar examples can easily be produced from earlier homiletical literature. A second difficulty is that every Hasidic teacher developed his own theology and ethics and his own list of priorities which may distinguish him or his group but never characterize all the hundreds of teachers and writers who created Hasidic literature. It is unfeasible to generalize from one or a group of Hasidic teachers to the movement as a whole. Every definition is therefore a necessarily subjective one. Thus only a few general outlines, qualified by the preceding statements, can be presented concerning Hasidic theology.

Relationship to Lurianic Qabbalah. Hasidism relies on qabbalistic terminology and is largely based on Lurianic Qabbalah. In many specific formulations, however, the Hasidim seem to have preferred the simpler symbolism of the *Zohar* (the main qabbalistic work written in northern Spain in the late thirteenth century) to that of Hayyim Vital (1543–1620), the disciple of Luria who wrote the main body of Lurianic teachings.

Hasidic theology, like other qabbalistic schools of the eighteenth century, downplayed the most dramatic mythical symbols of Lurianic mysticism, especially that of *shevirat ha-kelim* ("the breaking of the divine vessels"), the description of the catastrophe within the divine world which is the origin of evil, according to Luria. The idea of *tsimtsum* (divine self-contraction) was elaborated by the Hasidim (especially by Dov Ber), but in a completely different manner than in Luria's original thought. According to Luria, this was the drastic process of divine contraction away from the world, which vacated the space in which the cosmos was going to be created from the divine light of the godhead, the first exile of God. According to Hasidism, however, this was a necessary process, for the world could not absorb the full power of the undiluted divine light. The act of *tsimtsum,* the contraction of that light, was intended to facilitate the acceptance of divine light, in a less concentrated form, by the righteous in the created world. Instead of the original Lurianic idea of a mythological catastrophe, the Hasidim presented a theology in which this process was the result of divine benevolence toward the faithful.

The Hasidim also deemphasized the Lurianic concept of *tiqqun* (restoration), the process by which messianic redemption is enhanced by the collective efforts of the Jewish people as a whole; they preferred instead the concept of *devequt* (communion with God), a process of individual redemption by which a person uplifts his own soul into contact with the divine powers. The description of the ten qabbalistic *sefirot,* the ten divine hypostases, is closer in Hasidic works to the thirteenth-century system of the *Zohar* than to the much more complicated system of Luria.

Extent of Messianism in Hasidism. There is an emphasis in Hasidic literature on personal religious achievement rather than on the general, national, and cosmic impact of religious life. The redemptive element, while still strong in Hasidism, often emphasizes the redemption of the individual's soul rather than that of the nation or of the cosmos as a whole. This is a slight departure from Lurianic Qabbalah, but not all Hasidic teachers shared this view, and some non-Hasidic writers, who either predated Hasidism or belonged to the opponents of Hasidism, also often stressed the emphasis on the individual in qabbalistic symbolism.

The place of the messianic element in Hasidic thought has been a subject of controversy among contemporary scholars. In a detailed study in 1955, Ben Zion Dinur tried to prove that the Hasidim, following the Besht himself, developed an esoteric messianic system that was hidden in most of their works but served as the main purpose and drive behind Hasidic preaching and the expansion of its influence. This approach was severely criticized by Gershom Scholem, who saw in Hasidism the neutralization of the Lurianic and Shabbatean acute messianism and a new emphasis on individual redemption through the process of communion with God. Isaiah Tishby recently analyzed early Hasidic texts and found that many of them include more messianic elements than Scholem suggested. There is no doubt that, on the whole, early Hasidism rejected the more extreme messianic tendencies; the works of Dov Ber can be characterized as neutralizing the messianic drive. But Hasidic teachers in their various works reveal differing attitudes, and some of them may have had stronger messianic inclinations than the Maggid and even the Besht.

In the early nineteenth century there was a renewed messianic enthusiasm with Hasidism. Nahman of Bratslav developed a messianic system (see below), and under the impact of Napoleon's invasion of Russia in 1812 we find several Hasidic leaders engaged in messianic activity. In contemporary Hasidism the Habad sect seems to be deeply motivated by an acute belief in an imminent messianic redemption, concentrating its activities on enhancing this process by strict adherence to religious commandments.

Hasidic Approach to God. In early Hasidic literature there is an emphasis on direct, emotional worship of God and a deemphasis on contact with God through constant study of the Torah and Talmud and diligent observance of the particulars concerning the performance of the *mitsvot*. This does not mean that the Hasidim did not study the Torah or that they disregarded the *mitsvot*, as their opponents often claimed; rather, the Hasidim stressed the importance of mystical contact with God through *devequt*, usually attained while praying but also achieved when a person is working for his livelihood or engaged in any other physical activity.

There are many precedents for this attitude in pre-Hasidic Jewish thought, and there are many exceptions to it among Hasidic teachers. Still, it seems that on the whole, Hasidim perceived a wider range of modes of worship as acceptable and commendable than did their detractors, and that the mystical aspect of everyday religious life is more prominent among the Hasidim. This attitude led to the prevailing conception of Hasidism as oriented toward the needs of the simple believers, the uneducated, and even the ignorant—a conception based primarily on very late (end of the nineteenth and early twentieth centuries) collections of stories and one that is considerably exaggerated.

Good and Evil. Hasidic teachers, more than non-Hasidim, contributed to the development of a conception of the way to fight evil within one's soul that is different from the prevailing Lurianic one. On the one hand, Lurianic theology described a common source for good and evil, claiming that both emanate from the godhead; but, according to Luria, evil cannot exist unless it is in close contact with the good and derives sustenance from it. In order to overcome evil, the righteous must separate good from evil, thus making the latter's existence impossible. Shabbatean thinkers, on the other hand, emphasized that evil can be overcome from within by correcting it. Dov Ber of Mezhirich and other Hasidic teachers insisted that evil can and should be overcome by absorbing it, uplifting and making it again a part of goodness, believing that the spiritual stature of the "corrected" or "repentant" evil is higher than that of the elements that were always good. In early Hasidic works this theory is presented as teachings accessible to everybody and offered to all righteous Jews; later it was merged with the doctrine of the *tsaddiq*.

Hasidism as Revival of Traditional Spirituality. The spiritual side of religious life holds a central place in Hasidic teachings, following the traditions of medieval Hebrew ethical and homiletical literature. Great emphasis is placed on the correct qabbalistic intentions in prayers *(kavvanot)*, on spiritual repentance, on the love and fear of God, and on social justice and love for fellow men. While very few new ideas on these subjects are to be found in the vast Hasidic literature, the movement undoubtedly represents a revival of these spiritual values within the framework of everyday religious life. In this respect, then, there is no basis to the frequent descriptions of Hasidism as an original phenomenon that changed the face of traditional Judaism; but it can be claimed that the Hasidim collected many spiritualistic ideas and practices from previous Jewish sources and brought them to the foreground of their teachings and Jewish worship in a more central way than before. In this sense their endeavor can be described as "revivalistic."

THE DOCTRINE OF THE TSADDIQ

While these ideas characterize Hasidism, they do not distinguish the Hasidic movement from previous Jewish religious movements or from the other religious movements of that time, even that of the *mitnaggedim*. Many of these ideas are found, and emphasized, in late eighteenth-century and early nineteenth-century non-Hasidic Jewish works of ethics and homiletics. Hasidism, however, can be defined as a separate movement, different from all others preceding or contemporary to it, because of its doctrine of the *tsaddiq* ("righteous man"), which sets clear boundaries, in theory and in practice, between Hasidim and non-Hasidim.

The theory of the *tsaddiq* presented Judaism with a new concept of religious leadership that was both charismatic and mystically motivated. According to this theory, in every generation there are some righteous persons who can and should, by their outstanding mystical worship, correct the sins and transgressions of lesser-endowed people. The Hasid (follower) has only limited ability to approach the godhead and to carry out difficult religious tasks, especially the correction of evil, including that in his own thoughts and deeds. The leader, the righteous *tsaddiq*, whose soul emanated from a very high place in the divine realm, is the one to carry out these tasks for his generation and especially for his followers, the members of the Hasidic community that he leads. Thus the *tsaddiq* is an intermediary between the Hasid and God, bringing before the heavenly powers (the qabbalistic *sefirot*) the prayers and religious achievements of his community. He receives forgiveness for the sins of his followers and effects the elevation of the evil within them, transmuting it into good at the common source of both in the divine realm.

The *tsaddiq* himself does not contain any evil; the sins he uplifts and corrects are those of his community. One description of this transaction—found in the works of the great formulator of this theory, Elimelekh of Lizhensk, a disciple of Dov Ber—is that the sins of the community appear to the *tsaddiq* as evil thoughts which he then uplifts and rehabilitates into good thoughts. This theory demands that the *tsaddiq* be in constant movement between good and evil, heaven and earth (*ratso' va-shov*, "ran and returned," after *Ezekiel* 1:14). He has to be close to the evil that he is to correct, subjecting himself to the process of a "fall" *(yeridah)* or "smallness" *(qatnut,* a term used in Lurianic theology only to refer to the divine powers when they descend from their high dominion). When he uplifts evil and turns it into goodness, he is united with the divine powers in a state of "greatness" *(gadlut).* This dynamism is the most characteristic aspect of the *tsaddiq* concept, and there is no difficulty in ascertaining the source from which the Hasidim, probably unwittingly, derived it.

Even before Shabbetai Tsevi's conversion to Islam, his "prophet," Natan of Gaza, described his messianic role as an intermediary between the godhead and evil on earth. The changing moods of Shabbetai Tsevi, probably caused by a manic-depressive state, were explained as resulting from his constant movement between his source and origin among the *sefirot* and the realm of the devil on earth. After his conversion, Shabbatean theologians explained that in order to overcome evil the Messiah had to merge with it and destroy or correct it from within. There are close parallels between the Shabbatean concept of the Messiah and the Hasidic concept of the *tsaddiq,* and there can be little doubt that the Hasidim created their system on the heels of Shabbatean theology.

Nevertheless, the Hasidic concept of the *tsaddiq* is not messianic in the same sense as its Shabbatean precursor. The *tsaddiq* is undoubtedly a quasi-messianic figure, but his influence is limited in time and place—he "redeems" only his own community in his own lifetime. The redemption that the *tsaddiq* accomplishes is not the general, national, and cosmic redemption of Shabbateanism. Rather, he effects individual redemption of the souls in his community—those of his followers—only while he is alive; after his death his successor (his son or relative) will continue in this task, while at the same time dozens of other *tsaddiqim* are performing the same task for other communities in other places. It may be stated that Hasidism broke down the Shabbatean concept of the messiah into small fragments, each of which is the *tsaddiq* for his own time and place. Instead of one messianic figure who inaugurates the historical redemption, Hasidism provides a process of constant redemption of the souls of the believers, a process carried out by every *tsaddiq* within the boundaries of his time and place. When viewed in terms of a messianic movement, Hasidism destroyed the basis for any large, messianic upsurge, replacing it with the small, everyday process of individual redemption. It is possible that the vehement opposition of the Hasidic movement as a whole, with very few exceptions, to modern Jewish nationalism and Zionism should be understood in this light. If individual redemption is assured by faithfulness to the *tsaddiq,* the importance of national redemption is diminished.

The theory of the *tsaddiq* was the focal point of Hasidic theology, shaping to a very large extent Hasidic social organizations and ways of worship as well. According to this theory, the *tsaddiq* not only provides the Hasidim with spiritual redemption for their souls but also promises them the basic earthly needs—their livelihood, delivery from illness, and assurances that they will have children *(banei, ḥayyei, mezonei;* literally, "my sons, my life, my food"). The Hasidim, for their part, have to give the *tsaddiq* spiritual support; their belief in his superhuman role enables him to achieve his spiritual tasks. They are also obligated to supply the *tsaddiq's* everyday needs so that he may support himself and his family.

The *tsaddiq* became the center of the Hasidic community. His court was their meeting place several times each year; his room became the place where they brought their complaints and requests; his blessing was believed to ensure both earthly and heavenly success. The Hasidim congregated to listen to the *tsaddiq*'s prayers and sermons, worshiped with him with great qabbalistic "intentions" *(kavvanot),* and practiced the religious commandments, often with joy and happiness. The task of uplifting evil was thus taken from the shoulders of the individual Jew and consigned to the *tsaddiq* as the representative of the community and the intermediary power between heaven and earth.

Not all the *tsaddiqim* accepted this role. There were several leaders who were uncomfortable with this mode of worship; they left their communities and secluded themselves. Notwithstanding these exceptions, the basic Hasidic attitudes to social organization and everyday worship were developed according to the lines drawn by the doctrine of the *tsaddiq.*

The most important variant to this doctrine grew out of Bratslav Hasidism, founded by Naḥman of Bratslav (1772–1810), the grandson of the Besht's daughter. Naḥman's life passed in conflict with other *tsaddiqim;* he refused to accept their authority even over their own communities. When he died his followers chose not to nominate another *tsaddiq* but continue, to this very day, to believe that Naḥman was the "true *tsaddiq*" *(tsaddiq ha-emet)* and that the Messiah, who will redeem Israel, will be his reincarnation. In the Bratslav doctrine of the *tsaddiq* there is, to a very large extent, a return to the Shabbatean concept of one redeemer for all; the redemption therefore assumes historical dimensions.

Another important variant is that of the Habad Hasidism, founded by Shne'ur Zalman of Lyady (1754–1813), a disciple of Dov Ber. From this school we have the most detailed information concerning the organization of a *tsaddiq*'s court. At the same time, Habad Hasidic works seem to minimize the redemptive role of the *tsaddiq,* especially as outlined in the works offered to the public as a whole, such as Shne'ur Zalman's *Tanya'.* Habad developed a highly centralized global organization headed by the *tsaddiq,* with an emphasis on the teaching of Jewish ethics and practice of the *mitsvot* and basic qabbalistic theology, relegating the more developed messianic and redemptive elements in their theology to esoteric groups among the Habad adherents. Habad is reputed to insist on a more intellectual version of Hasidism, but many other communities share this same trend.

The doctrine of the *tsaddiq* also contributed to the emergence of a special kind of hagiographic literature, for the *tsaddiq* could easily serve as a religious hero to stories of this kind. A body of legends in which the Besht was a central hero was collected early in the nineteenth century under the title *Shivḥei ha-Besht* (In Praise of the Besht), following the earlier example of *Shivḥei ha-Ari,* which was about Isaac Luria. The tales told by Naḥman of Bratslav in his last years were published as *Sippurei ha-ma'asiot le-rabbi Naḥman,* stories describing in a veiled manner the spiritual conflicts and messianic drives of Naḥman. Many stories were told by the Hasidim about their leaders, but these began to be published only in the last third of the nineteenth century, mostly by non-Hasidic authors, editors, and publishers, and later by some Hasidic publishers. Many of these stories are nothing but adaptations of ancient Jewish folktales in which the specific *tsaddiqim* are inserted as heroes. Hasidism throughout its history, including contemporary Hasidism, chose the sermon to be its basic literary genre and mode of expression. This vast body of homiletical literature is the basic and often the only source for Hasidic theology and practice. Some *tsaddiqim* prepared, or their disciples collected, brief anthologies of the sayings of the leaders, and a few *tsaddiqim* wrote ethical works, such as *Tanya'*, but the dominance of homiletical literature in authentic Hasidic literature is uncontested.

MISCONCEPTIONS ABOUT HASIDISM

In popular works about Hasidism that focus on material derived from late Hasidic hagiography and collections of sayings of Hasidic teachers culled from their homiletical works and sermons, Hasidism is often described as a popular movement concentrated around charismatic leaders who impress their believers by various miracles and exemplary ethical behavior, without any theological or mystical basis. In some accounts even the strict adherence of Hasidim to the commandments of Judaism is missing, and Hasidism appears as a kind of "ethical Judaism" based on enthusiastic celebration of festivals and social ethics.

This erroneous image of Hasidism is the product of the literature written by Jewish writers in Hebrew and Yiddish in the early twentieth century, such as Shalom Asch, Yitshaq Loeb Perez, and Yehudah Steinberg, who portrayed Hasidism in nostalgic terms after having left traditional Judaism and embraced Western ways of life. Some scholars and writers, from Martin Buber to Elie Wiesel, followed them to an extent, perpetuating the image of Hasidism as pure, spiritual Judaism which expresses love of Israel, love of God, and love toward every human being. In their descriptions, modern writers have tended to emphasize public behavior in the Hasidic courts and to neglect the mystical, quabbalistic theology and the theoretical basis of the worship of the *tsaddiq* in Hasidism.

The studies of scholars such as Gershom Scholem, Joseph G. Weiss, Isaiah Tishby, Mendel Pierkaz, and others in the last generation restored the serious study of Hasidism and based it on philological, historical, and ideological scrutiny of the Hasidic texts themselves. Hasidism is the latest chapter in the history of Jewish mysticism, in which qabbalistic symbols became central to a wide, popular movement that produced a new type of religious leadership and introduced religious-mystical values to modern Orthodox Judaism.

BIBLIOGRAPHY

Several important book-length studies of Hasidism are to be found in English. Simon Dubnow's classic *Geschichte des Chassidismus,* 2 vols. (Berlin, 1931), is still the best factual description of the development of early Hasidism. A brief but profound description of Hasidic mysticism is to be found in "Hasidism: The Last Phase," the last chapter in Gershom Scholem's *Major Trends in Jewish Mysticsm,* 2d ed. (New York, 1954), pp. 325–350; the reader may use previous chapters in this book to study main qabbalistic terminology and symbols. Scholem's studies of Hasidic concepts of communion with God and messianism can be found in his collection of essays, *The Messianic Idea in Judaism and Other Essays on Jewish Spirituality* (New York 1971), pp. 176–250.

The Hasidic idea of the intermediary between God and man is studied in Samuel H. Dresner's book *The Zaddik* (London, 1960), and the biography of one of the creators of this idea, Nahman of Bratslav, is presented in a profound book by Arthur Green, *Tormented Master* (University, Ala., 1980). An anthology of early Hasidic texts in English translation is to be found in my book *The Teachings of Hasidism* (New York, 1983). A selection from the works of an early Hasidic master has been translated and edited by Arthur Green in *Upright Practices: The Light of the Eyes, by Menahem Nahum of Chernobyl* (New York, 1982). The most important collection of Hasidic stories about the Besht is *In Praise of the Baal Shem Tov,* translated and edited by Dan Ben-Amos and Jerome R. Mintz (Bloomington, Ind., 1970).

Many articles about specific problems in Hasidic history and thought were written in English. The most important ones are those of Joseph G. Weiss, especially "Via Passiva in Early Hasidism," *Journal of Jewish Studies* 11 (1960): 137–155, and "The Kavvanoth of Prayer in Early Hasidism," *Journal of Jewish Studies* 9 (1958): 163–192. A recent study of the theory of Hasidic leadership is to be found in Arthur Green's "The Zaddiq as *Axis Mundi* in Later Judaism," *Journal of the American Academy of Religion* 45 (September 1977): 327–347.

Most of the scholarly work concerning the history and theology of Hasidism was written in Hebrew. Among the most important books are Rivka Schatz Uffenheimer's *Hasidism as Mysticism* (in Hebrew with English summary; Jerusalem, 1968) and her *Maggid devarav le-Ya'aqov* (Jerusalem, 1976), a critical edition of Dov Ber's collection of sermons. A general survey of the works of the main Hasidic teachers is presented in Samuel A. Horodetzky's *He-hasidut veha-hasidim,* 4 vols. in 2 (Tel Aviv, 1951). The history of the controversies around the Hasidic movement, and scholarly edition of the relevant texts, is included in Mordecai Wilensky's *Hasidim ve-mitnaggedim,* 2 vols. (Jerusalem, 1970). The relationship between Hasidism and its sources in earlier Hebrew ethical and homiletical literature is studied in detail in Mendel Piekarz's *Bi-yemei tsemihat he-Hasidut* (Jerusalem, 1978). A study of Nahman of Bratslav's life, works and main ideas is to be found in Joseph G. Weiss's *Mehqarim be-Hasidut Breslav* (Jerusalem, 1970) and Mendel Piekarz's *Hasidut Breslav* (Jerusalem, 1972). A theological discussion of the theology of Habad Hasidism in the second generation is presented in Rachel Elior's *Torat ha-elohut ba-dor ha-sheni shel Hasidut Habad* (Jerusalem, 1982). A detailed study of Hasidic narrative literature is to be found in my book *Ha-sippur he-Hasidi* (Jerusalem, 1975).

A selection of articles on Hasidic history and thought in Hebrew (some with English summaries) is listed below.

Elior, Rachel. "The Controversy over the Leadership of the HaBad Movement." *Tarbiz* 49 (1979–1980): 166–186.

Etkes, Emanuel. "Shitato u-fa'alo shel R. Hayyim mi-Volozhin Ki-teguvat ha-hevah ha-mitnaggdit he-Hasidut." *Proceedings of the American Academy for Jewish Research* 38/39 (1970–1971): 1–45.

Gries, Z. "The Hassidic Conduct *(Hanhagot)* Literature from the Mid-Eighteenth Century to the 1830s." *Zion* 46 (1981): 199–236, 278–305.

Scholem, Gershom G. "New Material on Israel Loebel and His Anti-Hassidic Polemics." *Zion* 20 (1955): 153–162.

Shmeruk, Chone. "Tales about R'Adam Baal Shem in the Versions of *Shivhei ha-Besht.*" *Zion* 28 (1963): 86–105.

Tishby, Isaiah. "The Messianic Idea and Messianic Trends in the Growth of Hassidism." *Zion* 32 (1967): 1–45.

Weiss, Joseph G. "Beginnings of Hassidism." *Zion* 16 (1951): 46–105.

Weiss, Joseph G. "Some Aspects of Rabbi Nahman of Bratzlav's Allegorical Self-Interpretation." *Tarbiz* 27 (1958): 358–371.

22 ORTHODOX JUDAISM

CHARLES S. LIEBMAN

Orthodox Judaism is the branch of Judaism that adheres most strictly to the tenets of the religious law *(halakhah)*. Its forebears may be identified in the eighteenth century, by which time the *qehillah*, the Jewish communal organization in each locality, had lost much of its authority in central and western Europe and its prestige in eastern Europe. This, in turn, undermined religious authority, which had heretofore relied not only on the faith of each Jew but also on communal consensus and the formal authority and prestige of communal leaders. The breakdown of the traditional community, coupled with the hope and expectation of political emancipation, encouraged new interpretations of Jewish life and new conceptions of appropriate relationships between Jews and non-Jews. These began to emerge by the end of the eighteenth century in central and western Europe and somewhat later in eastern Europe. Orthodoxy was born as the ideological and organizational response to these new conceptions.

The major tenets of Orthodoxy, like those of traditional Judaism, include the dogma that the Torah was "given from Heaven," that the *halakhah* derives directly or indirectly from an act of revelation, and that Jews are obligated to live in accordance with the *halakhah* as interpreted by rabbinic authority. But unlike traditional Judaism, Orthodoxy is conscious of the spiritual and cultural challenges of the modern world and especially of rival formulations of the meaning and consequences of being Jewish. Orthodoxy, in all its various manifestations and expressions, has never recognized any alternative conception of Judaism as legitimate. But it is aware of itself as a party, generally a minority party, within the Jewish world.

Orthodox Judaism received its earliest formulation in Hungary (then part of the Austro-Hungarian empire) in the first quarter of the nineteenth century and in Germany in the middle of the century. In both countries it constituted a response to the efforts of reformers to adapt the *halakhah* in general and the synagogue service in particular to currents in nineteenth-century culture. The reformers maintained that this was a condition for Jewish emancipation and civil equality. Orthodoxy developed in France and England at about this same time but in far less explicit and rigorous a manner. A major reason, no doubt, was that the challenge of Reform Judaism was so much weaker. The weakness of Reform Judaism in France and England may be attributable to the fact that it developed after, rather than before, the Jews had more or less obtained civil equality in those countries.

Orthodoxy arose in eastern Europe at the end of the nineteenth century, primarily in response to secular interpretations of Jewish life rather than in opposition to religious reform. The most important centers of Orthodoxy today are in Israel and the United States.

HUNGARIAN ORTHODOXY

The ideological and programmatic outlines of Hungarian Orthodoxy were formulated by Rabbi Mosheh Sofer (1762–1839), better known as the Hatam Sofer, the title of his seven-volume *responsa* to halakhic questions. This earliest variety of Orthodoxy is best described by the term *neotraditionalism* because it rejects any attempt at change and adaptation of the tradition. According to the Hatam Sofer, "all that is new is forbidden by the Torah"; the phrase is a play on the words of an injunction prohibiting consumption of "new" grain from each year's harvest until a portion is offered in the Temple in Jerusalem. Unlike some of his followers, the Hatam Sofer did not oppose all forms of secular education. A knowledge of some secular subjects, for example, is helpful in resolving certain halakhic problems. But in characteristically neotraditional fashion, he legitimated secular education in utilitarian terms, not as an end in itself.

The basic strategy of neotraditionalism was the sanctification of the rabbinic tradition in its entirety. Whereas traditional Judaism recognized different levels of sanctity and degrees of importance of halakhic injunctions (for example, acts prohibited by the Torah were in a more stringent category than acts prohibited by rabbinic legislation), neotraditionalists blurred the differences insofar as obligations to observe the injunctions were concerned. The tradition was self-consciously projected as woven of a single cloth, all parts of which were equally binding and sanctified. The two major instruments that the neotraditionalists fashioned to socialize the community to their ideology and values were a greatly expanded rabbinic authority and a new type of *yeshivah* (pl., *yeshivot*), or academy for intensive Talmudic study. These new and larger *yeshivot* were designed to exist in economic and ideological independence from the increasingly fragile local Jewish communities in which they were located. The *yeshivah* of the Hatam Sofer in Pressburg, where he served as communal rabbi from 1806 until his death, was the most important *yeshivah* in central Europe. His students, in turn, served as community leaders throughout Hungary, Galicia, and Bohemia-Moravia and in the Land of Israel (Erets Yisra'el), strengthening neotraditional influences in all these places.

The Hatam Sofer favored immigration to the Land of Israel. Many who favored immigration in those days were reacting to the reformers' rejection of nationalist elements in Judaism. The Hatam Sofer's espousal of an early form of Jewish nationalism and his projection of the importance of the Land of Israel in the Jewish tradition may also have been related to his negative attitude toward political emancipation. He feared its threat to religious authority. His followers believed they could establish a pure Jewish society, insulated from secularist modernizing influences, in the Land of Israel. They established a Hungarian subcommunity in the Land of Israel that played a major role within the old *yishuv* (the nineteenth-century settlement of religiously observant Jews, as distinct from the new *yishuv* of late-nineteenth- and twentieth-century settlers motivated by secular Jewish nationalism).

The distinctive instrument of Hungarian Orthodoxy in furthering its neotraditional objectives was the independent communal organization. In 1868 the Hungarian government convened a General Jewish Congress in order to define the basis for the autonomous organization of the Jewish community. The majority of the delegates were sympathetic to religious reform (Neologs), and most of the Orthodox delegates withdrew from the Congress. In 1870 the Hungarian parliament permitted the Orthodox to organize themselves in separate communal frameworks, which might coexist in the same locality with a Neolog community or a Status Quo community (the latter was composed of those who refused to join either the Orthodox or the Neolog community). Orthodox communities provided their members with the full gamut of religious services (kosher food, schools, religious courts, and, of course, synagogues) and represented Orthodox political interests to the government. Orthodox leaders discouraged contacts with members of the rival communities and prohibited entering their synagogues, and many Orthodox rabbis even enjoined intermarriage with them.

Hungarian Orthodoxy included both Hasidic and non-Hasidic elements. Hasidism, which originated in the eighteenth century, was bitterly opposed by the traditional religious elite, who feared that its folkishness, pietism, and ambivalence toward the central importance of Talmudic study undermined the tradition itself. Orthodoxy might have been born in opposition to Hasidism if not for leaders like the Hatam Sofer who sought a *modus vivendi*, recognizing that Hasidic leaders were no less antagonistic to basic changes in tradition than were the traditional religious elite. In fact, by the end of the century, the centers of Hasidic influence in the smaller Jewish communities remained least compromising in their attitude toward modernity. In the larger, more urbanized communities, one found signs of the growing attraction of German Orthodoxy with its more accommodating attitude toward modernity.

Even in an earlier period, not all Hungarian Orthodox rabbis were neotraditional in orientation. A minority were attracted by aspects of modern culture and/or believed that a more moderate approach might prove more attractive to potential deviators. Outstanding among such rabbis was German-born Esriel Hildesheimer, who served as a rabbi in Hungary until 1869. Although Hildesheimer was no less opposed to reform than his Hungarian colleagues, he aroused their particular antagonism when he established in the Austro-Hungarian community of Eisenstadt a *yeshivah* whose curriculum included secular studies. After leaving Hungary, Hildesheimer accepted the post of rabbi in an independent Orthodox congregation in Berlin. In 1873 he established a new rabbinical seminary in the more hospitable climate of German Orthodoxy.

GERMAN ORTHODOXY

The year 1850 marks the emergence of German Orthodoy, with the establishment of the Israelitische Religionsgesellschaft in Frankfurt am Main, a congregation led by Samson Raphael Hirsch from 1851 until his death. But the distinctive ideological formulation of German Orthodoxy (often known as Neo-Orthodoxy) dates, at least in embryo, from the publication of Hirsch's *Nineteen Letters on Judaism* in 1836.

The publication a few years later of an Orthodox weekly by Ya'aqov Ettlinger (1798–1871) is also of significance.

Hirsch was the foremost proponent of the idea that Torah-true Judaism (to borrow a popular phrase of German Orthodoxy) was compatible with modern culture and political emancipation. Hirsch envisaged a divine order revealed in nature in which Jews could and should participate. But the divine order was also revealed in the Torah, many of whose commands were speficif to Jews. The effect of Hirsch's conception, though not his intent, was the compartmentalization of life for the Orthodox Jew. Modern culture, patriotism, civil law—all became legitimate spheres for Jewish involvement since they were perceived as falling outside the realm proscribed by *halakhah*.

Hirsch and his followers directed their antagonism not at the gentile world or its culture, but raather at religious reform, and in this respect they shared the outlook of the most intransigent of the Hungarian Orthodox. Reform Judaism, as a self-conscious movement in Jewish life, began in Germany with the establishment of the Hamburg temple in 1818. In the first few decades of the century it seemed that Reform conceptions of Judaism would replace those of traditional Judaism in Germany. Indeed, the major intellectual battle lines seemed to be drawn between the moderate reformers who sought changes in Jewish practice through the reinterpretation of Jewish law and the generally younger second generation of reformers who would abrogate the authority of the law entirely. Hirsch made no distinctions between moderate and radical reformers. Although in his *Nineteen Letters on Judaism* he was critical of traditional as well as Reform Judaism and seemed to advocate a position equidistant from both, some of his early endorsement of change was mitigated with the passage of time. What Hirsch never forgot was that the attraction of reform was an outgrowth of Jewish desire for emancipation and acceptance, the traditional Judaism appeared to be an obstacle to this goal, and that unless it could be reformulated as compatible with emancipation and modern culture, it had no future in Germany.

In addition to its educational system—day schools, religious schools, and seminaries around which Germany Orthodoxy united—the distinctive instrument that traditional Judaism forged to socialize its adherents to its values and conceptions was the autonomous congregation, even though it was only effective in a small number of localities. The heart of the congregational activity was the synagogue service itself, where the weekly or biweekly sermons by the rabbi, in German, represented a dramatic innovation. The traditional rabbi preached only afew times a year and never in the language of the state. The german Orthodox rabbi was likely to possess a university degree, an acquisition that distinguished him from his Hungarian and, as we shall see, his eastern European and Israeli counterparts. German Orthodox Jews were most attentive to the form of the service. Many Reforms innovations, influenced in turn by the Christian churches, were adopted. German Orthodox rabbis, to the dismay of their traditional colleagues in other countries, Officiated in clerical gowns, encouraged the participation of choirs (all male), and paid careful attention to musical arrangements in the service. In fact, some of their innovations would have been enough to identify a synagogue in Hungary as Neolog.

In addition to the synagogue itself, the autonomous congregation might sponsor a school, assume responsibility for the supervision of kosher foods, and provide opportunity for study and semisocial activity. Only political activity and sometimes welfare services remained outside its sphere of Jewish responsibilities, remaining the prerogatives of the more inclusive *Gemeinde* (the local Jewish community).

After the passage of a Prussian law in 1876 permitting Jews to secede, Hirsch insisted, as a matter of *halakhah,* that members of his congreation resign from the Frankfurt *Gemeinde*. Most of his congregants and certainly most Orthodox Jews in Germany refused to separate themselves and establish their own *Austrittsgemeinde* (seceded community).

Hirsch's demand for secession met opposition from traditionalists such as Rabbi Seligmann Ber Bamberger of Würzburg (1807–1878), probably the greatest contemporary Talmudist of Germany. It has recently been suggested that Bamberger harbored animosity toward the "modernizing ways" of Hirsch and his followers. The secession issue may have been a convenient opportunity to rebuke him and challenge his mastery of textual soruces. Hirsch himself, in his lengthy response to Bamberger's opinion agains secession, noted that the latter had never accepted Hirsch's ideal of *Torah 'im derekh erets* (Torah and worldliness), which was the slogan of German Orthodoxy. Hildesheimer also favored secession and was no less antagonistic to Reform Judaism. Nevertheless, he differed from Hirsch, to whom he was personally close, on other issues. He was more favorable than Hirsch to integrating secular and sacred study. He and his followers did participate with non-Orthodox Jews in organizations dedicated to defending Jews agains anti-Semitism. He was an enthusiastic supporter of the settlement of Jews and the establishment of Jewish institutions in the Land of Israel. To the chagrin of neotraditionalists, he sought means to raise the educational and vocational standards of Jews in the old *yishuv* and fought with them over this issue.

By the end of the century, Orthodocy in both Germany and Hungary was well established, albeit with minority status within the Jewish world. Its exclusionary form of organization, its emphasis on those forms of observance that distinguished it from Reform Judaism, and its insistence that the core component of the authentic Jew's faith was the belief that God dictated the Torah to Moses suggested, in fact, that Orthodoxy was content to survive as a minority party in Jewish life, more concerned with maintaining its purity than extending its boundaries. The Orthodox camp in each country was reasonably well integrated and possessed its own organizational structure, periodicals, and schools. Its acknowledged leaders commanded deference in the general as well as the Jewish commu nity. In fact, conservative governments, wary of radicals in general and aware of the attraction of political radicalism to so many Jews, often favored Orthodoxy, which it associated with tradition, law, and stability, over Reform. In short, by the end of the century it appeared that Orthodoxy, in one way or another, had withstood the challenge of modernity and emancipation and the blandishments of Reform. Jews and Hungary and Germany were increasingly assimilating and intermarrying. But this was a matter of greater immediate threat to Reform than to Orthodoxy.

In retrospect, Orthodoxy's strength was its ability to create small, meaningful, integrated communities that provided its adherents with a sense of identity and stability and mediated their involvement with the infinite. But Orthodoxy built upon certain assumptions. It was organized in a milieu in which one anticipated continued political and social freedom and in which the major threat to the tradition stemmed from religious reform. Its insularity from non-Orthodox Jews ill equipped it for a role in the defense of Jewish rights against a rising tide of anti-Semitism. Second, it had not yet developed ideological defenses against secular conceptions of Judaism. These, unlike Reform, argued not for religious alternatives to the tradition but for a totally new conception of the meaning of Jewishness. The most influential of these conceptions was Zionism, the notion that the Jews are a nation like other nations whose *sancta* are language, territory, and people rather than God and Torah. It was this last threat more than any other that led to the emergence of an international Orthodox organization—Agudat Yisra'el. Before such an organization could emerge, however, the level of Orthodox consciousness in eastern Europe had to undergo development.

ORTHODOXY IN EASTERN EUROPE

The vast majority of eastern European Jews continued to live in accordance with the religious tradition throughout the nineteenth century, although the institutions of traditional Judaism were severely undermined. Government law had destroyed many of the traditional privileges and responsibilities of the Jewish community. The charismatic authority of the *rebeyim* (Hasidic leaders) had further undermined the status of communal leaders. At the margins of society, the small party of radical *maskilim* (adherents of Jewish enlightenment) challenged traditional patterns of Jewish life. By the middle of the nineteenth century, changing economic conditions afforded new opportunities for a few, but further impoverished the masses and shook the moral consensus within the community. They also highlighted the importance of secular education, thereby undermining the alliance of the wealthy and the religious elite. They undermined the *battei midrash* ("houses of study"), once found in virtually every Jewish locality. There, small numbers of men had spent their day in study, supported, however meagerly, by the local householders.

Traditional Judaism responded, however feebly and tentatively, to these developments, but the response cannot be labeled Orthodoxy, because it lacked one major distinguishing feature—self-awareness as one party among others in Jewish life. Traditional Jewish leaders who saw their authority questioned, Torah study abandoned, and new modes of behavior and belief increasingly legitimated differed among themselves as to how to meet the crisis. Their first concern tended to be the challenge to the primacy of textual study in the hierarchy of religious commandments. Hasidism had stressed the importance of religious experience and intention—adapting from earlier mystical Jewish conceptions the notion that in performing the commandments with true devotion and proper intent, the Jew was repairing the torn fabric of the cosmos. This stress on intention rather than behavior introduced a potential antinomianism and, no less seriously, suggested that the study of Talmud was of secondary importance in the hierarchy of religious injunctions.

The traditionalists' response was the establishment of central *yeshivot* supported by contributions solicited throughout the Jewish world. The first such *yeshivah* was established in 1802 in Volozhin (near Vilnius) by Rabbi Hayyim of Volozhin from hs own funds. During the course of the century, *yeshivot* were founded throughout Lithuania and Belorussia (then still part of Russia). Leadership of a *yeshivah* rather than service as a communal rabbi marked one as a preeminent scholar automatically meriting deference and authortiy.

The *yeshivot* trained the Orthodox elite but generally failed to strengthen traditional Judaism among the masses. The Hasidic *rebeyim* filled a more important role in maintaining traditional norms, at least among their followers. But the decline of traditional patterns of observance until the last decades of the century must not be exaggerated, Rabbis such as Naftali Tsevi Yehudah Berlin (1817–1893), known as the Netsiv, Yisra'el Me'ir ha-Kohen (1838–1933), known as the Hafets Hayyim; and Yitshaq Elhanan Spektor (1817–1896) retained authority and enormous prestige among the masses.

One measure of the continuing strength of the tradition was the failure of Rabbi Yitshaq Ya'aqov Reines (1839–1915), who later founded Mizrahi, the Religious-Zionist movement, to establish a *yeshivah* in the 1880s. In 1881 Reines published a sharp critique of the method of study in traditional *yeshivot* and called for the reorganization of the institutions of eastern European Judaism. Jewish society, he maintained, was undergoing as ideological and institutional crisis. *Yeshivot* were crumbling, the rabbinate was weakended, and its authority was undermined because of its economic dependence on the wealthy. This, he argued, was a result of the loss of Jewish respect for the traditional leader. His solution was the establishment of a new *yeshivah* to include secular studies in its curriculum and to produce graduates who would fill positions of Jewish leadership. Reines's view was supported by wealthy Russian Jews and Orthodox leaders from central Europe. But the opposition of the heads of the traditional *yeshivot* was enough to prevent the establishment of the new *yeshivah*.

A more successful effort at the reform of *yeshivot,* known as the Musar (ethical) movement, was initiated by Rabbi Yisra'el (Lipkin) Salanter (1810–&1883). His call for ethical renewal was first addressed to the Jewish masses, businessmen and traders in particular, but failed to attract much enthusiasm. His doctrines were more influential in the *yeshivot.* While many of the heads of these academies initially resited the introduction of the study of moral literature or discussions of moral issues at the expense of Talmudic study, the Musar movement was eventually co-opted. A limited amount of time was dedicated to the study of an ethical tract, and the custom of a weekly talk by the moral supervisor (a new position created in the *yeshivot* in response to the demands of the Musar movement) was introduced.

What traditional religious leaders did not do until the end of the century, either because they saw no need or because they did not know how to do it, was oppose the organization of rival parties with alternative conceptions of Judaism. But by the end of the nineteenth century this need was becoming apparent. In the 1870s an organization of Hasidic and non-Hasidic elements was formed to oppose the founding of a rabbinical seminary and the introduction of organizzational changes in the community. In 1912 Agudat Yisra'el (Agudah for short) was established under the impetus of German Orthodox leaders, uniting the Orthodox leaders of central and eastern Europe in defense of the tradition.

Agudat Yisra'el never spoke for all religious Jews. Its greatest following was in Poland, the heartland of eastern European Jewry. Within Poland it functioned as a political party after World War I, rivaling the Zionists and the Bund (General Jewish Workers Union, a socialist Jewish party founded in 1897) for control of the Jewish street. Even within Poland it was opposed by the minority of religious Zionists and by the larger group of traditionalists, who remained indifferent to the needs that had led to its creation.

Agudah's primary strength came from the union of the Hasidic *rebe* of Ger (Avraham Mordekhai Alter, 1866–1948), whose followers numbered in the hundreds of thousands, with the leaders of the Lithuanian *yeshivot,* the most prominent of whom included Rabbi Hayyim 'Ozer Grodzinski of Vilnius (1863–1940). The latter carried enormous status in the world of religiousJewry. Nevertheless, in the Galician and Lithuanian regions, the masses remained aloof. The region around Warsaw and Lodz attracted Jews from the countryside. The struggle between religion and its opponents was most obvious and intense there, and Agudah prospered. In the older Jewish communities of Galicia, however, the Jewish tradition was less threatened, and religious Jews were content to leave political activity to non-Jews and secularists.

Agudah's own rabbinical authorities were, at best, tolerant of the necessity for political activity. Agudah was established to protect the traditional way of life, but political activity has an acculturating impact of its own. The Agudah press carried warnings from rabbis not to regard partisan politics as more than a temporary expedient.

Traditional religious leaders outside Agudah's ranks were impatient with the notion that some adaptation to modernity was necessary in the very defense of the tradition. Rabbi Yosef Yitshaq Schneersohn (1880–1950), leader of the Habad branch of Hasidism (better known as Lubavitcher Hasidism), attacked Agudah schools for including secular studies, accusing them of behaving no differently than the enemies of the tradition.

In addition to sponsoring schools whose curriculum included secular studies, Agudah established reading rooms where secular books were to be found, published a newspaper (though adherents were cautioned against reading it on the Sabbath), and organized a youth movement in which *yeshivah* students were warned not to spend too much time. Most damaging of all, Agudah's political survival required alliances with nonreligious parties, and when Agudah was the majority party in the local Jewish community, it bore at least indirect responsibility for nonreligious and even antireligious activity which the community funds supported.

Agudah, certainly in Poland, began as a neotraditionalist response to modernity. But its own efforts to defend the tradition through political instrumentalities and its own concern to control the environment within which the tradition had to function forced it into compromises that became particularly noticeable in the 1930s.

World War II brought the end to Agudah activity in eastern Europe. By the late 1930s it was apparent to many within Agudah itself that Jewish life in Poland was heading for catastrophe and that traditional responses were ineffective. Settlement in the Land of Israel became an increasingly attractive option, and Agudah muted its opposition to Zionism. Voices were increasingly heard, from within, for constructive efforts in the Land of Israel and for cooperation with the Zionists at the tactical level. Isaac Breuer (1883–1946), grandson of Samson Raphael Hirsch, a leading ideologue of German Orthodoxy, led the call for a reassessment of the Land of Israel in Agudah's program and ideology. The Balfour Declaration and the modern Zionist settlement of the land revealed, Breuer believed, the hand of providence. The Jews, he claimed, were a nation formed by Torah, but as a nation they required their own land in order to renew themselves. In 1936 Breuer settled in Jerusalem. By the time other Agudah followers were prepared to reevaluate their position, the British had closed the gates of the land to world Jewry.

ORTHODOXY IN ISRAEL

Most Orthodox Jews today reside in Israel or the United States. Religiously observant Jews make up 15 to 20 percent of the Jewish population of Israel. The neotraditionalists, once quite marginal to Israeli society, play an increasingly important role. The most colorful and controversial group within their ranks is the successor to the old *yishuv,* the 'Edah Haredit (Community of the Pious), consisting of a few thousand families with thousands of sympathizers located primarily in Jerusalem and Benei Beraq (on the outskirts of Tel Aviv). These are the most intransigent of the neotraditionalists. They relate to the state of Israel with varying degrees of hostility. They refuse to partic ipate in its elections, the more extreme refuse to bear Israeli identification cards or utilize the state's ser vices (their schools, for example, refuse government support), and the most extreme seek the imposition of Arab rule.

A more moderate neotraditionalism is found in Israeli Agudah circles. They are dominated by the heads of *yeshivot* and a number of Hasidic *rebeyim.* The most prominent continues to be the *rebe* of Ger. Agudat Yisra'el generally obtains from 3 to 4 percent of the vote in Israeli elections. Although it has been a party to the ruling coalition, it continues to condemn ideological Zionism, that is, secular Jewish nationalism. It maintains that Israel's constitution must be based upon Torah and *halakhah* as interpreted by rabbinical authority. The leading rabbinical authorities, Agudah further claims, constitute its own Mo'etset Gedolei ha-Torah (Council of Torah Sages), to whom it turns for direction on basic policy issues.

Agudat Yisra'el maintains its own network of elementary schools. Following graduation, boys continue their studies in *yeshivot qetannot* (minor *yeshivot*), whose curriculum consists almost exclusively of sacred text. They do not receive a high school degree. At the age of sixteen or seventeen they generally move on to advanced *yeshivot,* where study is devoted entirely to sacred writ, almost exclusively to Talmud. Girls pursue their high school studies in Beit Ya'aqov, a network of girls' schools first established in Poland. The tendency is to prepare the girls to assume housewife-mother roles.

Beneficent government subsidy, largely for political reasons, has resulted in relative prosperity among Agudah-oriented institutions. Although the party itself is seriously troubled by personal and institutional conflicts and rivalries, and while it is the object of vociferous condemnation by more extreme neotraditionalists who charge it with selling out to the Zionists, the Agudah world appears relatively secure. It sponsors or supports a number of institutions for *ba'alei teshuvah,* Jews raised in nonreligious homes who have embraced Orthodoxy and are attracted by neotraditionalism rather than religious Zionism. Its *yeshivot* attract students from all over the world. Whereas a short time ago they were considered generally inferior to their counterparts in the United States, this is no longer true. The Agudah world is an international community with centers in New York, Montreal, London, Antwerp, and Zurich, to mention the major locations, but Jerusalem plays an increasingly important role. The young seem easily socialized to the values of the community, and their large families (seven and eight children are not at all uncommon) apparently assure continued communal growth. In fact, Israeli observers are rather surprised, given the size of Agudah families, that the party has not increased its proportion of the vote in recent elections—an indication that all may not be as well as it appears on the surface. One problem is Agudah's inability to integrate Sefardic Jews (Jews originating from Muslim countries) in their leadership groups. Sefardic Jews represent an important constituency of Agudah voters (some claim almost half), and in the summer of 1984 they bolted the party because they were excluded from its leadership. Another threat is economic. Agudah's educational institutions play a major role in the socialization of the Agudah community. The extended period of study for the men, often into their mid-twenties and beyond (they are exempted from Israeli army service as long as they remain in the *yeshivot*), requires public and/or private sources of support, which may not necessarily continue in the case of economic depression or a radical change in the Israeli political climate.

The Agudah world is in, but lives apart from, Israeli society. The religious Zionists are in a different category. They make up roughly 10 percent of the Jewish population but are in some sense the symbol of contemporary Israel. Israel's political culture, particularly since the 1970s, focuses on the Jewish people, the Jewish tradition, and the Land of Israel as objects of ultimate value. Symbols of traditional religion, though not traditional theology, pervade Israeli life. Religious Zionists are viewed by many of the nonreligious as most committed to and most comfortable with these values and symbols. The political elite, in particular, has been strongly influenced by the religious Zionists and their personal example of idealism and self-sacrifice. In fact, the success of religious Zionism makes the National Religious Party (their political organization) less attractive to voters, who no longer feel they need be as defensive about threats to religion from the secular parties.

In no other society do Orthodox Jews, religious Zionists in particular, feel quite so much at home. They are separated from the non-Orthodox population by their distinctive cultural and educational institutions (in the advanced religious Zionist *yeshivot,* students are required to fulfill their military obligations but generally do so in selected units) and their own friendship groups. There are political tensions between religious and nonreligious Israelis over issues such as "Who is a Jew?," whether marriage and divorce law should be left to the rabbinate, Sabbath closing laws, and the sense of many secularists that they are subject to religious coercion. But most religious Zionists not only feel that they fully participate as equal members of the society but also sense a wholeness to their lives that they find missing outside of Israel. Nevertheless, they, too, confront the tension between tradition and modernity.

The founders of religious Zionism were influenced by modern currents of nationalism and the desire for political emancipation. Religious Zionists shared a concern for the physical as well as the spiritual welfare of Jews and an identification with nonreligious as well as religious Jews. Most of them believed that the modern settlement of the Land of Israel pointed to the beginning of divine redemption of the Jewish people. Unlike the neotraditionalists, they did not believe that Jews must patiently await the coming of the Messiah but rather that redemption was a process that Jews could initiate themselves. In other words, it was not only their espousal of Zionism that distinguished religious Zionists from the neotraditionalists, but also their acceptance of so many of the assumptions and values of modernity. Compartmentalization was an inadequate alternative. Although compartmentalization was and always will be a temptation for religious Jews who want to participate in worldly activity without compromising their religious principles, it is an inadequate ideology for religious Zionists. The establishment of the state of Israel and its public policies are to them matters of metaphysical significance intimately related to their religiously formed conceptions of reality. The reconciliation of tradition and modernity, therefore, requires other strategies.

One such strategy is adaptationism, sometimes labeled modern Orthodoxy. It affirms that the basic values of modernity are not only compatible with Judaism but partake of its essence. Freedom, the equality of man, rationalism, science, the rule of law, and nationalism are all found to be inherent in the Jewish tradition. Secular study is affirmed as a positive religious value—an instrument whereby man learns more about the divinely created world and therefore more about God. Adaptationism includes the effort to reinterpret the tradition, including those aspects of the *halakhah* that seem to stand in opposition to modern values. Adaptationism was a popular strategy among American Orthodox Jews. There are very few Israeli halakhic authorities whose rulings are adaptationist, and they lack the ideological self-consciousness or philosophical underpinning that is found among American Orthodox.

There are limits to the extent to which Orthodoxy can affirm every aspect of modernity, and there is an apologetic as well as an adaptive side to this strategy in practice. As in other religions, family law and relations between the sexes evoke the most conservative sentiments, though even here adaptationism has proved far more accommodating of modernity than other Orthodox strategies.

An alternative strategy for religious Zionism is expansionism. Expansionism affirms modernity by reinterpreting it through the prism of the Jewish tradition. It aspires, in theory, to bring all aspects of life under the rubric of its interpretation of Judaism. The program of religious Zionism, almost by definition, is expansionist. Since religious Zionism calls for a Jewish state in accordance with Jewish law, its adherents must believe, at least in theory, that Jewish law is a suitable instrument to guide a modern state. Me'ir Berlin (1880–1949), a major political leader of religious Zionism, claimed that the religious Zionist program was "not to content itself with a corner even if the Torah was there, but to capture Judaism, Jewish life, to impose the spirit of the Torah on the market, on the public, on the State." Anyone who reflects upon this statement must wonder whether, if this is indeed the task of religious Zionists, they would not have to reinterpret major motifs in the religious tradition and introduce rather radical changes in Jewish law. In other words, expansionism of this type bears within it the seeds of adaptationism. The leadership of the religious Zionist labor movement, the religious *kibbutsim* in particular, were prepared, at least in theory and sometimes in practice, for some halakhic adaptation. But they shied away from the final step that the realization of their goal would have required—the legitimation of religious changes through their adoption by the religious public rather than the assent of rabbinical authority. The ambivalent attitude toward adaptation by the leaders may help account for the permissive interpretation that many of their followers gave to *halakhah*. It may also help to account for the failure of this branch of expansionism to develop. It made no real effort to realize in practice its theoretical pretensions to adaptation, and it never legitimated the halakhic deviations that occurred under its roof.

Expansionism today is associated with the personality and philosophy of Rav Kook (Avraham Yitshaq Kook). This branch of expansionism, like neotraditionalism, is halakhically uncompromising. Unlike neotraditionalism, it abjures social and cultural isolation. Its goal is to sanctify all of life. The characteristic features of expansionism that support such a worldview and make its realization feasible, in addition to its commitment to Jewish nationalism, are a redefinition of secular-religious distinctions and a belief that divine redemption is imminent.

Expansionism is necessarily nationalistic since it argues that Jews must live a natural life in all its physical manifestations in order to invest all of life with the divine spirit. In the expansionist conception, as it has worked itself out in the last few years, the state itself assumes a special sanctity, its very creation being a sign of God's favor and a harbinger of the imminent redemption.

The religious conception of the state is challenged by three facts: that Israel was established by Jewish secularists, that the avowedly nonreligious constitute a majority of the population, and that the institutions of the state are controlled by secularists. The expansionists overcome this objection by their redefinition, following Rav Kook, of secularism. They blur distinctions not only between holy and profane but also between ostensibly religious and ostensibly secular Jews. This enables the expansionists to break out of the traditional Orthodox perception, which viewed religious Jews as a beleaguered minority surrounded by hostile Jewish secularists with whom they might at best, and even then at their peril, cooperate at an instrumental level. The belief in imminent redemption that characterizes the expansionists' viewpoint reinforces their confidence in the eventual triumph of their position despite the apparent absence of support in the international arena. It also serves as a caution against any retreat or compromise that might interrupt and delay divine redemption. Finally, the belief in imminent redemption permits the evasion of troubling questions about the suitability of the *halakhah*, in its present state, to direct a modern society.

In addition to the neotraditionalists and religious Zionists, one still finds vestiges of pre-Orthodox traditionalism among some elderly Sefardic Jews of North African origin. They arrived in Israel before their own societies underwent modernization. They have no successors. Their descendants, in turn, tend to be deferential toward the tradition; they observe many of its customs and practices but are neither as punctilious or knowledgeable about the religion as are most Orthodox Jews. They categorize themselves and are categorized by others as "traditional," as distinct from the "religious" and "secular" segments of the population. They constitute a hinterland for Orthodox Jewry, though only time will tell whether they will continue to do so.

The state of Israel provides basic religious services such as religious schools, supervision over the *kashrut* of foods, religious courts, an established rabbinate with responsibility for marriage and divorce of Jews, ritual baths, and subsidies for synagogue construction and rabbis' salaries. The religious political parties act as intermediaries in the provision of welfare and educational services. Hence, the role of the synagogue is relatively minor. Though synagogues proliferate in Israel, there is probably no country in the world where they play a less important role in the life of the Orthodox Jew.

ORTHODOXY IN THE UNITED STATES

American Orthodoxy bears the mark of two waves of immigrants and a native generation that combines characteristics of each. Many of the eastern European immigrants who came to the United States during the great wave of Jewish immigration between 1881 and 1924 were traditionalists. In the confrontation with American culture and the challenge of finding a livelihood, they abandoned many traditional patterns of religious observance. The dominant Orthodox strategy that emerged in the United States was adaptationism. In fact, in the first few decades of the century it appeared as though the difference between American Orthodox and Conservative Judaism was really the degree or pace of adaptation. The institutions and ideology of American Orthodoxy were severely challenged by neotraditionalist immigrants who arrived just prior to and immediately following World War II. They established their own *yeshivot,* Hasidic *rebeyim* among them reestablished their courts of followers, and they expressed disdain for the modern Orthodox rabbi. He was likely to be a graduate of Yeshiva University, the major institution for the training of Orthodox rabbis in the United States, where rabbinical students are required to have earned a college degree.The neotraditionalists were zealous and very supportive of their own institutions. In addition, they clustered in a few neighborhoods of the largest cities. Their concentration and discipline provided their leaders with political influence, which, in the heydays of the welfare programs of the 1960s and 1970s, was translated into various forms of government assistance.

The neotraditionalist challenge to modern Orthodoxy has had a decided impact on the native generation raised in modern Orthodox homes, and the American environment has left its mark on the generation raised in neotraditionalist homes. The American-born Orthodox Jew, regardless of the home in which he was raised, tends to be punctilious in religious observance, more so than his parents, and hostile to what he considers deviant forms of Judaism (i.e., Conservative or Reform). But he is sympathetic to many aspects of contemporary culture and accepting of secular education, if only for purposes of economic advancement. With the exception of pockets of neotraditional extremists who recall the ideology and attitudes of the 'Edah Haredit in Israel, the American Orthodox Jew, even the neotraditionalist, is familiar with, if not at home in, modern culture. Finally, there is a general willingness among most American Orthodox Jews to work with the non-Orthodox on behalf of general Jewish interests, those of Israel in particular.

Among the outstanding Orthodox figures in the United States is Rabbi Menahem Mendel Schneersohn (b. 1902), the present leader of Habad Hasidism. Habad is the Hasidic group with the largest number of sympathizers in the world. It is really a *sui generis* variety of Orthodoxy because it combines a neotraditional outlook with a conversionist impulse (toward other Jews, not non-Jews) and a unique belief system centering on the charismatic figure of the *rebe*.

Rabbi Moshe Feinstein (b. 1895), who came to the United States in 1937, is renowned in the Orthodox world as the outstanding *poseq* (adjudicator of religious law). Another significant Orthodox personality is Rabbi Joseph B. Soloveitchik (b. 1903), scion of a prominent rabbinical family and considered by many the greatest living Talmudic authority in the Orthodox world. Soloveitchik, who arrived in the United States in 1932, is particularly revered in modern Orthodox circles. He has a doctorate in philosophy and can communicate in the language of the world of ideas. His thought, which only began appearing in print in the last two decades, is characterized by sensitivity to the tension between man, possessed of feelings and ideas connected to the divine within him, and the objective and demanding *halakhah* to which God also commands the Jew to subject himself.

The increasing importance of the neotraditional *yeshivot* has challenged the central role of the synagogue, but it is still the crucial mediator between most Orthodox Jews and their religious identity. Certainly, the synagogue plays a critical role in the lives of its members and recalls the importance of the autonomous congregations of German Orthodoxy. However, unlike the German congregations, the rabbi's role in the American Orthodox synagogue is more limited, though by no means negligible. The real strength of the Orthodox synagogue, which tends to be much smaller than the average Conservative or Reform synagogue, rarely exceeding 200 to 250 members, lies in the sense of community and mutual support that it offers rather than the network of services that it provides.

ORTHODOX JUDAISM TODAY

The dominant trend in Orthodoxy throughout the world, since the end of World War II, has been increased religious zealotry, punctiliousness in religious observance, and, with some exceptions, less explicit accommodation to modern values and contemporary culture. This is, at least in part, a result of the direction in which modern values and culture have moved. Increased permissiveness; challenges to authority, order, and tradition in general; and affirmation of self are inimical to all historical religions. But Orthodoxy has become far more skilled, after a century of experience, in developing institutions—such as schools, synagogues, political organizations, a press, and summer camps—to mute the threats of secularism and modernity. In some respects this means that Orthodoxy is more at ease with the world and tolerates certain forms of accommodation (advanced secular education is the outstanding example) that many Orthodox circles denounced in the past. But it also means an increased self-confidence and an absence of fear on the part of Orthodoxy to challenge and reject some of the basic behavioral and ideological assumptions upon which most of modern culture rests.

[*See also* Judaism, *article on* Judaism in Northern and Eastern Europe since 1500; Yeshivah; Musar Movement; Agudat Yisra'el; Zionism; *and the biographies of Sofer, Hirsch, and other influential figures mentioned herein.*]

BIBLIOGRAPHY

Hebrew items are included only where English sources are inadequate and/or the Hebrew source is of major importance.

Hayim Halevy Donin's *To Be a Jew* (New York, 1972) is a practical guide to what it means to be an Orthodox Jew.

There is very little scholarly material in any language on most aspects of the social and religious history of Orthodox Judaism. The best material has been written recently; much is available only in the form of articles or doctoral dissertations.

On the background to Orthodoxy, see the last five chapters in Jacob Katz's *Tradition and Crisis: Jewish Society at the End of the Middle Ages* (New York, 1961) and *Out of the Ghetto: The Social Background of Jewish Emancipation* (Cambridge, Mass., 1973), particularly chapter 9, "Conservatives in a Quandary."

There is no general history of Orthodox Judaism. An outline of the topic is found in two articles by Moshe Samet, "Orthodox Jewry in Modern Times," parts 1 and 2, *Mahalakhim* (in Hebrew), nos. 1 and 3 (March 1969 and March 1970). Much can be learned from the two volumes of uneven biographical chapters edited by Leo Jung entitled *Jewish Leaders, 1750–1940* (New York, 1953) and *Guardians of Our Heritage, 1724–1953* (New York, 1958).

The best history of Hungarian Jewry covering the nineteenth and twentieth centuries and devoting considerable attention to Orthodoxy is Nathaniel Katzburg's "History of Hungarian Jewry" (in Hebrew), a lengthy introduction and bibliography to *Pinqas Qehillot Hungariyah* (Jerusalem, 1975). His article "The Jewish Congress of Hungary, 1868–1869," in *Hungarian Jewish Studies,* vol. 2, edited by Randolph Braham (New York, 1969), is the most significant study of a crucial aspect of the topic. The Hatam Sofer is the subject of Jacob Katz's major essay,

"Contributions toward a Biography of R. Moses Sofer" (in Hebrew), in *Studies in Mysticism and Religion Presented to Gershom G. Scholem on His Seventieth Birthday, by Pupils, Colleagues and Friends,* edited by E. E. Urbach et al. (Jerusalem, 1967).

The English-language material on German Orthodoxy is more plentiful. Robert Liberles's *Between Community and Separation: The Resurgence of Orthodoxy in Frankfort, 1838–1877* (Westport, Conn., 1985) treats Hirsch and his community in detail. *Judaism Eternal: Selected Essays from the Writings of Rabbi Samson Raphael Hirsch,* vol. 2, translated from the German by I. Grunfeld (London, 1956), is probably the best place to start in reading Hirsch himself. On understanding some other leaders of German Orthodoxy, see David Ellenson, "The Role of Reform in Selected German-Jewish Orthodox Responsa: A Sociological Analysis," *Hebrew Union College Annual* (Cincinnati, 1982).

For a selection from Isaac Breuer, considered the most profound thinker of twentieth-century German Orthodoxy, see his *Concepts of Judaism,* edited by Jacob S. Levinger (Jerusalem, 1974).

There is no history of eastern European Orthodoxy. Emanuel Etkes's *R. Yisra'el Salanter vere'shitah shel tenu'at ha-musar* (Jerusalem, 1982) is an important source for understanding the Musar movement and the world of eastern European *yeshivot.* Eliyahu E. Dessler's *Strive for Truth* (New York, 1978), edited and translated by Aryeh Carmell, is an excellent example of Musar thought. *The Teachings of Hasidism,* edited by Joseph Dan (New York, 1983), provides some flavor of Hasidic literature.

On Zionism and Orthodox Judaism, see Ben Halpern's *The Idea of the Jewish State,* 2d ed. (Cambridge, Mass., 1969), pp. 65–95. On mainstream religious Zionism, see *Religious Zionism: An Anthology,* edited by Yosef Tirosh (Jerusalem, 1975).

The best study of the old *yishuv* and its confrontation with modern Zionism is Menachem Friedman's *Society and Religion: The Non-Zionist Orthodox in Eretz-Israel, 1918–1936* (Jerusalem, 1977; in Hebrew with English summary). An expression of the extreme neotraditionalist position is I. I. Domb's *The Transformation: The Case of the Neturei Karta* (London, 1958). On Rav Kook, see Avraham Yitshaq Kook's *The Lights of Penitence, The Moral Principles, Lights of Holiness, Essays, Letters, and Poems,* translated by Ben Zion Bokser (New York, 1978).

Charles S. Liebman and Eliezer Don-Yehiya's *Civil Religion in Israel: Judaism and Political Culture in the Jewish State* (Berkeley, Calif., 1983) reviews the role of traditional Judaism in Israel and devotes a chapter to the variety of Orthodox responses to Israel's political culture.

On American Orthodoxy, Charles S. Liebman's "Orthodoxy in American Jewish Life," *American Jewish Year Book* 66 (1965): 21–97, is the most extensive survey. An adaptation of Rabbi Soloveitchik's lectures is Abraham Besdin's *Reflections of the Rav* (Jerusalem, 1979), but Soloveitchik's work "The Lonely Man of Faith," *Tradition* 7 (Summer 1965): 5–67, is a better example of his speculative effort. Norman Lamm's *Faith and Doubt: Studies in Traditional Jewish Thought* (New York, 1971) illustrates the approach of a leading American Orthodox rabbi to problems of contemporary concern.

The halakhic literature remains the heart of the Orthodox enterprise. This literature is virtually closed to the nonspecialist, but the regular feature "Survey of Recent Halakhic Responses," appearing in each issue of *Tradition: A Journal of Orthodox Jewish Thought* (New York, 1958–), provides the nonspecialist with a good sense of that world. At a more academic level, see *The Jewish Law Annual* (Leiden, 1978–).

23 CONSERVATIVE JUDAISM

Herbert Rosenblum

Conservative Judaism is one of the major religious movements in modern Judaism. Founded in central Europe in the middle of the nineteenth century, it proved attractive, first in Europe and later in the Americas, to those who preferred a Jewish expression that avoided the extremes of ultraliberalism on the one hand and right-wing traditionalism on the other. By affirming the valid claim of Jewish tradition upon modern Jews, Conservative Judaism acquired the allegiance of many Jews who sought to remain psychologically and culturally loyal to their image of the relgion of their predecessors. In addition, by accepting the necessity of coming to grips with the new climate of modernity, the movement placed itself firmly on record as willing to mediate between the claims of the tradition on the one hand and the radically new circumstances of modern Jewish life on the other. In the process, it has required that both its leaders and its rank and file become vitally concerned and knowledgeable about the central values inherent both in the tradition and in modern culture. Today, its academic center and professional training school is the Jewish Theological Seminary of America in New York, and it has several branches around the world: the University of Judaism in Los Angeles, the American Student Center (Neve Schechter) in Jerusalem, and the Seminario Latinamericano in Buenos Aires.

BACKGROUND AND INSTITUTIONAL HISTORY

Conservative Judaism originated in the conviction that the earlier Reform Jewish movement had simply gone too far in its efforts to accommodate modern Judaism to the visible models of Christian church society. In 1845, at the (Reform) Rabbinical Conference in Frankfurt am Main, Zacharias Frankel grew concerned about the increasingly radical tenor of the discussions and finally decided that he could not agree with his Reform colleagues' decision that the Hebrew language was only an "advisable," not a "necessary," feature of Jewish worship. He withdrew from the meeting and issued a widely circularized public denunciation of the extremist departures from tradition that had been countenanced by the participants.

While Frankel did not see fit to launch a new movement, he did insist on periodically expounding his new theological approach to modern Judaism, which he named positive-historical Judaism. This approach accepted the "historical" dimension that had been so enthusiastically embraced by the Reformers, and which emphasized the evolutionary character of the change from generation to generation. It also insisted, however, that the "positive" dimensions of Jewish religion and ritual, the ones that offer continuity and recognizability, needed to be afforded greater emphasis than was being granted to them by the radical Reformers.

Frankel's approach to modern Judaism was widely propagated through his *Monatsschrift* journal and received a warm reception in many quarters in central and western European Jewish communities, particularly among scholars and communal leaders. It was not surprising, therefore, that when the first modern Jewish theological seminary was established in Wrocław (Breslau) in 1854, its founders turned to Zacharias Frankel to be its dean in preference to the other major candidate, Abraham Geiger, the leading Reform rabbi of the period. This school attracted some of the great nineteenth-century scholars, including Heinrich Graetz, Isaak Markus Jost, Moritz Steinschneider, and David Hoffmann, and through its graduates it became a powerful traditionalizing influence in central and western European Jewry throughout the nineteenth and twentieth centuries, until it was closed by the Nazis in 1938.

Origins in the United States. In the United States, Conservative Judaism was formally launched in 1886 with the founding of the Jewish Theological Seminary of America, eleven years after the establishment of the (Reform) Hebrew Union College in Cincinnati (1875). The new seminary was organized in direct reaction to the issuance of the Pittsburgh Platform by a representative group of Reform rabbis in 1885, which set forth their ideological commitment to a Judaism of morality and ethics, but one that was devoid of its national and ritual dimensions and that entertained only a God "idea," not a deep-rooted conviction in a "personal" God. In the ensuing reaction, a broad coalition of moderate Reform rabbis (Benjamin Szold, Frederick de Sola Mendes, and Marcus Jastrow) together with several traditionalist rabbis (Sabato Morais, Alexander Kohut, and Henry Pereira Mendes) joined together to establish the new seminary.

These founders of the new seminary had earlier sought to cooperate with the organizers of the Hebrew Union College until it became clear that the young institution had been turned essentially into a training school for Reform rabbis. In their efforts to maintain unity, the traditionalists had followed in the path of Isaac Leeser, the Philadelphia rabbi who had sought since the beginning of his ministry in 1827 to steer a moderate path between the ultraorthodox and the radical reformers. Leeser's mainstream thrusts were exemplified by his monthly publication *The Occident*, by his organization of the Board of Delegates of American Israelites, and by his founding of Maimonides College, the first rabbinical training school in America. Most of his innovations did not survive his death, in 1868, and left the field clear for the Reform leaders, led by Isaac Mayer Wise, as they established the Union of American Hebrew Congregations in 1873 and their Hebrew Union College two years later.

The Jewish Theological Seminary began its classes in 1886 in rooms provided by the Shearith Israel congregation in New York. It was largely staffed and funded by its founding volunteers during its early years and was led by its president, Sabato Morais of Philadelphia. Its initial broad constituency, however, did not long endure; the polarization of American Jewry between the German Jews, who inclined toward Reform, and the recent immigrants from eastern Europe, inclined toward Orthodoxy, made the new seminary's search for a moderate constituency an increasingly difficult task. By the time Sabato Morais died, in 1897, the prospects for the Conservative seminary's survival seemed increasingly dim.

Reorganization of the Jewish Theological Seminary. At that low point, a new and powerful coalition appeared on the seminary's horizon, possessing both the intellectual energy and the material resources necessary to reverse its decline. Organized by Cyrus Adler, librarian of the Smithsonian Institution, this strong cadre of cultured philanthropists included the renowned attorney Louis Marshall, the eminent banker Jacob Schiff, the judge Mayer Sulzberger, and industrialists like Adolph Lewisohn and Daniel and Simon Guggenheim. Adler successfully persuaded them that the Jewish Theological Seminary of America could become a powerful americanizing force for the thousands of Jews who were beginning to arrive from eastern Europe. Through respect for their traditions, it could provide a healthful synthesis of learning and observance, while drawing them into the modernist world of new ideas and open horizons. Above all, it could produce rabbis who would combine the wisdom of the Old World with the disciplines and skills of the New World and facilitate the generational transition from Yiddish-speaking immigrant to upstanding American citizen.

The key to the successful reorganization of the seminary in the minds of these philanthropists and community leaders was the appointment of a world-renowned Jewish scholar and personality to oversee the new institution, who could chart appropriate goals and methods for the accomplishment of their ambitious program. The person they sought was Solomon Schechter (1850–1915), then professor at Cambridge University, who had acquired international acclaim with his discovery of the long-lost literature of the Cairo Genizah (a depository for discarded Jewish books) and whose academic and communal pronouncements in England had attracted wide attention. It was expected that Schehter, a product of eastern European piety and learning coupled with western European academic accomplishments, would be able to communicate equally well with the new immigrants and the established Jewish populations in the United States.

After considerable negotiation, Schechter agreed to undertake the new challenge, and Adler, Schiff, and Marshall proceeded with the reorganization of the Jewish Theological Seminary, appropriating the main administrative positions. Schechter arrived in 1902 and as dean proceeded in systematic fashion to develop a curriculum, engage a faculty, establish a library, recruit students, and to implement the type of academic standards for the seminary to which he had become accustomed in the graduate schools with which he had been associated in England and the continent.

Schechter's initial efforts were widely hailed as important contributions to the strengthening of American Jewry, and indeed their influence has been of such long-lasting quality that until the 1970s the seminary was widely referred to as Schechter's seminary. By 1909–10, Schechter had become convinced that the mere excellence of his institution's academic programs was not sufficient to acquire and retain the type of lay support that would be necessary to continue the intellectual and spiritual breakthroughs that would be required to redirect American Jewry. This was particularly so since the organized Reform and Orthodox movements were becoming increasingly defensive and even hostile toward his seminary and its program. He therefore spearheaded the establishment of a consortium of congregations that could lay the framework for a national organization in support of the seminary. After considerable negotiation, the United Synagogue of America was organized in 1913, with Schechter as its first president, and it began pioneering the establishment of organizations and programs that eventually coalesced into the Conservative movement.

Launching the new organization was not an easy task. Many of the ideological issues that would later beset the Conservative movement were discussed emotionally at the founding meeting. Schechter, Adler, and some of their foremost colleagues on the faculty of the seminary preferred to view the new organization as an "Orthodox-Conservative Union" whose major mandate would be to stem the persistent tide toward Reform Judaism. The younger leaders, who were alumni of the seminary, including Mordecai Kaplan, Jacob Kohn, and Herman H. Rubenovitz, tended to prefer a clearly defined "Conservative" federation of congregations. A smaller, fringe group, led by Judah Magnes, insisted that the new organization proclaim itself as a new, third denomination in Jewish life, distinct from Orthodox and Reform. Eventually the alumni position would prevail, but at the founding meeting a temporizing compromise was struck, and the title of the new organization was voted as the United Synagogue of America, modeled on the British organization, whose chief rabbi, Joseph Hertz, was a seminary alumnus and took part in the proceedings.

Upon Schechter's death in 1915, Cyrus Adler succeeded him as president of both the seminary and the United Synagogue of America until his death, in 1940. This era was characterized by the progressive strengthening of the seminary and its affiliated arms, the United Synagogue and the Rabbinical Assembly, and by the establishment of such significant organizations as the Women's League for Conservative Judaism and the National Federation of Jewish Men's Clubs.

Growth of the Movement. Adler's successor in 1940 as titular head of the Conservative movement was Louis Finkelstein, a seminary alumnus who had studied under Schechter and had become a mainstay of the seminary faculty and administration during the Adler era. Finkelstein almost immediately launched a broad-based expansion of the seminary's programs during the wartime and postwar periods, an expansion that was carried forward with vision, energy, effectiveness, and a large measure of success. These efforts coincided with several important developments in the maturation of the American Jewish community, all of which combined to produce a heightened readinenss for the "message" that was being advanced by the seminary. The proliferating suburban congregations in the major metropolitan areas were all seeking a new meaningful structural identity; the virtual disappearance of Europe as a reservoir of new Jewish leadership and ideas compelled the emerging American Jewish leadership to accept far more responsibility; the returning war veterans felt far more at home in America than had their parents, and were better prepared emotionally to experiment and build the types of institutions that would more fully meet their needs. The changing American Jewish community of those traumatic years seemed to be ready for exactly the type of organizational outreach that was coming from the seminary leadership.

The Finkelstein era (1940-1972) was characterized by enormous growth in the number of congregations affiliated with Conservative Judaism, a sharp escalation in the number of programs offered by the institutions of the movement, and greater recognition of the responsibilities that devolved upon the movement in view of its newfound preeminence in American and world Jewish affairs. Having grown from about 200 affiliated congregations in 1940 to some 830 congregations by 1965, the movement had become the largest federation of synagogues in the Diaspora.

To respond properly to its enormously enlarged responsibilities, the Conservative movement proceeded to establish the types of agencies that would seek to adequately serve its new constituency. In 1940 the National Academy for Adult Jewish Studies was founded; in 1947 the first in the network of Ramah summer camps was established; in 1951 the United Synagogue Youth movement was organized; in 1956 the first Solomon Schechter Day School was launched; in 1958 the American Student Center in Jerusalem (Neve Schechter) was dedicated and in 1959 the World Council of Synagogues was initially convened and the Seminario Latinamericano was opened in Buenos Aires.

The phenomenal growth of Conservative Judaism tapered off in the mid-1960s. By then the movement had established a full network of professional and lay organizations designed to enhance its local, national, and international functioning. Its California branch, the University of Judaism, had become a major force in the growth of West Coast Jewry. The Mesorati ("traditional," i.e., Conservative) movement was launched to establish Conservative congregations in Israel. The Cantors Institute, the Teachers Institute, and the seminary's various graduate schools were seeking to meet the perennial shortage of qualified Jewish professionals. The burgeoning Association for Jewish Studies, serving the academic community, was heavily populated by scholars trained in the Conservative Jewish institutions. Prayer books for the Sabbath, festivals, High Holy Days, and weekday services had been published by the United Synagogue and the Rabbinical Assembly. While not departing radically from the form and substance of the traditional prayer books, these "official" publications of the Conservative movement made several highly symbolic changes. They eliminated references to the future restoration of the sacrificial system, sought to inject a more gender-egalitarian tone into the prayers, and eliminated what were seen as anti-gentile passages.

In 1972 Finkelstein announced his retirement. His successor, Gerson D. Cohen, also a seminary alumnus, had served with distinction as a professor of Jewish history at Columbia University and at the seminary. He became chancellor of an institution that was now in the forefront of American Jewish institutional life and titular head of the largest of the Jewish religious movements. The agenda for the new administration included resolving some of the lingering ideological issues that had been brushed aside during the rapid expansion period of Conservative Judaism, consolidating the many activities of the movement, and addressing the capital improvement projects that had become increasingly imperative as the movement had grown.

During the chancellorship of Gerson Cohen (1972–1986), therefore, the attention of the Conservative movement was drawn to the intensified decision making that took place in the Committee on Jewish Law and Standards (on matters involving marriage and divorce, women's right, Sabbath and festival observances, etc.); to the enhancement of relationships between the seminary and its partners in the movement, the Rabbinical Assembly and the United Synagogue, and its associated groups, such as the Women's League for Conservative Judaism, the Educators Assembly, and the Cantors Assembly; and, most strikingly, to the mammoth undertaking of completing the seminary's physical facilities, with the building of its new Boesky Library, which was dedicated in 1983.

A major accomplishment of this period was the expansion of the Conservative movement in Israel. By 1985 there were some forty Mesorati congregations in Israel, up from the two or three that had been functioning two decades earlier. An additonal highlight was the major decision, laboriously arrived at, to admit women into the seminary's rabbinical school. In 1984, women were admitted for the first time, and in 1985 the seminary ordained its first female rabbi, Amy Eilberg, a woman who previously had achieved considerable advanced credit and training before being admitted.

The election of Ismar Schorsch, then a professor of Jewish history at the seminary, to succeed seminary chancellor Gerson D. Cohen in July 1986, followed a year-long search process and marked the beginning of a new period in the development of the Conservative movement and its central institution. The announced perception of both the search committee and the new chancellor was that the new era was to begin with a period of mending rifts and healing organizational wounds. At this time it was hoped that the women's issue and the related strains in the interpretation of Jewish law would be resolved in a more consiliatory vein, allowing the movement to unite more fully in pursuit of its central mandates.

MAJOR ORGANIZATIONS

Over the course of the century, the Conservative movement spread from the Jewish Theological Seminary of America into a web of religious and social institutions which are herewith described.

The United Synagogue of America. Founded by Solomon Schechter in 1913, the United Synagogue is the national association of Conservative congregations, responsible for the coordination of activities and services of the Conservative movement on behalf of its constituent congregations. Divisions of the the United Synagogue created for this purpose include some of the most important bodies of the movement. The Commission on Jewish Education provides for the publication of textbooks, in-service training of educators, guidance on educational policies, and mobilization of the resources of the movement on behalf of afternoon schools and the Solomon Schechter Day Schools. The Department of Youth Activities oversees the development of the broad programs of the United Synagogue Youth movement (USY) with its regional and local chapters, as well as its summer and year-round activities in Israel. The National Academy for Adult Jewish Studies seeks to stimulate the entire movement to intensify its programs in the area of adult Jewish education. The Israel Affairs Committee plans projects to place the Israel dimension more actively on the agenda of the United Synagogue affiliates via periodic news alerts to its constituent congregations and by promoting the organizational development of MERCAZ, the Conservative Zionist membership movement within the World Zionist Organization. In addition, the United Synagogue coordinantes the activities of several professional organizations and their placement services—the Educators Assembly, the Cantors Assembly, and the National Federation of Synagogue Administrators.

The Rabbinical Assembly. The Rabbinical Assembly (RA) is the organization of Conservative rabbis and has a membership of over eleven hundred rabbis. The Rabbinical Assembly has historically served as the religious policy-making body in the

Conservative movement; its Committee on Jewish Law and Standards (CJLS) has been recognized as the authoritative forum for the development of Jewish legal precedents for the movement. Its placement director serves as the chief administrator of the Joint Placement Commission for the referral of rabbinical candidates to individual congregations. It has become a major publisher of the liturgical texts used in religious services in Conservative congregations. The annual *Proceedings* of its conventions provide important source material for the historical, ideological, and organizational developments in Conservative Judaism. Its quarterly journal, *Conservative Judaism*, provides a popular and literary forum for the exchange of ideas, innovations, and creative writing.

The Women's League for Conservative Judaism. More than eight hundred synagogue sisterhoods are affiliated with the Conservative movement through the coordinating body of the Women's League. Founded by Mathilde Schechter in 1918, the Women's League has historically proven to be one of the pioneering organizations in Conservative Judaism in the development of social, educational, and philanthropic programs for the entire movement. In addition, the Women's League spearheaded the expansion of the seminary's facilities and the building of the Mathilde Schechter student dormitory, and it continues to provide important support to the seminary's programs through its annual Torah Fund drives.

The National Federation of Jewish Men's Clubs. The four hundred men's clubs affiliated with the Conservative movement plan joint ventures for the advancement of Conservative Judaism. The National Federation of Jewish Men's Clubs is particularly active in the areas of social action, youth activities, and Israeli affairs.

The World Council of Synagogues. The international arm of the Conservative movement, the World Council of Synagogues was established in 1959 to assist in bringing the message of Conservative Judaism to the attention of world Jewry outside the borders of North America. It maintains offices in Jerusalem, Buenos Aires, and New York and meets in convention every two years in Jerusalem.

CONCEPTUAL COMPONENTS OF THE MOVEMENT

Throughout its relatively brief history, the leadership and members of the movement have striven to understand and define the role of Conservative Judaism in its increasingly important place in the Jewish organizational world. A close analysis of the ideological stands taken by its major cultural leaders generally reveals the central concepts that have served to unify the rank and file of the movement's propounders, both in Western Europe and now in the United States, and can therefore be considered central to Conservative Judaism.

Positive-Historical Judaism. The philosophical approach of Zacharias Frankel, described above, became the rallying cry of the nascent Conservative movement. As Frankel explained it, and as it was later interpreted by Solomon Schechter, modern Judaism did indeed require an appreciation of the "historical" dimension, which accounted for evolution and changeability in Jewish life, as insisted upon by the Reform leaders. However, what the Reform movement did not adequately appreciate, he felt, was the fact that Judaism's integrity and survival required an enduring commitment to the "positive" dimension—the ritual commandments, personal observances, and communal structures—that had characterized all ages of Jewish history.

How this "positive-historical" balance was to be struck, and just who would be empowered to make the necessary adaptations, was a subject addressed a generation later by Solomon Schechter, writing first in England and then in the United States. In his introduction to *Studies in Judaism: First Series* (rev. ed., Philadelphia, 1945), Schechter speaks of *Catholic Israel,* the collective spirit and body of the Jewish people throughout the world that evolutionarily decides which aspects of the tradition are worthy of perpetuation and which can be safely discarded. More recently, both Conservative leaders and their opponents have noted that contemporary world Jewry is far less observant than the Jewry of Schechter's day and warn that "catholic Israel" is a concept that today would support radical Reform hypotheses. The response of Conservative leaders has been that it is not the general community but rather that of the observant and the learned that comprises the policy-making and guidance-offering body of "catholic Israel" and its evolutionary dimension.

Zionism. Zionism was embraced as a major component of the Conservative Jewish ideology at an early stage of its development. As a result of the encouragement of Solomon Schechter, several of his most active associates (among them Israel Friedlander, Mordecai Kaplan, Henrietta Szold, and Judah Magnes) became pioneers in the development of American Zionism. Ideologically, the founders of the Conservative movement found themselves deeply moved by the Zionism inherent in the Bible and prayer book and not overly affected by the hostility toward secular nationalism that pervaded the religious thinking of both the Reform and Orthodox leadership of the nineteenth and early twentieth centuries. Historically, American Zionists have been able to count upon Conservative Judaism as their most reliable ally in building the strength of their movement.

Revelation. Along with its corollary, the authority of the *halakhah* (Jewish law), revelation has been one of the central ideological issues in the evolution of Conservative Judaism. As a coalition movement of traditionalists and liberals, Conservative Judaism has swung pendulum-fashion, cyclically, in its several generations of existence. Traditionalists, such as Louis Finkelstein, Cyrus Adler, and Abraham Joshua Heschel, have tended to emphasize the literal aspects of the covenant of Sinai and the consequent obligation upon Jews to adhere closely to the classic formulations of Jewish law. Liberals, such as Mordecai Kaplan, Robert Gordis, and Gerson D. Cohen, have stipulated that revelation was more of an evolutionary process and that the evidence of adaptations in tradition and *halakhah* throughout the centuries is sufficient to allow responsibly continued adjustments and innovations. Consequences of this ongoing debate have been the departure of the ultraliberal wing of the movement in 1966 to establish the Reconstructionist Rabbinical College and the debates within the CJLS on issues such as *kashrut,* marriage and divorce, conversion and intermarriage, Sabbath and festival observances, and, most recently, the rights of women.

Religious Education. Jewish culture has been spread through education in Hebrew, Jewish history, and religious and literary texts has been at the center of the program of the Conservative movement since its inception. Solomon Schechter founded the Teachers Institute in 1909 and chose Mordecai Kaplan to develop its program, faculty, and horizons. The Rabbinical Assembly has repeatedly convened major conferences to intensify the educational offerings of the Conservative movement, with large measures of success. The United Synagogue has in recent decades been the prime mover in educational advances through its high priority Commission on Jewish Education. The Ramah camps have become one of the most remarkable achievements of the Conservative movement; thousands of elementary and high-school students have savored the educational, recreational, and inspirational atmosphere of these remarkable summer camps. For the past twenty years, a great deal of the movement's educational energy and resources have been invested in the development of the Solomon Schechter Day Schools, with gratifying results both in numbers and in quality education. Educational philosophy, methodology, and textual materials have been among the major mandates of the Melton Research Program in Jewish Education of the Teachers Institute.

ISSUES AND DEBATES WITHIN THE CONSERVATIVE MOVEMENT

From its very inception, the Conservative movement has been comprised of a broad coalition of liberal, moderate, and traditional Jewish constituencies. The Rabbinical Assembly until the 1960s routinely alternated its presidential nominations, traditionalist succeeding a liberal and a liberal succeeding a traditionalist; it thus recognized *de facto* its committment to safeguarding the prerogatives of both elements of the movement. It gradually became clear to the centrists that they had been left out of the rotation, and they felt that the movement had become paralyzed by the concessions granted regularly to the right and the left. They thereupon demanded, and received, the right to high office that their preponderant numbers warranted. With their accession, the mood of the Rabbinical Assembly began to change noticeably.

Halakhic Revision. The Rabbinical Assembly's Committee on Jewish Law and Standards is generally recognized as the movement's governing body on matters of ritual decision-making. As a result, it has been the focus of some of the major policy controversies that have arisen within the leadership of the movement during the latter half of the twentieth century. Despite considerable frustration and soul-searching, the committee stayed within the limits acceptable to the traditionalists during the 1930s and 1940s, and only in 1950 did it cross the so-called "Halakhic Rubicon," by declaring it acceptable (by majority decision) to drive to the synagogue on the Sabbath, and similarly, to use electricity on the Sabbath.

These symbolically significant decisions were followed by a period of relative quiescence on the part of the CJLS while it negotiated intensively with the seminary Talmud faculty on matters affecting marital and divorce procedure. By 1967, however, under the leadership of its chairman Benjamin Kreitman, it initiated several far-reaching modifications of Jewish ritual practice. The committee approved (religious) court-ordered annulment of marriages in cases where civilly-divorced spouses refused to grant the *get* (divorce document) necessary for religious remarriage. It further liberalized several laws of *kashrut* and granted to congregations the option of eliminating the second day of the three pilgrimage festivals, Sukkot, Passover, and Shavu'ot. The procedural questions raised by these halakhic questions and revisions brought a revamping of the committee's internal regulations in 1970 to keep the Rabbinical Assembly responsive to the new largely centrist thrust. Whether these rabbinical decisions play any decisive role in the daily life and decision-making activities of the Conservative membership and laity remains an open question.

Women's Rights. The newly reorganized committee became preoccupied in the 1970s with the unavoidable issue of women's rights. Although in 1955 the committee had approved the right of women to receive 'aliyyot (the honor of ascending to the pulpit to read from the Torah) its approval had largely been overlooked. It now reaffirmed this right and in 1974 voted to give women the right to be counted toward a minyan (religious quorum of ten). The issue of admitting women into the rabbinical program at the seminary was now raised with more frequency and pressure, especially since the Reform and Reconstructionist movements had been ordaining women regularly since the early 1970s. After the seminary faculty, upon the repeated urging of the chancellor, Gerson Cohen, finally agreed in 1984 to accept female students, the Rabbinical Assembly voted to accept its first woman into membership in 1985. It remains to be seen, of course, whether this constitutional acceptance will be accompanied in the near future by a functional and social acceptance of women into the ranks of recognized candidates for major congregational appointments. There remain, in addition, lingering religious issues that have not as yet been resolved, such as the right of women to serve as judges on batei din (religious courts), or to serve as witnesses for religious documents, or to serve as shelihei tsibbur, the congregational leaders who represent the community in worship.

Communal-Congregational Tensions. The model of the Conservative congregation that evolved during the rise of the movement was that of the "institutional synagogue." The congregation was to undertake any and all functions that were useful in educating Jews, facilitating worship, fostering Jewish sociability, encouraging interfaith activities, promoting youth activities, and so forth. In short, the synagogue, by definition, was to become the central institution in the Jewish community. This mandate, when exercised to its fullest extent, made inevitable a broad variety of tensions between its existing agencies and institutions in the Jewish community. Synagogues became embroiled in "jurisdictional" disputes with groups such as Jewish community centers, communal Hebrew schools, Jewish federations, and Jewish community relations councils. These tensions are more frequently encountered by Conservative congregations than by their Orthodox and Reform counterparts, since the former rarely venture beyond ritual and education, and the latter concentrate most often on social action and liturgical innovation.

THE FUTURE OF THE MOVEMENT

Sociological trends seem to indicate that the Conservative movement will not long continue to enjoy the numerical preeminence that it has experienced during the past two decades. Surveys taken by various communities as well as the National Jewish Population Study indicate that the percentage of Jews who identify themselves as Conservative, while still high, has been decreasing for some time. Gerson Cohen suggested in a 1977 address entitled "The Present State of Conservative Judaism" that "what is immediately required, therefore, is a strong emphasis on mass learning within our movement, so that the canard that only Conservative rabbis identify with the principle of 'tradition and change' can finally be put to rest" (Judaism: A Quarterly 26, no. 3, Summer 1977: p. 272).

An address entitled "Unity in Diversity" given by Mordecai Kaplan to a United Synagogue convention in the 1950s caught the imagination of its audience. It seemed to capture the essence of the appeal of the Conservative movement to its broad constituency. Conservative Judaism offered modernity to the American born generations seeking to establish themselves in the new suburbs surrounding America's cities in the postwar era; and it offered the flavor of tradition to those whose roots in the Old World, or ties to traditional parents and grandparents, remained of strong concern. Making few demands and simulating an "all things to all men" approach, the movement grew rapidly in the 1950s and 1960s. By the 1970s not only had the Orthodox experienced an upsurge in popularity, but the Reform had begun to introduce far larger measures of traditional material into their liturgical and educational programs. The situation in the 1970s was reminiscent of the haunting analysis made by Israel Goldstein to his colleagues in the Rabbinical Assembly at their 1927 convention: "As Orthodoxy becomes more and more de-ghettoized and Reform becomes more and more Conservatized, what will be left for the Conservative Jew to do? How will he be distinguished from the other two? With both his wings substantially clipped he will surely be in a precarious position" *(Proceedings of the Rabbinical Assembly of America,* 1927, p.35*)*. In the meanwhile, Jews continue to flock to the educational and cultural programs sponsored by the movement, the quality of academia at the seminary and related institutions remains impressive, and both men and women are eagerly entering the Conservative rabbinate.

[*Related entries include* Jewish Thought and Philosophy, *article on* Modern Thought; Judaism, *article on* Judaism in the Western Hemisphere; Zionism; *the biographies of Frankel, Heschel, Kaplan, Schechter, and Szold; and* Reconstructionist Judaism; Reform Judaism; *and* Orthodox Judaism.]

BIBLIOGRAPHY

The standard works on the origins of the Conservative movement are Moshe Davis's *The Emergence of Conservative Judaism* (Philadelphia, 1963), Herbert Parzen's *Architects of Conservative Judaism* (New York, 1964), and my own *Conservative Judaism: A Contemporary History* (New York, 1983). The definitive sociological study of the movement is Marshall Sklare's revised and augmented *Conservative Judaism: An American Religious Movement* (New York, 1972). Conservative views of Jewish tradition can be found in *Tradition and Change* (New York, 1958), an anthology of essays by leading Conservatives edited by Mordecai Waxman, and in a special issue of the magazine *Judaism* 26 (Summer 1977). Conservative approaches to Jewish law are intensively described in Isaac Klein's *A Guide to Jewish Religious Practice* (New York, 1979) and in *Conservative Judaism and Jewish Law,* edited by Seymour Siegel (New York, 1977). Journals published by various arms of the Conservative movement include the following: *Conservative Judaism* (New York, 1945–), published quarterly by the Rabbinical Assembly; *The Outlook* (New York, 1930–), published quarterly by the Women's League for Conservative Judaism: the *Torchlight* (first published as *The Torch* in 1941, renamed in 1977), published quarterly by the National Federation of Jewish Men's Clubs; *The United Synagogue Review* (New York, 1945–), published quarterly by the United Synagogue of America; and *Proceedings of the Rabbinical Assembly* (New York, 1927–), published annually.

Important aspects of Conservative ideology are explored in Simon Greenberg's *A Jewish Philosophy and Pattern of Life* (New York, 1981) and in Elliot N. Dorff's *Conservative Judaism: Our Ancestors to Our Descendants* (New York, 1977). In addition, shorter treatments of Conservative Judaism have been written by Robert Gordis, Simon Greenberg, and Abraham Karp, and there are important chapters on the Conservative movement in large works by Joseph Blau, Arthur Hertzberg, Mordecai Kaplan, Gilbert Rosenthal, and David Rudavsky, among others.

RECONSTRUCTIONIST

24 JUDAISM

HAROLD M. SCHULWEIS

Reconstructionism, the youngest of the four main religious movements in contemporary Judaism, is the only one indigenous to America. Its ideology remains the creation of its founder and theoretician, Mordecai Kaplan (1881–1983); it can be summarized as an appreciation of the unifying elements of the Jewish past, a critical discontent with the present ideological and institutional responses to the posttraditional Jewish situation, and an activist resolve to advance Judaism through conscious and deliberate planning. Both the Reconstructionist ideology and movement thus grew in partial response to other Jewish movements in America.

FOUNDATION OF THE MOVEMENT

In January 1922, Kaplan established in New York the Society for the Advancement of Judaism, which functioned as a synagogue center and gathering place for rabbis, educators, and laity sympathetic to Kaplan's philosophy of Judaism. The influential magazine *The Reconstructionist* was launched in 1935 in collaboration with Kaplan's closest associates Eugene Kohn, Milton Steinberg, and Ira Eisenstein, all rabbis ordained at the Conservative movement's Jewish Theological Seminary of America, as was Kaplan himself. Kaplan's magnum opus, *Judaism as a Civilization*, first published in 1934, laid the architectural frame of the Reconstructionist approach to the institutional structure, theology, and ritual of Judaism.

Kaplan remained affiliated with the Conservative movement, but late in his teaching career at the seminary, ideological differences led to the transformation of Reconstructionism from a school of thought to a fourth movement. Ira Eisenstein, who assumed the leadership of the Reconstructionist Foundation in 1959 and founded the Reconstructionist Rabbinical College (RRC) in 1968, was the driving force behind this denominational change.

JUDAISM AS AN EVOLVING RELIGIOUS CIVILIZATION

Kaplan's social pragmatism argues for the right and obligation of a people to use its discriminating intelligence in adapting to the changing conditions that confront it. The Jewish people are a living organism whose will to live and fulfill itself often necessitates theological and institutional changes, a process that characterizes Judaism, in Kaplan's definition, as the evolving religious civilization of a living organism, the Jewish people. Kaplan's sociological and theological proposals are rooted in the matrix of the Jewish people and are responsive to its needs and aspirations. Jewish theology is responsible for the salvation, or self-fulfillment, of the Jewish people. For Kaplan, there is no paradox in maintaining that continuity requires change. The new is no less sacred than the old, and reverence for the creative innovation expresses no less a piety than does veneration of the past. Kaplan's sociological bent carries with it a pragmatic intent. His descriptive analysis of the condition of Judaism and the Jewish people lays the groundwork for his program to reconstruct.

Kaplan's Social Existentialism. Reconstructionism is thus an amalgam of philosophy, sociology, and ideology. As its founder and architect, Mordecai M. Kaplan functioned as both its statesman and theologian; he was concerned with preserving the identity, unity, and continuity of the Jewish people and its civilizational superstructure, Judaism. At the core of Kaplan's universe of discourse lies a social existentialism: the existence of the Jewish people is prior to any attempt to define its essence. If any characterization of Judaism can be made, it is in its overriding concern with the preservation and fulfillment of the Jewish people. The matrix out of which the civilizational complex of Judaism emerges is the Jewish people. In Kaplan's self-declared "Copernican revolution," Judaism is for the sake of the Jewish people, not the Jewish people for the sake of Judaism. His inversion of the traditionalist formulation of the relationship between people and religion entails both descriptive and prescriptive elements. The centrality of the Jewish people, consciously or not, has been the guiding motivation of Jewish thought.

The primacy of peoplehood explains the evolutionary character of Judaism, which, according to Kaplan, has passed through three major stages: the national era, while the First Temple stood; the ecclesiastical era of the Second Temple; and the rabbinic era, from then until the modern age. Judaism at the end of the eighteenth century entered the democratic state, and therein lies the uniqueness of its internal challenge. Judaism as a civilization refers to that which unites the millennial generations of Jews into one people. It is expressed through language, art, history, music, culture, ethics; the variety of sancta manifests a people's collective will to find meaning in its life. Judaism is not a set of dogmas, doctrines, or ritual prescriptions, nor is it a philosophy. It is the expression of a people's instinctual will to live, according to a postulate articulated by Ahad ha'Am (Asher Ginzberg, 1856–1927), one of Kaplan's cultural heroes, and used by Kaplan to counter a purely ideational rationale of Jewish existence. As a civilization, Judaism neither requires justification as an indispensable means to some universal good nor needs rely on claims of supernatural election and design. Ahad ha-'Am could find no more meaning in the question "Why be Jewish?" than in the question why he remained his father's son. For Kaplan, as well, the ties of belonging are prior to the justification of believing. Nevertheless, "since Judaism not only exists for the sake of the Jews but has been fostered by the Jews themselves, who, for thousands of years, have devoted their best energies to its preservation, obviously the Jews are badly in need of Judaism and cannot get along without it" (Kaplan, 1967, p. 427). In this sense, the relationship between the Jewish people and Judaism, described in Kaplan's Copernican inversion, is not linear but dialectical. Judaism exists for the sake of a people who develop a sacred social heritage that, in turn, affects the character and choices of a people.

In Kaplan's analysis, the threat to the status of Jewry and the continuity of Judaism in the modern era is unique. The emancipation in the late eighteenth century offered Jews entry into a publicly neutral society, freer of economic restraints and religious barriers than any in its history. No analogy with Jewish communities in the premodern past properly applies to the condition of this old-new people who were offered citizenship in open societies. Jews who in traditional societies functioned quasi-autonomously as an *imperium in imperio* were now asked to surrender their corporate interests for the rights of individual, cultural, and socioeconomic advantages. Modern nationalism sought to melt down the cultural and ethnic individualities of minority groups and to relegate Judaism to a religion of private affairs. Post-emancipation Jewish efforts to accommodate the imperatives of modern nationalism—for example, Reform Judaism, Neo-Orthodoxy, and Zionism—threatened, in Kaplan's view, to sever the organic religio-ethnic cord and result either in an inauthentic spiritualization and intellectualization of Judaism or in a nationalism devoid of all religious memory. Accompanying the threat of nationalism was the challenge of naturalism, which shook the plausibility of traditionalism shared by Muslims, Jews, and Christians alike. The supernaturalist worldview of miraculous divine intervention, literalistic divine revelation, and otherworldly reward and punishment is confronted by a this-worldly naturalism. Nationalism and naturalism present a two-pronged challenge to the status of Jewry and the continuity of Judaism.

The unity of the Jewish people in modern times cannot be retained by the imposition of uniform religious or secular ideologies. The new condition of Jewish status and the fragmentation of traditional faith requires acceptance of a voluntaristic and pluralistic Jewish society and the ideal of unity in diversity. It demands a discriminating assimilation of the values of nationalism and naturalism. The democratic character of modern nationalism, the separation of church and state, and the unprecedented opportunities offered to citizens of an open society are to be absorbed into Judaism without abandoning the fidelities and attachments to Jewish peoplehood. While extolling the values of naturalism, Kaplan warns against the reductionism, scientism, and desacralization that frequently accompany secular naturalism and humanism. The creative adaptation of the values of naturalism, pragmatism, and functionalism calls for genuine alternatives for Jews who can no longer accept the inherited presuppositions and authority of supernaturalism. The artful integration of naturalism and tradition promises to expand the circle of Jewish identity and introduce a new nexus for Jewish continuity. Kaplan's pragmatic statesmanship and theology were designed to offer no excuse for Jewish apostasy. His inclusive project aims at Jewish unity without creedal uniformity and Jewish continuity without the conceit of immutability.

God and the God Idea. The major adjective characterizing Kaplan's definition of Judaism as an evolving civilization is *religious*. The Jewish religion expresses the self-consciousness of a people's quest for meaning, purpose, or salvation. The God idea of a people is the apogee of religion. The Jewish conceptualization of God does not spring from instant revelation or metaphysical speculation. The Jewish idea of God develops out of the transactions of a particular people with its historical environment. "Divinity" and "peoplehood" are correlative concepts in much the same manner that "parent" and "child" are correlative terms. To paraphrase George Santayana, to speak of religion in general is as meaningful as speaking in general without using any language in particular. Judaism is the particular language through which the Jewish people articulate their spiritual meaning. While God ideas are cultural expressions and, as such, are subject to various formulations, belief in God refers to the intuitive experiences that point to the cosmic power upon which we depend for our existence and self-fulfillment. Belief in God is not a logical but a soteriological inference. It expresses the psychic manifestation of the will to live and fulfill one's life. Belief in God, thus, is not a reasoned but a "willed" faith.

Such faith is not acquiescence to a supernatural subject who orders the world on our behalf. It is trust in the energies within the world that must be properly understood and used to transform the world in quest of salvation. This-worldly salvation is conditional. It depends upon the proper exercise of human intelligence, responsibility, and will. When physical and human nature are understood and responsibly cultivated, the salvific processes of divinity are revealed. When we are sustained in our tragic losses, find strength to overcome the paralysis of despair, and are propelled toward life, we discover the power within and beyond us that is transnatural but not supernatural. According to Kaplan, the meaning of the God idea is grasped pragmatically by observing the behavioral and attitudinal consequences that flow to it from commitment. "All we can know about God is what happens to human life when men believe in God, and how much improvement in their mode of life and thought is reflected in their belief concerning God" (Kaplan, 1948, p. 181).

Change and Continuity. Kaplan's widely quoted aphorism "The past has a vote but no veto" articulates his insistence that the modern era calls for conscious choices in revitalizing Judaism and selectively assimilating those features of naturalism, humanism, and pluralism that further the advancement of Jewish life. Creative interaction between the values of tradition and modernity requires restructuring the institutions of Judaism and the reconstruction of its theological, ritual, and liturgical expressions. As religious statesman and ideologue, Kaplan was aware of the need for structure and stability. He identified the "sancta" of Judaism as those constants that Jews share together though they may be differently interpreted and celebrated: the heroes, events, places, celebrations, and commemorative holy days that function as unifying factors in Judaism. Kaplan's own liturgical reconstruction demonstrates the struggle to hold on to continuity and change in a pluralistic society.

Large public interest in Reconstructionism was not aroused through the publication of Kaplan's sociological and theological writings. The movement gained mass attention through the publication of two of its liturgical texts. The first was the *New Haggadah* (1941), edited by Kaplan, Eugene Kohn, and Ira Eisenstein, which sought to integrate the traditional and contemporary meanings of democracy and freedom and eliminated such items from the Seder as the enumeration of the Ten Plagues and the imprecation of the psalmist against the nations that do not know God and consume his people. The publication of the *Reconstructionist Sabbath Prayer Book* in 1945, edited by Kaplan and Kohn with assistance by Eisenstein and Milton Steinberg, led to its denunciation by the Union of Orthodox Rabbis. At a special meeting that year in New York, the 200 members of the Orthodox Union voted unanimously to issue a *herem,* a writ of excommunication against Kaplan. A copy of the "new heretical prayer book" was placed on the speaker's table and burned by Joseph Ralbag, then rabbi of Congregation Oheb Shalom in New York.

Kaplan sought to express liturgically what he sensed many Jews believed privately. He argued that Jewish religiosity is not exhausted in its supernaturalist formulation. God is one, but God ideas are many. Accordingly, there are many ways to express one's relationship to God in prayer. Moreover, if prayer is poetry, it is poetry believed in. The compartmentalization of theological convictions and liturgical nostalgia is to be overcome by a liturgy that can be followed with both heart and mind. Those theological obstacles that blocked some Jews from serious prayers were to be either reinterpreted, replaced, or removed.

The changes in the Reconstructionist prayer book had to exhibit, in the language of the editors, the "courage as well as reverence" to set aside or modify such prayers or ideas unacceptable to moral and intellectual sensibilities of modern people. Unlike other modern prayer books, the Hebrew text was deleted or altered wherever changes were made in the English translation. Thus, the *Reconstructionist Sabbath Prayer Book* substituted prayers in praise of Jewish uniqueness for those proclaiming the exclusive divine choice of the Jewish people, omitted references to the hope for restoration of the Temple and animal sacrifices there, and deleted prayers in praise of the physical resurrection of the dead and God's reward and punishment of Israel by granting or withholding the rainfall. Prayers that discriminated against women, slaves, and gentiles were replaced by positive affirmations of freedom and the celebration of the divine image in all human beings.

It was Reconstructionism's rejection of the literal meaning of God's election of the Jewish people that created the deepest controversy. For Kaplan the idea of divine election could be explained functionally as a belief that compensates for a people's sense of isolation and persecution; but exclusivity raises questions not only about the nature of a God who chooses and rejects but about the morality of a divine favoritism, which tends to inflame rivalry among sibling religions, each contending superiority. Kaplan replaced the notion of God choosing a people with the idea of "vocation," the calling to serve God that religious civilizations claim. No religion is precluded from serving God according to its own concept of salvation.

LATER DEVELOPMENT OF THE MOVEMENT

In 1963, with the impending retirement of Kaplan from the faculty of the Jewish Theological Seminary of America in New York, where he had been teaching since 1909, and the reluctance of the seminary to appoint a Reconstructionist successor, Kaplan faced increased pressure to institutionalize Reconstructionism. Throughout his career, Kaplan had resisted the efforts to turn Reconstructionism into a fourth religious movement. He warned against the centrifugal forces of congregationalism and denominationalism. Reconstructionism was to transcend institutional privatism and not further fragment Jewish life. When the Reconstructionist Federation of Congregations was created in 1955, it insisted that the associating congregations retain or acquire membership in the Union of American Hebrew Congregations (the main body of the Reform movement, UAHC) or the United Synagogue (which unites Conservative congregations). But by 1968, when it became the Federation of Reconstructionist Congregations, its transdenominational character was transformed into another wing of American Judaism. Under the vigorous leadership of Ira Eisenstein, the Reconstructionist Rabbinical College was founded in Philadelphia also in that year. Under Eisenstein, its first president, men and women were accepted for a five-year program of graduate study. Reflecting Kaplan's concept of Judaism as an evolving religious civilization, the curriculum was divided into the study of five major periods of Jewish civilization: biblical, rabbinic, medieval, modern, and contemporary. In 1982, Ira Silverman succeeded Eisenstein as the college's president. In the same year, the federation was restructured as the Federation of Reconstructionist Congregations and Havurot under the guidance of its first full-time executive director, David Teutsch, and three years later numbered over fifty affiliated groups. *The Reconstructionist* magazine, first published in 1935, was renewed in 1983 under the editorship of Jacob Staub. After a decade, the members of the Reconstructionist Rabbinical Association, founded in 1975, numbered nearly one hundred and included as well a number of student members of RRC and faculty members. In 1980, the association established for the first time in Jewish history a procedure for an egalitarian *get* (a Jewish divorce).

Reconstructionism, after Kaplan and his immediate successor Ira Eisenstein, evidences a "softer" naturalism, a greater hospitality to the mystical and emotional elements in Judaism. This openness and responsiveness to the changing needs of a community is compatible with the latitudinarian spirit of Reconstructionism. No one can *a priori* know precisely how the living organism of a dynamic people may express its vitality; the essence of Judaism, and of Reconstructionism, is continually redefined.

[*See also the biography of Kaplan.*]

BIBLIOGRAPHY

Berkovits, Eliezer. "Reconstructionist Theology." *Tradition* 2 (1959): 20–66.
Eisenstein, Ira, ed. *Varieties of Jewish Belief.* New York, 1966.
Eisenstein, Ira and Eugene Kohn, eds. *Mordecai M. Kaplan: An Evaluation.* New York, 1952.
Kaplan, Mordecai. *Judaism as a Civilization* (1934). Reprint, Philadelphia, 1981.
Kaplan, Mordecai. *The Meaning of God in Modern Jewish Religion* (1937). Reprint, New York, 1974.
Kaplan, Mordecai. *The Future of the American Jew.* New York, 1948.
Kaplan, Mordecai. *Questions Jews Ask.* New York, 1956.
Kaplan, Mordecai. *Judaism without Supernaturalism.* New York, 1958.
Kaplan, Mordecai. *The Greater Judaism in the Making* (1960). Reprint, New York, 1967.
Liebman, Charles S. "Reconstructionism in American Jewish Life." *American Jewish Yearbook* 71 (1970): 1–99.
Meyer, Michael A. "Beyond Particularism: On Ethical Culture and the Reconstructionists." *Commentary* 51 (March 1971): 17–76.
Schulweis, Harold M. "The Temper of Reconstructionism." In *Jewish Life in America,* edited by Theodore Friedman and Robert Gordis, pp. 54–74. New York, 1955.

25 REFORM JUDAISM

MICHAEL A. MEYER

Reform Judaism is the branch of the Jewish faith that has been most adaptive, in belief and practice, to the norms of modern thought and society. It is also sometimes called Liberal Judaism or Progressive Judaism. By *Reform* is meant not a single reformation but an ongoing process of development. Over one million Reform Jews live in the United States and Canada, with about another one hundred thousand in Europe, Latin America, South Africa, Australia, and Israel. Internationally, all Reform congregations are united in the World Union for Progressive Judaism, which holds biennial conferences usually in Europe or in Israel. In the United States some 750 independent congregations constitute the Union of American Hebrew Congregations (UAHC), and more than 1,300 rabbis—some of them serving abroad—make up the Central Conference of American Rabbis (CCAR). Rabbis, as well as scholars, educators, community workers, and cantors, are trained at the Hebrew Union College–Jewish Institute of Religion (HUC-JIR), which has branches in Cincinnati, New York, Los Angeles, and Jerusalem. The most influential role of organizational leadership in Reform Judaism is the presidency of the UAHC, in recent years a professional position held by a rabbi.

BELIEFS AND PRACTICES

Unlike more traditional forms of the Jewish faith, Reform Judaism does not hold that either the written law (Torah) or the oral law (Talmud) was revealed literally by God to Moses at Sinai. It accepts biblical and other historical criticism as legitimate, understanding scripture and tradition as a human reflection of revelation rather than its literal embodiment. While theologies among Reform Jews vary greatly, from the traditional to the humanistic, concepts of God strike a balance between universal and particular elements, with somewhat more stress upon the former than among other religious Jews. Like other branches of Judaism, Reform recognizes the close connection between religion and ethics. It especially emphasizes the prophetic message of social justice and seeks to act upon it both congregationally and as a united movement. Judaism is seen to exist for a higher universal purpose, which aims messianically at the biblical vision of world peace. Traditionally in Reform Judaism, this sense of purpose has been known as the "mission of Israel."

The doctrine that most significantly sets Reform Judaism apart from more traditional currents is the conception of progressive revelation. Reform Jews hold that revelation is ongoing with the progress of human knowledge and religious sensitivity. This represents a reversal of the Orthodox belief whereby the theophany at Sinai, as interpreted by the rabbis, constitutes the authoritative, permanent expression of God's will, which must therefore remain normative for all time. The Reform conception of progress in understanding of the divine does not necessarily imply the continuous moral advance of the Jews or of Western civilization, although Reform Judaism before the Holocaust was prone to draw that conclusion.

The freedom of the individual Jew to be selective, to draw from Jewish tradition those elements of belief and practice that he or she finds the most personally meaningful, is far greater among Reform Jews than among either Orthodox or Conservative. Religious anarchy, while always a danger, is restrained by a common though theologically diverse liturgy, general agreement on basic commitments, and a well-structured organizational framework. Reform Jews do not accept the Jewish legal tradition as binding but have always—and especially in recent years—turned to it for guidance in ritual matters. The CCAR currently issues both a manual for Sabbath observance and a guide to the Jewish life cycle.

At most Reform congregations in America the main religious service of the week is held after dinner on Friday evenings; men and women sit together, participating equally in the service. Only in recent years have many rabbis, some male congregants, and a much smaller number of women begun to wear the ritual head covering (*kippah* or *yarmulke*) during worship. In nearly all Reform synagogues (or temples, as they are often called) the liturgy is accompanied by an organ, while musical responses are led or performed by a choir and/or a cantor. Most of the prayers are spoken in English, except for those of central significance, which are rendered in Hebrew; the ratio varies from congregation to congregation. Especially under the impact of the state of Israel, the relative amount of Hebrew in the service has generally increased and its pronunciation has been altered from the Ashkenazic (central and eastern European) to the Sefardic (Spanish and Near Eastern) accent used in the Jewish state. Formality and decorum have been hallmarks of the Reform temple, but in recent years some congregations have sought to regain some of the informality and emotion of the traditional synagogue through greater congregational involvement in the service and experimentation with alternative musical instruments such as the guitar. The influence of worship services conducted in the summer camps of the National Federation of Temple Youth has been an appreciable factor in this regard.

Outside the synagogue Reform Jews practice their faith by attempting to guide their lives according to the moral precepts of Judaism. A large percentage practices some Jewish rituals in the home, especially the lighting of the Sabbath candles on Friday evening, the Passover eve ceremony, or Seder, and the celebration of Hanukkah. Once especially aware of their religious differences from traditional Jews, today Reform Jews emphasize to a greater extent their common ethnic identity and the faith shared by all religious Jews, limiting the significance of denominational differences.

Reform Jews remain more favorably inclined to proselytism than other branches of religious Judaism. The largest portion of converts to Judaism become Reform Jews, often as the result of marriage with a Jewish partner. Such "Jews by choice" today comprise a small but growing percentage of the membership of most Reform congregations. Reform Judaism has recently given much attention to issues concerning procedures for conversion as well as the Jewish legal status of children born from mixed marriages in which the father, but not the mother, is Jewish. According to the *halakhah* (traditional Jewish law), such children are not Jewish unless formally converted. The Reform rabbinate is unique in that some Reform rabbis will conduct weddings for mixed couples in which the non-Jewish partner does not intend to convert to Judaism. Usually in such instances, however, the couple promises to raise its children as Jews.

THE MOVEMENT IN EUROPE

Reform Jews have often pointed out that religious reform was inherent in Judaism from its beginnings. They have noted that the prophets were critics of contemporary religious practices, that the Talmud includes reforms of earlier biblical legislation, and that even later legal scholars were willing to alter received beliefs and practices. Such willingness to adjust to historical change waned only under the pressure of persecution and the isolation of the ghetto. Latter-day Jews seeking religious reform thus sought, and to a degree found, precedent for their programs in earlier layers of Jewish tradition. However, they soon became aware that most of their fellow Jews, and especially the established rabbinical leadership, did not share such views. The result was a movement for reform, originally intended to harmonize all aspects of Jewish life with the modern world into which European Jews increasingly entered beginning with the later eighteenth century. Only gradually did the movement come to focus specifically on the religious realm, and only after a generation did it separate itself as a differentiable religious current with a more or less fixed religious philosophy. In discussing origins, it is therefore more accurate to speak of the "Reform movement in Judaism" than of Reform Judaism. Even this terminology, however, requires the qualification that self-conscious awareness of being a movement with definite goals came only gradually with the coalescence of various elements of belief and practice.

Beginnings. The background for the emergence of the Reform movement is the changing political and cultural situation of central and western European Jewry in the last decades of the eighteenth century and the beginning of the nineteenth. For numerous generations Jews had been physically and intellectually excluded from the surrounding, largely Christian civilization. With occasional exceptions, they lived within their own spiritual world. Their communities possessed corporate status; they were allowed to conduct their internal affairs according to Jewish law. The curriculum of their schools was confined almost exclusively to study of traditional Jewish texts. Secular knowledge was gained only informally and only to the extent necessary for the conduct of daily affairs. This medieval situation of the Jews was undermined by two novel elements: political centralization and the universalism of the Enlightenment. As European states sought greater concentration of power, they found it necessary to remove the divisive elements of medieval corporatism. Jews were brought more directly under state control; their autonomous jurisdiction and the coercive power of their rabbis were curtailed. Hopes were raised among Jews that political integration would lead as well to abolition of political, economic, and social disabilities. At the same time a more friendly attitude to Jews, which regarded them foremost as creatures of the same God rather than as Christ-killers, began to pervade enlightened circles, drawing Jews to respond with their own broader, more universal identifications. In increasing numbers they now began to learn modern European languages, to read contemporary literature, to absorb the prevalent aesthetic sensibilities, and to regard themselves culturally as Europeans no less than religiously as Jews.

Gradually a gap was created between Jewish traditions, harmonious with medieval realities, and the new economic, social, and cultural status of a portion of western Jewry. To be sure, this modernizing process did not affect all Jews at once or to the same degree. Well into the nineteenth century most Jews in eastern Europe remained virtually untouched by the norms of modern civilization, while even in western Europe modernization among Jews was a slow process, more so in the religious sphere than in the cultural sphere. However, as early as the turn of the nineteenth century, there began, especially in Germany, a pronounced falling away from Jewish belief and observance on the part of those Jews most exposed to the currents of modernity. Fears arose that unless Jewish traditions could be brought into harmony with the intellectual canons and the social norms of the surrounding society, Judaism might find itself relegated to the dustbin of medievalism. The Reform movement arose as an attempt to reconcile Jewish religious tradition with cultural and social integration, to stem the rising tide of religious apathy and even conversion in certain circles, and to reshape Judaism in such a way as would make it viable under radically novel circumstances.

The first religious issue to arouse major controversy was burial on the very day of assumed death, as required by Jewish law. The famed Jewish philosopher of the Enlightenment, Moses Mendelssohn (1729–1786), who remained an Orthodox Jew, broke with established practice in 1772 when he advocated temporary "burial" above the ground and graveyard vigil until actual death could be determined with certainty. Mendelssohn based his view both on the precedent of an ancient custom and on current medical experience. For decades thereafter this question served as a touchstone separating traditionalists from modernists, those who held that all customary practice was sacred and inviolable from those who believed that at least in some instances criteria external to the Jewish tradition should be invoked to determine religious obligation.

A new theoretical religious position, which thereafter was largely, if not directly, absorbed by the Reform movement, first appears in a work entitled *Leviathan* (1792), by Saul Ascher (1767–1822), a Jewish book dealer living in Berlin. Ascher rejected the Mendelssohnian dichotomy between natural religion (that shared by all rational human beings) and revealed law (that given exclusively to the Jews and the basis for their separation as a religious community). For Ascher the distinguishing feature of Judaism was not its legal corpus but its unique religious faith. Thus Judaism was not dependent on political or judicial autonomy; it could take its place alongside Protestantism and Roman Catholicism, differentiated from them as one faith from another. In contrast to Mendelssohn, Ascher held that Judaism does indeed possess specific dogmas that set it apart from natural religion. These include belief in the God of love, who revealed himself to the patriarchs, who rewards and punishes, and who guides the world through divine providence. Likewise essential to Judaism are certain practices, including circumcision, observance of Sabbaths and holidays, and atonement as a way of seeking God's favor. Ascher's arbitrary selectivity marks a sharp departure from traditional Jewish thought. In the fashion of non-Jewish thinkers of the eighteenth century, it makes religion largely a means to the end of personal spiritual happiness (*Glückseligkeit*) rather than, as in Judaism, the fulfillment of God's will as expressed in divinely ordained commandments. Though Ascher's specific program remained idiosyncratic, his subjectivization of the Jewish faith and its confessionalization soon became characteristic for the Reform movement. In later literature the differentiation is repeatedly made between what is essential to Judaism and what has been added by historical accident, "the kernel and the husk." In Jewish education the concomitant to this endeavor to isolate the basic tenets and distinctive practices of the faith was the catechism, now increasingly introduced in place of, or supplementary to, traditional texts.

The reform of synagogue ritual under modern cultural influence was undertaken for the first time by the Adath Jeshurun congregation of Amsterdam in 1797. This synagogue was established in separation from the general community, following the grant of emancipation to Dutch Jewry by the French-controlled Batavian Republic the previous year. The congregation buried its dead only on the third day, shortened its liturgy, made aesthetic "improvements" in the worship service, introduced a regular sermon on a moral theme, and eliminated a prayer that asked for vengeance against those who had martyred Jews at the time of the Crusades. The congregation had existed for only about a decade when the new king of Holland, Louis Bonaparte, required it to rejoin the general Jewish community.

Although France preceded other European states in giving its Jews complete political equality at the time of the French Revolution, its Jewish community did not lead the movement for religious reform. The Assembly of Jewish Notables (1806) and the Sanhedrin (1807), called by Napoleon, committed French Jewry to the fulfillment of all civic obligations and to the official acceptance of the superiority of the law of the state over Jewish law. However, the delegates were not required to undertake liturgical reforms, to give up any religious practices, or to alter their theological conceptions. The centralized Jewish consistory system, which emerged in France shortly thereafter, militated against individual initiative in religious matters, favoring a superficially modernized official orthodoxy.

It was in the kingdom of Westphalia that a program of religious reforms for an entire Jewish community was first undertaken by an officially constituted body enjoying government support. Under the leadership of the wealthy and influential financier Israel Jacobson (1768–1828), a Jewish consistory, composed of three rabbis and two laymen, was created there in 1808. It introduced the confirmation ceremony, which it borrowed from Christianity, removed secular elements from the sacred space of the synagogue, and generally sought to impose a more dignified and decorous mode of worship. One of the rabbinical members of the consistory, Menachem Mendel Steinhardt (1768–1825), attempted to justify some of its reforms by reference to Jewish law and tradition as well as to the variant customs of Sefardic Jewry.

Some months after Jacobson moved to Berlin following the demise of the Westphalian kingdom and its Jewish consistory in 1813, he established regular weekly worship in his home for those members of the community who desired a service modeled on that of Westphalia. Like the services that Jacobson had instituted at the chapel of a school that he sponsored in the small Westphalian town of Seesen, the worship here was enhanced by the use of an organ and by a boys' choir. Later moved to larger quarters, these services attracted as many as four hundred worshipers. There were hymns and regular edifying sermons in the German language. However, the liturgy—for which a special prayer book was published—remained mostly traditional in content, if not in form. As long as the prayer gatherings remained a private venture, the Orthodox faction of the community was willing to tolerate them. However, once it seemed that some of these reforms would be introduced into the community synagogue, traditionalist opposition, combined with Prussian government hostility to religious innovations, led to a royal edict in 1823 prohibiting any and all Jewish religious reform. This was the first of many disputes and polemical exchanges between reformers and traditionalists that thereafter punctuated the history of the Reform movement.

In 1817 a "New Temple Association" was formed in the independent city of Hamburg. Its members, who represented a broad economic and social cross section of the city's Jewry, succeeded in establishing and maintaining their own synagogue, despite Orthodox opposition, on account of the more indulgent attitude of the city's senate. The Hamburg temple, which lasted until the Holocaust, remained for a generation the model for the movement. In 1819 it issued a prayer book which, for the first time, made substantial changes in the liturgy. Intensely particularist passages were removed or altered. While references to Zion were not wholly excised, the prayer book reflected the members' abandonment of the desire to return to the Land of Israel and to reestablish the ancient sacrificial service. Two lay preachers gave regular German sermons on the Christian model and prepared both boys and girls for the confirmation ceremony.

Ideologists. The next two decades may be described as a period of latency in the history of the Reform movement. The climate of political reaction in Europe was not conducive to religious innovation. Orthodox opposition, moreover, had proven to be pervasive and united. No new Reform prayer books were published between 1819 and 1840, and no new congregations were established. Aside from the Hamburg temple, Reform of any more than a minimal variety flourished only in those modern Jewish schools that, as in Berlin and Frankfurt am Main, offered a modified worship service for the children and their parents.

However, during this same period a new generation of rabbis came to maturity, some of them eager to institute religious reforms. Schooled not only in traditional Jewish texts but also at German universities, this younger rabbinical generation was able to provide spiritual leadership for what heretofore had been basically a lay movement. Gradually these men received rabbinical positions, first in the smaller Jewish communities and then in the larger ones. A number of them possessed considerable scholarly abilities and applied themselves to the task of creating a historical theology for the Reform movement. The most prominent was Abraham Geiger (1810–1874), who rapidly became the leading ideologist of the movement in Europe. Employing the new critical approach to Jewish texts, an approach known as *Wissenschaft des Judentums,* Geiger wrote scholarly studies and delivered lectures that showed Judaism as an evolving entity, subject to the forces of history. The essence of Judaism, Geiger argued, was not its legal system but its religious spirit, reflected and symbolized in its rituals. This Jewish spirit was the product of revelation, creating in turn the great literary monuments of Judaism. Geiger stressed the universal message of Judaism, setting its rational ethical monotheism into sharp contrast with Christian trinitarian dogma and pagan materialism. Under the influence of the early Romantic thinker Johann Gottfried Herder, who conceived spiritual epochs succeeding one another in nondialectical fashion, Geiger saw Judaism as a spiritual historical entity, which in the modern world was entering a new epoch in its history. It bore within it the combined heritage of previous stages of its development and was moving toward yet undetermined forms of historical existence. For Geiger, it was the task of the Reform rabbi to press the wheel of history forward with a program of modernizing and rationalizing reforms.

Geiger's colleague, Zacharias Frankel (1801–1875), the rabbi of Dresden, took a more conservative position. He maintained the centrality of Jewish law, though he recognized its historical development and believed that the rabbinical leadership should rather be responsive to the present collective will and spiritual situation of the community than attempt to direct and hasten its course of development. In 1845 Frankel broke with fellow reformers on the issue of Hebrew in the worship service, and in 1854 he became the head of the new conservatively oriented rabbinical seminary in Breslau. The most prominent radical reformer in this period was Samuel Holdheim (1806–1860), who believed the revolutionary new situation of Western Jewry demanded a thoroughgoing transformation of Judaism. Holdheim favored the transfer of the Jewish Sabbath to Sunday and the abolition of all legal elements in Judaism. He regarded his own age as representing a clearly higher level of religious evolution and hence argued that contemporary Jews had the right to reshape Judaism in messianic, universal terms without overmuch regard for preserving continuity with the past. Holdheim eventually became the rabbi of a separatist Reform congregation in Berlin, which radically abbreviated and altered the traditional liturgy, retained only a minimum of Hebrew, and conducted its principal weekly service on Sunday.

Collective Activity and Diffusion. In the 1840s the Reform movement in Germany underwent a major revival. After considerable opposition, Geiger was able in 1840 to assume his tasks as one of the rabbis in the influential Breslau community. A year later the Hamburg temple issued a new version of its prayer book on the occasion of its move to more spacious quarters. Lay societies seeking more radical reforms sprang up in Frankfurt am Main, Berlin, and Breslau. Led for the most part by university-educated, highly acculturated German Jews, these societies proposed elimination of national symbols and ritual prescriptions from Judaism in favor of a highly spiritualized and universalized faith, anchored in a humanistic understanding of the Hebrew Bible and virtually excluding later rabbinic tradition. In their religious radicalism they paralleled similar contemporary movements in German Protestantism and Catholicism.

The rabbis inclined to religious reform now undertook a collective initiative for the first time. Three conferences were held in the years 1844–1846, in which a total of forty-two rabbis participated. Most of them were still in their thirties and possessed doctorates. Although they represented a spectrum of opinion, the tenor of these conferences reflected a middle position among German reformers, dissatisfying both conservatives like Frankel, who favored only the slightest revisions in existing law and custom, and radicals like Holdheim, who urged strict conformity to the demands of the *Zeitgeist*. Among the conclusions reached were that the use of Hebrew in the service was a subjective but not an objective necessity, that prayers for the return to Zion and the reinstitution of the sacrificial service should be eliminated from the prayer book, and that it was permissible to accompany the service with an organ even on the Sabbath. Plans for a new common liturgy and a committee report favoring equality of women were not acted upon when the annual conferences ceased after the third year, in part because of the agitated political situation preceding the Revolution of 1848.

In the second half of the nineteenth century the Reform movement in Germany continued to make inroads in the Jewish communities, but generally with less éclat and polemic than heretofore. Increasingly, the larger Jewish communities provided for modified services (with organ accompaniment and a modified liturgy) as well as traditional ones. Religious reform became institutionalized in Germany as "Liberal Judaism," one of two religious currents or trends (*Richtungen*) within the general community, and it soon won over the majority of German Jews. Synods, including laity as well as rabbis, were held to discuss further reforms in 1869 and 1871. At the end of the century a permanent union of Liberal rabbis was established, with a similar national organization for all Liberal Jews coming into existence in 1908. However, a common prayer book for the German Liberal congregations—quite traditional in character—was not issued until 1929.

While the Reform movement in Europe remained centered in Germany, which had the largest Jewish population west of the tsarist empire, it spread to other countries as well. The Vienna community as early as 1826 adopted a number of aesthetic reforms, as did some congregations in Hungary, Galicia, Holland, and Denmark. Even in Russia certain circles of *maskilim* ("enlightened" Jews) or immigrants from the West introduced decorum, choirs, and vernacular sermons. In the 1860s some Russian Jewish intellectuals argued, as did reformers in the West, that religious reform was indigenous to Jewish tradition from ancient times and that Orthodoxy in fact reflected stagnation.

In England a Reform congregation, called the West London Synagogue of British Jews, was founded in 1840. Generally conservative in character, its most pronounced reform was the abolition of the second days of certain holidays, which were celebrated only according to rabbinic, not biblical, precept. Similar congregations were established elsewhere in England. After the turn of the century a more radical religious movement emerged, which soon adopted the term *Liberal* to differentiate itself from the earlier *Reform*. British Liberal Judaism, which was patterned largely upon the American Reform Judaism of the time, sought to win back to the synagogue the large mass of English Jews who had become alienated from all religious Judaism. Its liturgy was largely in English, and men and women sat together.

In France the centralized consistory long militated against religious division. Some, mostly cosmetic, reforms were undertaken by the chief rabbis, and proposals for more radical change were aired with some regularity in the Jewish press. However, a viable, independent Reform congregation, the Union Israélite Liberale, was established only after the separation of church and state in France in 1905.

European Liberal Judaism—together with its counterpart in America—finally achieved international organizational unity with the establishment of the World Union for Progressive Judaism in London in 1926. Until World War II, the work of the Union and of Reform Judaism in Europe generally was particularly influenced by Leo Baeck (1873–1956), a Liberal rabbi in Berlin and a teacher at the seminary of the movement, the Hochschule für die Wissenschaft des Judentums, which had been established there in 1872. As a religious thinker, Baeck elaborated an antiromantic theology, greatly indebted to Kant, which stressed the revealed moral commandment that emerges out of the mystery of revelation. Under the influence of Rudolf Otto, Baeck's theology later became less rationalistic while his perspective grew more particularistic as he came to focus his attention on the unique religious history of the people of Israel.

AMERICANIZATION

Reform Judaism has enjoyed its greatest success in the United States. In Europe it was repeatedly forced to assert itself against an entrenched Orthodoxy, sometimes supported by the government; in the New World it faced no such established institutions. The United States lacked officially recognized Jewish communities, like the German *Gemeinde* with its powers of taxation and centralized control over Jewish affairs. The complete separation of church and state, the numerous Christian denominations existing side by side, and the prevalent notion that religious activity was strictly a matter of free choice created an atmosphere most conducive to Jewish religious fragmentation. Moreover, it was difficult for an immigrant Jew in nineteenth-century America to make a living while still observing all the inherited traditions. Given also the large influx of Jews from Germany in the second third of the nineteenth century—among them some who had had experience with religious reform, as well as a number of Reform rabbis—it is understandable that until the massive Jewish immigration from eastern Europe in the last decades of the century, Reform Judaism should play the dominant role in American Jewry. In the freer atmosphere of America, Reform soon took on a considerably more radical character than its counterpart in Europe.

Classical American Reform. With the exception of an isolated and short-lived attempt to create a Reform congregation in Charleston, South Carolina, in 1824, somewhat on the model of the Hamburg temple, Reform Judaism took hold in the United States only toward the middle of the nineteenth century. Beginning in 1842 with Har Sinai in Baltimore, and during the next twenty years, liturgical reforms were gradually introduced into existing congregations or new Reform congregations founded in New York City, Albany, Cincinnati, Philadelphia, and Chicago. Jewish periodicals favoring religious reform made their appearance, as did new prayer books embodying various degrees of liturgical revision. When a rabbinical conference, held in Cleveland in 1855, reaffirmed the authority of the Talmud, it aroused protests from the more thoroughgoing reformers, whose influence was to increase in the following decades.

During the second half of the nineteenth century, American Reform was dominated by two immigrant rabbis representing, respectively, a consistent, separatist ideological position and a pragmatic, relatively more conservative stance, which sought to make Reform Judaism most broadly acceptable. David Einhorn (1809–1879), a rabbi in Baltimore and later in New York, stressed the priestly mission of the Jewish people and vigorously opposed mixed marriages, but he saw little value in most Jewish ceremonials and was a firm believer in the progress of Judaism beyond its ancient sacred texts. His influence was dominant at a meeting of Reform rabbis held in Philadelphia in 1869. Following debate held in the German language, this conference declared that the dispersion of Israel providentially served its universal messianic aim. It also rejected the traditional dogma of bodily resurrection in favor of belief only in the immortality of the soul.

Isaac Mayer Wise (1819–1900) was the founding father of organized Reform Judaism in the United States. Unlike Einhorn, whose intellectual stature he did not rival but whom he far excelled in practical energy, Wise sought to create an Americanized Judaism that could appeal to the widest spectrum of Jewry in the United States. Eschewing consistency, Wise sometimes took one position on religious issues, sometimes another, concerned more with momentary effect than with crystallized ideology. However, unlike the radicals, he consistently rejected pentateuchal criticism as undermining the foundations of Judaism. As a rabbi in Cincinnati, Wise came to represent the more moderate midwestern wing of Reform Judaism, which differentiated itself from the more thoroughgoing Reform of the East Coast. It was largely due to Wise's efforts that the national organizations of Reform Judaism were created: the UAHC in 1873, HUC in 1875, and the CCAR in 1889.

In 1885 Wise served as president of a rabbinical conference that formulated the Pittsburgh Platform, a document that was to represent the ideological position of American Reform Judaism for the next half century. The key figure at the conference, however, was not Wise but Kaufmann Kohler (1843–1926), a son-in-law and spiritual heir of David Einhorn, who became the movement's leading theologian and, after a short interval, succeeded Wise as president of the Hebrew Union College. Under Kohler's influence the Pittsburgh conference declared that "Judaism presents the highest conception of the God-idea as taught in our holy Scriptures and developed and spiritualized by the Jewish teachers in accordance with the moral and philosophical progress of their respective ages." It recognized in the Bible "the record of the consecration of the Jewish people to its mission as priest of the One God" but found only the moral laws of the Pentateuch to be binding, while ritual precepts were to be subjected to the criterion of their continuing capacity to sanctify life and to be harmonizable with modern civilization. Jews were defined as a religious community, not a nation, their religion as progressive, "ever striving to be in accord with the postulates of reason." A final paragraph expressed commitment to seek social justice in American society by reducing the "contrasts and evils" in its present organization.

For the next fifty years Reform Judaism adhered to the Pittsburgh Platform. During this period the movement increased in numbers, reaching a high point of about 60,000 families in 285 congregations before the Great Depression temporarily halted its growth. In 1892 the CCAR published the first edition of the *Union Prayer Book,* which with only relatively minor revisions remained standard in Reform Judaism until 1975. However, during this same half century the movement was forced to give up its hopes of becoming the norm for American Jewry. Increasingly it was associated specifically with the German Jewish immigrants and their descendants. Eastern Europeans, concentrated in New York, either remained Orthodox, dissociated themselves from religion entirely, or in the second generation were attracted by the more ethnic and nostalgic appeal of Conservative Judaism. Most Reform Jews until the late thirties were opposed to Jewish nationalism and saw in Zionism a retreat from the universal mission of Judaism. Nonetheless, a small percentage, especially among the rabbis, played active roles in Zionist affairs from the beginning of the century.

Reorientation. It was only in the late 1930s that Reform Judaism in the United States began to lose its identification with the German immigrants. Reform rabbis, and then increasingly the laity as well, were now coming from eastern European backgrounds. During this same decade awareness of the lot of Jews in Nazi Germany created stronger national ties among all Jews. Gradually Reform Judaism began a process of transformation from which it would emerge with a much more significant ethnic and ceremonial component than heretofore. Eventually the earlier period came to be designated Classical Reform Judaism, and while its particular emphases continue to be represented in some congregations even down to the present, a reoriented Reform Judaism began to displace or modify it at an increasing pace.

The first major indication of this shift in position was the Columbus Platform, adopted by the CCAR in 1937. This document was largely the work of Samuel Cohon (1888–1959), an eastern European Jew who served for many years as professor of Jewish theology at the Hebrew Union College. It spoke of a "living God" rather than a "God idea," described Torah, in its broad sense as both written and oral law, as enshrining Israel's "ever-growing consciousness of God," and declared that it was the task of all Jews to rebuild Palestine as a Jewish homeland, both as a "refuge for the oppressed and a center of Jewish culture and spiritual life." In contrast to the Pittsburgh Platform, it stressed the use of Hebrew in worship and the importance of customs, symbols, and ceremonies. Like its predecessor, the platform declared the movement's commitment to social justice, a dominant concern of Reform Judaism during those years of economic distress in the United States.

DEVELOPMENTS SINCE WORLD WAR II

In the immediate postwar years Reform Judaism in the United States enjoyed remarkable growth. New congregations were established in the suburbs of major cities as increased Jewish affluence made possible higher levels of support for religious institutions both locally and nationally. The Christian religious revival of the 1950s produced renewed interest in Jewish theology. In 1951 the UAHC moved its offices from Cincinnati to New York, the center of Jewish life in the United States. From 1943 to 1973 the congregational union was headed by Rabbi Maurice Eisendrath, a talented organizer and impressive public speaker. The well-known biblical archaeologist Nelson Glueck, as president of the Hebrew Union College from 1947 to his death in 1971, was able to achieve a merger with the Jewish Institute of Religion, founded by the Zionist Reform rabbi Stephen S. Wise in 1922, and to bring about considerable expansion of the combined institution.

Reform Judaism now engaged itself vigorously with the moral issues troubling American society. Rabbis and laity participated actively in the civil rights movement and later in the organized opposition to the Vietnam War. In 1961 the UAHC established the Religious Action Center in Washington, D.C., with the intent of making a direct impact on legislation of Jewish and general religious or moral concern, as well as educating the Reform constituency as to questions under current legislative consideration. In the spirit of ecumenism, the UAHC developed a department dealing with interfaith activities, supplementing the long-standing work of individual congregations and of the National Federation of Temple Brotherhoods in this area.

Reform theology in this recent period grew increasingly diverse. A group of Reform rabbis, who became known as "covenant theologians," favored a more personalist and existential grounding of their faith. Influenced by the twentieth-century European Jewish thinkers Franz Rosenzweig and Martin Buber, they eschewed the earlier idealist theology based on progressive revelation in favor of the notion of divine-human encounter as represented both by the testimony of the Torah and by contemporary religious experience. At the same time, however, there arose a significant rationalist and even humanist faction within the movement. Its members stressed the impact of biblical criticism and psychoanalysis upon religion, as well as the difficult theological questions that the Holocaust had raised for Jewish theism.

While theological positions in Reform Judaism generally moved apart, religious practice, for the most part, became more traditional. The postwar period witnessed a renewal of interest in Jewish law, not as authoritative in the Orthodox sense but as a guide for the religious life. Over three decades Solomon Freehof of Pittsburgh, one of the most influential Reform rabbis, published half a dozen collections of Reform *responsa* on issues ranging from aspects of synagogue ritual to matters of individual observance. The publication of these *responsa*, as well as guides for religious observance, was due in part to the feelings of most of the religious leadership that Reform Judaism needed to reengage itself with traditional symbols and practices if it was not to dissipate in the absorptive social climate of postwar America. It was also prompted by a heightened ethnicism and personalism in Reform Judaism. The individual *bar mitsvah* ceremony for boys reaching the age of thirteen, and later the equivalent *bat mitsvah* ceremony for girls, were increasingly adopted by Reform congregations, preceding the group ceremony of confirmation. The rabbinical role, which in Reform Judaism had principally been that of prophetic preacher, now became more priestly, as congregants especially sought rabbis whose personal warmth would enhance life-cycle ceremonies. Reform synagogues introduced more Hebrew into the liturgy and encouraged greater congregational participation.

Jewish education among Reform Jews became more comprehensive in the 1970s. In place of the customary two hours per week of Sunday school instruction, most temples now offered twice-weekly classes, supplemented by weekends or summer sessions at a camp. A handful of Reform day schools came into existence for those children whose parents desired them to obtain more extensive Jewish knowledge and depth of Jewish commitment. The National Federation of Temple Youth introduced study programs for Reform teenagers beyond religious-school age, and rabbinical education was extended to women, the first woman (Sally Preisand) being ordained by HUC-JIR in 1972. In 1981 the UAHC published its own Torah commentary, encouraging lay study of the Pentateuch according to the liberal approach of Reform.

The commitment of Reform Judaism to Zionism deepened in the postwar period. Reform Jews welcomed the establishment of the state of Israel in 1948, shared feelings of crisis and relief during its Six Day War, and increasingly appropriated its cultural impact. Israeli melodies entered the synagogues, religious schools, and summer camps. The CCAR declared Israeli Independence Day a religious holiday, and beginning in 1970 HUC-JIR required all entering rabbinical students to spend the first year of their study at its campus in Jerusalem. Reform Jews organized the Association of Reform Zionists of America (ARZA) in order to give Reform Judaism an individual voice in the world Zionist movement.

In the state of Israel itself, the first successful Progressive congregation was established, mostly by German Jewish immigrants, in Jerusalem in 1958. It was followed by congregations in the other major cities, attendance reaching about five thousand for the High Holy Days. The congregations and their rabbis united as the "Movement for Progressive Judaism in Israel," a regular constituent of the World Union for Progressive Judaism, the latter moving its headquarters to Jerusalem in 1974. In the seventies Israeli Reform also established its first *kibbuts* (collective agricultural settlement) in the southern desert and a youth movement with groups in various cities. In 1980 HUC-JIR for the first time ordained an Israeli Reform rabbi in Jerusalem. However, Reform Judaism (and also Conservative Judaism) remained unrecognized by the Israeli rabbinate and was forced to wage a continuous, and as yet very incompletely successful, struggle for equal rights with Orthodoxy. In general, Israeli Reform emerged as considerably more traditional than its counterpart in the United States, finding the positions taken by the American radical wing on such matters as rabbinical officiation at mixed marriages and conversion procedures to be embarrassing in the Israeli milieu.

The centrality of Jewish peoplehood, symbolized by the state of Israel, found clear expression in the most recent platform of Reform Judaism. Called "A Centenary Perspective" because it was composed about one hundred years after the creation of the first national institutions of American Reform Judaism, it was adopted by the CCAR in 1976. The statement was the work of a committee chaired by Rabbi Eugene Borowitz, a professor at the New York school of HUC-JIR and one of the most influential contemporary theologians of the movement. Unlike previous platforms, it does not seek to define Judaism as a whole dogmatically, but only to give a brief historical account of Reform Judaism—what it has taught and what it has learned—and to describe its present spiritual convictions. Recognizing and affirming the diversity of theology and practice in contemporary Reform, it points to those broad conceptions and values shared by most Reform Jews. In the wake of the Holocaust and recognizing the physically precarious situation of Israeli Jewry and the assimilatory forces operative on American Judaism, the statement gives prominence to the value of ethnic survival, an element not highlighted in earlier platforms. It affirms the reality of God, without setting forth any specific theology, and defines the people of Israel as inseparable from its religion. Torah is seen as the product of "meetings between God and the Jewish people," especially, but not only, in ancient times. Rejecting the optimism of nineteenth-century Reform Judaism, the statement nonetheless reaffirms the religious significance of human history and the moral obligations of Jews, both particularly in Jewish matters and in the pursuit of universal messianic goals.

[*See also* Judaism, *article on* Judaism in Northern and Eastern Europe since 1500, *and the biographies of the principal figures mentioned herein.*]

BIBLIOGRAPHY

Although outdated in many respects, the standard work on Reform Judaism remains David Philipson's *The Reform Movement in Judaism*, 2d ed. (1931), reissued with a new introduction by Solomon Freehof (New York, 1967). W. Gunther Plaut has brought together a good selection of primary sources, abbreviating the lengthier ones and translating into English those in other languages. The material in two volumes edited by him, *The Rise of Reform Judaism* and *The Growth of Reform Judaism* (New York, 1963 and 1965), extends to 1948. More general, but valuable for the European context, are Heinz Moshe Graupe's *The Rise of Modern Judaism*, translated by John Robinson (Huntington, N.Y., 1978), and the older Max Wiener's *Jüdische Religion im Zeitalter der Emanzipation* (Berlin, 1933), translated into Hebrew (Jerusalem, 1974) but not, regrettably, into English. The specific matter of liturgical change is comprehensively treated, with extensive quotation of primary sources, in Jakob J. Petuchowski's *Prayerbook Reform in Europe* (New York, 1968). The initial phases of Reform Judaism in the United States are best understood from Leon A. Jick's recent study, *The Americanization of the Synagogue, 1820–1870* (Hanover, N.H., 1976). Sefton D. Temkin has chronicled the history of the Union of American Hebrew Congregations in "A Century of Reform Judaism in America," *American Jewish Year Book* 74 (1973), pp. 3–75, and the story of the movement's seminary is told in my article, "A Centennial History," in *Hebrew Union College-Jewish Institute of Religion at One Hundred Years,* edited by Samuel E. Karff (Cincinnati, Ohio, 1976), pp. 3–283. The more significant speeches delivered at meetings of the Central Conference of American Rabbis have been collected by Joseph L. Blau in *Reform Judaism: A Historical Perspective* (New York, 1973), while some of the more thoughtful members of the CCAR themselves reflect on various aspects of the history of their organization in *Retrospect and Prospect: Essays in Commemoration of the Seventy-Fifth Anniversary of the Founding of the Central Conference of American Rabbis,* edited by Bertram Wallace Korn (New York, 1965). The variety in Reform Jewish theology after World War II is well reflected in *Contemporary Reform Jewish Thought,* edited by Bernard Martin (Chicago, 1968). Two sociological analyses based on surveys taken at the beginning of the last decade present the state of belief and practice among Reform rabbis and laity: Theodore I. Lenn's *Rabbi and Synagogue in Reform Judaism* (West Hartford, Conn., 1972) and Leonard J. Fein et al., *Reform Is a Verb: Notes on Reform and Reforming Jews* (New York, 1972). Contemporary Reform Judaism can best be followed through its current major publications. *Reform Judaism* is a popular UAHC magazine circulated to all members four times a year; the *Journal of Reform Judaism,* a quarterly, is the official organ of the CCAR; and the occasional *Ammi* presents news of the World Union for Progressive Judaism.

26 ZIONISM

David Biale

The origin of the word *Zion* is unclear. It most likely derives from a word meaning "rock" or "stronghold" or perhaps "a dry place." The first occurrence of the name is in *2 Samuel* 5:7, where David captures the Jebusite city of Jerusalem. The "fortress of Zion" appears to have been the Jebusite name for the place that was henceforth to be called "the citadel of David." But although Jebusite in origin, the name *Zion* (Heb., *Tsiyyon*) was assimilated into the Israelite vocabulary and became associated with the Davidic monarchy and its capital in Jerusalem. In writings of such prophets as "First Isaiah" and Jeremiah and in *Psalms,* the name *Zion* is used as a synonym first for the Temple in Jerusalem, then for the kingdom of Judah, and finally, in postexilic literature, for the Land of Israel. In the Babylonian exile, the psalmist wrote: "By the waters of Babylon / There we sat down, yea, we wept / When we remembered Zion" (*Ps.* 137:1). Thus, what was first a specific place-name came to represent symbolically the whole Land of Israel whose people had been exiled. The particular associations between Zion and the Davidic monarchy gave the word a special resonance in later messianic literature that expressed longing not only for the return of the people to their land but also for the reestablishment of the kingdom of David.

A particular tension has informed the Jewish relationship to Zion since biblical times. On the one hand, the Land of Israel is regarded as a "holy land" specially promised to the ancient Israelites and their descendants. According to this position, the Israelite God can be worshiped only on this sanctified territory. Thus, when David flees from Saul to the land of the Philistines, he laments that "[men] have driven me out this day that I should have no share in the heritage of the Lord, saying 'Go and serve other gods' " (*1 Sm.* 26:19). In Psalm 137, the writer wonders, "How shall we sing the song of YHVH in a foreign land?" In both biblical and rabbinic law, much of the agricultural, ritual, and even civil law applied only to the Land of Israel.

On the other hand, a strong universalist tendency already developed in biblical times held that God rules over all the world and can be worshiped anywhere. This tendency became particularly prominent as a result of the Babylonian exile and found expression in such exilic writers as "Second Isaiah" (*Is.* 40ff.). In some of this literature, there is even a hint of criticism against those who wished to limit worship of God to Zion: "Thus says YHVH: with heaven my throne and earth my footstool, what house could you build me, what place could you make for my rest?" (*Is.* 66:1).

The realities of Jewish life during and after the Second Temple period (538 BCE–70 CE) made a combination of these positions necessary. From the time of the Babylonian exile, a large Jewish community developed outside the Land of Israel and became particularly prominent during the Hellenistic and Roman empires. Even before the destruction of the Second Temple in 70 CE and the Bar Kokhba Revolt (132–135), the Jews of the Diaspora probably constituted a majority of the Jewish people. Nevertheless, these Jews maintained a strong connection with the Land of Israel and its religious institutions. They made regular pilgrimages to the Temple and contributed money to it for sacrifices. After the Temple was destroyed, the Palestinian community remained important until the late third century, when it began to decline, and following the Muslim conquest in the seventh century, it ceased to play a significant role in Jewish life. Yet the centrality of the Land of Israel, which was accepted by all the Diaspora communities, owed much to the fact that the Palestinian authorities were so important for such a long period after the Temple was destroyed.

The rabbis developed rituals that could be practiced anywhere and yet were designed to preserve the memory of the Temple *(zekher le-ḥurban)*. Such ceremonies include the breaking of a glass at weddings and leaving a small area of wall unfinished in one's house. It was during this period that prayers were added to the daily service that pleaded with God:

> *Sound the great shofar for our freedom; raise the standard for the gathering of our exiles, and assemble us from the four corners of the earth. . . . Restore our judges as of old. . . . And to Jerusalem thy city return in mercy and dwell therein as thou has spoken, rebuild it soon in our days as an everlasting building, and speedily set up therein the throne of David.*

Theologically, the rabbis held that the *Shekhinah,* the aspect of God that dwelt in the Temple, had gone into exile with the Jews (e.g., B.T., *Meg.* 29a). God himself was therefore in exile from his land. Not only was God universal, but that aspect of him that specially protected the Jews was close at hand wherever they might wander. This position maintained the tension between God as universal and the hope for the reestablishment of his cult in the Temple in Zion.

MEDIEVAL PERIOD

The spiritual connection to Zion was kept alive during the Middle Ages primarily through literature, although through the centuries there were also individual Jews who made pilgrimages or actually settled in the Land of Israel. The theme of Zion played an important role in the medieval liturgical poems *(piyyuṭim)* and especially in the lamentation poem *(qinot)* recited on the Ninth of Av (the day, according to tradition, on which the First and Second Temples were destroyed).

The best examples of secular poetry devoted to longing for Zion can be found during the "classical age" of the Spanish Jews (900–1200). Two themes intermingle in this poetry: descriptions of the beauty of Zion and lamentations for her ruin. Some of the Spanish Jewish writers achieved high positions in Spanish society, but their work reflects persistent attachment to the land of their forefathers. Shemu'el ha-Nagid (933–1055/6) was the vizier of Granada and the commander of its army.

One of his poems, entitled *My Heart Waxes Hot within Me,* celebrates victory over his enemies, but the first part is a lament over the destruction of Zion. Thus, Shemu'el's pride over his military accomplishments was tempered by the feeling that they were incomplete as long as the Jews lived in exile.

Perhaps the most outstanding representative of this school of poets was Yehudah ha-Levi (c. 1075–1141) whose *Shirei Tsiyyon* (Songs of Zion) inspired many imitations later in the Middle Ages. One of his poems (*Zion, will you not seek the welfare of your prisoners?*) was included in the liturgy of the Ninth of Av. In another, he wrote:

> My heart is in the East and I am at the edge of the West
> How then can I taste what I eat, how can I enjoy it?
> How can I fulfill my vows and pledges, while
> Zion is in the domain of Edom [i.e., the Christian Crusaders]
>   and I am in the bonds of Arabia [i.e., Muslim Spain]?
> It would be easy for me to leave behind the good things
>   of Spain, just as
> It would be glorious to see the dust of the ruined Shrine.

Many of these songs describe ha-Levi's trip to Israel, which he undertook in 1140. However, he never reached his goal and died in Egypt in 1141. Ha Levi represents one important pole of medieval thought that emphasized the centrality and sanctity of the Land of Israel. Another medieval Spanish writer, one who succeeded in emigrating to the Land of Israel, was Nahmanides (Mosheh ben Naḥman, c. 1194–1270), exegete, philosopher, and qabbalist. Nahmanides interpreted the verse in *Numbers* 33:53 ("And you shall take possession of the land and settle in it, for I have given the land to you to possess it") to be a positive commandment incumbent on all Jews. In this, he followed certain Talmudic dicta (see B.T., *Ket.* 11b) that, among other things, call a wife rebellious who does not follow her husband to the Land of Israel. This notion of the religious duty of living in Israel inspired numerous waves of immigration throughout medieval Jewish history, including, for example, a group of rabbis in 1211 and the messianic circle led by Yehudah Hasid ha-Levi around 1700. In the sixteenth century, following the expulsion of the Jews from Spain, the community of Palestine increased and a number of "proto-Zionist" efforts were undertaken to establish Jewish agricultural colonies and reestablish the ancient Sanhedrin.

This proto-Zionist sentiment cannot be dissociated from medieval Jewish messianism. All messianic thinkers in the Middle Ages considered the return to Zion to be among the primary tasks of the Messiah. Even as messianic expectations were embroidered with supernatural fantasies, such as the belief in the resurrection of the dead, the core of Jewish messianism remained political and nationalistic: the Messiah would return the Jews to Zion, reestablish the kingdom of David, and rebuild the Temple in Jerusalem. The movements mentioned here were all attempts to spark the messianic process by encouraging human beings to take the first steps of resettling the Land of Israel. In the seventeenth century, the Shabbatean movement caused Jews throughout the world to prepare themselves for the imminent return to Zion, a hope largely dashed when the putative Messiah, Shabbetai Tsevi, converted to Islam in 1667.

On the other hand, another group of medieval thinkers deemphasized the importance of immigration to Zion. Some, such as Hayyim Kohen (twelfth century), saw no obligation to live in the Land of Israel since the commandments pertaining to the land could not be observed until the coming of the Messiah. Meir ben Baruch of Rothenburg (c. 1220–1293) argued that it is permissible to leave the Land of Israel in order to study the Torah. Similarly, Maimonides (Mosheh ben Maimon, 1135/8–1204), the most renowned of medieval Jewish philosophers and legal scholars, gave greater emphasis to the study of the Torah than to awaiting or hastening the coming of the Messiah. For Maimonides, the central event in Jewish history was at Mount Sinai, and the return to Zion in messianic times would be a means toward uninterrupted study of the law revealed at Sinai. Although Maimonides clearly believed in the coming of the Messiah (which he understood as a realistic and not solely supernatural process), he subordinated Zion to Sinai.

This trend of thought became even more pronounced in eighteenth-century Hasidism, which, as Gershom Scholem has argued, frequently played down expectations of the imminent coming of the Messiah. Dov Ber, the Maggid of Mezhirich (1704–1772), believed that the qabbalistic task of "raising the sparks" might be more effectively accomplished in the lands of the exile. Naḥman of Bratslav (1772–1810), who was perhaps the most messianic of the Hasidic masters, stretched the holiness of the Land of Israel to encompass all the lands in which the Jews lived, thus spiritualizing what had hitherto been a concrete concept. [For further discussion, see Messianism, article on Jewish Messianism.]

THE NINETEENTH CENTURY

In the nineteenth century the forces of modern nationalism, released by the French Revolution, awakened nationalist hopes among the Jews throughout Europe. Although emancipation and assimilation caused many Jews, particularly in western and central Europe, to identify with the national aspirations of the countries in which they lived, increases in anti-Semitism and the failure of emancipation to fulfill its promises refocused attention on Zion. The nineteenth century thus witnessed a fusing of traditional messianism with modern nationalism that culminated in the emergence of modern Zionism at the end of the century.

Two important intellectual developments in the nineteenth century, among both modernizing and traditional Jews, prepared the ground for Zionism. The first was the movement of Jewish Enlightenment (Haskalah), which began in Germany in the late eighteenth century and spread to eastern Europe in the nineteenth. The Haskalah developed in two directions with respect to Zion. On the one hand, there was a general tendency to promote the emancipation of the Jews in Europe by glorifying the European nations. The Reform movement in Germany, which was one product of Enlightenment, deleted references to Zion in the prayer book and emphasized the patriotic attachment of Jews to their native countries. Some Haskalah writers used messianic language to describe European rulers such as Joseph II of Austria and Alexander II of Russia, who were perceived as particularly sympathetic to the Jews.

On the other hand, much of the new Hebrew literature written by Haskalah authors, especially in eastern Europe, harkened back to the land of the Bible. Avraham

Mapu (1808–1867), the first Hebrew novelist, placed the plots of two of his novels, *Ahavat Tsiyyon* (Love of Zion) and *Ashmat Shomron* (Guilt of Shomron), in romantic biblical settings. Hebrew newspapers such as *Ha-shahar* and *Ha-maggid* also fostered interest in the Land of Israel, and countered assimilationist tendencies by arguing for a Jewish national consciousness. In addition, the activities of western European Jewish philanthropists such as Adolphe Crémieux and Moses Montefiore in settling Jews in Palestine fostered the beginnings of the modern settlement in the country. Thus, both in literature and philanthropy, modern "enlightened" Jews created the basis for a Zionist movement.

One secular Jewish thinker of particular importance was Moses Hess (1812–1875). Hess was one of the early leaders of European socialism. Following the 1848 revolutions, he withdrew from political activity and became interested in the history of national groups. He rediscovered his Jewish origins and became a fervent advocate of Jewish nationalism. In his *Rome and Jerusalem* (1862), he advanced a proposal for the renewal of the Jewish state, arguing that the continuation of the Jewish people could be justified only on national, rather than religious, grounds.

The second important nineteenth-century development was among traditional Jews. Tsevi Hirsch Kalischer (1795–1874) appealed to Meyer Anschel Rothschild to buy the Land of Israel from Muhammad 'Alī, the ruler of Egypt. Kalischer developed a plan to reinstitute the ancient sacrifices on the Temple mount as a way of hastening the coming of the Messiah. He based his messianic doctrine, which called for human initiative, on Moses Maimonides, who had argued that certain human actions might precede the actual coming of the Messiah. Later, following the Damascus Blood Libel Affair of 1840 and the attempt by Western philanthropists to rescue the Damascus Jews, Kalischer advocated agricultural settlement in the Land of Israel. However, even in his later writings, which put forward this kind of practical suggestion, Kalischer never abandoned his messianic expectations, nor did he give up his hope that the sacrifices might be reinstituted by the new settlers.

A similar kind of religious "Zionism" can be found in the writings of Yehudah ben Shelomoh Alkalai (1798–1878), who, until the Damascus Affair, was an obscure preacher in the Balkans. Like Kalischer, Alkalai argued in numerous pamphlets for Jewish settlement in the Holy Land as a means toward bringing the Messiah.

The writings of Kalischer and Alkalai had little immediate effect, although there was an increase in immigration to Palestine by Orthodox Jews throughout the nineteenth century. New communities of religious Jews were established outside the walls of Jerusalem, in some cases with the help of philanthropists like Montefiore. In 1878 a group of Orthodox Jews established the first agricultural colony, Petach Tikva. Scholars have come to appreciate the contribution that these religious Jews made in laying the groundwork for the later Zionist settlement.

MODERN SECULAR ZIONISM

The rise of anti-Semitism in France, Germany, and Russia in the last quarter of the nineteenth century raised serious questions about the prospects of Jewish integration into European society. Under the influence of modern nationalist ideas, a number of secular or partially secular Jews in several countries began to conceive of a Jewish homeland as the only answer to the Jewish situation. In addition to the political problem of anti-Semitism, many of these thinkers felt that the growing problem of Jewish assimilation could be addressed only by the creation of a Jewish society with its own national culture.

The new Zionist thinkers attempted to combine the ideas of secular nationalism with the messianic aspirations still cultivated by the large population of traditional Jews. Indeed, it might be argued that Zionism emerged when it did as a result of the influence of modern nationalism, but that it emerged at all was a result of the persistence of the age-old religious longing for Zion. Yet the tensions between these seemingly similar national ideals were evident from the inception of modern Zionism, and they continue to characterize the conflict between the secular and the religious in modern Israel.

Following the pogroms in Russia in 1881, a group of eastern European intellectuals formed the Hibbat Tsiyyon ("love of Zion"). The members of this movement came from both of the groups previously mentioned: followers of the Haskalah and religious figures. Hibbat Tsiyyon was primarily a practical movement that sought to foster settlement and agricultural development in Palestine. It borrowed its ideology of "productivization" of the Jews from the earlier Haskalah. The Hibbat Tsiyyon was a response to the mass emigration of Jews from Russia that began in the wake of the pogroms, and it tried to direct the immigration to Palestine instead of to western Europe and America. Although the Hibbat Tsiyyon sponsored a number of colonies in Palestine, it never became a mass movement, and its impact was largely on Russian Jewish intellectuals.

Modern Zionism really began with Theodor Herzl (1860–1904). The term *Zionism* was coined in 1890 by Nathan Birnbaum in his journal *Selbstemanzipation* and was adopted by Herzl and his followers at the first Zionist Congress in 1897. Although some rabbis supported Herzl, most members of the movement, including Herzl himself, were secular and westernized. Nevertheless, Herzl was greeted by many eastern European Jews as a messianic figure. The first substantial Zionist emigration from eastern Europe to Palestine started after the pogroms of 1903 and 1905–1906 and was largely made up of young secular Russian Jews, many of whom were influenced by the Russian radicalism of the period.

The attitude toward religion among the early secular Zionist thinkers was frequently quite hostile. Traditional Judaism was viewed as the religion of the exile and the Zionists saw themselves as a movement to "negate the exile" *(shelilat ha-golah)*. This position received its sharpest expression in the writings of M. Y. Berdichevsky (1865–1921), J. H. Brenner (1881–1921), and Jacob Klatzkin (1882–1948). Berdichevsky, for example, saw the whole religious Jewish tradition, going back to Mount Sinai, as being opposed to a proud national life, and he wished to create a "new Hebrew man" based on a "Nietzschean" countertradition of strength and naturalism. Berdichevsky traced this countertradition back to the biblical period when, he believed, the ancient Hebrews followed a revelation from Mount Gerizim, mentioned in *Deuteronomy* 27:11–26, that was opposed to the "ethical" Torah of Mount Sinai. The prophets, and later the rabbis, suppressed this Torah of nature, but it persisted in heretical movements and splinter sects such as the first-century Zealots and the eighteenth-century Hasidim. This idea, that the Jews had been misled by the rabbis and had followed a tradition alien to their roots, had an important influence on the secular Zionist attitude toward the Jewish religion and especially on extreme secular groups such as the "Canaanites" of the 1940s.

Nevertheless, there were other secular Zionists who tried to base the new Zionist culture on elements from the religious tradition. Aḥad ha-'Am (the pen name of Asher Ginsberg, 1856–1927) tried to develop a secular Judaism based on certain principles from the Jewish heritage. He believed that the Jewish religion was one expression of a wider Jewish national culture. The elements that a secular Judaism might borrow from the tradition varied in Aḥad ha-'Am's writings (sometimes "absolute monotheism" was stressed, other times "liberal ethics"), but he held that the development of this culture was possible only in a Jewish national home. This national cultural center would in turn revitalize the Jewish Diaspora, which had been spiritually weakened by assimilation and the decline of the Jewish religion.

A number of the leaders of the secular Zionist labor movement also tried, with varying degrees of success, to incorporate a more positive attitude toward the Jewish religion into their secular ideologies. Aharon David Gordon (1856–1922), who was one of the pioneers of the early agricultural settlements, developed a religion of labor based on a mystical bond between the Jew and the Land of Israel. Physical labor on the national soil is a way of renewing the self and bringing it into harmony with the cosmos. Although Gordon was not a practicing Orthodox Jew, his philosophy relied heavily on Jewish mysticism and Hasidism as well as on Tolstoyan ideals.

Another labor leader, Berl Katzenelson (1887–1944), argued for the adaptation of traditional Jewish holidays and rituals to the new national home. Katzenelson, who was enormously influential as a cultural and ideological writer, laid the groundwork for a secular national culture that had its roots in Jewish tradition. Similarly, the first prime minister of Israel, David Ben Gurion (1886–1973), sought to base the new national culture on a return to the Bible, a theme that had precedent among the Haskalah writers of the nineteenth century.

The ambivalence toward the Jewish tradition that one finds in many of these early secular Zionists had much to do with their biographies. In most cases, they came from traditional homes and were educated in the *yeshivot* (rabbinic academies) of eastern Europe. Zionism was a radical revolution for them against the world of their childhood, but they never fully broke with their positive memories of this religious culture. Even if their way of life was secular, they wished to recreate an authentic Jewish culture on a new, national basis.

If the labor Zionists were ambivalent at best toward the Jewish religion, their counterparts in the Revisionist Zionist party (organized in 1925) were militant. The Revisionists were led by Vladimir Jabotinsky (1880–1940), the Russian-Jewish journalist and poet, and they acquired the reputation of a right-wing, nationalist movement. Although Jabotinsky had a few religious followers, his movement was generally adamantly secular and opposed to religion. In the 1940s, a splinter group under the poet Yonatan Ratosh broke off from the Revisionists and formed the Young Hebrew, or "Canaanite," movement (the latter term was originally used by their opponents). The Canaanites saw the Jews as a religious group whose history was in the exile, whereas the new Hebrew community in Palestine was to break from the religious past and develop its own indigenous culture. The Canaanites were inspired by the myths of the ancient Canaanites that were uncovered in the Ras Shamra excavations of the 1930s. Although the Canaanites were an extreme nativist movement, their thought points to an important trend in Israeli culture away from traditional Jewish religion and toward a new national culture that might incorporate ancient Near Eastern myths.

RELIGIOUS ZIONISM

Although the majority of the Orthodox Jewish world was either indifferent or opposed to Herzl's Zionist movement, there was a significant group that responded favorably to the idea of a Jewish state. Among the first rabbis to join Herzl were Isaac Reines and Shemu'el Mohilever, who was perhaps the most prominent rabbi in the Hibbat Tsiyyon movement. In 1902, Reines formed Mizrahi, a religious faction within the World Zionist Organization (the name is a composite of some of the Hebrew letters from the words *merkaz ruhani,* "spiritual center"). Mizrahi consisted of two groups: one that opposed the introduction of any "cultural" issues into the Zionist movement, for fear that the secularists would set the tone in such endeavors, and another that saw that Zionism could not avoid confronting cultural issues and demanded that Mizrahi try to influence the Zionist movement in a religious direction. Although the "political" faction was initially predominant, the Mizrahi movement ultimately saw as its *raison d'être* the fostering of religious education and public religious practice in the Zionist settlement in Palestine and, later, the state of Israel.

Mizrahi played a major role in mustering support for Zionism among Orthodox Jews in Europe and the United States. It created a network of schools in which Zionism was taught together with traditional religious subjects. At the same time, Mizrahi established schools in Palestine that formed the backbone of the religious educational system that is an important part of the general educational system in the state of Israel. The Mizrahi youth movements, Young Mizrahi and Benei Akiva, began establishing agricultural settlements in Palestine in the 1920s.

The Mizrahi joined three other religious parties to create a religious faction in the first Israeli governing coalition. In 1956 they formed the National Religious Party (NRP) and Po'el Mizrahi ("Mizrahi workers"). The NRP has sat in every Israeli government (with the exception of one year) and regularly receives approximately 10 percent of the vote. However, this percentage dropped in the 1981 and 1984 elections with the defection of more nationalist elements to other, nonreligious, parties. Despite its relatively small share of the national vote, the NRP has constituted an important "swing" element in all Israeli governments since neither the Labor Alignment nor the Likud Party has been able to win a clear majority. Thus the NRP has been able to exert disproportionate influence on Israeli politics and on the role of religion in Israeli society.

Since their inception the Mizrahi have sought to avoid the problem of the relationship of Zionism to Jewish messianism. Much opposition to Zionism in the religious world stemmed from the belief that human beings should not "force the end" (i.e., initiate messianic times by secular means). Instead of answering this position with a new messianic theory, the Mizrahi took a cautious stance, claiming that the Zionist movement constituted a "beginning of redemption." They saw their role as guaranteeing that the future redemption would not be ruined by the heretical actions of the secular Zionists.

There were, however, certain elements among the religious Zionists who took a bolder approach to the question of messianism. Primary among these was Avraham Yitshaq Kook, who was chief rabbi of Jaffa from 1904 and then chief Ashkenazic rabbi of Palestine from 1921 until his death in 1935. Kook held that redemption had begun with the Zionist movement and, in anticipation of imminent messianic times, he fostered study of the sacrificial laws in his *yeshivah.* Unlike other religious Zionists and religious anti-Zionists, Kook believed that the secular pioneers were a necessary force to prepare the material foundation for messianic times. He argued dialectically that the profane was necessary for subsequent emergence of the sacred. Kook met frequently with leaders of the labor Zionist movement and developed close ties with them. As chief rabbi of Jaffa he played a central role in 1909 in the attempt to solve the problem of the *shemiṭṭah,* the agricultural sabbatical during which land owned by Jews in the Land of Israel is supposed to lie fallow. Kook arranged for sale of such land to a non-Jew, thus allowing it to be worked by Jews, which permitted the continuation of the agricultural settlements. Kook's unusually positive attitude toward the secular Zionist movement was based on his belief that when Zionism succeeded, messianic times would come and the Zionist movement would itself return to its unconscious religious roots.

Kook's messianic philosophy had little direct impact on the religious Zionist parties, but it did influence a new generation of religious Israelis, particularly through the Merkaz ha-Rav Yeshivah in Jerusalem, established by Kook and headed by his son Tsevi Yehudah Kook until the latter's death in 1982. This new generation did not accept the compromise position of the older leaders of Mizraḥi, who believed that the religious parties should primarily guard the religious status quo in the state of Israel. The young religious Zionists, who grew up after the creation of the state in 1948, believed strongly in Zionism as the fulfillment of traditional Jewish messianism. This belief took political expression after the Six Day War of 1967. Young religious Israelis reestablished the settlements in the Etsion bloc south of Jerusalem and created a Jewish outpost in Hebron in 1968. (This illegal settlement was later recognized by the government and developed into the town of Qiryat Arba outside of Hebron.) In 1974, following the Yom Kippur War, these religious activists founded the Gush Emunim ("bloc of the faithful") movement, which advocated the incorporation of Judea and Samaria (the West Bank of the Jordan River) into Israel. The Gush Emunim led a settlement drive in these areas, sometimes with the support of the Israeli government and sometimes illegally. They constituted a significant messianic force in Israeli politics and formed alliances with secular nationalist forces.

RELIGIOUS INSTITUTIONS IN THE STATE OF ISRAEL

Under both the Ottoman empire and the British Mandate, Jewish religious courts enjoyed official jurisdiction over matrimonial and inheritance law. The office of the *ḥakham baṣi* in the Ottoman empire was succeeded by the Ashkenazic and Sefardic chief rabbis under the British Mandate. These functions were carried over to the rabbinic courts and the chief rabbinate of the state of Israel, which were given jurisdiction over matters of personal law by a Knesset enactment of 1953. Rabbinical judges were given the same status as district court judges and their decisions were enforced by the civil authorities. Thus, in matters of marriage, divorce, and child custody, rabbinic courts—ruling according to Jewish law *(halakhah)*—have state sanction. Civil marriage and divorce do not exist, although civil marriages are recognized if contracted abroad. A Ministry of Religious Affairs deals with the needs of the various religious communities in Israel and funds the construction and maintenance of synagogues, *yeshivot,* and other religious facilities.

Although both the Conservative and Reform movements have followings in Israel, their rabbis are not authorized by the rabbinate to perform marriages and they do not benefit from the budgets available through the Ministry of Religious Affairs. Conversion to Judaism is supervised by the rabbinate, and thus Conservative and Reform conversions are not recognized as valid.

Although the majority of the Jewish citizens of Israel are secular or quasi-traditional, a religious status quo is maintained. The Sabbath is the national day of rest and Jewish holidays are national holidays. Sabbath rules apply in public places at the discretion of local municipalities, but the various political parties have undertaken to maintain the practices that have existed since the creation of the state. In the 1977 and 1982 coalition agreements, the Agudat Yisra'el party, which represents some of the most orthodox elements, demanded certain changes in the status quo such as cancellation of Sabbath flights by the national airline, El Al. [*See* Agudat Yisra'el.]

The problem of religion in the state of Israel is connected more generally to the question of a Jewish state. According to the Orthodox interpretation, a Jewish state would have to be a "theocratic" state governed by Jewish law *(halakhah)*. At the opposite extreme, the secular nationalist argument holds that Israel should be a secular state in which church and state are strictly separated and whose Jewish character is determined purely by the sociological makeup of its population. For the Orthodox, the identity of the Jews can only be determined by the *halakhah:* one is a Jew only if born of a Jewish mother or converted by a halakhic procedure. For the secular Zionists, anyone who declares himself a Jew should be considered as such. Moreover, some secular nationalists argue that a new Israeli identity should take the place of Jewish identity, which they regard as a religious relic of the years of exile. In a case in the 1960s, the Israeli Supreme Court ruled that Jewish identity is not determined by the *halakhah.* The case concerned a Carmelite monk, Brother Daniel, who was born a Jew and had fought against the Nazis as a partisan. He requested Israeli citizenship under the Law of Return, arguing that, according to the *halakhah,* he remained a Jew even though he professed another religion. The Court ruled against him with the argument that the conventional understanding of who is a Jew contradicted the *halakhah* in such a case and, since Israel is not a halakhic state, that the common definition should prevail. Similarly, in 1970, the Court ruled that a child born of a Jewish father and a non-Jewish mother might be registered as of "Israeli" rather than "Jewish" national identity. This decision would have set aside the concept of a corporate Jewish state in favor of a new secular Israeli identity. As a result of pressure from the religious Zionist parties and of discomfort on the part of many secular Zionists, the Knesset passed a law providing that only persons recognized as Jews by the *halakhah* might be registered as Jews by nationality. In 1980 the Knesset passed a law stipulating that in matters in which there is no specific law or precedent, judges should be guided by "Hebrew jurisprudence" *(mishpat 'ivri)*. Judges were directed to follow traditional Jewish law, but by avoiding the term *halakhah,* the Knesset was able to satisfy the secular refusal to accept a theocratic state. Thus, the judicial system has generally attempted a secular definition of Jewish identity, whereas the legislative system, responding to religious sentiments, has avoided such a break with tradition.

ANTI-ZIONISM

There are a number of expressions of anti-Zionism based on religious motivations. In both Europe and America, nineteenth-century Reform Judaism was unalterably opposed to a national definition of Judaism. The Pittsburgh Platform of 1885 specifically rejected any expectation of a return of the Jews to Zion. By 1937, however, the

Reform movement had moved to a more neutral position and adopted the Columbus Platform, in which the "group loyalty" of the Jews is recognized and the upbuilding of Palestine is supported "not only [as] a haven of refuge for the oppressed but also [as] a center of Jewish culture and spiritual life." Nevertheless, a wing of the Reform movement, which formed the American Council for Judaism, actively opposed the creation of Israel in the 1940s. Following the Six Day War, the Reform movement became explicitly Zionist and joined the World Zionist Organization. Reform Jews established several *kibbutsim* and congregations in Israel.

Among the Orthodox, Zionism was initially greeted with skepticism or hostility. The initial plan to hold the first Zionist Congress in Munich was canceled as a result of opposition by the German rabbis. In 1912, Agudat Yisra'el was formed by rabbis from Germany, Hungary, and Poland as an organization to advance orthodoxy in Jewish life. The Agudah opposed secular Zionism, but maintained an ambivalent attitude toward settlement in the Land of Israel. Following the establishment of the state, the Agudah became a political party advocating a state based on the *halakhah*. The ideology of the movement opposes participation in Zionist governments, although its representatives have nevertheless from time to time held cabinet seats and although they provided coalition support for the government after 1977. The Agudah has used its political influence to strengthen its educational and religious institutions and has sought religious concessions from the Knesset such as exemptions for religious girls from national service and stricter adherence to Sabbath rules. As opposed to the National Religious Party, the Agudah considers itself non-Zionist and does identify with the national goals of the state.

A more extreme anti-Zionist group is the Neturei Karta ("guardians of the city"), which broke off from Agudat Yisra'el in 1935. The Neturei Karta are largely followers of the Satmar Hasidic sect. Neturei Karta opposed the creation of the state of Israel and regarded Zionism as a heinous sin that prevents the coming of the Messiah. They believe that the Nazi Holocaust was punishment for secular Zionism and they declared their willingness to participate in an Arab government in Palestine. They clashed violently from time to time with the Israeli police when they demonstrated against what they regard as violations of Jewish law in the state. The members of Neturei Karta live for the most part in Jerusalem, where they govern themselves, taking no services from the state and paying no taxes. They also have significant support from certain ultra-Orthodox Jews in the United States.

CONCLUSION

Modern Israel is the product of both secular and religious tendencies that have their origins in modern nationalism and in the traditional messianic connection to Zion. With the exception of the small anti-Zionist group, most Jews in the world, representing virtually the whole religious spectrum, support the basic aspirations of Zionism. Thus, the character of the Jewish state—religious, secular, or some combination of both—remains an issue of political conflict among Zionists, but this conflict is also emblematic of the larger question of the relationship of religion to nationalism in the modern world.

BIBLIOGRAPHY

The only book devoted specifically to the subject of Zion in Jewish thought is *Zion in Jewish Literature,* edited by Abraham S. Halkin (New York, 1961), which contains essays on the biblical and rabbinic periods, medieval secular and religious poetry, and nineteenth-century Hebrew poetry and prose. For additional articles on the biblical period, see Shemaryahu Talmon's "The Biblical Concept of Jerusalem," *Journal of Ecumenical Studies* 8 (1971): 300–316, and Ben Zion Dinaburg's "Zion and Jerusalem: Their Role in the Historic Consciousness of Israel" (in Hebrew), *Zion* 16 (1951): 1–17. Gerson D. Cohen has given the best treatment of the rabbinic period in his essay "Zion in Rabbinic Literature," included in Halkin's *Zion in Jewish Literature,* mentioned above. See also in Halkin's collection the discussions of medieval writings by Chaim Z. Dimitrovsky and Nahum Glatzer. Other valuable discussions of medieval writings are Yitzhak F. Baer's "Erez Yisrael and the Diaspora in the View of the Middle Ages" (in Hebrew), *Zion Yearbook* 6 (1946): 149–171, and H. H. Ben-Sasson's "Exile and Redemption through the Eyes of the Spanish Exiles" (in Hebrew) in *Yitzhak F. Baer Jubilee Volume,* edited by Salo W. Baron and others (Jerusalem, 1960). A nationalist argument about the relationship between the Jews and Zion in Jewish history and especially the modern period can be found in Ben Zion Dinur's *Israel and the Diaspora* (Philadelphia, 1969). For the relationship of the Jewish Enlightenment to Zion, see Isaac F. Barzilay's "National and Anti-National Trends in the Berlin Haskalah," *Jewish Social Studies* 21 (1959): 165–192, and Jacob S. Raisin's *The Haskalah Movement in Russia* (Philadelphia, 1913), an old but still useful work. The attitude of nineteenth-century Reform is treated in W. Gunther Plaut's *The Rise of Reform Judaism* (New York, 1963).

On the origins and history of the Zionist movement, see David Vital's *The Origins of Zionism* (Oxford, 1975) and *Zionism: The Formative Years* (Oxford, 1982). A good general history of Zionism is Walter Laqueur's *A History of Zionism* (New York, 1972). The history of Zionist thought has been treated by Shlomo Avineri in *The Making of Modern Zionism: Intellectual Origins of the Jewish State* (New York, 1981) and by Ben Halpern in *The Idea of the Jewish State* (Cambridge, Mass., 1961). A good anthology of Zionist thought with a superb introductory essay is *The Zionist Idea,* edited by Arthur Hertzberg (Philadelphia, 1959). The specific issue of religion in the state of Israel is discussed by Ervin Birnbaum in *The Politics of Compromise: State and Religion in Israel* (Rutherford, N.J., 1970) and by S. Zalmon Abramov in *Perpetual Dilemma: Jewish Religion in the Jewish State* (Rutherford, N.J., 1976). An anthology of anti-Zionist thought can be found in *Zionism Reconsidered,* edited by Michael Selzer (New York, 1970). A semischolarly treatment of religion in Israel from the viewpoint of Neturei Karta is Émile Marmorstein's *Heaven at Bay: The Jewish Kulturkampf in the Holy Land* (London, 1969).

CONTRIBUTORS

MOSHE BARASCH, Hebrew University of Jerusalem

DAVID BIALE, State University of New York at Binghamton

EUGENE B. BOROWITZ, Hebrew Union College—Jewish Institute of Religion, New York

MARK R. COHEN, Princeton University

MARTIN A. COHEN, Hebrew Union College—Jewish Institute of Religion, New York

JOSEPH DAN, Hebrew University of Jerusalem

SHLOMO DESHEN, Bar-Ilan University

JANE S. GERBER, Graduate School and University Center, City University of New York

ROBERT GOLDENBERG, State University of New York at Stony Brook

JUDAH GOLDIN, University of Pennsylvania

LAWRENCE A. HOFFMAN, Hebrew Union College—Jewish Institute of Religion, New York

LOUIS JACOBS, Leo Baeck College, London

LEON A. JICK, Brandeis University

PETER S. KNOBEL, Beth Emet, The Free Synagogue, Evanston, Illinois

CHARLES S. LIEBMAN, Bar-Ilan University

IVAN G. MARCUS, Jewish Theological Seminary of America

MICHAEL A. MEYER, Hebrew Union College—Jewish Institute of Religion, Cincinnati

JACOB NEUSNER, Brown University

DAVID NOVAK, Congregation Darchay Noam, Far Rockaway, New York

ELLIS RIVKIN, Hebrew Union College—Jewish Institute of Religion, Cincinnati

HERBERT ROSENBLUM, Temple Israel, Wilkes-Barre, Pennsylvania

HAROLD M. SCHULWEIS, Valley Beth Shalom, Encino, California

E. E. URBACH, Israel Academy of Sciences and Humanities, Jerusalem

MOSHE WEINFELD, Hebrew University of Jerusalem

STEVEN J. ZIPPERSTEIN, Wolfson College, University of Oxford

ROBERT M. SELTZER is professor of History at Hunter College and the Graduate School, City University of New York

FINDING LIST OF ARTICLE TITLES

The following table lists the article titles (in parentheses) as they originally appeared in *The Encyclopedia of Religion*. Titles not listed below are unchanged.

Judaism in the Middle East and North Africa to 1492 (Judaism: Judaism in the Middle East and North Africa to 1492)

Judaism in the Middle East and North Africa since 1482 (Judaism: Judaism in the Middle East and North Africa since 1492)

Judaism in Southern Europe (Judaism: Judaism in Southern Europe)

Judaism in Northern and Eastern Europe to 1500 (Judaism: Judaism in Northern and Eastern Europe to 1500)

Judaism in Northern and Eastern Europe since 1500 (Judaism: Judaism in Northern and Easter Europe since 1500)

Judaism in the Western Hemisphere (Judaism: Judaism in the Western Hemisphere)

Jewish Worship (Worship and Cultic Life: Jewish Worship)

The Structure of Halakhah (Halakhah: The Structure of Halakhah)

The Religious Year (Jewish Religious Year)

Rites of Passage (Rites of Passage: Jewish Rites)

Domestic Observances (Domestic Observances: Jewish Practices)

Iconography (Iconography: Jewish Iconography)

Hasidism (Hasidism: An Overview)

SYNOPTIC OUTLINE

Elisha' ben Avuyah
Eliyyahu ben Shelomoh Zalman
Feinstein, Moshe
Frankel, Zacharias
Gamli'el of Yavneh
Gamli'el the Elder
Geiger, Abraham
Gershom ben Yehudah
H'ai Gaon
Heschel, Abraham Joshua
Hildesheimer, Esriel
Hillel
Hirsch, Samson Raphael
Hoffmann, David
Holdheim, Samuel
Huna'
Hutner, Yitshaq
Ibn Daud, Avraham
Ibn 'Ezra', Avraham
Ibn Gabirol, Shelomoh
Isserles, Mosheh
Josephus Flavius
Kagan, Yisra'el Me'ir
Kalischer, Tsevi Hirsch
Kaplan, Mordecai
Karo, Yosef
Kaufmann, Yehezkel
Kimhi, David
Kohler, Kaufmann
Kook, Avraham Yitshaq
Kotler, Aharon
Krochmal, Nahman
Leeser, Isaac
Levi ben Gershom
Levi Yitshaq of Berdichev
Luria, Isaac
Luria, Shelomoh
Maimonides, Moses
Malbim
Me'ir
Me'ir ben Barukh of Rothenburg
Mendelssohn, Moses
Mohilever, Shemu'el
Montagu, Lily

Nahmanides, Moses
Nahman of Bratslav
Philo Judaeus
Rabbah bar Nahmani
Rashi
Rav
Rava'
Reines, Yitshaq Ya'aqov
Revel, Bernard
Rosenzweig, Franz
Sa'adyah Gaon
Salanter, Yisra'el
Schechter, Solomon
Schenirer, Sarah
Scholem, Gershom
Shabbetai Tsevi
Shemu'el the Amora
Sherira' Gaon
Shim'on bar Yoh'ai
Shim'on ben Gamli'el II
Shim'on ben Laqish
Shne'ur Zalman of Lyady
Sofer, Mosheh
Spektor, Yitshaq Elhanan
Spinoza, Barukh
Szold, Henrietta
Tam, Ya'aqov ben Me'ir
Tarfon
Vital, Hayyim
Wise, Isaac M.
Wise, Stephen S.
Wittgenstein, Ludwig
Ya'aqov ben Asher
Yehoshu'a ben Hananyah
Yehoshu'a ben Levi
Yehudah bar Il'ai
Yehudah bar Yehezqe'l
Yehudah ha-Levi
Yehudah ha-Nasi'
Yehudah Löw ben Betsal'el
Yishma'e'l ben Elisha'
Yohanan bar Nappaha'
Yohanan ben Zakk'ai
Yose ben Halafta'

Israelite Religion